WILLIAM J. SEYMOUR AND THE ORIGINS OF GLOBAL PENTECOSTALISM

WILLIAM J. SEYMOUR AND THE ORIGINS OF GLOBAL PENTECOSTALISM

A BIOGRAPHY AND DOCUMENTARY HISTORY

Gastón Espinosa

With a Foreword by Harvey Cox

Duke University Press
Durham and London
2014

© 2014 Duke University Press
All rights reserved

Text designed by Chris Crochetière
Typeset in Galliard and Trade Gothic type by BW&A Books, Inc.

Library of Congress Cataloging-in-Publication Data
William J. Seymour and the origins of global Pentecostalism :
a biography and documentary history / Gastón Espinosa, ed.
pages cm
Includes bibliographical references and index.
ISBN 978-0-8223-5628-8 (cloth)
ISBN 978-0-8223-5635-6 (pbk.)
1. Seymour, William Joseph, 1870–1922. 2. Pentecostalism.
3. Pentecostals—Biography. 4. Pentecostal
Churches—Clergy—Biography. I. Espinosa, Gastón.
BX8762.Z8S49 2014
289.9'4092–dc23
[B]
2013048705

Cover photos, top: William J. Seymour, author's collection;
bottom: Azusa Street Mission, used by permission of Flower
Pentecostal Heritage Center.

This book is dedicated to Birgit Dickerman—"a Mother in Israel"
—Judges 5:7

CONTENTS

FOREWORD xiii
PREFACE xix
ACKNOWLEDGMENTS xxi
SEYMOUR TIMELINE xxiii

INTRODUCTION
Definitions and One Hundred Years of
Historiography on Seymour 1

PART I
BIOGRAPHY

Chapter 1 American Pentecostal Origins: Parham and Seymour 41

Chapter 2 Holy Awe and Indescribable Wonder: The Azusa Street Revival 53

Chapter 3 Moses and Mecca: Seymour, Azusa, and Global Origins 69

Chapter 4 God Makes No Difference in Color: Azusa's Transgressive Social Space 96

Chapter 5 Wrecking the Spirit of Azusa: Grumbling and the Road to Decline 109

Chapter 6 Race War in the Churches: Promoting Peace by Taking the Initiative 126

Chapter 7 We Don't Believe in Relics: Seymour in Ignominy 143

Conclusion Holy Restlessness and Cracking Bottles 149

PART II
DOCUMENTARY HISTORY OF WILLIAM J. SEYMOUR, THE AZUSA STREET REVIVAL, AND GLOBAL PENTECOSTAL ORIGINS

A. Seymour's Spiritual Writings from the *Apostolic Faith*, 1906–08

Introduction   161

1. Letter from William J. Seymour to Warren Faye Carothers   161
2. Letter from William J. Seymour to Charles Fox Parham   162
3. Bro. Seymour's Call   163
4. The Apostolic Faith Movement   163
5. The Precious Atonement   165
6. The Way into the Holiest   166
7. River of Living Water   167
8. In Money Matters   169
9. Counterfeits   170
10. "Behold the Bridegroom Cometh!"   172
11. Gifts of the Spirit   174
12. "Receive Ye the Holy Ghost"   176
13. Rebecca; Type of the Bride of Christ—Gen. 24   177
14. The Baptism with the Holy Ghost   180
15. [Good-Bye]   182
16. The "Latter Rain" in Zion, Ill.   184
17. The Holy Spirit Bishop of the Church   185
18. Letter to One Seeking the Holy Ghost   188
19. Testimony and Praise to God   189
20. "The Marriage Tie"   190
21. Questions Answered   194
22. Christ's Messages to the Church   201
23. Portsmouth and Richmond, VA   206
24. "To the Married"   207
25. Sanctified on the Cross   210
26. The Baptism of the Holy Ghost   211
27. The Holy Ghost and the Bride   215

B. Seymour's *Doctrines and Discipline* Minister's Manual (1915)

Introduction   216

28. The *Doctrines and Discipline* of the Azusa Street Apostolic Faith Mission of Los Angeles, Cal.   217

C. Azusa Street Revival Accounts in the *Apostolic Faith* (1906–08)

Introduction   301

29. Pentecost Has Come   302

30. The Old-Time Pentecost   303
31. The Same Old Way   303
32. The Promise Still Good   304
33. The Pentecostal Baptism Restored   304
34. Bible Pentecost   306
35. Pentecost with Signs Following   306
36. Beginning of World Wide Revival   307
37. Pentecostal Missionary Reports   308
38. Who May Prophesy?   308

D. Historical Overviews and Testimonies of Seymour and the Azusa Revival
Introduction   309

—Historical Overviews

Introduction   309
39. Charles Shumway, "A Critical Study of 'The Gift of Tongues'"   309
40. J. C. Vanzandt, Speaking in Tongues   314
41. Frank Bartleman, Azusa Street   316
42. Arthur Osterberg, Oral History of the Azusa Street Revival   319
43. Glenn Cook, The Azusa Street Meeting   320
44. Seymour Obituary, "Brother Seymour Called Home"   322

—Euro-American Testimonies

Introduction   323
45. William Durham, A Chicago Evangelist's Pentecost   324
46. Gaston Barnabas Cashwell, "Came 3,000 miles for His Pentecost"   325
47. F. M. Britton, "In Alvin, S.C."   326
48. A. E. Robinson [and J. H. King], Report on the Fire Baptized Holiness Church   327
49. A. W. Orwig, "'Tongues' the Great Stumbling Block"   327
   "My First Visit to the Azusa Street Pentecostal Mission"   328
50. Rachel Sizelove, "Pentecost Has Come"   329
51. Florence Crawford, "Testimony"   330
   "A Cheering Testimony"   331
52. Clara Lum, "Miss Clara Lum Writes Wonders"   331

—African-American Testimonies

Introduction   332
53. Jennie Evans Moore (Seymour), Music from Heaven   333
54. Emma Cummings, Ye Are My Witnesses   333

55. "Mother" Emma Cotton, Inside Story of the Outpouring of the Holy Spirit   334
56. Julia Hutchins, Testimonies of Outgoing Missionaries   336
57. Charles Mason, Tennessee Evangelist Witnesses   337
58. D. J. Young, Pentecostal Meetings in Little Rock, Ark.   339
59. Mack Jonas, Testimony   339
60. Garfield Haywood, Notice about G. T. Haywood   340

—Euro-American Immigrant Testimonies
Introduction   341
61. Louis Osterberg, [Swedish Immigrant] Filled with God's Glory   341
62. Owen "Irish" Lee, "A Catholic That Received Pentecost"   342

—Mexican-American and Native American Testimonies
Introduction   343
63. Arthur Osterberg, Mexican Conversion and Healing at the Azusa Street Revival   343
64. Abundio and Rosa López, Spanish Receive the Pentecost   345
65. Brigido Pérez, Preaching to the Spanish   346
66. *Apostolic Faith* Editorial, Mexican Indian Prays for White Woman's Healing   347
67. Adolfo Valdez, Mexican-American Account of Azusa Street   347
    Mexican-American Ministry among Native Americans   349
68. Thomas Hezmalhalch, Among the Indians at Needles, California   350

—Africa Missionary Testimonies
Introduction   351
69. Lucy Farrow, Report on Lucy Farrow's Ministry in Liberia   351
70. George and Daisy Batman, En Route to Africa   352
71. Edward and Molly McCauley, Molly McCauley Testimony   353
72. John Lake, Origin of the Apostolic Faith Movement   353
73. Thomas Hezmalhalch, Pentecost in Denver   354
74. Samuel and Ardell Mead, New-Tongued Missionaries for Africa   355
75. Henry Turney, Alaska Brother Proves Acts 1:8   356
76. Ansel Post, Testimony of a Minister   357

—Europe and Middle East Missionary Testimonies
Introduction   358
77. Andrew Johnson, Letter from Bro. Johnson   358
    "In Sweden"   359

"Salvation in Sweden" 359
"Sweden" 359
78. Thomas Ball Barratt, Baptized in New York 360
"In Norway" 361
79. Alexander Boddy, A Meeting at the Azusa Street Mission, Los Angeles 361
80. Lucy Leatherman, "Pentecostal Experiences" 362

—Asia: India Missionary Testimonies

Introduction 363
81. Florence Crawford and Clara Lum, "How India Received Pentecost" 363
82. Lillian Garr, "Testimony and Praise to God" 366
"In Calcutta, India" 367
83. Max Wood Moorhead, Pentecost in Mukti, India 367

—Asia: China Missionary Testimonies

Introduction 368
84. Florence Crawford and Clara Lum, "How Pentecost Came to China" 369
85. Bernt Bernsten, Came from China to America for Pentecost 370
86. Antionette Moomau, China Missionary Receives Pentecost 371

E. Critics of Seymour and the Revival

Introduction 372
87. *Los Angeles Times*, "Weird Babel of Tongues" 372
88. A. Sulger, "Delivered from the 'Tongue' Heresy" 374
89. *Indianapolis Star*, "Negro Bluk Kissed" 376
90. Oswald Chambers, "Gift of Tongues" 377
91. William Durham, "The Great Revival at Azusa Street Mission— How It Began and How It Ended" 377

F. Writings of Charles Fox Parham

Introduction 380
92. Parham's Theological, Social, and Racial Views 380
93. Letter from Bro. Parham [to Azusa Mission] 381
94. Letter from Charles Parham to Mrs. Sarah Parham / Apostolic Faith 382
95. "A Note of Warning" 382
96. "The Sealing" 383
97. Hell 383
98. Source of Disease 383
99. Baptism of the Holy Ghost 384

100. Criticisms of Azusa Street   384
101. "Leadership"   385
102. "Unity"   386
103. "Free-Love"   386
104. E. N. Bell, Notice about Parham   387

NOTES   389
BIBLIOGRAPHY   411
INDEX   429

FOREWORD

HARVEY COX,
HOLLIS RESEARCH PROFESSOR OF DIVINITY,
HARVARD UNIVERSITY

When a travel-weary itinerant Jewish preacher walked into Athens sometime around 52 CE, no one who spotted him would have guessed that an epochal spiritual transformation was underway and that he was its harbinger. But what the Apostle Paul said there on Mars Hill marked just such an upheaval. When a young Augustinian monk from the nether regions of northern Germany came to Rome in 1510 no one could have known that he would return home to tack some theses on a church door and launch a historic reformation. Likewise, anyone waiting to board a train at the Los Angeles railway station on February 22, 1906, who even noticed a somewhat disheveled black man climbing out of a train from Houston would probably not have favored him with a second look. But the appearance in the City of the Angels of a Holiness preacher named William Joseph Seymour ranks with these other arrivals as the beginning of an epochal turning point in the religious history of the world. Before Seymour left Los Angeles, the present day Pentecostal movement was to be born, a spiritual tsunami that would eventually engulf the entire globe.

It was not that Los Angeles was in a welcoming mood for this kind of newcomer. At the very moment Seymour climbed down the ladder to the platform one Joseph Widney, later to be president of the University of Southern California, was writing an opus entitled *Race Life of the Aryan People*. Widney predicted that despite the takeover of some eastern cities by immigrants, Los Angeles would become a stronghold of Protestant Caucasian power and influence. But history had other plans for the city. It was already becoming the destination for a wide variety of people—black, brown, and yellow—who would hardly count as Aryan. The city would become the cradle and manger of a spiritual New Jerusalem radically at variance from Widney's xenophobic vision.

St. Paul, Martin Luther, and William Joseph Seymour all had certain things in common. St. Paul had utterly no intention of "founding a new religion." He crisscrossed the Mediterranean area speaking to both Jews and Gentiles, trying to convince the former that the Messiah they had been expecting for centuries had in fact come and that the ancient promise that the Gentiles would one day enter into the commonwealth of Israel had been accomplished. He did not ask them to leave their inherited faith but to recognize this new and final stage of its history. His message to Gentiles was that because of God's action in Jesus Christ they were no longer "outsiders" to the divine promises. The wall had been broken down, and they were now fellow citizens with Jews in a new and inclusive spiritual covenant.

Nor did Luther have any intention of founding a church or a denomination, least of all one that would bear his name. Like many of his contemporaries, he insisted that the Catholic Church needed to be radically reformed and rescued from what he considered the fabricated and malicious leadership of the papacy. For his part, Seymour was convinced that God was pouring down a new shower of blessings, a "latter rain," on the whole church, cleansing it from its sinful divisions along racial and denominational lines. All three men had the whole church, the entire people of God, indeed the whole world in mind.

None of these three singular men foresaw what the results of their labors would be, and perhaps that is just as well since all three would surely have been both pleased and deeply disappointed. After some two centuries of porous borders between what would eventually be called "Christian" and Jewish congregations a certain parting of the ways took place, although current historical research indicates the split was never as severe as earlier scholars believed. When eventually the prelates of the Roman Catholic Church responded to Luther's effort to reform it, they excommunicated him, and the reformation was ultimately confined to the northern regions of Europe. Its universal hopes were dashed. Likewise William Joseph Seymour would have been horrified to think that the revival he encouraged, beginning at Azusa Street, would one day be viewed as a congeries of separate "denominations." His fond hope was that those who were touched by the new outpouring of the Holy Spirit, with gifts of prophecy, tongues, and healing would return to their own congregations as joyful bearers of this good news. The sad fact is that when they tried to, most of them were ridiculed, shunned, and expelled. When they eventually went their separate ways it was with bitter disappointment and great reluctance.

There is another fascinating parallel. St. Paul, Luther, and Seymour were not lone rangers. There were evidently other messengers spreading the gospel in places like Ephesus and Corinth at the time of Paul. He respected some of them. They "sowed and watered," he writes. Some of them he distrusted and opposed. His epistles warn against teachers of false doctrine. Still, when the dust of history settled it became clear that St. Paul played a preeminent role, a first among equals. Luther had other reformers to contend with too. Acting on the same stage at the same time were such formidable figures as Bucer,

Melanchton, Karlstadt, Muntzer, and of course, John Calvin. Some had ideas close to Luther's. Some were to his right and some to his left. Luther engaged with many of them, cooperated when he could, disagreed when he thought he had to, and sometimes lashed out with fierce polemic. In one sense there were multiple "reformations" going on in early sixteenth-century Europe. All these figures played their parts in the drama. But, again, it is hard to imagine what we now call "the" Reformation without the towering person and driving inspiration of the monk from Wittenberg.

One of the finest features of this volume is that Espinosa boldly enters the heated arguments about Seymour's role in the birth of Pentecostalism, gives all parties their due, but still persuades at least this reader that both Seymour and the Azusa revival played a central role in the appearance of the modern Pentecostal movement. He does this in three ways. First, he includes here all the confirmed writings on spiritual and theological topics that researchers agree come from Seymour's own hand. Second, he includes other invaluable sources from the early days and years of the movement. Third, and perhaps most important, he sketches out a biography of Seymour himself, filling out his portrait with a cautious and evenhanded examination of the theses and theories advanced by other serious scholars. He explains and respects their contributions, but comes out with an assessment of the critical place of Seymour that any subsequent writer must contend with.

Still, after all is said and done, the question remains: Does William Joseph Seymour belong in this gallery of spiritual giants and world changers? I think the answer is yes, but the issue is still disputed. Do numbers count for anything? Religious demographers now estimate the count of Pentecostals and Charismatic Christians as approximately 630 million. That places them as the second most numerous Christian family, just behind Roman Catholics, but ahead of Protestants and Eastern Orthodox. Yet, despite their astonishing growth, especially during the past half century, scholarly attention to them was pathetically sparse until the past two decades. Just as inexplicable has been the lack of attention paid to Seymour. Wander the aisles of any library and you will find whole shelves, often whole sections, devoted to St. Paul and to Martin Luther. This is as it should be, but the wholesale discounting of Seymour is hard to explain. It is painful to think that such patent disregard might stem, at least in part, from racism. Does a one-eyed Black man, a son of former slaves, with no formal education really belong in this Christian pantheon? Now, however, with this present volume, and with others appearing, the gap is being filled.

Remember the parable of the mustard seed. Momentous things sometimes spring from small beginnings, and the advent of the Pentecostal wave was surely one of these. Espinosa conjures the scene on Bonnie Brae Street and later at 312 Azusa Street in fascinating detail. Picture a leaky frame building, formerly an AME church but recently converted to a stable, nestled among a tombstone store, a lumberyard, and stockyards. It was an edifice where the scent of horses rather than incense perfumed the air. Picture maids and chauffeurs, laundry workers and garbage collectors, men and women, all crowded into what was sometimes a stifling space to welcome the cooling downpour of blessings. Many, but not all, were poor or bordering on poor. But there was also a sprinkling of middle-class attendees. And imagine, at the cruel nadir of Jim Crow and lynching elsewhere in America, a tiny oasis where black and white, Latino and Asian seekers sang, prayed, and hugged each other at one makeshift altar.

Quietly presiding over it all was William Joseph Seymour, surveying the scene with his one good eye (the other had been blinded by smallpox). Sometimes black or white women stood to preach or testify. Often many of the worshippers repaired to a small cottage behind the main building where they ate in the same mixed company. Together these unlikely candidates for history-making created what Espinosa calls a "transgressive space." As Espinosa writes, Azusa was multi-racial-ethnic from the first day it opened its doors on April 15, 1906. In the power of the Spirit they were crafting a new and radically inclusive human community in which man-made barriers were erased, a foretaste of the Kingdom of God.

But others found their way to Azusa Street as well. Attracted by the sensational, sometimes salacious, coverage of the "holy rollers" in the secular press, the curious, the ridiculers, and the just plain nosy descended on the little chapel in which services continued three times a day, seven days a week for three years. Some left disgusted. They were enraged by the open flaunting of customary racial boundaries. But others, as Pentecostals like to say, "Came to scorn and stayed to pray." In any case, the movement grew and spread . . . and eventually, sadly, fragmented, but still continued to grow.

It is important to note that for Seymour, racial integration and justice were not merely items on a "social action" agenda as they have become for many churches and denominations since. These ideals were theological. As mentioned above, he believed that God was sending the Holy Spirit in these latter days to purge the church of its sinful man-made divisions and to present her as a spotless bride, prepared for the coming of the divine bridegroom whose descent was expected soon. Here we have another intriguing comparison with St. Paul and Luther, both of whom also believed, though in somewhat different terms, that they were living in the end times. This in turn points to a deeper theological enigma. If radical renewal upheavals often come in response to eschatological expectations, what happens to them when the expected fulfillment does not come to pass, at least in the manner in which it had been anticipated? The fruits of St. Paul's preaching and teaching did not evaporate even after the Lord did not descend on a cloud.

Five hundred years after Luther defied Rome, the denominations that trace their roots to the sixteenth century are still with us. And after the longed-for consummation Seymour proclaimed in the early years of the twentieth century did not appear, Pentecostalism is thriving. Furthermore in one of its multiple expressions it is flourishing in "faraway places" like China and Africa to which he had dispatched missionaries, and wanted to send more.

From a historical perspective it is virtually impossible to sort out just how much of the Pentecostal explosion stems exclusively or mainly from Azusa Street. There were demonstrably other very similar revivals, some including tongue-speaking, prophecy, and healing, already in progress when the news from Azusa Street arrived. Espinosa gives these movements careful and balanced attention. But in the end he insists, and I think rightly, on the indispensable role of Seymour and Azusa Street. Indeed, I know of no other volume that deals so comprehensively with just how the Azusa DNA found its way to all corners of the earth.

Finally, what about Seymour's theology? Seymour himself has not made it easy for later generations to know what he thought. A modest person, he often did not attach his name to the articles he wrote for the weekly newspaper, *The Apostolic Faith*, which he began publishing right away in 1906. But by now careful students of the paper have confirmed the pieces written by Seymour himself from 1906 until 1908, and as I have pointed out above, Espinosa has included them all in this volume. In doing so he has rendered a remarkable service to ordinary readers and scholars alike. Now, one can study what Seymour wrote on a wide variety of topics, from the new birth and the plan of salvation to the nature of God and the human soul. In incorporating these precious writings, along with other key documents, in this volume Espinosa has not only greatly strengthened the value of the book, he has also provided a model of how future studies should be prepared. The format itself suggests a kind of Pentecostal spirit. It is anti-elitist, inviting the reader not just to accept the judgment of the expert but to join in the process of historical reflection.

Who can say what a future evaluation of Seymour and Azusa Street, written, say, in 2106 at the two hundredth anniversary, might conclude about their place in Christian and world history? But whatever future scholars decide on these matters, this evocative portrait of the one-eyed preacher and this collection of key writings will have to be taken into consideration.

Harvey Cox, Hollis Research Professor of Divinity at Harvard, is the author of *Fire from Heaven: The Rise of Pentecostal Spirituality and the Reshaping of Religion in the Twenty-first Century* and *The Future of Faith*.

PREFACE

This book analyzes the life and ministry of William J. Seymour, the Azusa Street Revival, and his influence on global Pentecostal origins through an introduction, biography, and documentary history. It is similar to and yet different from Larry Martin's very fine theologically framed and self-published eight-volume "Azusa Street Library." The first volume is a biography followed by seven short primary source books. As a Pentecostal "revival evangelist," he stated that he created the series to inspire "a hunger in the hearts of the people of God."[1]

This present book covers much of the same material in half of Martins' eight volumes. It differs because it is the most comprehensive collection of materials on Seymour, Azusa, and his influence on Pentecostal origins in one volume that is academic in tone, critical in analysis, comprehensive in scope and vision, and yet also written for the general public. It also takes a historical and phenomenological approach to the study of Pentecostalism that seeks to—in the words of Mircea Eliade—interpret religious traditions, experiences, and practitioners on their own plane of reference from a critical but fair-minded scholarly perspective. Drawing on Ninian Smart's methodological notion of bracketed realism, it seeks neither to affirm or deny the truth claims of its subjects, but rather to understand them in light of their larger socio-religious context.[2] Despite its comprehensiveness, it is not a general history of Pentecostal origins and development in every single country around the world, but rather a study that focuses exclusively on Seymour's life, Azusa Street revival, and influence on global Pentecostal origins from 1906 to 1912 in select countries like England, Norway, Sweden, Liberia, South Africa, India, and China.

This book begins by defining key theological terms and phrases and explains the differences between Pentecostals, Charismatics, and Neo-Charismatics, and then provides a historiographical overview of how Seymour has been interpreted over the past one hundred years. Next it provides a short biography that analyzes Seymour's life and ministry, his relationship with Charles Fox Parham, both of their views on race relations, and

Seymour's influence on global Pentecostal origins from 1906 to 1912 in the aforecited countries. The 104 primary-source documentary history that follows provides brief introductions to each entry and insight into Seymour, his influence, and how his followers and critics viewed him. It is divided into six sections: Seymour's Spiritual Writings, Seymour's *Doctrines and Discipline* minister's manual, Azusa Street Revival accounts in the *Apostolic Faith*, histories and testimonies of Seymour and the Azusa Revival, critics of Seymour and the Revival, and Parham's writings. Included are selections in whole or part from letters, testimonies, diaries, autobiographical accounts, editorials, reports, newspaper articles, and oral histories. Since Seymour's authorship of other unsigned editorials cannot be unequivocally confirmed, they are not included.

This book also differs from others because it includes in one volume all of Seymour's extant writings in full and without alteration or abbreviation. No changes have been made to his grammar, punctuation, or syntax. In select cases, brackets have been provided to clarify to whom the author is referring. Eyewitness and early secondary accounts about Seymour have been abbreviated due to strict space limitations. However, the content of the reproduced portions is identical to the originals.

Parham's writings are included because they reveal how he viewed Seymour, race relations, tongues and the spiritual gifts, his split with Seymour in 1906, and their differing theological, social, and racial views. To ensure a critical, comprehensive, and well-rounded understanding of Seymour, highly critical accounts of Seymour and the Azusa Revival are also included.

Unlike other reprintings of Seymour's *Doctrines and Discipline* manual, the version in this book has not been altered. The verb tenses, punctuation, grammatical and spelling errors, and order, structure, and arrangement are identical to the 1915 original.

To capture the rich racial-ethnic diversity of the Revival and its influence globally, this book includes African-American, Latino, Swedish, and Irish immigrant testimonies, and reports by Azusa evangelists preaching to Native Americans along with their reported responses. Also included are testimonies by missionaries, evangelists, and lay leaders who were influenced by Seymour and spread his vision and version of Pentecostalism around the world. Finally, this book provides a chronology, a bibliography, thirty-five photographs and illustrations, and an index that cross-references all primary and secondary sources.

ACKNOWLEDGMENTS

My interest in William J. Seymour was sparked while a master's student at Harvard University. In 1992–93, I took a pivotal graduate seminar with Harvey Cox and Eldin Villafañe on Pentecostalism and liberation theology, and learned that little had been published about Seymour and the Latino contributions to the Azusa Street Revival. This set me on a journey to explore the historical origins of the North American Latino Pentecostal movement. For my doctoral dissertation, I tracked down every available source on Seymour, the Revival, and Latino Pentecostal origins. I canvassed archives and private collections in the United States, Mexico, Puerto Rico, and Europe and wrote one chapter on Seymour and another on the Mexican contributions to Azusa. This along with twenty years of ongoing research gave birth to two books. The first is this present volume and the second is *Latino Pentecostals in America: Faith and Politics in Action* (Harvard University Press, 2014). I decided to publish this short biography and comprehensive collection of sources about Seymour's life and work for scholars and the general public. This final version is half its original length.

I am indebted to Glenn Gohr of the Assemblies of God (AG) Archives. An excellent archivist and grammarian, Gohr tirelessly tracked down key documents and read through all of Seymour's sermons and *Doctrines and Discipline* minister's manual to make sure that the retyped texts were identical to the originals, though I take responsibility for any mistakes or omissions. I also want to thank Wayne Warner and the Flower Pentecostal Heritage Center staff for their kind assistance. A heartfelt thank you is due to my family for their support and to assistants Lois Gundry and Karen Gluck for transcribing the primary sources from the originals and Ulrike Guthrie for editing the manuscript. I also want to thank Harvey Cox, Catherine Albanese, David Daniels, Candy Gunther-Brown, Amos Yong, Michael McClymond, Jan-Åke Alvarsson, Jason Stevens, David Yoo, Mario T. García, and others for their critical feedback on various drafts of this manuscript over the years or more recently and Michael McGowan, Bryan Cottle, and Benji Rolsky for assisting in its production. Finally, this project would not have been completed without the generous support over the years of Jim Lewis and the Louisville Institute for the Study of American Religion, James Leech and the National Endowment for the Humanities (NEH), Kent Mulliken and the National Humanities Center (NHC), and Presidents Pamela Gann and Hiram Chodosh and deans William Ascher and Gregory Hess of Claremont McKenna College. Finally, I thank Valerie Millholland, Miriam Angress, Sara Leone, and Duke University Press for their enthusiastic support.

SEYMOUR TIMELINE

ca. 1841	Simon Seymour born in St. Mary Parish, Louisiana
1844	Phillis Salabar born on Adilard Carlin Plantation, St. Mary Parish
1867	Simon and Phillis married by white Methodist Reverend R. K. Diossy on July 27
1870	Seymour baptized on September 4 by Father M. Harnais at the Catholic Church of the Assumption, Franklin, Louisiana
1891–1905	Travels throughout South and Midwest
1905	Meets Lucy Farrow and attends Parham's Houston Bible School
1906	Arrives in Los Angeles on February 22, Spirit falls on April 9, Azusa Mission begins services on April 15
1906	Sends missionaries to Sweden, Liberia, South Africa, China, and India
1908	Prints fifty thousand copies of his *Apostolic Faith* newspaper per month with 405,000 total copies printed; tensions with Crawford, Carpenter, Lum
1909	Ordains Abundio López; tension between an Azusa leader and Mexicans
1911	Durham leads second Azusa Revival and fails to take over Azusa Mission
1913	Oneness controversy splits Second Pentecostal Camp Meeting in Pasadena
1914	Revises Azusa Mission Constitution and Articles of Incorporation
1915	Publishes *Doctrines and Discipline* minister's manual
1916–17	Promotes racial reconciliation and unity
1918	Visits Aimee McPherson's Los Angeles revival as a quiet spectator
1919	Promotes Christian unity at Church of God in Christ (COGIC) Convention
1920	Promotes Christian unity across races at fourteenth Azusa Anniversary
1921	Promotes Christian unity across races and at COGIC Convention
1922	William Seymour dies from heart attack on September 28
1931	Azusa Mission torn down
1936	Jennie Seymour dies on July 2

William Seymour. Used by permission of the Flower Pentecostal Heritage Center.

Introduction
DEFINITIONS AND ONE HUNDRED YEARS OF HISTORIOGRAPHY ON SEYMOUR

GASTÓN ESPINOSA

The Pentecostal movement is one of the most powerful and fastest growing grassroots religious movements in the world today. This book explores William J. Seymour, the Azusa Street Revival, and his influence on global Pentecostal origins across the U.S. and around the world from 1906 to 1912 in select countries like England, Norway, Sweden, Liberia, South Africa, China, and India.[1] The following chapter will set the context for the biography and documentary history by defining key terms, phrases, and movements and by providing an historical overview of how Seymour has been interpreted over the past one hundred years.

Most scholars break the global Pentecostal movement into three main groupings: Denominational Pentecostals (Classical Pentecostals/ Pentecostals) (16 percent), Charismatics (Protestant, Catholic, Orthodox) (39 percent), and Neo-Charismatics (Independents/Postindependents/ Nondenominationals) (45 percent). In this study, denominational and classical Pentecostals will simply be referred to as Pentecostals. Pentecostalism's proliferation into twenty-three thousand denominations has understandably led some to question whether it's even possible to define a Pentecostal and a global Pentecostal movement.[2] While clearly there are many streams and combinative theological traditions that feed into the larger global movement, there are nonetheless two salient beliefs and experiences that tend to unite most Pentecostals, Charismatics, and Neo-Charismatics around the world. The first is the necessity of having a personal, born-again conversion experience with Jesus Christ and the second is a desire to be baptized and filled with the Holy Spirit—or being "born-again and Spirit-filled." Contrary to stereotypes, a person does not have to speak in tongues to be considered a Pentecostal or Charismatic Christian, but they normally desire to do so. These core beliefs reportedly helped unite forty-five thousand Pentecostals, Charismatics, and Neo-Charismatics from 113 countries around the world in spiritual unity across races, languages, denominations, and nationalities at the Azusa Street Revival Centennial Celebration in Los Angeles on April 25–29, 2006, where participants claimed there was no confusion about the movement's main identity and core distinctives, despite their own unique denominations, customs, and theological traditions.[3]

TONGUES AND THE BAPTISM WITH THE HOLY SPIRIT

Pentecostals take their name from Acts 2:4, where on the "Day of Pentecost" the Holy Spirit reportedly fell on the Apostles and they began to speak in unknown tongues. They affirm all of the spiritual gifts listed in the New Testament, including tongues, prophecy, service, evangelism, wisdom, knowledge, pastoring, teaching, exhortation, faith, healing, working miracles, distinguishing/discerning spirits, casting out evil spirits, contributing, giving aid, mercy, administration, interpretation of tongues, and apostleship (I Cor. 12:8–10, 28–30; Ephesians 4:11; Rom. 12:6–8; 1 Pet. 4:11; Mark 16:17). Today many Pentecostals, Charismatics, and Neo-Charismatics teach that all of the above gifts are available except apostleship, which they believed was reserved for the New Testament period—though a small but growing sector of the movement argues that this gift is also available today.

Pentecostals teach that the baptism in the Holy Spirit is normally evidenced by speaking in tongues. Tongues are considered a supernatural manifestation of the Holy Spirit (Acts 2:4, 10:46, 19:6; I Cor. 12:10) that is available to all born-again Christians (John 3:3) regardless of a person's race, class, gender, nationality, or Christian denominational affiliation. For this reason, the Pentecostal/Charismatic movement often transcends these boundaries. There are two types of tongues: a divinely given human language one has never studied (xenolalia—Acts 2) and a divinely given language known only to God (glossolalia—in all other accounts in Acts 8:17–19, 10:44–46, 19:1–6).

The modern classical Pentecostal movement in the United States was born in the wake of Charles Fox Parham's Topeka Bible School revival in 1901 and William J. Seymour's Azusa Street Revival in Los Angeles from 1906 to 1909. Pentecostalism was influenced by nineteenth-century Protestant evangelicalism, the Holiness and Keswick movements, revival and divine healing movements, and African American spirituality.[4] Parham and Seymour (for a short time) taught that the baptism in the Holy Spirit *must* be evidenced by speaking in unknown tongues, which they believed was a divinely given human language one had never studied. This developed into the initial evidence theory and has been adopted by the Assemblies of God, Church of God (Cleveland), Foursquare, Pentecostal Assemblies of the World, and other denominations. However, by October 1906 Seymour and later F. F. Bosworth, Charles Mason, G. A. Cook, and most global Pentecostals taught that tongues was just one of the evidences of the Spirit baptism and that it could manifest itself as xenolalia or glossolalia. Parham never changed his view that it must always be xenolalia.[5]

The main purposes of tongues are to empower people to carry out cross-cultural missionary work, to communicate a divine message for the Christian community, and to serve as a private prayer language known only to God. Pentecostals teach that tongues should only be spoken in a public setting when someone is present to interpret them for the edification of the congregation. For these reasons, Paul stated: "Do not forbid speaking in tongues," but practice them "decently and in order" (I Cor. 14:4, 12, 33, 39–40)—something Seymour never forgot.

Despite Paul's admonition, Protestants like Benjamin Warfield, Cyrus Scofield, and more recently Hank Hanegraaff and John MacArthur, teach that the spiritual "sign" gifts like tongues, healing, exorcism, and prophecy noted in Mark 16:17–18 and elsewhere ceased to be practiced and needed after the death of the Apostles.[6] This "cessationist" conviction led some conservative evangelicals—often conservative Baptists and Presbyterians—to break off fellowship with Pentecostals. However, some softened their views and joined forces with white Pentecostals to form the National Association of Evangelicals (NAE) in 1942 to exercise a national voice in American public life.[7]

PENTECOSTALS IN THE U.S.

Protestant Pentecostals in the U.S. trace their roots back to Parham, Seymour, Ambrose Tomlinson, Charles Mason, G. T. Haywood, F. M. Britton, J. H. King, and others before 1950 and attend classical Pentecostal denominations like the Assemblies of God, Church of God in Christ, United Pentecostal Church, Church of God (Cleveland), International Pentecostal Holiness Church, Foursquare Church, and other denominations and independent churches.

They generally come in two theological varieties: Trinitarian and Oneness. Most affirm the Trinity (God as one essence in three distinct persons) and the fundamentals of the Protestant evangelical faith: biblical inerrancy, the virgin birth, the deity of Christ, Jesus's bodily resurrection from the dead, salvation through Christ alone, and Jesus's second coming. Oneness Pentecostals affirm these doctrines except the traditional Christian view of the Trinity, which they deem tri-theistic or the belief in three separate Gods. Instead, they argue the Trinity is three modes of the same one person—Jesus. They argue that Matthew 28:19–20 teaches people to baptize in the "name" of the Father, the Son, and the Holy Spirit. That "name," they reason from the context, is Jesus. They also teach that Acts 2:38 proves the apostles baptized people in the name of Jesus only. Therefore, all Trinitarians must be rebaptized in only Jesus's name. The largest U.S. Oneness denominations are the United Pentecostal Church (white), Pentecostal Assemblies of the World (black), and Apostolic Assembly of the Faith in Christ Jesus (Latino).[8]

EVANGELICAL, FUNDAMENTALIST, AND MAINLINE PROTESTANTS IN THE U.S.

Because many evangelical and mainline historic Protestants do not believe that speaking in tongues is the main or only evidence of the baptism with the Holy Spirit or a vital part of the Christian life, it is important to define all three groups. The English word *evangelical* comes from the Greek *evangelion*, which means "good news." An evangelical is therefore someone who preaches the Good News about Jesus's life, death, and resurrection from the dead, his sacrificial love for all of humanity, and the need for people to repent of their sins and have a personal born-again conversion experience and relationship with Jesus Christ (John 3:3, 3:16; Romans 3:23, 6:23, 10:9–10). Although born-again Christians can be found in every denomination, the term *evangelical* is largely applied to politically, theologically, and morally conservative Protestants. While most Pentecostals are "born-again" and thus "evangelical," not all evangelicals are Pentecostal/Charismatic because they don't believe the spiritual sign gifts should be practiced in the church today.[9]

In this book, "evangelical" will generally refer to socially progressive but theologically conservative Protestants who affirm the fundamentals of the faith, but who are not Pentecostal, Charismatic, Neo-Charismatic, or Fundamentalist. Evangelical denominations include the Southern, Conservative, and Freewill Baptists; Free Methodists; Evangelical Free; Evangelical Covenant; Presbyterian—EPC and PCA, and independent non-Charismatic churches. However, one can find Charismatic Christians who believe in the gifts of the Holy Spirit in almost all Evangelical denominations and churches as well.

"Fundamentalist" refers to socially and theologically conservative anti-modernist militant Protestants who fought to preserve the fundamentals of the faith from skeptics and liberal Protestants. They generally hold to a premillennial dispensationalist and/or a cessationist position on the gifts of the Holy Spirit. In 1928, the World Christian Fundamentalist Association rejected Pentecostals as a "fanatical" "menace" to Christians for promoting tongues, divine healing, the ordination of women, and the sign gifts.[10] For these reasons and others, Pentecostals/Charismatics should not be strictly classified as fundamentalists.

"Mainline" or "historic" Protestants trace their roots back to Martin Luther, John Calvin, and the Protestant Reformation in Europe after 1517. Although originally evangelical in theological orientation, most mainline Protestants today are moderate-liberal in their theology and social ethics, though some conservatives remain. The largest mainline denominations include the Presbyterians (PCUSA), United Methodists (UMC), Episcopalians, United Church of Christ (UCC), Lutherans (ELCA), Disciples of Christ, and American Baptists.

CHARISMATICS

Charismatics are Christians in non-Pentecostal/Charismatic denominations (Protestant, Catholic, Orthodox) who believe the spiritual gifts are available to all Christians today, though some exclude the gift of apostleship because they believe it was reserved only for Jesus's Apostles. They affirm a born-again, Spirit-filled life but normally do not mandate that a person must speak in tongues after conversion. Most believe that one receives all of the Holy Spirit at conversion. Charismatics are found in almost all Christian denominations and nondenominational and interdenominational churches. The modern Charismatic movement in the U.S. began in the 1960s when Episcopalian Dennis Bennett; Lutheran Larry Christenson; Catholics Kilian McDonnell, Francis McNutt, Edward O'Connor, and others promoted the spiritual gifts within their traditions. The movement quickly spread and today there are Charismatics in Presbyterian, Baptist, Episcopalian, Methodist, Catholic, Orthodox, Anglican, and many other Christian denominations and independent churches around the world.[11]

NEO-CHARISMATICS

Neo-Charismatics in the United States grew out of classical Pentecostal bodies, but left to form their own independent Charismatic churches and denominations during the countercultural movement of the 1960s and 1970s. They generally affirm many classical Pentecostal beliefs, but tend to deemphasize speaking in tongues, public manifestations of the spiritual gifts, strict dress codes, and social prohibitions against dancing, wearing cosmetics, and other non-essentials. Few require affirmation of the initial evidence theory. Leaders of the Jesus Movement in the U.S. reached out to hippies, youth, and others in the 1960s and 1970s. Neo-Charismatics emphasize evangelism, expository Bible teaching, guitar- and band-led worship services, and a relaxed, "laid-back," and "come as you are" informal style and atmosphere, which has appealed to youth, families, and the unchurched. The most popular Neo-Charismatic leaders and traditions include Chuck Smith and Calvary Chapel (Costa Mesa, California), John Wimber and the Vineyard Christian Fellowship, Hope Chapel, and Sonny Arguinzoni and Victory Outreach International (La Puente, California), among others. Many were birthed in Southern California and have spread globally.[12]

There are other Neo-Charismatic movements around the world today with no structural ties to the U.S. They often emerged during this same period out of indigenous Pentecostal or Charismatic churches and traditions in their own countries. They range in style from very formal to very casual and tend to be theologically conservative-moderate, though some can be moderate-progressive on social justice, race, and separation of church and state issues, because in Latin America, Africa, and Asia they are often a working-class religious minority. Others can be quite socially and politically conservative and can manifest themselves through megachurches and prosperity Gospel-oriented churches, which have brought much ill repute on the movement.

However, Donald Miller and Tetsunao Yamamori note that other progressively oriented Pentecostal and Charismatic megachurches defy such simplistic stereotyping since many are relatively nonpolitical and are providing some of the most innovative grassroots social programs in the developing world today. In fact, when he sent letters to four hundred denominational, mission, and other experts around the world to name the fastest growing self-supporting indigenous churches in the developing world that have active social programs, he found that 85 percent of those nominated were Pentecostal or Charismatic. He argued that they were not trying to reform society or challenge the political system like liberation theology or the social gospel movement, but rather attempting to build "from the ground up" and an "alternative social reality." All of this, they contend, puts "one more nail in the coffin of secularization theory," which predicted the growing privatization of religion and that supernatural healing would be replaced by medical science. They argue that neither took place and that people are moving in and out of both worlds and that Pentecostals—reportedly among the most otherworldly of all Christian groups—are increasingly involved in community development and other social programs that are attracting the allegiances of the masses and making religion a vital force in the world today.[13]

Neo-Charismatics have contributed to a growing evangelical pop subculture around the world with evangelistically oriented Christian rock, rap, R&B, hip-hop, and pop bands and innovative worship groups like Hill Song and Jesus Culture. They have also generated their own clothing styles, videos, books, sports teams, music bands, magazines, art, plays, and musicals. They attract large numbers of racial-ethnic minorities and urban youth via evangelistic campaigns like Greg Laurie's "Harvest Crusades" at Anaheim Stadium in California, which has attracted 4.4 million people over the past decade.[14] The thread that binds Pentecostals, Charismatics, and Neo-Charismatics together is their common born-again and Spirit-filled experiences. This is why scholars often call it the Pentecostal/Charismatic movement.

SEYMOUR AND THE ORIGINS OF THE GLOBAL PENTECOSTAL MOVEMENT

Contrary to recent claims, Seymour played a critical role in global Pentecostal origins. The movement he helped originate has blossomed into 612 million people attending twenty-three thousand Pentecostal/Charismatic/Neo-Charismatic denominations around the world. While there has been substantial growth over the past century, it is important to avoid statistical triumphalism and to recognize that only slightly more than half of these people see themselves as part of the classical Pentecostal and Charismatic traditions, the two strands of the movement Seymour and his spiritual progeny most directly and indirectly influenced. Despite Seymour's importance, most people know surprisingly little about his life and ministry and fewer still have read his writings. His story is important not only for understanding American religion and Pentecostalism, but also global Christianity and the rise of Pentecostal/Charismatic movements in the global South.[15]

Seymour's quiet influence is not only evident in his current spiritual descendants like Church of God in Christ bishop Charles Blake, the Potter's House bishop T. D. Jakes, Assemblies of God superintendent George O. Wood, German evangelist to Africa Reinhard Bonnke, and countless others, but also increasingly in American politics through hitherto unknown African-American leaders such as Reverend Joshua DuBois and Reverend Leah Daughtry. DuBois was ordained in the heavily African American Trinitarian United Pentecostal Council of the Assemblies of God, headquartered in New England. During the 2008 U.S. election, DuBois ran Barack Obama's outreach to all faith communities across the United States and Reverend Daughtry ran the Democratic National Convention. They reflected Seymour's spirit by helping Obama reach out across religious and racial divides to win the election. As a result, DuBois was appointed director of the White House Office of Faith-Based and Neighborhood Partnerships, the highest office in the nation assigned with a task that Seymour himself promoted a century earlier—to build bridges across the religious, class, and racial divides in society. DuBois continued this influence by writing Christian devotional reflections for President Obama every day during his first five years in office. In each devotional entry for President Obama, he quoted a Bible passage, wrote a spiritual reflection, and then provided a short prayer. The purpose was to challenge President Obama to follow Jesus Christ and to "live a life of purpose and joy."[16]

Seymour's influence through his spiritual descendants has been bipartisan. Pentecostal evangelist Arthur Blessitt prayed with then Texas governor George W. Bush to receive Jesus Christ as his personal Savior; presidential candidate John McCain selected Alaska governor Sarah Palin to serve as his vice presidential running mate in 2008; and President George W. Bush appointed Missouri senator John Ashcroft U.S. Attorney General. Palin and Ashcroft attended Assemblies of God churches, which are members of a denomination based in Springfield, Missouri, that traces its roots back to Seymour, Parham, and the Azusa Street Revival. The Pentecostal influence in public life is a global trend that reflects Seymour's socially liberative message that the Spirit baptism breaks down all human-made racial, class, educational, and national barriers and unites all born-again, Spirit-filled Christians into one body of believers.[17]

HISTORIOGRAPHY ON WILLIAM J. SEYMOUR AND GLOBAL PENTECOSTAL ORIGINS

SEYMOUR IN FIRST-GENERATION HISTORIES

Despite Seymour's growing importance today, his life, ministry, and influence have been downplayed and diminished over the past one hundred years. This is because many books on Pentecostalism, American religious history, and world Christianity have until recently argued that Parham was the father, founder, or originator of Pentecostalism, or Parham and Seymour were cofounders with Seymour serving as Parham's popularizer, or that Seymour was one among many founders.

One of the first leaders to criticize Seymour's message was none other than his former teacher Charles Fox Parham. After Parham broke fellowship with Seymour in October 1906, he argued that Seymour promoted a "counterfeit" revival. He claimed that Seymour's success was due to the residual "element" of truth he had received at Parham's Houston Bible School, but which was soon overshadowed by the "fanaticism" and "fleshly" "Negro" practices at Azusa, which were "pawned off on people all over the world as the working of the Holy Spirit."[18]

Despite Parham's criticisms, Sarah—his wife—argued after her husband's death that Seymour "received all of the truths and teachings" that we "held from the beginning" and implied that he popularized Parham's views to the masses. As a result of her reconstruction and others like B. F. Lawrence, Parham was largely hailed the "father," "founder," and/or "originator" of Pentecostalism. This subtle shift from calling Seymour a counterfeit propagator to a Parham popularizer has been overlooked by writers seeking to emphasize their spiritual continuity and unity. From 1916 to 1970 writers also tended to overlook Parham's controversial theological, social, and racial views, allegations of misconduct, and the Parham-Seymour split in October 1906.[19]

First- and second-generation Pentecostal writers like B. F. Lawrence, Frank Bartleman, Stanley Frodsham, and others promoted one of four explanations for Pentecostal origins: Holy Spirit as originator, Parham as originator, Seymour as nominal leader, and/or spontaneous outpouring of the Spirit on multiple leaders and centers.[20] Many writers saw Parham as the founder and driving human force behind Pentecostal origins. Perhaps because some were embarrassed by Seymour's race and limited education and Parham's alleged misconduct, most simply claimed God was the founder.

So Lawrence wrote in *The Apostolic Faith Restored* (1916): "Many have made the claim that this blessed revival originated among the colored associates of Bro. Seymour. These reports . . . are unfounded in fact. The . . . doctrines were communicated to Bro. Seymour by the [white] brethren [e.g., Charles Parham and W. F. Carothers] in Houston."[21] Disagreeing with Parham and Lawrence, Bartleman wrote in *Azusa Street* (1925) that "we prayed down our own revival" and that "it came from Heaven." Seymour was the "nominal leader."[22] Frodsham wrote in *With Signs Following* (1926), "The Pentecostal revival of the twentieth-century has had no outstanding leader such as Luther or Wesley."[23]

SEYMOUR IN SECOND-GENERATION HISTORIES

By the 1940s–1950s, as white Pentecostals began to enter the evangelical mainstream through organizations like the National Association of Evangelicals (NAE), second-generation historians sought to construct a respectable human genealogy. Parham was rehabilitated by overlooking his controversial views and Seymour was assigned a duly noted secondary role.

Klaude Kendrick wrote in *The Promise Fulfilled* (1961) that Parham was the human founder and "recognized leader" of the movement and "largely determined its direction." Seymour was the humble and unpretentious "Godly" "leader in the early months," but was "superseded by men of greater natural ability"—a view adopted in African-American and Latino Pentecostal histories by Morris Golder and Miguel Guillén.[24]

In *Suddenly . . . From Heaven* (1961), Carl Brumback stated that Pentecostalism did "not begin in a back alley mission but in a mansion!" The "back alley mission" was Seymour's "mission" and the "mansion" was Parham's Topeka Bible School, which first met at "Stone Mansion." This was to be expected because "no one seemed to be in charge of the [Azusa] service . . . most of the time!" Brumback blamed the Parham-Seymour split on the latter's unwillingness to accept Parham's "corrective ministry." Yet Brumback was no fan of Parham because he criticized the Assemblies of God. However, to protect a seamless genealogy he says nothing about Parham's controversial views or Parham's split. Brumback acknowledges that Seymour was often overlooked in histories but still argued that "AZUSA" (no reference is made to Seymour) became a hallowed name in Pentecostalism. He concluded: "So, we in Pentecost glory in the fact that we have no earthly 'father.' There is no individual so outstanding that the entire Movement instinctively turns to. . . . It was not conceived in the mind of a religious genius. . . . It is . . . a 'child of the Holy Ghost.'"25

William Menzies reflected this view a decade later in *Anointed to Serve: The Story of the Assemblies of God* (1971). He approvingly cites Donald Gee's statement that Pentecostalism did "not owe its origin to any outstanding personality or religious leader, but was a *spontaneous revival*." Although Seymour was the "ostensible leader" of Azusa at least at first, it "transcended any individual human leadership." Seymour was simply one spiritual "cog" in a "chain of [divine] events" that linked the Topeka revival in 1901 with the Azusa revival in Los Angeles in 1906. However, he admitted that "Azusa" (again Seymour is not mentioned) was the "center from which the Pentecostal message rapidly spread around the world."26

Despite the fact that Seymour led the Azusa revival for three years and pastored the Azusa Mission until 1922, he is not credited as the decisive leader of the revival or as a key leader in global Pentecostal origins. In all, Seymour was assigned a noted secondary role. Furthermore, nothing was said about the ways he and Parham differed in their theological, racial, and social views on central issues like the Holy Spirit baptism, white supremacy, and annihilationism; their October 1906 split; or how Seymour uniquely contributed to the movement's origins. Downplaying these factors enabled them to preserve the movement's orthodoxy and white racial pedigree and provided a seamless genealogy from the Holy Spirit to Parham to Seymour on down to their own traditions. It also enabled them to keep white leadership as the driving human force behind their origins.

SEYMOUR IN THIRD-GENERATION HISTORIES

These theories dominated Pentecostal historiography until the early 1970s, when scholars began to criticize them in light of newly discovered sources, the civil rights movement, and the new social, racial-ethnic, and Two-Thirds World histories. Walter Hollenweger, Vinson Synan, James Tinney, Leonard Lovett, Douglas Nelson, Cecil Robeck, and more recently Harvey Cox, David Daniels, and Estrelda Alexander, spotlighted Pentecostalism's black origins. Robert Mapes Anderson, James Goff, and others reaffirmed Parham's primacy, though also duly acknowledging Seymour's contributions.

Hollenweger argued that Seymour's contributions "were shamefully hidden away" by whites and that his message carried within it African-American cultural sensibilities and practices including: (1) oral liturgy, (2) narrativity of theology and witness; (3) maximum participation in reflection, prayer, and decision-making and a community that is reconciliatory; (4) inclusion of dreams and visions in worship; and (5) an understanding of the close body/

mind relationship. Although these practices were at risk of being diluted into white "evangelical middle class religion," they are alive and well in the Two-Thirds world, where "oral modes of communication" are usually the most effective way to spread the Christian message, he argued.[27]

Vinson Synan steered a middle path in his *The Holiness-Pentecostal Movement* (1971), arguing for the biracial origins—though with Parham as the doctrinal originator. Both "share roughly equal positions as founders" because Parham laid the "doctrinal" foundations and Seymour served as the catalytic agent. "It was Parham's ideas preached by his followers that produced the Azusa revival of 1906 and with it the worldwide Pentecostal movement." Synan affirms Seymour's pivotal role, yet rejects Hollenweger's notion that Pentecostalism began as a "Negro phenomenon." Synan also broke ranks with previous writers by pointing out Parham's racial attitudes and his sympathy for the Ku Klux Klan. However, he argued that southern tradition and mores rather than white supremacy per se were to blame. Like Brumback, he argued that Parham's conflict with Seymour was not due to racism but to his corrective ministry and his denunciations of "hypnotists" and "spiritualists" "who seemed to have taken over the [Azusa] service[s]."[28]

James Tinney disagreed with previous interpreters and argued that Azusa was largely an African-American "event" that "originated as a Black religious development . . . springing from African and Afro-American impulses in the most immediate sense."[29] Leonard Lovett criticized scholars for failing to make a clear-cut distinction between precursors and the mainstream movement and for hailing Parham as the "Father" of Pentecostalism while "fail[ing]" to fully recognize black contributions: "The exponents of the interracial view are so eager to make their point that they fail to see that Parham's efforts, at best, were a continuation of [previous] sporadic light showers [of glossolalia that had already taken place in history], while Seymour's Azusa Street Revival was the torrential downpour that created a major worldwide flood."[30]

In the *Vision of the Disinherited: The Making of American Pentecostalism* (1979), Robert Mapes Anderson argues that Hollenweger's black origins thesis was "inaccurate" because Parham was the true "founder" and "originator" of Pentecostalism. Anderson admitted Parham's racism, moral failings, and unique theological views. However, he contends that Seymour preached a simplified version of Parham's views and that although Seymour's own vision was potentially "revolutionary," it was later domesticated and "transformed into social passivity, ecstatic escape, and finally, a most conservative conformity."[31]

Douglas Nelson challenged Anderson in his 1981 dissertation, "'For Such a Time as This': The Story of William J. Seymour and the Azusa Street Revival." Seymour, he argued, was a "great leader directly responsible for a revolutionary Christian renewal movement," which overcame the color line in the church. The movement would not have happened without Seymour's leadership. Whites tried to hide "the black origins of the movement while establishing an imagined basis for its alleged superiority over all others." Instead, "Seymour's farsighted leadership harnessed the power released in glossolalic worship to break the color line barrier—along with other serious divisions in humanity." Prejudice and racial separation returned "the morning after" because people lost the inclusive vision, became preoccupied with glossolalia, bowed to social pressure, and refused to follow Seymour's model.[32]

In *Fields White unto Harvest: Charles F. Parham and the Missionary Origins of Pentecostalism* (1988), James Goff challenged Tinney, Lovett, and Nelson's views: "Parham, more than Seymour, must be regarded as the founder of the Pentecostal movement" because he "first formulated the theological definition of Pentecostalism by linking tongues with the Holy Spirit baptism." The black origins and interracial theories were somewhat problematic, he contends, because they obscure Parham's primacy of theological formulation. While both men may properly be considered pioneers, "only Parham can chronologically be labeled founder" of Pentecostalism. Goff wrote although Parham affirmed white supremacy, abhorred interracial marriage, segregated blacks and whites, praised the Ku Klux Klan, and taught that interracial marriage caused Noah's flood, he was "far from a ranting," "card-carrying" racist, but rather someone whose views reflected those of many Midwesterners in his day.[33]

Edith Blumhofer argued in *The Assemblies of God: A Chapter in the Story of American Pentecostalism* (1989) that Parham's temperament, spiritual and emotional immaturity, financial irregularities, "unique" theological views, and alleged sexual misconduct became something of an embarrassment to early Pentecostals who wanted to prove their respectability. She insisted that, despite Parham's denials, "his worldview nurtured racist assumptions." She also argued that although Seymour disavowed Parham's racial views, "Seymour later allowed explicit racial prejudice to surface in his own ranks" because he "reserved for 'people of color' the right to be officers of his mission, limiting whites to membership."[34]

Cecil Robeck argued in *The Colorline Was Washed Away in the Blood* (1995) that despite Seymour's call for racial equality, racial separation eventually emerged in the Church of God (Cleveland) and the Assemblies of God. The Assemblies of God, for instance, carefully noted "colored" in its list of ministers so those concerned about race could avoid inviting blacks to speak. However, to their credit, he notes that both denominations continued to allow blacks to receive credentials.[35]

Harvey Cox argues in *Fire From Heaven: The Rise of Pentecostal Spirituality and the Reshaping of Religion in the Twenty-First Century* (1995), that although Azusa's interracial character and ethos attracted seasoned Christian leaders and the masses, defections by white leaders along with latent racial animosity led Seymour to become defensive and restrict the movement's top three leadership roles to "people of color." Although he had more right than any other single person to be called the "father of Pentecostalism," he died with little fanfare from white colleagues. Despite this, Azusa's message swept around the world because its restorationist message spoke to the spiritual emptiness and longing of our time by promoting a kind of primal spirituality, which manifested itself in primal speech (ecstatic utterance/glossolalia), primal piety (visions, healing, spirit possession, and archetypal religious expressions), and primal hope in a future millennial kingdom where their wrongs would be righted. This once despised and ridiculed group is now quickly becoming one of the preferred religions of the global poor.[36]

In "Visions of Glory: The Place of the Azusa Street Revival in Pentecostal History" (1996), Joe Creech popularized the modern multiple centers theory of Pentecostal origins. He claims that early eyewitnesses, denominational historians, "Azusa boosters," and modern scholars like Hollenweger uncritically adopted Bartleman's (alleged) claim that Azusa was the "starting point" for global Pentecostalism, thus creating the "myth" of Azusa's influence. Aside from a condescending tone throughout and suggestion that past scholars were driven more by ideology than the facts, Creech claims (a) there were many other centers and points of origin that were equally important and independent such as William Durham's Mission in Chicago and Gaston Barnabas Cashwell's Mission in North Carolina; (b) that they not only rivaled but in Durham's case arguably surpassed Azusa in theological influence and leadership development; (c) that because these Azusa-influenced leaders did not maintain "institutional" and "structural" ties with Azusa and because they often kept their preexisting Protestant institutional structures, theological tendencies, and social dynamics, this "demonstrates" that "Azusa played only a limited substantive role in the institutional, theological, and social development of early Pentecostalism"; and (d) that "only a handful" of people and "a few congregations" adhered to Seymour's interracial message. The idea that Azusa's "spiritual ethos" and interracial vision and message of equality were part of the "marrow" of Pentecostal theology and spirituality is a myth invariably perpetuated by black Pentecostal scholars, Douglas Nelson, Harvey Cox, and others, Creech implies. He further claims, "It is also unclear whether or not racial equality, even where it existed, was a core theological tenet" at all in early Pentecostalism. Without showing precisely how, he further claims that Donald Dayton, James Goff, Gary McGee, Grant Wacker, and Edith Blumhofer demonstrate that Pentecostal origins "arose from multiple [preexisting] pockets of revival" and that even Azusa-influenced leaders like Durham and Florence Crawford worked "in direct opposition to Seymour." He argued Pentecostalism's theological "*raison d'être* came not from Azusa but from . . . Parham." He claims that Seymour and Azusa were one of many leaders and centers and that they played a "limited substantive role" in Pentecostal origins.[37]

In Gastón Espinosa's dissertation on the origins of the North American Latino Pentecostal movement (1999), he argues that although Parham influenced some of Seymour's theological views on the spiritual gifts and tongues, they ultimately created two overlapping but still competing visions and versions of Pentecostalism that differed in some of their key theological, social, and racial views. Seymour created a "transgressive social space" at Azusa from 1906 to 1909 wherein people could invoke pneumatic experiences to cross some (though not all) of the social, racial, and gender boundaries of the day. Espinosa challenged the biracial interpretive paradigm of Azusa, arguing that Latinos and other immigrants helped transform a largely black and then biracial, American, English-language prayer meeting on 214 Bonnie Brae Street into a multi-racial-ethnic, multilinguistic, and international revival on 312 Azusa Street.[38]

Larry Martin argues in *The Life and Ministry of William J. Seymour* (1999) that Seymour was critical to Pentecostalism. He traces how the fires of the Pentecostal movement passed from Parham to Seymour, who popularized the movement and also promoted racial equality. He links Seymour to Parham's Apostolic Faith Mission and argues that Seymour only severed these ties after Parham's incendiary remarks in October 1906. He concludes that Parham was a "racist" whose support for the Ku Klux Klan "amounted to little less than white supremacy." He points out a number of important and hitherto unreported facts about Seymour's family and early life.[39]

Rufus Sanders challenged previous writers by arguing in *William Joseph Seymour: Black Father of the 20th Century Pentecostal/Charismatic Movement* (2001) that Seymour was the black founder and "Father" of Pentecostalism. Although Parham "planted the seed" and "help[ed] to formulate . . . Pentecostal theology," it was Seymour's experiences that served as the bedrock for the new faith—though he does credit Parham as "Seymour's father in this new-found faith." Despite the fact that "white historians deliberately denied Seymour's title of 'Father,'" Sanders contends that he was the "main architect of modern Pentecostalism" and that "every ritual and practice of Pentecostalism had a precedent in African-American traditional religion."[40]

Grant Wacker suggests in *Heaven Below: Early Pentecostals and American Culture* (2001) that the genius of Pentecostalism lay in its ability to balance "two seemingly incompatible impulses in productive tension . . . the primitive and pragmatic . . . idealism versus realism, or principle versus practicality." Pentecostals were thus able to "capture" the proverbial "lightning in a bottle and, more importantly, keep it there, decade after decade, without stilling the fire or cracking the vessel [bottle]." He argued that the deeper problem with race relations was that Pentecostal leaders (black and white) and newspaper editors were "indifferent about race" because "on the whole, pentecostal culture failed to provide a sustained theology of racial reconciliation for whites and blacks alike" because it only played a "slight role in their theological thinking." He notes this inability was not due to a lack of desire, but rather to a resignation that whites were simply unwilling to acknowledge and accept black leadership and racial reconciliation.[41]

Grant Wacker and Augustus Cerillo questioned the "Edenic" theories of race relations—that race relations went from good to bad after "the snake of white racism" entered the movement—in their essay on Pentecostal historiography (2002). They criticized Parham's racial views and recognized Seymour's leadership role, but also contend that Parham was the primary founder and initiator. They noted recent "multicultural" approaches to Pentecostal origins and argued "a convincing black interpretation of Pentecostal origins awaits further research and must successfully answer . . . Blumhofer's charge [following Creech] that it derives not from the primary sources but from the presentist-driven creation of the 'myth of Azusa Street.'"[42] Exactly why they are called "multicultural" approaches and "black interpretations" while other views are not called "white" approaches and interpretations is unclear.

SEYMOUR IN CONTEMPORARY HISTORIES

Cecil M. Robeck Jr.'s important book, *The Azusa Street Mission and Revival* (2006), steers a middle path by blending the black origin account's commitment to spotlighting Seymour's contributions with Goff's view that Seymour was largely Parham's disciple who was organically and spiritually tied to his Apostolic Faith Movement. He noted that Parham held racist assumptions about white superiority and would not allow blacks to mingle with whites at the altars. Azusa was "first and foremost an African American congregation" for the first couple of months, he contends.[43] The fact that Seymour hid his head behind a makeshift pulpit at Azusa set the norm for Christian humility, Robeck noted. He successfully challenges the notion that the revival declined precipitously after newspaper coeditor Clara Lum left the mission in 1908.[44]

Craig Borlase's popular account, *William J. Seymour: A Biography* (2006), largely follows Nelson, Martin, and others by laying the burden of the conflict on Parham. He portrays Seymour as the "father of the modern Pentecostal movement" and argues that his vision for racial acceptance did not succeed because "within years" the movement split along racial lines" due to "bigotry and racial oppression." Although he rejects the nominal leader theory, he echoes the divine origins theory stating that Azusa "neither started nor finished with . . . Seymour. It . . . [was] scripted by a larger hand."[45]

In *Spreading Fires: The Missionary Nature of Early Pentecostalism* (2007), Allan Anderson argues that an American bias in Pentecostal historiography has led scholars to uncritically accept the claim that Parham and Seymour are the sole founders of global Pentecostalism. He contends that the literature finds multiple leaders and centers (e.g., Ellen Hebden, Levi Lupton, Ivey Campbell, Marie Burgess, Pandita Ramabai, Minnie Abrams at Mukti). While not wanting to underestimate Azusa's importance, he asserts that Pentecostalism "was not a movement that had a distinct beginning in the USA or anywhere else, or a movement based on a particular doctrine," but rather was "a series of . . . historically related movements where the emphasis is on the exercise of spiritual gifts." He challenges the American missionary "origins" view of the global movement by focusing on early Pentecostal missionaries from outside the United States. However, he does not emphasize the fact that most of the first pioneers (and those they influenced) prior to 1907 were white missionaries from western Europe—thus displacing Seymour's multi-ethnic band of pioneer missionaries and their converts for a largely homogenous band of white western Europeans and their converts. Unlike Creech, who downplays Seymour's decisive influence, Anderson carefully acknowledges that Seymour's Azusa revival was the main center in North America from 1906 to 1909 and that it directly contributed to the birth of classical Pentecostalism.[46]

The most recent articles and dissertations on Seymour focus on his theology, ethics, and racial practices. Derrick Rosenior argues in his dissertation (2005) on reconciliation that although Seymour held to racial equality after the various divisions, he became "very skeptical of the intentions of whites who came to Azusa" and as a result curtailed their leadership—though largely as a rearguard reaction to past attempted takeovers.[47]

Cephas Omenyo (2006) traces Seymour's influence on West African, Liberian, and Ghanaian Pentecostalism and argues contrary to Ogbu Kalu for a link between Seymour, Lucy Farrow (who preached Seymour's message in Africa), and William Wade Harris because Farrow and other Azusa missionaries ministered among Harris's people, the Kru. He implicitly critiques the theological a priori behind some recent multiple centers theories when he points out that human movements cannot have spontaneous multiple global origins: "The Pentecostal experience 'does not drop from heaven,' but is usually experienced through human agency."[48]

Stephen Dove (2009) argues that although Seymour and Azusa "eschewed traditional" lectionaries and set schedules from 1906 to 1908, they nonetheless created their own unique form of music and liturgy that actually emphasized the Christological rather than pneumatological aspects of Pentecost.[49] Similarly, Charles R. Fox Jr.'s dissertation (2009) analyzes Seymour's soteriology, pneumatology, and ecclesiology. He unpersuasively argues that some scholars accuse Seymour of "rejecting the Hispanic contingency [sic]" and of engaging in "blatant discrimination" against Latinos, a topic that will be thoroughly discussed in chapter five. Although Fox claims to move beyond apologetics, his stated goal was to "write Seymour's contribution back into the ongoing discussion" of theology.[50]

Rene Brathwaite (2010) attempted to challenge Cecil Robeck's purported view that Seymour rejected "the Bible evidence" theory of the baptism with the Holy Spirit, arguing that he instead "made certain clarifications in light of personal and pastoral concerns," which was a "commendable biblical balance to the issue." He also states that because Seymour revised his Apostolic Faith Mission *Constitution* to state that only people of color could occupy the top three leadership posts, Seymour "was now guilty of racial discrimination." However, he fails to demonstrate from Seymour's own statements that this decision was motivated by racial prejudice. In fact, Seymour explicitly stated that his decision to restrict leadership posts to people of color "is not for discrimination," but "for peace" and to "keep down the race war" and "friction" in the churches.[51]

Marne Campbell (2010) insists that Azusa was an "accidental revival" and a "working class insurgency that challenged the racial order dominated by wealthy Anglo-Americans committed to the maintenance of white supremacy." Although Los Angeles promised racial equality to new migrants, "it was actually Seymour and . . . Azusa that delivered it."[52] Likewise, John Foxworth argues in his dissertation (2011) that Raymond T. Richey kept alive Seymour's vision of divine healing and the use of material objects like handkerchiefs in passing on healing power in early American Pentecostalism.[53]

Estrelda Alexander writes in her path-breaking book *Black Fire: One Hundred Years of African American Pentecostalism* (2011) that despite Seymour's efforts to create a racially inclusive and unified church, he failed to bring long-term unity because of white-led divisions, which led to disenchantment and prompted him to restrict white leadership roles. However, Seymour's shortcomings were not due primarily to a lack of desire or will power, she notes, but to "a conspiracy of silence by white religionists [who] relegated Seymour to a footnote" and to "petty sectarian attitudes in early African American Pentecostalism."[54]

Vinson Synan and Charles R. Fox Jr.'s book *William J. Seymour: Pioneer of the Azusa Street Revival* (2012) examines Seymour's theological views on sin, salvation, the Holy Spirit, and ecclesiology. The first biographical section is based on Fox's slightly revised doctoral dissertation written at Regent University, Virginia, under Synan's direction. Their book seeks to "discover the implications of his theology for Pentecostals and Charismatics today" and to promote "a more robust understanding of the Holy Spirit baptism and Spirit-empowered life." Unlike other biographies, the second section of their book also contains Seymour's extant writings. However, it not does include sections C (Seymour's *Apostolic Faith* accounts of the Azusa revival), D (historical overview and testimonies of Seymour and the revival), E (critics of Seymour), and F (Parham's writings) of this present volume.[55]

NEW PENTECOSTAL HISTORIOGRAPHY

SEYMOUR AND AZUSA: ONE IMPORTANT LEADER AND CENTER AMONG MANY?

It is important to assess Creech's claims because they've influenced scholars around the world and because they flatten out and often contradict the earliest evidence.[56] Aside from implying that he is more objective and driven by the facts than previous "Azusa boosters," what further claims and compelling evidence does he provide? He asserts (a) that Bartleman and his Azusa "colleagues" constructed a revisionist narrative that "cast Azusa as the starting point" of Pentecostal origins rather than other "multiple points of origin" in Kansas, Chicago, and North Carolina; (b) that Pentecostalism arose from a number of other important and independent centers led by Cashwell, Durham, Crawford, and others who were not significantly influenced in their theological and social development by Seymour and Azusa, and (c) that "Azusa only played a limited substantive role" in Pentecostalism. Because the last point was not qualified, it would also imply this was also true prior to Durham's death in 1912.[57]

However, after a careful review of the primary sources, I have not come across any compelling evidence that Bartleman colluded with Seymour's followers to fabricate this alleged narrative. Who—precisely—did Bartleman collude with? When? In what documents? How were they distributed? Where? By whom? There's also no compelling evidence that all or even most Pentecostal writers from 1906 to 1925 had read—let alone adopted—Bartleman's alleged narrative. Furthermore, as we have already seen, prior to 1970 most early and mid-century writers didn't credit Seymour and in some cases even Azusa for Pentecostal origins. Finally, why would Bartleman want to solely promote Azusa and Seymour when he acknowledged other revival centers around the world, was an outspoken critic of Seymour, sided with Durham in the 1911 Durham-Seymour schism, helped Durham find an alternative meeting place to set up a rival Azusa mission, acknowledged other centers, and stated that Seymour was a "nominal leader" whom God left after the 1911 split with Durham?[58]

But isn't it true that Cashwell, Durham, and Crawford led equally important centers that were independent of Seymour and Azusa? Again, the evidence indicates otherwise. Cashwell, Durham, and Crawford (among others) acknowledge Seymour and Azusa's influence not only in their spiritual outlook, but also in some of their theological, social, and racial views. Cashwell said he crucified his racial views at Azusa, encouraged and preached to interracial audiences in the South, taught Seymour's Pentecostal theological views in his newspaper, and reportedly led the "Azusa of the South" during his revival in Dunn, North Carolina. He also preached Seymour's message to scores of pneumatically oriented independent, Holiness, Methodist, Baptist, and Presbyterian leaders like F. M. Britton, J. H. King, A. J. Tomlinson, M. M. Pinson, H. G. Rodgers, G. F. Taylor, H. A. Goss, and others.[59] They received it, brought many of their denominations into Pentecostalism or splintered off to form their own, and often added to their denominational name "Pentecostal," a term popularized by Seymour. This, rather than Bartleman's alleged influence, is why—much to Creech's puzzlement—they credit Azusa as *one* of the main sources of and/or influences on their movements.

This is also why, despite Cashwell's defection from Pentecostalism in 1909, leaders like F. M. Britton and S. D. Page of the Pentecostal Holiness Church (PHC) made the arduous and expensive trip from North Carolina to Los Angeles to visit Azusa and even take a keepsake photo of themselves standing in front of the "312 Apostolic Faith" door sign in coat and tie with their Bibles and songbooks in hand. They did this long after the Azusa revival had ended in 1909 and after they had developed their own denominations. Just a novelty photo? Perhaps, but believing that they just happened to travel more than two thousand miles west to Los Angeles and just happened to show up at Azusa in coat and tie along with their Bibles, songbooks, and a large box camera just to take a novelty photo stretches credulity.[60] Their spiritual ties to Azusa were taught by Cashwell and others and transcended their ties to Cashwell alone as evidenced by the fact that they still revered Azusa long after he left the PHC in 1909. Clearly Cashwell had passed on to them more than just a few stories for they felt a deep spiritual and genealogical connection to Seymour and Azusa, even if their denominations did not maintain "structural" ties. So did many others.

Even if Cashwell, Durham, and Crawford didn't maintain *any* "institutional" and "structural" ties with Azusa and even if some later broke with Seymour on one key point or another, this doesn't prove he didn't have a pivotal and paradigmatic influence on their general theological, social, and racial outlook. The primary reasons why they didn't establish "institutional" and "structural" ties with Azusa prior to 1914 are several: because almost everyone (including Seymour himself) saw it as an interdenominational revival and renewal center (a phrase used by Crawford and her followers to describe Azusa), the Azusa Mission wasn't yet a denomination (that took place in 1914), and because they went to Azusa with the hopes of bringing the fires of revival back to their own denominations and traditions.

In fact, the extant testimonies and evidence challenge Creech's claims. After Durham visited Azusa in 1907 he persuaded his North Avenue Mission to accept Seymour's theological, social, and racial outlook, he taught many of Seymour's views in his newspaper, and patterned aspects of his own revival after Azusa. This is why his already diverse congregation became even more multiethnic and global-mission minded. Most revealing, Durham also preached at Azusa for a lengthy two-and-a-half months in 1911, promising Seymour he'd usher in a "Second Great Azusa," something Seymour would have never allowed if they weren't close friends with strong organic ties. He also stated he was one of Seymour's closest allies from 1906 to 1911.[61] In fact, there is no major compelling evidence that Durham's split with Seymour over sanctification in the summer of 1911 also led him and his followers to repudiate the rest of Seymour's doctrinal, social, and racial teachings.

The same is true for Florence Crawford—even after her departure from Seymour in 1907. She not only credits Seymour and Azusa for teaching her about the outpouring and baptism with the Holy Spirit but also adopted his mission name (Apostolic Faith) for her own denomination and newspaper. She certainly wasn't taking her cues from Parham, whom she disliked and did not recognize as the founder of Pentecostalism. She and her movement made the rather bold claim that although others changed their Azusa-influenced theology, "they hold on to the Bible doctrines as originally embraced by the Apostolic Faith at the time of the outpouring of the Holy Spirit in 1906" at the "Azusa Street Revival Center." They viewed Azusa as a "revival center," not a denomination, and the place that taught them their core Pentecostal doctrines, which they still clung to half a century later.[62]

The documentary evidence makes it clear that Seymour and Azusa had a profound impact on these and other leaders across the United States. Azusa-influenced evangelists were the thread that connected many of these independent pockets of Spirit-oriented revivals into an identifiable movement prior to 1912, however variegated, unruly, and loosely connected. Seymour's message, theology, and followers provided them with a common theological grammar, spiritual outlook, and social-racial framework that they in turn incorporated, developed, revised, and made distinctively their own.

SEYMOUR AND AZUSA—RELATIVELY SMALL IMPACT ON GLOBAL PENTECOSTAL ORIGINS?

In an understandable and laudable desire to spotlight the meteoric rise of Pentecostalism in the non-Western world, some scholars have applied Creech's claims (and in some cases his tone) globally and as a result downplay and almost dismiss Seymour and Azusa's decisive contributions to global Pentecostal origins. Those who disagree are often labeled "Azusa Boosters" and accused of a pro-American bias. Michael Bergunder, who published an otherwise excellent book on Indian Pentecostalism in South Asia, contends that Seymour and Azusa were a "prelude" that had a "relatively small impact at that time" on global Pentecostal origins for some of the reasons Creech gave in the United States; because other centers didn't have formal institutional ties with Seymour and Azusa and also because they allegedly didn't reflect Seymour's theological and social views. Instead, and without stating how, he argues that Pentecostalism was created by the emergence of "a vast and vague international network." Precisely when, where, how, and *who* created and transformed this "pneumatically oriented" "vast and vague international network" that at some unspecified point in history birthed a definable classical Pentecostal movement around the world is not fully explained, explored, or proven. At what point did they become Pentecostal? Due to what Pentecostal message and which human actors? Which precise non-Azusa Pentecostal leaders transformed this vast and vague international network into a classical Pentecostal movement independent of Azusa?

Bergunder argues that Azusa became prominent in the historiography largely because it engaged in a kind of global marketing campaign wherein "they" claimed "to be the definitive formula for and sure beginning of the end-time revival."[63] Just who the "they" at Azusa are, is unstated. Perhaps it's Bartleman, because Bergunder later cites his claim that while the Pentecostal revival was rocked in the "cradle of little Wales," and "brought up" in India, it became "full-blown" in Los Angeles.[64] However, this isn't a claim about Seymour and Azusa being the exclusive, sole, or only historical starting point of global Pentecostal origins, but rather a statement about Seymour and Azusa as the single most important force and voice behind the articulation of a more fully developed Pentecostal theology—one that we now call classical Pentecostalism. There's a difference. Furthermore, even if it was true, Bartleman's alleged propaganda cannot and should not be read as synonymous with a claim by Seymour and Azusa itself. Overlooking and flattening out these distinctions in the early sources is theoretically and methodologically problematic and results in underestimating Seymour and Azusa's influence.

Even if one entertains Creech's and Bergunder's point, just how Bartleman and other unnamed leaders colluded to fool an entire generation of international leaders and global eyewitnesses like Alexander Boddy of England, T. B. Barratt of Norway, and others is unclear and unproven. How could they have fooled them when they not only traveled to many of these other centers around the world, but also organized the first international Pentecostal conferences and had contact with leaders in forty-six countries?[65] Despite these problems, Bergunder is correct that Azusa's success was tied (at least in part in *some* countries) to the ability of its missionaries to work within preexisting evangelical missionary networks.[66] Allan Anderson also argues for the influence of other global centers, but unlike Creech and Bergunder he credits Azusa as the most important center in North America and one of the most important globally.

Although there is a general hermeneutics of suspicion about Seymour and the U.S.'s contribution to global Pentecostal origins, one wonders why this same hermeneutic is not as vigorously applied to their own nationalistic, hemispheric, and socio-historical-racial locations, or to the largely white Western European missionary origins story they seek to replace it with? The problem is theoretical and methodological. For despite claims about focusing on the non-Western origins, one wonders why they draw almost exclusively on white European missionary sources, testimonies, leaders, and their subsequent converts and newspapers. The exceptions—like Pandita Ramabai in India—prove the rule. In essence, by non-Western they largely mean non-American and geographical centers outside of the United States. However and somewhat ironically, their non-Western origins story is still largely that of white Western missionaries (in this case the first generation being almost entirely European or whites from other parts of the world like Minnie Abrams in India and Dennis Hoover in Chile) in non-Western contexts giving birth to indigenous Pentecostalism—precisely what Seymour's multi-ethnic group of missionaries also did in the non-Western world. Although the distinctions have been conflated, there's a difference between being non-Western in location and non-Western in origin. To the historian who seeks to trace the source of ideological and theological change over time, the distinction matters. The documentary evidence indicates that while white European missionaries and native evangelists may have been the first to plant the Pentecostal message in many countries and provinces around the world beginning in 1908, prior to that time Seymour's Azusa-influenced missionaries and their converts along with his *Apostolic Faith* newspaper were nonetheless the first to spread and in some cases via missionaries to plant (though often not fully develop) the classical Pentecostal message and movement in key countries like England, Sweden, Norway, India, China, Japan, Liberia, South Africa, and other select countries and provinces around the world.

This move to disestablish Seymour and Azusa as the major catalyst in global Pentecostal origins from 1906 to 1912 also reflects a quiet theological a priori, which implies that a "vast and vague international network" can both spontaneously erupt around the world and come together to form a broad series of overlapping revivals that at some later point of time coalesce on their own into a definable movement. This theological a priori and lack of human actors is ironic because one of their chief criticisms of early writers is that they were driven by a theological a priori and nationalistic (i.e., American) ideology. However, unlike church history, the academic discipline of history does not allow for deus ex machina—God's hand in history—in this case a spontaneous and simultaneous outpouring of the Holy Spirit around the world. While this is normatively acceptable in traditional church histories and theological seminaries and departments wherein one's readers can affirm God's handiwork in history, secular historians are constrained by their discipline and method to look for all too human actors and causal agents. They are bound by a craft that is theoretically and methodologically agnostic with respect to the truth claims of its subjects. Instead, historians scrutinize the archival sources, newspapers, and interviews for historical actors, interconnecting chains of events—no matter how loosely connected—and people who originate and propagate ideas in order to trace historical change and the development of ideas and social movements over time. For this reason, in secular histories there are no spontaneous outpourings and movements that erupt simultaneously in the United States, Canada, Europe, Africa, and Asia. However rich and valuable to the community of faith, that's another kind of theological history and story altogether.

So in all fairness, just as some scholars have in fact overstated the influence of America and Azusa (though ironically not normally Seymour) on global Pentecostal origins, it appears that some other scholars have swung the pendulum too far in the opposite direction. They have gone beyond the evidence and engaged in a little of the very theoretical and methodological shortcomings and hyperbole they accuse others of engaging in. Although Walter Hollenweger believed that the debate over Azusa's influence is a theological and ideological rather than an historical and factual one, Allan Anderson and I both agree that there's enough evidence to make an argument for the historical origins of the movement. After carefully wading through tens of thousands of pages of primary and secondary source material about the origins of the Pentecostal movement around the world over the past two decades, I am convinced there's compelling evidence to argue for Seymour and Azusa's primal and primary, though not exclusive or total, influence on American and global Pentecostal origins from 1906 to 1912 in the aforecited countries, though not for the movement's later development (an important distinction) and origins in other places.

While Creech's and Bergunder's theories are an important and helpful correction to some writers who do in fact overemphasize America and Azusa's contributions, their push for "non-Western," non-American, and/or non-Azusa origins has arguably gone beyond and in many cases contradicted the earliest eyewitness reports. Like early U.S. Pentecostal historians they criticize, some have flattened out the evidence and distinctions and reinscribed Seymour's marginalization in global Pentecostal origins, albeit for different reasons and no doubt without malicious intent.

Still, it is important to take a moment to address their main charge that Seymour and Azusa are not as important to global Pentecostal origins as some hitherto argued. Why aren't these other leaders and centers as important to Seymour and Azusa? First, Bartleman never said Azusa was the "sole" and thus only starting point of American and global Pentecostal "origins." Throughout his book, Bartleman acknowledged other revival centers in Topeka, Wales, and India that predated or developed concurrently with Azusa. What Bartleman and other first-generation eyewitnesses stated is that Seymour and Azusa were for a period of time the single most important leader, center, and catalyst (among many) in the crystallization of the Pentecostal message and origins prior to 1912, though not necessarily the only leader, center, and catalyst in the movement's subsequent spread and development.[67]

Second, some make a faulty leap in logic concerning historical agency and the spread of ideas by assuming that the only way a person, center, and ideology can have a life-changing paradigmatic influence on someone is if the latter maintains "institutional" and "structural" ties with the former. As any teacher, student, and revolutionary realizes, ideas can take on a life of their own in people's minds and spirits even without structural and institutional ties. For this reason, few would deny the influence of revolutionary thinkers like Marx on Vladimir Lenin, Chairman Mao, Ho Chi Minh, Fidel Castro, and countless other "Marxist" revolutionaries who kept no personal or structural ties to Marx. What they adopted were his core ideas and then rearticulated and indigenized them in light of their intellectual and social conditions in Russia, China, Vietnam, and Cuba. So too it was with Seymour and Azusa. Their ideas and influence gave birth to and shaped global Pentecostal origins around the world among people who embraced, blended, and rearticulated them with other movements in light of their own context and conditions.

Even if Creech's point is granted in theory, as we have seen and will see in the biography and documentary history that follows, there is strong countervailing evidence that Durham, Cashwell, Mason, Cook, Johnson, Boddy, and others adopted Seymour's rather than Parham's or someone else's Pentecostal theological, racial, and social outlook. As the rest of this book documents, they spoke at one another's missions (Durham, Cook, Boddy), spoke at one another's conferences (Lake, Mason), praised Seymour's and/or

Azusa's influence on them (Garrs, Bernsten, Crawford, Bartleman, Sizelove, Johnson), and patterned their revivals (Cashwell, Durham, Cook, Mason, Johnson, Barratt) and based their theological explanations for tongues, the spiritual gifts, divine healing, sanctification (in some cases), and other beliefs on Azusa and Seymour's teachings via his newspaper and followers. In South Africa, for example, some complained that some Azusa-influenced missionaries were trying to put blacks on an equal playing field with whites like in Los Angeles.[68]

Third, many of these so-called "independent" leaders and centers had upon closer inspection clear and in some cases deep ties to Seymour and Azusa. As the biography and sources that follow indicate, G. B. Cashwell, William Durham, T. B. Barratt, Andrew Johnson, A. A. Boddy, and others were clearly influenced by Seymour's theological, social, and/or racial beliefs and practices, commented on them in their writings, patterned aspects of their own revivals and/or missions after Azusa, and/or claimed (e.g., Boddy) that Azusa is sort of a Mecca still of global Pentecostalism. For example, T. B. Barratt was converted to Pentecostalism through Azusa missionaries, read Seymour's *Apostolic Faith*, and wrote letters to Seymour about the progress of his work in Norway. A similar pattern was true for others like Durham, Johnson, and Cashwell. Eyewitness Max Moorhead wrote in 1907 that Minnie Abrams, who reportedly led an independent Pentecostal revival that predated and equaled Azusa in global influence, was brought into a fuller understanding of Pentecostalism after coming into contact with Seymour's writings and missionaries. And Alexander Boddy, who supposedly led an independent Pentecostal center of international significance in England, stated that he was brought into Pentecost by the Azusa-influenced pastor T. B. Barratt. Boddy also made the rather astounding assertion in 1912 that Seymour's Azusa Mission was the "Mecca" and thus sacred center of global Pentecostalism, which seems to challenge some contemporary claims that Seymour and Azusa were just one of many important leaders and centers of global Pentecostalism. This was no minor assertion since he had contacts with Pentecostal leaders and/or centers in forty-six countries and in fact had visited many of them in his global travels. He was perhaps the most globally minded and internationally oriented and traveled Pentecostal in his day.[69]

Fourth, the fact that some of Seymour's followers held onto their previous Protestant denominational superstructure is not surprising and is not convincing evidence—as Creech contends—that Seymour did not have any significant influence on their ministries, denominations, and theological outlook. As any teacher or media expert realizes, influence is not solely determined by ongoing institutional and structural ties. Furthermore, the fact that their denominational histories traced their origins back to Azusa, they called themselves "Pentecostals" (a term that Seymour popularized and that had—and still has in some circles—a negative social stigma), sometimes used "Pentecostal" in their denominational title, and often made unique Pentecostal beliefs that tended to follow Seymour's rather than Parham's teachings a requirement for ordination while also affirming Seymour's social practices on race all attest to his quiet influence. For example, after Cashwell brought A. H. Butler and others into the Pentecostal experience, in 1909 Butler and the Holiness Church of North Carolina changed their name to the Pentecostal Holiness Church (PHC) and added speaking in tongues to their denomination's articles of faith.[70] The fact that leaders kept some or most of their pre-Azusa evangelical Protestant beliefs isn't surprising because Seymour and his message were also evangelical and because he led an interdenominational spiritual renewal and revival center that was not transformed into a denomination until around 1914—by which time most other Pentecostal groups had or were in the process of forming their own denominations (e.g., Assemblies of God in 1914). This mitigated against keeping or developing any official structural ties to Seymour and Azusa. For these reasons, there simply wouldn't be any reason for a denominational leader to keep structural ties with an interdenominational renewal center—let alone another denomination. However, this does not mean that they did not see their own ministries as influenced to varying degrees by the Seymour's theology, vision, and revival, which most tend to imply when they note the influence of the Azusa Street Revival on their denominational origins, theology, and early history.

Fifth, if one maps out the influence of these supposedly equally important leaders and centers (e.g., Glad Tidings, Lupton, Hebden, and Mukti missions) in the aforementioned countries, they were not by any objective standard *individually*, or even *all four collectively in this case*, as important to global Pentecostal *origins* as Seymour and Azusa from 1906 to 1909 and globally from 1906 to 1912. Even if all four Pentecostal centers had never existed, Seymour and his followers still would have birthed and developed the movement in these countries (United States, Canada, India) at almost the same speed, depth, and breadth without them not only because of Azusa's pioneer missionaries, but also because of the steady stream of Azusa missionaries that continued to visit centers like the Mukti Mission year after year in the first decade of the movement—something overlooked by most scholars. The reverse is not true—these four movements would not have developed with the same speed, depth, and breath in the aforementioned countries without the Azusa-influenced missionaries, newspaper, and their converts and followers. Alfred and Lillian Garr and George Berg, for example, converted scores of Protestant missionaries, mission centers, and natives to Pentecostalism throughout India and China and planted Pentecostal works independent of these other leaders and centers. And as we shall see in chapter 3, they also influenced many of the reportedly independent missionaries and centers to embrace Seymour's Pentecostal theology and teachings.

Sixth, the fact that pneumatically oriented revivals arose prior to Azusa does not mean that they would have all fully developed into classical Pentecostalism on their own and without any influence from Seymour or Azusa Street. In many cases, stories and testimonies about Azusa and/or its daughter revivals were one of the key triggering mechanisms that prompted pneumatically interested and predisposed leaders and centers to adopt the Azusa-influenced Pentecostal message and theology, after which they were grafted into a growing network that shared in common a recognition of Azusa's critical (though not exclusive) influence and articulation of Pentecostal teachings from 1906 to 1912. Seymour's and Azusa's Pentecostal message also provided these pre-Azusa pneumatic manifestations with a carefully and cogently articulated biblical explanation, theological grammar, and social framework, which leaders and centers incorporated, developed, revised, and indigenized to varying degrees as their needs dictated.

Seventh, some of these allegedly equally important centers for global Pentecostal origins left Pentecostalism and/or created no lasting denominations to continue their work. Although Seymour, Azusa, and those leaders and centers they influenced contributed to the origins of literally hundreds if not thousands of denominations through their spiritual progeny around the world, Allan Anderson rightly points out that the Mukti Mission, which is held up as the chief exemplar of an alternative independent center and rival to Azusa, did not found *any* Pentecostal denominations. This is probably because Pandita Ramabai (who Anderson notes may have never spoken in tongues) took the Mukti Mission *out* of Pentecostalism to join the Christian and Missionary Alliance (CMA), despite having plenty of Pentecostal alternatives to join. She did this even though—or perhaps because—the CMA (and perhaps she herself) adopted a "seek not, forbid not" position on tongues, repudiated the initial evidence theory, and in 1914 declared tongues and the gifts were not "*essentially* connected with the baptism with the Holy Spirit."[71] Why this mission is held up as a rival on par with Azusa's global influence is unclear, especially when one remembers that Azusa missionaries continued to stream through Mukti and other missions in India and around the world for at least a decade (see chapter 3), thus reinforcing Seymour's and Azusa's influence. The reverse was not (to the same degree) true.

Eighth, some writers conflate originators and developers. Not every originator is a developer and not every developer is an originator. A person can spread an idea or theological outlook to another country and plant it in the minds of converts and followers without fully developing a center and/or movement to propagate it. Likewise a person can propagate an idea and worldview that he or she did not create or develop. The fact that a person modifies an existing idea should not deny its originator's first paradigmatic and foundational influence on subsequent thinkers and in their theological explanations.

Ninth, some also conflate cause and effect. They assume that if non-Azusa-influenced indigenous evangelists and missionaries spread and developed Pentecostalism (i.e., effect) within a particular country or place then they must have also created its original message and/or evangelistic impulse (i.e., cause). However, it was Seymour's publications and missionaries who, along with their followers (e.g., Durham), planted most if not all of the *first* seeds and articulations of classical Pentecostalism in the aforementioned countries prior to 1912, which were often subsequently incorporated and developed by non-Azusa-influenced native evangelists.

Tenth, some argue that pneumatic experiences and references to tongues and Pentecost prior to or concurrent with Seymour's revival (e.g., Abrams and Mukti) prove these leaders and centers developed their own unique brand of classical Pentecostalism completely independent of Seymour, Azusa, and their followers. However, pre-Azusa pneumatic experiences and references do not a classical Pentecostal make. There are many people and movements in history that affirmed pneumatic experiences, tongues, and/or even used the word *pentecostal* (e.g., Joseph Smith and Mormonism; A. B. Simpson and CMA; Pentecostal Church of the Nazarene—which later dropped "Pentecostal" from its name to disassociate itself from Pentecostalism), but that never took that next step to self-identify as Pentecostal or join the movement.

Next, a careful examination of the dates of some of the explanations of "pre-Azusa" pneumatic manifestations in centers like Mukti, India, reveal that they actually postdate the 1906 start of Seymour's revival (April), the arrival of Seymour's *Apostolic Faith* (September/October) newspaper in that country/region, and/or in some cases the arrival of Azusa missionaries (Garrs, December), to say nothing of Parham's 1901 Topeka revival and newspaper reports. This conflation has led some to reread, through a presentist lens, pre-Azusa experiences in light of post-Azusa language and explanations.[72] As a result, pre-Azusa manifestations are conflated with their post-Azusa explanations as evidence of a pre-Azusa "Pentecostal" experience and movement.

Twelfth, notwithstanding the important role of pre-Azusa revivals and theological developments, word of the Azusa outpouring through word-of-mouth and the 405,000 copies of Seymour's *Apostolic Faith* newspaper in circulation around the world (to say nothing of countless other papers that also promoted his teachings and/or followed Seymour's revival from a distance) also helped create a common predisposition,[73] theological grammar, and spiritual receptivity to Pentecostal practices and explanations prior to the arrival of the first Azusa missionaries in places like India, China, and South

Africa. As will be discussed in chapter 3, in all three countries Seymour's newspaper arrived and influenced people prior to and independent of Azusa's first missionaries. This was no doubt true in other countries as well. Some now want to claim that this predisposition is exclusively evidence of a pre-Azusa and/or non-Azusa-influenced independent Pentecostal movement, but this view overlooks Seymour's influence through his paper and missionaries who provided more fine-tuned and in-depth explanations for those already predisposed to and perhaps who even had limited experiences with pneumatic manifestations.

Finally, while some have tried to point to the existence of Pentecostal newspapers around the world as evidence of independent non-Azusa-influenced Pentecostal leaders and centers, many fail to point out that most of those created prior to 1912 were actually founded or re-envisioned by Azusa missionaries, their converts, and/or those they influenced (2nd–4th generation). This is true of papers founded by William Durham (Chicago), Gaston Cashwell (Atlanta), Elmer Fisher (Los Angeles), Alexander Boddy (England), T. B. Barratt (Norway), Mok Lai Chi (China), Max Wood Moorhead (India), and M. L. Ryan (Japan), among others. Their papers helped spread Seymour's core theological views and some of his social practices along with their own combinative distinctives, which in turn led to the birth of other Pentecostal papers that to varying degrees did the same.

Seymour's newspaper along with those of his daughter and granddaughter missions are important because they facilitated the rapid transfer of his vision and version of Pentecostalism and a common theological and socio-cultural grammar that knit them together into an admittedly loose but still clearly definable transnational global movement from 1906 to 1912. These definitions and boundaries were so crystal clear for some Christian leaders and denominations that some began to adopt—even before the Azusa Street Revival ended—anti-Pentecostal statements, platforms, or positions that rejected the modern promotion and practice of the spiritual gifts and speaking in tongues. This strong Pentecostal identity and sense of community and shared pneumatic experiences are the main reasons why there was such a high degree of cooperation, pulpit sharing, and combinative blending between Seymour's followers and other classical Pentecostal centers. It also explains why so many aforementioned pioneers and founders stated—to the puzzlement of some modern interpreters—that Azusa was the single most important influence (among many) in global Pentecostal origins prior to 1912.

Noting Seymour's and Azusa's paradigmatic and catalytic influence on global Pentecostal origins is not a zero-sum game. It does not deny or diminish in any way the major contributions that European, indigenous, and non-Azusa-influenced missionaries and native leaders made to global Pentecostal origins. Furthermore, it also does not deny the importance that other Pentecostal leaders and centers may have played in spreading Pentecostalism to other countries and regions around the world, and especially in states or regions never reached by the Azusa newspaper or missionaries. Although beyond the purview of this study, but thankfully explored by Anderson, Bergunder, and others, native and non-Azusa leaders clearly developed their own independent and combinative theological centers that preached elements of Seymour's Azusa message along with their own native understandings of Pentecostalism. While some learned Seymour's message firsthand through his newspapers and/or missionaries, many learned it through second-generation followers and secondary sources who—despite their being one step removed—still articulated Seymour's and the Azusa Street revival's message about the Spirit baptism, race relations, and theological world view, rather than that of Parham or one of his followers. The result was a dynamic combinative spiritual movement that helps explain Pentecostalism's adaptability and rapid growth around the world.

CONTRIBUTIONS OF THIS BOOK

This book challenges a number of previous theories and notions about Seymour, the Azusa Street revival, and global Pentecostal origins. First, it challenges the multiple origins theory of Pentecostalism by arguing that although Seymour and Azusa were *not* the only leader and center responsible for classical global Pentecostal origins, they were the single most important leader, center, and catalyst among many for its *origins* (i.e., first classical Pentecostal newspaper source, preaching event, and/or mission) though not its subsequent development in the United States from 1906 to 1909 and around the world in countries like England, Norway, Sweden, Liberia, South Africa, India, and China from 1906 to 1912. During this foundational period (1906 to 1912), Seymour directly contributed to Pentecostalism's core doctrinal foundation and its fidelity to classical Protestantism, racial equality and integration, and numerical growth. He did so through the Azusa revival; his theological, racial, and social teachings in the 405,000 copies of his *Apostolic Faith* newspaper in circulation in the United States and around the world; his cross-country preaching tours to Pentecostal and non-Pentecostal missions; and through his daughter, granddaughter, and sister missions along with their innumerable followers.[74]

Second, it revises the static and almost hagiographic accounts of Seymour as a nominal leader who simply popularized Parham's beliefs to the masses. Rather than freeze Seymour's personality and theological development to the pre-October 1906 period when he was under Parham's influence, it analyzes the various ways Seymour changed over his twenty-plus-year ministry, why he promoted his own vision and version of Pentecostalism, and how and why he used it to challenge and supplant Parham's theological, social, and racial influence at home and abroad. It contends that Seymour and Parham promoted two similar visions and versions of Pentecostalism that differed on key theological, racial, and social points. These differences came into sharper focus after Parham repudiated Seymour, his Azusa revival, and their theological views and social practices starting in October 1906, something downplayed by later writers seeking to emphasize their spiritual continuity and unity. Parham not only charged that Seymour's revival was a "counterfeit," but lamented in 1912 that it had superseded his own "true" revival around the world.[75]

Third, this book challenges the notions that Seymour allowed explicit racial prejudice to enter into his ranks, that he was guilty of racial discrimination because in 1914 he restricted the top three leadership director positions to people of color, and that early leaders were oblivious to race matters. Instead, it contends that while some Pentecostal leaders may have been oblivious to race matters, Parham and Seymour actively promoted their own views on race matters in a clear, systematic, and sustained way throughout much of their ministries. In fact, at times race matters seemed to consume them. Parham invoked British Israelism to justify his racial views and white supremacy and Seymour stated that the outpouring of the Holy Spirit united followers across racial lines into "one lump" and body of believers. Furthermore, Seymour explicitly repudiated racial prejudice, forbade his followers from discriminating against whites, and stated that Blacks must love their white brothers and sisters even if they discriminated against them. He further stated that the decision to reserve the top three leadership posts to people of color was "not for discrimination," but for peace and to keep down racial division, friction, and race war in the churches.[76]

Fourth, this book challenges the theory that the genius of Pentecostalism lay in its ability to hold the primitive and pragmatic impulses in productive tension and by so doing "capture lighting in a bottle and . . . keep it there . . . decade after decade . . . without . . . cracking the vessel [bottle]." Instead, it argues that the genius of Pentecostalism and the key to its growth and splintering into almost innumerable denominations is due to its built-in tendency to fragment and crack the bottle of denominationalism precisely because of its leaders' *inability* to balance these competing impulses. This is because its aspiring leaders tend to emphasize the primitive impulse for direct, unmediated revelatory experiences with God, that they invoke to justify breaking out of their existing traditions (i.e., cracking and fragmenting the bottle of denominationalism) to form their own new "Apostolic" ministries.[77]

This fragmentation process and thesis is evident in the lives of Parham, Seymour, Crawford, Durham, Mason, and countless indigenous leaders around the world. It may help to explain why this one tradition has developed into 60 percent of all Protestant denominations in the United States and 56 percent (23,000) globally. While some may lament this development, some could look at it from a theological point of view as a vehicle for fulfilling the Great Commission to make disciples of all nations and ethnic groups and as an indigenization of the movement into the local rhythm, cadence, and vernacular of the people.[78]

Fifth, this book argues that the power and attraction of the Azusa Street revival lay in Seymour's ability to create a Christian transgressive social space wherein people from diverse backgrounds could watch, cross, and selectively engage in otherwise socially, racially, theologically, and denominationally prohibited and/or stigmatized practices in American society. These practices included speaking in unknown tongues; interracial and interdenominational mixing; touching, hugging, and laying hands on people for prayer and divine healing across race, class, and gender lines; exorcising evil spirits; engaging in enthusiastic worship and Negro spirituals; and testifying and prophesying, all reportedly, under the power the Holy Spirit. Seymour justified these practices by citing the Bible (e.g., Joel 2:28 and Acts 2:17—"in the last days your sons and daughters shall prophesy . . . and see visions . . . ") and by allowing people to have direct, unmediated revelatory experiences with God, which they invoked to transgress some—though clearly not all—of the social borders and boundaries of the day. Seymour stated the Holy Spirit was key to this Christian transgressive social space because He was, in Seymour's words, a "means to be flooded with the love of God and power for Service" and foster "a love for the truth in God's word."[79] Regardless of the claim's veracity, practically speaking the invocation of the Holy Spirit provided precisely the kind of divine pretext that people needed to override many of the unbiblical social boundaries and conventions of the day.

This transgressive dimension was not just a short liminal moment limited to a few weeks or months as some have suggested, but rather ran continuously for three years at Azusa and spread around the world throughout the twentieth century, despite the racial retrenchment that took place among some white Pentecostals in the United States by the 1920s. In response to external criticism and his own concerns about emotional excess, Seymour began to gently rein in some unbridled charismatic practices by 1909 and run his services decently and in order like a conventional church. Although it lost some of its transgressive racial, social, and transdenominational appeal as a result, it never lost all of it because he still promoted direct experiences with God, the Spirit baptism, revival, and a desire to be flooded with divine love for Christian service and community. By the time Seymour created the Azusa Street Apostolic Faith Mission denomination in 1914, most of his followers had already long since spread his theology and social practices around the world where they founded their own denominations and combinative transgressive Christian social spaces, wherein they selectively blended core Pentecostal beliefs along with local cultural (usually nontheological) practices.

Sixth, Seymour's revival, theology, and transgressive Christian social space were important because they fostered, stimulated, and released transformational leaders and religious founders around the world. They not only attracted a disproportionate number of seasoned missionaries and Christian workers seeking spiritual renewal, but also those seeking a transformational breakthrough in their visions and leadership styles. His theology, revival, and Christian transgressive social space fostered and generated highly effective transformational leaders. Herein lay one of the secrets of the revival and its propensity to generate visionaries that break out of the bottle of denominationalism to spread their message among the masses.

In his classic study on leadership, James MacGregor Burns argues that there are two types of leaders: transactional and transformational. While transactional leaders can be effective because they provide a service or goods in exchange for their follower's support (e.g., politicians provides jobs in exchange for votes or clergy provide ministerial services in exchange for regular church attendance, loyalty, and support), Burns argues that transformational leaders are generally the most effective and influential type of leaders because they help their followership "release" their human potential now "trapped in ungratified needs and crushed hopes and expectations."[80] Burns, Bernard Bass, and Ronald Riggio believe they are also highly effective because they transform their followers into agents of change by uplifting and empowering them to reach their goals and by paying particular attention to their individual needs (i.e., "individualized consideration") and gifts (i.e., in this case their spiritual gifts). Finally, they are transformational because they are intellectually (i.e., in this case doctrinally) stimulating, creative, motivate ordinary people to do more than they thought originally possible (i.e., in this case via the Holy Spirit), and because they provide a compelling vision of the future (i.e., in this case to help fulfill the Great Commission to spread the Christian message to all nations in order to help usher in Christ's Second Coming). In short, they encourage followers to try new approaches and achieve extraordinary outcomes, all of which uplift and enhance their self-worth. Their innovative ideas and creative visions and experiences are not discouraged or criticized because they differ with the leaders' views, something that seems to resonate naturally with Pentecostalism's emphasis on empowering its followers via the Holy Spirit to unleash their spiritual gifts to build up the church and transform their world.[81]

Seymour role modeled transformational leadership through a host of activities, including in his individualized consideration, mentoring, and promotion of each person's spiritual gift(s). He and his revival stimulated transformational leadership by encouraging veteran missionaries and new converts from socially marginal locations in life (poor, working class, female, young, old, immigrants) to receive direct, unmediated revelations from God, to use their revelations and spiritual gifts to benefit others in the church and society, and by allowing them to experiment with their newfound callings, gifts, and emerging leadership skills during revival services without having to worry about or navigate the scoffing and skepticism they might encounter in traditional churches. This created a transgressive social space that empowered people to reimagine their often debilitating historical identities and invoke the Bible and divine revelation to authorize, commission, and grant them the authority they needed to carry out their visions. Going beyond just verbal encouragement, Seymour also provided his followers with the funds, resources, mentoring, and spiritual/moral support (often via letters) they needed to start and carry out their newfound visions. This individualized consideration is not only evident in little actions like Seymour's decision to buy G. B. Cashwell—a former white supremacist—a new suit before he went back to North Carolina to start what many called the Azusa Revival of the South, but also in his raising over $7,000 to meet the material needs of the missionaries and their families he sent to Europe, the Middle East, Africa, India, and China. Moving beyond transactional leadership into a mentoring role, Seymour also wrote to many of these leaders and visited their missions during his preaching tours. He encouraged and publicly praised his followers and published their testimonies in his *Apostolic Faith* newspaper, which not only reinforced their self-worth, but also their loyalty to Seymour and Azusa. This individualized consideration made them more effective than some other leaders at exercising social, emotional, and spiritual intelligence, which contributed to their charisma and ability to create a loyal followership.[82]

Despite facing serious financial and family hardships, they were able to carry out their visions with tenacity because in the words of William James, their ecstatic experiences generated ideas and visions that possessed them until they could work them off though action. In *Varieties of Religious Experience*, James argues that the religious life and vision exclusively pursued tends to make a person eccentric and exceptional. However, this is not so for ordinary believers—who tend to inherit and follow the conventional beliefs and practices of others—but for those future leaders who reportedly have supernatural experiences that in turn become the foundation and basis for their charismatic authority and alternative vision. They use these supernatural experiences and newfound authority to divinely authorize their break out of the confines of institutional religion (i.e., bottle of denominationalism) to become the pattern setters for the church and society. For these religious founders (whom he likens to "religious geniuses" on par with geniuses in other fields), religion is not a "dull habit," but an "acute fever" characterized by exalted emotional sensibility, nervous instability, and abnormal psychological visitations (in this case we might argue divine and supernatural experiences). Many of these characteristics, by the way, were noted by early writers like Charles Shumway in their descriptions of Pentecostal leaders.[83]

As a result of these "original experiences," James notes, they are liable to obsessions, fixed ideas, trances, imbalance, voices, and visions, all of which give them the confidence, resilience, religious authority, and perception of exalted spiritual insight they need to win over the allegiances of the masses to their newfound ideas and movement. Unlike regular followers, this type of leader cannot find rest "until he proclaims it, or in some way 'works it off,'" James stated. Instead of saying, "what shall I *think* about it?" they instinctively ask what "must I *do* about it?" They do not remain mere critics of society, but are people whose ideas they "inflict," for better or worse, "upon the companions of their age" until they work them out in action. Although he cites Quaker founder George Fox as an example of this type of leader (he wrote this in 1902 before Seymour's revival), one could also argue that these insights help explain not only Pentecostal leaders like Seymour, Parham, Crawford, Durham, and others, but also why the larger movement has a built-in tendency to generate religious leaders and founders that crack the bottle of denominationalism and start their own upstart religious movements. In short, Seymour's focus on a vibrant and experiential relationship with Jesus Christ rooted in the outpouring and baptism of the Holy Spirit as manifested through the spiritual gifts helped birth and foster leaders that seek to work out their visions through action. These above factors perhaps as much as any other explain not only the attraction and appeal of Pentecostalism, but also its tendency to fragment, especially in countries and societies where native religions still actively encourage direct, unmediated experiences with the supernatural. This is one of the reasons why Pentecostalism has thrived in highly tribalized and religiously unregulated societies and why most of the fragmentation has taken place in the Two-Thirds World.[84]

However, we should be remiss were we not also to note that there is a darker side to fragmentation and charisma. The Pentecostal tendency to invoke direct unmediated experiences with God to justify their alternative visions can and in many cases has led to schism and division—at least from the point of view of the mother tradition. It can also contribute to a separatist mentality and a lack of unity over seemingly minor doctrinal details and social practices. However, there are also larger macro level unifying experiences like being born-again and Holy Spirit-filled that seem to create a platform and vehicle for interdenominational cooperation and activities like conferences, revival services, evangelistic crusades, pro-life activism, social programming for the poor, women, and at-risk youth, and events like the International March for Jesus and organizations like the Society for Pentecostal Studies.

Despite these unifying experiences, Jay Conger notes that the darker side of charisma is evident when leaders use their platform to aggrandize their own personal needs at the expense of their followers. Charismatic leaders can also seriously miscalculate the material, emotional, and financial resources they need to realize their vision, create unrealistic assessments of the situation and the market demand for their vision and message, and can fail to adapt their vision to the changing times. All of this can lead to a failure to recognize their own flaws, an exaggerated sense of self-importance, blind ambition, and to the manipulation of their followers. Despite being prone to strong visions, charismatic leaders are equally prone to dysfunctional management practices like poor management of followers and secondary leaders, unconventional behavior, the creation of rivalries with in and out groups, and autocratic leadership styles. Just as many of the positive traits of transformational charismatic leaders are evident in the lives of Seymour, Parham, Crawford, Durham, Mason, and others, so too are some of the flaws. These flaws can lead to succession problems because it is difficult for younger followers to fully blossom into leaders of similar authority and power because the charismatic leaders in charge are often not willing to share the stage and necessary resources for their protégés to reach their maximum potential. As a result, this can give birth to new and alternative visions and callings that can ultimately lead to expulsion from the mother movement and fragmentation. This process is evident in the interactions between Parham and Seymour, the latter of whom left Parham's Apostolic Faith after Parham made it difficult for him to develop the Azusa Street revival on his own recognizance and because the former tried to take over and eventually repudiated Seymour's leadership. Thus charismatic qualities and leadership can be both a positive and a negative factor in leadership development and in creating smooth successions. However, Conger also points out that it is possible to train, socialize, and develop future leaders so that these drawbacks can be minimized by intentionally mentoring and empowering people to develop and foster their own unique gifts and visions.[85]

Finally, this book argues that Azusa's decline and loss of transformative power was not due to Seymour's nominal leadership, but rather to a series of overlapping factors such as the loss of his newspaper in 1908; a series of white-initiated conflicts from 1906 to 1911; a conflict between an Azusa leader (not necessarily Seymour) and the Mexican contingent in 1909; the Oneness controversy and rise of other denominations by 1914; and to Seymour's three decisions to rein in the socially experiential and transgressive nature of his once free-flowing revival, to restrict the top three leadership posts at Azusa to people of color in order to end the racial strife in the churches, and to form his own Azusa Street Apostolic Faith Mission denomination. In all of these endeavors, Seymour's ministry went through a very modest but important shift from being a highly transformational to a slightly more transformational-transactional environment that was increasingly bound and routinized by his new church government and guidelines prescribed in his minister's manual.

However, there was never a complete loss of Seymour's transformational vision and style because this routinization was always reportedly tempered by a focus on the work of the Holy Spirit, which kept the doors open to transformational experiences, revelations, and new visions. Still, as a result of these developments and this subtle shift along with the other reasons outlined above (especially losing his newspaper, white-initiated divisions, birth of other denominations), Seymour and Azusa were soon eclipsed by other leaders, centers, and denominations as the most important catalysts for global Pentecostal origins, development, and expansion. However, by this time in 1912 his doctrinal, social, and racial DNA was already deeply infused in the movement's genetic code around the world, even among those that left him since many still clung to many of his core beliefs and social practices, however selectively and episodically practiced. Ironically, the loss of Seymour's newspaper, white support, and influence helped ensure that his original, free-flowing transformational vision and version of Pentecostalism was the one that was exported globally, which explains why some of his later modifications after 1914 were never mainstreamed to the same degree into the larger global Pentecostal movement.

I
BIOGRAPHY

Los Angeles Daily

WEDNESDAY MORNING, APRIL 18, 1906.

WEIRD BABEL OF TONGUES.

New Sect of Fanatics Is Breaking Loose.

Wild Scene Last Night on Azusa Street.

Gurgle of Wordless Talk by a Sister.

Breathing strange utterances and mouthing a creed which it would seem no sane mortal could understand, the newest religious sect has started in Los Angeles. Meetings are held in a tumble-down shack on Azusa street, near San Pedro street, and the devo- for his church, head down, eyes absently fixed on his coming sermon. Suddenly his book went flying one way; his hat another. His two arms widely clutched the empty air. With a furious sprawl, he measured his length along the gravel walk.

From behind a neighboring hedge came very suspicious snickers.

Mr. Gould brushed himself off as best he could and proceeded sorrowfully to church.

He had just started in on his "firstly" when here came an ominous thump and a startling ker-bang on the roof; everyone in the congregation jumped with a start; then smiled and resumed attention to the sermon.

Another thump sounding like Vesuvius getting busy! One of the deacons ran outside. Snorts of laughter, but the thumping ceased.

But just as the congregation was getting rapt in attention to the sermon, there came a most dismal sound, seemingly from the regions under the earth. It was a most lonely, piercing and doleful howl!

The sermon came to a dead stop.

Out from under one of the pews crawled the most forlorn-looking kitten that ever existed. It was not happy and it desired the world to know of its state of mind. Scared by the sudden stillness it searched its

"Weird Babel of Tongues," Los Angeles Daily Times, April 18, 1906. Courtesy of Gastón Espinosa Collection.

1
AMERICAN PENTECOSTAL ORIGINS
PARHAM AND SEYMOUR

GASTÓN ESPINOSA

"As I brushed the sand out of my eyes to wake up, she began talking fast in some language I had never heard before. . . . ," A. C. Valdez recounted of his mother's first visit to the Azusa Street Revival in 1906. "Then the language stopped, and she said: 'Son, I have had the most glorious experience! I have just been baptized in the Holy Ghost and have been given the gift of tongues! . . . These are blessed times. . . . The Holy Ghost is here on earth—like at Pentecost. Thank God we are alive to see fulfillment of the promises of the Bible!"[1]

By contrast, the *Los Angeles Times* declared Seymour's revival a "Weird Babel of Tongues." The "night is made hideous . . . by the howlings of the worshipers, who spend hours swaying back and forth in a nerve-racking attitude of prayer and supplication." The reporter claimed Seymour preached the wildest theories and mad excitement and that although Los Angeles was home to almost numberless creeds, that this new sect of fanatics surpassed them all.[2]

SOCIAL AND RELIGIOUS CONTEXT

Although Seymour's revival took A. C. Valdez's working-class Mexican-American Catholic family by storm and his mother and her entire family converted, the reporter's reaction reflected the rationalistic sentiment of the age. The rise of Enlightenment rationalism, science, and a new urban middle class and the decline of isolated rural communities and experiential religion created an impersonal society. Industrialization, mechanization, the mass production of the pocket watch and the Model T Ford, along with the influx of millions of immigrants and African Americans fleeing the South in the wake of a failed Reconstruction created a period of tremendous social upheaval. The middle-class response was a search for order that stressed uniformity and rationality, administration and management, Americanization and assimilation, and the centralization of authority. Rationality and emotional control were key ingredients in the psychosocial makeup of the era.[3] Seymour and his revival seemed to challenge these ingredients.[4]

Many of the nation's leading Protestant denominations embraced this new middle-class ethos. New scientific interpretations of the Bible and Christianity were gaining ground not only in liberal Protestant but also in fundamentalist-evangelical circles, with its emphasis on Scottish commonsense realism.[5] Scholars sought to demythologize the Bible of its premodern superstitious talk of miracles, healings, and exorcisms in light of human reason and scientific discoveries. While Christian liberalism was outright skeptical of most supernatural truth claims, some fundamentalists and evangelicals targeted select supernatural manifestations such as tongues and miracles. This criticism is best captured in Princeton Seminary's Benjamin Warfield's classic book, *Counterfeit Miracles*. His rationalistic interpretation of history and religion denigrated what he considered primitive social arrangements and religious practices, especially those associated with supernatural, miraculous, and ecstatic experiences.[6]

Those unready or unwilling to embrace this new ethos found solace and meaning in a growing number of metaphysical, occult, and new religious movements, and in upstart Holiness missions advertising their wares in the national religious marketplace. In short, people had choices.[7]

Generally, however, their choices lay between a more orderly and rationalistic approach to religion and an intensely personal and supernatural one represented by metaphysical traditions like spiritualism and theosophy.[8] Pentecostalism provided a third way that navigated between the polarities of hyperrationality and ecstatic supernaturalism, one that combined historic Christianity and experiential religion.

ORIGINS

The exact origins of Pentecostalism are hotly debated.[9] Scholars agree that it was shaped by nineteenth-century slave religion, revivalism, black and white Holiness theology, the Keswick movement, the Reformed idea of power for Christian living, dispensational premillennialism, and divine healing movements. It was also indirectly influenced by Evans Robert's Welsh revival of 1904.[10] Most believe the modern movement in the U.S. began in the early twentieth century.[11] Many credit the slightly built, eccentric evangelist Charles Fox Parham (1873–1929) and the sturdy black Holiness minister William J. Seymour (1870–1922) as two of its key founders.[12]

CHARLES FOX PARHAM

Parham was one of the first persons to teach the classical Pentecostal doctrine that speaking in unknown tongues (xenolalia) was the physical evidence of the baptism with the Holy Spirit. His pre-Pentecostal religious experiences greatly influenced his theology. He was born in Muscatine, Iowa, on June 4, 1873. As a child he suffered from an ailment that affected his growth. He was a bright and precocious lad of strong convictions. Plagued by rheumatic fever, heart trouble, and stomach disorders, Parham and his mother moved to the golden wheat fields of Kansas in 1878. Upon his mother's death in 1885, Parham vowed to see her in heaven and despite being raised in the church later converted to Protestantism in a Congregational church near Cheney. He became an earnest and genuinely pious youth who stressed holy living and personal purity. He also wrestled with the idea of becoming a minister.[13]

Pushing this idea aside in favor of becoming a medical doctor, the feisty but self-conscious teenager entered the Methodist-sponsored Southwest Kansas College around 1890. This took tremendous fortitude given his physical handicap. His medical condition left his feet dangling from his ankles "like tin cans." Despite long stares from his peers, he courageously hobbled from class to class on the sides of his feet. A critical turning point came after another severe bout of rheumatic fever left him at death's door. He interpreted his illness as divine chastisement for refusing God's calling to the ministry. Sitting under a gigantic oak tree at Southwest Kansas in December 1891, he promised God that if he was healed that he would drop out of college and give himself 100 percent to preaching the Gospel. At that moment, his ankles were "instantly healed," he reported. Charles stood up and walked away from college and a medical career and decided to become an evangelist. In 1893, he joined the Methodist Episcopal Church, North. In March, he was licensed as a "local preacher," later pastored two small Methodist churches in Eudora and Linwood, Kansas, and became enamored with the Holiness movement and divine healing.[14]

The Holiness movement began as a renewal movement in the Methodist Church and grew rapidly during Parham's youth from the 1870s to the 1890s. It emphasized complete sanctification and moral perfection in this life and was popularized by the writings of Phoebe Palmer and Hannah Whitall Smith. Parham's growing involvement left him disenchanted with the bishop-driven Methodist Church. He was particularly horror-struck that candidates for ordination had to preach from a script rather than simply by divine inspiration. After the Methodist Church expelled the Holiness movement from its ranks around 1895, Parham and 100,000 others fanned out across the nation to create their own ministries. Parham wrote that God called him to leave the Methodist Church and "set others right"—a sentiment he kept his entire life.[15]

In 1896, Parham married Sarah Thistlethwaite, a Quaker. Her grandfather, an Englishman named David Baker, persuaded Parham to reject the traditional beliefs in hell as a place of eternal torment, water baptism, and

Charles Fox Parham. Used by permission of Flower Pentecostal Heritage Center.

mandatory church membership. This led Parham to later argue that hell was a "Pagan-Catholic doctrine" "concocted by Augustine and adopted by Protestants" for anyone who would not join their churches.[16]

Parham also embraced the British-Israelism theory, which claimed that the Anglo-Saxon race were the lineal descendants of the ten lost tribes of Israel and therefore God's chosen people. He adopted a sacred genealogy that traced Queen Victoria's ancestral pedigree all the way back to the Tribe of Judah, the ten lost tribes of Israel, and Adam and Eve. He believed that the Stone of Scone, on which the kings of England, Scotland, and Ireland had been crowned for a thousand years, was brought to Ireland by the prophet Jeremiah and the ten lost tribes.[17]

In his theological treatise, *Kol Kare Bomidbar: A Voice Crying Out in the Wilderness* (1902, 1910), he argued that Adam and Eve were a white race of people created by God on the eighth day of creation and were morally and spiritually superior to blacks, Latinos, Native Americans, and Asians, who were all created on the sixth day. Despite centuries of white missionary efforts, sixth day people were "nearly all heathen still." For this reason, Parham believed it was important to segregate the races and avoid interracial marriage because miscegenation had caused Noah's Flood and the destruction of the world. He warned that if the present intermarriage between the races did not cease it would dilute the Anglo-Saxon race and lead to the eventual downfall of America. His Anglo-Saxon British Israelism theory gave him a sacred genealogy by which to support Manifest Destiny, Jim Crow segregation, and white supremacy.[18]

Parham also embraced aspects of Zionism and Theodore Herzl's Jewish Congress's work in Vienna to reclaim Palestine and turn it into a Jewish state. He did not believe that orthodox Jews had to convert to Christianity. In order to help hasten Christ's Second Coming, he set out on a journey to find the Ark of the Covenant (and later Noah's Ark) in order to attract the Jewish Diaspora back to Jerusalem, where they would rebuild the Temple, though without success. This series of events would usher in the Armageddon and the Second Coming of Christ to set up His thousand-year millennial kingdom prophesied in Revelation 20:1–6. Anglo-Saxon Americans played a special role by fighting against the Anti-Christ, a view Parham based on the Apocrypha (II Esdras 11–12), despite also arguing that most Roman Catholics were not true Christians.[19]

Parham developed these views during a tumultuous period in his life. In 1897 his first child was born and Parham was "miraculously" healed of heart disease. As a result, the former premed student preached that medicine was from the devil not because he didn't recognize its positive impact, but rather because he believed that people placed their trust more in medicine than God. To help spread his message on healing and prepare people for the mission field, in 1898 he opened Beth-el Healing Home in Topeka, Kansas, and started the *Apostolic Faith* newspaper.

Two years later Parham and eight students traveled cross-country, visiting prominent Holiness centers like John Alexander Dowie's Zion City, Illinois; A. B. Simpson's Nyack College in New York; Frank Sandford's Shiloh commune in Maine; and others. He was particularly inspired by Dowie's attempt to replicate the Apostolic Church in the United States and practice the spiritual gifts, especially divine healing.[20]

After soaking up Sandford's Holiness teaching for six months in Maine and hearing stories about students and missionaries speaking in real languages they had never studied—as in Acts 2:4—what they called "tongues" (xenolalia), Parham became convinced that tongues enabled people to preach to "pagans" globally in their own language. Energized by his newfound conviction, Parham returned to Kansas, where he opened Beth-el Bible School in Topeka on October 16, 1900. He rented Stone Mansion from the American Bible Society for sixteen dollars per month and enrolled forty nonpaying students to prepare them for the outpouring of the Spirit and missionary work.[21] They were about to make history.

The American Pentecostal movement began after Parham challenged his students to search the Bible for evidence of the baptism with the Holy Spirit. In his absence, they concluded that speaking in tongues (xenolalia) was the initial, physical evidence of the baptism with the Holy Spirit—later refined as the Initial Evidence Theory.

According to Pentecostal tradition, on New Year's Day 1901, Parham laid his hands on Miss Agnes Ozman (1870–1937) and prayed that she might receive the Holy Spirit.[22] As a result, she reportedly received it and spoke Chinese. On January 3, nineteen more students were reportedly baptized. Fanciful accounts claimed that—like on the Day of Pentecost in Acts—tongues of fire rested over their heads. Parham himself finally received the baptism and reportedly spoke in German.[23] As a result, he became convinced and possessed by the idea that speaking in tongues (xenolalia, not glossolalia) was the true physical, initial evidence of the baptism with the Holy Spirit—though the initial evidence doctrine was not crystalized until a number of years later.[24]

Parham's controversial beliefs and aggressive proselytism attracted sharp criticism from the otherwise mild-mannered Kansans. The local press ridiculed his Bible school, calling it "the Tower of Babel." Some of Parham's former students called him a fake. The storm that erupted over his newfound beliefs prompted him to flee Topeka in April 1901. With his Bible school disintegrating and his foes attacking him on all sides, Parham retreated from the world he sought to convert for a short time. During this respite, he published *Kol Kare Bomidbar* in 1902. His ministry was reignited by his powerful revivals two years later in Galena, Kansas, and in Joplin and Carthage, Missouri. The rough and tumble mining region of Galena was ripe for Parham's message of divine healing and spiritual empowerment. Thousands converted to his Apostolic Faith Movement. A new Christian denomination was born.

Emboldened by his recent campaigns, Parham cast his eyes south to the horizonless prairies of Texas. He and his followers "invaded" the state on July 4, 1905, and made preparations to "lay siege to the city of Houston in the name of the Lord." On July 10, he held revival services at Bryan Hall, where they put on native Bible Lands costumes and walked down the street carrying banners with slogans like "Victory" and "Unity" to advertise their services. He also hosted "fashion shows" and marches as strategies to attract people to their nightly revival meetings, even wearing a plumed hat.[25]

Parham and Apostolic Faith Workers, Bryan Hall, Houston, July–August 1905. Used by permission of Flower Pentecostal Heritage Center.

In August, he persuaded a young lawyer named Warren Faye Carothers to receive the baptism with the Holy Spirit and to join his fledgling movement. In December, Parham claimed the title of "Projector" of the Apostolic Faith Movement and opened his tuition-free Houston Bible School. It served as the headquarters and training ground for his Apostolic evangelists. Not long thereafter, a soft-spoken black Holiness preacher from Louisiana Bayou Teche country named William J. Seymour expressed interest in attending the all-white school.[26]

WILLIAM JOSEPH SEYMOUR

Seymour was an unlikely prophet and even more unlikely founder of a global religious movement. The five-foot nine-inch tall Seymour was born to former slaves named Simon and Phyllis Salabar Seymour in Centerville, Louisiana, on May 2, 1870. He was baptized by Father M. Harnais on September 4 at the Roman Catholic Church of the Assumption in nearby Franklin and brought up in the steaming hot Louisiana bayous during Reconstruction with his seven brothers and sisters—Rosalie, Simon, Amos, Julia, Jacob, Isaac, and Emma. They soon attended New Providence Baptist Church right next to their home in Centerville. Sugarcane, cotton, and other plantation-grown crops and Jim Crow segregation dominated the economy and their lives.[27]

Seymour was keenly aware of his theoretical Fourteenth Amendment "freedoms" and the ugly reality of Southern racism. Louisiana had one of the highest lynching rates in the nation. He grew up hearing stories about black men being tarred, feathered, and branded and perhaps even witnessed a charred black body dangling from a lynchman's rope. Although little is known about his childhood, he was raised on a four-acre farm that his father, a Union Civil War veteran, had purchased in 1883. Despite the land, the Seymours lived in poverty. With only a few years of primary school education, William could read and write, but only with difficulty until later in life.[28]

Seymour was not part of W.E.B. Du Bois's (1868–1963) "Talented Tenth," that elite corps of African-American college-educated leaders that would raise the black community out of the misery and the legacy of slavery. Du Bois, a Harvard trained PhD in history and a contemporary of Seymour, wrote: "from the very first it has been the educated and intelligent Negro people that have led and elevated the mass." This new corps were called on to be the "missionaries of culture" and to exercise the "vision of seers." Du Bois believed they would "leaven the lump" and "inspire the masses" in the black community and through them the nation.[29]

Although Seymour and Du Bois probably never met, Seymour was part of the "lump," and he knew it. Yet he became convinced that God also used ordinary prophets (that is, ordinary people led by the Spirit of God to promote God's will on earth), and not just those blessed with a formal education, to make a difference in this world. Indeed, Seymour's story represents how some of the other 90 percent of the black masses tried to "leaven the lump" and elevate, empower, and inspire the masses.[30]

Like Parham, Seymour resisted his divine calling to the ministry. In the 1890s, and for reasons that are unclear, Seymour left the South and journeyed north to Memphis, Tennessee; St. Louis, Missouri; Indianapolis, Indiana; Chicago, Illinois; then back to Louisiana before moving on to other locales like Cincinnati, Ohio. Whether or not he was specifically running away from his divine calling is uncertain, though possible. What is clear is that he wanted to escape the stifling oppression of southern racism along with its reign of terror, which from 1880 to 1920 resulted in the political disenfranchisement and grisly torture and lynching of more than twenty-five hundred blacks throughout the nation, but especially in the South.[31]

FINDING FAITH AND A DIVINE CALLING: AFRICAN-METHODIST EPISCOPAL AND HOLINESS MOVEMENT INFLUENCES

In the north, Seymour found respite from the terror but still faced racial prejudice, albeit in a more genteel Yankee form. A critical turning point came when he moved to Indianapolis in 1895, where although he continued to visit other states for brief periods, he stayed until 1900. He attended the all-black Simpson Chapel Methodist Episcopal Church, which was part of the larger white Northern Methodist Episcopal denomination. There he answered the evangelist's call, gave his life to Jesus Christ, and became a born-again Christian.[32]

During his travels, Seymour was influenced by Daniel S. Warner's Evening Light Saints, later called the Church of God Reformation Movement. This socially progressive, radical Holiness group preached racial equality and reconciliation around the beginning of Jim Crow segregation and actively reached out to blacks. During this time, Seymour claimed to be instantaneously sanctified and felt a divine calling to the ministry, but refused it. The Saints provided him with one of his first visions of a racially egalitarian church—a vision he remained true to the rest of his life. Next he journeyed to Cincinnati, Ohio, in search of a new life and a color-blind society, and a land of plenty—Beulah Land (Isaiah 62:4). He lived in Ohio from 1901 to 1902. In Cincinnati, Seymour experienced racial equality and integration when he associated with Martin Wells Knapp's God's Bible School. There he soaked up holiness teachings and radical social views on racial integration and unity, something he clung to the rest of his life.[33]

Seymour only gave in to his divine calling to the ministry after suffering a bout with small pox that nearly cost him his life. With his face now permanently scarred and blind in his left eye, Seymour was ordained an evangelist by the Evening Light Saints. As a sign of his fresh start, he grew a beard to cover the scars of what he believed was God's just chastisement for his disobedience. He traveled to Texas in search of ministry opportunities and his relatives. In the winter of 1904–5, he was led by "special revelation" to Jackson, Mississippi, where he visited the famous black Holiness leader Charles Price Jones (1864–1949) and possibly met Charles Mason (1866–1961). He sought Jones's spiritual advice and probably participated in his pastors' conference from January 15–25, 1905, and thus left the South with an even stronger commitment to the Bible, premillennial theology, prophecy, holiness, and special revelation.[34]

SEYMOUR MEETS PARHAM IN HOUSTON

Seymour traveled to Houston where he found his lost relatives and joined a Holiness church led by a former Virginia slave named Lucy Farrow, the niece of Frederick Douglass. She had received the Spirit baptism at Parham's revival in Columbus, Ohio, on September 6, 1905, and worked as Parham's governess. When the Parhams decided to travel briefly to Kansas, Farrow asked Seymour to serve as interim pastor. Upon her return, she introduced Seymour to Parham. He then asked Seymour to conduct joint evangelistic

Houston Bible School, 1905. Used by permission of Kansas State Historical Society.

services among blacks. Parham was, in his own way, a nonconformist who welcomed blacks, Indians, and Mexicans to his services, though always segregated from whites. He believed every soul mattered to God.[35]

Impressed by Parham's outreach to blacks, Seymour asked him in late 1905 or early 1906 if he could attend his Houston Bible School. Parham agreed but only on the condition that Seymour take notes in the hallway or in an adjacent room. This move affirmed the letter but violated the spirit of the Jim Crow segregation laws in Houston. This took courage on Parham's part, for he risked not only alienating potential students but also the very society he sought to convert. Parham, however, was his own man. He counted the cost and adjusted the boundaries of law and society as his worn Bible and conscience dictated.[36]

Seymour soaked up Parham's teachings about the outpouring and baptism with the Holy Spirit and divine healing and he became convinced by the idea they were long forgotten biblical truths. They conducted joint evangelistic services in the black community. While he wholeheartedly agreed with Parham's teaching on the Spirit baptism, he was increasingly disturbed by some of his theological, social, and racial views. Although Sarah Parham wrote that Seymour "received all the truths and teachings we had held from the beginning" and memorized many of Parham's teachings "word for word," she failed to note that he only spent two to eight weeks at Parham's School, left before his studies were complete, didn't receive the Spirit baptism under Parham's ministry because he would not allow blacks and whites to mix at the altar, and that within less than a year he'd repudiate almost all of Parham's controversial theological, social, and racial views.[37]

GROWING DOUBTS ABOUT PARHAM

Seymour embraced Parham's views on tongues and divine healing, yet realized that Parham's segregation views were not simply a matter of social convention but his genuine theological convictions about race relations. In *Kol Kare Bomidbar: A Voice Crying in the Wilderness*, Parham taught racial separation, Eighth-Day Creationism, white supremacy, and the idea that miscegenation caused Noah's flood. Parham also promoted British Israelism, which posited that the Anglo-Saxon race were the lineal descendants of the ten lost tribes of Israel and therefore God's chosen race.[38] Seymour was surprised by Parham's controversial belief on annihilationism, rejection of hell as a place of eternal punishment, Zionism, use of the Apocrypha, and his notion that America would play a key role in Bible prophecy by waging war against the Anti-Christ and would emerge "seemingly victorious, though horribly punished."[39] Many of these beliefs perplexed Seymour. After careful reflection, he decided neither to repudiate nor affirm Parham's controversial views but join another church outside of Parham's control.

Seymour's break came in late January or early February 1906 when a visitor to Farrow's congregation named Neely Terry asked him to candidate for the pastorate of her home Holiness Mission in Los Angeles. Seymour jumped at the chance, even though Parham and Carothers strongly admonished him to remain in Texas and preach among his "own color." A classic opportunist and careful propagandist, Parham saw the hard-working and mild-mannered Seymour as a way to reach the vast throngs of blacks in Texas and the Deep South. For this reason, Parham and Carothers were surprised when the normally compliant Seymour "suddenly announced that he was called of God to go to California"—against their expressed wishes.[40]

Seymour gently stood up to Parham and insisted that he had to follow God's calling. He used the divine pretext to "pull rank" on Parham and alter the otherwise unequal power relationship, much as Parham himself had done several years earlier with the Methodists. Although not happy about Seymour's "calling" to a mission outside of his control, Parham relented and even financed part (though not all as claimed by Sarah Parham) of Seymour's trip after he learned that he would be preaching to blacks.[41] Carothers and his friends organized a farewell party. Parham's patronage left Seymour in his debt—one that he would call in soon enough. For the time being, Seymour boarded the train for Los Angeles and a new life in California.[42] Had Parham known the future, he would have done all he could to stop Seymour from going west.

Richard and Ruth Asberry's home, 214 (later 216) North Bonnie Brae Street. Used by permission of Flower Pentecostal Heritage Center.

2
HOLY AWE AND INDESCRIBABLE WONDER
THE AZUSA STREET REVIVAL

GASTÓN ESPINOSA

On February 22, 1906, William Seymour arrived in Los Angeles hopeful but practically broke. Two days later he began preaching at Mrs. Julia Hutchins's Holiness Mission near Santa Fe Avenue and Ninth Street. He planned to spend the next ten days preaching about salvation, sanctification, healing, and the Holy Spirit baptism. His hopes for a vibrant ministry were dashed after he taught that although he had never personally spoken in tongues, they should eventually be spoken by all true Christians in his day. Hutchins, the interim leader, was shocked by Seymour's outlandish claims. Without warning, on March 4 she padlocked the church door. He was expelled from the mission and, by implication, the ministry in his new Holiness Mission.[1]

Now penniless and without a place to stay, Seymour turned hat-in-hand to Edward Lee, a member of Hutchins's all-black congregation. Lee let him stay at his home until he could raise the train fare back to Texas. He did so despite his skepticism about the "strange" claims of his "unwelcome guest." Over the next few days Seymour's spirituality, humility, grasp of theology, and persuasive abilities impressed the Lees. Seeking to discern the will of God, Seymour called for a prayer meeting at the Lee's cottage on 114 South Union Street. After it quickly grew too large, Seymour moved it to Richard and Ruth Asberry's home at 214 (now 216) North Bonnie Brae Street, in the heart of the small but lively African-American community.

By mid-March, whites began to attend the meetings, including Swedish immigrants like Louis, Anna, and Arthur Osterberg and future Azusa Street historian Frank Bartleman—who first visited the prayer meeting on March 26. Louis later became a trustee and Arthur later merged his own independent mission with Seymour's Azusa Mission.[2] As the services grew, Seymour realized he needed to secure ministerial credentials to legally incorporate the work, perform his ministerial duties like marriages and funerals, and send out missionaries. With his newfound convictions about tongues rejected by all Protestants, he took a second look at Parham's Apostolic Faith. Although he had already outgrown some of Parham's unique views, he returned because he was still firmly convinced of Parham's teaching about the outpouring and baptism with the Holy Spirit. Thus the decision to return to Parham—and more accurately to the Apostolic Faith—is not as surprising as it might sound, since it was operationally run by Carothers and was growing rapidly beyond Parham's control. In fact, not long thereafter Carothers and others expelled Parham from the Houston-based Apostolic Faith faction. The physical distance between Los Angeles and Houston also provided Seymour maximum freedom to run his ministry as he felt led by the Spirit.

However, this same distance also made communication slow. Seymour made multiple requests to Parham, almost pleading to him to send his promised credentials. Parham promised them back on April 1, but still hadn't sent them. In fact, he didn't respond to any of Seymour's letters. Seymour finally wrote Carothers on July 12, three-and-a-half months later. Almost as if to prove his worth, Seymour wrote about the spectacular growth of the revival and the fact that he was sending missionaries to China, India, Africa, and Jerusalem. He needed credentials right away to legally ordain them in the State of California and also for railroad travel discounts to visit the growing number of missions that invited him to speak. Parham continued to drag his feet, thus keeping Seymour firmly under his control and from fully developing his ministry. As his frustration grew, the normally patient Seymour asked Parham to "please answer soon."[3]

As an incentive, Seymour shrewdly invited Parham to hold a citywide revival in Los Angeles that would unite all of the "little revivals" throughout the city. The strategy worked and Parham finally authorized Carothers to send him the credentials.[4] Parham then wrote Seymour promising that he would unite "all of the little revivals" into one grand revival under his leadership during his visit on September 16. Parham, however, never showed. This could have been due to a genuinely busy schedule, as his biographer argues, or as a way of putting Seymour and his followers in their place, or some combination thereof. More than likely, Parham had bigger fish to fry. For several months he had been trying to wrest control of Alexander Dowie's Zion City, Illinois, from Wilbur Viola, Dowie's outspoken successor and Parham's sworn enemy. Despite Parham's delay, Seymour's prayer meeting was now bursting at the seams and excitement was in the air. Full-blown revival was just around the corner.[5]

ORIGINS AND SETTING OF THE AZUSA STREET REVIVAL IN LOS ANGELES

On April 6, 1906, Seymour led the all-black prayer group on a ten-day fast for revival. He tapped into this widespread theme popularized the preceding year throughout Los Angeles by Frank Bartleman, Joseph Smale, and other white and black Holiness leaders inspired by Evan Robert's 1904 Welsh revival.[6]

Louis, Terry, Esther, Arthur G., and Emma Osterberg, Chicago, ca. 1895. Used by permission of Flower Pentecostal Heritage Center.

Three days later on April 9, Seymour laid hands on Lee and prayed for him to receive the Spirit baptism. Lee immediately spoke in tongues. At the prayer meeting that night a little before 7:30 PM in the Asberrys' living room, Seymour preached from Acts 2:4 about the Spirit baptism. Before he finished, Pentecostal tradition has it that "the fire came down," meaning that God poured out His Spirit on Bonnie Brae like on the Day of Pentecost in Acts 2:4 and people erupted in tongues. The Azusa Street Revival was ignited. Like at Parham's Topeka School five years earlier, embellished reports later claimed that tongues of fire swirled above the heads of the band of "prayer warriors." Jennie Evans Moore was the first woman to reportedly speak in tongues—Spanish, French, Latin, Greek, Hebrew, and Hindustani—none of which she knew prior to that evening. She reportedly played the piano under the divine inspiration and thereafter served as the mission's worship leader.[7]

Seymour received the Holy Spirit baptism on April 12. In direct opposition to Parham's practice, he and a white man went to the makeshift altar in the Asberrys' living room and after a long night of tarrying together received the baptism side-by-side—black and white. These events attracted a growing throng of curious and spiritually "hungry" washerwomen, cooks, laborers, janitors, ministers, and housewives.[8] More miraculously it seemed to outsiders, blacks and whites were worshipping together—and at the same altar. The color line that divided America, Frank Bartleman quipped, was washed away by the blood of Jesus.[9]

The revival's popularity was due not only to Seymour's creative leadership but also to a number of large historical, social, and spiritual developments that paved the way. Seymour and his followers saw their movement in continuity with previous Protestant Evangelical movements led by Martin Luther, Charles and John Wesley, Charles Finney, Dwight Moody, Evans Robert, and others.[10] They also recognized a number of other pre- and proto-Azusa revivals around the world.[11]

Seymour was convinced that the outpouring at Azusa was the latest in a series of revivals among the French Protestants, the Quakers, the Irvingite Church around 1830, in the Swedish Revival of 1841–43, the Irish Revival of 1859, Parham's Topeka revival of 1901, the Welsh revival of 1904–5, and even among certain missionaries in Africa—a reference not without significance given Seymour's African heritage.[12] They also wrote about similar manifestations of the Spirit in the work of Minnie Abrams, Pandita Ramabai, and their students at the Mukti Mission, India.[13] They interpreted these manifestations and others as precursors and contemporary developments that paved the way for the Latter Rain Holy Spirit Outpouring prophesied in Joel 2.[14]

Seymour and his followers began printing their own *Apostolic Faith* newspaper in Los Angeles in September 1906 and used it to argue that the Spirit baptism brought people together in Christian unity across all man-made racial, social, and ecclesiastical boundaries. As a result, people from twenty races and nationalities reportedly worshipped together in one accord and laid hands on each other for prayer to receive the baptism with the Holy Spirit and for divine healing. Men not only prayed for men, but also for women—and across racial and class lines. For some outsiders, this created a socially, racially, and spiritually transgressive social space wherein people engaged in behavior and practices (blacks and whites laying hands on one another for prayer or greetings) that were deemed socially inappropriate (i.e., socially sinful) by many in society. It was also a place where worshippers could reimagine their often socially debilitating historical (i.e., racial, social, gender) identities and interact on a more even playing field. A black man could now expect to be treated like a white man and a white man was allowed to worship like a black man and women could preach to both.

The socially transgressive nature of Seymour's message and revival practices is clear when compared to the race riots that erupted that same month in Springfield, Missouri. On April 14, 1906, the day before Azusa opened its doors, three African Americans named Horace Duncan, Fred Coker, and Will Allen were dragged by an angry club-wielding mob of seven thousand whites to the town square and hung until their lifeless bodies dangled in the air. Five months later in September 1906, Atlanta newspapers claimed that black men had assaulted white women on four separate occasions. This ignited the Atlanta race riots—among the worst in U.S. history—that left at least twenty-five African Americans and two whites dead. By contrast, that same September in Los Angeles, God was "melting" all races together in Christian unity.[15]

At Azusa blacks, whites, and other nationalities worshipped together in racial harmony in a black person's home in the black section of Los Angeles. Their interracial meetings, reports of supernatural healings, and powerful singing attracted the masses. The weight of the attendees overflowing onto the Asberrys' front porch was so great that it caused the porch to collapse, though without injury.[16]

The growing throngs of parched souls, skeptics, and curious onlookers forced Seymour to make the historic decision to move his growing flock to the former Stevens African Methodist Episcopal (AME) Church at 312 Azusa Street. Although Stevens was founded in the home of Biddie Mason in 1870, the church was not finally completed until 1888. It was abandoned in 1903 after a fire destroyed the pitched roof. Seriously damaged, the dilapidated forty by sixty foot, two-story whitewashed building was converted into a horse stable and storage room on the first floor and tenement apartments on the second. The cobweb-lined low ceilings, sawdust-covered dirt floor, and rough-hewn redwood pews made it feel like old Methodist and Holiness camp meetings on the frontier—but now twenty-five hundred miles west in the former Mexican pueblo of Los Angeles. Indeed, the old mission looked and smelled more like a barn than a church, participants reported. Located on a short dead-end street half a block long, not far from the Los Angeles railroad terminal, the mission was surrounded by a lumberyard, a tombstone shop, stockyards, and other shops. The "barn-like" atmosphere was not lost on attendees, who later compared it to Jesus's humble manger in Bethlehem.[17]

The fact that Seymour chose Stevens has historical and social significance, though often overlooked in past histories. Stevens was part of the oldest black denomination in the United States. Richard Allen and Absalom Jones founded the AME in 1814. The spark that ignited the founding took place in 1787 after Jones was asked to get up from the altar where he was kneeling in prayer with whites at St. George's Methodist Episcopal Church in Philadelphia and pray in the segregated seating at the rear of the church. Instead, he walked out and never returned.[18] Now, over a century later, blacks and whites still prayed at segregated altars. However, at Azusa—and in direct contrast with Parham's practices—blacks and whites transgressed this social prohibition and prayed together at the front altar.

Seymour chose the former AME church because people in his prayer group had been members of Stevens and because he wanted to avoid complaints about noise. He was keenly aware of the controversy that might arise if news broke of a black man leading a loud multiracial revival in a white church. Perhaps—more presciently—he also realized it would simply be a matter of time before whites assumed control, something that other black leaders like W.E.B. Du Bois—among others—also struggled with even in progressive organizations like the NAACP.[19]

While Seymour and the AME shared a common desire to save souls, by 1906 he parted company with it because it focused almost exclusively on the black community. In contrast, Seymour decided to share power and the highest leadership positions with whites. He asked whites like Hiram Smith—a Methodist—to serve as founding copastor, and Louis Osterberg and Edward Doak to serve on the Board of Trustees, though he also named African Americans to his pastoral staff (Joseph Warren) and board as well. Although it's true that his prayer meeting began as an all-black event on Bonnie Brae Street, by the time it arrived at Azusa and opened its doors on April 15, it was a multiracial-ethnic rather than a black only congregation. This is evident in the Articles of Incorporation and decisions to appoint whites to his pastoral staff, business staff, trustee board, ordination committee, and newspaper editorial team.[20]

Despite his differences with the AME, Seymour clearly drew on AME and black church hymnody, spirituality, theology, social practices, and progressive attitudes on racial equality. He also "prayed down" revival the way he and his black colleagues knew best. The Bonnie Brae meeting was birthed and nurtured in the womb of the black church and was transformed by Seymour into a multiracial-ethnic revival on Azusa Street.[21]

MEXICANS AND THE FIRST SUPERNATURAL MANIFESTATIONS OF THE HOLY SPIRIT AND DIVINE HEALING

Despite the church's location and dilapidated state, scores of curious spectators and spiritual vagabonds from all over the city and walks of life descended on it, where "freedom in the Spirit" prevailed. This freedom was evident in the first reported manifestation of the Spirit, which took place the day before the first service. Eyewitness and future Assemblies of God leader Arthur G. Osterberg stated that on Friday, April 13, 1906, a Mexican-American day worker clearing the Azusa Mission of debris was struck by the power of the Spirit after a black woman from the Bonnie Brae prayer group pulled him aside and, after an energetic discussion, prayed for him. As a result, he reportedly fell to his knees amidst the clutter and burst into tears. Osterberg stated this was the first manifestation of the Spirit at Azusa.[22]

Indeed, the revival began as an enthusiastic prayer meeting with sixty to one hundred "prayer warriors." They prayed for a revival that would shake the city, nation, and world. They got more than they bargained for when on April 18 the San Francisco earthquake's aftershocks rolled through the city and rattled the dust off the old rafters. A *Los Angeles Times* reporter also ripped into Azusa on April 18 as a place where a "colored" minister with a "big fist" preached the "wildest theories" and "mad excitement."[23]

Despite the negative press in the English-speaking community, in the Spanish-speaking community the Mexican day laborer invited other Latinos to Azusa. Osterberg reports that "hundreds" of Catholics attended the revival, "many" of them "Spanish" (Mexican Americans) and "Mexican" (Mexican immigrants). Abundio and Rosa López; Susie, José, and Adolfo C. Valdez; Brigido Pérez; Juan Navarro Martínez; Luís López; and possibly Genaro and Romanita Carbajal Valenzuela were among the many. Abundio and Rosa began attending on May 29 and received the Holy Spirit baptism on June 5. They preached Seymour's message in downtown Los Angeles (La Placita) and throughout California and probably northern Mexico. The growing Latino response to the revival was significant enough to prompt them to publish the López's testimony in English *and* Spanish in October 1906. Abundio faithfully assisted Seymour and was ordained by him in 1909. He and Rosa attended Maria Woodworth-Etter's healing ministry and Abundio went on to serve in the Spanish ministry until the 1940s in southern California as the photograph below indicates. They ministered at Azusa and Victoria Hall before Rosa passed away and Abundio remarried.[24]

Mexicans were not only involved in the first supernatural manifestation of the Spirit at Azusa, but also in its first healing.[25] Osterberg stated that the first person healed at Azusa was a Mexican man with clubfoot. The Sunday after Azusa began, Osterberg and his family sat toward the front of the mission along with a Mexican family from San Bernardino. He knew they were Catholic because the man, his wife, and two daughters knelt in front of their seats and then crossed themselves. After Seymour called on people to stand up and pray, the clubfooted Mexican began to haltingly walk up and down the aisle in an attitude of prayer. As he walked back and forth, he began clapping his hands with his face tilted heavenward. His wife joined him. They walked up and down the aisle until gradually he ceased to limp. After he returned to his seat and the service was over, Osterberg asked: "Your foot—did something

Reverend Abundio López (front center, wearing the pinstripe suit) is seated with a Pentecostal congregation in Southern California between 1920 and the 1940s. Courtesy of Gastón Espinosa Collection.

happen to your foot?" Surprised, the Mexican man looked down and began moving his foot and realized he had been healed. He shouted "Hallelujah!" Afterward, the other Mexicans explained to him the Holy Spirit baptism, and he immediately went to the front of the altar, knelt down, and received it, something that amazed Osterberg because he still hadn't received it.[26]

He was not the last Mexican to be healed at Azusa. A. C. Valdez reported many healings, including that of his father, José, who traced his ancestry back to the founding of the California Spanish missions after 1769. Abundio and Rosa also stated that divine healing was part and parcel of their ministry.[27] Latino participation along with that of other immigrants helped transform a largely biracial, national, English-language prayer meeting on Bonnie Brae Street into a multiracial, international, and multilinguistic revival on Azusa.[28]

CADENCE AND SPIRITUALITY OF THE REVIVAL

Azusa's daily schedule was mind-boggling by today's standards. Seymour or one of his associates led services three times a day seven days a week from 1906 to 1909. Services took place in the morning, midday, and evening, often blending into one another. In contrast to highly liturgical services, the

The Shakarians were Russian immigrants of Armenian heritage who attended Seymour's revival and started their own Pentecostal mission in Los Angeles. Demos Shakarian founded the Full Gospel Businessmen's Association. Photo: Demos and Grace Shakarian. Dau, Hamas, Erchen, Illy, Isaac, Margaret, Esther, Sirron. Used by permission of Flower Pentecostal Heritage Center.

revival was reportedly led by the Spirit. However, people regularly kneeled in front of their seats, prayed, and then sat with their eyes closed to hear the voice of God, listened to a sermon and testimonies, and finally prayed for the manifestation of the Holy Spirit. Conversion, Spirit baptism, exorcising demons, and miraculous healings reportedly took place on a regular basis. One could also expect to see fervent prayer, quiet reflection, songs, and testimonies, words of exhortation, and preaching at almost every service—in addition to singing in tongues (aka "singing in the spirit").[29]

After services, blacks, whites, Mexicans, Swedes, Irish, English, Russians, Armenians, Chinese, South Asians, and other immigrants trod upstairs to the Upper Room where they sought the baptism with the Holy Spirit, the gift of tongues, and spent more time in prayer and quiet meditation—sometimes for days. Racial-ethnic minorities, men, and women often intermingled, prayed for each other, lay prostrate on the floor, or knelt in an attitude of prayer and supplication. This "tarrying room" was also the place where people normally received the Spirit baptism. These activities also took place in the little cottage behind Azusa, where they shared meals across racial, class, and gender lines. Working-class immigrants like the Russian origin but ethnic Armenian Demos Shakarian family, for example, were convinced by Seymour's message and were so possessed by the desire to promote the outpouring and baptism with the Holy Spirit that they even started their own mission. Swedes, Mexicans, and other immigrants followed suit.[30]

To avoid accusations of sexual impropriety, men generally prayed for men and women prayed for women, although exceptions were made provided other women were present. Still, the fact that a man might lay his hands on a woman other than his wife to pray for her to receive the Spirit baptism or to be healed—especially when it was a black man praying for a white upper-class woman—was considered a transgressive social act.

Although not emphasized in contemporary Pentecostalism, most early "saints" equated tongues with the God-given ability to speak a human language (xenolalia) they had never studied. This was Parham's stated teaching and one from which he never wavered.[31] These "missionary tongues" were reportedly confirmed by immigrants, eyewitnesses that had formally studied the language, and missionaries on furlough.[32] However, many went to the mission field only to find that they didn't in fact speak the language. As a result, Parham and others were quick to criticize Seymour's teachings and practices as "counterfeit," since he believed that true tongues must always evidence real human languages. Most scholars argue there is not enough decisive historical evidence to confirm or deny these missionary tongues.[33]

While some left the movement, Seymour and other veterans like Alfred and Lillian Garr simply rationalized that it was a misunderstanding of the biblical purpose of tongues. They taught that tongues did not always have to be a real human language (xenolalia), but could also be a divine language (glossolalia) known only to God.[34]

WORSHIP

It wasn't tongues but the powerful singing that stood out most to visitors. Bartleman wrote: "In the beginning in 'Azusa' we had no musical instruments. In fact we felt no need for them. . . . All was spontaneous. We did not ever sing from hymnbooks. All the old well-known hymns were sung from memory quickened by the Spirit of God. We sang it from fresh, powerful heart experience." Glenn Cook wrote that the worship services created a "holy awe" and "indescribable wonder" and a place where "evil speaking and evil thinking was all departed."[35]

Contrary to criticisms of the revival as a wild time of loud and ecstatic experiences, there was a quieter side. Seymour's sermons were almost never shrill. Most were short and simple. Eyewitnesses tell of soft singing, hushed prayers, and long periods of quiet meditation on Scripture, especially in the Upper Room. Bartleman claims that the Upper Room was "sacred, a kind of 'holy ground.'" It was here that "men sought to become quiet from the activities of their own too active mind and spirit, to escape from the world for the time, and get alone with God. There was no noisy, wild, exciting spirit

Frank and Anna Bartleman family. Used by permission of Flower Pentecostal Heritage Center.

there.... It was a sort of 'city of refuge'... a 'haven of rest,' where God could be heard, and talk to their souls."[36]

In 1925, after traveling to many of the leading Pentecostal centers around the world, Bartleman wrote that although Wales was "the cradle" of the modern revival movement and India "the Nazareth" where it was developing, Los Angeles was the place where it became "full grown" Pentecostal and one of the main centers from whence it spread globally. This is why he stated Azusa and the Upper Room were its sacred center and "holy of holies."[37]

THEOLOGY AND MESSAGE OF THE REVIVAL

Indeed, the revival was a place where people integrated body, mind, and spirit. Although some critics accused Seymour and Pentecostals of being "ignoramuses," many leaders were keen students of the Bible, doctrine, and church history.[38] Seymour, Parham, Bartleman, Alfred Garr, Charles Mason, Elmer Fisher, and others had attended college and/or Bible school.[39] They saw the Pentecostal movement in spiritual, theological, and historical continuity with Martin Luther's doctrine of justification and John Wesley's Arminian teaching on sanctification and salvation,[40] and with popular Christian thinkers like Charles Finney, Dwight Moody, G. Campbell Morgan, Charles Spurgeon, A. J. Gordon, A. B. Simpson, and A. T. Pierson.[41] Frequent references to theologians, church historians, Bible scholars, figures in church history, "Siniatic manuscripts," and fine-tuned theological distinctions over the spiritual gifts, tongues, eschatology, annihilationism, along with critiques of occult traditions all indicate a level of theological literacy and sophistication not often ascribed to early Pentecostals.[42] Still some Pentecostals were poorly educated and gloried in it because they believed their ministries rested not on class-bound education and human knowledge but on the power of the Holy Spirit.

Seymour's theological world was shaped by his Holiness, AME, and Arminian backgrounds. He placed a tremendous emphasis on the Great Commission (Matthew 28:19–20), evangelism, and a personal born-again conversion experience with Jesus Christ. He said, "We must remember that every man that is born . . . [is] lame in his intellect, will, and affections" and for this reason needs to be born-again and filled with the illumination of Holy Ghost. In addition, he preached the Second Coming of Jesus Christ. After conversion, he called on Christians to live a holy and pure life. He declared the Bible the infallible Word of God and that the baptism with the Holy Spirit brought Christian unity. He called on people to never speak lightly of each other and to in all earnestness love and build up each other. He called on believers to "do no harm" and "avoid every kind of evil." He also actively encouraged preachers to attend Spirit-filled Bible schools, colleges, and seminaries and to even start their own schools. He insisted that men must lead their families in regular Bible devotions and that they must treat their families with kindness and gentleness so their children would grow up loving God.[43]

Despite his openness to the Spirit's leading, it was precisely his commitment to "sound doctrine" that prompted him to condemn vigorously other religions such as spiritualism, theosophy, Christian Science, Mormonism, and the Jehovah's Witnesses. He also publicly repudiated heterodox theological views like annihilationism, conditional immortality, and British Israelism. For these traditions and beliefs, he offered no quarter. Seymour's magnanimous spirit had limits. He drew the line deeply at historic Protestant orthodoxy. The Bible was his standard. His sternness was probably because some spiritualists and occultists had tried to infiltrate the revival. He and his trustees either converted or expelled them.[44]

Gaston Barnabus Cashwell. He spread Pentecostalism throughout the American South, especially among Holiness leaders. Used by permission of Flower Pentecostal Heritage Center.

While Seymour's message had a loud sectarian ring to it, he and his followers did not originally see themselves as ushering in a new movement, but rather as spiritual reformers seeking to restore existing denominations to their Apostolic roots. They stated: "We are not fighting men or churches, but seeking to displace dead forms and creeds and wild fanaticism's [sic] with living, practical Christianity."[45]

Pentecostal emphasis on tongues often led to ridicule and expulsion. With no place to go, the homeless Pentecostals began to band together to form their own missions, councils, and associations, which developed into denominations. Still others like Gaston Barnabas Cashwell in 1907 and 1908 persuaded other Holiness leaders such as A. J. Tomlinson, A. H. Butler, F. M. Britton, and J. H. King to embrace Seymour's message and bring their denominations into the movement.[46]

While many attendees were converted by Seymour and his followers through their street corner preaching, door-to-door outreach, and evangelistic social work, most who attended were seasoned Christian workers who came from traditional churches in search of renewal. Bartleman wrote, "One reason for the depth of the work at 'Azusa' was the fact that the workers . . . were largely seasoned veterans. . . . They . . . were pioneers, 'shock troops,' the Gideon's three hundred, to spread the fire around the world."[47] And so they did.

Seymour's main message was not tongues, missions, nor end times eschatology, but rather that a person must be born-again to go to Heaven. His desire to convert and transform the lump of the masses to a vibrant, active faith in Jesus Christ drove his vision of Pentecost. He was first and foremost a Pentecostal pastor, evangelist, and revivalist.[48]

AZUSA'S REVOLT AND PROTESTANT PERSECUTION OF SEYMOUR'S "NEGRO REVIVAL"

Seymour and his followers shared a deep conviction that revival was needed to awaken the church from its slumber. Bartleman, Valdez, Osterberg, and others wrote that Azusa was a "spiritual revolt" and a "climactic war" against the "perversion" of biblical Christianity brought about by human creeds and traditions. They hoped that the present outpouring would restore the church to its Apostolic origins.[49]

Protestant leaders became alarmed when they saw their churches dwindle and Azusa and its daughter missions grow. In June 1906, the Los Angeles Ministerial Association attempted to silence Seymour and the revival. It filed a complaint with the Los Angeles Police Department against the "negro revival" (thus injecting race into the complaint) on the grounds that it was disturbing the peace. The police investigated the charges and decided against their request because it was located in an industrial, not residential, section of the city.[50] The race card did not work.

Perhaps the fact that prominent Angelenos like Los Angeles City Hospital surgeon Henry S. Keyes, Women's Christian Temperance Union leader Florence Crawford (who worked closely with the police to help ex-cons integrate back into society), and a number of prominent ministers had joined Azusa or one of its daughter missions may have also quietly and collectively protected Seymour and Azusa. Seymour and his flock believed, however, that God protected them.[51]

Criticism did not end here. Seymour and the revival were criticized by Methodists, Holiness folks, Nazarenes, Baptists, and liberal Protestants as the latest brand of a long-prophesied biblical plague of end-time false prophets decimating the land and ravaging the spiritually undiscerning and malnourished.[52] Some charged that Seymour's revival was nothing more than foolishness, fanaticism, and the work of the devil.[53]

The press coverage, although negative, continued to attract skeptics and

Charles Mason. He brought the Church of God in Christ into the Pentecostal movement, and today it is the largest Pentecostal denomination in the United States. Used by permission of Flower Pentecostal Heritage Center.

scoffers and people seeking a deeper Christian faith, spiritual renewal, or the latest religious fad. It also reportedly attracted people hungry for more of God and the salvation of souls and those seeking to bridge the racial divide. Rather than lament the barrage of criticism, Seymour spiritualized it as proof the revival was challenging the very "gates of hell."[54]

Preaching "waves of power," Azusa attendees fanned out like a flash flood across a sun-scorched Los Angeles and the nation.[55] The revival not only attracted African Americans and Mexicans, but also prominent Angelenos like Rabbi Gold and railroad aristocracy Mr. Huntington.[56] They were drawn in by stories of supernatural manifestations of the Spirit, divine healing, and heavenly music along with newspaper reports, street preaching, and people like Bartleman passing out seventy-five thousand evangelistic tracts. It attracted seasoned leaders from as far away as places like Memphis, Tennessee.

Garfield T. Haywood. Through the ministry of Glenn Cook, he later embraced and became a leader in the Oneness Pentecostal Assemblies of the World (PAW). Used by permission of Flower Pentecostal Heritage Center.

After Charles Mason soaked up Seymour's revival for five weeks in 1907, he spread his message throughout the South. His ministry transformed a small faction of the Church of God in Christ (COGIC) into what is today the largest Pentecostal denomination in the United States. That same year, Azusa veteran Henry Prentiss traveled to Indianapolis, Indiana, and brought Garfield T. Haywood into the Pentecostal movement. Haywood joined the Pentecostal Assemblies of the World (PAW) and later led the Oneness movement. Together Mason and Haywood spread the movement throughout the South, Midwest, and East Coast.[57]

At its peak in the fall–winter of 1906–7, crowds at the mission grew to as many as 800 to 1,500 people on Sundays, though the core membership remained around 150–200. Eyewitness Glenn Cook reported that, reflecting the cosmopolitan mix of the city itself, twenty nationalities sat under Seymour's teaching,[58] many of whom went on to pioneer the work around the world.[59] All of this underscored one important fact: Seymour's vision of a racially integrated ministry was now a vibrant reality.

3
MOSES AND MECCA
SEYMOUR, AZUSA, AND GLOBAL ORIGINS

GASTÓN ESPINOSA

SEYMOUR'S PENTECOSTALISM SPREADS ACROSS THE U.S.

The hordes who descended on Azusa came from across the nation. Many were seasoned pastors and evangelists. Christian leaders like Charles Mason, William Durham, F. F. Bosworth, John Lake, Glenn Cook, A. D. Adams, Thomas Hezmalhalch, Ophelia Wiley, Lucy Farrow, F. W. Williams, Josie and Rachel Sizelove, Gaston Barnabas Cashwell, Ernest Williams, and countless others spent several days to months seeking the Spirit baptism before Seymour sent them out to pioneer their newfound Pentecostal faith at home and abroad.

Although there were many reasons for the revival's appeal, Cook wrote it was Seymour's gentle and quiet spirit and "wonderful character" that was the real secret and drawing power of Azusa. "No amount of confusion or accusation seemed to disturb him. He would sit quietly behind the makeshift pulpit and smile at us until we were all condemned by our own activities," Cook wrote. Drawing upon an African American motif, white leaders like Bartleman compared Seymour to Moses leading His people by a pillar of fire. The Sizeloves similarly extolled: "the Lord gave Seymour wisdom to rule the people as he did to Moses." Durham wrote: "Seymour was the meekest man I ever met. He seems to maintain a helpless dependence on God and is as simple-hearted as a little child, and at the same time is so filled with God that you feel the love and power every time you get near him." Like the ocean breeze, their opinions would change.[1]

For now, they spread Seymour's Pentecostal theology and practices to New York City (Robert and Marie Burgess, Farrow, Leatherman), Chicago (Durham, Seymour, Cook), Oregon (Crawford, Ryan, Wiley), Washington (Thomas Junk), Oklahoma (Cook), Ohio (Ivey Campbell, Frank Bartleman, Haywood, Cook, Seymour), Tennessee (Cook, Mason, Young, Jeter), Missouri (Rachel and Joseph Sizelove), Alabama (Williams), Virginia (Farrow, Seymour), and North Carolina and the southern United States (Cashwell,

Photo of future U.S. and global Pentecostal leaders John Adams, F. F. Bosworth, Thomas Hezmalhalch, Seymour, and John Lake at the Azusa Mission, ca. 1907.

Mason). Many patterned their missions after Azusa, especially in promoting socially transgressive racially integrated services and in sending out missionaries. By 1914, Seymour and others had spread Pentecostalism to almost every U.S. city with a population over three thousand. A new Protestant tradition was born.[2]

AZUSA STREET: THE MECCA AND SACRED CENTER OF GLOBAL PENTECOSTALISM

Although there were other centers of Pentecostalism,[3] Seymour and Azusa along with those they influenced were the single most important catalyst for its origins and spread prior to 1912 globally in England, Norway, Sweden, Liberia, South Africa, China, India, and Japan. The centrality of Seymour and the Azusa Street Revival were driven home by none other than Anglican vicar Alexander Boddy of England, who wrote in November 1912 that Azusa is sort of a "'Mecca' still to Pentecostal travelers . . . [who] like to kneel where

Alexander A. Boddy. He embraced Seymour's message and spread it throughout Europe, Asia, and through his newspaper Confidence, *around the world. Used by permission of Flower Pentecostal Heritage Center.*

the Fire fell."[4] This was no minor claim since Boddy had contacts with Pentecostal leaders and centers in 46 countries, followed and documented the spread of Pentecostalism around the world in his periodical *Confidence,* and had traveled to many of the leading Pentecostal centers around the world. Boddy's claim was not unique. Charles Shumway noted in 1914 that Azusa was the single most important center of global Pentecostalism and B. F. Lawrence wrote in 1916 that Azusa "became the center" (though not the "sole" or "only" center) of a movement that "swept around the world" because "almost every country on the globe has been visited by them" (i.e., Azusa missionaries and their followers).[5] Bartleman wrote that in the earliest years of the revival Los Angeles was the American Jerusalem and Azusa's Upper Room was "held sacred, like a 'holy ground'" for visitors from around the world.[6] What these eyewitness claims all share in common is the view that Seymour and Azusa were the single most important catalyst and sacred center of the global Pentecostal movement prior to 1912. They are not claiming that Seymour and

Azusa were the only leader or center or that Azusa missionaries went to every single country and province around the world, but rather that they were the single most important among many prior to 1912.

These were no minor compliments from provincial leaders. Almost all of them had traveled around the world to North America, Europe, India, and Asia or had contacted people from around the world and were thus in a good position to judge any competing claims. There were none. No rival mission was ever afforded such accolades from 1906 to 1912. Their statements undermine later claims that they were simply one among many important leaders and centers of early Pentecostalism.[7]

PAVING THE WAY FOR GLOBAL PENTECOSTAL GROWTH

A number of factors paved the way for Pentecostalism's rapid growth. The first was the conviction that Pentecostals must use tongues and the Great Commission to help usher in Christ's Second Coming by preaching the Gospel to all nations, thus fulfilling Matthew 28:19–20, Acts 1:8, 2:4, and Joel 2.[8] This conviction gave them the divine mandate and courage to leave behind their homes and often families to make the perilous journey overseas—often, like the Batman family and Daniel Awrey, never to return.[9]

Seymour and his followers were well aware of pre- and proto-Pentecostal revivals in Sweden (1841–43), Ireland (1859), Australia (1901), Keswick, England (1902), Sweden (1903), Wales (1904), Mukti, India (1905), and elsewhere that created a receptive environment for their own Pentecostal message, which served as a kind of finishing theology. They even contributed to the multiple outpouring and centers theory by re-reading these previous revivals through a presentist lens in light of their post-Azusa Pentecostal experiences.[10]

Seymour spread his message globally through approximately 405,000 copies of his *Apostolic Faith* newspaper in circulation from 1906 to 1908 and still others did the same in their own papers, reports, books, and periodicals.[11]

One of the reasons why Seymour's message was so effectively spread was because he sent out veteran missionaries already fluent in the native language. Pentecostals rode the wave of the Protestant missionary impulse popularized by Cecil Polhill's Cambridge Seven, John Mott's Student Volunteer Movement for Foreign Missions, Moody Bible Institute's missionary training school, and Hudson Taylor's China Inland Mission.[12]

On the foreign mission fields, Seymour's followers and newspaper swept many seasoned missionaries into the Pentecostal experience. By July 1908, Seymour's paper and followers had swept up sixty veteran Protestant missionaries in twenty-eight centers in India and a large number of missionaries and centers in China.[13]

Pentecostals also benefitted from British, American, and European colonialism, which provided political stability, religious freedom, and protection for their proselytism. This also gave them the time and freedom to plant deep roots in Africa, Asia, and India, where they were especially successful in tribal and animist-based cultures that emphasized spirits, healing, and the supernatural.[14]

Seymour's message that God was no respecter of a person's race, ethnicity, class, education, income, age, or nationality was attractive to many, especially in the Two-Thirds world suffering under the weight of ethnic division, conflict, and imperialism.[15]

Their affirmation of women in ministry was also relatively congruent with the growing women's movement in the United States, with its emphasis on independence, personal calling, and fulfillment. It also afforded non-Western women agency by enabling them in some cases to exercise a public and religious voice in societies were it was otherwise regulated by men.[16]

African-American missionaries like Hutchins and Farrow created what amounted to a de facto Pentecostal version of the "Back to Africa" movement, which began among historically black denominations like the AME to spur on the Christianization and moral, economic, and social uplift of Africans.[17] Between 1820 and the early 1900s, African Americans and Africans in the Diaspora sent more than two thousand missionaries back to Africa. Seymour and Azusa missionaries were part of this trend.[18]

It also grew because many indigenous religions were naturally predisposed to Pentecostalism's worldview, especially with its emphases on the supernatural, healing, exorcisms, and experiential spirituality.[19] Although most Pentecostals rejected any kind of theological syncretism on core doctrines, native healing prophets and evangelists like William Wade Harris, John Swatson, Samson Oppong, Simon Kimbangu, and Garrick Braide blended Pentecostal and indigenous cultural practices, although reinscribing their theological meaning with various strands of biblical and largely (in some cases) Protestant evangelical beliefs, imagery, and practices.[20]

Finally, Seymour's vision and version of Pentecostalism was attractive to missionaries and indigenous converts because it navigated between the polarities of Western hyperrationalized Christianity on the one hand and popular ecstatic beliefs on the other. On its best days, Pentecostalism was able to soften the hardest edges of American nationalism, rationalism, and exceptionalism by not only affirming supernaturalism, but also by preaching a universal message of love, salvation, forgiveness, healing, equality, and spiritual unity across racial, tribal, and nationality lines. However, as Allan Anderson and others rightly note, some Pentecostal missionaries also reflected all of the same Western colonial, paternalistic, and ecclesiastical and racial-ethnic prejudices they and their message claimed to transcend. This helps to explain why Pentecostalism was more successful in some countries than in others.[21]

SEYMOUR'S PENTECOSTALISM SPREADS AROUND THE WORLD

LIBERIA

The critical role that Seymour, Azusa, and his followers played in the spread of global Pentecostalism undermines the claim that they were just one of many substantive leaders and centers around the world. The first place Seymour's message planted deep roots was in Africa, something that challenges the claims by scholars like Ogbu Kalu, who argued that Azusa missionaries did not first birth the Pentecostal movement on the African continent. In fact, Seymour sent Azusa missionaries to Liberia in the summer of 1906. Lucy Farrow, Mr. and Mrs. Julia Hutchins, and others arrived in August and spent the next seven months preaching in Johnsonville, twenty-five miles outside of Monrovia. Farrow wrote Seymour that God gave her the ability to preach in the Kru language and as a result baptized twenty-five natives and converted and healed others.[22]

In January 1907, Farrow and Hutchins were joined by Edward and Mollie McCauley, Rosa Harmon, and others. They held services for three months until March 26 when they began a ten-day revival in a nearby school. On the tenth day, the Spirit fell and five were baptized with the Spirit, including one Liberian man and his entire household. This Liberian believed God called him to the ministry. He may have been the first African Pentecostal minister on the continent. The McCauleys reported to Seymour that at their packed meetings many were healed of diseases.[23] Harmon stated: "It is marvelous at times to see the manifestations of the Spirit and to feel the power . . . they are in such earnestness when they pray . . . you can hear them a block away."[24] They established the first permanent Azusa-influenced Pentecostal mission in Africa.

In December–January 1906–7 another band of six Azusa missionaries arrived in Liberia. Samuel and Ardella Mead, George and Daisy Batman, and Robert and Myrtle Schideler pioneered a work near Lincoln Station in Caconda, Benguella. The Meads joined the Pentecostal movement while on furlough in August 1906 and by September or October had received the Holy Spirit baptism. They helped pioneer the 1885 Methodist Episcopal work in Melange, Angola, under Bishop William Taylor. In Liberia, they evangelized, opened schools, and supervised large farms, where their converts lived, worked, and studied, and adopted several children.[25] They also inspired the Shideler family to remain in the mission field.[26]

The Meads influenced the Batmans' decision to go to Liberia. After hav-

Daniel Awrey seated with his wife Ella and their children, possibly at one of the Azusa or missionary camp meetings around 1913. He served as ruling elder of the Tennessee based Fire-Baptized Holiness Church and became principal of Emmanuel Bible College in Beulah, OK. After attending Azusa, he spread Seymour's message around the world. Used by permission of Flower Pentecostal Heritage Center.

ing difficulties raising the funds and working through concerns about Africa being a missionary graveyard, the Batmans set sail with the Meads and Shidelers in 1906, where they too preached Pentecost, converted natives, and led people into the Holy Spirit baptism. Their fears were not unfounded: the entire Batman family, plus a Mrs. Cook and a Mrs. Lee, all died of pestilence not long after they arrived in Liberia.[27]

Their work was joined by additional Azusa missionaries from the U.S. and England, including Daniel Awrey. Awrey left his young family for Liberia around September 1913. He carried out itinerant preaching through the work of other Azusa missionaries like the McCauleys in the capital of Monrovia until he died that December of malaria before he could return home to his family.[28] These missionaries laid the foundation for and probably influenced Kru evangelists like William Wade Harris (ca. 1865–1929). Harris preached throughout West Africa and reportedly converted and baptized upwards of 100,000 West Africans to Pentecostalism between 1913 and 1914.[29] The pioneer Azusa work in Liberia spread throughout Western and Central Africa.

SOUTH AFRICA

Seymour's Pentecostal message also planted deep roots in British-controlled South Africa among Dutch Reformed, Anglican, and Holiness missionaries, the latter of which helped pave the way. Alexander Dowie's Zion City sent Daniel Bryant to pioneer an "Apostolic Mission" in 1903 and thus created a predisposition to Pentecostal talk about tongues, healing, and the Holy Spirit.

Thomas Hezmalhalch and John Lake, along with the latter's wife and seven children, and three other adults arrived in South Africa in 1908. They maintained regular correspondence with Seymour. Lake effectively bridged the Zion City and Azusa movements because he himself had once been an elder under Alexander Dowie. Lake faced many hardships, including the death of his first wife, yet he converted hundreds before leaving around 1913, but not before he and Afrikaners Pieter Le Roux and another leader named "Bucher" organized the Apostolic Faith Mission of South Africa (AFMSA) on October 13, 1913.[30]

The reception for Seymour's vision and version of Pentecostalism was not always warm. Lake noted that Seymour's daughter missions caused problems because their missionaries promoted "brand new America ideas" about "social equality between the white people and the [black African] natives."[31] Another Pentecostal wrote how "American missionaries make a great mistake in trying to put the natives on an equality [sic] with the white man." This was a mistake because these "unchristianized" natives could be emboldened through Pentecostal power to "extinguish the whites altogether" in a revolt, he feared.[32]

The result of Azusa evangelism was that Pieter Le Roux, a Dutch-origin Afrikaner pastor, embraced the Pentecostal message in 1908 and brought scores of native black Africans into the movement, among them Daniel Nkonyane, who replaced Le Roux as the future leader of the now Pentecostal-Zionist movement. They in turn brought Paul Mabilitsa, Elias Mhlangu, and Eduard Lion into Pentecostalism, who helped spread Seymour's revival message throughout Zionist Pentecostalism and African Instituted Churches (AICs).[33]

A white South African named Rodney "Gipsy" Smith read about the Azusa revival and Pentecostal beliefs through copies of Seymour's *Apostolic Faith* circulating in Cape Town. He wrote how he wanted to receive the Spirit baptism. After Lake arrived, Smith received the baptism, and they along with another Azusa missionary Henry Turney organized a work that later became the Assemblies of God (AG) in Cape Town and Johannesburg.[34]

Turney had attended Azusa where he met Seymour and received the Spirit baptism on October 5, 1906. He departed for South Africa on February 12, 1908.[35] He teamed up with eleven missionaries by May 1908. They arrived in South Africa around 1909, where they and Hanna James ministered in Pretoria. In 1911, they opened up a mission in the Transvaal, which became affiliated with the Assemblies of God in 1917.[36]

Seymour's decision to send Turney and his associates to Cape Town was in response to yet another letter from someone in the city who had read copies of Seymour's *Apostolic Faith* newspaper and invited Azusa missionaries to South Africa. In a comment that could be duplicated many times over in the early literature, they stated that Seymour's newspapers were "setting afire the hearts of . . . Christians . . . [who] have been led to pray for the . . . Holy Ghost and fire . . . [a phrase used by Seymour and Minnie Abrams in India] both in Cape Town and in Johannesburg." Thus Seymour's newspaper as well as missionaries played a critical role in spreading Pentecostalism in South Africa, where it led to the conversion of Dutch Afrikaners, Africans, and South Asian Hindus and Muslims.[37]

Seymour's message of racial equality and integration was promoted in South Africa despite their historic racial separation (apartheid developed later). In November 1908, Azusa missionaries wrote that more than forty blacks and whites were baptized in the Spirit and that many were healed, though "the natives . . . get the blessing so much sooner than whites."[38]

In September 1909, two native Basuto evangelists from Le Roux's church walked 183 miles from Wakkerstroom to Johannesburg. They held special meetings among the Zulus for two or three days. Many were saved and sixteen were baptized with the Spirit. Because people had heard reports that a child had been raised from the dead, the meetings were so packed that a hundred people could not enter into the building.[39] Another unnamed African evangelist reportedly raised four people from the dead, including a fifteen-year-old girl. While one might question the veracity of such claims, their larger importance among the native population in promoting and spreading Pentecostalism should not be overlooked.[40]

In July 1908, the Holy Spirit reportedly fell on 250 native Africans and about 60 were converted. By October 1909, Pentecostal revivals were being held in Johannesburg, Cape Colony, Doornfontein, and Pretoria. Scores were reportedly saved, healed, and baptized in the Spirit. Near Johannesburg, Pentecostals were evangelizing the 250,000 Africans in the diamond mines and local jails.[41] Many Zulus and Dutch Afrikaners in the Orange River Colony also received the baptism, including a Basuto chief and his entire village. Within a few years, Pentecostals claimed 250 plus native black

Ansel and Henrietta Post. They spread Seymour's Pentecostal vision and work to Africa, Asia, and the Middle East, especially Egypt. Courtesy: Flower Pentecostal Heritage Center.

preachers, 12 ordained ministers, and 6 places of worship. From these pioneer works and others, Pentecostalism spread throughout Africa, all of which undermine the claims by Kalu that Seymour and Azusa did not significantly contribute to African Pentecostal origins.[42]

EGYPT, ISRAEL, AND THE MIDDLE EAST

Meanwhile on August 10, 1906, Seymour sent out a missionary team to Palestine made up of Lucy Leatherman, Andrew Johnson, and Louise Condit. Although Johnson went to Sweden, Leatherman arrived in Jerusalem in late 1906 and later preached in Beirut, Lebanon. She was joined by the T. J. McIntosh family and in 1909 "brother and sister Murray." She reported that near half a dozen received the Spirit baptism. In May 1908, more than three hundred people attended the convention she organized in the Palestinian village of Ramallah, including Egyptian Ghali Hanna and a Syrian Protestant named Zarub, both of whom were Spirit baptized and later pioneered the work in Egypt and Syria.⁴³ Leatherman reported "the 'latter rain' is falling" in Palestine and that CMA missionary Miss Elizabeth Brown had received the baptism.⁴⁴ By July 1908, they published an English-Arabic Pentecostal paper. Leatherman wrote Seymour in January 1909 that many had been saved and baptized. She continued evangelistic work in Palestine, Lebanon, Syria, and Egypt from 1909 to 1921.⁴⁵

Ansel Howard and Henrietta Post (d. 1931) spread Seymour's message to Egypt. Ansel arrived at Azusa in mid-June 1907 and was Spirit baptized. A Baptist minister with more than thirty years' experience, they left Azusa on August 1, 1907, for South Africa, England, Wales, India, Sri Lanka, and finally Egypt, where they began work in 1909. The Posts' story is not only important for their primary pioneer work in Egypt, but also because it highlights how Azusa missionaries continued to reinforce Seymour theology around the world.⁴⁶

In March 1909, George Brelsford arrived in Egypt, and opened the first mission. H. E. Randall, a Canadian Holiness minister who had received the Spirit baptism while on furlough, soon joined him. Post and Randall evangelized Egyptians, opened a mission in Cairo, and started an Arabic newspaper called *The Message of God*.⁴⁷

Their ministries grew slowly. Most of their converts were Coptic Orthodox Christians or Western missionaries. In March 1910, they wrote that many had been baptized with the Spirit and healed, including one woman who had not walked in seven years. Lillian Trasher arrived in 1910. She opened an orphanage in Assiout, where she labored for fifty years. The Assiout work sponsored a mission in Cairo, pastored by an Egyptian and his wife, perhaps the first Egyptian Pentecostal ministry team in Egypt.⁴⁸ In 1912, the Crouch and C. W. Doney families joined them, the former of whom ministered in Egypt for nearly fifty years. Many of these missionaries later affiliated with the Assemblies of God.⁴⁹

SWEDEN AND NORWAY

One of the first Azusa missionaries to Europe was Andrew G. Johnson. Like the Osterbergs, Johnson was a Swedish immigrant. Seymour helped raise seven thousand dollars to send him and others overseas.⁵⁰ Seymour and Johnson had a warm and loving friendship. This was evident when Johnson wrote on August 31, 1906: "Tell Bro. Seymour that I am one with him and all the other saints in Los Angeles. I love my dear Bro. Seymour so much."⁵¹

Johnson arrived in Skövde, Sweden, on November 19, 1906. He gave his testimony in several home Bible studies, but found the Swedish soil "rocky." On December 15, he prayed that "fire from heaven" would fall on his mission like at Azusa—which served as his model: "I am praying every day for the

Andrew Johnson, 1907. He spread Seymour's vision and message to Sweden, the Middle East, and Asia, but especially in his native Sweden. Courtesy of Jan-Åke Alvarsson. Used by permission of Gudren Johnson Noonan.

Lord's work in Los Angeles. . . . This is not [the] Azusa Street Mission here, but I am praying that the Lord would grant us [the same] fire from heaven and give life to half-dead Christians."⁵²

The fires of Azusa broke out in Sweden in late December 1906 in Skövde and spread to the Free Church region of Örebro through Reverend John Ongman. Within two months it had spread to Stockholm and Göteborg and within a year Seymour's message spread south to Malmö and north to Lulea via itinerant evangelists. Johnson wrote Seymour that by February 1907 several hundred Swedes were converted and sanctified. Over one hundred had received the Spirit baptism and some were healed. His ministry met with strong opposition, but he reported that God was giving him victory.⁵³ By April a dozen preachers had received the Spirit baptism. He received invitations from across Sweden and was going from place to place almost daily, although not without opposition.[54]

As a result, Johnson declared in June 1907 that a spiritual "tidal wave" was washing over Stockholm, with hundreds saved and seeking Pentecost. Although most histories argue the first Swedish Pentecostal "church" was created in 1912, Johnson wrote that by September 1906, "The church in Skofde [i.e., Skövde] is growing. I think there are about 40 now who are baptized with the Holy Spirit and speaking and singing in new tongues there." The same paper reported that Seymour sent "Sister Johnson" and "Sister Jacobson" to help Johnson, though nothing is known about their work. Seymour sent Swedish immigrants Eric Hollingsworth and his wife to Sweden by December 1906 and by March 4, 1907 they reported many baptized in the Spirit in Stockholm.[55]

In May 1908, Johnson reported that a number of recently arrived Azusa missionaries were reinforcing his work.[56] After nearly two years, Johnson organized the first Swedish Pentecostal Conference at his mission at Ostra Larmgatan 6 in Göteborg in December 1908 or January 1909, where he met up again with T. B. Barratt. Contrary to most books on Swedish Pentecostal origins, new evidence reveals that Johnson directly influenced the future leader of the Swedish Pentecostal movement Lewi Pethrus by no later than 1911 and probably much earlier. By that time, Johnson and other Seymour-influenced missionaries had birthed the national Swedish Pentecostal movement.[57]

While Johnson was busy preaching in Sweden, T. B. Barratt was pioneering the work next door in Norway. Barratt was a minister in the Methodist Episcopal Church of Norway, pastored various churches in Oslo, and founded the Christian newspaper, *Byposten*. After reading copies of Seymour's *Apostolic Faith*, engaging in extensive correspondence with Azusa, and meeting Azusa missionaries Andrew Johnson, Lucy Leatherman, and Louise Condit in New York City in August 1906, he received the Spirit baptism on November 15, 1906. He said all of this along with letters from Glenn Cook and other Azusa leaders "had a great influence on my mind." Beginning on December 23, 1906, he patterned his revivals in Oslo after reports about Azusa in the *Apostolic Faith*. Within just a few days ten people had received the Spirit baptism, and by January 19 he had moved into a large gymnasium that seated fifteen hundred to two thousand people. The result: revival broke out. Thousands attended the meetings. Barratt reported to Seymour, "God is wonderfully demonstrating his power here in the Norwegian capital. . . . Hundreds are seeking. . . . The fire is spreading very rapidly. Glory to God!"[58]

Barratt organized a number of international Pentecostal conferences and reinforced Seymour's theological views in England, Sweden, Finland, Denmark, Iceland, Poland, Estonia, and India. He sent missionaries to India

Lewi Pethrus (far left), unknown person, Andrew Johnson (far right) in Vienna, Austria, attending a Pentecostal conference in the early twentieth century. This photo establishes a direct tie between Seymour, Azusa, Johnson, and Pethrus. Courtesy of Jan-Åke Alvarsson. Used by permission of Gudren Johnson Noonan.

T. B. Barratt, ca. 1906. He spread Seymour's Azusa Street message to Norway, Europe, and around the world. Courtesy of Jan-Åke Alvarsson. Used by permission of Gudren Johnson Noonan.

(Dagmar Gregersen Engstrøm and Agnes Telle Beckdal) and China (Parley Gulbrandsen) in 1910 and South Africa (Anna Østreng) in 1915, all of whom were influenced by Seymour's teachings and Barrett's interpretation of them.[59] Azusa's influence on Barratt was also reinforced by other Azusa missionaries like Marie Iverson, who left Los Angeles in the summer of 1908 for Bjerka, Norway, and another Azusa missionary named Berger Johnson. Iverson wrote that many had been saved, healed, and baptized in the Holy Spirit through their ministries.[60]

ENGLAND, SCOTLAND, AND IRELAND

Seymour's vision and version of Pentecostalism was spread from Barratt to Alexander Alfred Boddy, rector of All Saints Anglican Church in Sunderland, England, in 1906. He was soon joined by C. H. Hook on Christmas Day 1907 after Boddy laid hands on him to receive the Spirit baptism.[61] Boddy had also heard about Seymour through his *Apostolic Faith*. A keen student of the Bible who had studied with the famous evangelical scholar J. B. Lightfoot at the University of Durham, Boddy became convinced that tongues and Seymour's revival were of God.[62] On September 11, 1908, Barratt laid hands on Boddy's wife Mary to receive the Spirit and shortly thereafter on their daughters, Janie and May.[63]

Boddy wrote Seymour and personally visited Azusa in 1912, which he described for his readers in *Confidence* as the "Mecca" of global Pentecostalism. He spread and reinforced many of Seymour's views throughout the Anglican, Methodist, and Baptist churches in Wales, Scotland, Ireland, and Western Europe and via major international Pentecostal conferences he directed and through his publication *Confidence*. In the summer of 1908, he organized a Pentecostal convention that attracted workers from Europe.[64] Likewise, Azusa stalwart Owen "Irish" Lee spread Pentecost to his native Ireland for a short time.[65] Alexander Boddy and others in turn spread Seymour's message to Germany, Denmark, Switzerland, France, Holland, Italy, and Russia. Although some scholars like to point to Boddy and Barratt as examples of Pentecostal leaders and missions that were completely independent of Seymour and Azusa, it is clear that the latter had a greater influence on them than hitherto recognized.[66]

INDIA

Seymour also influenced the origins of Indian Pentecostalism through his newspaper and missionaries. At the same time Seymour raised a love offering to send Leatherman, Conduit, and Johnson overseas, he also sent Alfred and Lillian Garr to India. They were surprised to learn that copies of Seymour's *Apostolic Faith* were already in circulation and that proto-Pentecostal revivals and manifestations of the Spirit had reportedly taken place at Tirunelveli (Tamil Nadu, 1860–61), Travancore (Kerala, 1874–75), and at Mukti Mission (Kedgaon) in 1905–6 through Methodist Minnie Abrams and Indian Pandita Ramabai.[67] The Mukti children's revival reportedly began after a student at the girls' school woke another girl, stating that one of the girls had been Spirit baptized. The event ignited a small revival at the school.[68]

The Mukti revival was influenced by stories of Evan Robert's 1904 Welsh revival and other renewal movements sweeping through a large number of Protestant missionary societies like the Church Missionary Society (CMS—Anglican), English Baptist Mission, American Baptist Mission, Mukti Mission, Peniel Mission, Open Brethren, Salvation Army, Scandinavian Alliance, Christian and Missionary Alliance, American Presbyterian, Tibet Mission, Poona and India Village Mission, Latter Rain Mission, and the Evangelical Mission.[69]

Alfred Garr. The Garrs spread the Azusa message around the world, but especially to India and later China. Used by permission of Flower Pentecostal Heritage Center.

They set the stage and receptivity for the arrival of the Seymour's message through his newspapers and Alfred and Lillian Garr's arrival in Calcutta in December 1906. Born in Danville, Kentucky, Garr was converted at a Baptist revival meeting and attended Asbury College, where he met and married Lillian Anderson. After college, they accepted the pastorate of a Holiness Burning Bush congregation in Los Angeles until they attended Azusa, where he met Seymour and received the Spirit baptism on June 14, 1906. Lillian followed suit. After the Garrs were expelled from the Burning Bush denomination, Seymour sent them to India.[70]

In Calcutta, the Garrs conducted revivals at a number of mission centers and conferences. At one, they were asked about Azusa, indicating that word of it had already arrived prior to December. Reverend C. H. Hook invited Garr to hold services at the historic Carey Baptist Chapel in Calcutta, which they did for two months. Many missionaries were Spirit baptized. Some had learned about Seymour's teachings through his newspaper prior to their arrival.⁷¹

Lillian wrote to Seymour in April 1907 that thirteen or fourteen missionaries and other workers had embraced the Spirit baptism and that copies of Seymour's *Apostolic Faith* had paved the way. Some even publicly read portions of Seymour's papers at the conferences and revivals.⁷²

By September 1907, the Garrs reported that five or six hundred people had been touched by Pentecost, including many seasoned Christian leaders. The Garrs wrote they were "laying the axe at the root of the tree, for they [existing missionaries] know all the customs of Indians and also the languages." This was good news because Alfred realized he didn't in fact have the gift of Bengali, something Charles Parham and critics pounced on to prove that Seymour's teachings and Azusa revival were a sham.⁷³ This embarrassing realization along with other developments and deep reflection led Seymour to modify Parham's view that tongues could only be xenolalia. He later taught it could be xenolalia or glossolalia, something that again Parham jumped on to argue that Seymour was preaching a counterfeit Pentecost since he believed it could only be xenolalia.⁷⁴

The Garrs spent time with Abrams and Ramabai before moving on to Sri Lanka and Calcutta. Contrary to the theory that Abrams and Ramabai had a fully developed independent understanding of classical Pentecostal theology prior to Azusa, eyewitness and former Presbyterian missionary turned Pentecostal leader Max Moorhead (who knew Abrams, Ramabai, Mukti, and the Garrs personally) wrote in 1907 that Abrams and Ramabai received a deeper understanding of the "Pentecostal" blessings *after* first hearing about reports from Seymour's revival through his newspaper. This understanding was reinforced not only through subsequent copies of the paper, but also after coming into contact with the Garrs in December 1906. Seymour's teaching in his newspaper along with the Garrs' further explanation helped bring them into a "deeper fullness of the outpouring of the Holy Ghost accompanied with the gift of tongues which had not yet been received . . . [in its fullness] *before* Christmas 1906." Charles Shumway confirmed this when he wrote in 1914 that after corresponding with more than one hundred foreign missionaries about the origins of Pentecostalism, including Minnie Abrams, the first instance of speaking in tongues in India in the modern Pentecostal movement took place *after* coming in contact with Seymour's paper and missionaries. He wrote that the Garrs' followers spread Seymour's message to an Episcopalian Girls' School in Bombay and shortly thereafter "news of the new doctrine reached Ramabai's [Mukti] school."⁷⁵ Even if this is incorrect, its highly unlikely that given their close following of global revivals in places like Wales that they wouldn't have also heard about and closely followed the Pentecostal outpouring at Azusa after April 1906, let alone Parham's revival after 1901.

Although Shumway and Moorhead date the birth of the modern "Pentecostal" movement in India to December 1906, it is abundantly clear that (later) reports also claim there were manifestations of the Spirit prior to the Garrs' arrival in India. Whether Moorehead's and Shumway's recollections were the result of a post-Azusa rereading of events is unclear, though possible. However, the motive is unclear since Shumway was no fan of Seymour and Moorhead had no obvious reason to promote recently arrived outsiders over long-term colleagues like Abrams and Ramabai.

These two views may not be entirely irreconcilable. What Shumway, Moorhead, and others seem to imply is that these prior pneumatic manifestations (which Seymour and others noted and viewed as genuine) were independent precursors to the modern Pentecostalism. They took place without a clearly defined and fully developed Pentecostal theology or sense of belonging to a larger global "Pentecostal" movement. They suggest this does not develop until *after* word of Seymour's revival and explanation of the outpouring and baptism with the Holy Spirit arrived in India. A careful examination of the language and timing of Seymour's and Abram's writings indicates that they used very similar expressions to describe the Pentecostal outpouring and restoration of tongues after the start of Azusa in April 1906. This is evident Abrams's booklet, *The Baptism of the Holy Ghost and Fire*. In the first edition issued in the spring or early summer of 1906, she encourages people to seek the Spirit baptism to help live a holy life, but after tongues were reported in June and July in Manmad and Bombay and especially after their manifestation at Mukti Mission in December 1906, she released a second edition that taught the restoration of tongues in a language similar to that used by Seymour in his newspapers and Azusa missionaries. Abrams also seems to confirm this view in September 1907 when she wrote that despite their own revival and manifestations of the Spirit two years earlier in 1905, they still "had not yet received a mighty Pentecost" (like at Azusa Street).[76]

Compared to Abrams and others, Ramabai was relatively quiet about her personal experiences with tongues. Allan Anderson has rightly noted that although her daughter received the Pentecostal baptism, Ramabai may have never received it. This may help to explain why she decided to merge her Mukti Mission with the Christian and Missionary Alliance (CMA) rather than with one of the emerging Pentecostal denominations, the former of which rejected initial evidence, took a "seek not, forbid not" position on tongues, and in 1914 officially declared that tongues and the spiritual gifts were not "*essentially* connected with the baptism with the Holy Spirit." Despite this, it is clear that Abrams and later Pentecostals reread and grafted some elements of the Mukti children's revival into the larger Pentecostal movement and glossed over Ramabai's later decision to lead Mukti into the CMA.[77]

Regardless, Seymour's influence in India on Abrams and others was reinforced by a steady stream of Azusa-influenced missionaries, leaders, and their converts who traveled there, such as the Garrs, George and Mary Berg, George and Carrie Judd Montgomery, J. H. King, Daniel Awrey, A. H. Post, Lucy Leatherman, Robert and Anna Cook, and T. B. Barratt. Notwithstanding Seymour's influence, it is clear that manifestations of the Spirit were reported in 1905 and that by 1907 Mukti was a robust center of Pentecostalism in its own right. Abrams visited Azusa-influenced missions like George and Carrie Judd Montgomery's Home of Peace in Oakland and Elmer Fisher's Upper Room Mission in Los Angeles while on a fundraising trip in 1908. Although Anderson points out that Abrams and Mukti never birthed Pentecostal denominations like Seymour and Azusa, it still became the most important base of operations for Pentecostal travelers in India and one of the top international centers until it joined the CMA.[78]

The Garrs and Abrams weren't alone. Mary Johnson, a "Sister Nelson," and a Miss Gammon soon joined them. The movement spread to Assam, Bombay, Allahabad, Khamgaon, Okola, Amraoki, Dholka, Dharangaon, Rhesqaon, Nasrapur, Pandharpur, and Dhond, where revival broke out among the mission stations and quickly spread to the native peoples.[79] In the Khassia Hills, by May 1908 revival was spreading like "a great prairie fire" and "nothing was able to withstand it." Many were converted as a result of divine healing.[80] By 1909, Pentecost had spread to native speakers of Badaga, Tibet (i.e., Pali), Tamil, Telugu, Marathi, Bengali, Gugerathi, Kanarese, and Hindi.[81]

The growth of the movement was so significant that one missionary wrote to Seymour (indicating it was a key center for South Asian Pentecostal missions) in July 1909, "India has ceased to be a pioneer field as touching Pentecost. Sixty missionaries are baptized and 14 or 15 missionary societies have witnesses to Pentecost in 28 stations scattered through Punjab, Bombay, Presidency, Bengal, and Madras Provinces [sic], the Northwest, and Nizams Dominion." He reported that God was bestowing raw power to prophesy, heal the sick, and cast out demons. Pentecost had fallen in India, he claimed.[82]

The growth came at a price. Because of the Garrs' Pentecostal theology and tenacious desire to persuade others to accept their newfound ideas, they were accused of practicing fanaticism. They also faced personal tragedy. Their memories of Azusa helped them weather the storms.[83] Lillian wrote: "The blessed reality of the experience received in dear old Azusa Street Mission. . . . [helped] as persecution arose in India." She continued, "Our hearts are knit with the dear Saints at Azusa street [sic] and we think with love of all."[84] Indeed, they had. By this time—and independent of Mukti, Azusa missionaries and others brought more than a thousand people into the Pentecostal movement in India, including sixty veteran missionaries at twenty-eight mission stations representing more than a dozen denominations and organizations.[85] Their ministry, which was reinforced by other Azusa-influenced missionaries and evangelists who followed, gave birth to a vibrant and combinative version of Pentecostalism that continued to spread throughout South and East Asia.

CHINA, JAPAN, AND KOREA

After the Garrs spread Seymour's message in India, they left to pioneer the work in China. They arrived in Hong Kong in early October 1907. As in India, they worked through preexisting Protestant missionary organizations and missions. M. L. Ryan, another Azusa participant, left Portland, Oregon, in September for Japan and China with a group of fifteen missionaries, many of whom later met up with the Garrs. The Garrs, Pittman, and others began preaching in Hong Kong at the American Board of Commissioners for Foreign Missions (ABCFM), a Congregationalist operation. The Garrs' reports about the Azusa Street Revival, divine revelation, and the baptism with the Holy Spirit, along with criticisms of the "methods of other Christian missionaries," and claims that God had given Lillian the ability to speak Chinese, led to dissension within the ABCFM mission and eventually a split over tongues. The director tried to silence and expel them, though without immediate success.[86]

The Garrs were told "if you get Mok Li [i.e., Mok Lai Chi], you will get the whole thing [i.e., Chinese Protestant work]." They persuaded Li to join their work and were able to win over his wife, three sons, and two daughters—probably the first Chinese family to embrace Pentecostalism. Li converted many Chinese and twenty-five were baptized in the Spirit. In January 1908, Mok published *The Pentecostal Truth*, the first such paper in China.[87] He also published Chinese tracts.[88] By the fall of 1909, Mok was printing six thousand copies per month and spreading Seymour's and Azusa's basic message to Protestant missionaries and native workers throughout China.[89] Ironically, Li is often cited as an example of a Pentecostal leader that was independent of Azusa's influence, but this is not so.

The Garrs also persuaded nine CMA missionaries and a hundred Chinese Christians to receive the Spirit baptism. Following the Azusa pattern, the Garrs held nightly services in CMA churches for weeks.[90] Their joy was tempered by the unexpected stillborn birth of their second child and death from smallpox of their daughter Virginia and her African-American nanny Maria Gardner.[91]

They left their sorrows behind for a short trip to Japan to visit M. L. Ryan before returning to Hong Kong to resume their work on October 4, 1909. After a lengthy furlough in the United States, the Garrs returned to China

This Azusa Street missionary team traveled to China and Japan in 1907. Children seated in front (l-r): Leonard Colyar, Maynard Colyar, Paul Ryan, Lester Ryan, Harland Lawyer, Beatrice Lawler. 2nd row (l-r): Mrs. Will Colyar, Mrs. M. L. Ryan (with baby in lap), M. L. Ryan, F. H. Lawler, Mrs. Emma B. Lawler. 3rd row (l-r): Will Colyar, Miss Rose Pittman, Cora Fritsch Faulkner, Edward Reilly, Mrs. May Law Michael, Lillian Callahan, Bertha Milligan, Vinnie McDonald, and Archie McDonald. Used by permission of Flower Pentecostal Heritage Center.

on April 9, 1911, where they stayed until they returned permanently to the United States in December 1911. Alfred continued his evangelistic work in the United States until his death in 1944.[92]

M. L. Ryan, F. H. and Emma Lawler, May Law Michael, Rose Pittman, Cora Fritsch Faulkner, and other adult missionaries and their children traveled to Japan and then China in the fall of 1907. They worked with other Azusa-influenced missionaries like Thomas and Annie McIntosh, A. E. Kirby, Mabel Evans, and S. C. Todd in 1907 and 1908. In letters to Seymour, Todd described how a revival was breaking out and people were being saved and baptized with the Holy Spirit in Hong Kong, Canton, and Macao. Another wrote that curious Chinese came to their homes at all times of the day and night,[93] and that by May 1908 more than a hundred people had received the baptism.[94]

To reinforce and spread his Pentecostal message, Seymour sent Bernt Bernsten and his family to China. Bernsten was a Protestant missionary in northern China who first learned about Pentecostalism in December 1906 through Seymour's *Apostolic Faith* circulating among missionaries. He and his wife traveled to Seymour's Mission, where on Sunday, September 15,

1907, he was baptized in the Spirit.[95] In the spring of 1908, Bernsten and thirteen missionaries, including the Roy Hess and George Hansen families and six workers from an Azusa Scandinavian daughter mission in Los Angeles, left for China. He corresponded regularly with Seymour,[96] and in the spring and summer of 1908, he and others opened missions and carried out evangelistic-social work by distributing free food in famine-struck Zhengding, Hebei Province, and Cheng Ting Fu, North China. In January 1909, they persuaded some Methodist missionaries and a reportedly "backslidden" Chinese teacher to receive the Spirit.[97]

In October 1906, Seymour sent Antionette Moomau to reinforce the Chinese work. She was a graduate of Moody Bible Institute and had been a Presbyterian missionary to Shanghai. After meeting Seymour and receiving the baptism, she pioneered Seymour's Pentecostal work in Shanghai with Leola Phillips until Leola died in a smallpox outbreak in October 1910. Moomau continued her work until her death on March 25, 1937, bringing hundreds of Chinese into Pentecost.[98]

To maximize their influence, the Azusa missionaries split up; some traveling to Shanghai, while Roy Hess and his family remained in Zhengding. Bernsten founded China's second Pentecostal paper, *Popular Gospel Truth*, in 1912, and used it to spread Seymour's theological views, encourage the scattered believers, and teach basic doctrine. The Garrs, Bernstens, Moomau, and others were soon joined by Azusa-influenced missionaries like the German immigrant Thomas Junk in mid-1908, Hector and Sigrid McLean and Anna Deane in 1909, Englishman Cecil Polhill (one of the Cambridge Seven) in 1910, and others Azusa missionaries like Daniel Awrey, Paul Bettex, J. H. King, and Frank Bartleman. They variously opened up Bible schools and/or evangelized in Canton and southern China at various periods between 1908 and 1916. Anna Deane attended Azusa and later joined the International Pentecostal Holiness Church. She had a highly successful ministry and girls' school in Hong Kong, which she helped run with Mok Lai Chi from 1909 to 1918. Like the Bernstens, the McLeans were seasoned missionaries, having served with Hudson Taylor's China Inland Mission (CIM) since 1901. They heard about Seymour's revival and sailed to Los Angeles where they met Seymour and received the Spirit baptism, before returning to China with their newfound Pentecostal message in 1909. By 1915, there were almost 150 missionaries and lay leaders in 30 cities, towns, and villages throughout China, many of them influenced in one way or another by Seymour, his missionaries, and/or their converts. Their work helped give birth to the house church movement, which in turn contributed in part to Christianity's rapid growth. Today there are an estimated 130 million Christians in China, many of whom can trace their spiritual genealogical roots back to these Azusa pioneers and their spiritual descendants.[99]

Anna Deane, Hong Kong, China, 1909. Courtesy of International Pentecostal Holiness Church.

The work in Japan was pioneered by M. L. Ryan and his band of twelve workers in 1908. Although progress in gaining converts was slow, in time a small number of Japanese and Western missionaries were brought into the Spirit baptism. Ryan organized a mission and school with S. Ishakawa before he left to evangelize expatriate Japanese in Shanghai, China, in 1910. While in Japan, he was joined by other missionaries like Robert Atchison and Estella Berrnauer. Korea, which was a Japanese colony at this time, was not formally evangelized until 1928 when Mary Rumsey, an Azusa Street participant, began the work and eventually opened a mission in Seoul in 1932 with Reverend Heong Huh. This mission affiliated with the Assemblies of God. There is little reason to doubt that the previous Korean revival of 1903 didn't help pave the way for Pentecostalism and its subsequent growth.[100]

AUSTRALIA AND NEW ZEALAND

In May 1908, Seymour's newspaper ran the front-page story: "Pentecost in Australia." Pentecostalism arrived by February 1907 in a cottage in Melbourne, where many were converted at an Easter service, including a police officer.[101] Former Azusa attendee George Studd wrote on August 3, 1908, that he received "many" letters from Australia and New Zealand asking for tracts, which indicates Pentecostal influence through solo missions or the Azusa newspaper.[102]

According to historians, Pentecostalism was formally organized in the 1920s through the brief evangelistic work of Smith Wigglesworth (1922–23),

A. C. Valdez is pictured here with H. H. Bruce, Wellington, New Zealand, 1925. He spread Seymour's vision of Pentecost to Australia and New Zealand from 1924 to 1927. Used by permission of Ian Johnson. Courtesy of Gastón Espinosa Collection.

Aimee Semple McPherson (1922), and especially A. C. Valdez (1924–27). Valdez, who attended the Azusa revival from 1906–1909, is credited with formally organizing the Pentecostal movement in both countries in the wake of his revivals and ongoing relationship with national leaders from 1924 to 1927. After receiving a prophecy in 1924 from Australian Mary Ayers, who was living at that time in northern California, to preach Pentecost in Australia, Valdez sailed that year to New Zealand. He arrived in Wellington in September, where he reportedly converted, healed, and brought many into the baptism with the Holy Spirit, including a wealthy merchant and later sponsor named H. H. Bruce. During his time in New Zealand, Valdez also sailed to Australia where he preached until he returned to New Zealand in June 1926. On March 29, 1927, Valdez contributed to the development of a national Pentecostal movement in New Zealand. He preached in Melbourne in February 1925 and in New Zealand and Australia until 1927, after which time he returned to California. Despite earlier Pentecostal evangelistic work, most scholars argue that Valdez was the first Pentecostal leader to appoint elders and deacons in the wake of his revivals and to organize the Pentecostal Church of Australia.[103]

U.S. SOUTHWEST, MEXICO, PUERTO RICO, AND LATIN AMERICA

The first Latinos converted to Pentecostalism did so through Seymour's Azusa revival. The Lópezes, Pérez, Navarro Martínez, Luis López, the Valdezes, Valenzuelas, and Euro-American Azusa attendees like George and Carrie Judd Montgomery and Cornelia Nuzum spread Pentecostalism to Latinos in the United States and Mexico from 1906 to 1915. Contrary to previous histories, Jennie Mishler first pioneered Pentecostalism in Puerto Rico from June 1909 to at least October 1910, though without any lasting results. She was sponsored by an Azusa daughter mission—Elmer Fisher's Upper Room Mission—in Los Angeles and complained about bitter Catholic opposition and criticism. Another seasoned missionary on furlough named Gerald A. Bailey attended Seymour's Azusa revival around 1907 and received the baptism with the Holy Spirit. Bailey preached Pentecostalism in Latin America, primarily in Venezuela and Puerto Rico (1910). Despite the preaching of Mishler and Bailey, no permanent missions were organized in Puerto Rico; that task would be left to another person influenced by Azusa—Juan Lugo.[104]

After George Montgomery was baptized with the Holy Spirit at Azusa in 1907, he spread Seymour's Pentecostal message to San José los Playitos, Sonora, Mexico, where he and his cohorts converted a number of Mexicans at a gold mine he owned. Back in Oakland, California, he influenced a Puerto Rican from the Hawaiian Islands named Juan Lugo. Lugo was first converted by Francisco Ortiz Sr. He along with a number of other Puerto Ricans had been converted to Pentecostalism by some Azusa missionaries who stopped off in Oahu in 1912 en route to China and Japan. Lugo came into contact and spent time with the Montgomerys during his stay in northern California from 1913–16 before going on to organize the first permanent Pentecostal work in Puerto Rico in August 1916. His missionary work was also sponsored by Bethel Church in Los Angeles, which was founded by another Azusa attendee named George Eldridge. Lugo was soon joined in Puerto Rico by others from the same Azusa-influenced Mission on Oahu.

In Oakland, George Montgomery persuaded Mexican Francisco Olazábal to receive the Pentecostal message after they prayed for and reportedly witnessed his wife Macrina's healing. Their influence was reinforced by A. C.

Valdez, who after returning from Australia met with Olazábal in East Los Angeles for fellowship, family potlucks, and to preach in each other's Spanish services in the late 1920s. They and their followers converted thousands through their evangelistic-healing services in the United States and Latin America.[105]

In addition to native Latino evangelists, Seymour's message and reports from his *Apostolic Faith* paper spread from Minnie Abrams and others in India to a Methodist missionary named Willis Hoover in Valparaiso, Chile, in early 1907, by which time she had embraced many of Seymour's views and met Azusa missionaries and their followers. Although indirect, Seymour's influence was also reinforced in Hoover through Azusa-influenced newspapers from Durham's mission in Chicago and from two young female evangelists from America, in addition to extensive correspondence about Pentecostalism with Alexander Boddy and T. B. Barratt—both influenced by Seymour, his newspaper, and followers. Hoover's ministry spread Pentecostalism throughout Latin America. They were soon joined in South America by Swedish-American Pentecostal missionaries Daniel Berg and Adolf Gunnar Vingren. Berg first heard about Pentecostalism during a visit to Sweden in 1909, where he came into contact with people influenced by Azusa's Andrew Johnson and after attending a Pentecostal conference at William Durham's church in Chicago, which was at that time still fraternally associated with Seymour and Azusa. Durham, who at this point in time was still one of Seymour's staunchest supporters and propagators, commissioned Berg and Vingren to Para, Belém, Brazil, on November 19, 1910.[106] Seymour's vision and version of Pentecostalism was planted around the world through his revival, 405,000 newspapers in circulation, and missionaries along with their countless spiritual children and grandchildren. Far from being just one among many leaders and centers and having just a small impact on global Pentecostal origins, Seymour and Azusa were the single most important leader and center of early Pentecostalism from 1906 to 1912.

Back home in the U.S., all of this missionary activity caught Parham's attention in the fall of 1906. He proposed uniting all of the little revivals throughout Los Angeles into one grand revival after he arrived. However, he wasn't pleased about stories of interracial mixing, African-American spiritual practices, rumors of spiritualist infiltration, and Seymour's Pentecostal teachings, which was increasingly at odds with his own. If the rumors held true, he planned to assume control of Seymour's mission and set him and Azusa right. The only question that remained was: would Seymour have the courage to stand his ground?

4
GOD MAKES NO DIFFERENCE IN COLOR
AZUSA'S TRANSGRESSIVE SOCIAL SPACE

GASTÓN ESPINOSA

PARHAM, RACE, AND THE BATTLE FOR PENTECOST

Seymour's multi-racial-ethnic revival was growing by leaps and bounds. He and his leadership team defiantly declared "God Makes No Difference in Nationality" because God was bringing all of the races and nations together into one body of believers.[1] Everyone was the same at the foot of the cross.

Seymour's practice of racial reconciliation and integration attracted criticism from the press and religious leaders. Reporters sensationalized stories about men and women from different races, classes, and nationalities kneeling alongside one another at the altar and laying hands on each other to pray for healing and the Spirit baptism. This interaction served as proof positive to some that Seymour's revival was—in their minds at least—a transgressive social space. Holiness leader Alma White charged that Seymour was a "devil-possessed," "religious fakir" whose revival in the "worst slums" of Los Angeles was the scene of kissing, witchcraft, and shocking familiarity between the sexes.[2]

"GOD IS SICK AT HIS STOMACH": THE FIRST SCHISM IN THE PENTECOSTAL MOVEMENT

However, the most scandalous accusation of all came from Parham. The revival had been running about six months when he finally arrived on October 26. After monitoring the revival and even preaching several times from the pulpit, Parham became incensed by what he saw. He later wrote: "To my utter surprise and astonishment I found conditions even worse than I had anticipated. . . . [There were] manifestations of the flesh," "spiritualistic controls," and "people practicing hypnotism" over candidates seeking the Spirit baptism.[3]

The next day as he walked toward the mission he reportedly "heard chatterings, jabberings, and screams." That was it. Without permission or

Azusa Street Revival Leadership Team, 1907. Seated in front (l-r): Sister Evans, Hiram W. Smith, William Seymour, Clara Lum. Second row, standing (r-l): Brother Evans (reportedly the first man to receive the baptism in the Holy Spirit at Azusa Street), Jennie Moore (later Mrs. William Seymour), Glenn A. Cook, Florence Crawford, and unidentified man. Florence Crawford's daughter, Mildred, is seated in front of Hiram Smith. Used by permission of Flower Pentecostal Heritage Center.

a formal introduction, he briskly walked to the pulpit and stated: "God is sick at his stomach!"[4] Silence. With an air of ownership, Parham told the now stunned onlookers that God would not "stand for any such animalism as was in progress." He was "disgusted" by all of the "fanaticism," he later wrote.[5] Seymour and the mission had to submit to his authority, or else. Seymour's hopes and dreams of receiving Parham's blessing were dashed on the bitter rocks of theological dogmatism and white privilege. Seymour had to make a decision: submit or stay true to his calling. After Seymour stood his ground and refused to repudiate the revival and interracial mixing, and hand over the mission's leadership to Parham, he publicly declared Seymour's revival "counterfeit."[6] Seymour's chief trustee Glenn Cook, along with another white trustee, told Parham he was no longer welcome and should leave—at once.[7]

Angry and humiliated that a black man had locked him out of a mission in his own movement and now worried about Seymour's growing popularity, Parham launched a vigorous campaign against him and the socially and racially transgressive conduct of the revival.[8]

His first step was to set up a rival mission at the Women's Christian Temperance Union (WCTU) to siphon off Azusa followers, thus initiating the first major schism in Pentecostalism. It worked. He advertised his services in the local paper on November 6 and attracted two hundred to three hundred white followers—at least at first.[9] He publicly accused Seymour of not accepting his direction, advice, and corrective ministry because he was "drunken with power and flattery" by whites like Glenn Cook. However, Seymour was his own man and possessed with the idea that the outpouring of the Holy Spirit infused the church with divine love and knit the Christian community together into one lump of believers across racial, class, and national boundaries to empower people to fulfill the Great Commission to evangelize all nation's in order to help usher in Christ's Second Coming.[10]

Seymour was "in bounds" for about four months and his followers "spoke in real languages" before that "confessed hypnotist" Cook arrived, Parham scolded. He accused Cook of bringing with him a "brutish, sensual, and devilish" spirit and "barking like dogs, crowing like roosters . . . trances, shakes, fits and all kinds of fleshly contortions with windsucking and jabbering."[11]

From 1906 to 1913, Parham unleashed a torrent of theologically, socially, and racially laced attacks to discredit Seymour, the revival, and its growing number of daughter missions. He called them "degenerate" and accused their "darky camp meetings" of practicing "crude Negroism" of the South.[12] In his spiritual war against Seymour and the Azusa revival, he declared, "Two-thirds of the Los Angeles work was of the flesh and devil" and "spook driven."[13]

The increasing urgency of Parham's attacks was due in part to Seymour's decision to publicly repudiate not only Parham's racial views but also his theological views on annihilation, conditional immortality, Eighth-Day Creationism, and British Israelism, for which he harbored serious concerns while at Parham's Bible School in Houston. These earlier concerns help to explain why Seymour left Houston after less than two to eight weeks in Parham's school and how he could so quickly publicly condemn Parham's views in his newspaper right after the October conflict.[14] Previous attempts by scholars to gloss over or downplay their differences and the criticisms Parham leveled at Seymour's ministry mask his profound disagreement with Seymour's Pentecostal spirituality and social and racial views. After Parham's public repudiation of Seymour and Azusa, they were forced to respond in kind since Parham's views were now laid bare and since the revival's integrity lay in the balance. Far from being a passive and tragic victim and nominal leader, Seymour exercised strong if gentle transformational leadership in publicly repudiating those views that he considered unbiblical and out of line with the Gospel principle of love and the beloved community.

Outsiders took notice. One Holiness leader wrote: "Mr. Parham cannot find English sufficient to express his contempt for the Seymour crowd, and Seymour, on the contrary, feels it his bounded duty to warn the country of the false doctrine which is be promulgated by the aforesaid Parham."[15] This hardly sounds like Seymour simply popularized Parham's views.

This point is driven home by Parham's accusation that Seymour used his Azusa Mission newspaper to challenge his "true" version of Pentecost and that he lied about the movement's origins.[16] He also accused Seymour of teaching "new doctrines" on the Holy Spirit: that the gift of tongues could be any of the nine spiritual gifts listed in I Corinthians 12–14 or a private prayer language and that a person didn't have to speak in a real language (xenolalia) to prove they were Spirit-filled.[17] Hogwash, Parham said. Seymour's views were "entirely unscriptural." "True" Holy Spirit baptism is always followed by a real human language—no exceptions, Parham wrote.[18]

"DARKY CAMP MEETINGS" AND "BIG BUCK NIGGERS": RACIALIZATION OF THE MOVEMENT

Although Parham said it was Seymour's false teaching and "fanaticism" that drove his rebukes, Seymour knew they were driven by a deeper reason—that he, a black man, was leading a highly successful and racially integrated revival beyond Parham's control. In what must have been a painful admission, Seymour confided to future Assemblies of God superintendent, Ernest S. Williams, that Parham repudiated his ministry because of his color.[19]

Parham's racial motivations became clear when he charged that Seymour allowed blacks and whites to crowd around the Azusa altar, "laying across one another like hogs" and that he allowed them to "get worked up into an animalism creating magnetic currents tending to lust and free love rather than purity."[20]

Parham viewed Seymour's Azusa Street Revival as a transgressive social space where different races, classes, and genders crossed the social borders and boundaries of the day—and with impunity. He publicly excoriated this mixing when he lamented: "frequently" a white woman, perhaps of wealth and culture, could be "seen thrown back in the arms of a 'big buck nigger,' and held tightly thus as she shook in freak imitation of Pentecost." This was a "horrible, awful shame!" Azusa, he wrote, was nothing more than "a hotbed of wildfire" where "religious orgies outrivaling scenes in devil or fetish worship" took place in its Upper Room. Most upsetting of all, these "disgusting" practices were "pawned off" on people *"all over the world"* as the work of the Holy Spirit, Parham noted.[21] It is abundantly clear that Parham did not see

Mr. & Mrs. Ernest S. Williams. Used by permission of Flower Pentecostal Heritage Center.

Seymour as popularizing his (Parham's) spiritual, racial, and social views and practices. From Parham's point of view, Seymour was preaching another vision and version of Pentecostalism—one inimical to his own.

Worse yet, Seymour's daughter missions were propagating the same nonsense, Parham charged. Parham wrote about how "the woman leader" of one Azusa daughter mission in Oakland took great pains to tell him how much blacks and whites "loved each other so MUCH!" Parham could hardly hide his contempt when he editorialized in his newspaper: "In speaking of a Negro who was visiting them, she told how 'they all loved him so, and just made him love them; in fact, we will not let anyone stay in our house unless they love us all, and we just love each other more and more all the time, etc. etc.'" This "lovey dovey went on until it was actually sickening." "An outsider," Parham declared, "would have said that this was just another bunch of nigger-lovers and free-lovers." "But they were not, oh no, but were a very esteemable class of Christians." He ended his lament by publicly calling on his newspaper readers to fight a spiritual war against "these forces" and "counterfeit Pentecost" and pray "that this BLIGHT be removed."[22]

The color line, which for six months had been reportedly washed away by the blood of Jesus, was now back with Parham—and with a vengeance. His scorching attacks were a reminder of one simple truth: race mattered.[23]

However, Parham's attacks along with other factors prompted even those who agreed with him to quietly slip away from his Los Angeles mission until by early 1907 just a handful remained.[24] Reading the handwriting on the wall, Parham left for Zion City, Illinois, in the ill-fated hope that he could still wrest control of Alexander Dowie's former kingdom from his arch nemesis, Wilbur Glenn Voliva.[25]

Despite Parham's best efforts, the Azusa revival moved full steam ahead. Parham was right. It grew precisely because it was a transgressive social space wherein racial-ethnic minorities, women, the working class, and others could cross some of the deeply inscribed unbiblical racial-ethnic, class, gender, and national borders and boundaries of the day. It was "transgressive" not because these interactions were biblically or theologically sinful—something Seymour would have never allowed—but rather because these racially integrated practices were considered "socially sinful" in a society dominated by white supremacy and Jim Crow racial segregation.

DEFINING PENTECOST: SEYMOUR, PARHAM, AND THE DEBATE OVER PENTECOSTAL ORIGINS

The wounds Parham inflicted on Seymour must have been deep because he never spoke of Parham again by name in his public writings. When asked if Parham was their leader, in December 1906 Seymour and his associates stated in their newspaper: "No he is not the leader of this movement of Azusa Mission."

However, they may have bent the truth when they wrote, "We thought of having him to be our leader and so stated in our paper," but this was before "waiting on the Lord." They explained that their earlier statements were rather hasty because they were very young, "just like a baby"—full of love—and "willing to accept anyone that had the baptism with the Holy Spirit as our leader." However, in time "we saw that the Lord should be our leader."[26]

Indeed, by invoking God as their founder and leader they effectively pulled rank on Parham. The Holy Spirit "made him [Seymour] *overseer*," a term hitherto applied to Parham and white leaders. This conflict over leadership was picked up by the secular and religious press, especially Holiness papers, which had a field day mocking Parham and Seymour, even publishing a cartoon of Seymour locking Parham out of the mission.[27]

Cartoon states: "The Foot [Seymour] Cannot Say to the Head [Parham], I Have No Need of Thee." The Burning Bush, January 24, 1906. Courtesy of Gastón Espinosa Collection.

SEYMOUR'S REWRITING OF AZUSA STREET AND PENTECOSTAL ORIGINS

In response to Parham's rewriting of Pentecostal origins, Seymour and his colleagues wrote their own competing history. They began to differentiate their "Pentecostal" (a term popularized by Seymour) movement from Parham's Apostolic Faith movement on a whole range of aforementioned doctrinal, racial, and social views.[28]

Until that time, Seymour had overlooked Parham's unique views. He did so no longer. In a sharp public repudiation of Parham's views, Seymour and his followers now boldly wrote on page one of the December 1906 issue of the *Apostolic Faith:* "Sinners, skeptics, and ungodly preachers . . . are trying to find consolation in the doctrine of no hell, annihilation, and universalism."[29] To underscore this criticism, in January 1907 Seymour himself wrote on the "Annihilation of the Wicked," which he roundly condemned. He exhorted those who affirmed annihilation (e.g., Parham) to "turn" from their "sin."[30] In defiance of Parham's teaching on racial separation, they also declared that the Spirit of God was "melting all of the races and nations together . . . into one body . . . and people."[31]

PARHAM'S REWRITING OF AZUSA STREET AND PENTECOSTAL ORIGINS

Parham was furious. He took issue with Seymour's selective reconstruction of the movement's origins and deviation from his theological beliefs. He mocked Seymour's commitment to "Protestant orthodoxy," which he saw as little better than Catholicism. Though he acknowledged proto-Pentecostal movements around the world, Parham argued that the first modern outpouring of the Spirit took place at his Topeka Bible School, not in "the sewage of Azuza [sic]." He implied that Seymour carried the fires of Topeka to Los Angeles under his banner. In Parham's account, Azusa was simply a continuation of a revival he'd begun five years earlier, a view adopted by most writers on Pentecostalism throughout the twentieth century.[32]

Parham also accused Seymour and his followers of pride and distorting the truth.[33] He and his wife Sarah singled out Seymour and stated that he "received all the truths and teachings that we had held from the beginning."[34] It was only after he "was made Pope by his followers" like Glenn Cook that Seymour began to change his doctrinal views and "used all his [*Apostolic Faith*] papers to prove that Azuza [sic] was the original 'crib' of this Movement and a Negro the first preacher."[35] This is important because it clearly establishes that Parham believed that Seymour changed his views over time and became the most important rival leader and that Seymour sought to prove the importance of black leadership in Pentecostal origins.

PENTECOSTAL ORIGINS: ASSESSING COMPETING CLAIMS

SEYMOUR'S INDEPENDENCE

There is some truth in both accounts. Parham was unwilling to fully acknowledge (perhaps because he was unaware of) the influence the Welsh revival had on people in Los Angeles who attended Seymour's prayer meeting; the influence that other Holiness leaders like Martin Wells Knapp, Daniel S. Warner, and Charles Price Jones had on Seymour; that blacks and whites were already praying for revival a year before Seymour arrived; that the prayer meeting began among blacks associated with Holiness, Baptist, and independent Protestant churches; and that other white leaders like Cook and Bartleman also repudiated Parham's claim of spiritual authority.[36]

In addition, Parham does not fully acknowledge that Seymour only attended Houston Bible school for two to eight weeks; that he sat in the hallway or in an adjacent classroom; that Seymour did not receive the Spirit baptism because Parham would not allow racial mixing at the altar; that he did not accept all of his doctrinal views; and that the Bonnie Brae Street prayer meetings did not begin under Parham's leadership, but rather as an all-black prayer group independent of his denomination and control. Neither does Parham acknowledge that Seymour left his denomination when he accepted the invitation to pastor a Holiness mission outside of Parham's control in Los Angeles.

Seymour and his followers argue that the Holy Spirit, black leaders, and a black mission were the primary catalysts for the Azusa revival and—by inference—the single most important center (among many) in the American and global movements. They implied that Parham's movement was like a light rain in comparison to Seymour's global revival now being poured out around the world.[37]

PARHAM'S INFLUENCE

Despite Seymour's reconstruction, it's also clear that Parham did influence him. Seymour clearly reestablished formal ecclesiastical ties with Parham's Apostolic Faith organization for six months from April to October 1906, though only because he was expelled from Julia Hutchins's Holiness Mission and because no other denomination affirmed tongues. In September, Seymour also called Parham "God's leader in the Apostolic Faith Movement" and wrote "this work [at Azusa] began about five years ago last January . . . under the leadership of Chas. Parham," though the latter was possibly meant to diplomatically placate Parham and get him to issue his ordination credentials, which were long overdue.[38]

Parham's influence is also evident in Seymour's belief that the baptism with the Holy Spirit was always evidenced by speaking in tongues (xenolalia), by which he meant a real human language—a view Seymour later modified, but that Parham never changed. He also named his mission and newspaper the *Apostolic Faith,* listed Parham as the "Projector" of the movement on early editions of his Azusa letterhead, published Parham's apostolic-style letter ("all my children . . ."), and sought his advice and assistance (feigned or not), most of which went unanswered.[39] The fact that after April he also sought ordination credentials from Parham demonstrates a direct tie to his movement.[40]

Finally, Parham also influenced him in one less flattering way. Parham's behavior and racial attacks prompted Seymour to later repudiate his views that speaking in unknown tongues was always a human language (xenolalia) and the main evidence of the baptism with the Holy Spirit. Why? Because Seymour believed that tongues could be physically counterfeited by spiritualists and occult practitioners and because he could not fully reconcile Parham's incendiary racial attacks and heterodox theological views on annihilation with a truly Holy Spirit–guided leader. Seymour concluded that tongues was only one of several important evidences of a Spirit-filled life, the chief of which were divine love, the fruit of the Spirit—and tellingly—how one treated fellow believers. However, Seymour did not reject speaking in tongues or the Spirit baptism, but rather argued that it was simply one of several important signs of a born-again, Spirit-filled life.[41]

All of this makes it clear that although Seymour sought to break out of Parham's sphere of influence after he learned about his racial, theological, and social views at his Houston Bible School, he later strategically chose to realign with his movement. However, it is also equally clear that he did so because it was the only denomination that affirmed tongues and because the Apostolic Faith was larger than Parham. He also needed workers to help minister to the growing crowds. His decision was both pragmatic and pastoral. It is also likely that after Seymour arrived in Los Angeles, the Protestant workers who joined Seymour's leadership team confirmed what he already knew, that some of Parham's racial, social, and theological views were—in their view—"unbiblical." Thus Parham's influence on Seymour was both real, but limited to select doctrines and his organizational title and apparatus, which Parham himself had borrowed from the Bible and other denominations and leaders. Regardless, by October 1906 Seymour had the divine calling, staff, and organizational apparatus to go independent—and so he did.

PARHAM'S DECLINING INFLUENCE

Like a summer storm, Parham's success and followers quickly receded. He went back to Illinois and Texas to face a tidal wave of accusations. Parham had gone to Azusa at the height of his glory, claiming thirteen thousand followers throughout the United States. His conflict with Seymour cost him dearly. Losing thousands of followers on the West Coast, he could no longer count on their support. This fact, along with his failed attempt to take over Dowie's Zion City after his demise, left Parham's public image seriously tarnished. However, the most crippling blow was the news that Parham had been arrested in San Antonio on July 18 and accused of sodomy with J. J. Jordan, a twenty-two-year-old Apostolic worker with a troubled past.[42]

In Parham's morally strict world this accusation was the kiss of death to any ministry. Parham insisted he'd been framed by Viola of Zion City and Carothers in Houston, with whom he had since parted company on hostile terms. Although the charges were mysteriously dropped, innuendo and whispering cast a long shadow over Parham's life.[43] This along with his growing conflict with other leaders and a general unwillingness to submit to church discipline, led E. N. Bell and other Apostolic Faith leaders in Houston to publicly repudiate Parham's leadership over the movement.[44]

As Parham's star dimmed, Seymour's was rising. Parham spent the rest of his life living in the shadow of what he called "the sewage" of Azusa Street.[45] By the time Parham died in 1929, Goff states that he was largely unknown among second-generation Pentecostals on either coast.[46]

WOMEN IN MINISTRY

Parham criticized not only Seymour's African-American spiritual practices and interracial mixing, but also the freedom he afforded women. Seymour held very progressive views on women in ministry. He based them on Acts 1–2 wherein on the Day of Pentecost God called men *and* women into the Upper Room and anointed them both with the Holy Ghost, thus qualifying them to preach. He also based it on Joel 2:28, which stated that in the last days of the world God would pour out His Spirit on young men and women and they both would prophesy.[47]

As a result, he promoted the ordination of women and their work as missionaries, evangelists, pastors, social workers, newspaper editors, and local and statewide directors. He supported Florence Crawford's evangelistic work on the West Coast and appointed her state overseer of the entire Azusa work in California—one of the highest leadership posts in his ministry. After Glenn Cook left for Indianapolis, he also invited Clara Lum to run the day-to-day operations of the newspaper. He also supported Rosa López's ministry at the altar during revival services, encouraged Susie Villa Valdez and Swedish immigrant Emma Osterberg to conduct joint evangelistic social work among prostitutes, alcoholics, single mothers, and farm laborers in Los Angeles, Riverside, and San Bernardino, and appointed Julia Hutchins, Lucy Farrow, and Lucy Leatherman to lead missionary teams to Africa and the Middle East.[48]

However, by 1907 Seymour's views began to change. The shift was driven by tensions that surfaced after Frank Crawford, Florence's husband, informed Seymour that she was using her divine calling to justify not taking care of her family. As a result, Frank and their daughter Mildrid were left to fend for themselves—even when their daughter was sick and had a broken arm. He tried to bring about reconciliation, but was unsuccessful, Frank claims. As a result, he filed for divorce. Seymour was genuinely divided about what to do. He had taught that a divorced person could remarry and remain in the ministry provided that they were not the cause of the divorce, did everything possible to maintain a biblical marriage, and met all of the biblical qualifications for the ministry. The straw that broke the camel's back was Frank's decision to divorce Florence because of "abandonment." Seymour now had a divorced woman on his pastoral staff—and one accused of abandoning their family to work in his Azusa Street Revival ministry. He knew that the holiness and reputation of the revival was at stake. After carefully restudying the Bible's teaching on marriage, divorce, and remarriage, Seymour concluded that a divorced person could not remarry if their spouse was still alive, because according to the Bible this forced both parties to commit adultery since God did not recognize the dissolution of the first marriage.[49]

Florence respectfully disagreed. Reading the writing on the wall, in 1907 she left Azusa for Portland, Oregon, where she started her own Apostolic Faith Mission denomination—one that remains to this day. To maintain her holiness standards, she never remarried. On her way up the coast she made it clear that she would accept any missions who felt divinely called to join her new movement. As a result, some of Seymour's daughter missions in Los Angeles, Oakland, and San Francisco joined Crawford's new denomination. Given the high profile, platform, and level of trust Seymour afforded Crawford, he must have felt deeply betrayed by her actions.[50]

Crawford's denominational history described her decision in language strikingly similar to Seymour's own rationale for leaving Parham several years earlier: "Everything seemed to be against her leaving Los Angeles at that time. [Seymour] . . . did not see how he could spare her from their meetings; but she remarked that . . . God was truly calling her." God reportedly stated in a vision to Crawford: "'I have set before thee an open door, and no man can shut it.'"[51] No man indeed. She was convinced and possessed by her divine calling and invoked her direct, unmediated revelation from God to pull rank on Seymour and start her own Apostolic movement. This fragmented the movement. A new denomination was born.

As a result, Seymour wrote a series of signed articles on marriage, divorce, and gender roles. In another surprising example of leadership, in January 1907 he stated in a veiled allusion to Crawford: "Many homes today have been wrecked and brought to naught through false teaching. Wives have left husbands and gone off, claiming that the Lord has called her to do mission work, and to leave the little children at home to fare the best they can."[52]

True to his egalitarian impulse, Seymour didn't cut wayward men any slack either. He stated: "Many precious husbands have left their wives and children at home, and their wives are working hard to support the little children, washing, ironing, scrubbing, and family, while their husband is claiming to be doing missionary work, and saying the Lord gave him that same Scripture in regard to forsaking."[53]

Seymour made it abundantly clear that leaving one's family in financial poverty or for long periods of time without mutual consent is "desertion" and something harmful to the spiritual vitality of one's children and family. He concluded: "Our mission station begins at home and with family prayer, until one by one the members of the family receive the Lord Jesus."[54] This is something he modeled with his adopted daughter, about whom we know nothing—not even her name.

This series of events led Seymour to rein in but not completely suppress the authority of women in the church.[55] In 1915, he wrote in his minister's manual: "All ordination must be done by men not women. Women may be ministers but not to Baptize and ordain in this work."[56] Women could not serve as bishop or vice bishop since they could change these guidelines.

Despite these modifications, Seymour strongly supported women in ministry until the day he died. They could serve as pastors, evangelists, missionaries, editors, state directors, and teachers. He also handed over the pastorate of his own mission and denomination to his wife before his death.

EMPOWERING THE WORKING CLASS

Seymour's egalitarian impulse on race and gender also shaped his views on class and education—brick ceilings for working-class men, women, immigrants, and racial-ethnic minorities. He argued that God "recognizes no man-made . . . classes of people, but 'the willing and obedient.'"[57] Bartleman wrote that "we [at Azusa] had no 'respect for persons.' The rich and educated were the same as the poor and ignorant, and found a much harder death to die. We only recognized God. All were equal."[58] A. G. Jeffries likewise declared "education and culture are at a discount in this great battle for souls. The [divine] call is not based on what we know, but what we have experienced."[59] To underscore his support, Seymour often made it a habit to avoid wearing flashy suits, hats, and ties during the revival, all signs of upper-class denominational clergy, though he later modified this practice when visiting other missions where they were customary.

As word about Seymour's revival spread, it continued to rage throughout 1907 and the spring of 1908. By May 1908, Seymour's team was sending out fifty thousand copies of the *Apostolic Faith* per month, missionaries were being sent across the United States and around the world, and God was reconciling and melting all of the races and nations together into one body of believers. Feeling on top of the world, he and his followers joyfully declared: "We are on the verge of the greatest miracle the world has ever seen."[60] Had they known the stony path that lay ahead, they might have said otherwise.

5
WRECKING THE SPIRIT OF AZUSA
GRUMBLING AND THE ROAD TO DECLINE

GASTÓN ESPINOSA

Seymour's strong leadership and committed co-workers enabled him to weather the storms and by 1908 his influence was increasing around the world. There was little Parham could do to stop him as long as he maintained the confidence of his co-workers and held on to the mission and its newspaper, the keys to his growing prominence. He employed them not only to defend himself, but to challenge Parham's views and check his influence.[1] He knew they were critical because they provided an international platform from which to promote his own vision and version of Pentecostal history, theology, and race relations, and because they enabled him to respond rapidly, directly, and publicly to criticisms, all of which helped him guide the movement.

Seymour also knew something else: the mission was on borrowed time. The Stevens AME Trustees wanted to sell the mission—preferably to Seymour. To show they meant business, they nailed a large "For Sale" sign across the side of the mission.[2] After much prayer and reflection, Seymour and his Trustees decided to purchase it in order to secure the revival's future. On February 2, 1907, he reluctantly took an offering for the down payment—the first he'd ever taken at Azusa not earmarked for missions. Prior to that, an offering box was put in the back and later center (due to pilfering) of the mission for free will tithes. Then on March 8, he and the congregation elected Trustees, adopted a Constitution, and later replaced the "For Sale" sign with one that read: "Apostolic Faith Mission."[3]

While many celebrated the decision, Frank Bartleman and Rachel Sizelove claimed that its purchase and sign smacked of worldly recognition and advertised their failure to get along with established churches.[4] He was transforming a Spirit-led revival into just one more man-made denomination—and without the approval of the "brethren," Bartleman chided.[5]

Although they were seemingly harmless internal observations, when combined with Parham's schism and Crawford's departure, they threatened to undermine Seymour's leadership and his co-workers' esprit de corps. The bickering and whispering quenched Seymour's spirit. The tension was

Azusa Street Mission with "For Sale" sign, 1907. Used by permission of Flower Pentecostal Heritage Center.

brought to an end—at least publicly—after Cecil Polhill, an Englishman of considerable means and a member of the Cambridge Seven missionary group in China,[6] gifted Seymour the $7,300 to pay off the mortgage.[7]

SEYMOUR SPREADING PENTECOST ACROSS THE NATION

As Azusa's fame grew, Seymour received a stream of invitations to hold little revivals across the United States. In response to one such invitation from Glenn Cook, on May 1, 1907, Seymour began a five-month tour across the country to Texas, Illinois, Indiana, Virginia, and other states. He was accompanied by the Frank Cummings family, who were on their way to Liberia, and an increasingly attractive Ms. Jennie Evans Moore.[8]

Seymour conducted a powerful revival at Cook's mission in Indianapolis. Cook had spread Seymour's message to Tennessee, Arkansas, Oklahoma, and Missouri, before settling in Indiana.[9] Hundreds attended, something that caught the attention of an insatiable press. Reporters were stunned by the interracial nature of the meetings and that a black man was in charge. On June 8, 1907, one fear-mongering reporter for the *Indianapolis Star* described Seymour in a menacing light: "This leader of the sect stands full six feet in height. He wears a rubber collar, decorated by no sign of a necktie. Adorning his mouth is one massive gold tooth, flanked by rows of other teeth, perfectly straight and white. The beard that he wears could be called a flowing one if it was longer. . . . His voice is like the roaring of a cannon and of all his most striking characteristics, he has but one eye."[10] Seymour was actually five feet nine.

More scandalous were salacious reports of white women and black men comingling. Hardly able to hide his contempt, the reporter wrote how Mrs. Tom Oddy publicly dropped to her knees before Seymour and allowed him to lay his hands on her for prayer. Seymour, Cook, and Cummings also laid hands on and baptized a number of blacks and whites in a local river, including soaking wet women like Oddy. As a result of the reporter's stories and others like it, an angry white mob formed outside the mission over the next few nights. So intense were the threats, the police were called out to protect the worshippers. It was an ominous reminder that race relations were far from harmonious even in the North.[11]

FIRST AZUSA STREET REVIVAL CAMP MEETING

While controversy raged on the revival trail, back home in California Seymour's faithful assistants, R. J. Scott, Clara Lum, Mae Mayo, Tom Anderson, and Rachel Sizelove were busy preparing the First Pentecostal Camp Meeting at Arroyo Seco in Pasadena. It began on June 1 and ran for six weeks. More than one thousand attendees from across the nation participated and left with Seymour's theological, social, and racial DNA stamped on their theological outlooks. It was a major success and continued to raise Seymour and Azusa's public profile and message throughout the Protestant subculture at home and abroad. However, it also birthed a growing independent spirit on the part of some Azusa workers, since the ever-trusting Seymour allowed them—even after splits with Parham and Crawford and grumblings from Sizelove—to direct and guide it in his absence.[12]

The revival continued unabated and was led by his white copastor Hiram Smith. Participants wrote that they were "saturated with the spirit in love and prayer," with the days passing "all too swiftly." Indeed, Seymour taught the baptism with the Holy Spirit was "a means to be flooded with the love of God and Power for Service, and a love for the truth as it is in God's word." He said that the Spirit baptism created a love for God and their fellow human beings. For Seymour, love was foundational to Pentecostal theology and practice and for this reason he stated, "Our colored brethren must love our white brethren and respect them in the truth."[13] This teaching and practice was non-negotiable.

As a result, white Holiness leaders from the South like Gaston Barnabus Cashwell from North Carolina testified how God enabled them to "crucify their racial prejudice" at the Azusa altar and were now worshipping with blacks in racial equality. Seymour's dream of racial equality, integration, reconciliation, and unity had come to pass and had now been in full swing for almost two years, despite claims that it was simply a short liminal moment in time.[14]

GRUMBLINGS

Despite Seymour's growing personal success—or perhaps because of it—some whites began to grumble about his management and leadership. In the past, Seymour could count on Cook and Crawford to set them straight. Now without them, this proved difficult given Seymour's passive-aggressive leadership style. He was also ever mindful that he was black and they were white.

In 1908, while Seymour was on a trip back East, he again put Reverend Hiram Smith rather than Reverend Joseph Warren or some other African American in charge of the mission, which led to grumbling among some blacks because they felt overlooked despite their unflinching loyalty. This was exacerbated after a new Azusa treasurer—a white Los Angeles high school teacher named "Mr. Carpenter"—called for a meeting to discuss the mission's finances. He wanted Seymour to give an account of all funds received and spent over the past two years since he didn't keep any systematic financial records. Seymour agreed to participate in the meeting Carpenter announced he would chair. Some blacks grew concerned that he and other whites were scheming to take over the mission in Seymour's absence. Carpenter denied the charges, but unwisely told blacks that although they had a part in God's program that "they should follow . . . the white people, and the white people with the colored." This "follow . . . the white people" phrase really raised a "rumpus" among blacks, eyewitness Arthur Osterberg noted.[15]

After Seymour returned, he tried to bring calm. At the meeting, Carpenter "insisted" that Seymour give an account of all of the money raised and spent. Although Seymour never kept financial books, he began to itemize from memory how he gave the Garrs one amount to travel to India, Johnson and others another amount to travel to the Middle East and Europe, and so on. Carpenter was unsatisfied. He kept on insisting that the mission had taken in more money than Seymour could account for. The questions were fair enough, but the tone, innuendo, and badgering crossed an invisible line. They seemed to question Seymour's integrity and spiritual leadership—besides being publicly humiliating.

When Seymour realized the seriousness of the matter and—possible accusations of fraud, a lawsuit, and scandal—it reportedly grieved his spirit deeply. He stood his ground, lamenting: "I sent it out as the Lord told me and as the need required, and before God I never misspent or kept a cent of it."[16]

Although Carpenter backed down and later left the mission, Osterberg said the accusations by another white leader "wrecked the spirit of Azusa Street." Even though a later revival helped somewhat, "it did not restore the spirit or give us the unity we had in the beginning" between blacks and whites, Osterberg lamented.[17]

The accusation by still another white began to weigh heavily on Seymour and blacks. The fact that Elmer Fisher opened up an Azusa daughter mission called "The Upper Room" in Los Angeles didn't help, as some whites now left Azusa. All of this chipped away at Seymour's leadership, message, and racial unity, and checked his growing influence.[18]

SEYMOUR, CLARA LUM, AND MARRIAGE, 1908

Despite these internal difficulties, externally the revival moved ahead throughout 1908. Oblivious to these internal conflicts, missionaries, pastors, evangelists, and spiritually hungry laity continued to arrive and depart from the mission like an international airport. Letters poured in asking Seymour to bring the fires of Azusa to prayer groups and churches across the country and around the world. Some even asked him to bless and mail out handkerchiefs for divine healing, a practice noted in Acts 19:12. Seymour often dictated his responses to these inquiries through his ever faithful assistant and newspaper coeditor Ms. Clara Lum. They made a great team—and she knew it. Together they helped published over 405,000 copies of the *Apostolic Faith* newspaper and used them to spread Seymour's vision and version of Pentecostalism around the world.

The smoldering embers of the Florence Crawford and Carpenter conflicts were still glowing when Seymour unexpectedly announced that he and Jennie Evans Moore had married on May 13, 1908. The private ceremony was conducted by Reverend Ed Lee and witnessed by his wife and Richard and Ruth Asberry—all black leaders. Seymour's other co-workers had not been invited, perhaps due to the cost and not knowing where to draw the line of whom to invite. Many were shocked and profoundly disappointed.[19]

Hardest hit was Clara Lum, the person Seymour spent more time with than any other white person on staff. Stunned by the decision, Lum and others interpreted his marriage as a betrayal of their "end-times" message of self-sacrifice and self-imposed celibacy. Some questioned Seymour's wisdom, virtue, and spirituality. Like a jilted lover, Lum, who Charles Mason stated wanted to marry Seymour, raised a hornet's nest of opposition.[20]

Some accused Seymour of having compromised on "sanctification," a serious accusation among the holiness-minded Pentecostals. The fact that Seymour was thirty-eight and Evans was twenty-five years old may have also

Seymour had a very close relationship with both Jennie Evans Moore and Clara Lum. Seated in front (left to right): Hiram W. Smith, Florence Crawford's daughter Mildred, William Seymour, Clara Lum. Second row, standing (left to right): Jennie Moore (later Mrs. William Seymour), Glenn A. Cook, Florence Crawford, unidentified man, 1907. Used by permission of Flower Pentecostal Heritage Center.

spiked the ire of the thirty-nine-year-old Lum. She left the mission in protest to join Florence Crawford's work in Portland, Oregon, but not before she grabbed Azusa's newspaper and the only copies of the national and international mailing lists, leaving only the local lists. Seymour and his Trustees demanded that she return them—at once. Lum not only defied their request, but began publishing the newspaper from Crawford's mission in Portland without notifying Seymour, the Trustees, or their readers. It wasn't until May/June 1909 that she finally notified the readers that she had moved the paper to Portland. However, she said nothing about taking the paper against the expressed wishes of Seymour and the Azusa Trustees.[21]

For the first time in almost two years, Seymour was without a newspaper and a voice to the nation and outside world.

Lum's actions shook Azusa to its core. As in slavery days, Seymour's tongue had been symbolically cut out. He had been symbolically castrated. Without the newspaper to spread his message and shape the movement, he was largely voiceless and powerless to guide and influence it across the United States and around the world. He had hoped that his admittedly close relationship with Lum could weather the news of his marriage to Jennie and that she might even be happy for her fellow co-workers. No such luck. Lum, the newspaper, and the national and international mailing lists were gone. The soft-spoken and now even quieter Seymour gained strength from his feisty and strong-willed wife. Jennie encouraged him to stand up for his rights. Ernest Williams and Arthur Osterberg said she helped put Seymour "in his place" at the "head of the movement."[22]

There was little time for a honeymoon. Not willing to give up on their dreams and recognizing the central importance of the paper to Seymour's future, the newlyweds traveled to Portland in hot pursuit of the mailing lists. Lum rejected Seymour's overtures for Christian reconciliation and refused to see him. With no other options and legal recourse out of the question since it went against the Bible and would scandalize the church and revival before an unbelieving world, Seymour left empty handed. Although he might win a legal battle on merit of ownership, he also recognized the racial calculus of a frail white woman defending herself against a big black man in an all-white courtroom. Seymour went back to Los Angeles disappointed, but not without hope.

Although he was the pastor and executive editor of the newspaper, it was generally Lum and others who ran the day-to-day operations. Her departure and decision to reissue the paper made it awkward for him to publish his own paper because he'd have to explain why the division happened in the first place—which could turn into a feeding frenzy for Parham and the revival's critics. Despite this burden, J. C. Vanzandt wrote in 1911 that Seymour managed to publish at least one more issue (perhaps one near completion before Lum left) that he himself (Vanzandt) had read before Seymour gave up the venture. Seymour, with only a primary school education, was no copyeditor and in no position to manage both the newspaper and burgeoning revival. The influence he was able to wield at home and abroad with the newspaper were now gone—something that Lum no doubt anticipated and considered a just reward for Seymour's actions.[23]

Seymour was now permanently hamstrung. He could no longer use the paper to respond to Parham's public criticisms or to guide the racial, social, and theological development of the American and global Pentecostal movements. His followers would have to carry on and build on the foundation he helped lay without him. Despite the devastating loss, he still held on to the world-famous Azusa Mission and had Pentecostal superstars like William Durham and John Lake backing him. They continued to defend Seymour and promote his vision of Pentecost. Though now without a newspaper to promote his views, he could still send letters and conduct revivals across the nation—something he did now with even greater frequency. This, however, invariably hurt the revival because it kept him away from the mission.

All of this points to the fact that Seymour's fall from influence and "nominal leadership" was not simply the result of his quiet nature, humble spirit, or "lack of leadership," but rather the actions of some of his closest white friends who not only betrayed his trust, but took what rightfully belonged to the mission he founded. As a result of Lum's actions, his influence was also diminished in the emerging Pentecostal historiography since he didn't have a vehicle through which to publish his own views and history after 1908. Seymour's moral, pastoral, and public authority had taken a devastating hit, one from which it would prove difficult to recover. This began the long and slow road to decline.

GROWING TENSIONS

Seymour's growing number of conflicts with Crawford, Lum, and Carpenter were part of a larger trend wherein Seymour spoke out and exercised pastoral oversight and spiritual discipline with people who questioned his leadership, defied his instructions, and joined one of his critic's missions. A Danish immigrant named A. Sulger wrote that after he handed in his Azusa ministerial credentials and rejected Pentecostalism as "heresy," Seymour told him that if he did not stop his sin against the Holy Spirit he would "lose" his "soul." When it became clear that he would not repent, Sulger claims that Seymour gave him "a bitter and hateful look" and publicly "denounced" him before the Azusa followers and told everyone that he had committed the "unpardonable sin." However, this is contradicted by Sulger's own claim that Seymour also later asked him to accept a new ministerial assignment, which Sulger promptly declined.[24]

Similarly, Ernest S. Williams reported that when he ran into Seymour in Portland, Oregon, he stated that if Williams continued to preach at Crawford's mission he would take back Williams' Azusa ministerial credentials and he'd lose his rail discount. After Williams continued his ties with Crawford, Seymour kept his word.[25]

All of these criticisms point to one inescapable fact: Seymour was changing. The days of the nominal leader who hid his head behind a shoe crate pulpit—if ever completely true—were now balanced by a still gentle person, but one who could preach with power, chastise critics, and rebuke incompliant and disloyal ministers. Indeed, he acted more like a denominational leader than just a quiet overseer.

"THE CITY IS . . . ELECTRIFIED WITH THE MOVEMENT": REVIVAL CONTINUES, 1909

Despite the conflicts, Seymour found solace in Jennie's love and the support of his white, black, Latino, and other ethnic leaders and friends that stood by him. Hundreds of people continued to pour into the mission on a regular basis, most completely oblivious to the conflicts. The services continued daily in early 1909. Despite these betrayals, the ever-trusting Seymour regularly shared his pulpit with guest speakers. He invited Reverend W. B. Godbey, an influential white New Testament scholar and Holiness leader, to speak. Rather than praise Seymour, Godbey later wrote that the revival's manifestations of the Spirit were "counterfeit." However, he also admitted that the city was "on tip-toe, all electrified with the movement" and that revival meetings were "running without intermission day and night." Visitors "arrived from every point of the compass at all hours" on "all of the trains."[26]

By late 1909, the meetings no longer ran seven days a week, due in part to Seymour's busy travel schedule, but also to the growing number of Azusa daughter missions. While not rivals per se, they had almost the same effect. Yet they still collaborated and maintained warm fellowship and freely visited each other's missions, often sharing pulpits. While Seymour's theology and Azusa still dominated the Pentecostal landscape for international visitors, after 1910 some three hundred people were attending Fisher's Upper Room, in addition to ethnic missions. The Upper Room quickly became the largest mission in Los Angeles, though invariably at Seymour's expense.[27]

Regardless, former Christian and Missionary Alliance minister George N. Eldridge confirmed Seymour's continuing influence. He wrote that after carefully watching Seymour and the revival for two years, he and his wife came to the conclusion they were of God. They eagerly attended the mission in 1910, where they received the baptism with the Holy Spirit. Eldridge said it was "like the outflowing of water from my inmost being according to Jesus' words in John 7:37, 38."[28] This newfound love for the outpouring and baptism with the Holy Spirit so moved him that he decided to found Bethel Temple there in Los Angeles, which in 1916 helped send Juan Lugo to pioneer Pentecostalism in Puerto Rico, thus establishing a direct connection between the Azusa Street Revival and the origins of Puerto Rican Pentecostalism.[29]

CONFLICT BETWEEN AN AZUSA LEADER AND THE MEXICAN CONTINGENT, 1909–11

The pattern of conflicts with his white "brethren" led Seymour to ask a growing number of faithful blacks and Latinos to exercise leadership along

> "Go ye therefore and teach all nations, baptizing them in the name of the Father, and of the Son, and of the Holy Ghost; teaching them to obrve all things, whatsoever I have commanded you."—MATT. 28: 19, 20.

Ministerial Credential
FOR THE YEAR 1909.

This is to Certify:
That the Bearr hereof *Abundio L. Lopez* of *Los Angeles* State of *California* having been called by the Holy Ghost as a Minister of the Word in

The Apostolic Faith Mission

has been ordained by us, n conjunction with the Church at Los Angeles, California, and is recommended to the saints as a *Minister* in good standing. This Credential to hold good so long as *he* has our confidence and keeps the unity of the Spirit with us.

J. A. Warren *W. J. Seymour*
                                          Pastor.

Abundio López's ordination certificate signed by William J. Seymour, 1909. Courtesy of Gastón Espinosa Collection.

with whites. As a result, he ordained at least three Mexicans to the ministry: Abundio López (1909), Juan Navarro Martínez, and Luís López. Abundio's ordination signaled the formal birth of the Latino Pentecostal movement in the Americas.[30]

Latinos began to exercise greater leadership and voice in the mission and to boldly testify. For reasons that are still unclear and perhaps due to past criticisms that the mission allowed for unbridled enthusiasm, Bartleman wrote in his history of the Azusa revival that "the leader" (whom he does not specify by name) of the Azusa Mission at that time deliberately refused to let some poor and illiterate Mexicans testify. This was, Bartleman claimed, like "murdering the Spirit of God" and was a foreboding of the decline that followed:

> The Spirit tried to work through some poor, illiterate Mexicans, who had been saved and "baptized" in the Spirit. But the leader deliberately refused to let them testify, and crushed them ruthlessly. It was like murdering the Spirit of God. Only God knows what this meant to those poor Mexicans. Personally I would rather die than to have assumed such a spirit of dictatorship. Every meeting was now programmed from start to finish. Disaster was bound to follow, and it did so.[31]

The exact date of this conflict is unclear. It is sandwiched between Bartleman's daughter's birth on October 15, 1909 and his trip around the world on March 17, 1910—and therefore before Durham arrived in February 1911—thus probably ruling out Durham unless Bartleman's chronology is inaccurate. Who this leader was is also unclear. Bartleman does not identify Seymour as the leader in that immediate paragraph. He does, nonetheless, identify him as the leader throughout the rest of the book. However, because he does not mention Seymour by name, it's possible he's referring to another leader like J. A. Warren, who was the African American co-pastor by that time and the person who also co-signed Abundio López's ordination certificate in 1909.[32]

Given that William and Jennie Seymour were increasingly invited to speak at Azusa Street daughter mission and sister churches across the nation and especially in the Midwest and South, Warren would have been regularly asked to step in to lead the mission in their absence since he was one of its senior co-pastors. For this reason, it is very possible that Warren may have been the leader in question. As already noted earlier, we do know that some black leaders were concerned about possible white takeovers and black marginalization in the mission, though it is unclear if Warren was one of these leaders. Regardless, there is no documentary evidence from any extant sources that Warren harbored any resentment towards Latinos or that they in return did the same towards Warren. In fact, the fragmentary evidence indicates that Warren at least publicly supported Latinos since he went along with Seymour's recommendation to ordain López to the ministry and sign his ordination certificate. This does not by itself rule out the possibility that Warren may have uncharacteristically lashed out against Latinos, but it does make it seem unlikely. Neither does Bartleman ever identify Warren as the leader of the mission.

Part of the problem with this passage is that Bartleman does not go into detail about who the leader was and why they refused to let the Mexicans testify. It is always possible that misdirected frustration with whites and/or blacks prompted the otherwise patient and conciliatory Azusa leader (Warren, Seymour, someone else) to uncharacteristically lash out at the enthusiastic Mexican contingent. While it was Douglas Nelson's argument that such behavior was entirely inconsistent with what we know about Seymour, we do know that the Azusa ministerial team began to rein in an overemphasis on the public manifestation of the gifts. They wrote: "We have learned to be quieter with the gifts . . . everything [will] be done decently and in order and without confusion."[33]

And so it was—and increasingly so by 1909. While control was the price of acceptance, loss of transgressive and transformative social power was the price of control. Seymour's leadership team had changed. Gone were the days of unfettered free-flowing, Spirit-led spontaneity. Now, due to the influx of overly enthusiastic worshippers and merciless criticism from friends and foes, Seymour and some of his associates began to gently regulate public expressions with the above episode being the exception that proved the rule. Although people continued to speak with conviction, enthusiasm, and raw joy, they now did so decently and in order and without confusion. If not, Seymour and other leaders would simply walk over and gently tap the overly enthusiastic person on the shoulder, and quietly say: "It's flesh, you can always tell—right away."[34]

Nelson and others dismiss Bartleman's accusation out of hand by stating that it was entirely inconsistent with Seymour's character to treat the Mexican contingent so harshly—which is true. However, even if it were true (which is doubtful), he would not be the first leader in church history who occasionally acted in a way that was inconsistent with his/her professed convictions. The fact is that prior to Nelson's 1981 dissertation not a single black or white person, not even Seymour's wife who died in 1936, ever came forward to challenge, revise, modify, call into question, or deny Bartleman's assertion, which was first printed in his widely read history in 1925. It is possible that Seymour's death a few years earlier may have prompted Bartleman not to mention Seymour (or an associate) by name out of respect for their memory. However, the most straightforward reason Seymour and his followers never challenged the claim is that it referred to Warren or some other Azusa leader and therefore they felt no reason to defend Seymour.

Although it probably was not Seymour, there is evidence to support Bartleman's claim of a conflict between an Azusa leader and the Mexican contingent. A. C. Valdez wrote that the revival came to an end (for him) in 1909, a statement at odds with the well-known fact that Seymour continued to hold services off-and-on until the 1920s. Furthermore, there are no *documented* reports of any Latinos *regularly* attending Azusa after 1909. Between 1909 and 1910, Finis Yoakim's Pisgah and Elmer Fisher's Upper Room missions reported the influx of a large number of *already* "Spirit-baptized" Mexicans. At this time there were no independent Mexican Pentecostal missions. The growth was so significant and unexpected that Fisher created a Spanish-language service and mission to accommodate them. Over forty Latinos attended the first service, though some no doubt were just visiting.[35]

This conflict could also help explain why despite ordaining at least three Mexicans to the pastoral ministry around 1909, Seymour and his largely black leadership team decided not to allow any Latinos to serve in the top three leadership posts after he revised the Constitution and Articles of Incorporation in 1914, unless he included them under the rubric "people of color." This, however, is doubtful since they are always referred to as Spanish (Mexican American) or Mexican (Mexican immigrants) in his newspaper. Alternatively, if the conflict took place before López's ordination, perhaps Seymour and Warren's decision to do so was to heal the conflict and affirm Latino leadership at Azusa and beyond. Regardless, several facts are clear: the last documentary evidence of Latinos at Azusa is Abundio López's ordination certificate from 1909. Furthermore, despite his ordination by Seymour, we know that within just a few years López decided to affiliate with other missions like Victoria Hall.[36] Whatever the cause, this conflict may have been a factor in Genaro Valenzuela's decision to open the Spanish Apostolic Faith Mission on North Alpine Street in 1911. Regardless, Seymour kept good if sporadic ties with Mexican Pentecostals like the Valenzuelas even if they didn't regularly attend his mission.[37] Because the evidence is unclear, people should not assume that the conflict with the Mexican contingent was with Seymour or that it was motivated by discrimination. Regardless of the conflict's details, Bartleman cites it to make the point that it signaled a larger shift toward routinization, loss of freedom in the Spirit, and a decline in the revival and its transformational spiritual and racial-ethnic social power.

CONFLICT WITH DURHAM AND THE ONENESS MOVEMENT, 1911–13

Seymour and Azusa forged ahead. While the internal conflicts had taken most of the wind out of the revival's sails, Azusa still attracted a small band of black and white followers and functioned like an interdenominational retreat center. In 1911, Seymour asked one of his most trusted white supporters—William Durham—to serve as visiting preacher during his revival tour back East. Durham gladly accepted and by February was preaching old-time Pentecostal power. He promised Seymour that he'd usher in a Second Azusa Street Revival. And so he did.

Durham ushered in not only a second great revival, but also a devastating schism. His dynamic preaching abilities and unbounded conviction attracted upward of a thousand people per night for approximately two-and-a half months. Azusa was filled to overflowing. The fire was back—but now with devastating results. Unbeknownst to Seymour, Durham was preaching his "Finished Work of Calvary," which denied Seymour's Wesleyan view of sanctification. He taught that the believer received complete sanctification at conversion and that it was not a second experience. After remaining quiet at first in the face of withering criticisms, Durham soon believed that God called him to set others right and used Seymour's pulpit to propagate the "Finished Work of Calvary." He ridiculed all other missions that disagreed, including The Upper Room, which saw its numbers decline.[38]

The Pentecostal community in Los Angeles was now divided. Unable to bite their tongues any longer, the Azusa Trustees wired Seymour and asked him to return home immediately. With the vast majority of the new parishioners loyal to Durham, including many who had left or turned on Seymour, Durham now threatened to take over the mission by popular acclaim. In an ironic twist of history, while Seymour was back East, Jennie persuaded

William H. Durham. Used by permission of Flower Pentecostal Heritage Center.

two (both black) of Azusa's seven trustees to padlock the mission. Seymour approved.[39]

Durham was locked out—and incensed. Like Parham before him, he set up a rival mission. The date was May 2, 1911.

After Seymour returned, he tried as best he could to find common ground with Durham and persuade him to reject the "Finished Work" position. True to his feisty nature and possessed by conviction about the "Finished Work," Durham wouldn't budge. Neither would Seymour. Durham began to berate Seymour for even making the request. He tried to pull rank on Seymour by invoking divine authority. He told Seymour that God made it clear that He wanted Seymour to embrace his "Finished Work" and to hand over Azusa. Seymour should step down as senior pastor—immediately.[40]

After Seymour would not yield, Durham spiritualized the revolt and tried to turn public opinion against him through his sermons and Durham's own newspaper. He broadcast his criticisms of Seymour across the nation. He sought the spiritual high ground by declaring that Seymour's decision to allow the mission to be locked was symbolic of locking out the Holy Spirit. It demonstrated that although God had once mightily used Seymour years ago "when he was humble," it was now clear that "the power of God had entirely left him" and that "he was no longer worthy of the confidence and respect of the saints." Taking on the mantle of the ever-loyal friend and suffering servant, Durham wrote in his own newspaper that he was the "last of all" of Seymour's (famous white) friends to "give him up." Although Durham had always "found an excuse for [Seymour's] failures and blunders," he was now "compelled" by the Holy Spirit to admit that the people were right. The most painful blow of all fell when he wrote: This once "mighty man . . . is such no longer." He asked his readers not to condemn him, but Seymour, for not submitting to divine revelation and the will of God.[41]

Seymour was devastated.

Durham's dogmatic zeal, "firm determination to rule or ruin," and nonstop campaigning to win Azusa and the Pentecostal world to his "Finished Work" was unstoppable. He brazenly called on Florence Crawford and Charles Parham to accept his new doctrine, though—unsurprisingly—without success. It seemed that only God could stop him. Durham's followers were thus shocked to hear of his sudden death on July 9, 1912, from pulmonary tuberculosis. He was thirty-nine years old. A powerful preacher and advocate was lost not only to the Pentecostal world, but also to Seymour.[42]

Durham's rival mission decimated Azusa. Rather than return to Seymour, after Durham's death most decided to join one of the growing number of white or ethnic daughter missions. By 1912, there were at least twelve Pentecostal missions in Los Angeles. This division led Alexander Boddy to lament that the Pentecostal community in the Los Angeles was "hopelessly" divided. The schism by still another white friend contributed to a growing perception among some blacks that "these white folks are going to try to take this property [i.e., Azusa Mission] away from us."[43]

Durham's highly publicized criticisms damaged Seymour's reputation—in some circles beyond repair. As a result of Durham's withering public criticisms and Seymour's inability to publicly respond via his own paper, after 1911 few white Pentecostals wanted to point to Seymour as one of the "fathers" of the movement. God had moved on. Bartleman captured this sentiment best when he wrote in his history *Azusa Street* that the "cloud" of the Holy Spirit that had once guided Moses in the Sinai desert and Seymour at Azusa had moved on to Durham and now others.[44] Seymour was quite literally history.

As a result, it's not surprising that Bartleman, a strong supporter of Durham and the one who helped him find an alternative meeting place after he was expelled from Azusa, later depicted Seymour as the "nominal" leader. In his own way and contrary to previous claims about Bartleman's promotion of Seymour and Azusa as the only center of Pentecostal origins,

Bartleman's perspective directly contributed to Seymour's marginalization in Pentecostal history. Durham's criticisms along with the emergence of new denominations after 1913 shifted the loyalties of many of his followers to their new traditions at home and abroad. This all contributed to Seymour's marginalization in the literature, though as shall be shown shortly, some like Charles Mason continued to afford him this dignity and honor.

SEYMOUR AND THE ORIGINS OF THE ONENESS CONTROVERSY, 1913

One of the final factors that blunted Seymour's influence was the Oneness controversy. The Pentecostal movement was permanently torn asunder at the second Worldwide Pentecostal Camp Meeting at Arroyo Seco. The meetings were again organized by R. J. Scott and ran from April 15 to June 1, 1913. In sharp contrast to the first camp meeting six years earlier, which Seymour superintended, this time he was not invited to speak or even sit on the stage—a traditional courtesy afforded even visiting clergy, perhaps because most had sided with Durham. As evidence of Seymour's unwillingness to hold a grudge, he attended the meetings anyway as a quiet spectator. Just as the one thousand plus white, black, Mexican, and other participants were about to proclaim Maria Woodworth-Etter's healing services a great victory, controversy erupted. Again over revelation and doctrine.[45]

Canadian evangelists Robert McAlister (1880–1953) and John Scheppe (1870–1939) argued that the Holy Spirit had directly revealed to them that the Apostles baptized in the name of Jesus only (Acts 2:38) and not in the triune formula as found in Matthew 28:19. They rejected as unbiblical the classic Trinitarian formula of God as one essence in three persons. The "Oneness" or "Jesus Only" Pentecostals required Trinitarians to be rebaptized in Jesus's name only. The new controversy permanently split the movement into two theological camps. Seymour was powerless to stop it. Not only did a large number of Durham's followers embrace the "Jesus Only" position, but so too did some of Seymour's strongest remaining black and white supporters like Glenn Cook and G. T. Haywood—all of which further isolated Seymour in the larger movement.[46]

The Oneness movement spread like a flashflood throughout emerging denominations like the Assemblies of God, which it almost destroyed as approximately one-third of its ministers defected to Oneness ranks, including Howard Goss and, for a short time, E. N. Bell. Seymour repudiated the Oneness doctrine, although he still maintained ties—though admittedly looser—with leaders like Cook and Haywood.[47]

Seymour's conflicts brought him to the painful and unhappy realization that human ambition, spiritual pride, white privilege, and desire to invoke new revelations made Azusa a Golden Apple that others might try to take by persuasion, spiritual pretext, or even legal means. Without the money, lawyers, and a formal education to stand up against white clergy and their powerful lawyers in white-ruled courtrooms during Jim Crow segregation, Seymour was now forced to take actions to protect the mission, his message, and the new Apostolic Faith denomination that he founded in 1914 that seemed to belie his interracial vision. However, few things in race-conscious America are seldom as they seem.

6
RACE WAR IN THE CHURCHES
PROMOTING PEACE BY TAKING THE INITIATIVE

GASTÓN ESPINOSA

Durham's revolt almost succeeded. Had he replaced Seymour's white and black Trustees with his own, they could have revised the Azusa Constitution and Articles of Incorporation and legally expelled Seymour. Only Jennie Seymour's prescient actions and support from the black Trustees saved Azusa from a white takeover.

By 1913, the steady stream of conflicts with Parham, Crawford, Carpenter, Lum, and Durham forced Seymour to realize that his dream of a racially unified church wherein blacks and whites shared power on an equal basis could not completely overcome four centuries of white privilege.[1] This privileging had spilled over into the church, even with well-intended friends. If this were not bad enough, Parham's recent attacks against Azusa, her daughter missions, and black spiritual practices led Seymour to believe that a spiritual "race war" had arisen within some sectors of Pentecostalism. He courageously declared that white racial prejudice led some whites to challenge and repudiate his leadership and the good work of the Azusa Street Revival itself. Seymour's decision demanded much soul searching and quiet and somber reflection with Jennie and his most trusted friends. However, after prayerful reflection he believed he had no other choice since the legacy of the revival, the already bruised black community, and what he believed was the genuine work of the Holy Spirit was at stake. It was a cross he would have to bear. Furthermore, as one of the founding fathers of the U.S. movement and presiding bishop of his newly created Azusa Street Apostolic Faith Mission denomination, he felt a pastoral responsibility to end the conflict before it tore apart the larger movement and destroyed the fruit of the Azusa revival. Seymour's charge of racially motivated division in Pentecostalism seemed confirmed by the decision in 1914 of 352 white clergy to leave Charles Mason's Church of God in Christ (COGIC) denomination to form the de facto all-white Assemblies of God. The growing separation across the nation was fanned into flames in February 1915 after D. W. Griffith released his explosive Hollywood film, *The Birth of a Nation*, which portrayed the Ku Klux Klan defending the honor of white women against the rapacious depredations of

The Birth of a Nation poster, *1915. Courtesy of Gastón Espinosa Collection.*

black men. Griffith's film fueled the racial ideology of a resurgent Klan across the nation, which did not reach its maximum strength until 1925—another ten years in the future.

REVISING THE CONSTITUTION—ALLOWING RACIAL DISCRIMINATION OR PURSUING PEACE?

To prevent future takeovers, in 1914 Seymour boldly revised the Constitution and Articles of Incorporation of the Azusa Street Apostolic Faith Mission (which was also the headquarters of his new denomination) to state that only "people of color" could serve as bishop, vice bishop, and trustees.[2]

This has understandably led some scholars to conclude that Seymour "allowed explicit prejudice to surface in his own ranks" because he restricted the "right to be officers" to "people of color," thus "limiting whites to membership."[3] Others contend that because of these actions Seymour was "guilty of racial discrimination."[4] On the one hand, it is true that he reserved the top three offices for people of color. However, whether he allowed explicit racial prejudice to enter his ranks and was motivated by racial prejudice and desire to discriminate against whites is misleading and inaccurate, especially when one takes into account the larger social context of his actions.[5]

Webster's dictionary defines prejudice with respect to race as "unreasonable feelings, opinions, or attitudes, esp. of a hostile nature, regarding a racial group."[6] Experts note that racial prejudice has three components: it is negative in nature (e.g., hatred), based on faulty information or unsubstantiated data, and is rooted in an inflexible generalization that monolithically essentializes a racial group.[7]

The historical record reveals that Seymour's motivations and actions do not fit the above definition and criteria. He did not restrict all whites from all leadership posts; did not base his decisions about whites on faulty knowledge, unsubstantiated data, and misinformation; did not hold any unreasonable and hostile feelings, opinions, or attitudes against all whites as an essentialized racial group; and did not root his views in inflexible generalizations that negatively essentialized all whites as inherently biologically, morally, and/or spiritually inferior to blacks. Instead, Seymour made this decision for a number of other practical pastoral and legal reasons.

Seymour's revised Constitution and Articles of Incorporation make it abundantly clear that whites and other ethnics could hold a number of leadership posts including superintendent, secretary, treasurer, deacon, evangelist, missionary, and youth leader. They were not restricted to membership only.[8]

Seymour also did not accuse all whites of being racist or troublemakers. Neither did he offer irrational generalizations about all whites based on faulty information or unsubstantiated data. He clearly differentiated between prejudiced and nonprejudiced whites when he wrote: "If *some* of our white brethren have prejudices and discrimination (Gal. 2:11–12), we can't do it." He further stated: "*Some* of our white brethren and sisters have never left us in all the division; they have stuck to us. We love our white brethren and sisters and welcome them."[9] These distinctions hardly sound like the comments of someone who essentialized and wanted to discriminate against all whites as a monolithic racial group. It is clear that he did not base his decision on a theory of black supremacy, white inferiority, or black racial prejudice against whites.

To make his own racial motivations crystal clear for posterity and to address future accusations of reverse discrimination, Seymour explicitly states in the first few pages of his minister's manual that his reason for reserving the top three posts for people of color was "not for discrimination," but to promote "peace" and racial harmony and "to keep down race war" and "friction" in the churches.[10]

Since there was not a literal race war in American Christianity and because Seymour refers to the "prejudices" and "discrimination" of "our white brethren" in the same passage, he was probably referring to Parham and some Pentecostals. This surmise is supported by the fact that from 1910 to 1913, Parham unleashed a torrent of racially laced attacks in his newspaper against Seymour, African-American spiritual practices, the Azusa revival, and his daughter missions—all right before Seymour made the revision in 1914.[11] Afterward the attacks drop off precipitously.

Seymour's talk about race wars is also confirmed by Parham himself, who also stated that a "bitter war was waged" against him by other Pentecostals, among whom Seymour was normally singled out as a ringleader.[12] After criticizing Seymour and "big 'buck' niggers" and "nigger lovers" at one of his daughter missions, Parham used militaristic language to describe his opponents: "I thank God we are gaining ground and victory against these forces."[13]

Seymour said he also made this decision so people would have "greater liberty and freedom in the Holy Spirit." Perhaps he was responding to black and white fears that outsiders might accuse them—like Parham did—of practicing "crude Negroisms of the Southland" and/or of having inappropriate physical contact.[14]

"Some of our white brethren," Seymour also argued, had created a lot of "trouble" by "causing division, and spreading wild fire and fanaticism." He did not link whites' divisiveness to an essentialist or innate biological disposition because he also added that "some of our colored brethren" had also caught the "spirit of division," he said.[15] Seymour was always careful to qualify what he wrote by saying "some" rather than "all" whites promoted division and wildfire and noted that blacks also promoted these things.

Parham confirms Seymour's view. He wrote that Azusa was "in bounds for four months" under Seymour's leadership until white leaders like Glenn Cook showed up and "made Azuza [sic] a hotbed of wildfire" and "fanaticism"—almost the exact words Seymour used a decade later in his above-cited manual.[16] Seymour believed that it was the dogmatism and fanaticism of Parham, Cook, Durham, and others (including blacks) that led to fanaticism, wildfire, and divisions in 1906, 1908, 1911, and 1913, something Bartleman and others confirm to varying degrees.[17]

This decision to reserve the top three posts to people of color was also a practical one. By 1914 the vast majority of the people at Azusa and its daughter missions in his new denomination—especially in the South—were African American.

In addition to these practical pastoral concerns, Seymour made the decision for a legal reason: to thwart any legal white takeovers. He became increasingly legal minded due to a number of events: Parham's attempt to take over the mission in 1906; Seymour's decision to purchase the mission; Lum's flight with the newspaper to Portland; Carpenter's interrogation of Seymour about the mission's finances; Seymour's incorporation of a new Azusa daughter mission in 1909 in Portland, Oregon; Durham's attempted takeover of the mission in 1911; and the decision of 352 white clergy to leave Charles Mason's interracial COGIC in 1913 to legally incorporate the Assemblies of God (AG) in 1914. The fact that Parham "spent a great deal of time" in southern California during some of Seymour's greatest crises (1908, 1911, 1912, 1913) and attempted in January 1908 to start a new mission at the same WCTU building he used in 1906 may have also contributed to his decision.[18]

Seymour knew that a black southerner with a limited education and his small interracial congregation would be hard pressed to fund and win a major legal battle against white clergy and their allies in a white-controlled courtroom. He also knew blacks had no real legal power in an American system that legally rationalized segregation and enforced separate schooling, dining, and housing facilities and that did little to stop the lynching of blacks across the nation. Race mattered. Seymour knew it and acted accordingly. That he did so in a preemptive manner in the best interests of his family, mission, and movement reveals that he was a wise and calculating leader.

Yet it grieved his spirit. This is evident in a short but painful statement often overlooked by scholars at the bottom of his *Doctrines and Discipline* Table of Contents:

> May none of us be like Ahab, to rob our brother of their vineyard. I Kings 21:14–20. Be sure your sin will find you out. Numbers 32:23. Judas's sin found him. Cain's sin found him.[19]

Indeed, Seymour believed that some of his brethren were trying to rob him of the vineyard God had given him to promote Pentecostal revival—the Azusa Street Mission. Given the loss of his newspaper and many of his white friends, Seymour needed to hold on to the mission for another practical reason: it was his last remaining internationally recognized platform from which to spread his vision and version of Pentecostalism.[20]

That Seymour apologized to his readers for his decision implies it was a forced concession and not due to any theory of black supremacy or white spiritual inferiority or desire to discriminate. Indeed, he lamented: "We are sorry for this, but it is best now and in later years in the work." His final comment also underscores his deeper pastoral motivation: "I hope we won't have any more trouble or division [of] spirit" in the Pentecostal churches.[21] Despite his decision, he also promised "people of all countries, climes and nations shall be welcome."[22]

Even more important, he continued to practice racial integration at Azusa until the day he died. Perhaps most compelling of all, not a single person from this period—white or black, friend or foe—not even Parham—ever accused Seymour of allowing racial prejudice or practicing racial discrimination.[23]

Finally, Seymour made the decision for another set of larger societal reasons: racial strife and division were ripping the nation and church apart. In 1915 Booker T. Washington died and W.E.B. Du Bois declared that Washington's policy of accommodation had failed. So too—at one level—had Seymour's.[24]

Past is prologue. On May 15, 1916, a crowd of ten thousand white spectators looked on as Jesse Washington, accused of assaulting a white woman, was lynched and burned in Waco, Texas—his charred body dangling from a lynch mob's rope. Some celebrated by selling postcards (like the following image) throughout the state.[25] The following year, four major race riots erupted across the United States and two years later seven more blazed through black communities in the "Red Summer" of 1919.[26]

More disheartening, President Woodrow Wilson, the pious son of a Presbyterian minister and Democrat, caved in to social pressure and decided to segregate all government facilities in order to—in language strikingly similar to Seymour's—reduce racial "friction" in society. Even Parham, who in his early years reached out to blacks and allowed Seymour to attend his Bible school, in his later years called on Pentecostals across the nation to work with the Ku Klux Klan to coordinate their "high ideals for the betterment of mankind" with . . . Pentecostal "Old Time Religion."[27]

In short, Seymour's decision was driven by a host of practical pastoral, social, and legal considerations, the most important being his genuine desire to promote peace and harmony in the churches, to end the race war and friction in the Pentecostal churches, to recognize that his primary ministry

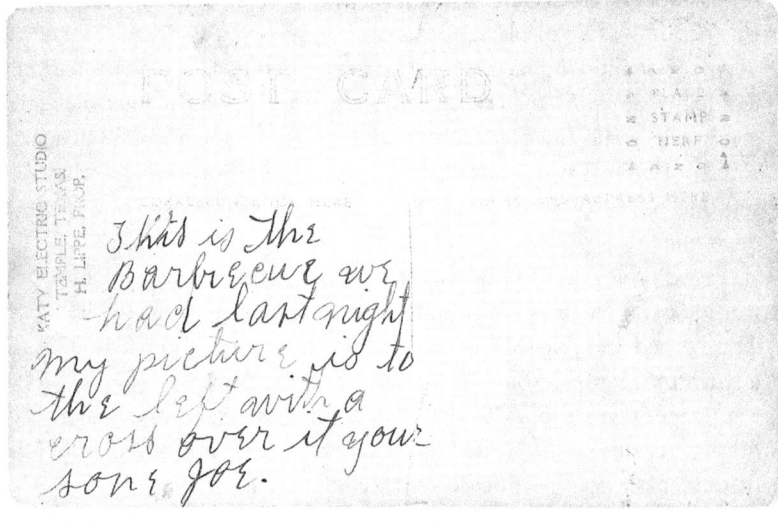

Jesse Washington was lynched on May 15, 1916, for reportedly assaulting a white girl in Waco, Texas. This postcard was made by a young man who witnessed the lynching and then sent the postcard to his parents. The back of the postcard reads: "This is the barbecue we had last night. My picture is to the left with a cross over it Your son Joe." This is the world in which Seymour had to live and negotiate his existence and ministry. Courtesy of Gastón Espinosa Collection.

was to African Americans (especially after Durham's 1911 schism), and to legally and economically protect his mission, family, and denomination from future lawsuits they could not afford to fight or expect to win.[28] Seymour's conviction that making this revision could help end the race war and friction appears right on target, because after he made it, Parham's public racial criticisms of Seymour, blacks, and Azusa stopped almost overnight. Did white supremacy win? No, Seymour still held the mission and continued to use it as a platform to promote his integrationist vision and racial equality, though at a considerable price. He knew that future writers might accuse him of racial prejudice and reverse discrimination, but hoped that they would weigh this one decision against his explicit statements against discrimination in his minister's manual (his last known publication) and a lifetime of teaching, preaching, and interracial practices.

PROMOTING RACIAL EQUALITY, RECONCILIATION, INTEGRATION, AND UNITY

This painful struggle over race relations has understandably led some to argue that "on the whole, pentecostal culture failed to provide a sustained theology of racial reconciliation for whites and blacks alike" because "the movement's working theologians offered little guidance in race matters" and white and black editors were largely oblivious or indifferent to race matters because it only "played a slight role in their theological thinking." In all of Seymour's signed *Apostolic Faith* articles, he allegedly refers to "race" only once—and in a rather generic manner.[29] Indeed, this general assessment is largely correct. The historical record indicates that many first- and second-generation leaders were seemingly indifferent to race matters. For some, race was a seemingly insoluble problem; for others the status quo was an acceptable if imperfect solution.

However, were Seymour and Parham indifferent to race? No, to the contrary. A careful review of the historical literature indicates that both Seymour and Parham—the Pentecostal movement's two most important founders, newspaper editors, and working theologians—used their newspapers, books, revivals, and followers to articulate their views on race matters in a clear, compelling, and sustained manner throughout much of their lives and ministries. This is because race relations mattered deeply to both of them.

Seymour used the Bible and the language and logic of the outpouring and baptism of the Holy Spirit to express both his grievances and desire to promote racial equality, reconciliation, integration, and unity in the church. Parham used them to air his grievances about Seymour's vision and version of Pentecostalism and to distinguish his "true" Pentecost from Seymour's "counterfeit" revival, which he believed was corrupted by some African-American spiritual practices, interracial mixing, and fanaticism.[30] They not

Apostolic Faith *newspaper, January 1907. Courtesy of Gastón Espinosa Collection.*

only addressed race matters in their writings, but vigorously and publicly disagreed with each other over the theological significance of the multiracial origins, character, purpose, and meaning of Azusa and the larger Pentecostal outpouring.[31] The literature has downplayed their disagreements in order to promote Christian unity, which has not only obscured their genuine differences but diminished Seymour's contributions to Pentecostal origins.[32]

The fact that Seymour provided guidance on race matters and promoted racial equality, reconciliation, integration, and unity throughout his ministry are evident in (1) the churches he chose to attend from 1895 to 1906, (2) his editorial statements and teachings in his *Apostolic Faith* newspaper, (3) his teaching on race relations, racial prejudice, and the origins of the racial conflict at Azusa and in early Pentecostalism in his *Doctrines and Discipline* minister's manual, (4) his teaching on racial separation in Galatians 2:11–22, (5) eyewitness testimonies by friends, foes, and observers, and (6) in statements by Parham.

The first piece of evidence that race played a major role in Seymour's theological thinking and that he was committed to racial reconciliation is his practice of attending and seeking ordination with the white-led interracial denominations that promoted (at least when he visited them) racial equality and reconciliation, such as the Evening Light Saints and Martin Wells Knapp's God's Bible School, and even—for a short while—Parham's Apostolic Faith.[33]

The next piece is the theological and spiritual guidance Seymour and his colleagues provided on race matters in his *Apostolic Faith*—often on the first page and sometimes in the lead article. The fact that he did not sign all or even most of them does not mean that he did not author, affirm, and/or promote their content. Even assuming he did not dictate or author them himself, it is implausible that his editorial team, right after the conflict with Parham and in the atmosphere of America's racial tensions, would have published statements on racial equality month after month—and often on the first page—without Seymour's knowledge and express approval. The fact that so many of these statements were lead articles or published as stand-alone exhortations with nothing else to compete with their impact only underscores their strategic significance.[34]

Furthermore, since he was the unrivaled founder and senior pastor of the Azusa Mission and its newspaper, everyone would have assumed his authorship and/or approval. The fact that he did not write a treatise on race relations like W.E.B. Du Bois or did not sign all of the editorials, does not mean he failed to promote—in his own modest and quiet way—racial harmony and offer sustained guidance on race relations, especially when one takes into account his background, limited education, social context, and goals. Seymour no doubt would have agreed with the old adage: less is more. This approach also reflected his quiet, laconic, and pastoral spirit and admonition to ministers to "converse sparingly."[35] He was a man of few words—fewer still when they could be perceived as self-promoting and were as potentially explosive as loudly banging the drum of racial equality and integration in Jim Crow America.

Contrary to previous assertions, Seymour did not resign himself to the status quo, but made his points crystal clear month after month and year after year not only in short, strategic statements in his newspaper but also in the way he practiced his beliefs at Azusa. Seymour believed that action mattered a whole lot more than words and was a more persuasive teacher. All of this, along with a general sense of Christian humility and southern modesty, dictated that he take a more subtle and gracious approach to race matters, though one that was still clear—as Parham's reaction illustrates.

Although the term *race* reportedly only occurs once in his signed articles, Seymour and his editorial team shrewdly used many other euphemisms and racial placeholders like "color," "Ethiopians," "classes of people," and "nationality," which together show that Seymour and his followers provided sustained guidance on race matters. This strategy is clearly evident in the very first issue of the *Apostolic Faith,* where they boldly declared: "God makes no difference in nationality, Ethiopians, Chinese, Indians, Mexicans, and other nationalities worship together" because "God recognizes no man-made creeds, doctrines, nor classes of people, but 'the willing and obedient.'"[36] "Nationalities" and later "Ethiopians" were often diplomatic euphemisms and placeholders for race-ethnicity and blacks. Jennie Seymour, for example, listed her race as "Ethiopian" on her 1908 marriage certificate.[37] The fact that Seymour and his followers referred to them as "man-made" racial categories sent a signal to the reader that they knew they were socially constructed, not divinely ordained—a point that directly challenged Parham's writings and racial geneology.

This approach stood in sharp contrast to the way Hoke Smith and Clark Howell, two newspaper editors turned Democratic gubernatorial candidates, used the press to stoke the flames of racial hatred. In the summer of 1906, they spread false rumors in the *Atlanta Constitution* and *Atlanta Journal* about black "brutes" sexually assaulting white women. As a result, in September ten thousand whites marched over to the black community, where they looted; burned down businesses; and chased, beat, stabbed, and lynched blacks. The riots left twenty-five blacks and two whites dead on the streets.[38]

In direct contrast, Seymour and his colleagues wrote on the front page of the November 1906 issue: "It is noticeable how free all nationalities feel. If a Mexican or German cannot speak English, he gets up and speaks in his own tongue and feels quite at home for the Spirit interprets through the face and people say amen. No instrument that God can use is rejected on account of *color*."[39] In an age when people did reject, beat, and kill people because of their color, his promotion of full racial equality and integration was why, in the minds of Seymour's supporters, "God has so built up the [Azusa] work."[40]

In a direct repudiation of Parham's view in *Kol Kare Bomidbar* (1902, 1910) that racial separation was divinely ordained, Seymour and his colleagues wrote in another front-page stand-alone editorial in December 1906: "This meeting has been a melting time. The people are melted together by the power of the blood and by the Holy Ghost. They are made one lump, one bread, all one body in Christ Jesus. There is no Jew or Gentile, *bond* [i.e., black slave] or free, in the Azusa street [*sic*] Mission."[41] African-American eyewitness Mattie Cummings similarly noted: "Everybody was just the same. It did not matter if you were black, white, green or grizzly. There was a wonderful spirit. Germans and Jews, blacks and whites, ate together in the little cottage in the rear. Nobody ever thought about color" as a dividing line at the Azusa revival.[42]

The multiple references to the Holy Spirit "melting" "all of the races together" "into one lump" of "bond" and "free" were racially loaded—and Seymour knew it. It was the Spirit of God who was breaking down the racial divide, they declared. These references also reveal that Seymour was using the outpouring of the Holy Spirit as a divine pretext to authorize their socially transgressive racial behavior of interracial mixing and touching (for the laying on of hands for divine healing and to receive the Spirit baptism) in Jim Crow America.

Seymour's "lump" resonated with W.E.B. Du Bois's statement about how the "Talented Tenth" of black educated elites would "leaven the lump" of black masses to raise them out of the mire of segregation and racism.[43] Rather than black elites alone, Seymour believed the Holy Spirit was ushering in a new Apostolic age wherein God would blend all of the races together into one "lump" (a word used multiple times by Du Bois and Seymour and may reveal Du Bois's influence on Seymour or vice versa) of believers that would leaven the church and society.[44] Indeed, Seymour's vision provided a divine mandate and strategy for how the other 90 percent of the "lump" could, in their own small ways, be ordinary prophets with—in the words of Du Bois—the "vision of seers."

Their promotion of full racial integration stands in sharp contrast to Boddy's description of the danger of blacks and whites mixing—even with other clergy—in the South:

> The back portion of the cars are generally filled with coloured people, who sit together—the white man may not sit there. At the railroad stations you see the words: "Waiting Room for Coloured People." No mixing of the two races is acceptable. If a white preacher speaks to a coloured congregation, he does not go home to the coloured pastor's house. If he was known to make a practice of doing such a thing, he would soon become what some term a "dead man" to both sides.[45]

Seymour and his colleagues continued this sustained teaching in their January 1907 lead article—once again on the first page. They declared: God "recognizes no flesh, no color, no names" because he was unifying "them . . . into one body" of believers.[46]

They interpreted this melting of the "colors" (i.e., "races") into one body of believers as evidence of Christ's Second Coming. In the February–March issue they similarly wrote: "One token of the Lord's coming is that He is melting *all races* and nations together. . . . He is baptizing by one spirit into one body and making up a people that will be ready to meet Him when He comes."[47]

The fact that these editorials were published after Parham's failed takeover in October reveals that Seymour was unwilling to roll over and allow Parham to dominate the movement's theological, social, and racial vision. Indeed, after Parham publicly criticized Seymour and the revival, Seymour and his staff felt they had no choice but to go on the offensive to correct the distortion and set the record straight.[48]

The third piece of evidence that race played a major role in Seymour's theological thinking and that he promoted racial reconciliation was his decision and explanation for revising the Constitution and Articles of Incorporation to state that only "people of color" could serve as bishop, vice bishop, and trustees.[49] He took this opportunity to openly and honestly discuss the racial conflict at Azusa and in the Pentecostal movement, the Bible's teaching on race matters, and then to provide clear guidance on race relations.[50]

Seymour stated that even if whites were prejudiced against blacks, blacks could not under any circumstances engage in reverse discrimination: "if some of our white [Pentecostal] brethren have prejudices and discrimination (Gal. 2:11–20), we can't do it, because God calls us to follow the Bible. We must love all men as Christ commands (Heb. 12:14)." While many black radicals called on their followers to only tolerate whites, Seymour commanded them to love whites. He also exhorted whites to "love their colored brethren and respect them in the truth so that the Holy Spirit won't be greaved [sic]." He underscored his commitment by declaring: "Jesus takes in all people in his Salvation [sic]. He is neither black nor white man, [sic] nor Chinaman, nor Hindoo, nor Japanese, but God. God is Spirit because without his spirit we cannot be saved."[51] In short, if you don't take in and *accept* all races as equals in Christ, then you can't be saved.

The next piece of evidence that race was central to Seymour's theological thinking and that he promoted racial reconciliation in a sustained manner is his citation and use of Galatians 2:11–20 in several places in his writings. In *Doctrines and Disciplines,* for instance, Seymour used this passage to teach that racial separation and segregation is unbiblical. After he said that blacks could not have prejudices and discrimination against whites, he cited Galatians 2:11–20 as his biblical support.[52]

Seymour took this position because in the Galatians passage Paul criticizes Peter for caving in to social pressure to avoid intermingling and eating (i.e., integrating) with Gentiles, despite his previous practices. Peter did this because James reminded him of long-standing Jewish traditions, dietary laws, and views on inter-racial-ethnic mixing, which taught that Gentiles were religiously impure. This required them to self-segregate. Paul, the younger convert to the movement, criticized Peter, the founder and leader of the Apostolic church, for buckling under social pressure. Paul argued that tradition and law—both civil and religious—were now superseded by their spiritual equality and unity in Christ, which overrode all socially constructed man-made racial-ethnic, cultural, national, and legal barriers. This passage provides insight into how Seymour viewed Parham's later racialization of the movement and his own repudiation of Parham's views. Seymour was Paul, and Parham was Peter.

> 11 When Peter was come to Antioch, I withstood him to the face, because he was to be blamed. 12 For before . . . James [came to Antioch], he [Peter] did eat with the Gentiles: but when they were come, he *withdrew* and *separated* himself, fearing them [Jewish legalists]. . . . 14 But when I saw that they walked not uprightly according to the truth of the gospel, I said unto Peter before them all. . . . 16

man is not justified by the . . . law, but by the faith of Jesus Christ . . . for by the works of the law shall no flesh be justified. . . . 18 For if I build again the things which I [God] destroyed [i.e., national/ethnic laws that justified separation and segregation by race-ethnicity/nationality, but not by faith/belief], I make myself a transgressor. For I through the law am dead to the law, that I might live unto God . . . [emphasis added]

Seymour used Paul's teaching to reject Parham's racial views because they were unbiblical and he also criticized those who attempted to hide behind the Old Testament and current laws and social practices to justify their socially constructed man-made racial and social conventions.

The fifth piece of evidence that race was central to Seymour's theological thinking and that he promoted racial reconciliation in a sustained manner are the many comments that his friends, foes, and other eyewitnesses made about him. For example, Bartleman wrote that at Seymour's revival, "The 'colorline' [of race] was washed away in the blood."[53] Orwig stated that Seymour's messages resulted in "removing prejudice."[54] And Cashwell wrote about how he "crucified" his racial prejudice at the Azusa altar.[55]

Even secular sources like the *Indianapolis News* confirmed this view when a reporter wrote that Seymour promoted complete racial equality, integration, reconciliation, and unity. Their headlines sensationalized his practices: "Whites and Blacks Mix in a Religious Frenzy" and "Crazed Girls in Arms of Black Men."[56] Another reporter wrote: "This is a religious sect in which the color line is not drawn [by their leaders] . . . and the Negro brother is accorded the same consideration in the meetings of the sect as the white man." They noted: "Incidentally, a Negro is the 'founder' of this faith."[57] In a highly provocative portrayal meant to portray Seymour's revival as a transgressive racial and social space, one reporter exclaimed:

> White women threw their arms about the dusky necks of negresses and went through performances that would put to shame the most accomplished "park spooning." Among the men, the conduct was much the same. Negroes and whites locked in each other's arms, kissed and patted each other's backs and caressed white faces against black faces and chocolate colored faces and coffee colored faces. . . .
>
> Sister Cripe walked clear down the line of women, kissing all. Negresses were not neglected. Sister Schurmann kissed, everybody kissed. In the far part of the room men were clasped in each other's arms. In fond embrace Osborn and Brother Cummings, colored, remained almost a full minute. It was real hugging, no beating around the bush about it. And nearly every other man was going through [a] similar process.[58]

Cartoon mocks Seymour's and Glenn Cook's baptism of people in the latter's mission in Indianapolis, Indiana. The Indianapolis Star, *June 1907. Courtesy of Gastón Espinosa Collection.*

The final and perhaps most compelling piece of evidence in support of Seymour's longstanding position and practice comes from none other than his former teacher, Charles Parham. He criticizes Seymour and his followers for proactively promoting racial equality, reconciliation, integration, and unity and—in his mind—another vision and version of Pentecostalism. He stated: "O, how many have been deceived by the Azuza [sic] mess" "where all this counterfeit Pentecostal was born."[59] Seymour and his followers spread his views "all over the country" and around "the world," Parham lamented.[60]

Indeed, Parham and Seymour both saw themselves as locked in a spiritual struggle over defining the theological, social, and racial significance of the outpouring of the Holy Spirit. Seymour's actions help explain why Parham lamented that "Seymour" "used all his papers to *prove* that Azusa was the original 'crib' of this Movement, and a Negro the first preacher,"[61] and that "in vain" Seymour (again) sought to "*prove* the fanaticism of Azuza [sic] as the original manifestation of Pentecost."[62] In all of the above cases, Parham singles out Seymour as the prime leader and originator of this alternative vision and version of Pentecostalism.

The simple and unvarnished truth is that Seymour and Parham were hardly indifferent about race matters. They both used the language of the Pentecostal outpouring to legitimize their own interpretations, grievances, and historical reconstructions, and to criticize—to varying degrees—each other's movement as unbiblical and in Parham's criticism of Seymour's revival—"spiritual prostitution" and satanically inspired.[63]

Parham's consistent attacks on Seymour, his Azusa Mission, and their racial practices only make sense if he was indeed a serious threat and formidable leader who promoted his beliefs in a compelling and sustained manner. Parham admitted as much when he lamented that Seymour's work had "superceded [sic] the true work [i.e., Parham's work]" and "filled the earth" with his counterfeit Pentecost.[64] This hardly sounds like a nominal leader who simply popularized Parham's views to the masses.

FINAL OUTCOME: INITIAL EVIDENCE, DIVINE LOVE, AND STRANGE RELIGION

The greatest casualty of this struggle was Seymour's belief that the baptism with the Holy Spirit is only evidenced by speaking in unknown tongues. Seymour could not square Parham's heterodox theological views and vicious racial attacks with the belief that speaking in tongues was the main true physical evidence of the Spirit baptism. There must be more. Where was the fruit of the Spirit and divine love for one another—the true hallmarks of the Spirit baptism?

As a result, in a veiled allusion to Parham, Seymour taught in his minister's manual: "Annihilation . . . is why we could not stand for tongues being the evidence of the Baptism in the Holy Ghost and fire." "If tongues was the evidence . . . then men and women that have received the tongues . . . could not believe contrary of the teachings of the Holy Spirit." However, his experience with Parham taught him just the opposite. This led him to teach: "Since tongues was not the [only] evidence of the Baptism in the Holy Spirit, men and women can receive it and yet [still] be destitute of the truth." He thus concluded that although tongues are one of the signs of being filled with the Holy Spirit, it's not the only evidence.[65] His other pastoral concern was that "wherever the doctrine of the Baptism in the Holy Spirit will only be known as the evidence of speaking in tongues, that work . . . will suffer, because all kinds of [counterfeit] spirits can come in."[66]

Seymour didn't reject the baptism with the Holy Spirit, just an overemphasis on it. He stated: "It is all right to have the signs following, but not to pin our faith to outward manifestations. We are to go by the word of God. Our thought must be in *harmony* with the Bible or else we will have a strange religion." He proposed that the true baptism in the Holy Spirit was a "means to be flooded with the love of God and Power for Service, and a love for the truth as it is in God's word"—a teaching he clung to throughout his ministry.[67]

LIMINAL MOMENT? SPREADING SEYMOUR'S VISION OF RACIAL RECONCILIATION

All of this reveals something deeper: Seymour had changed.[68] In fact, as this study has documented, Seymour changed some of his views and practices via divine inspiration and as the circumstances demanded. This challenges the static pre-October 1906 portrayal of Seymour as a humble, soft-spoken, and nominal leader. Although eyewitnesses claim that Seymour still walked to the pulpit with his head bowed low, he also now taught his ministers that they had a responsibility to "tell everyone under your care what you think wrong in his conduct and temper" as "lovingly and plainly" and as soon as possible lest it "fest in our heart"—perhaps a festering that he knew all too well from experience. In contrast to Pentecostal stereotypes, Seymour wrote that a minister's deportment should be "serious, weighty and solemn."[69] He should have a deep prayer life, preach, visit members at their homes, pray for the sick, youth, and elderly, meditate on the Bible, love his family, and be diligent, converse sparingly, and believe evil of no one without good evidence. In a comment loaded with double meaning and no doubt painful memories, he also admonished his ministers—most of whom were black, economically impoverished, and no doubt mocked as "Holy Rollers"—to "be ashamed of nothing but sin." Their only task was to "save souls"—Seymour's life-long goal.[70]

In the end, the problem of race relations at Azusa and in early Pentecostalism was not due to a lack of leadership, sustained guidance, and understanding about the theological, social, and racial implications of the outpouring of the Holy Spirit, but rather to a lack of will on the part of some whites and blacks to implement Seymour's teachings and practices, and later attempts to deny or diminish them in the historiography. However, the real story is not with those who lacked the courage to implement his vision, but rather with those like leaders in the COGIC and other denominations and independent churches who fought to keep it alive over the past century.[71] In this respect, Seymour's vision and version of Pentecostalism was not a liminal moment restricted to a few weeks or months in 1906, but rather a three-year revival and an ongoing practice that has been kept alive in some segments of the movement by countless working-class prophetic preachers and teachers around the world.

7
WE DON'T BELIEVE IN RELICS
SEYMOUR IN IGNOMINY

GASTÓN ESPINOSA

Seymour survived. And his once powerful revival had, like the rains in a desert storm, given way to a flood of ideas, social practices, and innovative combinative spiritual experiences around the world. Despite the thousands touched by Seymour and the revival, by 1915 Azusa was reduced to a small group of about twenty black and white participants, largely the original Bonnie Brae Street prayer group. Nightly meetings were reduced to just one Sunday meeting a week, in large part because of the Seymours' busy travel schedule.[1]

Seymour did not give up. He continued to preach racial reconciliation and unity and to pastor his flock for almost another decade, though now in the shadow of emerging Pentecostal giants like Aimee Semple McPherson. Despite his optimistic spirit, he may have been discouraged by the news of Pentecostal evangelists like Raymond T. Richey allowing delegations of the Ku Klux Klan to march down the aisles of his revivals in Houston—the place Seymour first heard about Pentecost more than a decade earlier.[2]

As the roaring twenties brought prosperity to millions of white Americans and remarkable growth to the scores of emerging Pentecostal churches that dotted the American landscape, Azusa struggled to survive. In contrast to glory days, when Seymour could raise $1,200 in fifteen minutes, he now asked his working-class congregation, hat clenched in hand, "Expenses, please, at least."[3]

Most of his annual income now came from the "love offerings" and other honoraria he received on his preaching tours across the United States. He visited black, white, and interracial missions in Indianapolis, Chicago, Cincinnati, New York, Washington, Baltimore, Houston, Tennessee, Virginia, Alabama, Texas, and storefronts across the nation. He spoke at Cook's mission in Indianapolis, at John Lake's revival in Washington, and at several of Mason's Church of God in Christ (COGIC) Annual Holy convocations.[4]

Around 1917, Seymour called on Pentecostal missions in Los Angeles to meet at Azusa to promote Christian unity. Two pastors attended.[5] In 1918, Seymour visited Sister Aimee Semple McPherson's Los Angeles campaign as

William J. Seymour, ca. 1915. Used by permission of Apostolic Faith, Portland, Oregon.

a silent spectator. Why she didn't acknowledge him from the pulpit is uncertain. Perhaps she didn't see him or overlooked him because of her friendship with William Durham.[6] Regardless, a new star was rising and Seymour's star was dimming.

However, in December 1919, Seymour was invited to speak again at the COGIC General Convocation in Memphis. Former Azusa attendees but now "Chief Apostle" Charles Mason and "Overseer" Mack Jonas introduced "Bishop" Seymour as "one of the founders" whose "noble sayings" continued to guide "this great movement." Seymour praised COGIC as one of the greatest Pentecostal movements on "earth" since they'd remained true to his vision. He challenged them to "contend for doctrine," repudiate "even the thought of [spiritual] fornication in the ministry," and to "show their fruits" by living a holy, Christ-centered life. Mason praised the "noble sayings" of "Elder Seymour" and concluded by singing a song of welcome to him in the Spirit.[7]

Seymour's superstar reception at COGIC encouraged him to press forward. He was a man of quiet action and firm resolve—and not easily dissuaded. Despite the low turnout at his last Los Angeles conference, because of the ongoing recognition of Azusa as a key center of the rapidly growing Pentecostal revival, he stubbornly decided to organize the Azusa Street Mission Fourteenth Anniversary celebration and Bible conference in 1920. We know nothing about who attended. However, he must have expected a strong turnout because he published a fifteen-page program that indicated he had financial support. At the conference, he promoted the Second Coming of Christ, Bible teaching, and sang twelve songs—one third of which were Negro spirituals, evidence that he continued to promote African American spirituality. The final hymn, "Lord, I couldn't hear nobody pray," captured Seymour's concerns about the church and commitment to prayer, which only grew with age, eyewitnesses noted.[8]

In 1921, Seymour went on another nationwide preaching tour. He conducted revivals at various churches, including Georgiana Aycock née Pepsico's church in Columbus, Ohio. At nightly services, he admonished hearers to live holy, Christ-centered lives. Touched by the sweet spirit of the racially mixed crowd, Seymour kept calling from the platform for Mrs. Aycock to sing his favorite hymn, "Is not this the land of Beulah?" For Seymour and many other Blacks, Mrs. Aycock's fully integrated service was indeed a taste a Beulah land, a place often sung about in Negro spirituals where God's blessing was realized. Seymour was so impressed by his hostess that he invited her to join his staff. She declined. As he parted he looked at her and said: "Whatever you do, be true to God."[9]

Unlike most superstar revivalists who demanded front row, if not front stage recognition, Seymour regularly attended conferences led by others as a quiet spectator to keep up with the latest trends, to hear the preaching of powerful revivalists, and to learn more about the Bible and Christian faith. In the summer of 1922 he attended a Bible convention in Los Angeles. He was not invited to sit on stage or to give a greeting; a practice normally afforded visiting ministers. There's no record that he held a grudge.[10]

HOMEGOING OF AN ORDINARY PROPHET

In the fall of 1922, William and Jennie Seymour planned another preaching tour across America. Their plans were cut short when, on September 28, 1922, Seymour suffered a minor heart attack that morning. After catching his breath, he stubbornly went back to work. He, Jennie, and his black and white co-workers spent the day in prayer, singing praise songs, and letter writing. At 5:00 PM while dictating a batch of letters to his followers, he suffered a second massive heart attack. He died in the arms of Jennie Seymour.

Foreshadowing Martin Luther King's message a half a century later and true to his focus on divine love and the beloved community, Seymour's last message was "a plea for love among the brethren everywhere" and to live a life of "love to all and malice to none." His last words to Jennie were: "I love my Jesus so."[11]

Despite the impact that Seymour and Azusa had on thousands of people around the world, only two hundred attended his funeral.[12] This number stood in sharp contrast to the twenty-five hundred people who waded through a snowstorm to attend Parham's funeral in 1929, a person his biographer said was largely forgotten by the larger Pentecostal world.[13]

At his funeral, people testified about the impact Seymour had on their lives and his faith, devotion, and love for God and people. While some sang his favorite hymns, others shed silent tears.

Although it's understandable why some might interpret his life and ministry as a tragedy, it's also possible to view his determination to hold on to his interracial message, the Azusa Mission, and his Christian faith as a story of steadfast determination in the face of forces that sought to destroy him, his message of Godly love and racial reconciliation, and break his quiet spirit. This determination was captured in his obituary:

> His departure is a grief and loss to many a heart that remembers how often his great understanding and loving heart had comforted and advised them and brought them to see Christ in a deeper way. . . . His life was a crowning example of . . . self-denial and whole consecration to God. . . . Brother Seymour was our father. . . . The world was his parish. . . . When asked so often the secret of his power he would say, 'Living free from sin and in the Word of God.'[14]

G. T. Haywood wrote that Seymour was "loved and respected," even by those in the Oneness movement who disagreed with him.[15] His body was laid to rest in a simple redwood coffin in Evergreen Cemetery, East Los Angeles.[16]

It was a fitting tribute that right above Seymour's obituary on the front page of the *Pentecostal Herald,* forty white and black leaders joined forces to announce, "A Great Unity Conference of the Pentecostal Movement of North America" for October 24, 1922. For despite Seymour's death, his spirit of racial reconciliation and unity was kept alive by his black and white followers such as Charles Mason, Frank Bartleman, G. T. Haywood, F. W. Williams, and others who helped lead this racially integrated conference. They sought to "promote a close bond of love and fellowship among God's Spirit-Baptized People," a sentiment Seymour heartily affirmed.[17]

"WE DON'T BELIEVE IN RELICS": JENNIE SEYMOUR AND AZUSA'S STRUGGLE TO SURVIVE, 1923-36

In light of her husband's wishes, Jennie Seymour assumed leadership of Azusa, though she refused the title of bishop out of respect for her husband and the mission's bylaws. The 1929 stock market crash and Great Depression made life difficult for her congregation. Still, she held on to their vision. Seymour's decision to revise the Constitution and Articles of Incorporation in 1914 proved prescient because in 1930 a white man claiming to be a Coptic bishop named R. C. Griffith attempted to take over the mission. After ministering there for several months, he persuaded a majority of the Azusa congregation (largely white) to elect him bishop. He pointed out that according the bylaws, Jennie could not lead the mission since only a man could be a bishop. Before the election took place, Jennie foiled the plot and the police padlocked the door shut until the dispute could be settled. After a costly legal battle, Judge Guerin reviewed the Constitution and Articles of Incorporation and decided in favor of Jennie against "the white faction." Azusa remained firmly in Seymour's control—at least for now.[18]

However, the costly legal battle put the mission in "receivership." The Azusa Trustees had to borrow two thousand dollars. On top of this, the City of Los Angeles scheduled the mission to be torn down in 1931 on the shoddy pretext of it being a "fire hazard"—perhaps called in by their opponents.[19]

After exploring every other possible option, Jennie's only hope was for one of her white brethren to save the now world famous Azusa Mission. In desperation, she turned to the Assemblies of God, since so many in it were ushered into Pentecost through her husband's ministry at Azusa—including its current General Superintendent—Ernest S. Williams. In response to her plea, it was conveyed to her that AG didn't believe in saving "relics."[20]

As the timbers of the Azusa Mission came crashing down, Jennie shed silent tears. After she walked over to the pile of rubble to pick up the mission address as a keepsake, she found that Bartleman had already picked up the numbers "312" for himself—which he proudly displayed on his living room wall.[21]

Jennie was left with only memories, but not without hope. With firm determination she took her now homeless Azusa flock back to the original Bonnie Brae Street house where she and William had begun twenty-five years earlier. The room that once overflowed now comfortably seated their small but energetic band of black and white saints. She preached, prayed for the sick, led worship services, and led people into the baptism with the Holy Spirit. She remained true to their vision. Aside from Jennie's encouragement and prayers, the other daughter missions in their denomination were now left largely to fend for themselves, and many developed into their own denominations.[22]

In June 1933, Jennie's failing health forced her to step down as pastor. On July 2, 1936, Jennie Seymour died. Her body was laid to rest in a simple redwood coffin next to William. In 1938, Security First National Bank foreclosed on the Azusa property and it was sold to the city of Los Angeles, who turned it into a parking lot. The Bonnie Brae house remains intact and is now a museum.[23]

Although the Seymours and the Azusa Mission are gone, their memories have been kept alive in the spirit of the living who continue to preach their vision and version of Pentecostalism around the world.

Conclusion
HOLY RESTLESSNESS AND CRACKING BOTTLES

GASTÓN ESPINOSA

Twentieth-century writers have tended to overlook or downplay Seymour's contributions to global Pentecostalism, arguing in favor of divine origins, Parham as founder, Seymour as nominal leader, and multiple founders/centers. Most assume that Parham largely founded or initiated modern Pentecostalism, created its theological corpus, and that Seymour popularized his views.

This book contends that although they shared much in common, after October 1906 Parham and Seymour saw themselves as promoting two *different* visions and versions of Pentecostalism that parted company on key theological, social, and racial points. These differences were deep enough for them to break fellowship and for Parham to charge Seymour with promoting a counterfeit revival, something downplayed in previous studies.

Rather than argue for "one" sole or only founder or leader of Pentecostalism, this book posits that there were many people, centers, and movements that contributed to global Pentecostal origins, but that Seymour and Azusa were the single most important leader, center, and catalyst in its origins (among many) in the United States from 1906 to 1909 and around the world to 1912 in the aforecited countries. His influence was shaped by the Azusa revival; 405,000 copies of his *Apostolic Faith* in circulation; cross-country preaching; and missionaries, missions, evangelists, and their innumerable daughter and granddaughter missions. Lum's taking the newspaper to Portland in 1908 and especially Durham's devastating schism in 1911 undermined and permanently hamstrung Seymour's spiritual authority, leadership, and ability to influence the emerging global movement. The Oneness controversy, growing racialization of society, and rise of new centers and denominations after 1913 shifted the loyalties of his remaining supporters at home and abroad. By the time the word got out about Seymour's own denomination, many Pentecostals were already ensconced in their new denominations.

Notwithstanding these developments, Seymour's teachings along with those he influenced were heavily responsible for the seventy thousand Pentecostals throughout the United States, missionaries in more than fifty countries on six continents, and literature being published in more than thirty languages.[1] Despite the growing racialization of American Pentecostalism, Charles Mason and the Church of God in Christ, A. J. Tomlinson and the Church of God, and many other black, white, Latino, and other racial-ethnic leaders at home and abroad continued to promote—however inconsistently applied—Azusa's theology and vision of racial equality and unity, albeit combined with their own distinctive beliefs and practices.[2] Seymour's death in relative obscurity should not diminish the very real contributions he made to American and global Christianity.

IRONIES

Seymour's story is full of ironies. Noting them offers a more complex and nuanced picture of his life, ministry, and relationship with Parham. They also pinpoint the various ways he changed and yet remained the same.

- Parham, who promoted white supremacy and racial separation, taught a black man who promoted racial equality and integration.
- Parham, who accused Seymour of false doctrine, promoted doctrinal irregularities.
- Parham, who accused Seymour of promoting Negroisms, promoted British Israelism.
- Parham, who accused Azusa of allowing orgies, was accused of sexual misconduct.
- Seymour, who promoted speaking in tongues, did so without having first done so himself.
- Seymour, who Parham claimed to train in doctrine, repudiated some of Parham's key doctrines.
- Seymour, who promoted women in ministry, was challenged by some of these women in ministry.
- Seymour, who had once been locked out of a mission, locked out Durham.
- Seymour, who was discriminated against, forbade racial discrimination.
- Seymour, who restricted whites from the top three leadership posts, allowed some whites to remain in their posts.
- Seymour, who preached that tongues were the main evidence of the baptism with the Holy Spirit, later said it was only one of the evidences.
- Seymour, who was called a nominal leader throughout most of the twentieth century, is now called one of the important figures in Christian history.

FINDINGS

These ironies and larger findings question a number of existing interpretations of Seymour, the Azusa revival, and global Pentecostal origins. They challenge the nominal leader and Parham as sole or primary founder theories. This book argues that Parham and Seymour largely coinitiated the classical Pentecostal movement in the United States and some of its first movements around the world.

This research challenges the notion that Seymour and Azusa were just one among many important leaders and centers of global Pentecostalism. Rather, they were the single most important leader, center, and catalyst (among many) in American (1906–9) and global Pentecostal origins until 1912. This is why international leaders like Anglican vicar Alexander Boddy, Frank Bartleman, and many others wrote that Los Angeles, Azusa, and the Upper Room were like the new Jerusalem, "Mecca," and the sacred center and holy of holies of global Pentecostalism. While Azusa wasn't the only center, it was the most important—both literally and symbolically prior to 1909 in the U.S. and prior to 1912 around the world. No rival center from 1906 until 1912 was ever afforded such recognition. This also helps to explain why Parham's views on xenolalia never became the sine qua non of the global movement and why his teachings on annihilation, conditional immortality, British Israelism, miscegenation, and other unique views never became mainstream. Seymour and his followers along with others checked their spread at the earliest and most critical paradigmatic stages of the movement's global development.

This book also challenges the widespread belief that Seymour accepted all of Parham's theological teachings and popularized them for the masses. Although they shared much in common, Seymour's repudiation of Parham's unique beliefs are why Parham so ferociously opposed him and why Parham claimed Seymour preached a "counterfeit" Pentecost—hardly the words one uses to describe two people working in tandem to promote the same message. Seymour intentionally used the revival, mission, newspaper, minister's manual, and his followers to spread his own vision and version of Pentecostalism. He did so at Parham's expense, and they both knew it. This is why Parham lamented that the true Pentecostal message was being superseded around the world by Seymour's Azusa message.[3] By publicly repudiating Parham's theological, social, and racial beliefs in the fall of 1906, Seymour and his followers along with others helped protect and reinforce the Protestant orthodoxy and racial egalitarianism of Pentecostalism, however inconsistently and episodically applied.

These findings also question the longstanding notion that Seymour didn't seek to break away from Parham's movement until after the conflict at Azusa in October 1906 and instead argue that Seymour broke away when he left

Houston but later rejoined Parham for practical reasons after being expelled from Hutchins's Holiness Mission in Los Angeles and having no place else to turn for the time being.

This book reveals that Parham's repudiation of Seymour had quite a bit to do with race, and that his racial criticisms were not simply a reflection of the social conventions of the day. It wasn't until after 1906 that Parham began to criticize interactions between "big 'buck niggers'" and white women of wealth and culture, openly praise the KKK, and mock and essentialize African-American spiritual practices as fanatical, counterfeit, and monkey-chattering crude Negroisms and chanting of the Southland.

It also challenges the largely biracial interpretations of Azusa and Pentecostal origins by noting the important if overlooked contributions of Latinos and other racial-ethnic minorities who helped transform a largely American national English-language revival on Bonnie Brae into a multiethnic, international, multilinguistic revival on Azusa.

The book challenges the claims that Seymour allowed explicit racial prejudice to surface within his own ranks and was guilty of racial discrimination. In fact, his decision to appoint people of color to the top three administrative posts in his new denomination was prompted by a number of factors such as a pastoral desire to promote peace and to end the race war and friction in the Pentecostal churches; a practical response to attempted takeovers; a recognition that by 1914 his denominational ministry was primarily to African Americans; a desire to protect his family, mission, and new denomination from frivolous lawsuits (which could adversely affect the long-term credibility and influence of his Azusa message and promotion of racial reconciliation); and a desire to hold on to the mission he founded because it was his last remaining platform from which to promote his message, in addition to serving as his living and denominational headquarters.[4]

The book challenges the notion that Seymour, as one of the movement's most important founders, working theologians, and newspaper editors, not only failed to provide a sustained theology of racial reconciliation, but was largely oblivious to race matters. While this was true for some leaders, it was not true for Seymour—who was all three. Similarly, although Parham did not promote racial reconciliation, he did write quite a bit on race matters and like Seymour was also a founder, working theologian, and newspaper editor. They promoted their racial views in a sustained manner through their sermons, revivals, books, and/or newspapers. Seymour's commitment to racial reconciliation and guidance on race matters is evident in the churches he attended from 1895 to 1906, his teaching on race relations, the editorial teachings and their placement in his newspaper, and his description of the origins of racial conflict in his minister's manual, his multiple citations of

Galatians 2:11–22, eyewitness testimonies by friends and outsiders, and even in statements by Parham and other critics.

This study indicates that the first major historiographical debate over Pentecostal origins was between none other than Parham and Seymour. Seymour was not simply a victim of Parham's historical reconstruction. Instead, he resisted Parham's mischaracterizations of his teachings, the revival, and African-American spiritual practices and used his newspaper to publicly repudiate Parham's history and unorthodox theological, social, and racial views.

Seymour's later marginalization in the movement and historiography was due not only to his social and racial views, but also to the loss of his newspaper and white support, Parham's and Durham's searing public criticisms from 1911 to 1912, and a number of white-initiated divisions. It may have also been due to Jennie Seymour, who courageously prodded him to be more assertive and to stand up for his rights, something that may have alienated some whites since both Ernest S. Williams and Arthur Osterberg seemed to imply it was a negative shift in William's personality. Her influence along with the changing demographics of the mission led Seymour to appoint more blacks and Latinos to his pastoral team and to speak his own mind with greater frequency after 1908. By 1909 J. A. Warren served as Seymour's main co-pastor and cosigned with William the ordination certificates of people like Abundio López.

At a larger level, this book contends that Pentecostalism's dynamic growth is due to its leaders' inability to balance the primitive and pragmatic impulses and thus keep the proverbial lightning in the denominational bottle. Why? Because Pentecostals' experience-oriented spirituality leads its people to a "holy restlessness" and natural propensity for more direct, unmediated revelatory experiences with God. This creates a desire in their spiritual orientation to place a premium on direct, unmediated revelatory experiences with God, which possess some of them until they can work them off through action. They invoke them to authenticate and justify their divine callings and to pull rank on their denominational leaders in order to crack the bottle of denominationalism and ecclesiastical authority structures so that they can create their own divinely sanctioned Apostolic movements. This fragmentation thesis and process is evident in the rationales that Parham, Seymour, Crawford, and Durham invoked to justify the creation of their own movements.

This invocation of direct revelation also leads to a kind of religious entrepreneurialism and transformational leadership that empowers ordinary people to become leaders and religious founders who are able to effectively reach their native cultures because they can more readily track and respond to current trends and make local micro- and macro-level adaptations quickly and under the sanction of divine authority. They were able to carry out their often difficult and arduous journeys because their ideas possessed them until they could work them off through action and because they were able to persuade others to believe in and embrace their revelations and visions. This fragmentation practice traces its roots directly back to Parham and Seymour and is part of the spiritual DNA of global Pentecostalism. It also helps explain the movement's propensity to fragment and why there are 3,300 Pentecostal/Charismatic denominations in the United States and 23,000 globally.[5]

This story revises the image of Seymour as a passive accommodationist and agentless victim who allowed himself and the African-American community to be marginalized by whites. Instead, it shows that Seymour was constantly adapting to his changing circumstances and was an active agent in his struggle for spiritual, social, and racial liberation. One could argue that he became more Afro-centric in his ministry as time went on and especially after he married Jennie Evans. He always (even before the split with Parham) sought to recognize the important contribution of blacks, even if he went the extra mile to accommodate whites by assigning them many prominent leadership posts—which was no doubt partly due to their often more senior ministry and work experience. James Cone argues in *Martin & Malcolm & America* that both the accommodationist/integrationist and nationalist/separatist approaches to race relations are resistance traditions. While it is tempting to identify Seymour as a strict accommodationist in the tradition of Booker T. Washington, a more careful analysis of his entire life and ministry (and not just the years from 1906 to 1909) reveals that Seymour shifted to just right of center in the direction of W.E.B. Du Bois, which although promoting integration, also sought to promote black leadership. Seymour increasingly used his faith to stand up for his rights, to speak out against racial prejudice and discrimination, and to reaffirm and protect African-American spiritual practices, traditions, and the community from false accusations by Parham and others. He did all of this while still holding firmly to his integrationist vision, much like W.E.B. Du Bois did in his balancing act with the white board of the NAACP and *The Crisis* newspaper during that same period.[6]

The evidence that Seymour stood up for blacks throughout his ministry and increasingly so after marrying Jennie is evident in his decisions to spotlight the black origins of Azusa in the first issues of his newspaper, allow blacks to lead mission teams to Africa and the U.S. South, and promote black equality and positive images of blacks in his newspaper and minister's manual. He did all this while allowing whites to continue to exercise disproportionate influence so that he could be a role model for racial integration and not be accused of favoring blacks over whites—which was the case in some black-led denominations and organizations. Seymour's decision to later promote black and Latino leaders did not so much privilege racial-ethnic minorities over whites as simply adapt to the changing racial-ethnic composition of the mission.

His call for racial inclusion was rooted in his understanding of divine and brotherly love and Christian brotherhood. He believed a true Christian must love their white brothers and sisters, even if they discriminated against them. In fact, he foreshadowed the ministry of Martin Luther King Jr., who also called on people to love whites. In 1915 Seymour forcefully stated that we "must love our white brethren" and "welcome them" in our churches even "if some of . . . [them] have prejudices and discrimination" against us. This call to love was a refrain echoed almost verbatim half a century later by Martin Luther King Jr. who said, "we most love our white brothers no matter what they do to us."[7]

Seymour, Du Bois, and Martin Luther King Jr. served at different locations in the same black intellectual tradition. While Du Bois pegged the salvation of the black community largely on the creative intelligence of its "Talented Tenth" and King on promoting full integration and civil rights, Seymour rooted it in the mind-altering events of becoming born-again and Spirit-filled. Seymour believed that a vibrant, living, and mind-altering Spirit-led relationship with Jesus Christ could alone truly elevate the masses and leaven the lump of American society.

While Seymour's Azusa was not a blatant protest against the racial and social order that people are used to seeing in the post–civil rights period, in Jim Crow America it was a profound populist critique and working-class revolt against the religious, social, and racial order. Changing hearts and minds at the grassroots level in a call for conversion of one's religious, social and racial views may be just as powerful and subversive a strategy for promoting social change as standing on the steps of the Lincoln Memorial in Washington, DC, to demand structural change. More important, in Jim Crow America it was one of the few real options open to economically and educationally limited but steadfastly determined southern black prophets like Seymour.

Rather than a tragic figure who remained silent in the face of insults and marginalization, Seymour as revealed in this study was a quiet man of action and resolve who both loved his followers and yet also resisted takeovers, challenged false accusations, rebuked apostates, dismissed incompliant clergy, and repudiated false doctrine—even when it came from his own teacher. Rather than become bitter about his loss of power and status after 1912, he was gracious and self-confident enough to sit silently in the audience of services led by others—often many years his junior in age and stature.

Far from being simply a liminal moment limited to a few weeks or months, Seymour's mission successfully created a Christian transgressive social space where people could reimagine their historical, racial, and social identities, and cross some of the social, gender, racial, and class borders and boundaries of the day for years. It was this version of Pentecostalism that was exported around the world prior to 1912 and arguably for many years thereafter in some segments of the movement.

As Seymour began to respond to white criticism and rein in unauthorized experiential and socially transgressive spiritual practices and run his services decently and in order, this restricted Azusa's ability to function as the same kind of transgressive social space it had once been in its heyday. However, it wasn't a zero-sum game, for even the more restrained Seymour continued to promote interaction that was religiously, racially, and socially inclusive and transgressive by many people's standards in society, though admittedly not with the same novelty, innovative spirit, and freedom as during its heyday.

Finally, this short biography documents how the other 90 percent of rank-and-file African Americans not part of W.E.B. Du Bois's "Talented Tenth" found ways to harness the power of faith to make a difference in society. Although it might be tempting to contrast Seymour with Du Bois, a more contextualized reading may view him as a populist expression just right of center in the same black intellectual tradition. Despite his limited education, Seymour functioned in his own way like a "missionary of culture" who had—in the words of Du Bois—the "vision of seers."[8]

Although by the 1920s and 1930s Parham's vision of a segregated society won the day in some denominations as they began to self-segregate along racial lines, there have always been preachers, churches, and denominations that have kept alive the spirit of racially and socially inclusive Seymour's message. For this reason it's not surprising that Charles Mason's Church of God in Christ denomination allowed Martin Luther King Jr. to deliver his famous "I've Been to the Mountain Top" sermon from Mason's well-worn pulpit in Memphis on April 2, 1968—almost sixty-two years to the month after Seymour began preaching racial equality and integration at Azusa. King's message and haunting words reflected Seymour's own heart not only for blacks, but for all Spirit-filled believers:

> Well, I don't know what will happen now. We've got some difficult days ahead. But it doesn't matter with me now. Because I've been to the mountaintop. . . . And I've looked over. And I've seen the promised land. I may not get there with you. But I want you to know tonight, that we, as a people will get to the promised land. And I'm happy, tonight. I'm not worried about anything. I'm not fearing any man. Mine eyes have seen the glory of the coming of the Lord.

The next day King was assassinated. But his vision lives on in the lives and memories of the millions he inspired. So too Seymour's vision now lives on among some of the millions of people around the world who, although they may have never heard his name, still share a desire for Spiritual power, divine love, and hope.

Seymour would have been profoundly humbled to learn that an unknown twenty-six-year-old African-American Pentecostal preacher named Joshua DuBois helped a then largely unknown black Senator from Illinois win the American presidency. The country has come a long way since Seymour's day, but still has far to travel to fully realize Seymour's bold declaration that "God recognizes no races or classes of people."

However, Seymour would have no doubt been happier to hear that the same outpouring of the Spirit that fell on Azusa Street over one hundred years ago is still reportedly falling afresh on people around the world and transforming the lives of ordinary people into one body of believers still hungry for more of God's love and the salvation of souls.

II
DOCUMENTARY HISTORY OF WILLIAM J. SEYMOUR, THE AZUSA STREET REVIVAL, AND GLOBAL PENTECOSTAL ORIGINS

A. SEYMOUR'S SPIRITUAL WRITINGS FROM THE *APOSTOLIC FAITH*, 1906–08

INTRODUCTION

The following letters, sermons, and teachings were written by Seymour or preached as sermons and then stenographically recorded by Clara Lum and others between 1906 and 1908. They provide rich insight into Seymour's theological thinking and social views. Several of the sources are unsigned by Seymour but there is no doubt that he wrote, co-wrote, or dictated them and/or agreed to their content. While I have included all of his extent letters and spiritual writings, they do not represent all of the documents he authored in the newspaper because his writing style and syntax is also evident in other unsigned sermons and newspaper editorials, but since I cannot definitively prove he wrote them, I have not included them.

1. LETTER FROM WILLIAM J. SEYMOUR TO WARREN FAYE CAROTHERS

(July 12, 1906)
Los Angeles, Cal.
July 12th, 1906.

Brother Carothers:
 Dear Brother in Christ Jesus: Grace and peace from God our Father and Christ our Redeemer be with you all saints. Amen. Dear Brother Carothers: We are having victory every night for 3 months. People are getting saved three times a day, justified, sanctified, Baptized with the Holy Ghost and the gift of tongues as a witness. Praise be Lord, Amen. Dear Brother Carothers, please send me my credentials for Bro. Parham said he was going to have them by the first of April. I was not at home, so I want you to please send it to me so I can have to show to get [railroad discount] rates. We have workers gone to India. God paid their way since they got the baptism with the Holy Ghost. Some going to Jerusalem—about 4 workers; their fare is paid. Some are going to Africa, some to China. The Lord is working mightily. God bless you all. I hope you will send me 100 [unreadable] for the workers. How is

Brother Parham and where is he? We have some of the finest singers in the world baptized with the Holy Ghost. The Holy Spirit sings through them and some interpret right along while singing is going on. God is working wonderfully in this City. I want to get you all to pray a special prayer for us on Tuesday night at 8 o'clock.

> Yours in Christ.
> W. J. Seymour
> North 214 Bonebra Street
> Los Angeles, Cal.

2. LETTER FROM WILLIAM J. SEYMOUR TO CHARLES FOX PARHAM

(August 27, 1906)
312 Azusa Street, Los Angeles, Cal.,
August 27, 1906

Dear Bro. Parham:—

Sister Hall has arrived, and is planning out a great revival in this city, that shall take place when you come. The revival is still going on here that has been going on since we came to this city. But we are expecting a general one to start again when you come, that these little revivals will all come together and make one great union revival.

Now please let us know about the date that you will be here, so we can advertise your coming and the date. I shall look for a large place, by God's help, that will accommodate the people. Hallelujah to God! Victory through the all cleansing blood of Jesus! I expect an earthquake to happen in Los Angeles when you come with other workers filled with the Holy Ghost; that God will shake this city once more.

Satan is working but God is mightier than satan for he is a conquered foe and a defeated creature. Glory be to God in the highest! God has been breathing on the dry bones with the Holy Ghost and the Word, until dry bones are coming together and flesh is coming upon them, life is put into them, until God has got a mighty host in this city standing for the faith that was once delivered unto the saints. Please answer soon, Yours in Christ and in the faith that was once delivered unto the saints.

> W.J. Seymour

3. BRO. SEYMOUR'S CALL

(*AF,* September 1906, 1)
Bro. W. J. Seymour has the following to say in regard to his call to this city:

> "It was the divine call that brought me from Houston, Texas, to Los Angeles. The Lord put it in the heart of one of the saints in Los Angeles to write to me that she felt the Lord would have me come over here and do a work, and I came, for I felt [it] was the leading of the Lord. The Lord sent the means, and I came to take charge of a mission on Santa Fe Street, and one night they locked the door against me, and afterwards got Bro. Roberts, the president of the Holiness Association, to come down and settle the doctrine of the Baptism with the Holy Ghost, that it was simply sanctification. He came down and a good many holiness preachers with him, and they stated that sanctification was the baptism with the Holy Ghost. But yet they did not have the evidence of the second chapter of Acts, for when the disciples were all filled with the Holy Ghost, they spoke in tongues as the Spirit gave utterance. After the president heard me speak of what the true baptism of the Holy Ghost was, he said he wanted it too, and told me when I had received it to let him know. So I received it and let him know. The beginning of the Pentecost started in a cottage prayer meeting at 214 Bonnie Brae."

4. THE APOSTOLIC FAITH MOVEMENT

(*AF,* September 1906, 2)
Stands for the restoration of the faith once delivered unto the saints—the old time religion, camp meetings, revivals, missions, street and prison work and Christian Unity everywhere.

> Teaching on Repentance—Mark 1:14, 15.
> Godly Sorrow for Sin, Example—Matt. 9:13. 2 Cor. 7, 9, 11. Acts 3:19. Acts 17:30, 31.
> Of Confession of Sins—Luke 15:21 and Luke 18:13.
> Forsaking Sinful Ways—Isa. 55:7. Jonah 3:8. Prov. 28;13.
> Restitution—Ezek. 33;15. Luke 19:8.
> And faith in Jesus Christ.
> First Work.—Justification is that act of God's free grace by which we receive remission of sins. Acts 10:42, 43. Rom. 3:25.
> Second Work.—Sanctification is the second work of grace and the last work of grace. Sanctification is that act of God's free grace by

which He makes us holy. John 17:15, 17.—"Sanctify them through Thy Truth; Thy word is truth." 1 Thess. 4:3; 1 Thess. 5:23; Heb. 13:12; Heb. 2:11; Heb. 12:14.

Sanctification is cleansing to make holy. The Disciples were sanctified before the Day of Pentecost. By a careful study of Scripture you will find it is so now. "Ye are clean through the word which I have spoken unto you" (John 15:3; 13:10); and Jesus has breathed on them the Holy Ghost (John 20:21, 22). You know, that they could not receive the Spirit if they were not clean. Jesus cleansed and got all doubt out of His Church before He went back to glory.

The Baptism with the Holy Spirit is a gift of power upon the sanctified life; so when we get it we have the same evidence as the Disciples received on the Day of Pentecost (Acts 2:3,4), in speaking in new tongues. See also Acts 10:45, 46; Acts 19:6; I Cor. 14:21. "For I will work a work in your days which ye will not believe though it be told you."—Hab. 1:5.

Seeking Healing.—He must believe that God is able to heal.— Ex. 15:26: "I am the Lord that healeth thee." James 5:14; Psa. 103:3; 2 Kings 20:5; Matt. 8:16, 17; Mark 16;16, 17, 18.

He must believe God is able to heal. "Behold I am the Lord, the God of all flesh; is there any thing too hard for me?"—Jer. 32:27

Too many have confused the grace of Sanctification with the enduement of Power, or the Baptism with the Holy Ghost; others have taken "the anointing that abideth" for the Baptism, and failed to reach the glory and power of a true Pentecost.

The blood Jesus will never blot out any sin between man and man they can make right; but if we can't make wrongs right the Blood graciously covers. (Matt. 5:23, 24.)

We are not fighting men or churches, but seeking to displace dead forms and creeds and wild fanaticisms with living, practical Christianity. "Love, Faith, Unity" are our watchwords, and "Victory through the Atoning Blood" our battle cry. God's promises are true. He said: "Be though faithful over a few things, and I will make thee ruler over many." From the little handful of Christians who stood by the cross when the testings and discouragements came, God has raised a mighty host.

5. THE PRECIOUS ATONEMENT

(*AF,* September 1906, 2)

Children of God, partakers of the precious atonement, let us study and see what there is in it for us.

First. Through the atonement we receive forgiveness of sins.

Second. We receive sanctification through the blood of Jesus. "Wherefore Jesus also said that he might sanctify the people with his own blood, suffered without the gate." Sanctified from all original sin, we become sons of God. "For both he that sanctifieth and they who are sanctified are all of one: for which cause he is not ashamed to call them brethren." Heb. 2:11. (It seems that Jesus would be ashamed to call them brethren, if they were not sanctified.) Then you will not be ashamed to tell men and demons that you are sanctified, and are living a pure and holy life free from sin, a life that gives you power over the world, the flesh, and the devil. The devil does not like that kind of testimony. Through this precious atonement, we have freedom from all sin, though we are living in this old world, we are permitted to sit in heavenly places in Christ Jesus.

Third. Healing of our bodies. Sickness and disease are destroyed through the precious atonement of Jesus. O how we ought to honor the stripes of Jesus, for "with his stripes we are healed." How we ought to honor that precious body which the Father sanctified and sent into the world, not simply set apart, but really sanctified, soul, body and spirit, free from sickness, disease and everything of the devil. A body that knew no sin and disease was given for these imperfect bodies of ours. Not only is the atonement for the sanctification of our souls, but for the sanctification of our bodies from inherited disease. It matters not what has been in the blood. Every drop of blood we received from our mother is impure. Sickness is born in a child just as original sin is born in the child. He was manifested to destroy the works of the devil. Every sickness is of the devil.

Man in the garden of Eden was pure and happy and knew no sickness till that unholy visitor came into the garden, then his whole system was poisoned and it has been flowing in the blood of all the human family down the ages till God spoke to his people and said, "I am the Lord that healeth thee." The children of Israel practiced divine healing. David, after being healed of rheumatism, (perhaps contracted in the caves where he hid himself from his pursuers,) testified saying, "Bless the Lord, O my soul, and all that is within me bless his holy name, who forgiveth all thine iniquities, who healeth all thy diseases." David knew what it was to be healed. Healing continued with God's people till Solomon's heart was turned away by strange wives, and he brought in the black arts and mediums, and they went whoring after familiar spirits. God had been their healer, but after they lost the Spirit, they turned to the arm of flesh to find something to heal their diseases.

Thank God, we have a living Christ among us to heal our diseases. He will heal every case. The prophet had said, "With his stripes we are healed," and it was fulfilled when Jesus came. Also "He hath borne our griefs," (which means sickness, as translators tell us.) Now if Jesus bore our sicknesses, why should we bear them? So we get full salvation through the atonement of Jesus.

Fourth. And we get the baptism with the Holy Ghost and fire upon the sanctified life. We get Christ enthroned and crowned in our hearts. Let us lift up Christ to the world in all His fullness, not only in healing and salvation from all sin, but in His power to speak all the languages of the world. We need the triune God to enable us to do this.

We that are the messengers of this precious atonement ought to preach all of it, justification, sanctification, healing, the baptism with the Holy Ghost, and signs following. "How shall we escape if we neglect so great salvation?" God is now confirming His word by granting signs and wonders to follow the preaching of the full gospel in Los Angeles.

W.J. Seymour

6. THE WAY INTO THE HOLIEST.

(*AF*, October 1906, 4)

A sinner comes to the Lord all wrapped up in sin and darkness. He cannot make any consecration because he is dead. The life has to be put into us before we can present any life to the Lord. He must get justified by faith. There is a Lamb without spot and blemish slain before God for him, and when he repents toward God for his sins, the Lord has mercy on him for Christ's sake, and puts eternal life in his soul, pardoning him of his sins, washing away his guilty pollution [*sic*], and he stands before God justified as if he had never sinned.

Then there remains that old original sin in him for which he is not responsible till he has the light. He hears that "Jesus, that He might sanctify the people with His own blood, suffered without the gate," and he comes to be sanctified. There is Jesus, the Lamb without blemish, on the altar. Jesus takes that soul that has eternal life in it and presents it to God for thorough purging and cleansing from all original and Adamic sin. And Jesus, the Son of God, cleanses him from all sin, and he is made every whit whole, sanctified and holy.

Now he is on the altar ready for the fire of God to fall, which is the baptism with the Holy Ghost. It is a free gift upon the sanctified, cleansed heart. The fire remains there continually burning in the holiness of God. Why? Because he is sanctified and holy and on the altar continually. He stays there and the great Shekina of glory is continually burning and filling with heavenly light.

W.J. Seymour

7. RIVER OF LIVING WATER.

(*AF,* November 1906, 2)

In the 4th chapter of John, the words come, "Jesus answered and said unto her, If thou knewest the gift of God and who it is that saith to thee Give me to drink, thou wouldest have asked of Him and He would have given the living water." Praise God for the living waters today that flow freely, for it comes from God to every hungry and thirsty heart. Jesus said, "He that believeth on me, as the Scripture hath said, out of his inmost being shall flow rivers of living waters." Then we are able to go in the mighty name of Jesus to the ends of the earth and water dry places, deserts and solitary places, until these parched, sad, lonely hearts are made to rejoice in the God of their salvation. We want the rivers today. Hallelujah! Glory to God in the highest!

In Jesus Christ we get forgiveness of sin, and we get sanctification of our spirit, soul, and body, and upon that we get the gift of the Holy Ghost that Jesus promised to His disciples, the promise of the Father. All this we get through the atonement. Hallelujah!

The prophet said that he had bourne [*sic*] our griefs and carried our sorrows. He was wounded for our transgressions, bruised for our iniquities, the chastisement of our peace was upon Him and with His stripes we are healed. So we get healing, health, salvation, joy, life—everything in Jesus. Glory to God!

There are many wells today, but they are dry. There are many hungry souls today that are empty. But let us come to Jesus and take Him at His word and we will find wells of salvation, and be able to draw waters out of the well of salvation, for Jesus is that well.

At this time Jesus was weary from a long journey, and He sat on the well in Samaria, and a woman came to draw water. He asked her for a drink. She answered, "How is it that thou being a Jew askest drink of me who am a woman of Samaria, for the Jews have no dealings with the Samarians?" Jesus said, "If thou knewest the gift of God, and who it is that saith to thee, give me to drink, thou wouldst have asked of him and he would have given thee living water."

O, how sweet it was to see Jesus, the Lamb of God that takes away the sin of the world, that great sacrifice that God had given to a lost, dying, and benighted world, sitting on the well and talking with the woman; so gentle, so meek, and so kind that it gave her an appetite to talk further with Him, until He got into her secret and uncovered her life. Then she was pricked in heart, confessed her sins and received pardon, cleansing from fornication and adultery, was washed from stain and guilt of sin and was made a child of God, and above all, received the well of salvation in her heart. It was so sweet and joyful and good. Her heart was so filled with love that she felt she could take in a whole lost world. So she ran away with a well of salvation and left the old water pot on the well. How true it is in this day, when we get the baptism with the Holy Spirit, we have something to tell, and it is that the blood of Jesus Christ cleanseth from all sin. The baptism with the Holy Ghost gives us power to testify to a risen, resurrected Saviour. Our affections are in Jesus Christ, the Lamb of God that takes away the sin of the world. How I worship Him today! How I praise Him for the all-cleansing blood!

Jesus' promises are true and sure. The woman said to Him, after He had uncovered her secret, "Sir, I perceive that Thou art a prophet." Yes, He was a prophet. He was that great prophet that Moses said the Lord would raise up. He is here today. Will we be taught of that prophet? Will we hear Him? Let us accept Him in all His fulness.

He said, "He that believeth on me, the works that I do shall he do also, and greater works than these shall ye do, because I go unto my Father." These disciples to whom He was speaking, had been saved, sanctified, anointed with the Holy Spirit, their hearts had been opened to understand the Scriptures, and yet Jesus said, "Tarry ye, in the city of Jerusalem, until ye be endued with power from on high." "John truly baptized with water, but ye shall be baptized with the Holy Ghost not many days hence." So the same commission comes to us. We find that they obeyed His commission and were all filled with the Holy Ghost on the day of Pentecost, and Peter standing up, said, "This is that which was spoken by the prophet Joel." Dear loved ones, we preach the same sermon. This is that which was spoken by the prophet Joel, and it shall come to pass in the last days, saith God, I will pour out of my Spirit upon all flesh, and your sons and your daughters shall prophesy, and your young men shall see visions, and your old men shall dream dreams; and on my servants and on my handmaidens I will pour out in those days of my Spirit, and they shall prophesy. . . .

There are so many people today like the woman. They are controlled by the fathers. Our salvation is not in some father or human instrument. It is sad to see people so blinded, worshiping the creature more than the Creator. Listen to what the woman said, "Our Fathers worshipped in this mountain, and ye say that in Jerusalem is the place where men ought to worship." So many people today are worshipping in the mountains, big churches, stone and frame buildings. But Jesus teaches that salvation is not in these stone structures—not in the mountains—not in the hills, but in God. For God is a

Spirit. Jesus said unto her, "Woman, believe Me, the hour cometh and now is when ye shall neither in this mountain nor yet at Jerusalem worship the Father." So many people today are controlled by men. Their salvation reaches out no further than the boundary line of human creeds, but praise God for freedom in the Spirit. There are depths and heights and breadths that we can reach through the power of the blessed Spirit. "Eye hath not seen, nor ear heard, neither have entered into the heart of man the things that God hath prepared for them that love him."

The Jews were the religious leaders at this time, and people had no more light upon salvation than the Jews gave them. The Jews were God's chosen people to evangelize the world. He had entrusted them to give all nations the true knowledge of God, but they went into traditions and doctrines of men, and were blinded and in the dark. Jesus came as the light of the world, and He is that light. "If we walk in the light as he is in the light, we have fellowship one with another, and the blood of Jesus Christ his Son cleanseth us from all sin." Let us honor the Spirit, for Jesus has sent Him to teach and lead us into all truth.

Above all, let us honor the blood of Jesus Christ every moment of our lives, and we will be sweet in our souls. We will be able to talk of this common salvation to everyone that we meet. God will let His anointing rest upon us in telling them of this precious truth. This truth belongs to God. We have no right to tax anyone for the truth, because God has entrusted us with it to tell it. Freely we receive, freely we give. So the Gospel is to be preached freely, and God will bless it and spread it Himself, and we have experienced that He does, We have found Him true to His promise all the way. We have tried Him and proved Him. His promises are sure.

8. IN MONEY MATTERS

(*AF,* November 1906, 3)

There have been teachers who have told all the people to sell out, and many of them have gone into fanaticism. We let the Spirit lead people and tell them what they ought to give. When they get filled with the Spirit, their pocket books are converted and God makes them stewards and if He says, "Sell out," they will do so. But sometimes they have families. God does not tell you to forsake your family. He says if you do not provide for your own you are worse than an infidel. Some are not called to go out and teach. We find some who have no wisdom nor faith, and the devil takes them to disgrace the work. Under false teaching, children have been left to go half naked, women have left their husbands, and husbands leave their wives to wash and scrub, and the Bible says that is worse than infidelity. Then they will go and borrow and cannot pay back. That person ought to go to work. The Bible says, "Let him labor, working with his hands the thing which is good, that he may have to give to him that needeth."

He sent those that were called out to preach the Gospel, to "take no thuogh [*sic*] what ye shall eat or drink." Get down and pray. Make your wants known unto God and He will send it in.

God does not expect all to sell out for He says in 1 Cor. 16:1, "Now concerning the collection for the saints, * * * upon the first day of the week, let everyone of you lay by him in store, as God hath prospered him." It does not mean for you to have great real estate and money banked up while your brothers and sisters are suffering. He means for you to turn loose because all that money is soon going to be thrown to the moles and bats. So it is better to spread the Gospel and get stars in your crown than to be holding it. But for us to go and tell you to do it, pick out somebody that has money and read the Word to them, would not be the Spirit of the Lord. The Spirit will tell you what to do. He makes you do it. When he wakes you up at night and tells you what to do, you cannot sleep till you obey. He says everyone shall be taught of God from the least to the greatest. God wants a free giver.

Annanias wanted to have a reputation that he sold out like the rest, so he plotted that he should give a portion and say he had sold out for the Lord. But the Holy Ghost told Peter that Annanias had told a lie. Peter told him the property was his. The Lord allows you to be the steward over it. The property was his and the sin was in lying to the Holy Ghost. It is right for you to have property, but if the Lord says, take $200 or $500 or $1,000 and distribute here or there, you do it.

We must know our calling. We can work when baptized with the Holy Ghost. Some think they have got to preach. Well, we do preach in testifying. Some think they must go out because they have the tongues but those are good for Los Angeles of anywhere else. The Lord will lead you by His small voice.

W.J. Seymour.

9. COUNTERFEITS

(*AF,* December 1906, 2)
God has told us in His precious word that we should know a tree by its fruit. Wherever we find the real, we find the counterfeit also. But praise God for the real. We find in the time of Peter, when men and women were receiving the power of the Holy Ghost, the counterfeit appeared in Annanias and Saphira. But God's power was mightier than all the forces of hell, so their sin found them out. Be careful, dear loved ones, for your sin will surely find

you out. "But if we walk in the light as He is in the light, we have fellowship one with another and the blood of Jesus Christ His Son cleanseth us from all sin."

In our meetings, we have had people to come and claim that they had received the baptism with the Holy Spirit, but when they were put to the test by the Holy Spirit, they were found wanting. So they got down and got saved and sanctified and baptized with the Holy Spirit and spoke in tongues by the Holy Spirit. And again people have imitated the gift of tongues, but how quickly the Holy Spirit would reveal to every one of the true children that had the Pentecostal baptism . . . heavy . . . till the counterfeits were silenced and condemned. God's promises are true and sure.

People are trying to imitate the work of the Holy Ghost these days, just as they did when the Lord sent Moses to Pharaoh in Ex. 7, 8, and gave him a miracle or sign to show before Pharaoh, that when Aaron should cast his rod before Pharaoh, it should become a serpent. So when Pharaoh saw that Aaron's rod had become a serpent, he called for his wise men and the counterfeit sorcerers and magicians [*sic*] of Egypt. They also did in like manner with their enchantments, for they cast down every man his rod, and they became serpents, but Aaron's rod swallowed up their rods. So the power of the Holy Ghost in God's people today condemns and swallows up the counterfeit. It digs up and exposes all the power of satan—Christian Science, Theosophy, and Spiritualism—all are uncovered before the Son of God. Glory to God.

Spiritualists have come to our meetings and had the demons cast out of them and have been saved and sanctified. Christian Scientists have come to the meetings and had the Christian Science demons cast out of them and have accepted the blood. Every plant that my heavenly Father hath not planted shall be rooted up.

People have come to this place full of demons and God has cast them out, and they have gone out crying with loud voices. Then when all the demons were cast out, they got saved, sanctified, and baptized with the Holy Ghost, clothed in their right minds and filled with glory and power.

Dear loved ones, it is not by might nor by power but by my Spirit, saith the Lord. "Tarry ye in the city of Jerusalem, until ye be endued with power from on high. John truly baptized with the Holy Ghost not many days hence." These were Jesus' departing words. May you tarry until you receive your personal Pentecost. Amen.

W.J. Seymour.

10. "BEHOLD THE BRIDEGROOM COMETH!"

(*AF*, January 1907, 2)

> "Then shall the kingdom of heaven be likened unto ten virgins, which took their lamps, [and went forth to meet the bride]groom. And five of them were wise and five were foolish. They that were foolish took their lamps and took no oil with them; but the wise took oil in their vessels with their lamps.
>
> "While the bridegroom tarried, they all slumbered and slept. And at midnight, there was a cry made, Behold the bridegroom: go ye out to meet him.
>
> "Then all those virgins arose and trimmed their lamps. And the foolish said unto the wise, Give us your oil, for our lamps are gone out (R. V. Going Out.) But the wise answered saying, Not so; lest there be not enough for us and you; but go ye rather to them that sell, and buy for yourselves.
>
> "And while they went to buy the bridegroom came; and they that were ready went in with him to the marriage: and the door was shut. Afterward came also the other virgins saying, Lord, Lord, open to us. But he answered and said, Verily I say unto you, I know you not.
>
> "Watch therefore, for ye know neither the day nor the hour wherein the Son of Man cometh." Matt. 25, 1–13

You know virgin in the scripture is a type of purity. Christ is speaking in this parable about the church and its condition at His coming. Many precious souls today are not looking for the return of their Lord, and they will be found in the same condition as the give foolish virgins. They started out to meet the bridegroom, and had some oil in their lamps but none in their vessels with their lamps. So when the cry was made to go forth, they were found wanting in oil, which is the real type of the Holy Ghost. Many of God's children are cleansed from sin and yet fight against getting more oil. They think they have enough. They have some of God's love in their souls, but they have not the double portion of it. The thing they need is oil in their vessels with their lamps. It is just as plain as can be.

Dearly beloved, the Scripture says, "Blessed are they which are called to the marriage supper of the Lamb." Rev. 19, 9. So they are blessed that have the call. Those that will be permitted to enter in are those who are justified, sanctified, and baptized with the Holy Ghost—sealed unto the day of redemption. O may God stir up His waiting bride everywhere to get oil in their vessels with their lamp that they may enter into the marriage supper. The Holy Ghost is sifting out a people that are getting on the robes of righteousness and the seal in their foreheads. The angel is holding the winds now till all the children of God are sealed in their foreheads with the Father's name. Then the wrath of God is going to be poured out.

"Behold the Bridegroom cometh!" O the time is very near. All the testimonies of His coming that have been going on for months are a witness that He is coming soon. But when the trumpet sounds, it will be too late to prepare. Those that are not ready at the rapture will be left to go through the awful tribulation that is coming upon the earth. The wise virgins will be at the marriage supper and spend the time of the great tribulation with the Lord Jesus. They will have glorified bodies. For we which remain unto the coming of the Lord will be changed in the twinkling of an eye.

Many precious souls believe today that in sanctification they have it all, that they have already the baptism with the Holy Ghost or enduement of power; but in that day, they will find they are mistaken. They say, Away with this third work. What is the difference, dear ones, if it takes 300 works? We want to be ready to meet the bridegroom. The foolish [sic] virgins said to the wise, "Give us of your oil." This thing is going to happen. Many that are saying they have enough and are opposing, will find their lamps going out and ask the prayers of God's people. God is warning you through His servants and handmaidens to get ready; but many are going to come back to get the oil from others. Dear ones, we cannot get more than enough for ourselves. You can grasp the saints' hands but you cannot squeeze any oil out. You have to get the vessel filled for yourself. Many are going to be marrying and giving in marriage, buying and selling, and the cares of this world are going to get in the way. Above all, we want to get the oil, the Holy Ghost. Every Christian must be baptized with the Holy Ghost for himself. Many poor souls in that day will be awfully disappointed. May we seek Him, today, the baptism with the Holy Ghost and fire. Now is the time to buy the oil; that is, by tarrying at the feet of the Lord Jesus and receiving the baptism with the Holy Spirit.

It seems that people will be able to buy oil during the rapture. It seems that the Spirit will still be here on earth and that they could get it, but it will be too late for the marriage supper. So the Lord warns us to be ready, for we know not the day nor the hour.

Those that get left in the rapture and still prove faithful to God and do not receive the mark of the beast, though they will have to suffer martyrdom, will be raised to reign with Christ. Antichrist will reign during the tribulation and everything will be controlled by him and by the false prophet, when they have succeeded in uniting the whole world in acknowledging the antichrist. Those that acknowledge him will be permitted to buy and sell, but those that stand faithful to the Lord Jesus and testify to the Blood, will be killed for the word of their testimony. But by proving faithful to death, they will be raised during the milennium [sic] and reign with Christ. But we that are caught up to the marriage supper of the Lamb will escape the plagues that are coming on the earth.

May God fit everyone of us for the coming of the Lord, that we may come back with him on white horses and help Him to execute judgment on the earth and make way for the millennial kingdom, when He shall reign from shore to shore, and righteousness shall cover the earth as waters cover the sea.

That is the time that Enoch prophesied of, "Behold the Lord cometh with ten thousand of His saints," Jude 14. "Then shall the Lord go forth and fight against these nations, as when He fought in the day of battle. And His feet shall stand in that day upon the mount of Olives," Zec. 14, 3, 4. The mountain shall be parted in two. Then shall the antichrist and the false prophet be cast into the lake of fire and brimstone and satan shall be bound a thousand years. Rev. 19, 20 and 20. 2.

We shall be priests and kings unto God, reigning with Him a thousand years in a jubilee of peace. Our Christ will be King of kings and Lord of lords over the whole earth. We shall reign with Him over unglorified humanity. Some will be appointed over ten cities and some over two, and the...................twelve tribes of Israel. "To him that overcometh will I grant to sit with me in my throne, even as I also overcame and am set down with my Father in His throne." Rev. 3. 21, 22.

W.J.S.

11. GIFTS OF THE SPIRIT

(*AF*, January 1907, 2)

"Now concerning spiritual gifts brethren, I would not have you ignorant."

Paul was speaking to the Corinthian Church at this time. They were like Christ's people everywhere today. Many of His people do not know their privileges in this blessed Gospel. The Gospel of Christ is the power of God unto salvation to everyone that believeth. And in order that we might know His power, we must forever abide in the Word of God that we may have the precious fruits of the Spirit, and not only the fruits but the precious gifts that Father has for His little ones.

Dearly beloved, may we search the Scriptures and see for ourselves whether we are measuring up to every word that proceedeth out of the mouth of God. If we will remain in the Scriptures and follow the Blessed Holy Spirit all the way, we will be able to measure up to the Word of God in all of its fullness [*sic*]. Paul prayed in Eph. 3.16, "That He would grant you, according to the riches of His glory, to be strengthened with might by His Spirit in the inner man; that Christ may dwell in your hearts by faith; that ye being rooted and grounded in love, may be able to comprehend with all saints, what is the breadth, and length, and depth, and height, and to know the love of Christ which passeth knowledge; that ye might be filled with all the fulness of God. Now unto Him that is able to do exceeding abundantly above all that we ask or think, according to the power that worketh in us."

Many people say today that tongues are the least gift of any that the Lord can give, and they do not need it, and ask What good is it to us? But by careful study of the Word, we see in the 14th of Corinthians, Paul telling the church to "follow after charity and desire spiritual gifts." Charity means Divine love without which we will never be able to enter heaven. Gifts all will fail, but Divine love will last through all eternity. And right in the same verse he says, "Desire spiritual gifts, but rather that ye may prophesy," that is to say, preach in your own tongue, which will build up the saints and the church.

But he says in the next verse, "For he that speaketh in an unknown tongue, speaketh not unto men, but unto God, for no man understandeth him, howbeit in the Spirit, he speaketh mysteries, (R. V., hidden truth.) But he that prophesieth speaketh unto man to edification, exhortation and comfort." He that prophesies in his own tongue edifies the church; but he that speaks in unknown tongues edifies himself. His spirit is being edified, while the church is not edified, because they do not understand what he says unless the Lord gives somebody the interpretation of the tongue.

Here is where many stumble that have not this blessed gift to use in the Spirit. They say, What good is it when you do not know what you are talking about?

Praise God, every gift He gives is a good gift. It is very blessed, for when the Lord gets ready, He can speak in any language He chooses to speak. You ask, "Is not prophecy the best gift?" Prophecy is the best gift to the church, for it builds up the saints and edifies them and exalts them to higher things in the Lord Jesus. If a brother or sister is speaking in tongues and cannot speak any English, but preaches altogether in tongues and has no interpretation, they are less than he that prophesies, but if they interpret they are just as great.

May God help all of His precious people to read the 14th of I. Cor., and give them the real interpretation of the Word. May we all use our gift to the glory of God and not worship the gift. The Lord gives us power to use it to His own glory and honor.

Many times, when we were receiving this blessed Pentecost, we all used to break out in tongues; but we have learned to be quieter with the gift. Often when God sends a blessed wave upon us, we all may speak in tongues for awhile, but we will not keep it up while preaching service is going on, for we want to be obedient to the Word, that everything may be done decently and in order and without confusion. Amen.

W.J.S.

12. "RECEIVE YE THE HOLY GHOST."

(*AF,* January 1907, 2)

1.—The first step in seeking the baptism with the Holy Ghost is to have a clear knowledge of the new birth in our souls, which is the first work of grace and brings everlasting life to our souls. "Therefore being justified by faith, we have peace with God." Every one of us that repents of our sins and turns to the Lord Jesus with faith in Him, receives forgiveness of sins. Justification and regeneration are simultaneous. The pardoned sinner becomes a child of God in justification.

2.—The next step for us is to have a clear knowledge, by the Holy Spirit, of the second work of grace wrought in our hearts by the power of the Blood and the Holy Ghost. Heb. 10.14, 15, "For by one offering, He hath perfected forever them that are sanctified, where of the Holy Ghost also is a witness to us.' The Scripture also teaches (Heb. 2.11), "For both He that sanctifieth and they who are sanctified are all of one; for which cause He is not ashamed to call them brethren." So we have Christ crowned and enthroned in our hearts, the tree of life." We have the brooks and streams of salvation flowing in our souls, but praise God, we can have the rivers. For the Lord Jesus says, "He that believeth on me, as the Scripture hath said, out of his innermost being shall flow rivers of living water. This spake He of the Spirit, for the Holy Ghost was not yet given." But, praise our God, He is now given and being poured out upon all flesh. All races, nations, and tongues are receiving the baptism with the Holy Ghost and fire, according to the prophecy of Joel.

3.—When we have a clear knowledge of justification and sanctification, through the precious Blood of Jesus Christ in our hearts, then we can be a recipient of the baptism with the Holy Ghost. Many people today are sanctified, cleansed from all sin, and perfectly consecrated to God, but they have never obeyed the Lord according to Acts. I. 4, 5, 8 and Luke 24. 39, for their real personal Pentecost, the enduement of power for service and work and for sealing unto the day of redemption. The baptism with the Holy Ghost is a free gift without repentance, upon the sanctified, cleansed vessel. II Cor. 1. 21–22, "Now He which stablisheth us with you in Christ, and hath anointed us, is God, who hath also sealed us, and given the earnest of the Spirit in our hearts." Praise our God for the sealing of the Holy Spirit unto the day of redemption.

Dearly beloved, the only people that will meet our Lord and Savior Jesus Christ and go with Him into the marriage supper of the Lamb, are the wise virgins—not only saved and sanctified, with pure and clean hearts, but having the baptism with the Holy Ghost. The others we find will not be prepared. They have some oil in their lamps but they have not the double portion of His Holy Spirit.

The disciples were filled with the unction of the Holy Spirit before Pentecost, that sustained them until they received the Holy Ghost baptism. Many people today are filled with joy and gladness, but they are far from the enduement of power. Sanctification brings rest and sweetness and quietness to our souls, for we are one with the Lord Jesus and are able to obey His precious Word, that "Man shall not live by bread alone, but by every word that proceedeth out of the mouth of God," and we are feeding upon Christ.

But let us wait for the promise of the Father upon our souls, according to Jesus' Word, "John truly baptized with water, but ye shall be baptized with the Holy Ghost not many days hence . . . Ye shall receive power after that the Holy Ghost is come upon you: and ye shall be witnesses unto me, both in Jerusalem and in all Judea, and in Samaria, and unto the uttermost part of the earth." Acts 1.5, 8. Glory! Glory! Hallelujah! O worship, get down on your knees and ask the Holy Ghost to come in, and you will find Him right at your heart's door, and He will come in. Prove Him now. Amen

–W.J.S.

13. REBECCA; TYPE OF THE BRIDE OF CHRIST—GEN. 24.

(*AF*, February–March 1907, 2)

"I pray thee is there room in thy father's house for us to lodge in?" These words were spoken by Eliezer, Abraham's eldest servant and steward of his house, to Rebecca when he had found her at the well in answer to his prayer. Eliezer (meaning "God's Helper") is a type of the Holy Spirit, and Isaac is a type of Christ. Now as Eliezer was seeking a bride for Isaac, the son of Abraham, so the Holy Spirit today is seeking a bride for the Lord Jesus, God's only begotten Son.

Eliezer was sent to Abraham's country and to his kindred to take a wife for Isaac. So God our Father has sent the Holy Spirit from the glory land down into this world, and He, the Spirit of truth, is convicting the world of sin, righteousness, and judgment, and is selecting out of the body of Christ His bride. He is seeking among His kindred, the sanctified, and Jesus is baptizing them with the Holy Ghost and fire, preparing them for the great marriage supper of the Lamb. Praise our God! Eliezer was under oath not to select the bride from the Canaanites but from Abraham's kindred. So God is not selecting a bride for Christ among the sinners, for a sinner must first get saved and sanctified before he can be one with the Lord Jesus. Heb. 2:11 says, "For both He that sanctifieth and they who are sanctified are all of one, for which cause he is not ashamed to call them brethren." So He is seeking a bride among His brethren, the sanctified.

"Christ so loved the church that He gave Himself for it; that He might sanctify and cleanse it with the washing of water by the Word; that He might present it unto Himself a glorious church, not having spot or wrinkle or any such thing; but that is should be holy and without blemish." Eph. 5:25–27. So Jesus today is selecting a sanctified people, baptizing them with the Holy Ghost and fire to greet Him at His coming. Rebecca was a virgin, the type of a sanctified soul. So the Holy Ghost today is standing at the heart of every pure virgin (sanctified soul) pleading, "I pray thee is there room in thy heart that I may come in and lodge?" O beloved, we see many of the sanctified people today rejecting the Holy Spirit, just as people rejected Christ when he was on earth here. It seems there is no room in their hearts for the baptism with the Holy Ghost and fire. May God help them to open their eyes and see that the time draweth nigh for His coming. O may Christ's waiting bride wake up and let the Holy Ghost come in.

Rebecca was a type of the wise virgins. When Eliezer met her at the well and asked her to let him drink a little water from her pitcher, O how sweet and ready she was. She answered and said, "Drink, my Lord." And she hastened and let down her pitcher upon her hand and gave him drink, and it pleased him. The Spirit is a person. He can be pleased, He can be quenched and He can be insulted, as we find Ananias insulted Him. We please Him when we accept the words of Jesus. Then Jesus sends the Holy Spirit to witness in our hearts.

When Rebecca had done giving him drink, she said, "I will also draw water for thy camels." Christ's bride must do everything without murmuring. O how sweet it is when we have the mighty Spirit in our hearts; we are ready for service; we are ready for watering the whole entire world with the precious well of salvation in our heart. Beloved, when the Holy Ghost comes, He brings the well of salvation and rivers of living water.

"And it came to pass, as the camels had done drinking, that the man took a gold earring of half a shekel weight and two bracelets for her hands of ten shekels weight of gold." Praise God. This is what our beloved sanctified people receive when they receive the witness of the anointing of the Holy Ghost upon their hears, as when Jesus breathed upon the disciples before Pentecost in the upper room, where He said, "Receive ye the Holy Ghost." The disciples had the witness in their hearts that very moment and "both He that sanctifieth and they who are sanctified are all of one." For He had opened the Scriptures to them, (Lu. 24:32) and their understanding was opened, (Lu. 24:45) and He had opened their eyes, (Lu. 24:31) "And their eyes were opened and they knew Him." So with us, when we receive sanctification and the witness of the Spirit in our hearts to our sanctification, the Scriptures are opened to us, we understand them, and our eyes are anointed. We see a picture of it in Rebecca. When she had received Eliezer and let him drink out of her pitcher and had watered the camels, he gave her the earrings and bracelets of gold. O beloved may we let the Holy Ghost sup out of our heart pitcher, for the Lord says, "Behold, I stand at the door and knock; if any man hear My voice and open the door, I will come in and sup with him and he with Me."

And when He comes in, He opens His precious treasures to us, bracelets and earrings, great weights of gold. O how blessed it is when the precious Spirit enters into our hearts like Eliezer. He tells us the great wealth of our Father and of our Christ, for He opens up our understanding, and enlightens our minds. His continual conversation is about the Father and Jesus. Eliezer was the very type of the Holy Spirit who takes the things of Christ and shows them unto us, for He told Rebecca of the wealth of Abraham and Isaac, giving her jewels. And she wore them, showing that she was the espoused of Isaac. Hallelujah! Jesus breathed the Holy Ghost on His disciples and said, "Whosoever sins ye remit, they are remitted unto them; and whosoever sins yet [sic] retain, they are retained." Thus they had the witness in their hearts that they were candidates for the baptism with the Holy Ghost and fire. He commanded them, "Tarry ye in the city of Jerusalem, until ye be endued with power from on high." Praise our God!

"I pray thee is there room in thy father's house for us to lodge in?" Beloved, is there room in your heart that God's blessed Spirit can come and lodge in? Rebecca was a wise virgin. She met Eliezer at the well and received the bracelets and earrings; but she did not receive them until she had allowed him to drink out of her pitcher and had watered the camels. Many others stood by, no doubt; but they did not do any watering of the camels. O may all of Christ's waiting bride be filled with the rivers of living waters that they may water the thirsty, parched hearts with the rivers of salvation.

Rebecca wore her jewels. She did not put them aside or into her pocket, for we read that Laban saw them on this sister's hands. When we have received the abiding anointing in our hearts, someone can always see it shining forth upon our faces. Praise God!

When Eliezer had fed the camels and had come into the house, and when meat was set before him, he said, "I will not eat until I have told mine errand." O beloved, we should be so zealous about the bride of Christ that nothing will be able to turn us aside. We find the first overthrow in the human soul was through the appetite; and when the Holy Spirit sends us on His mission, may we not be satisfied until we have told it, and of His coming back to earth again.

Then he told his mission how that Abraham had send him to his kindred to take a wife for his son, and he said, "And now if ye will deal kindly and truly with my master, tell me, and if not, tell me." They said, "The thing proceedeth from the Lord" and gave Rebecca to be his master's wife. When people are living under the guidance of God's Holy Spirit, it does not take them very long to hear the voice of God, and they are willing to obey. Praise God! Then Eliezer ate and tarried with them that night, because he had received the desire of his master's heart and his heart.

But on the morrow, her brother and mother said, "Let the damsel abide with us a Few days, at least ten days." But he said, "Hinder me not." It is best, when we hear the words of God and the Spirit is upon us, to receive now the baptism with the Holy Spirit, instead of waiting two or three days and meeting friends and meeting the devil, who will try to persuade us out of it. If Rebecca had remained, perhaps her friends might have talked her out of going with Eliezer over the plains away off to that distant land to her husband Isaac.

Eliezer said, "Hinder me not." O may we do nothing to hinder the entrance of the baptism with the Holy Ghost. We should see that everything is out of the way and nothing to stand between us and this glorious blessing. Then they called Rebecca and said to her, "Wilt thou go with this man?" And she said, "I will go." To receive the baptism with the Holy Ghost, we must forsake all and follow Jesus all the way. For the Lord Jesus says, "For this cause shall a man leave his father and mother, and cleave to his wife." So we that are Christ's bride must forsake all and cleave to Christ, as Rebecca left father and mother, brother and sister, and rode on the camel to meet Isaac.

"And Isaac went out to meditate in the fields at eventide; and he lifted up his eyes and saw, and behold the camels were coming. And Rebecca lifted her eyes, and when she saw Isaac, she lighted off the camel" to meet him. Now we are living in the eventide of this dispensation, when the Holy Spirit is leading us, Christ's bride, to meet Him in the clouds.

–W.J.S.

14. THE BAPTISM WITH THE HOLY GHOST

(*AF*, February—March 1907, 7)

Dear one in Christ who are seeking the baptism with the Holy Ghost: do not seek for tongues but for the promise of the Father, and pray for the baptism with the Holy Ghost, and God will throw in the tongues according to Acts 2.4.

We read in Acts 1.4, 5, "And being assembled together with them, commanded them that they should not depart from Jerusalem, but wait for the promise of the Father, which, saith He, ye have heard of me. For John truly baptized with water; but ye shall be baptized with the Holy Ghost not many days hence."

This promise of the Father was preached unto the disciples by John the Baptist. And Jesus reminded the disciples about this baptism that John had preached to them in life. In England we find the same thing. Matt. 3.11. John, after warning the Jews and Pharisees against sin and hypocrisy, preached the doctrine of the baptism with the Holy Ghost. He said first, "Bring forth therefore, fruits meet for repentence [*sic*]." God is sending our precious His [*sic*] ministers to preach repentance to the people and turn them from their sins and cause them to make restitution according to their ability, and to have faith in the Lord Jesus Christ and be saved. Glory to God!

And then they must get sanctified through the precious Blood of Jesus Christ, for He says in John 17.14–19, "I pray not that Thou shouldst keep them from the evil. They are not of the world, even as I am not of the world. Sanctify them through Thy truth; Thy Word is truth. As Thou hast sent Me into the world, even so have I also sent them into the world. And for their sakes I sanctify Myself, that they also might be sanctified through the truth." God wants His people to be sanctified, because He says again in Heb. 13.12. "Wherefore Jesus also that He might sanctify the people with His own Blood, suffered without the gate. Let us go forth therfore [*sic*] unto Him without the camp, bearing His reproach."

Then Jesus taught the disciples to tarry at Jerusalem. They obeyed Him and waited for the promise of the Father. "And when the day of Pentecost was fully come, they were all with one accord in one place. And suddenly there came a sound from heaven as of a rushing, mighty wind, and it filled all the house where they were sitting. And there appeared unto them cloven tongues like as of fire, and it sat upon each of them. And they were all filled with the Holy Ghost, and began to speak with other tongues, as the Spirit gave them utterance." Acts 2, 1–4.

Wind is always typical of the Spirit or of life. "And it filled all the house where they were sitting." The rivers of salvation had come and had filled the whole place, and they all were immersed or baptized in the Holy Spirit. Praise God!

"And there appeared unto them cloven tongues like as of fire." Beloved, when we receive the baptism with the Holy Ghost and fire, we surely will speak in tongues as the Spirit gives utterance. We are not seeking for tongues, but we are seeking the baptism with the Holy Ghost and fire. And when we receive it, we shall be so filled with the Holy Ghost, that He Himself will speak in the power of the Spirit.

"And they were all filled with the Holy Ghost, and began to speak with other tongues, as the Spirit gave them utterance." Now, beloved, do not be too concerned about your speaking in tongues, but let the Holy Ghost give you utterance, and it will come just as freely as the air we breathe. It is nothing worked up, but it comes from the heart. "With the heart man believeth unto righteousness; and with the mouth, confession is made unto salvation." So when the Holy Ghost life comes in, the mouth opens, through the power of the Spirit in the heart. Glory to God!

"There were, dwelling at Jerusalem, Jews, devout men, out of every nation under heaven. Now when this was noised abroad, the multitude came together, and were confounded, because that every man heard them speak in his own language. And they were all amazed and marveled, saying one to another, 'Behold, are not all these which speak, Gallileans. And how hear we every man speak in our own tongue wherein we were born?" Acts 2.5–8.

Beloved, if you do not know the language that you speak, do not puzzle yourself about it, for the Lord did not promise us He would tell us what language we were speaking, but He promised us the interpretation of what we speak.

In seeking the baptism, first get a clear, definite witness in your soul that you have the abiding Christ within. Then there will be no trouble in receiving the Pentecostal baptism, through faith in our Lord and Savior, Jesus Christ, for it is a free gift that comes without repentance. Bless His holy name!

–W.J.S.

15. [GOOD-BYE]

(*AF*, April 1907, 2)

Bro. W. J. Seymour then started the congregation singing:

> Jesus, Jesus, how I trust Thee,
> How I've proved Thee o'er and o'er;
> Jesus, Jesus, blessed Jesus,
> Oh, for grace to trust Thee more.

He then said: "Glory! Beloved, I want to say 'Goodnight' to you all for a short while. It has now been over a year ago since I left Texas and came up in this portion of the country to labor and work for the Lord, and I am going back there through that old state where the Lord called me from a year ago. I am going to pass through there and see those precious children that prayed with me for Pentecost, and while I am gone I want you all to pray that God may use me to His own honor and glory.

"I want to read some of God's own precious Word in the first chapter of the book of Isaiah. (He read to verse 9 and then said:) I am so glad the Lord

God has raised up a people right in Los Angeles, and San Francisco, they seem like Sodom and Gomorrah, but out of these cities the Lord God has raised up a people for His holy name. He has cleansed them from sin, He has scanctified [sic] them, and has baptized them with the Holy Ghost and sealed them unto the day of Redemption. Glory to His holy name! I can go and rejoice with the people in Texas, telling them of the wonderful things that God has done in Los Angeles. They said I should be back in a month's time, and now this is the first chance I have had to get back.

(He then read to the end of verse 20). "'But if ye refuse and rebel ye shall be devoured with the sword: for the mouth of the Lord hath spoken it.' Every man, every church, every home, that rejects the full Gospel of the Lord and Savior, Jesus Christ, shall be devoured. We are living in a time when the Holy Ghost is working—bless God,—convincing men and women of sin and righteousness and judgment, and every man and every women [sic] that hardens their heart against the Word of God shall fall. If the men and women of this city will repent and turn from their sin and accept our Lord and Savior, Jesus Christ, 'ye shall eat the good of the land.' Glory to His holy name! God has fat things to feed all His hungry people. Oh, He will fill you tonight. Oh, the music will be singing in your soul and, oh, the love of Christ that passes all understanding will be dwelling in your heart. Just read what He says: 'If ye be willing and obedient ye shall the good of the land.' Jesus says: 'Abide in me, as the branch cannot bear fruit of itself except it abide in the vine, no more can ye except yet abide in Me.' Oh, beloved, if we abide in the words of the Lord Jesus Christ and feed off Christ, I'll tell you, we shall live off the good of the land,—bless His holy name. We will have the fat—bless God,—we will have everything to cheer our heart, we shall have healing and health and salvation in our souls. Oh, glory to His holy name. Oh, do not refuse the Word of God; oh, accept it, accept all the doctrine of our Lord and Savior, Jesus Christ, and oh, beloved, it will fill your hearts with good things.

"But just listen to what he says: 'If ye refuse and rebel, ye shall be devoured with the sword: for the mouth of the Lord hath spoken it.' Beloved, if you reject Christ, if you reject His precious Blood, if you reject the Holy Ghost, ye shall be devoured with the sword; but if you accept Jesus Christ He will prepare a table before you, and the Lord God Himself will spread it and He will feed you Himself. When Jesus had gotten through feeding His disciples He told His disciples to feed His lambs and sheep. What are we going to feed them with? We are going to feed them with the precious Word of God; we are going to teach them to accept Jesus Christ as their Savior and as their Sanctifier to destroy the root of sin, and then we are going to teach them to accept the Holy Ghost. He shall baptize them with the Holy Ghost and fire, and when He comes He is going to speak through them, and He says 'In the last days I will pour out of My Spirit on all flesh.' Glory to His holy name. I want to say 'Goodnight' to you."

"God be with you till we meet again" was then sung as Brother Seymour shook hands with as many as possible and left for the train. Brother Anderson spoke a few words of encouragement to the saints on the necessity of continuing faithful in the pastor's absence."

16. THE "LATTER RAIN" IN ZION, ILL.

(*AF,* June–September 1907, 1)

God is doing a mighty work in Zion City among those heart-broken and crushed people. First they started meetings in the Edina Hospice, now a faith home called "The Haven" then they had the large auditorium in the college and now have the large tabernacle.

One morning in the upper room of "The Haven," the Holy Ghost fell, as they were praying for Him to come and manifest Himself. First one began to drop and then another until the floor was covered. The first to speak in unknown tongues was a young man who spoke in Chinese, Italian, and Zulu, which were identified. Then it was not long till the flood of joy began and all over the room they were praising and glorifying God in different tongues. Some were justified and sanctified. About twenty came through speaking in tongues.

God is using the children, young men and young women, in a marvelous manner. It is the most wonderful demonstration of the power of God upon human hearts. Denounce it as they will, when they see these little children under the power of the Holy Spirit, preaching, singing and speaking in different languages (which are many times identified by foreigners) they will in our meetings confess that their fighting has come to an end, and say that they have never seen anything after this manner.

Brother Seymour when he was in Zion City wrote. "People here receive the baptism in their pews while the service is going on and sometimes scores of them receive it. It is the sweetest thing you want to see. It reminds me of old Azusa tens [*sic*] months ago. The people that receive the baptism seem so happy, they remind me of our people at home. There are little children from six years and on up who have the baptism with the Holy Ghost, just as we have it in Los Angeles. Praise our God. This is another Azusa. It would do you good to hear these people speak under the power of the Holy Ghost. Some of them converse in tongues. Brother Tom has never lost the spirit of the Azusa. He is still fired up the same as ever. Everywhere I have traveled among our baptized souls, they seem to have such joy and freedom in the Holy Ghost."—Address "The Haven," Zion City, Ills.

17. THE HOLY SPIRIT BISHOP OF THE CHURCH

(*AF*, June–September 1907, 3)

It is the office work of the Holy Spirit to preside over the entire work of God on earth.—John 10: 3. Jesus was our Bishop while on earth, but now He has sent the Holy Ghost, Amen, to take His place, not men.—John 14:16; 15: 26; 16: 7–14. Praise His Holy name!

The Holy Ghost is to infuse with divine power, and to invest with heavenly authority. No religious assembly is legal without His presence and His transaction. We should recognize Him as the Teacher of teachers.

The reason why there are so many of God's people without divine power today without experimental salvation, wrought out in their hearts by the Blood, by the power of the blessed Holy Spirit, is because they have not accepted Him as their Teacher, as their Leader, as their Comforter. Jesus said in His precious Word that if He went away He would send us another Comforter. The need of men and women today in their lives, is a Comforter[.] Praise our God! We have received this blessed Comforter, and it is heaven in our souls. We can sing with all our hearts: "What matter where on earth we dwell On mountain top, or in the dell, In cottage or a mansion fair, Where Jesus is, 'tis heaven there."

Bless His holy name! May God help every one of His Blood bought children to receive this blessed Comforter. Glory to His name! Hallelujah! Hosannah to his omnipotent name! Oh, He is reigning in my soul! Hallelujah! I just feel like the song which says:

> Oh, spread the tidings round
> Wherever man is found,
> Wherever human hearts
> And human woes abound,
> Let every Christian tongue
> Proclaim the joyful sound,
> The Comforter has come!

Many people today think we need new churches, (that is to say church buildings,) stone structures, brick structures, modern improvements, new choirs, trained singers right from the conservatories, paying from seven to fifteen hundred dollars a year for singing, fine pews, fine chandeliers, everything that could attract the human heart to win souls to the meeting house is used in this twentieth century. We find that they have reached the climax, but all of that has failed to bring divine power and salvation to precious souls. Sinners have gone to the meeting house, heard a nice, fine, eloquent oration on Jesus, or on some particular church, or on some noted man. The people have been made glad to go because they have seen great wealth, they have seen people in the very latest styles, in different costumes, and loaded down with jewelry, decorated from head to foot with diamonds, gold and silver. The music in the church has been sweet, and it is found that a good many of the church people seem to be full of love, but there has always been a lack of power. We wonder why sinners are not being converted, and why it is that the church is always making improvements, and failing to do the work that Christ called her to do. It is because men have taken the place of Christ and the Holy Spirit.

The church had the right idea that we need bishops and elders, but they must be given authority by our Lord and Savior Jesus Christ, and their qualifications for these offices must be the enduement of the power of the Holy Ghost. Jesus, after choosing His disciples, said, in John 15:16 "Ye have not chosen me, but I have chosen you and ordained you, that ye should go and bring forth fruit, and that your fruit should remain, that whatsoever ye shall ask of the Father, in my name, He may give it to you." Praise our God! The Lord Jesus ordained His disciples with His own blessed hands, before going back to glory, but He put the credentials in their hearts on the day of Pentecost, when they were baptized with the Holy Ghost and fire. Hallelujah! This was the authority that made them His witnesses unto the uttermost parts of the earth, for without the blessed Holy Spirit, in all of His fullness, we are not able to witness unto the uttermost parts of the earth. We must be co-workers with Him, partakers of the Holy Ghost. Then, when He is in us, in all of His fullness, He will manifest Himself. Signs and miracles will follow. This is the office work of the Holy Spirit in the churches. Amen!

I pray God that all Christ's people and ministers everywhere will please stop by the headquarters, the Jerusalem before God, for their credentials. Then they are entitled to receive credentials from the visible church. But the main credential is to be baptized with the Holy Ghost. Instead of new preachers from the theological schools and academies, the same old preachers, baptized with the Holy Ghost and fire, the same old deacons, the same old plain church buildings will do. When the Holy Ghost comes in He will cleanse out dead forms and ceremonies, and will give life and power to His ministers and preachers, in the same old church buildings. But without the Holy Ghost they are simply tombstones.

We must always recognize that a meeting house is simply a place, where Christ's people gather to worship, and not the church. The church is planted in our hearts, through the Blood of Jesus Christ, for Christ said, in Matthew 16:16. "Upon this rock will I build my church, and the gates of hell shall not prevail against it." We see, if these meeting houses and such buildings were really churches of Christ, the storms, cyclones, and fire could not harm them; but we see them blown down by storms and burned down. But, through the precious Blood of Christ, this church that He plants in our souls will stand throughout eternity.

The first thing in every assembly is to see that He, the Holy Ghost, is installed as the chairman. The reason why we have so many dried up missions and churches today, is because they have not the Holy Ghost as the chairman. They have some man in His place. Man is all right in his place, that is when he is filled with the power of the Holy Ghost, for it is not man that does the work, but the Holy Ghost from the glory land, sent by Jesus to work through this tabernacle of clay. Wherever you find the Holy Ghost as the chairman in any assembly, you will find a fruitful assembly, you will find children being born unto God.

Just as it takes a father and a mother to bring forth children of this natural life so it takes the Word and the Spirit to bring forth children of the spiritual birth. There must be a father and there must be a mother. God chooses human instruments to preach the Word unto the people, and the Holy Ghost gives birth to everyone who receives the Word of Christ, which means the new birth. Praise our God. Where a Holy Ghost man preaches the Word of God, the Lord will bring forth sons and daughters unto his administration.

Jesus Christ is the archbishop of these assemblies, and He must be recognized. Also we must recognize the Holy Spirit in all of His office work. He takes the members into the church, which is the body of Christ. Through repentance to God, and faith in Jesus, they become the members of the church of Christ. And they remain members as long as they live free from sin. When they commence sinning, the Holy Ghost, the chairman and bishop, the presiding elder, turns them out, and they know when they are turned out of this church. They don't have to go and ask their pastor or their preacher, for they feel within their own soul that the glory has left them—the joy, the peace, the rest and comfort. Then when they feel the lack in their souls, if they will confess their sins, God, the Holy Ghost, will accept them back into the church.

Oh, thank God for this holy way. I am so glad that sham battles are over. Men and women must live straight, holy, pure lives, free from sin, or else they have no part with Christ Jesus. When men and women are filled with the Holy Ghost, everywhere they go, living waters will flow. The Lord promised that out of our innermost being living rivers of water should flow. This is the Holy Ghost. Amen! The mighty Pison, the Gihon, the Hiddekel, the Euphrates of our soul will flow, representing the rivers of salvation. Amen!

W.J.S.

18. LETTER TO ONE SEEKING THE HOLY GHOST

(*AF,* June–September 1907, 3)

Dear Beloved in Christ Jesus:—

The Lord Jesus has said in His precious Word, "Blessed are they which do hunger and thirst after righteousness, for they shall be filled." Matt. 5,6. God's promises are true and sure. We can rest upon His promises. He says, "Blessed are the pure in heart, for they shall see God." Matt. 5, 8. "Blessed are the poor in spirit, for theirs is the kingdom of heaven." Matt. 5, 3.

The Lord Jesus is always ready to fill the hungry, thirsty soul, for He said in His precious Word, "He that believeth on Me as the scripture hath said, out of his innermost being shall flow rivers of living water. (But this spake He of the Spirit which they that believe on Him should receive: for the Holy Ghost was not yet given; because that Jesus was not yet glorified.)" John 7, 38, 39. But, praise God. He is given to us today.

All we have to do it [*sic*] to obey the first chapter of Acts, and wait for the promise of the Father upon our souls. The Lord Jesus said in His precious Word, "Behold I send the promise of My Father upon you; but tarry ye in the city of Jerusalem until ye be endued with power from on high. (Luke 24,49.) For John Truly baptized with water; but ye shall be baptized with the Holy Ghost not many days hence. * * * Ye shall receive power after that the Holy Ghost is come upon you; and ye shall be witnesses unto Me both in Jerusalem and in all Judea, and in Samaria and unto the uttermost part of the earth." Acts 1.5, 8. They tarried until they received the mighty power of the baptism with the Holy Spirit upon their souls. Then God put the credentials in their hearts, and put the ring of authority on their finger, and sealed them in the forehead with the Father's name, and wrote on their heart the name of the New Jerusalem, and put in their hand the stone with the name written that no man knoweth save he that receiveth it. Praise the Lord, for His mercy endureth forever. Let us stand upon His promises. They are sure, they will not break.

The Lord Jesus says, "Behold, I give you power to tread upon serpents and scorpions and over all the power of the enemy; and nothing shall by any means hurt you." Luke 10,19. Dear loved one, the Lord Jesus when He rose from the dead, said "All power is given unto me in heaven and in earth. Go ye therefore, and teach all nations, baptizing them in the name of the Father, and of the Son, and of the Holy Ghost. (Matt. 28,19) He that believeth and is baptized shall be saved; but he that believeth not shall be damned. And these signs shall follow them that believe; in My name shall they cast out devils; they shall speak with new tongues; they shall take up serpents; and if they drink any deadly thing, it shall not hurt them; they shall lay hands on the sick and they shall recover." Mark 16:16–18. And they went forth and preached everywhere, the Lord working with them, and confirming the Word with signs following. Praise His dear name, for He is just the same today.

The first thing in order to receive this precious and wonderful baptism wit [*sic*] the Holy Spirit, we want to have a clear knowledge of justification by faith according to the Bible. Rom. 5:1, "Therefore being justified by faith, we have peace with God through our Lord Jesus Christ," faith that all our actual sins may be washed away. Actual sin means committed sin.

And then the second step is to have a real knowledge of sanctification, which frees us from original sin—the sin that we were born with, which we inherited from our father Adam. We were not responsible for that sin until we received light, for we could not repent of a sin that we did not commit. When we came to the Lord as a sinner, we repented to God of our actual sins, and God for Christ's sake pardoned us and washed our sin and pollution away, and planted eternal life in our souls. Afterwards we saw in the Word of God, "This is the will of God, even your sanctification." I Thess. 4:3, also John 17:15–19. We consecrated ourselves to God, and the Lord Jesus sanctified our souls and made us every whit clean.

Then after we were clearly sanctified, we prayed to God for the baptism with the Holy Spirit. So He sent the Holy Spirit to our hearts and filled us with His blessed Spirit, and He gave us the Bible evidence, according to the 2nd chapter of Acts verses 1 to 4, speaking with other tongues as the Spirit gives utterance.

Praise our God, He is the same yesterday, today, and forever. Receive Him just now and He will fill you. Amen. Don't get discouraged but pray until you are filled, for the Lord says, "Men ought always to pray and not to faint." Don't stop because you do not receive the baptism with the Holy Ghost at the first, but continue until you are filled. The Lord Jesus told His disciples to tarry until they were endued with power from on high. Many people today are willing to tarry just so long, and then they give up and fail to receive their personal Pentecost that would measure with the Bible. The Lord Jesus says, "Ye shall be filled." He says that to the person that hungers and thirsts after righteousness, and He says they are blessed. So if there is a hunger and thirst in our souls for righteousness, we are blest of Him. Praise His dear name!

Yours in Christ, W.J.S.

19. TESTIMONY AND PRAISE TO GOD

(*AF*, June–September 1907, 4)

"O, I feel the coming of our Lord and Savios [*sic*] Jesus Christ drawing nigh. Hallelujah! Glory to His name! I am so glad that the Lord is holding the winds until the angel has sealed all of the saints of the living God in their foreheads, the baptism of the Holy Ghost. The midnight cry will soon be made, when the morning and the night shall come. It will be morning in our souls, to those that are waiting for His coming; but the awful black night of tribulation as the black night of Egypt will come upon all the world. May God help all of His precious waiting bride to be watching, waiting until our Lord shall come.

"Oh, I am so thankful that I can work for my Christ and my God. The time is short when our blessed Jesus shall return to this earth, and snatch away His waiting bride. After six thousand years of toil and labor, we are going to have one thousand years of rest with our Lord and Saviour, Jesus Christ. Glory to His holy name!"

Bro. Seymour, 312 Azusa St.,
Los Angeles.

20. "THE MARRIAGE TIE"

(*AF*, September 1907, 3)

Marriage is a divine institution which God Himself has instituted. Gen. 2:18, 24. "And the Lord God said, It is not good that man should be alone; I will make him an help meet for him. Therefore shall a man leave his father and his mother and shall cleave unto his wife; and they twain shall be one flesh." I Cor. 11:9. "Neither was the man created for the woman, but the woman for the man."

God commended it. Gen. 2:18 and Prov. 18:22. "Whoso findeth a wife findeth a good thing, and obtaineth favor of the Lord."

God is in it. Matt. 19:4, 6. "And He answered and said unto them, Have ye not read that He which made them at the beginning made them male and female. Wherefore they are no more twain but one flesh. What therefore God hath joined together let not man put asunder."

It is honorable in all. Heb. 13:4. "Marriage is honorable in all and the bed undefiled, but whoremongers and adulterers God will judge."

Christ attended a wedding in Canaan. He went to adorn it, to beautify it with His presence. John 2:1, 2. "And the third day there was a marriage in Cana of Galilee, and the mother of Jesus was there. And both Jesus was called and His disciples to the marriage."

The forbidding to marry is the doctrine of devils. I Tim. 4:1, 3. "Now the Spirit speaketh expressly that in the latter times some shall depart from the faith, giving heed to seducing spirits and doctrines of devils; * * * forbidding to marry."

MARRIAGE BINDING FOR LIFE

God has approved of but one wife and one husband. Gen. 2: 24. "Therefore shall a man leave his father and his mother, and shall cleave unto his wife; and they twain shall be one flesh." Matt. 19: 3–6. "The Pharisees also came unto Him tempting Him, and saying unto Him, Is it lawful for a man to put away his wife for every cause? And He answered and said unto them, Have ye not read that He which made them at the beginning made them male and female, and said, For this cause shall a man leave father and mother, and shall cleave to his wife; and they twain shall be one flesh? Wherefore they are no more twain but one flesh. What therefore God hath joined together, let not man put asunder."

The husband and wife are bound together for life. Rom. 7:2. "For the woman which hath an husband is bound by the law to her husband so long as he liveth: but if the husband is dead, she is loosed from the law of her husband." I Cor. 7:39. The wife is bound by the law as long as her husband liveth; but if her husband be dead, she is at liberty to be married to whom she will, only in the Lord."

No court of man should sever the marriage tie. Matt. 19:6. "Wherefore they are no more twain but one flesh. What therefore God hath joined together let not man put asunder." Death alone severs the marriage tie. Heb. 13:4.

MOSES' LAW OF DIVORCE

Under Moses' law, he suffered men to divorce their wives and marry again, because of the hardness of their hearts Matt. 19:7, 8. "They say unto Him, Why did Moses then command to give a writing of divorcement, and to put her away? He saith unto them, Moses, because of the hardness of your hearts suffered you to put away your wives; but from the beginning it was not so." Under Moses' law they had been accustomed, for any uncleanness, adultery, fornication or some cause not as much as that, to put away the wife by giving her a bill of divorcement, and she could go and be another man's wife. But under the New Testament law, the law of Christ, she is bound by the law to her husband till death.

THE EDENIC STANDARD OF MATRIMONY

Jesus did away with the divorce law, and restored matrimony back to the Edenic standard. Under Moses' law, the sacredness of matrimony was lost through the hardness of hearts. But under the law of grace, it is restored back as in the beginning of grace. Praise God. God's promises are true and sure. Hallelujah! Amen.

Under the New Testament law, the law of Christ, there is but one cause for which a man may put away his wife, but no right to marry again. This cause is fornication or adultery. Matt. 5:31, 32. "It hath been said, Whosoever shall put away his wife, let him give her a writing of divorcement; but I say unto you that whosoever shall put away his wife, saving for the cause of fornication, causeth her to commit adultery; and whosoever shall marry her that is divorced committeth adultery." Matt. 19:9. "And I say unto you, Whosoever shall put away his wife, except it be for fornication, and shall marry another committeth adultery; and whosoever marrieth her which is put away doth commit adultery." These two scriptures are just the same in meaning. Matt. 5:31, 32 is just the key to the whole subject. It settles the question.

FORBIDDEN TO MARRY AGAIN

After a man has lawfully put away his wife, or a wife has lawfully put away her husband, they are positively forbidden to marry again, under the New Testament law, until the former companion is dead. Mark 10:11, 12. "And He saith unto them Whosoever shall put away his wife, and marry another, committeth adultery against her. And if a woman shall put away her husband, and be married to another, she committeth adultery." Luke 16:18. "Whosoever putteth away his wife and marrieth another, committeth adultery; and whosoever marrieth her that is put away from her husband committeth adultery." Rom. 7:2, 3. "For the woman which hath an husband is bound by the law to her husband so long as he liveth; but if the husband be dead, she is loosed from the law of her husband. So then if while her husband liveth, she be married to another man, she shall be called and adulteress; but if her husband be dead, she is free from that law; so that she is no adulteress though she be married to another man."

ADULTERY AND FORNICATION

The act of adultery is between a married person and another who is not the lawful companion. Both parties may be married or only one. When only one is married, the act is called fornication. Matt. 19, 9 and 5, 32. Jesus said, "Whosoever shall put away his wife, saving for the cause of fornication causeth her to commit adultery." These sins are just the same, only one is committed while living with a husband and the other is when one has separated and married again.

No man can enter the kingdom of heaven without confessing and forsaking adultery and fornication. Gal. 5, 19, 21, "Now the works of the flesh are manifest which are these, adultery, fornication, uncleanness, lasciviousness, evyings [*sic*], murders, drunkenness, revelings, and such like; of the which I tell you before, as I have also told you in time past, that they which do such things shall not inherit the kingdom of God." Isa. 55, 7, "Let the wicked forsake his way and the unrighteous man his thoughts; and let him return unto the Lord, and He will have mercy upon him; and to our God for He will abundantly pardon."

THE INNOCENT PARTY

If Jesus had intended that the innocent party should marry, He would have said so, and would not have said, Moses suffered it because of the hardness of your hearts. Jesus makes it very plain. If the innocent party marries, they are living in adultry. Jesus is showing the sacredness of matrimony. Dear beloved, let us obey God in spite of everything. There is one Scripture where many people are tied up, it is Matt. 19:9, where Jesus said, "But I say unto you that whosoever shall put away his wife, except for the cause of fornication, and shall marry another committeth adultery, and whosoever marrieth her that is put away committeth adultery." Now dear loved ones, let us stop and pray over this. "Except it be for fornication and marrieth another." Some think that this party would be entitled to marry again, but let us stop and see what Jesus is teaching here. If he puts away his wife except for the cause of fornication, he committeth a sin, because he will cause her to commit adultery. Therefore he is bound by the law as long as she lives, bound right to the Edenic standard. Amen.

Dear loved ones, if Jesus had instituted that the innocent party could get another wife, He would be instituting the same thing that was permitted by Moses, and would have the church filled with that today.

Now the reason Jesus gave him permission to put away his wife for the cause of fornication was that she is already adulterous, so her adultery gave him a lawful right to separate. While it gives him that right, yet it does not give him the right to get another wife while she lives.

Paul in I Tim. 3–2 says, "A bishop then must be blameless, the husband of one wife. He also says, I Tim. 5:9, "Let not a widow be taken into the number under threescore years old, having been the wife of one man." This shows plainly that they recognized in the church that a man was to have one wife and a woman one husband.

AFTER LIGHT HAS COME

Rom. 7:2, 3 and I Cor. 7:39 give us very clear light. O may God help us to accept Bible salvation, instead of having our opinion and losing our souls. Dear beloved, you that have two wives or two husbands, before you had light on it, you lived that way and had no condemnation. God did not condemn you until you received the light upon His Word on this subject; but now God holds you responsible for the light. If you continue in the old life after light has come upon you, then you will be in the sight of God an adulterer or an adulteress, and you are bound to lose your experience or substitute something in the place of what God hath wrought. "If we walk in the light as He is in the light we have fellowship one with another and the Blood of Jesus Christ His Son cleanseth us from all sin." Let us obey God's Word if it takes our right eye or right hand.

So we find under the New Testament there is no putting away the first wife and getting another. Death is the only thing that severs the marriage tie. Rom. 7.2 and Cor. 7.39.

W.J. Seymour.

21. QUESTIONS ANSWERED

(*AF,* October to January 1908, 2)

SHOULD A PERSON SEEK SANCTIFICATION BEFORE THE BAPTISM WITH THE HOLY GHOST?

Yes. Sanctification makes us holy, but the baptism with the Holy Spirit empowers us for service after we are sanctified, and seals us unto the day of redemption. Sanctification destroys the body of sin, the old man Adam. Rom. 6:6, 7, "Knowing this, that our old man is crucified with Him, that the body of sin might be destroyed, that henceforth we should not serve sin." When a man has been saved from actual sin, then he consecrates himself to God to be sanctified, and so his body of sin is destroyed or crucified. Then the resurrection life of Christ rises in this soul according to the Scriptures, Rom. 6:8, "Now if we be dead with Christ, we believe that we shall also live with Him."

IS IT NECESSARY FOR A PERSON TO LEAVE THEIR HOME DUTIES IN ORDER TO WAIT AT SOME PLACE FOR THE HOLY GHOST?

No; you can wait right in the kitchen or in the parlor or in the barn. Some have received the baptism of the Spirit in their barns, some in the kitchen, some at family worship, some on their porch, some about their business.

MUST PEOPLE GIVE UP THEIR PROPERTY AND HAVE ALL THINGS IN COMMON, IN ORDER TO RECEIVE THE PENTECOST?

No; God has made us stewards over all that we have, and He lays on our hearts to give as He prospers us. At the beginning of Pentecost, there was a great awakening in Jerusalem, and many people were waiting for salvation. Numbers of them were poor and had no home, and were in need of food and raiment. And God laid it on the hearts of as many as were possessors of lands or houses that they sold their possessions and brought the price and laid the money at the apostles' feet, to help supply food and to spread the World of God, that it might be preached over the world. But they did not do this in order to get salvation. God laid it on their hearts to do this for a special need. So those that were sent to preach the Gospel found favor with all the people and their needs were supplied, and they all were in one accord in the Spirit. But God does not mean that we should today, wherever the baptism is poured out, just sell our homes and come and wait for salvation, and expect to receive salvation simply because we have sold out our homes and our business and given up our talents. We can have positions that are decent and get salvation also, and can be called to a special business and can keep saved.

We read God's word in I. Thess. 4:11, "And that ye study to be quiet and to do your own business and work with our own hands as we commanded you: that ye may walk honestly toward them that are without, and that ye may have lack of nothing."

People that have large families have become so enthused over this wonderful salvation that they have sometimes sold out their homes, when God has not said so. We believe that people can have homes and still be in God's order. We bless God for everyone to whom He has given homes. We tell them not to run ahead of the Spirit in selling their homes, except God has really laid it on their hearts to do so. We have seen many that did so and regretted it afterwards.

WHAT IS THE REAL EVIDENCE THAT A MAN OR WOMAN HAS RECEIVED THE BAPTISM WITH THE HOLY GHOST?

Divine love, which is charity. Charity is the Spirit of Jesus. They will have the fruits of the Spirit. Gal. 5:22. "The fruit of the Spirit is love, joy, peace, longsuffering, gentleness, goodness, meekness, faith, temperance; against such there is no law. And they that are Christ's have crucified the flesh with the affections and lusts." This is the real Bible evidence in their daily walk and conversation; and the outward manifestations; speaking in tongues and the signs following: casting out devils, laying hands on the sick and the sick being healed, and the love of God for souls increasing in their hearts.

CAN A PERSON LOSE THE PENTECOSTT [*sic*] AND BE RESORED [*sic*]?

Yes; if they have not sinned willfully [*sic*]. A wilful [*sic*] sin means to deny the Blood of Jesus Christ and insult the Spirit of truth, which is the blessed Holy Ghost. Then there is no more remission of sin. But the person that has been snared by satan [*sic*] and will confess their sin and turn to God will find saving power in the Blood to cleanse them. There is a great difference between denying the Blood of Jesus Christ or doing despite the Spirit, and just simply falling into temptation and being overcome by satan [*sic*]. If they repent and do the first works, and consecrate to receive sanctification, and wait for the baptism, they can get it again.

DO YOU TEACH THAT IT IS WRONG TO TAKE MEDICINE?

Yes, for saints to take medicine. Medicine is for unbelievers, but the remedy for the saints of God we will find in Jas. 5:14, "Is any sick among you, let him call for the elders of the church, and let them pray over him, anointing him with oil in the name of the Lord, and the prayer of faith shall save the sick, and the Lord shall raise him up; and if he have committed sins, they shall be forgiven him."

DOES THE LORD JESUS PROVIDE HEALING FOR EVERYBODY?

Yes; for all those that have faith in Him. The sinner can receive healing.

DOES A SOUL NEED THE BAPTISM WITH THE HOLY GHOST IN ORDER TO LIVE A PURE AND HOLY LIFE?

No; sanctification makes us holy, Heb. 2:11, "For both He that sanctifieth and they who are sanctified are all of one, for which cause He is not ashamed to call them brethren." The Holy Ghost does not cleanse anyone from sin. It is Jusus' [Jesus'] shed Blood on Calvary. The Holy Ghost never died for our sins. It was Jesus who died for our sins and it is His Blood that atones for our sins. The Scripture says, I. John 1:9, "If we confess our sins, He is faithful and just to forgive us our sins and to cleanse us from all unrighteousness." And the 7th verse says, "If we walk in the light as He is in the light, we have fellowship one with another, and the blood of Jesus Christ His Son cleanseth us from all sin." It is the Blood that cleanses and makes holy, and through the Blood we receive the baptism of the Holy Spirit. The Holy Ghost always falls in answer to the Blood.

DO WE NEED TO STUDY THE BIBLE AS MUCH AFTER RECEIVING THE HOLY GHOST?

Yes; if not we become fanatical or many times will be led by deceptive spirits and begin to have revelations and dreams contrary to the word, and begin to prophesy and think ourselves some great one, bigger than some other Christians. But by reading the Bible prayerfully, waiting before God, we become just little humble children, and we never feel that we have got more than the least of God's children.

IS IT NECESSARY TO HAVE HANDS LAID ON IN ORDER TO RECEIVE THE HOLY GHOST?

No; you can receive Him in your private closet. The gift of the Holy Ghost comes by faith in the word of God. You may receive the Holy Ghost right now, that is if you are sanctified. Take your Bible, turn to the first chapter of Acts, 5th verse, "For John truly baptized with water, but ye shall be baptized with the Holy Ghost not many days hence." Just read this verse of Scripture and cry out to the Father, "Lord Jesus, baptize me with the Holy Ghost," and believe the Lord with all your heart and the power will fall.

The baptism of the Spirit is a gift of power on the sanctified life, and when people receive it, sooner or later they will speak in tongues as the Spirit gives utterance. A person may not speak in tongues for a week after the baptism, but as soon as he gets to praying or praising God in the liberty of the Spirit, the tongues will follow. Tongues are not salvation. It is a gift that God throws in with the baptism with the Holy Spirit. People do not have to travail and agonize for the baptism, for when our work ceases, then God comes. We cease from our own works, which is the very type of the millennium.

IS THE SPEAKING IN TONGUES THE STANDARD OF FELLOWSHIP WITH THE PENTECOST PEOPLE?

No; our fellowship does not come through gifts and outward demonstrations but through the Blood by the Spirit of Christ. There is nothing more loving than the Blood of Jesus Christ in our hearts. The Lord Jesus says, "If we walk in the light as He is in the light, we have fellowship one with another, and the Blood of Jesus Christ, His Son, cleanseth us from all sin." If a man is saved and living according to the word of God, he is our brother, if he has not got the baptism with the Holy Spirit with tongues.

HOW ARE WE TO KEEP THE ANOINTING OF THE SPIRIT AFTER RECEIVING THE PENTECOST?

By living in the word of God with perfect obedience.

IN MEETINGS, SHOULD A NUMBER SPEAK IN TONGUES AT THE SAME TIME?

No; except as God sends a wave of the Spirit over the saints. Sometimes the Spirit will come as a shower or a rushing wind and everybody may speak that has the power. But it is not in order or Bible regulation for all to speak in tongues at once. I. Cor. 14: 23, 24. Yet sometimes God works in ways that we do not just understand. But for the edification of all, there comes a time when we have to get back to the 14th chapter for First Corinthians from the 26th to the 40th verses. Paul says, "Let all things be done decently and in order."

IS THIS MOVEMENT A NEW SECT OR DENOMINATION?

No; it is undenominational and unsectarian. We believe in unity with Christ's people everywhere, in the Word of God. It is the old-time apostolic assembly, the same old teaching of 1900 years ago. It is new to the world in these last days, but its teaching and doctrine is old as the New Testament.

DOES ANY MAN CONTROL THE MISSIONS OF THE APOSTOLIC FAITH?

No; every mission will have its own elders and teachers as the Holy Ghost shall appoint and teach the pure word of God. Every mission will be in harmony and work in unity. The Lord has deacons, elders, and teachers for the perfecting of the ministry in His saints, until we all become a perfect man in Christ Jesus.

WHAT IS THE BIBLE WAY FOR A PREACHER TO GET SUPPORT AND TO RAISE THE EXPENSES OF THE CHURCH?

To pray to the Lord God and by free will offerings and donations, as God lays it on the hearts of the people that he is laboring with. God will graciously supply all needs, if you simply will trust Him and look to Him. He will pay off expenses.

DO YOU TEACH THAT DIVINE LOVE IN THE HEART WOULD MAKE ANY FAMILIARITY BETWEEN MEN AND WOMEN SAFE AND RIGHT?

No, every precious child that is getting the baptism of the Holy Spirit should be watchful and avoid all appearance of evil. Satan is transformed as an angel of light to deceive many precious souls that receive great spiritual blessing; and not understanding the cunning devices of the enemy, people have been led by satan into freeloveism. Some have taught that a baptism of love would make you so holy that you could overstep [t]he [*sic*] bounds of propriety. May God help us to keep free from anything that is impure. If a person happens to get under the influence of these powers, they must denounce their doctrine and get these spirits cast off from them and get under the Blood. The doctrine of freeloveism is satan's counterfeit of genuine salvation through the Blood of Jesus.

ON WHAT GROUNDS DID THE LORD JESUS TEACH THAT A MAN AND WIFE COULD SEPARATE?

On the ground of fornication. These are the words of Jesus, "It hath been said, whosoever shall put away his wife, let him give her a writing of divorcement; but I say unto you that whosoever shall put away his wife, saving for the cause of fornication, causeth her to commit adultery; and whosoever shall marry her that is divorced committeth adultery."—Matt. 5.31, 32. Notice He says, "It hath been said, let him give her a writing of divorcement." This used to be the teaching before the great Teacher came, but in Christ's church there is no divorcement. Now a man has a right by Scripture to put way his wife for fornication, but he has no right to marry another, according to the Scripture, while she lives. "For the woman which hath a husband is bound by the law to her husband, so long as he liveth; but if her husband be dead, she is loosed from the law of her husband; so then if while her husband liveth, she be married to another man, she shall be called an adulteress."—Rom. 7:2, 3.

If a man puts away his wife, except for fornication, he exposes her to get another husband and send her soul to hell, so it will pay every man and every woman to live with their companion for the salvation of their soul, except for the cause of fornication. He has a right to put away but not a right to get another again.

DO YOU HAVE PREACHERS AND EVANGELISTS OF THE APOSTOLIC FAITH THAT HAVE TWO WIVES OR TWO HUSBANDS?

No, we did allow it before we became settled down and searched the Scriptures and compared scripture with scripture. We allowed those that were divorced and remarried to preach the Gospel, thinking that everything was under the Blood, and if they did not have more light it did not condemn them. But after searching the Scriptures, we found it was wrong; that the widow was to be the wife of one man and the bishop was to be the husband of one wife. We found no scripture where the preacher could be engaged in this blessed Gospel ministry with two living companions.

IF PEOPLE NEVER HAD LIGHT ON THE DIVORCE QUESTION AND HAVE THE SECOND COMPANION, HOW SHALL THEY REGULATE THEIR LIVES IN HARMONY WITH THE SCRIPTURES?

"If any man come to Me, and hate not his father and mother and his wife and children and brethren and sisters, yes, and his own life also, he cannot be My disciple."—Luke 14:26. That does not mean to desert a lawful wife, but it means to let nothing stand between you and Christ. "And whosoever doth not bear his cross and come after Me, cannot be My disciple."—Luke 15: 27. "And if thy right eye offend thee, pluck it out and cast it from thee; for it is profitable for thee that one of thy members should perish, and not that thy whole body should be cast into hell. It hath been said, whosoever shall put away his wife, let him give her a writing of divorcement, but I say unto you, that whosoever shall put away his wife, saving for the cause of fornication, causeth her to commit adultery; and whosoever marrieth her that is divorced, committeth adultery."—Matt. 5: 29, 32.

CAN A CHILD OF GOD BE POSSESSED BY EVIL SPIRITS?

No; evil spirits cannot come under the Blood, any more than the Egyptians could pass through the Red Sea—the Red Sea represents the blood of Jesus Christ. The Blood gives you power over all the power of the enemy. But we must have Christ within us. If the soul is left empty and no "strong man" within, then the evil spirit can just take the house. (Luke 11:21–26.) Some say that when the soul is sanctified the house is empty and clean, and if he does not get the Holy Ghost, a wicked spirit can come in. Don't you ever believe that. That empty house represents a man that had a demon cast out (as we see plainly in the 24th verse); and he did not get Christ within. But a man that is sanctified, has Christ ruling within. People that are living under the Blood live free from demons and satanic powers. They live pure and holy before the Lord. A man might be a Christian and oppressed by a demon, but that is altogether different from being possessed. Wicked spirits are driven out and repentance and faith wrought in the heart, when a man is justified. Then Christ comes in and keeps them out. A demon might be in the flesh as in the case of a cancer. The devil may oppress the body with sickness but that is very different from possessing the soul.

22. CHRIST'S MESSAGES TO THE CHURCH

(*AF,* October–January 1908, 3)

The last message given to the church was by the Holy Ghost, from our Lord and Savior Jesus Christ through Brother John on the Isle of Patmos. Dear beloved, we read in Revelations 1:5–7, these words, "Unto Him that loved us and washed us from our sins in His own Blood." Hallelujah to His name. "And hath made us kings and priest unto God and the Father: to Him be glory and dominion for ever and ever. Amen. Behold He cometh with clouds; and every eye shall see Him, and they also which pierced Him; and all kindreds of the earth shall wail because of Him. Even so, Amen."

This is the beginning of this wonderful and blessed message given to our beloved Apostle John while he was suffering for the word of God and for the testimony of Jesus Christ. Jesus knew all about His servant, though He had been living in Heaven more than half a century after His ascension. And He came and visited that beloved apostle, the disciple who loved Jesus and leaned on His bosom. He now was old but had been faithful to the trust that Jesus had given him. He had passed through awful trials and tribulations for this precious Gospel, even being boiled in a caldron of oil, tradition tells us; but, blessed be God, they were not able to kill him. And when they got tired of this precious Holy Ghost Gospel messenger, preaching to them the faith of Jesus, they banished him to the Isle of Patmos. And while he was in the Spirit on the Lord's day, our blessed Jesus Christ, the Son of the living God, our great Redeemer, came and gave him this wonderful revelation, and introduced Himself to John as, "I am Alpha and Omega, the beginning and the ending, said the Lord, which is, and which was, and which is to come, the Almighty." Hallelujah.

O beloved, the Lord Jesus knows all about our trials and tribulations, because He was a man of sorrows and acquainted with grief. His whole life was a life of suffering. We read in Heb. 5:7, 8, "Though He were a son, yet learned He obedience by the things which He suffered. And being made perfect, He became the author of eternal salvation unto all them that obey." O bless our God. Just to think that Jesus was God's Son, and all things were made by Him and for Him; yet He was foreordained before the foundation of the world that He should die. He was slain before the foundation of the world. So the Word of God became flesh and dwelt among men and was handled by men, and lived in this world. And at the age of 33 years, He paid the debt on Calvary's cross. O beloved, if we expect to reign with Him, we must suffer with Him—not that people must be sick or unhealthy or go with a long face, but we must bear all things and keep the faith of Jusus [sic] in our hearts. Our lives now are with the suffering Christ; and "it doth not yet appear what we shall be, but we know that when He shall appear, we shall be like Him: for we shall see Him as He is." Glory to Jesus.

After Jesus introduced Himself, He gave John these blessed messages to the church. John was permitted to see from the beginning of the church age on down to the white throne judgment, the final winding up of the world. He was permitted to see the overcomers. He was permitted to see the millennial reign with Jesus in triumph over the kingdoms of satan; to see this old world pass away, to see the new heavens and new earth, and the New Jerusalem coming down from God out of Heaven. John saw things past, things present, and things in the future. He had witnessed the glory and power of the apostolic church, and saw the falling away of the church, and God sent him to the church with this blessed message: that she should come back to her first love.

THE VISION OF JESUS IN HIS CHURCH

The most striking passage of Scripture in the first chapter is where John was permitted to see Jesus walking among the golden candlesticks, which represent the church. Christ is in His church today to fill men and women, to heal their bodies, save and sanctify their souls, and to put His finger upon every wrong and mean thing in the church. His rebuke is against it, for He hates sin today as much as He ever did when He walked by the sea of Gallilee [sic]. Glory to His name. Jesus hates impure doctrine just as much as when He rebuked the Pharisees for their impure doctrine.

John beheld Jesus in His glorified body. What a holy scene it was: the Son of God clothed with a garment down to the foot and girt about the paps with a gold girdle. "His head and His hairs were white like wool, as white as snow." Hallelujah. There is nothing but purity and holiness in our Saviour. And "His eyes were as a flame of fire." Glory to Jesus. "And His feet like the fine brass, as if they burned in a furnace. And His voice as the sound of many waters," which represents many people. Bless God.

"And He had in His right hand seven stars." This represents His Holy Ghost ministers. Jesus has them in His hand, that is to say that He gave them the authority to preach the Gospel and power over devils. All of our authority and power comes from Jesus. It is so sweet when we know that we have authority from Jesus. Bless His holy name. O beloved, when we know Jesus Christ has His minister in His hand, we know that minister is a live preacher. Glory to Jesus. Hallelujah. A live minister represents one that is saved, sanctified and filled with the Holy Spirit. Then the same life, the same authority that Jesus promised we will find in his life.

"And out of His mouth went a sharp two-edged sword, and His countenance was as the sun shineth in his strength," the glory of God shining through the blessed Christ. "And when I saw Him, I fell at His feet as one dead. And He laid His right hand upon me, saying unto me, Fear not; I am the first and the last." Praise God, Jesus is alive and because He lives everyone that gets Christ is alive in the blessed Holy Spirit. The Blood of Jesus Christ does give life, power and fire, joy, peace, happiness and faith. Hallelujah to His name.

"I am He that liveth and was dead, and behold, I am alive for evermore." Bless His holy name. He wanted John to know that He was the same One that hung and bled and died and shed His precious Blood on Calvary's cross, went down into the grave, and rose again. This ought to make the whole of Christ's people everywhere happy to know that Jesus is alive for evermore. Hallelujah to His name.

Then He said, "And have the keys of hell and of death." Bless God. No wonder Bro. David said, "Though I walk through the valley of the shadow of death, I will fear no evil, for Thou are with me." When we get Jesus Christ in our hearts, we can use the word and it is a comfort to us to know that we have passed from death to life.

Then He told John particularly, "Write these things which thou hast seen, and the things which are, and the things which shall be hereafter."

THE MESSAGE TO THE CHURCH OF EPHASUS [sic]

Then He gave him the messages to the seven churches. "And to the angel of the church at Ephesus write, "These things saith He that holdeth the seven stars in His right hand, who walketh in the midst of the seven golden candlesticks." Hallelujah to His name. Ephesus was a city of Asia, quite a commercial city, a city of wealth, refinement, culture and great learning. It was where John preached and where Paul had labored. Many people there had been saved and baptized with the Spirit. Paul had witnessed a great scene in Ephesus where he had preached the Gospel of the Son of God and of the doctrine of the baptism with the Holy Spirit, and 12 men after hearing of this blessed doctrine, received water baptism, and when Paul laid his hands on them, they received the baptism with the Holy Ghost and spake with tongues and prophesied. Acts. 19:6. So Ephesus was a favored place, but the message was sent to it and to all the churches of Asia. This is a true picture of the Lord Jesus' eyes upon the church ever since its beginning, and will be unto the end. We are living near the close of the Gentile age down in the Laodicean period, when the church has become as formal as the Laodiceans. This message was first to the church at Ephesus.

I KNOW THY WORKS

The Lord Jesus said, "I know thy works." God knows our works, He knows our hearts. "And thy labor and thy patience, and how thou canst not bear them which are evil; and thou has tired them which say they are apostles, and are not, and hast found them liars; and hast borne and hast patience, and for My name's sake hast labored and hast not fainted." Bless our God. That is more than many churches today could receive from the Master. Jesus commended them for what they had done. He commended them for their faithfulness. He is not like men. He knows our hearts, our trials, our conditions. But Bless God, He does not make any allowance for sin. He hates sin today as much as He ever did. Yet He does not come to destroy us or condemn us, but to seek and to save us.

"Nevertheless I have somewhat against thee, because thou hast left thy first love." The Lord does not want anything to get between us and Him. O may every precious child in these times that are getting the Holy Spirit not go into apostasy, but may they be a burning and a shining light for God, just as we were when we first received the baptism with the Holy Spirit. God wants us to keep the same anointing that we received and let nothing separate us from Christ.

REPENTANCE

We find Jesus still preaches the same doctrine of repentance that He preached while on earth. In order to get right with God, He says, "Remember from whence thou art fallen and repent and do the first works, or else I will come unto the thee quickly, and will remove thy candlestick out of his place, except thou repent." Dear beloved, if there is anything wrong in your life and Jesus has His finger upon it, O may you give it up, for Jesus is truly in His Church today. This is the Holy Ghost dispensation and He does convince men of sin, righteousness and the judgment, and if we will be honest, God will bless us.

TO THE CHURCH TODAY

When a church or mission finds that the power of God begins to leave, they should come as a whole and confess, and let all get down before God and repent and pray to God until the old time fire and power and love come back again. Many times the Holy Spirit will leave an assembly, mission or church because the pastor grieves Him, and sometimes not only the pastor but the whole body commences backbiting, whispering, tattling, or prejudice and partiality creep in, until the whole becomes corrupted and Jesus is just ready to spew them out of His mouth. But, O beloved, let us then come to the 2nd chapter of Revelation and see what Jesus says to the assembly. He expects to find the church, when He comes back to earth again, just as full of fire and power and the signs following, as it was when He organized it on the day of Pentecost. Bless His holy name. May God help all His precious praying children to get back to the old Pentecostal power and fire and love. The church at that time was as terrible as an army with banners. She conquered every evil. Hypocrites were not able to remain in it any more than Annanias and Sapphira. God gave such wonderful love to His people.

Then He gave messages to every church, showing that Jesus' eyes are upon every church. His finger this day is upon every heart that does not measure to the fulness of holiness. God wants a holy church and all wrong cleansed away—fornication and adultery, two wives, two husbands, not paying grocery bills, water bills, furniture bills, coal bills, gas bills, and all honest bills. God wants His people to be true and holy and He will work. Nothing can hinder. Bless His holy name.

I thank God for this wonderful message to the church, a message from heaven, given by Jesus to show that He is in the church, that He does walk among the golden candlesticks. He is in heaven, but through the power of the Holy Spirit, He walks in the church today. Nothing can be hidden from His pure eyes. He wants people to live the highest and deepest consecration to Him. He does not want their love for him divided. Their first love is to Him.

IMPURE DOCTRINE

We find many of Christ's people tangled up in these days, commiting [sic] spiritual fornication as well as physical fornication and adultery. They say, "Let us all come together; if we are not one in doctrine, we can be one in spirit." But, dear ones, we cannot all be one, except through the word of God. He says, "But this thou hast that thou hatest the deeds of the Nicolaitanes [sic], which I also hate." I suppose that the apostolic church at Ephesus allowed people that were not teaching straight doctrine, not solid in the word of God, to remain in fellowship with them; and Jesus saw that a little leaven would leaven the whole, and His finger was right upon that impure doctrine. It had to be removed out of the church or He would remove the light and break the church up. When we find things wrong, contrary to Scripture, I care not how dear it is, it must be removed. We cannot bring Agag among the children of Israel, for God says he must die. Saul saved Agag, which represented saving himself, the carnal nature or old man; but Samuel said Agag must die, and he drew his sword and slew him. Christ's precious word, which is the sword of Samuel, puts all carnality and sin to death. It means perfect abedience [sic] to walk with the Lord. There are many people in these last days that are not going to live a Bible salvation, they are going to take chances. But may God help everyone, if their right hand or right eye offend them to cast it from them. It is better to enter into life maimed, than for soul and body to be cast into hell fire.

The Lord says, "He that hath an ear, let him hear what the Spirit saith unto the churches; To him that overcometh will I give to eat of the tree of life which is in the midst of the paradise of God." O beloved, if we expect to reign with the Lord and Saviour Jesus Christ, we must overcome the world, the flesh, and the devil. There will be many that will be saved but will not be full overcomers to reign on this earth with our Lord. He will give us power to overcome if we are willing. Bless His holy name.

W.J. Seymour.

23. PORTSMOUTH AND RICHMOND, VA.

(*AF,* January 1908, 1)

PORTSMOUTH AND RICHMOND, VA.

—Brother Seymour wrote from these places while he was visiting the missions in the East: "God is working in Portsmouth. Souls were baptized in Richmond and God is working in mighty power. The saints are just as sweet as can be. Glory to God for this Gospel. The saints are so simple here, that is the reasons they receive the Pentecost so quickly. They are ready for the power."

24. "TO THE MARRIED."

I Cor. 7.

(*AF,* January 1908, 3)

In these days, so many deceptive spirits are in the world, that we have felt impressed by the blessed Holy Spirit to write a letter on the seventh chapter of First Corinthians, that blessed letter which Paul has sent to the church.

The Corinthian church was one of Paul's most gifted churches, and just as it is today, where a church is very gifted, the only safeguard from deceptive spirits is by rightly dividing the Word of God, to keep out fanaticism. We may let down on some lines and rise on others, but God wants everything to be balanced by the Word of God. Paul writing to Timothy (II Tim. 1: 13, 14) says, "Hold fast the from of sound words which thou has heard of me in faith and love which is in Christ Jesus. That good thing which was committed unto thee keep by the Holy Ghost which dwelleth in us." And again he says (II Tim. 3:14): "But continue thou in the things which thou hast learned and hast been assured of, knowing of whom thou hast learned them; and that from a child thou hast known the holy Scriptures, which are able to make thee wise unto salvation through faith which is in Christ Jesus. All Scripture is given by inspiration of God, and is profitable for doctrine, for reproof, for correction, for instruction in righteousness: that the man of God may be perfect, thoroughly furnished unto all good works." So the Lord God wants us to search and compare scriptures with scriptures.

This Corinthian church had run into freelovism, and a good many isms. Great division had arisen in it; it had split into several parts, and Paul had to settle them down into the Word of God. He writes this letter to them, for they had got into awful trouble.

Paul tells them in the first verse of this chapter to avoid immorality. He says, "Now concerning the things whereof ye wrote unto me, it is good for a man not to touch a woman. (He does not mean a married man here, he means a man that is single, as verses 8 and 26 show.) He says in the 7th verse, "Every man hath his proper gift of God." And to those that can receive this gift, Paul writes in verse 8, "I say therefore to the unmarried and widows, It is good for them if they abide even as I." That is to say, by living a single life, they would have more power in the Spirit. He writes this to the church, to any who are saved, sanctified and filled with the Holy Spirit. Paul thought it was best, but he showed that everyone had his proper gift of God. So he did not put any bondage upon the people of Christ, because he had no scripture for it.

He says in the second and third verses, "Nevertheless to avoid fornication, let every man have his own wife, and let every woman have her own husband. Let the husband render unto the wife due benevolence: and likewise also the wife unto the husband." This of course means conjugal intercourse between man and wife. "The wife hath not power of her own body, but the husband: and likewise also the husband hath not power of his own body, but the wife." That is to say, that the husband has no authority to live separated, without the consent of his wife; and the wife has no authority of herself to live separated without the husband. Then he says in the 5th verse, "Defraud ye not one another, except it be with consent for a time, that ye may give yourselves to fasting and prayer; and come together again, that satan tempt you not for your incontinency [sic]." That is to say that every wife and husband should abstain from impurity, and give themselves to fasting for a time. It should be by mutual agreement between the two to fast for power and blessing, and many times to avoid impurity. But he advised them to come again, "that satan tempt you not for your incontinency [sic]." Paul here does not make this a law, but as one that had the Holy Spirit, he gives them this advice. He adds in the 6th verse, "But I speak this by permission and not of commandment." In Romans 1:26, 27, Paul shows there is a natural use for a wife, which is not lust. Speaking of the ungodly, he says, "For this cause God gave them up unto vile affections: for even their women did change the natural use into that which is against nature." May God help us to be clear teachers of His Word.

"I would that all men were even as I myself. But every man hath his proper gift of God, one after this manner and another after that." Paul is referring here to Matthew 19:12, where Jesus told the Pharisees that there were some men that were born eunuchs from their mother's womb (that is to say, unable to have wives), some have been made eunuchs of men (for other advantages in life) and there were some eunuchs for the kingdom of Heaven's sake. Men had prayed to God for this gift or blessing, just as Paul who said he wished all men were like him: he became no doubt a eunuch for the kingdom of Heaven's sake. Jesus Himself said (Matt. 19:11), "All men cannot receive this saying, save they to whom it is given." So Jesus did not put any bondage on men and women, but a man today that has received the power to become a eunuch for the kingdom of Heaven's sake can live a single life with all holiness and purity. Praise our God!

We must rightly divide the Scriptures and compare scripture with scripture so that there be no confusion and no deceptive spirit or wrong teaching may creep in.

Paul says in verses 29 to 31, "But this I say brethren, the time is short: it remaineth that both they that have wives be as though they had none; and they that weep as though they wept not; and they that rejoice as though they rejoiced not; and they that buy as though they possessed not; and they that use the world as not abusing it: for the fashion of this world passeth away." Bless the Lord! Now Paul in speaking this, did not put any bondage on mothers to fear that they would not be able to meet Jesus in His coming, because they were bringing forth children. Mothers and fathers that are saved and sanctified, to whom the Lord has given this gift of bringing forth children can live a pure and holy life before God and be of the bride of Christ, just as the bishop that teaches this holy Gospel can be the husband of one wife and raise his children in the fear of God.

Married couples who are mutually agreed, having received from the Lord power over both body, soul and spirit, God does not ask them to desire; but may they live as God has called them. Many times God gives this power to the husband before to the wife. Many times the wife has it; but in order to save the husband she has to submit to the husband. For God is not the author of confusion. This brings us back to the third verse of this same chapter. Also in Ephesians 5th chapter and 22nd verse we read, "Wives, submit yourselves unto your husbands, as unto the Lord." Please read on down to the 33d [sic] verse. God does not make the husband the tyrant or cruel sovereign over the wife, neither does He make the wife to exercise tyranny over the husband, but He makes both one. God knows our hearts and our lives.

Someone may ask what Jesus meant in Matt. 24:19, "And woe unto them that are with child, and to them that give suck in those days." Well, beloved, here Jesus' heart was upon the people that would suffer in the awful tribulation that was coming to Jerusalem forty years after His ascension. He says to them, "But pray ye that your flight be not in the winter, neither on the Sabbath day." Jesus was the Son of God but He was a man of prayer. He asked His disciples to pray with Him in the Garden of Gethsemane. He knew that in the destruction of Jerusalem, if they prayed to God, the Father would not permit it to come to pass in the winter, neither on the Sabbath day. He knew if it was on the Sabbath day, the Jews would be keeping the old Mosaic law (Col 2: 16) "Of new moons and of Sabbath days, which were a shadow of things to come, but the body of Christ." (The greatest thing that people need in this day is Christ, and then all the days will come in their order and in their place.) Jesus knew if their flight occurred on the Sabbath day, all the gates of Jerusalem would be shut and the Christians could not get out, and the mothers could not escape; so His heart went out for the precious women. The Lord Jesus Christ knows all about our struggles. He knows all about our sufferings and our trials. He is touched with every infirmity and He remembers us. Bless His holy name.

May God help everyone that is getting saved to stay within the lids of God's word and wait on God, and He will make all things right. Now we can give up anything that we see is really of self gratification. The Lord wants us to be temperate in all things. Bless His holy name. People that are desiring to get the victory over spirit, soul and body, can have it if they will trust God.

I have been asked so much on this question, and I can only give what God has revealed to me through His precious Word. Bless His holy name!

W.J.S.

25. SANCTIFIED ON THE CROSS

(*AF*, May 1908, 2)

"I pray not that Thou shouldst take them out of the world, but that Thou shouldst keep them from the evil. They are not of the world even as I am not of the world. Sanctify them through Thy truth, Thy word is truth." Jesus is still praying this prayer today for every believer to come and be sanctified. Glory to God! Sanctification makes us one with the Lord Jesus. (Heb. 2:11.) Sanctification makes us holy as Jesus is. Then the prayer of Jesus is answered, and we become one with Him, even as He is one with the Father. Bless His holy name.

He says again in I Thess. 4:3, "For this is the will of God even your sanctification." So it is His will for every soul to be saved from all sin, actual and original. We get our actual sins cleansed away through the Blood of Jesus Christ at the cross; but our original sin we get cleansed on the cross. It must be a real death to the old man. Rom. 6:6, "Knowing this that our old man is crucified with Him, that the body of sin might be destroyed, that henceforth we should not serve sin: for he that is dead is freed from sin." So it takes the death of the old man in order that Christ might be sanctified in us. It is not sufficient to have the old man stunned or knocked down, for he will rise again.

God is calling His people to true holiness in these days. We thank God for the blessed light that He is giving us. He says in II Tim. 2:21: "If a man therefore purge himself from these, he shall be a vessel unto honor, sanctified and meet for the Master's use." He means for us to be purged from uncleanness and all kinds of sin. Then we shall be a vessel unto honor, sanctified and meet for the Master's use, and prepared unto every good work. Sanctification makes us holy and destroys the breed of sin, the love of sin and carnality. It makes us pure and whiter than snow. Bless His holy name!

The Lord Jesus says, "Blessed are the pure in heart." Sanctification makes us pure in heart. Any man that is saved and sanctified can feel the fire burning in his heart, when he calls on the name of Jesus. O may God help men and women everywhere to lead a holy life, free from sin, for the Holy Spirit seeks to lead you out of sin into the marvelous light of the Son of God.

The Word says, "Follow peace with all men and holiness without which no man shall see the Lord." So, beloved, when we get Jesus Christ our King of Peace in our hearts, we have the almighty Christ, the everlasting Father, the Prince of Peace. "Thou wilt keep him in perfect peace whose mind is stayed on Thee, because He trusteth in Thee." We shall have wisdom, righteousness and power, for God is righteous in all His ways and holy in all His acts. This holiness means perfect love in our hearts, perfect love that casteth out fear.

Brother Paul says in order to become holy and live a holy life, we should abstain from all appearance of evil. Then the apostle adds, "And the very God of peace sanctify you wholly, and I pray God your whole spirit and soul and body be preserved blameless unto the coming of our Lord Jesus Christ." (I Thess. 5:22, 23.) "To the end He may establish your hearts unblameable in holiness before God, even our Father, at the coming of our Lord Jesus Christ with all His saints." (I Thess. 3:13.) Bless His holy name. O beloved, after you have received the light, it is holiness or hell. God is calling for men and women in these days that will live a holy life free from sin. We should remain before God until His all-cleansing Blood makes us holy, body, soul, and spirit.

W.J.S.

26. THE BAPTISM OF THE HOLY GHOST

(*AF,* May 1908, 3)

The Azusa standard of the baptism with the Holy Ghost is according to the Bible in Acts 1:5, 8; Acts 2:4 and Luke 24:49. Bless His holy name. Hallelujah to the Lamb for the baptism of the Holy Ghost and fire and speaking in tongues as the Spirit gives utterance.

Jesus gave the church at Pentecost the great lesson of how to carry on a revival, and it would be well for every church to follow Jesus' standard of the baptism of the Holy Ghost and fire.

"And when the day of Pentecost was fully come, they were all with one accord in one place." O beloved, there is where the secret is: **one accord, one place, one heart, one soul, one mind, one prayer**. If God can get a people anywhere in one accord and in one place, of one heart, mind, and soul, believing for this great power, it will fall and Pentecostal results will follow. Glory to God!

Apostolic Faith doctrine means one accord, one soul, one heart. May God help every child of His to live in Jesus' prayer: "That they all may be one, as Thou, Father, art in Me and I in Thee; that they all may be one in us; that the world may believe that Thou hast sent Me." Praise God! O how my heart cries out to God in these days that He would make every child of His see the necessity of living in the 17th chapter of John, that we may be one in the body of Christ, as Jesus has prayed.

When we are sanctified through the truth, then we are one in Christ, and we can get into one accord for the gift or power of the Holy Ghost, and God will come in like a rushing mighty wind and fill every heart with the power of the Holy Spirit. Glory to His holy name. Bless God! O how I praise Him for this wonderful salvation that is spreading over this great earth. The baptism of the Holy Ghost brings the glory of God to our hearts.

THE HOLY GHOST IS POWER

There is a great difference between a sanctified person and one that is baptized with the Holy Ghost and fire. A sanctified person is cleansed and filled with divine love, but the one that is baptized with the Holy Ghost has the power of God on his soul and has power with God and men, power over all the kingdoms of Satan and over all his emissaries. God can take a worm and thresh a mountain. Glory to God. Hallelujah!

In all Jesus' great revivals and miracles, the work was wrought by the power of the Holy Ghost flowing through His sanctified humanity. When the Holy Ghost comes and takes us as His instruments, this is the power that convicts men and women and in serving Jesus Christ. O beloved, we ought to thank God that He has made us the tabernacles of the Holy Ghost. When you have the Holy Ghost, you have an empire, a power within yourself. Elijah was a power in himself through the Holy Ghost. He brought down fire from heaven. So when we get the power of the Holy Ghost, we will see the heavens open and the Holy Ghost power falling on earth, power over sickness, diseases and death.

The Lord never revoked the commission He gave to His disciples: "Heal the sick, cleanse the lepers, raise the dead," and He is going to perform these things if He can get a people in unity. The Holy Spirit is power with God and man. You have power with God as Elijah had. God put man over all His works; but we know that when Adam sinned, he lost a great deal of his power; but now through the Blood of Jesus, He says, "Behold, I give you power to tread on serpents and scorpions, and over all the powers of the enemy." The Lord Jesus wants a church, when He comes back to earth, just like the one He started when He left the earth and organized it on the day of Pentecost.

TARRY IN ONE ACCORD

O may every child of God seek his real personal Pentecost, stop quibbling and come to the standard that Jesus laid down for us in Acts 2: "And suddenly there came a sound from heaven as of a rushing mighty wind, and it filled all the house where they were sitting." Glory to God! O beloved, if you wait on God for this baptism of the Holy Ghost just now, and can get two or three people together that are sanctified through the Blood of Christ, and all get into one accord, God will send the baptism of the Holy Ghost upon your souls as the rain falls from heaven. You may not have a preacher to come to you and preach the doctrine of the Holy Ghost and fire, but you can obey Jesus' saying in the passage, "Where two or three are gathered together in My name, there am I in the midst of them." This is Jesus' baptism; and if two or three are gathered together in His name and pray for the baptism of the Holy Ghost, they can have it this day or this night, because it is the promise of the Father. Glory to God!

This was the Spirit that filled the house as a rushing mighty wind. The Holy Ghost is typified by wind, air, breath, life, fire. "And there appeared unto them cloven tongues like as of fire, and it sat upon each of them; and they were all filled with the Holy Ghost and began to speak with other tongues as the Spirit gave them utterance." So, beloved, when you get your personal Pentecost, the signs will follow in speaking with tongues as the Spirit gives utterance. This is true. Wait on God and you will find it a truth in your own life. God's promises are true and sure.

THE BAPTISM FALLS ON A CLEAN HEART

Jesus is our example. "And Jesus being full of the Holy Ghost, returned from Jordan, and was led by the Spirit." We find in reading the Bible that the baptism with the Holy Ghost and fire falls on a clean, sanctified life, for we see according to the Scriptures that Jesus was "holy, harmless, undefiled," and filled with wisdom and favor with God and man, before God anointed Him with the Holy Ghost and power. For in Luke 2:40, we read, "Jesus waxed strong in spirit, filled with wisdom, and the grace of God was upon Him"; and in Luke, 2:52, "And Jesus increased in wisdom and stature, and in favor with God and man."

After Jesus was empowered with the Holy Ghost at Jordan. He returned in the power of the Spirit into Gallilee [*sic*], and there went out a fame of Him through all the region round about." Glory to God! He was not any more holy or any more meak [*sic*], but had greater authority. "And He taught in their synagogues, being glorified of all."

Beloved, if Jesus who was God Himself, needed the Holy Ghost to empower Him for His ministry and His miracles, how much more do we children need the Holy Ghost baptism today. O that men and women would tarry for the baptism with the Holy Ghost and fire upon their souls, that the glory may be seen upon them just as it was upon the disciples on the day of Pentecost in the fiery emblem of tongues. The tongues of fire represented the great Shekina glory. So today the Shekina glory rests day and night upon those who are baptized with the Holy Ghost, while He abides in their souls. For His presence is with us. Glory to His name. I thank Him for this wonderful salvation. Let us ring His praises through all the world that all men may know that the Comforter has come. Bless His dear name!

JESUS' FIRST SERMON AFTER HIS BAPTISM

"And He came to Nazareth where He was brought up; and as His custom was, He went into the synagogue on the Sabbath day and stood up for to read. And there was delivered unto Him the book of the prophet Esaias. And when He had opened the book, He found the place where it is written: The Spirit of the Lord is upon Me because He hath anointed Me to preach the Gospel to the poor; He hath sent me to heal the broken-hearted, to preach deliverence [sic] to the captives, and recovering of sight to the blind, to set at liberty them that are bruised, to preach the acceptable year of the Lord." (Luke 4:18, 19). Hallelujah. Glory to God! This is Jesus' sermon after His baptism with the Holy Ghost, preaching in the synagogue. He acknowledged that the Spirit of God was upon Him.

Jesus was the Son of God and born of the Holy Ghost and filled with the Holy Ghost from His mother's womb; but the baptism with the Holy Ghost came upon His sanctified humanity at the Jordan. In His humanity. [sic] He needed the Third Person of the Trinity to do His work. And He could truly say that His fingers became instruments of the Holy Ghost to cast out devils.

THE HOLY GHOST FLOWS THROUGH PURE CHANNELS

If men and women today will consecrate themselves to God, and get their hands and feet and eyes and affections, body and soul, all sanctified, how the Holy Ghost will use such people. He will find pure channels to flow through, sanctified avenues for His power. People will be saved, sanctified, healed and baptized with the Holy Ghost and fire.

The baptism of the Holy Ghost comes through our Lord and Savior Jesus Christ by faith in His word. In order to receive it, we must first be sanctified. Then we can become His witnesses unto the uttermost parts of the earth. You will never have an experience to measure with Acts 2:4 and 16, 17, until you get your personal Pentecost or the baptism with the Holy Ghost and fire. (Matt. 3:11.)

This is the latter rain that God is pouring out upon His humble children in the last days. We are preaching a Gospel that measures with the great commission that Jesus gave His disciples on the day when He arose from the dead. (Matt. 28:19, 20): "Go ye therefore and teach all nations, baptizing them in the name of the Father, and of the Son, and of the Holy Ghost: teaching them to observe all things whatsoever I have commanded you: and lo, I am with you alway [sic], even unto the end of the world. Amen!" They received the power to measure with this commission on the day of Pentecost. (Acts 2:4.) Bless the Lord. O how I bless God to see His mighty power manifested in these last days. God wants His people to receive the baptism with the Holy Ghost and fire.

W.J.S.

27. THE HOLY GHOST AND THE BRIDE

(*AF,* May 1908, 4)
We read in Rev. 22:17, "The Spirit and the bride say come." O how sweet it is for us to have this blessed privilege of being a co-worker with the Holy Ghost. He inspires us with faith in God's word and endues us with power for service for the Master. Bless His dear name!

Every man and woman that receives the baptism of the Holy Ghost is the bride of Christ. They have a missionary spirit for saving souls. They have the spirit of Pentecost. Glory to God!

"And let him that heareth say, come; and let him that is athirst, come; and whosoever will, let him take the water of life freely." O What a blessed text. The bride of Christ is calling the thirsty to come to Jesus, because this is the work of the Holy Ghost in the believer. He intercedes for the lost; He groans for them.

The Spirit also calls the believer to come to Jesus and get sanctified. He points the sanctified to Jesus for his baptism with the Holy Ghost. When you are baptized with the Holy Ghost, you will have power to call sinners to Jesus, and they will be saved, and sanctified, and baptized with the Holy Ghost and fire. Amen!

Christ's bride is pure and spotless. "Thou art all fair, my love, there is no spot in thee." (Sol. Songs, 4:7.) Christ's bride is clean, free from sin and all impurity. He gave Himself for her, that He might sanctify and cleanse the church with the washing of water by the word. That He might present it to Himself a glorious church, not having spot or wrinkle or any such thing, but that it should be holy and without blemish. (Eph. 5:25, 27.)

Christ's bride has but one husband. (2 Cor, 11:2.) She is subject to Him. (Eph, 5:25.) The Bridegroom is the Son of God. (2 Cor, 11:2.)

We are married to Christ now in the Spirit. (Rom. 7:2, 4.) Not only when He comes are we married to Christ but right now, if you are sanctified and baptized with the Holy Ghost and fire, you are married to Him already. God has a people to measure up to the Bible standard in this great salvation. Bless His holy name. Amen!

W. J. S.

B. SEYMOUR'S *DOCTRINES AND DISCIPLINE* MINISTER'S MANUAL (1915)

INTRODUCTION

Seymour's *Doctrines and Discipline* minister's manual draws on his sermons and articles previously published in the *Apostolic Faith* newspaper, the African Methodist Episcopal (AME) Church's *Book of Discipline,* on the Anglican Church's *39 Articles of Religion* (with modifications), and additional apostolic letters and doctrinal statements. It is important for a number of reasons. It summarizes Seymour's theological, social, and racial beliefs and documents how and why he changed his views on tongues, the baptism with the Holy Spirit, marriage and divorce, and other topics. It further explains why Seymour rejected Parham's unique theological views (e.g., annihilationism, conditional immortality, British Israelism) and other theological traditions (e.g., Oneness, Calvinism). It also documents Seymour's views on race relations, his condemnation of white discrimination and prejudice, who was to blame for the conflicts, and his justification for black-white racial equality and reconciliation. It shows that although Seymour chose to move from a congregational to an Episcopal-style polity, he still promoted an integrated ministry. It also explains why he reserved the top three leadership posts for people of color. Finally, it reveals that Seymour drew on black and white Protestant traditions to articulate a Pentecostal theology that affirmed historic Protestantism and the reported outpouring of the Holy Spirit at Azusa Street and elsewhere around the world.

28. THE *DOCTRINES AND DISCIPLINE* OF THE AZUSA STREET APOSTOLIC FAITH MISSION OF LOS ANGELES, CAL.

With Scripture Readings by W. J. Seymour
Its Founder and General Overseer
1915

Corrected Index
[Page numbers in parentheses represent original pagination.]

Preface	(5)
Proposition and Statements	(7)
New Birth	(8)
The Character of the Church	(9)
Church Membership	(10)
The Tabernacle, a Type of Full Salvation	(11)
Apostolic Address and History	(12–13)
Sound Doctrine	(13)
Rules for the Ministry	(13–14)
How Sacred Is the Marriage Tie	(14–17)
Separation	(17–18)
Adultry [*sic*]	(17–18)
Unscriptural Marriage	(18–19)
Melchizedek	(19–20)
Articles of Religion	(21–26)
Catechism on Faith	(27–35)
Reception of Members	(35–37)
Form for Receiving Persons into the Church after Probation	(37–38)
Membership	(39)
Admission into Full Membership	(39)
Qualifications and Work	(39–40)
The Call to Preach	(40)
Rules for a Preacher's Conduct	(40–41)
Spiritual Qualification	(41–43)
The Necessity of Union Among Ourselves	(43)
Deportment at the Conference or Convention	(43)
Where and How to Preach	(43–44)
The Trial of an Accused Member	(44)
Imprudent and Unchristian Conduct	(44–45)
Neglect of the Means of Grace	(45)
Causing Dissension	(45)
Disagreement in Business; Arbitration	(45–46)

Insolvency	(46)
General Directions Concerning Trials	(46)
Amended Articles of Incorporation, the Apostolic Faith Mission	(46–48)
Constitution of Apostolic Faith Mission	(49–51)
The Support of the Ministry	(51–52)
Annihilate	(52–56)
The State of Man between Death and the Judgment	(56)
Future State	(56–58)
God	(58–59)
The Saved Souls Are at Rest	(59)
The Nature of Man in His Present State	(59–60)
The Lord's Supper Night	(60)
Consecration and Ordination of Our Elders and Bishops	(60)
Consecration and Ordinations	(60–72)
The Form of Ordaining Deacons	(72–74)
Solemnization of Matrimony	(75–78)
Burial of the Dead	(78–82)
Amended Articles	(82–83)
Marriage	(83)
Slavery	(83)
Educational Institutions	(84)
The Ordinance of Feet Washing	(84)
The Church and Its Mission	(85)
Duty of Parents	(85)
Duty to Children	(85–86)
A Christian Home	(86–87)
The Soul of Man	(87–88)
Man a Trinity	(88–90)
Plan of Salvation	(91)
The Apostolic Faith	(92–95)

May none of us be like Ahab, to rob our brother of their vineyard. I King 21:14–20. Be sure your sin will find you out. Numbers 32:23. Judas's sin found him. Cain's sin found him.

PREFACE

Thy testimonies are very sure: holiness becometh thy house, Lord, forever. Psa. 93:5. God's church is Holy. Holiness is her only ornament Isa. 23:18. And her merchandise and her hire shall be Holiness to the Lord: it shall not be treasured nor laid up: for her merchandise shall be for them that dwell before the Lord to eat sufficiently and have durable clothing. Bless his name, salvation lies in the Blood of Jesus. He says, "Abide in me and I in you. The same will bring forth much fruits. If you love me, keep my commandments." Jn. 15. That is, abide in his word and if we abide in his word we are under the Blood and it cleanses us from all sin. Bless God forever. Amen! Sanctification means Holiness. Holiness means purity. To be pure means to be sanctified. There is no life sweeter than Holiness unto the Lord, for he is holy and therefore commands us to be holy. We must keep holy unto the Lord. This work must stand for everything that is in the word of God. The power of the Holy Ghost (Acts 2:1–4; Acts 10:44–48; Acts 19:1–6.) Ye shall know the truth and the truth shall make you free. St. John 8:31–32.

We take members in our church on probation, but not unconverted persons. They must know God and have a desire to go on to perfection. Heb. 6:1–4.

Wherever the doctrine of the Baptism in the Holy Spirit will only being known as the evidence of speaking in tongues, that work will be an open door for witches and spiritualists, and free loveism. That work will suffer, because all kinds of spirits can come in. The word of God is given to Holy men and women, not to devils. God's word will stand forever. 1 Pet. 1:22–23.

When we leave the word of God and begin to go by signs and voices we will wind up in Spiritualism. God's word is God's law. The Holy Spirit came to give us power to stand on the infallible word and overcome these false spirits.

I know since God has given me strength to write these rules we will understand each other better, trusting so by the good Lord.

After much work God has enabled me to put forth this book with the rule and Doctrine of our church. Many things put in this little book have done me good by studying them[.] I hope in the name of the Lord it may do all the readers of our work good.

W.J. SEYMOUR

CHAPTER 1.

PROPOSITIONS AND STATEMENTS.

Prop. 1. The Bible is a Divine Revelation given of God to men, and is a complete and infallible guide and standard of authority in all matters of religion and morals; whatever it teaches is to be believed, and whatever it commands is to be obeyed; whatever it commends is to be accepted as both right and useful; whatever it condemns is to be avoided as both wrong and hurtful; but what it neither commands nor teaches is not to be imposed on the conscience as of religious obligation.

Prop. 2. The New Testament is the constitution of Christianity, the charter of the Christian Church, the only authoritative code of ecclesiastical law, and the warrant and justification of all Christian institutions. In it alone is life and immortality brought to light, the way of escape from wrath revealed, and all things necessary to salvation made plain; while its messages are a gospel of peace on earth and of hope to a lost world.

We must take the Bible as the infallible word of God. Luke 24:25–31; Luke 24:44–45; John 5:39.

Prop. 3. None but regenerated persons ought to be, or properly can be, members of a Christian Church, which is a spiritual body separate from the world and distinct from the state, and to be composed of spiritual members only.

Prop. 4. Christ is the only Head over, and Lawgiver to, His church. Consequently the church cannot make laws, but only execute those which He has given. Nor can any man, or body of men legislate for the church. The New Testament alone is their statute book, by which, without change, the body of Christ is to govern itself.

THE NEW BIRTH.

St. John 3:5,6; Rom. 8:7, 8; Tit. 3:5; Salvation comes through the blood of Jesus Christ. When we get it, we will know it, and if we lose it we will know it. There is only one way to get it: It is by repenting and believing the Gospel. St. Mark 1:15.

Salvation is not feeling; it is a real knowledge by the Holy Spirit, bearing witness with our spirit. Rom. 8:14–16. Jesus said to Pontius Pilate, when Pilate asked him if he then was a King. Since Jesus told him that he had a Kingdom, but his Kingdom was not of this world, so Pilate believed if he was a King then he had a Kingdom.

Jesus told him his Kingdom was not of this world. He said, "if my Kingdom was of this world then would my servants fight, that I should not be delivered to the Jews; but now is my Kingdom not from hence." Pilate asked Him about His Kingdom and Kingship, so he confessed he was a King over his people in the Holy Spirit, for he said: "To this end was I born, and that I should bear witness unto the truth." So when we get the Salvation of God into our hearts we will bear witness to the truth; not lies, but like the disciples on their wal [sic] to Emmaus when Jesus met them and spoke about the truth, their hearts bared witness to the truth, Luke 24:13–32.

Some people to-day cannot believe they have the Holy Ghost without some outward signs: that is Heathenism. The witness of the Holy Spirit inward is the greatest knowledge of knowing God, for he is invisible. St. John 14:17. It is all right to have the signs following, but not to pin our faith to outward manifestations. We are to go by the word of God. Our thought must be in harmony with the Bible or else we will have a strange religion. We must not teach any more than the Apostles. 1 Cor. 12:1–34; 1 Cor. 13:1–13; 1 Cor. 14:1–40.

1. The Character of the Church.—A church constitutes a kind of spiritual kingdom in the world, but not of the world; whose king is Christ; whose law is his word; whose institutions are his ordinances; whose duty is his service; whose reward is his blessing.

In all matters of faith and conscience, as well as in all matters of internal order and government, a church is "under law to Christ:" (1 Cor. ix. 21) but as men and citizens, its members must "submit themselves to governors," (1 Peter ii. 14) like other men, so far as shall not interfere with, or contravene, the claims of the divine law and authority upon them—they must "render unto Cesar the things that are Cesar's, and unto God the things that are God's." (Matt. 22:21) remembering that God's claims are supreme, and annihilate all claims that contradict or oppose them.

2. The Design of Church.—The evident design of our Saviour in founding and preserving the church in the world, was, that it should be a monument in the midst of guilty men, bearing perpetual witness against the wickedness of the world, and to the goodness of God. But especially that she should be living testimonies to the work of redemption, "the light of the world," and "the salt of the earth." Matt. 5:13, 14.

The Church constitutes the effective instrumentality by which the will of God and the knowledge of salvation through Christ are made known to men; at the same time she forms homes for the saints on earth; sheep-folds for the safety of the flock, and schools for the instruction and training of the children of the covenant; while she encourages the penitent and warn[s] the careless. The church should well understand her "high calling," and seek to accomplish it, "according to the will of God." Gal. 1:4.

3. The Authority of the Church.—The authority of a church is limited to

its own memmbers [*sic*], and applies to all matters of Christian character, and whatever involves the welfare of religion. It is designed to secure in all its members a conduct and conversation "becoming godliness."

This authority is derived directly from God; not from states, nor princes, nor people; not from its own officers, nor its members, nor from any other source of ecclesiastical or civil power or right. But Christ is "head over all things to the church." (Eph. 1:22) and also as of right, "the church is subject to Christ (Eph. 5:24).

CHURCH MEMBERSHIP

The character of a building depends very much on the materials of which it is constructed. Christian disciples "are builded together for a habitation of God, through the Spirit." Eph. 2:21–22; 1 Pet. 2:1–15.

Some times the material of the church is in such a shape until it limit God in his great salvation. In order for a church to prosper, she must obey Jesus' teaching in all things. Jesus can not put his approval on a church that won't obey his teachings. In the Book of Revelation, the church had backslided so far from Jesus' teaching until we find him knocking at the door for admittance, so when a church has backsliden [*sic*] so far from God it can not demand anything from God until it repent of its sin. Rev. 2:1–8.

The proper material for the character of the church, is men and women saved from sin and hate sin, and living free from fornication and adultery. Acts 15:29. And all uncleanness and having faith in God's word, believing for the Faith that was once delivered to the Saints. Jude 1–3.

The church would have to believe in Healing the Sick, Casting out Demons and believe in all the signs following the church, as Christ said would follow. Acts 4:29–31; Acts 2:1–4.

Our colored brethren must love our white brethren and respect them in the truth so that the word of God can have its free course, and our white brethren must love their colored brethren and respect them in the truth so that the Holy Spirit won't be greaved [*sic*]. I hope we won't have any more trouble and division spirit.

W.J. SEYMOUR.

APOSTOLIC ADDRESS AND HISTORY

To the Members of the Apostolic Faith Church.

Dearly Beloved Brethern [*sic*]: We esteem it our privilege and duty most earnestly to recommend to you this volume, which contains the Doctrines

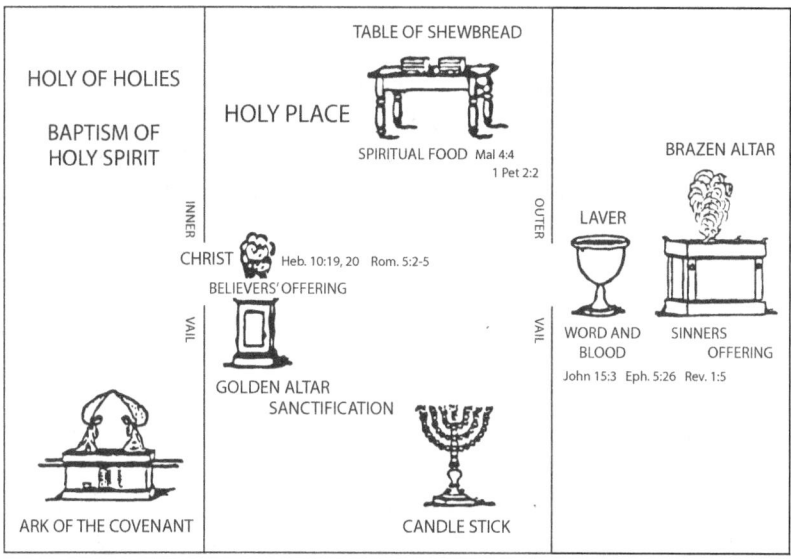

THE TABERNACLE, A TYPE OF FULL SALVATION

and Discipline of our Church, both of which, as we believe, are agreeable to the word of God, the only and the sufficient rule of faith and practice. Yet the Church, using the liberty given to it by its Lord, and taught by the experience of a long series of years and by observations made on ancient and modern Churches, has from time to time modified its Discipline so as better to secure the end for which it was cofounded [*sic*].

We believe that God's design in raising up the Apostolic Faith Church in America was to evangelize over these lands. As a proof hereof we have seen since 1906 that time of an extraordinary work of God extending throughout all the United States and Territories, and throughout the whole world.

In 1906, the colored people of the City of Los Angeles felt they were led by the Holy Spirit that they decided to have Elder W. J. Seymour, of Houston, Texas, to come to Los Angeles, Cal., and give them some Bible teaching. He came Feb. 22nd, and started Feb. 24th, 1906. From his teaching one of the greatest revivals was held in the city of Los Angeles. People of all nations came and got their cup full. Some came from Africa, some came from India, China, Japan, and England.

Very soon division arose through some of our brethren, and the Holy Spirit was grieved. We want all of our white brethren and white sisters to feel free in our churches and missions, in spite of all the trouble we have had with some of our white brethren in causing division, and spreading wild fire and fanaticism. Some of our colored brethren [*sic*] caught the disease of this spirit of division also. We find according to God's word to be one in the Holy Spirit, not in the flesh; but in the Holy Spirit, for we are one body. 1 Cor. 12:12–14. If some of our white brethren have prejudices and discrimination (Gal. 2:11–20), we can't do it, because God calls us to follow the Bible. Matt. 17:8; Matt. 23. We must love all men as Christ commands. (Heb. 12:14). Now because we don't take them for directors it is not for discrimination, but for peace. To keep down race war in the Churches and friction, so they can have greater liberty and freedom in the Holy Spirit. We are sorry for this, but it is the best now and in later years for the work. We hope every one that reads these lines may realize it is for the best; not for the worse. Some of our white brethren and sisters have never left us in all the division; they have stuck to us. We love our white bretherns and sisters and welcome them. Jesus Christ takes in all people in his Salvation. Christ is all and for all. He is neither black nor white man, nor Chinaman, nor Hindoo, nor Japanese, but God. God is Spirit because without his spirit we cannot be saved. St. John 3:3–5; Rom. 8:9.

We don't believe in the doctrine of the artificial dancing that lots of people are calling the Holy Ghost dancing. David danced before the Lord. He danced with all his might. The Ark was a type of the Presence of Christ. David, laying aside his royal majesty, and girdled himself with a linen ephod; this represent that he had come in the immediate Presence of God as a sinner to Humble himself; it represented that he was naked before the Lord, in his heart. He felt he could not be to be humbled, because God had been merciful to them in returning His Presence on the Ark which meant His Glory, so David danced before the Lord, not before the people, for a show or form, but before the Lord; the people saw him and his wife, but it was in God's Presence, so everything we do must be do the Glory of God.

We believe in rejoicing in the Holy Spirit. We believe in shouting and leaping as the New Testament endorses.

SOUND DOCTRINE

We must have sound doctrines in our work. We don't believe that the soul sleeps in the grave until the resurrection morning. The next we don't believe in being baptized in the name of Jesus only. We believe in baptizing in the name of the Father, and the Son, and the Holy Ghost, as Jesus taught his disciples (Matt. 28:19–20). We do not believe in keeping Saturday as the Christian Sabbath, we do not believe in dipping a person three times in order that he may be properly baptized. We believe in burying the candidate once in the name of the Father, and in the Son, and in the Holy Ghost, Amen. We don't believe in the Fleshy Doctrine of the male and female kissing and calling it the Holy Kiss. It hurts the cause of Christ, and caused our good to be evily [*sic*] spoken of. We believe in the Holy Brethren greeting the Brethren, and the Holy Sisters greeting the Holy Sisters with a kiss.

RULES FOR THE MINISTRY.

Discipline

The Discipline of the Azusa St. Apostolic Faith Mission is the New Testament which is the perfect law of government.

1. We must have government in all things.
    2 Tim. 3:17:
    Psa. 119:142
    John 1:17
    Gal. 6:2:
2. The Bible teaches the qualification of the ministry.
    Luke 24:49.
    Acts 1:5, 8
    Acts 2:4
    Titus 1:9, 11
    1 Cor. 3:6
3. It teaches the character of a true minister.
    1 Tim. 3:1–7
    1 Tim. 4:12.
    Titus 2:7, 8.
4. It teaches the duties of a true minister.
    Acts 20:28
    John 21:15
5. It gives the circuit for the ministry.
    Matt. 28:19.
    Mark 16:15, 16.
6. It gives instructions as to their ordination.
    Acts 13:2, 4.
    Titus 1:4, 9.
7. It gives instructions how to proceed in case a ministry goes astray.
    Gal. 6:1, 2.
    2 Thes. 3:15.
    2 Tim. 2:24, 26.
    1 Tim. 5:19, 20.
    2 Thes. 3:16.
8. It teaches how to deal with the members. It teaches their duty to each other.
    James 4:11.
    Col. 3:16.

1 Peter 1:22.
1 Thes. 5:11, 14, 15.
Matt. 14:15.
Heb. 13:1. Heb. 13.1.
Rom. 13:1
Rom. 13:10

9. It teaches them how to proceed in case of trespass.
Luke 18:3, 5.
Matt. 18:15, 18.
Col. 3:12, 14.
Eph. 4:31, 32.

10. A disciple that contains more than the New Testament is faulty, and it contains too much; if less than the New Testament it is faulty; it contains too little.
Deut. 4:2.
Prov. 30.5, 6.
Rev. 22:18.

Christ governs his church which he purshesed [*sic*] with his own blood, through his word by the operation of the spirit.

HOW SACRED IS THE MARRIAGE TIE

No remarriage while the first part of the first covenant are living.

And the third day there was a marriage in Cana of Galilee; and the mother of Jesus was there; and both Jesus was called, and his disciples, to the marriage.

And when they wanted wine, the mother of Jesus saith unto him, They have no wine. Jesus saith untod [*sic*] her, Woman what have I to do with thee? mine hour is not yet come.

His mother saith unto the servants, Whatsoever he saith unto you do it.

And there were set there six waterpots of stone, after the manner of the purifying of the Jews, containing two or three firkins apiece. Jesus saith unto them, Fill the waterpots with water. And they filled them up to the brim. And he saith unto them, Draw out now, and bear unto the governor of the feast. And they bare it.

When the ruler of the feast had tasted the water that was made wine, and knew not whence it was: (but the servants which drew the water knew); the governor of the feast called the bridegroom, and saith unto him, Every man at the beginning doth set forth good wine; and when men have well drunk, then that which is worse, but thou hast kept the good wine until now. Jesus has the best wine, His Spirit.

This beginning of miracels [*sic*] did Jesus in Cana of Galilee, and manifested forth his glory; and his disciples believed on him.

And after this he went down to Capernaum, he, and his mother, and his brethren, and his disciples: and they continued there not many days.

And the Lord God said, It is not good that the man should be alone: I will make him a help-meet for him.

And out of the ground the Lord God formed every beast of the field, and every fowl of the air; and brought them unto Adam to see what he would call them: and whatsoever Adam called every living creature, that was the name thereof.

And Adam gave names to all cattle, and to the fowl of the air, and to every beast of the field; but for Adam there was not found an help meet for him.

And the Lord God caused a deep sleep to fall upon Adam, and he slept: and he took one of his ribs, and closed up the flesh instead thereof; and the rib, which the Lord God had taken from man, made he a woman, and brought her unto the man. And Adam said, This is now bone of my bones, and flesh of my flesh: she shall be called Woman, because she was taken out of Man.

Therefore, shall a man leave his father and his mother, and shall cleave unto his wife: and they shall be one flesh.

Matt. 19:

The Pharisees also came utno [*sic*] him, tempting him, and saying utno [*sic*] him, Is it lawful for a man to put away his wife for every cause?

And he answered and said unto them, Have ye not read, that he which made them at the beginning made them male and female, and said, For this cause shall a man leave father and mother, and shall cleave to his wife: and they twain shall be one flesh?

Wherefore they are no more twain, but one flesh. What therefore God hath joined together, let not man put asunder. They say unto him, Why did Moses then command to give a writing of divorcement, and to put her away?

He saith unto them, Moses because of the hardness of your hearts suffered you to put away your wives: but from the beginning it was not so.

And Jesus answered and said unto them, For the hardness of your heart he wrote you this precept.

But from the beginning of the creation God made them male and female.

For this cause shall man leave his father and mother, and cleave to his wife; and they twain shall be one flesh: so then they are no more twain, but one flesh.

What therefore God hath joined together, let not man put asunder.

And in the house his disciples asked him again of the same matter.

And he saith unto them, Whosoever shall put away his wife, and marry another, committeth adultery against her.

If a woman shall put away her husband, and be married to another, she committeth adultery.

Wives, submit yourselves unto your own husbands, as unto the Lord; for the husband is the head of the wife, even as Christ is the head of the church; and he is the saviour of the body.

Terefore [sic] as the church is subject unto Christ, so let the wives be to their own husbands in everything. Husbands, love your wives, even as Christ also loved the church, and gave himself for it; that he might sanctify and cleanse it with the washing of water by the word, that he might present it to himself a glorious church, not having spot, or wrinkle, or any such thing; but that it should be holy and without blemish.

So ought men to love their wives as their own bodies. He that loveth his wife loveth himself, for no man ever yet hated his own flesh; but nourisheth and cherisheth it, even as the Lord the church: for we are members of his body, of his flesh, and of his bones.

For this cause shall a man leave his father and mother, and shall be joined unto his wife, and they two shall be one flesh.

This is a great mystery: but I speak concerning Christ and the church.

Nevertheless let every one of you in particular so love his wife even as himself; and the wife see that she reverence her husband.

Wives, submit yourselves utno [sic] your own husbands, as it is fit in the Lord. Husbands, love your wives, and be not bitter against them.

SEPARATION.

Mat. 19:6.

I. Concerning Divorcement.
  1. There were no divorces in the beginning
      Mat. 19:3–8.
  2. Moses allowed men to put away their wives for any cause. If she found no favor in her husband's eyes, if he saw any unbecoming thing in her he could give her a bill of divorcement, send her away, and she might become another man's wife.
      Deut. 24:1–4, LXX.
      Mat. 19:7, 8.
  3. Moses suffered men to divorce their wives and marry again because of the hardness of their hearts.
      Mat. 19:7, 8.
  4. Jesus did away with the divorce law, and restored matrimony back to the Edenic standard.

Mat. 19:3–8.
5. Under the New Testament no court on earth should dissolve the marriage relation.
    Mark 10:2–9.
    Mat. 19:5, 6.
6. Under the New Testament Husband and wife are bound together for life, death alone severs the marriage tie.
    Rom. 7:2, 3.
    1 Cor. 7:39.
7. Under the New Testament there is but one cause for which a man can put away his wife.
8. After a man has lawfully put away his wife, or a wife has lawfully put away her husband, they are positively forbidden to marry again until the former companion is dead.
    Mark 10:11, 12.
    Luke 16:18.
    Rom. 7:2, 3.
II. Concerning Departing.
    1. Let the wife not depart from her husband.
        1 Cor. 7:10.

ADULTERY.

Heb. 13:4.
I. Under the New Testament, Adultery Implies.
    1. An act of Adultery.
        John 8:4.
    2. A hidden lust of the heart.
        Mat. 5:28.
    3. A state.
        Mat [sic]. 19:9.
II. The Act of Adultery is
    1. Coition between a married person and the opposite sex who is not the lawful companion. Both parties may be married, or only one.
    2. This act is also called fornication.
        1 Cor. 5:1–13.
        Mat. 19:9.
        Mat. 5:32.
III. Secret Adultery is as follows:
    1. Looking on a woman to lust after her.
        Mat. 5:28.
        2 Pet. 2:14.

2. The secret lust and thought of the heart.
>Gen 6:5.
>Mark 7:21–23.

IV. The state of adultery is as follows:
1. After putting a companion away, if the husband or wife marries another, while the first one lives, they are guilty of adultery.
>Mark 10:11, 12.
>Luke 16:18.
>1 Cor. 7:39.
>Rom. 7:2, 3.

2. Whosoever marries a man or woman who has been put away is guilty of adultery.
>Mat. 5:32.
>Luke 16:18.

V. No man in adultery can enter Christ's Kingdom without confessing and forsaking his sin.
>Gal. 5:19–21
>Isa. 55:7.

UNSCRIPTURAL MARRIAGE

I. To marry a second companion while a former lives is adultery—sin—and is forbidden.
>Mark 10:11, 12.
>7:2, 3.

II. To marry a person who has a living companion is adultery—sin—and is forbidden.
>Mat. 5: 23.
>Luke 16:18.
>1 John 3:4.

1. The above is the law of Christ, and sin is the transgression of the law.
>1 John 3:4.

2. To transgress God's law, man must have a knowledge of that law.
   (a) Where no law is, there is no transgression.
   >Rom. 4:15.
   (b) Sin is not imputed where there is no law.
   >Rom. 5:13.
   (c) When men have no knowledge of God's law, they have no sin.
   >John 15:22–24.
   >John 9:39–41.
   (d) Light brings condemnation, but where no light is there is no condemnation.

John 3:19.

3. From the foregoing scripture we learn that sin is a wilful [sic] transgression of God's law. To commit sin men must have a knowledge of God's law, and transgress it knowingly—either the written law or the law of their conscience.

Rom. 2:14–16

III. Men who have a knowledge of the teachings of Christ's law regarding marriage, and then with that knowledge marry a second living companion, or a divorced wife or husband while their former companion lives, willfully transgress the law, 1 John 3:4, are guilty before God of sin—adultery—and must forsake their sin, 1 John 1:9. If we confess our sins, He will pardon us. All such unscriptural marriages must be dissolved to get clear from the sinful state of adultry [sic].

Prov. 28:13.
Isa. 1:16, 17.
Gal. 5:19–21.
1 Cor. 6:9, 10.

IV. If men entered the unscriptural marriages, even though ignorant of the written law, yet condemned by the law of their conscience, such are not clear before God.

Rom. 2:12, 14–16.

V. People who have entered unscriptural marriages in total ignorance of the teachings of Christ, and whose conscience did not condemn them because of the general low plane of teaching on this subject throughout the world, such individuals committed no sin—until the light came and they fail to walk in the light. St. John 3:19.

The Bible says: "He that covereth his sin shall not prosper: but whosoever confesseth and forsaketh them shall have mercy. Prov. 28:13, 1 John 1:9.

MELCHIZEDEK

I. He was a man—A priest.
> Gen. 14:18.

II. He was a type of Christ.
> Heb. 5:6.

III. Neither Melchizedek nor Christ were united to the Jewish priesthood.
> Psa. 110:4.
> Heb. 7:21.
> Zech. 6:13.

1. He was ordained direct from heaven.
> Gen. 14:18.

2. Christ our high priest came into office the same way.
>   John 8:54.
>   Heb. 5:5.
>   Acts 3:13.
3. Melchizedek's descent was not counted from Levi and Aaron.
>   Heb. 7:6.
4. Neither was Jesus Christ's.
>   Heb. 7:11, 19.
>   Gal. 2:21.
>   Heb. 8:7.
5. Christ was not of the tribe of Levi, nor of the family of Aaron, but of Judah.
>   Heb. 7:10–14.
6. There was no record kept of Melchizedek's or Christ's birth, parentage, and death, according to the Jewish custom.
>   Heb. 7:3.

IV. The Lord had a people on earth before he called Abraham from or of the Chaldeans.
>   Gen. 12:1.
>   Gen. 15:7.
>   Gen. 5:22.

V. The calling of Abraham was for a special purpose.
>   Gen. 17:6.
>   Gen. 12:1, 2.
>   Gen. 22:18.
>   Gen. 26:4.
>   Gal. 3:8.

VI. There was no Mosaical law when God called Abraham.
>   Heb. 11:9.
>   Gal. 3:17.
>   Rom. 5:13, 14.
>   Deut. 5:2, 3.

VII. The plan of Salvation did not come through the Sinaiatic code.
>   Gen. 17:4.
>   Rom. 4:13.
>   Gal. 3:27.

VIII. The law of Grace is separate from the law of Moses.
>   Rom. 4:14–18.
>   John 15:22.
>   John 1:17.

ARTICLES OF RELIGION

I. Of Faith in the Holy Trinity.
   1. There is but one living and true God, everlasting, without body or parts, of infinite power, wisdom, and goodness: the maker and preserver of all things, visible and invisible. And in unity of this Godhead there are three persons, of one substance, power, and eternity—the Father, the Son, and the Holy Ghost. Matt. 28:19–20; 1 John 5:6–9.
II. Of the Word, or Son of God, who was made very Man.
   2. The Son, who is the Word of the Father, the very and eternal God, of one substance with the Father, took man's nature in the womb of the blessed Virgin: so that two whole and perfect natures, that is to say, the Godhead and Manhood, were joined together in one person, never to be divided; whereof is one Christ, very God and very Man, who truly suffered, was crucified, dead, and buried, to reconcile his Father to us, and to be a sacrifice, not only for original guilt, but also for the actual sins of men.
II. [III.] Of the Resurrection of Christ.
   3. Christ did truly rise again from the dead, and took again his body, with all things appertaining to the perfection of man's nature, wherewith he ascended into heaven, and there sitteth until he return to judge all men at the last day.
IV. Of the Holy Ghost.
   4. The Holy Ghost, proceeding from the Father and the Son, is of one substance, majesty, and glory with the Father and the Son, very and eternal God.
V. The Sufficiency of the Holy Scripture for Salvation.
   5. The Holy Scriptures contain all things necessary to salvation; so that whatsoever is not read therein, nor may be proved thereby, is not to be required of any man that it should be believed as an article of faith, or be thought requisite or necessary to salvation. In the name of the Holy Scriptures we do understand those canonical books of the Old and New Testament of whose authority was never any doubt in the Church. The names of the canonical books are:

   Genesis, Exodus, Leviticus, Numbers, Deuternonomy [sic], Joshua, Judges, Ruth, The First Book of Samuel, The Second Book of Samuel, The First Book of Kings, The Second Book of Kings, The First Book of Chronicles, The Second Book of Chronicles, The Book of Ezra, The Book of Nehemiah, The Book of Esther, The Book of Job, the Psalms, The Proverbs, Ecclesiastes or the Preacher, Cantical or Song of Solomon, Four Prophets the greater, Twelve Prophets the less.

All the books of the New Testament, as they are commonly received, we do receive and account canonical.

VI. Of the Old Testament.

6. The Old Testament is not contrary to the New; for both in the Old and New Testament everlasting life is offered to mankind by Christ, who is the only Mediator between God and man, being both God and Man. Wherefore they are not to be heard who feign that the old fathers did look only for transitory promises. Although the law given from God by Moses as touching ceremonies and rites doth not bind Christians, nor ought the civil precepts thereof of necessity be received in any commonwealth; yet, notwithstanding, no Christian whatsoever is free from the obedience of the commandments which are called moral.

VII. Of Original or Birth Sin.

7. Original sin standeth not in the following of Adam (as the Pelagians do vainly talk), but it is the corruption of the nature of every man, that naturally is engendered of the offspring of Adam, whereby man is very far gone from original righteousness, and of his own nature inclined to evil, and that continually.

VIII. Of Free Will.

8. The condition of man after the fall of Adam is such that he cannot turn and prepare himself, by his own natural strength and works, to faith, and calling upon God; wherefore we have no power to do good works, pleasant and acceptable to God, without the grace of God by Christ preventing us, that we may have a good will, and working with us, when we have that good will.

IX. Of the Justification of Man.

9. We are accounted righteous before God only for the merit of our Lord and Saviour Jesus Christ, by faith, and not for our own works or deservings. Wherefore, that we are justified by faith only is a most wholesome doctrine, and very full of comfort.

X. Of Good Works.

10. Although good works which are the fruits of faith, and follow after justification, cannot put away our sins, and endure the severity of God's judgments; yet are they pleasing and acceptable to God in Christ, and spring out of a true and lively faith, insomuch that by them a living faith may be as evidently known as a tree is discerned by its fruit.

XI. Of Works of Supererogation.

11. Voluntary works—besides, over, and above God's commandments—which are called works of supererogation, cannot be taught without arrogancy and impiety. For by them men do declare that they do not

only render unto God as much as they are bound to do, but that they do more for his sake than of bounden [sic] duty is required: whereas Christ saith plainly. When ye have done all that is commanded of you, say, We are unprofitable servants.

XII. Of Sin after Justification.

12. Not every sin willingly committed after justification is the sin against the Holy Ghost, and unpardonable. Wherefore, the grant of repentance is not to be denied to such as fall into sin after justification: After we have received the Holy Ghost, we may depart from grace given, and fall into sin, and by the grace of God, rise again and amend our lives. And therefore they are to be condemned who say they can no more sin as long as they live here; or deny the place of forgiveness to such as truly repent.

XIII. Of the Church.

13. The visible Church of Christ is a congregation of faithful men in which the pure word of God is preached, and the Sacraments duly administered according to Christ's ordinance, in all those things that of necessity are requisite to the same.

XIV. Of Purgatory.

14. The Romish doctrine concerning purgatory, pardon, worshiping and adoration, as well as images as of relics, and also invocation of saints, is a fond thing, vainly invented, and grounded upon no warrant of Scripture, but repugnant to the word of God.

XV. Of Speaking in the Congregation in such a Tongue as the People understand.

15. It is a thing plainly repugnant to the word of God, and the custom of the primitive Church, to have public prayer in the Church, or to administer the Sacraments, in a tongue not understood by the people. 1 Cor. 14:1–33.

XVI. Of the Sacraments.

16. Sacraments ordained of Christ are not only badges or tokens of Christian men's profession, but rather they are certain signs of grace, and God's good will toward us, by the which he doth work invisibly in us, and doth not only quicken, but also strengthen and confirm, our faith in him.

There are three Sacraments ordained of Christ our Lord in the Gospel; that is to say, Baptism and the Lord's Supper, and Feet Washing.

The Sacraments were not ordained of Christ to be gazed upon, or to be carried about; but that we should duly use them. And in such only as worthily receive the same they have a wholesome effect or operation; but they that receive them unworthily, purchase to themselves condemnation, as St. Paul saith, 1 Cor. xi, 29.

XVII. Of Baptism.

17. Baptism is not only a sign of profession and mark of difference whereby Christians are distinguished from others that are not baptized; but it is also a sign of regeneration or the new birth.

XVIII. Of the Lord's Supper

18. The Supper of the Lord is not only a sign of the love that Christians ought to have among themselves one to another, but rather is a Sacrament of our redemption by Christ's death; insomuch that, to such as rightly, worthily, and with faith receive the same, the bread which we break is a partaking of the body of Christ; and likewise the cup of blessing is a partaking of the blood of Christ.

Transubstantiation, or the change of the substance of bread and wine in the Supper of our Lord, cannot be proved by Holy Writ, but is repugnant to the plain words of Scripture, overthroweth the nature of a Sacrament, and hath given occasion to many superstitions.

The body of Christ is given, taken, and eaten in the Supper, only after a heavenly and spiritual manner. And the means whereby the body of Christ is received and eaten in the Supper is faith.

The Sacrament of the Lord's Supper was not by Christ's ordinance reserved, carried about, lifted up, or worshiped.

XIX. Of both Kinds.

19. The Cup of the Lord is not to be denied to the Lay People; for both the parts of the Lord's Supper, by Christ's ordinance and commandment, ought to be administered to all Christians alike.

XX. Of the one Oblation of Christ, finished upon the Cross.

20. The offering of Christ, once made, is that perfect redemption, propitiation, and satisfaction for all the sins of the whole world, both original and actual; and there is none other satsfaction [*sic*] for sin but that alone. Wherefore the sacrifice of masses, in the which it is commonly said that the priest doth offer Christ for the quick and the dead, to have remission of pain or guilt, is a blasphemous fable and dangerous deceit.

XXI. Of the Marriage of Ministers.

21. The Ministers of Christ are not commanded by God's law either to vow the estate of single life, or to abstain from marriage; therefore it is lawful for them, as for all other Christians, to marry at their own discretion, as they shall judge the same to serve best to godliness.
1 Tim. 4:1–7.

XXII. Of the Rites and Ceremonies of Churches.

[22.] Whosoever, through his private judgment, willingly and purposely doth openly break the rites and ceremonies of the Church to which he belongs, which are not repugnant to the word of God, ought to be rebuked openly (that others may fear to do the like), as one that offendeth against the common order of the Church, and woundeth the consciences of weak brethren.

XXIII. Of Christian Men's Goods.

23. The riches and goods of Christians are not common, as touching the right, title, and possession of the same, as some do falsely boast. Notwithstanding, every man ought, of such things as he possesseth, liberally to give alms to the poor, according to his ability.

XXIV. Of a Christian Man's Oath.

24. As we confess that vain and rash swearing is forbidden Christian men by your Lord Jesus Christ and James his Apostle; so we judge that the Christian religion doth not prohibit, but that a man may swear when the magistrate requireth, in a cause of faith and charity, so it be done according to the Prophet's teaching, in justice, judgment, and truth.

CHAPTER III.

CATECHISM ON FAITH

I. Question 1. What is it to be justified?

Answer. To be pardoned and received into God's favor, into such a state, that if we continue therein, we shall be finally saved.

Ques. 2. Is faith the condition of justification?

Ans. Yes, for every one that believeth not, is condemned; and every one who believes, is justified. Rom. 5:1–3.

Ques. 3. But must not repentance and works meet for repentance, go before this faith?

Ans. Without doubt; if by repentance you mean conviction of sin, and by works met from repentance, obeying God, forgiving our brother, leaving off from evil, doing good, and using his ordinaces [*sic*] according to the power we have received.

Ques. 4. What is faith?

Ans. Faith in general is a divine, supernatural evidence, or conviction of things not seen—not discoverable by our bodily senses, as being either past, future or spiritual. Justifying faith implies not only a divine evidence or conviction, that God was in Christ, reconciling the world to himself, but a sure trust and confidence that Christ died for my sins, that he loved me and gave himself for me. And the moment a penitent sinner believes this, God pardons and absolves him.

Ques. 5. Have all Christians this faith? May not a man be justified and not know it?

Ans. That all true Christians have such faith as implies assurance of God's love, appears from Rom. viii.15; 2 Cor. xiii.5; Eph. iv.32; Heb. viii.10; 1 John iv.10; v.19. And that no man can be justified and not know it, St. John 3:11; first John 5:10, appears further from then ature [sic] of the thing; for faith after repentance, is ease after pain, rest after toil, light after darkness. It appears also from the immediate, as well as the distant fruits thereof.

Ques. 6. But may not a man go to heaven without it?

Ans. It does not appear from Holy Writ that a man who has heard the gospel can; Mark xvi, 16 whatever a heathen may do, Rom. ii.14, 15, 16.

Ques. 7. What are the immediate fruits of justifying faith?

Ans. Peace, joy, love, power over all outward sin, and power to keep down inward sin.

Ques. 8. Does any one believe who has not the witness in himself, or any longer than he sees, loves and obeys God?

Ans. We apprehend not seeing God being the very essence of faith; love and obedience being the inseparable properties of it.

Ques. 9. What sins are consistent with justifying faith?

Ans. No wilful sin [sic]. If a believer wilfully [sic] sins, he casts away his faith. Neither is it possible he should have justifying faith again without previously repenting. Heb. 6.1, 4.

Ques. 10. Must every believer come into a state of doubt or fear, or darkness? Will he do so unless by ignorance or unfaithfulness? Does God other wise withdraw himself.

Ans. It is certain a believer need never come again into condemnation. It seems he need not come into a state of doubt or fear, or darkness, and that (ordinarily at least) he will not unless by ignorance or unfaithfulness. Yet it is true, that the first joy seldom lasts long; that it is followed by doubts and fears; and that God frequently permits great heaviness before any large manifestation of himself.

Ques. 11. Are works necessary to the continuance of faith?

Ans. Without doubt; for many forfeit the free gift of God, either by sins of omission or commission.

Ques. 12. Can faith be lost for want of works?

Ans. The more we exert our faith, the more it is increased. To him that hath shall be given. Matt. 25:29.

[break in numeration in original]

Ques. 14. St. Paul says, Abraham was not justified by works; St. James, he was justified by works. Do they not contradict each other?

Ans. No; 1st, Because they do not speak of the same justification. St. Paul speaks of that justification which was when Abraham was seventy-five years old, about twenty-five years before Isaac was born. St. James of that justification, which was when he offered up Isaac on the altar; 2nd, Because they do not speak of the same works: St. Paul speaking of works that precede faith; St. James, of works that spring from it.

Ques. 15. In what sense is Adam's sin imputed to all mankind?

Ans. In Adam all die, i.e., Rom. 5:12. 1st, Our bodies then become mortal; 2nd, Our souls died, i.e., were disunited from God. And hence, 3d, We are all born with a sinful, devilish nature, by reason whereof; 4th, We are children of wrath, liable to death eternal. Rom. v.18; Eph. ii.3.

Ques. 16. In what sense is the righteousness of Christ imputed to all mankind, or to believers?

Ans. We do not find it expressly affirmed in Scripture, that God imputes the righteousness of Christ to any; although we do find that faith is imputed to us for righteousness. The text, "As by one man's disobedience, many were made sinners, so by the obedience of one, many were made righteous," we conceive, means, by the merits of Christ all men are cleared from the guilt of Adam's actual transgression. We conceive further, Through the obedience and death of Christ, 1st., The bodies of all men become immortal after the resurrection; 2nd, Their souls receive a capacity of spiritual life; and 3d, An actual spark or seed thereof; 4th, All believers become childred [sic] of grace reconciled to God, and 5th, made partakers of the divine nature.

Ques. 17. Have we, then, unawares, leaned too much towards Calvinism?

Ans. We are afraid we have.

Ques. 18. Have we not also leaned too much towards Antimonianism [sic]?

Ans. We are afraid we have.

Ques. 19. What is Antinomianism?

Ans. The doctrines which make void the law through faith the Doctrine of Antinomianism is so close to the perfect law of grace until we have to look closely to know the difference it says all Jesus, therefore Christians are not obliged to observed [sic] it; 3d, That [sic]

Ques. 20. What are the main pillars thereof?

Ans. 1st, That Christ abolished the moral law; 2d, That one branch of Christian liberty is liberty from obeying the commandments of God; [No 3rd] 4th, That it is bondage to do a thing because it is commanded, or forbear because it is forbidden; 5th, That a believer is not obliged to use the ordinances of God to do good works; not unbelievers, because it is hurtful; not believers, because it is needless.

Ques. 21. What was the occasion of St. Paul's writing his epistle to the Galatians?

Ans. The coming of certain men amongst the Galatians, who taught, "Except ye be circumcised and keep the law of Moses, ye cannot be saved."

Ques. 22. What is the main design herein?

Ans. To prove 1st, That no man can be saved, or justified by the works of the law, either moral or ritual; 2d, That every believer in Christ is justified by faith without the works of the law.

Ques. 23. What does he mean by the works of the law? Gal. ii.16, etc.

Ans. All works which do not spring from faith in Christ.

Ques. 24. What by being under the law? Gal. iii.23.

Ans. Under the Mosaic dispensation.

Ques. 25. What law has Christ abolished?

Ans. The Ritual law of Moses; not the moral law, for every believer keeps this moral law in his heart.

Ques. 26. What is meant by liberty? Gal. v.1.

Ans. Liberty, 1st, from the law, 2d, from sin.

II. Ques. 1. How comes what is written on justification to be so intricate and obscure? Is this obscurity from the nature of the thing itself, or from the fault or weakness of those who generally treated about it?

Ans. We apprehend this obscurity does not arise form the nature of the subject; but partly from the extreme warmth of most writers who have treated it.

Ques. 2. We affirm that faith in Christ is the sole condition of justification. But does not repentance go before that faith? Yea, and, supposing that there be opportunity for them, fruits or works meet for repentance?

Ans. Without doubt they do.

Ques. 3. How then can we deny them to be conditions of justification? Is not this a mere strif [sic] of words?

Ans. It seems not, though it has been grievously abused. But so the abuse cease, let the use remain.

Ques. 4. Shall we read over together Mr. Baxter's aphorisms concerning justification?

Ans. By all means.

Ques. 5. Is an assurance of God's pardoning love absolutely necessary to our being in his favor? Or may there possibly be some exempt cases?

Ans. Yes.

Ans. We dare not possibly say there are not.

Ques. 6. Is such an assurance absolutely necessary to inward and outward holiness?

Ans. Yes.

Ques. 7. Is it indispensably necessary to final salvation?

Ans. Love hopeth all things. We know not how far any man may fall under the case of invincible ignorance.

[break in numeration in original]

Ques. 9. Does a man believe any longer than he feels reconciled to God?

Ans. We conceive not. But we allow there may be infinite degrees of seeing God; even as many as there are between him that sees the sun, when it shines on his eyelids closed, and him who stands with his eyes wide open in the full blaze of his beams.

Ques. 10. Does a man believe any longer than he loves God?

Ans. In no wise. For neither circumcision nor uncircumcision avails, without faith working by love.

Ques. 11. Have we duly considered the case of Cornelius? Was he not in the favor of God when his prayer and alms came up for a memorial before God, i.e. before he believed in Christ?

Ans. It does seem that he was in some degree. But we speak not of those who have heard the Gospel.

Ques. 12. But were those works of his splendid sins?

Ans. No; nor were they done without the grace of Christ.

[break in numeration in original]

Ques. 16. Can faith be lost through disobedience?

Ans. It can. A believer first inwardly disobeys, inclines to sin with his heart; then his intercourse with God is cut off, i.e., his faith is lost. And after this he may fall into outward sin, being now weak and like another man.

Ques. 17. How can such a one recover faith?

Ans. By repenting and doing the first works. Rev. ii.5; Hebrews 6:1–3.

Ques. 18. Whence is it that so great a majority of those who believe, fall more or less in doubt or fear?

Ans. Chiefly from their own ignorance or unfaithfulness; often from their own not watching unto prayer; perhaps from some defect or want of the power of God in the preaching they hear.

Ques. 19. Is there not a defect in us? Do we preach as we did at first? have we not changed our doctrines? I am afraid we have preached too much on tongues being the evidence of the gift of the Holy Spirit instead as one of the signs following the believer. Mark 16:16–18.

Ans. 1st. At first we preached almost wholly to unbelievers. To those, therefore, we spake almost continually of remission of sin through the death of Christ and the nature of faith in his blood. And so we do still among those who need to be taught the first elements of the Gospel of Christ.

2d. But those in whom the foundation is already laid, we exhort to go on to perfection. Heb. 6:1–6; Heb. 10:26–27.

3d. Yet we now preach, and that continually, faith in Christ as our prophet, priest, and king; as least as clearly, as strongly and as fully, as we did several years ago.

Ques. 20. Do not some of our preachers preach too much of the wrath, and too little of the love of God?

Ans. We fear that they have leaned to that extreme, and hence some of their hearers have lost the joy of faith.

Ques. 21. Need we ever preach the terrors of the Lord to those who know they are accepted of him?

Ans. No; it is folly so to do, for love is to them the strongest of all motives.

Ques. 22. Do we ordinarily represent a justified state so great and happy as it is?

Ans. Perhaps not; a believer walking in the light is inexpressibly great and happy.

Ques. 23. Should we not have a care of depreciating justification, in order to exalt the state of Holy sanctification?

Ans. Undoubtedly we should beware of this, for one may insensibly slide into it.

Ques. 24. How should we avoid it.

Ans. When we are going to speak of entire sanctification, let us first describe the bless of a justified state, as strongly as possible.

Ques. 25. Does not the truth of the Gospel lie very near both Calvinism and Antinomianism?

Ans. Indeed it does, as it were within a hair's breadth; so that it is altogether foolish and sinful, because we do not altogether agree with one or the other, to run from them as far as we can.

Ques. 26. Wherein may we come to the very verge of Calvinism?

Ans. 1st. In ascribing all good to the free grace of God. 2d. In denying all natural free-will, and all power antecedent to grace; and, 3d. In excluding all merit from man even for what he has or does by the grace of God.

Ques. 27. Wherein may we come to the edge of Antinomianism? Antinomianism was a sect originated by John Abricola of Germany about the year 1535.

Ans. 1st. In exalting the merits and love of Christ. 2nd. In rejoicing evermore.

Ques. 28. Does faith supersede (set aside the necessity of) holiness or good works?

Ans. In nowise. So far from it that it implies both as a cause does its effects.

III. Ques. 1. Can an unbeliever (whatever he be in other respects) challenge anything of God's justice?

Ans . . . He cannot, nothing but hell; and this is a point on which we cannot insist too much.

Ques. 2. Do we exempt men of their own righteousness, as we did at first? Do we sufficiently labor, when they begin to be convinced of sin, to take away all they lean upon? Should we not then endeavor, with all our might, to overturn their false foundation? Yes.

Ans. This was at first one of our principal points; and it ought to be so still; for till all other foundations are overturned, they cannot build on Christ. 1 Cor. 3:1–16.

Ques. 3. Did we not then purposely throw them into convictions; into strong sorrow and fear? Nay, did we not strive to make them inconsolable, refusing to be comforted?

Ans . . . We did. And so should we do still: for the stronger the conviction the speedier is the deliverance. And none so soon receive the peace of God, as those who steadily refuse all other comfort.

Ques. 4. What is sincerity?

Ans. Willingness to know and do the whole will of God. The lowest species thereof seems to be faithfulness in that which is little.

Ques. 5. Has God any regard for man's sincerity?

Ans. So far, that no man in any state can possibly please God without it; neither in any moment wherein he is not sincere.

Ques. 6 But can it be conceived that God has any regard to the sincerity of an unbeliever?

Ans. Yes, so much that if he perseveres therein God will infallibly give him faith.

Ques. 7. What regard may we conceive him to have to the sincerity of a believer?

Ans. So much that in every sincere believer he fulfill all the great and precious promises.

Ques. 8. Whom do you term a sincere believer.

Ans. One that walks in the light, as God is in the light.

Ques. 9. Is sincerity the same with a single eye?

Ans. Not altogether: the latter refers to our intentions, the former to our will or desires.

Ques. 10. Is it not all in all?

Ans. All will follow persevering sincerity. God gives everything with it; nothing without it.

Ques. 11. Are not then sincerity and faith equivalent terms?

Ans. By no means. It is at least as nearly related to works as it is to faith. For example; who is sincere before he believes? He that then does all he can; he that, according to the power he has received, brings forth fruits meet for repentance. Who is sincere after he believes? He that from a sense of God's love, is zealous of all good works.

Ques. 12. Is not sincerity what St. Paul terms a willing mind? 1 Cor. viii. 12.

[Ans.] Yes, if the word were taken in a general sense; for it is a constant disposition to use all the grace given.

Ques. 13. But do we not then set sincerity on a level with faith?

Ans. No; for we allow a man may be sincere and not be justified, as he may be penitent and not be justified (not as yet) but he cannot have faith and not be justified. The very moment he believes he is justified. Rom. 5:1:12.

Ques. 14. But do we not give up faith and put sincerity in its place as the condition of our acceptance with God.

Ans. We believe it is one condition of our acceptance, as repentance likewise is. And we believe it is a condition of our continuing in a state of acceptance with God. Yet we do not put it in the place of faith. It is by faith the merits of Christ are applied to my soul. But if I am not sincere they are not applied.

Ques. 15. Is not this that going about to establish your own righteousness, whereof St. Paul speaks?

Ans. St. Paul there manifestly speaks of unbelievers who sought to be accepted for the sake of their own righteousness. We do not seek to be accepted for the sake of our sincerity; but through the merits of Christ alone. In deed, so long as any man believes he cannot go about (in St. Paul's sense) to establish his own righteousness.

Ques. 16. But do you consider that we are under the covenant of grace; and that the covenant of works is now abolished?

Ans. All mankind are under the covenant of grace, from the very hour that the original was made. If by the covenant of works you mean that of unsinning obedience [sic] made with Adam before the fall; no man but Adam was ever under that covenant, for it was abolished before Cain was born. Yet it is not so abolished, but that it will stand, in a measure, even to the end of the world: that is if we do this, we shall live; if not, we shall die eternally; if we do well we shall live with God in glory; if evil, we shall die the 2nd., death. For every man shall be judged in that, and rewarded according to his works.

Ques. 17. What means then; to him that believeth, his faith is counted for righteousness?

Ans. That God forgives him that is unrighteousness as soon as he believes, accepting his faith instead of perfect righteousness. But then observe Universal Righteousness follows though it did not precede faith?

Ques. 18. But is faith thus counted to us for righteousness, at whatever time we believe?

Ans. Yes. In whatsoever moment we believe all our past sins vanish away. They are as though they never had been, and we stand clear in the sight of God.

Ques. 19. Are not the assurance of faith, the inspiration of the Holy Ghost, and the revelation of Christ in us, terms of nearly the same import?

Ans. He that denies one of them, must deny all; they are so closely connected.

Ques. 20. Are they ordinarily, where the pure gospel is preached, essential to our acceptance?

Ans. Undoubtedly they are, and as such to be insisted on in the strongest terms.

Ques. 21. Is not the whole dispute of salvation by faith, or by works, a mere strife of words?

Ans. In asserting salvation by faith we mean this: 1st. That pardon (salvation begun) is received by faith, producing works. 2d. That holiness (salvation continued) is faith working by love. 3d. That Heaven, (salvation finished) is the reward of this faith.

If you assert salvation by works, or by faith and works, mean the same thing, (understanding by faith, the revelation of Christ in us, by salvation, pardon, holiness, glory,) we will not strive with you at all. If you do not, this is not a strife of words, but the very vitals, the essence of Christianity is the thing in question.

Ques. 22. Wherein does our doctrine now differ from that preached by Mr. Wesley at Oxford?

Ans. Chiefly in these two points: 1st, He then knew nothing of that righteousness of faith in justification; nor 2d. Of that nature of faith itself, as implying consciousness of pardon.

Ques. 23. May not some degree of the love of God go before a distinct sense of justification?

Ans. We believe it may.

Ques. 24. Can any degree of holiness or sanctification?

Ans. Many degrees of outward holiness may; yea, and some degrees of meekness, and several other tempers which would be branches of Christian holiness, but that they do not spring from Christian principles. For the abiding love of God cannot spring but from a faith in a pardoning God. And no true Christian holiness can exist without that love of God for its foundation.

Ques. 25. Is every man as soon as he believes a new creature, sanctified, pure in heart? Has he then a new heart? Does Christ dwell therein? And is he a temple of the Holy Ghost?

Ans. All these things may be affirmed of every believer in a true sense. Let us not, therefore, contradict those who maintain it. Why should we contend about words?

RECEPTION OF MEMBERS

Form For Receiving Persons into the Church as Probationers

Those who are received into the church as probationers shall be called forward by name, and the minister, addressing the congregation shall say:

Dearly Beloved Brethren: That none may be admitted hastily into the church, we receive all persons seeking fellowship with us on profession of faith into a preparatory membership on trial; in which proof may be made, both to themselves and to the church of the sincerity and depth of their convictions and of the strength of their purpose to lead a new life in Christ.

The persons here present desire to be so admitted. You will hear their answers to the question put to them, and if you make no objections they will be received. Acts 6:4.

It is needful, however, that you be reminded of your responsibility, as having previously entered this holy fellowship, and as now representing the church into which they seek admission. Remembering ther [sic] inexperience and how much they must learn in order to become good soldiers of Jesus Christ, see to it that they find in you holy examples of life and loving help in the true serving of their Lord and ours. I beseech you so to order your own lives that these new disciples may take no detriment from you, but that it may ever be cause for thanksgiving to God that were led into this fellowship.

Then, addressing the persons seeking admission on probation, the minister shall say: Dearly beloved, you have, by the grace of God, made your decision to follow Christ and to serve him. Your confidence in so doing is not to be based on any notion of fitness or worthiness in yourselves, but solely on the merits of our Lord Jesus Christ, and on his death and intercession for us.

That the church may know your purpose, you will answer the questions I am now to ask you.

Have you an earnest desire to be saved from all your sins? Do you desire to be Holy and wholly sanctified to God? Do you desire to be filled with the Holy Spirit?

Ans. I do.

Will you guard yourselves against all things contrary to the teaching of God's word, and endeavor to lead a Holy Life, following the commandments of God?

Ans. I will endeavor so to do by His grace.

Are you purposed to give reverent attendance upon the apointed [sic] means of grace in the ministry of the word, and in the public and private worship of God?

Ans. I am so determined, with the help of God.

No objection being offered the Minister shall then announce that the candidates are admitted as probationers and shall assign them to the watch care of the Church. Then shall the Minister offer extemporary prayer for the people that are coming into the church. As the Holy Spirit move [sic] on Him to pray.

FORM FOR RECEIVING PERSONS INTO THE CHURCH AFTER PROBATION.

On the day appointed all that are to be received into the church shall be called forward and the Minister addressing the congregation shall say: Dearly Beloved Brethren: The Scriptures teach us that the Church is the household of God, the body of which Christ is head; and that it is the design of the Gospel to bring together in one all who are in Christ. The fellowship of the church is the communion that its members enjoy one with another. The ends of this fellowship are, the maintenance of sound doctrine and of the ordinances of Christian worship, and the exercise of that power of godly admonition and discipline which Christ has committed to his church for the promotion of holiness. It is the duty of all men to unite in this fellowship, for it is only those that "be planted in the house of the Lord" that "shall flourish in the courts of our God." Its more particular duties are, to promote peace and unity; to bear one another's burdens; to prevent each other's stumbling; to seek the intimacy of friendly society among themselves; to continue steadfast in the faith and worship of the gospel; and to pray and sympathize with each other. Among its privileges are, peculiar incitements to holiness from the hearing of God's word and the sharing of God's ordinances; the being placed under the watchful care of pastors; and the enjoyment of the blessings which are promised only to those who are of the Household of Faith. Into this holy fellowship the persons before you who have already received the Sacrament of the Lord's Supper and of Baptism and the ordinance of footwashing, and have been born of the spirit and have been under the care of proper leaders for six months on trial, come seeking admission. We now purpose in the fear of God to question them as to their faith and purposes, that you may know that they are proper persons to be admitted into the church. Acts 20:28–32.

Then addressing the applicants for admission the Minister shall say: Dearly beloved, you are come hither seeking the great privilege of union with the church our Saviour has purchased with his own blood. We rejoice in the grace of God vouchsafed unto you in that he has called you to be his followers, and that thus far you have run well. You have heard how blessed are the privileges, and how solemn are the duties of membership in Christ's Church; and before you are fully admitted thereto, it is proper that you do here publicly renew your vows, confess your faith, and declare your purpose, by answering the following questions:

Do you here, in the presence of God and of this Congregation, renew the solemn promise contained in the Baptismal Covenant, ratifying and confirming the same, and acknowledging yourselves bound faithfully to observe and keep that Covenant?

Ans. I do.

Have you saving faith in the Lord Jesus Christ?

Ans. I know I have in his blood.

Do you believe in the doctrines of the Holy Scriptures as set forth in the Articles of Religion of the Apostolic Faith Church?

Ans. I do.

Will you cheerfully be governed by the rules of the Apostolic Faith Church? Hold sacred the Ordinances of God, and endeavor, as much as in you lies, to promote the welfare of your brethren and the advancement of the Redeemer's Kingdom?

Ans. I will by his grace.

Will you contribute of your earthly substance, according to your ability, to the support of the Gospel and the various benevolent enterprises of the church?

Ans. I will.

Then the Minister addressing the Church shall say: Brethren, these persons have given satisfactory responses to our inquiries, have any of you reason to allege why they should not be received into full membership in the church?

No objections being alleged the Minister shall say to the candidates: We welcome you to the communion of the church of God; and, in testimony of our Christian affection and the cordiality with which we receive you, I hereby extend to you the right hand of fellowship; and may God grant that you may be a faithful and useful member of the church militant until you are called to the fellowship of the church triumphant, which is without fault before the throne of God.

Then shall the Minister offer extemporary prayer, for the members received into the church and have members to shake their hands.

MEMBERSHIP

Chapter I. Reception on Probation.

No one to be taken on probation except he is born of God or on watch care; except he or she knows the Lord.

In order to prevent improper persons from gaining admission into the church of Jesus Christ, and in order to the exercise of the power of the godly admonition and discipline. Matthew 16:13–18; Acts 5:1–11; Acts 8:18–24.

1. Let great care be taken in receiving persons on probation and let no one be enrolled as a watch care member unless he give satisfactory evidence of an earnest desire to be saved from all sin and enjoy the fellowship of God's people. Let the pastor and the deacon and elders see that all persons on probation be early made acquainted with the doctrine, and rules and regulations of the Apostolic Faith Church.

2. Probationers are expected to conform carefully to all the rules and usages of the church. They are entitled to all its spiritual privileges and aids; but they may not be members in full until they have proven themselves to be true in every way.

ADMISSION INTO FULL MEMBERSHIP

1. Let no one be admitted into Full Membership in the Church until he has been at least six months on probation, has been recommended by the leaders and elders meeting or, where no such meeting is held, by his leader. If he has been born of the Spirit and baptized, and on examination by the pastor before the church, has given satisfactory assurances both of the correctness of his faith and of his willingness to observe and keep the rules of the church.

2. Nevertheless, a member in good standing in an Orthodox Evangelical Church desiring to unite with us may, on giving satisfactory answers to the usual inquiries, be received at once into full membership, if they have been born of the spirit and believe our doctrine.

3. Let the pastor and the committee on church records be careful to see that the names of all persons received into the church are duly recorded, and the pastor shall report at each monthly meeting all changes that have occurred in the membership during the monthly meeting.

QUALIFICATIONS AND WORK.

No one in our church shall be known as a preacher because he or she speaks in tongues; no one in our work shall be known as receiving the Holy Ghost simply because he or she speaks in tongues alone. 1 Corinthian [sic] 13.

CHAPTER I.

THE CALL TO PREACH

In order that we may try those persons who profess to be moved by the Holy Ghost to preach, let the following questions be asked, namely:

1. Do they know God as a pardoning God? Have they the love of God abiding in them? Do they desire nothing but God? Are they holy in all manner of conversation? Have they been sanctified wholly unto God? John 17:15–17; 1 Thess. 4 and 3, 5, 22–24; Acts 2–4; Acts 19:6.

2. Have they gifts, as well as grace, for the work? Have they, in some tolerable degree, a clear, sound understanding; a right judgment in the things of God; a just conception of salvation by faith? Has God given them any degree of utterance? Do they speak justly, readily, clearly? Have they been annointed [sic] by the Holy Ghost? Have any been truly convinced of sin and converted to God under their preaching? Have any been sanctified and healed and baptized in the Holy Ghost through their preaching? And are believers edified by their preaching?

3. As long as these marks concur in any one we believe he is called by God to preach. These we receive as sufficient proof that he is moved by the Holy Ghost.

RULES FOR A PREACHER'S CONDUCT

Rule 1. Be diligent. Never me [sic] unemployed. Never be triflingly employed. Never trifle away time. Neither spend any more time at any place than is strictly necessary.

Rule 2. Be serious. Let your motto be "Holiness to the Lord." Avoid all lightness, jesting and foolish talking.

Rule 3. Converse sparingly, and conduct yourself prudently with women. 1 Tim 5:2.

Rule 4. Believe evil of no one without good evidence; unless you see it done take need [sic] how you credit it. Put the best construction on everything. You know the judge is always supposed to be on the prisoner's side.

Rule 5. Speak evil of no one, because your word especially, would eat as doth a canker. Keep your thoughts within your own breast till you come to the person concerned.

Rule 6. Tell every one under your care what you think wrong in his conduct and temper, and that lovingly and plainly, as soon as may be; else it will fester in your heart. Make all haste to cast the fire out of your bosom.

Rule 7. Avoid all affectation. A preacher of the gospel is the servant of all.

Rule 8. Be ashamed of nothing but sin.

Rule 9. Be punctual. Do everything exactly at the time. And do not mend our rules, but keep them; not for wrath but for conscience' sake.

Rule 10. You have nothing to do but to save souls; therefore sppend [*sic*] and be spent in this work; and go always not only to those that want you, but those that want you most.

Observe! It is not your business only to preach so many times and to take care of this or that Mission but to save as many as you can; to bring as many sinners as you can to repentance, and with all your power to build them up in that holiness without which they cannot see the Lord. And remember! an Apostolic Faith Preacher is to mind every point, great and small, in the Discipline. Therefore you will need to exercise all the wisdom and grace you have.

Rule 11. Act in all things not according to your own will, but as a Son in the Gospel. As such, it is your duty to employ your time in the manner in which we direct; in preaching and visiting from house to house; in reading, meditation and prayer. Above all, if you labor with us in the Lord's vineyard, it is needful you should do that part of the work which we advise, at those times and places which we judge most for his glory.

Smaller advices which might be of use to us are perhaps these: First, Be sure never to disappoint a congregation. Second, Begin at the time appointed. Third, Let your whole deportment be serious, weighty and solemn.

SPIRITUAL QUALIFICATION

The duty of a preacher is: First, To preach. Second, To meet the members of the church. Third, To visit the sick.

A preacher should be qualified for his charge by walking closely with God and having his work greatly at heart and by understanding and loving discipline, ours in particular.

We do not sufficiently watch over each other. Should we not frequently ask each other: Do you walk closely with God? Have you now fellowship with the Father and the Son? Do you spend the day in the manner with which the Lord would be pleased? Do you converse seriously, usefully and closely? To be made particular: Do you use all the means of grace yourself and enforce the use of them on all other persons?

The means of grace are instituted or prudential.

Instituted are:

Prayer: private, family and public, consisting of deprecation, pretition [*sic*], intercession and thanksgiving. Do you use each of these? Do you forcast [*sic*] daily, wherever you are, to secure time for private devotion? Do you practice it everywhere? Do you ask everywhere: Have you family prayer? Do you ask individuals: Do you use private prayer every morning and evening in particular?

Searching the Scriptures. First: Reading; constantly some part of every day; regularly, all the Bible in order; carefully, with prayer; seriously, with prayer before and after; fruitfully, immediately practicing what you learn there. Second: Meditating; at set times; by rule. Third: Hearing, at every oportunity [*sic*], with prayer before, at, after. Have you a Bible always about you? Footwashing. Do you use this ordinance at every opportunity?

The Lord's Supper. Do you use this at every opportunity? With solemn prayer before? With earnest and deliberate self-devotion?

Fasting. Do you use as much abstinence and fasting every week as your health, strength, and labor will permit?

Christian Conference. Are you convinced how important and how difficult it is to order your conversation aright? Is it always in grace? Seasoned with salt? Meet to minister grace to the hearers? Do you not converse too long at a time? Is not an hour commonly enough? Would it not be well always to have a determined end in view? And to pray before and after it?

PRUDENTIAL means we may use either as Christians as Apostolics or as preachers.

1. As Christians: What particular rules have you in order to grow in grace? What arts of holy living?

2. As Apostolic: Do you ever miss your prayer meeting?

3. As Apostolics: Have you thoroughly considered your duty—And do you make a conscience of executing every part of it? Do you meet every meeting and the leaders?

These means may be used without fruit. But there are some means which cannot, namely: watching, denying ourselves, taking up our cross, exercise of the presence of God.

1. Do you steadily watch against the world? Yourself? Your besettinf [*sic*] sin? Heb. 12:1–2.

And we are not more knowing because we are idle. We forget our first rule. "Be diligent." Never be unemployed. Never be triflingly employed. Neither spend any more time at any place than is strictly necessary. We fear there is altogether a fault in this mater [*sic*], and that few of us are clear. Which of us spend as many hours a day in God's work as we did formerly in man's work. We talk—talk—or read what comes next to hand. We must, absolutely must cure this evil, or betray the cause of God. But how? First: Read the most useful books and that regularly and constantly.

THE NECESSITY OF UNION AMONG OURSELVES

Let us be deeply sensible (from what we have known) of the evil of a division in principle, spirit or practice, and the dreadful consequences to ourselves and others. If we are united, what can stand before us? If we divide, we shall destroy ourselves (Gal. 5:15–17), and the work of God, and the souls of our people.

In order to a closer union with each other. First: Let us be deeply convinced of the absolute necessity of it. Second: Pray earnestly for, and speak freely to each other. Third: When we meet let us never part without prayer. Fourth: Take great care not to despise each other's gifts. Fifth: Never speak lightly of each other. Sixth: Let us defend each other's character in everything so far as in consistent with truth. Seventh: Labor in honor each to prefer the other before himself. We recommend a serious perusal of The Causes, Evils and Cures of Heart and Church Divisions.

DEPORTMENT AT THE CONFERENCE OR CONVENTION

It is desired that all things be considered on these occasions as in the immediate presence of God. That every per-ELEVEN—SEYMOUR [*sic*] speak freely whatever is in his heart.

In order, therefore, that we may best improve our time at the Convention. First: While we are conversing let us have an especial care to set God always before us. Second: In the intermediate hours let us redeem all the time we can for privat [*sic*] exercise. Third: There let us give ourselves to prayer for one another, and for a blessing on our labor.

WHERE AND HOW TO PREACH

It is by no means advisable for us to preach in as many places as we can without forming any mission. We have made the trial in various places, and that for a considerable time. But all that seed has fallen by the wayside. There is scarcely any fruit remaining.

We should endeavor to preach most. First: Where there is the greatest number of quiet and willing hearers. Second: Where there is most fruit. Let us walk so close to God that his spirit will direct us. Acts 8:26.39.

We ought diligently to observe in what places God is pleased at any time to pour out his Spirit more abundantly, and at that time to send more laborers than usual into that part of the harvest.

The best general method of preaching is: First, To convince. Second: To offer Christ. Third: To invite. Fourth: To build up. And to do this in some measure in every sermon.

The most effectual way of preaching Christ is to preach him in all his offices, and to declare his law, as well as his Gospel, both to believers and unbelievers. Let us strongly and closely insist upon inward and outward holiness in all its branches.

THE TRIAL OF AN ACCUSED MEMBER.

I. Immoral Conduct.

A member of the church accused of immorality shall be brought to trial before a Committee of not less than five members of the church who are in good standing. They shall be chosen by the preacher in charge, and, if he judge it to be necessary, he may select them and the parties may challenge for cause. The preacher in charge shall preside in the trial, and shall cause a correct record of the proceedings and evidence to be made.

If the accused person be found guilty by the decision of a majority of the committee and the crime be such as is expressly forbidden in the word of God, sufficient to exclude a person from the kingdom of grace and glory, let the preacher in charge expel him.

But if in view of mitigating circumstances and of humble and penitent confession the committee find that a lower penalty is proper, it may either impose censure on the offender or suspend him from all Church privileges fo ra [sic] definite time, at its discretion.

IMPRUDENT AND UNCHRISTIAN CONDUCT

In cases of neglect of duties of any kind, imprudent conduct, indulging sinful tempers or words, the buying, selling or using intoxicating liquors as a beverage, signing petitions in favor of granting lcense [sic] for the sale of intoxicanting [sic] liquors, becoming bondsmen for persons engaged in such traffic, renting property as a place in or on which to manufacture or sell intoxicating liquors, dancing, playing at games of chance, attending theatres, horse races, circuses, dancing parties, or patronizing dancing schools, or taking such other amusements as are obviously of misleading or questionable moral tendency, or disobedience to the order and Discipline of the Church—first, let private reproof be given by the pastor or leader, and if there be an acknowledgement of the fault, and proper humiliation, the person may be borne with. On the second offense the pastor or leader may take one or two discreet members of the church. On a third offense let him be brought to trial, and if found guilty, and there be no signs of real humiliation, he shall be expelled.

NEGLECT OF THE MEANS OF GRACE

When a member of our church habitually neglects the means of grace, such as the public worship of God, the Supper of the Lord, family and private prayer, searching the Scriptures, praise meetings and prayer meetings:—

1. Let the preacher in charge, whenever it is practicable, visit him and explain to him the consequence if he continue to neglect.

2. If he do not amend, let the preacher in charge bring his case before a committee of not less than five who are members in good standing before which he shall be cited to appear. And if he be found guilty of wilful [sic] neglect by the decision of a majority of the members before whom the case is brought, let him be excluded.

Disobedient members have ruled the preacher in this church before. Tit. 1:5–14; 1 Thes. 5:12–23.

CAUSING DISSENSION

If a member of our church shall be accused of endeavoring to sow dissension in any of our churches by inveighing against either our Doctrines or Discipline, the person so offending shall first be reproved by the preacher in charge; and if he persist in such pernicious practice, he shall be brought to trial, and, if found guilty, shall be expelled.

DISAGREEMENT IN BUSINESS; ARBITRATION

On any disagreement between two or more members of our church concerning business transactions which cannot be settled by the parties, the preacher in charge shall inquire into the circumstances of the case, and shall recommend to the parties a reference, consisting of two arbiters chosen by one party, and two chosen by the other party, which four arbiters so chosen shall choose a fifth; the five arbiters being members of our church. The preacher in charge shall preside, and the disciplinary forms of trial shall be observed.

If either party refuse to abide by the judgment of the arbiters, he shall be brought to trial, and if he fail to show sufficient cause for such refusal, he shall be expelled.

If, in the case of debt or dispute, one of the parties is a minister, one of the duties laid on the preacher in charge in the foregoing paragraph shall be performed by the presiding elder of the minister concerned. If both are ministers, the presiding elder of either may act in the case.

INSOLVENCY

The preachers in charge are required to execute all our rules fully and strenuously against all frauds and particularly against dishonest insolvencies, suffering none to remain in our church on any account who are found guilty of any fraud.

To prevent scandal, when any member of the church fails in business, or contracts debts which he is not able to pay, let two or three judicious members of the church inspect the accounts, contracts and circumstances of the supposed delinquent; and if they judge that he has behaved dishonestly or borrowed money withoua [sic] a probability of paying, let him be brought to trial, and, if found guilty, expelled.

GENERAL DIRECTIONS CONCERNING TRIALS

In all cases of trial of members let all witnesses for the church be duly notified by the preacher in charge.

The order concerning absent witnesses and witnesses from without shall be the same as the observed in the trial of ministers. The accused shall have the right to call to his assistance as counsel any member or minister in good and regular standing in the Apostolic Faith Church.

AMENDED ARTICLES OF INCORPORATION, THE APOSTOLIC FAITH MISSION

WHEREAS, at a meeting of the members of the Apostolic Faith Mission, a corporation, regularly and legally called and held at the office of said Corporation at 312 Azusa Street, City of Los Angeles, County of Los Angeles, State of California, on the 19th day of May, 1914, at the hour of 7:30 P.M. all of the members of said Apostolic Faith Mission in good standing being present and voting, it was determined by resolution passed and adopted by unanimous vote, duly recorded, to amend the Articles of Incorporation of said corporation which were heretofore, to-wit: on the 24th day of April, 1907, duly filed in the office of the County Clerk of Los Angeles County, State of California; that said Amended Articles and the Constitution which is a part of these Articles of Incorporation, as hereinafter set forth were read, duly considered and adopted by the members of said Apostolic Faith Mission; that at said time and place the said Board of Trustees of said Apostolic Faith Mission, at its meeting duly and regularly called, unanimously adopt said hereinafter ammendments [sic] including said Constitution which are a part of these amended articles of incorporation.

NOW, THEREFORE, These Amended Articles of Incorporation and Constitution, Witnesseth:

I.

That the name of this corporation shall be the APOSTOLIC FAITH MISSION and shall be carried on in the interests of and for the benefit of the colored people of the State of California, but the people of all countries, climes and nations shall be welcome.

II.

That the purposes for which this corporation is formed are to do evangelistic work, conduct, maintain, control, carry on, supervise and found missions and also Revivals, Campmeetings, street and prison work in the State of California and elsewhere, by its members, and those who become members by compliance with the Constitution and By-Laws and the tenets and beleifs [sic] of the Apostolic Faith Missions; to establish Sunday Schools, supervise and carry on Apostolic Endeavors. It shall have the power to acquire such real and personal property as may be necessary for its use in carrying out its purposes and objects, and dispose of the same when no longer necessary for its use. It shall have the power to encumber all property, both real and personal, owned by it, when deemed advisable so to do; and generally to perform all acts requisite and necessary to more fully carry out its purposes aforesaid.

III.

That the same place where the principal business of the corporation is to be transacted is the City of Los Angeles, County of Los Angeles, State of California.

IV.

That the term for which this incorporation is to exist is fifty (50) years from and after the date of the original incorporation.

V.

The number of its Trustees shall be three or five, and the names and addresses of the undersigned, who are hereby named as trustees of the corporation for the first year after the filing of these articles are:

Spencer James, 1632 West 35th Place, Los Angeles, Cal.
James Ross, 312 Azusa St., Los Angeles, Cal.

And the name and residence of the one appointed for the first two years is:

Richard Asbery [sic—Asberry], 312 Azusa St., Los Angeles, Cal.

And the names and residences of the ones appointed for the first three years are:

Rev. W. J. Seymour, 312 Azusa St., Los Angeles, Cal.
Jennie E. M. Seymour, 312 Azusa St., Los Angeles, Cal.

That the said Trustees are to be selected in the manner provided for in the Constitution and By-Laws of the Apostolic Faith Church.

VI.

That on the 19th day of May, 1914, in the City of Los Angeles, County of Los Angeles, State of California, an election was held for Trustees: that the said election was held in accordance with a resolution at the last regular prior meeting of the said Apostolic Faith Mission, held on the 12th day of June in the office of said Corporation at the City of Los Angeles, County of Los Angeles, State of California: that notice of such meeting for the election of directors or trustees was given to the members of said Apostolic Faith Mission; that a majority of the members of said corporation who were present voted at such election, and that the result thereof was that the trustees hereinbefore named were duly elected for the respective terms.

VII.

That this Corporation has no capital stock and is not formed for profit.

CONSTITUTION OF APOSTOLIC FAITH MISSION

Article A.

Section 1. The name of this corporation shall be the "APOSTOLIC FAITH MISSION."

Sec. 2. The objects of this corporation are set in "II." of the Amended Articles as above set forth.

Sec. 3. There shall be no political discussions or any other discussions contrary to the Law of God. The Bishop shall decide what discussions shall take place in the Mission.

Article B.

This mission shall have jurisdiction over all Subordinate Missions that may hereafter be formed or come under the supervision of this Mission. It shall have the right and power of granting charters to subordinate missions hereafter formed, or of suspending or annulling or revoking the same for proper cause.

Article C.

This Mission shall be composed of one Bishop, one Vice Bishop, one Secretary, one Treasurer, five Trustees, three Deacons, two Deaconesses, two Elders, one Superintendent of Sunday Schools, one Superintendent of Apostolic Endeavor. The Bishop, Vice-Bishop and Trustees must be people of Color.

Article D.

The Mission shall hold its annual meeting on the first Monday in April at 7:30 P.M. of each and every year. There shall be such other meetings as the Bishop may elect.

Article E.

The elective officers shall be the Board of Trustees who are elected as follows: Two for one year, one for two years and two for three years. All to be elected by ballot or the yea or no. That said Trustees have been elected as hereinbefore set forth.

After the first year there shall be three trustees only.

The Bishop and wife shall be Trustees for life.

Article F.

The Founder and Organizer of the Mission shall be the Bishop. He shall be a colored person, thoroughly converted and sanctified.

Article G.

The other officers. Trustees and Bishop, shall be appointed by the Bishop and hold office during such time as the Bishop may direct and be subject to removal by the Bishop.

The Bishop shall approve all members taken into this Mission, grant charters, revoke charters, establish rules and discipline for the guidance of the Mission. Preside and lead at all meetings. Appoint all officers except the Trustees. Remove all officers except Trustees and perform any and such other and further duties that may devolve upon him from time to time. The Bishop and wife shall be Trustees for life time. The Bishop and wife shall be Head Trustees of the church. The Bishop shall remove trustees only for failing to obey the laws and doctrines of the church.

The Vice Bishop shall be appointed by the Bishop and he shall be a colored man who has served the Mission faithfully and well. His duties are as follows: Upon the death, removal, resignation or disqualification of the Bishop, the Vice Bishop shall succeed the Bishop. The Vice Bishop shall assist the Bishop as he may direct. Help the Bishop ordain preachers of the Gospel as well as Missionaries.

The duties of the other officers shall be as the Bishop may provide.

Article H.

There shall be such other committees as the Bishop may provide and from time to time select, all to serve under the direction of the Bishop and in the interests of the Mission.

Article I.

There may be such other subordinate Missions as may from time to time be established.

That upon the written request of not less that Twenty-Fve [sic] persons who are converted, a Mission may be founded and established. There must be passed a resolution by said twenty-five persons to the effect that they desire to found an Apostolic Faith Mission. The resolution expressing their desire must be forwarded to this Mission. If the Bishop is satisfied with the resolution he may then proceed to grant a charter to said Mission, which is all times under the control and supervision of this Mission. When the said charter is granted, the said Mission becomes a part of this Mission.

Article J.

The Bishop shall have power to hear all matters pertaining to the expulsion of any member of said Mission and of any Subordinate Mission.

The Bishop shall have power to expell or suspend any member for any misconduct or for any violations of the Scriptures. Every member against whom any charge is filed shall have a hearing before the Bishop and two other members or officers chosen by the Bishop. If after hearing the evidence the said member may be expelled or suspended from the Mission if the Bishop and one member so order. But no one shall be expelled or suspended from the membership without the Bishop's consent.

Article K.

This Constitution may be amended in the manner provided by the consent of the Bishop or by law.

THE SUPPORT OF THE MINISTRY

Our ministers that labor in the work of the Lord and give all their time to the Gospel should be supported by the Gospel. 1 Tim. 5:17–18. Those that labor in Doctrine and giving the word should be nicely carried, for they are worthy of it. 1 Cor. 9:7–11. We must support the Gospel or the Gospel will die in our hands and the enemy will get in and destroy the flock of God. How would a man know that he was born of the Spirit, if he did not have the inward witness? He would have to look for some outward sign. But God's word says he that believeth on the son of God, hath the witness in himself. 1 John 5:10. How do we take the gift of tongues? We believe that all God's children that have Faith in God can pray to God for an out pouring of the Holy Spirit upon the Holy sanctified life and receive a great filling of the Holy Spirit and speak in new tongues, as the spirit gives utterance. But we don't base our Faith on it as essential to our salvation. Some one will ask: How do you know when you will get the Holy Ghost? He, the spirit of truth, will guide you into all truth. St. John 16:13. The gift of the Holy Ghost is more than speaking in the tongues. He is wisdom, power, truth, holiness. He is a person that teaches us the truth.

How does our doctrine differ with the other Pentecostal brethren? First, they claime [sic] that a man or woman has not the Holy Spirit, except they speak in tongues. So that is contrary to the teaching of Christ. Matt 7:21–23. If we would base our faith on tongues being the evidence of the gift of the Holy Ghost, it would knock out our faith in the blood of Christ, and the inward witness of the Holy Spirit bearing witness with our spirit. Rom. 8:14–16.

ANNIHILATE

To reduce to nothing or non-existence; to destroy the existence of; to cause to cease to be.

We don't believe in the doctrine of Annihilation of the wicked. That is the reason why we could not stand for tongues being the evidence of the Baptism in the Holy Ghost and fire. If tongues was the evidence of the gift of the Holy Spirit, then men and women that have received the gift of tongues could not believed [sic] contrary to the teachings of the Holy Spirit. Since tongues is not the evidence of the Baptism in the Holy Spirit, men and women can receive it and yet be destitute of the truth. It's one of the signs, not the evidence. Mark 16:16–18. The Holy Spirit came from heaven to guide us in to all truth. So Annihilation of the soul is not the Holy Spirit, nor Jesus' teaching, for both the Holy Spirit and Jesus' teaching are all the same. Annihilation of the wicked, or the Annihilation of a soul is contrary to Scripture. Matt. 10:28. Jesus said in Matt. 10:28: "And fear not them which kill the body, but not able to kill the soul." Jesus showed that our soul or inner spirit is immortal. Matt. 10:28; Rev. 6:9–11; 1 Pet. 3:3–4. Annihilation means to reduce to nothing or non-existence: to destroy the existence of; to cause to cease to be. If man's soul was not immortal, he would be no higher than the beast or the apes and monkeys, but not so. Our body's [sic] are the only thing that are mortal.

The Doctrine of Materialism was advocated by The Ancient Sect of the Sadducees. Act. 23:8.

The Sadducees was a sect that did not believe in the doctrine of the resurrection of the dead; they did not believe in Angel or Spirit. But the Pharisees confess both. Acts 23:8. Now many people of to-day that deny the Immortality of the soul is nothing but modern Sadducees, saying man's soul is just his breath. Man has a spirit. God only hath Immortality. 1 Tim. 6:15–16.

Materialism is the doctrine that denies the Immortality of the soul. They maintain that the soul of man is not a spirit substance distinct from matter:

1. God only hath immortality. 1 Tim. 6:15, 16.
   (a) This text has direct reference to Jesus Christ and not to the Father. 1 Tim. 6:14–16.
   (b) Jesus Christ is King of kings and Lord of lords. Rev. 17:14. Rev. 19:16.
   (c) To take this text in an exclusive unqualified sense would deny the immortality of the Father and of angels. Mat. 22:29, 30.
   (d) We yet inhabit mortal flesh, mortal bodies, which are subject to physical death; while Christ has already received his immortal, resurrected body, and death hath no more dominion over him. In this sense he only hath attained immortality. Rom. 6:9.
   (e) This text referring to the resurrection of these bodies has not a feathers weight of evidence against the immortality of the soul.
2. Seek for immortality. Rom. 2:7.
   (a) We are mortal in body. Rom. 6:12. 2 Cor. 4:11.
   (b) Our soul or spirit is immortal. Mat. 10:28. Rev. 6:9–11. 1 Pet. 3:3, 4.
   (c) Our bodies are the only part of us that will put on immortality in the resurrection. Phil. 3:20, 21. 1 Cor. 15:42–44.
   (d) To seek for immortality is to so live that we may have a glorious resurrection in an immortal and glorified body to eternal rewards in heaven. Again, this proves nothing against the immortality of the soul. 1 Cor. 15:51–55.
3. The dead know not anything. Eccl. 9:5, 6.
   (a) This applies to the outer man—the body—that part of us which returns to dust. Gen. 3:19. Psa. 104:29. Dan. 12:2.
   (b) It can not apply to the real inner man—the soul—for that remains conscious after death. Luke 16:19–31. 2 Cor. 5:1–9. 1 Thes. 5:10. Rev. 6:9, 10.
4. In the day of death our thoughts perish. Psa. 146:4.
   (a) The mind is one thing, and its thoughts, schemes, purposes, and intentions quite another. Isa. 59.7. Jer. 4:14. Mark 7:21.
   (b) While the schemes, plans, and thoughts of worldly hearts are

cut off by death, and perish, the heart lives forever. Psa. 146:4. Psa. 22:26.

II. Against Eternal Punishment

1. The wages of sin is death. Rom. 6:22. Ezek. 18:4.

    (a) Sin produces death to the soul the very day that man transgresses God's law. Gen. 2:17; Rom. 7:9.

    (b) Sin separates from God now. Isa. 59:1.

    (c) All sinners are now dead, yet have a conscious existence. Eph. 2:1. Rom. 8:6. 1 John 3:14. 1 Tim. 5:6.

    These scriptures plainly show that the death of the soul is incurred by sin is not the destrucion [sic] of its consciousness.

    The sinner still lives. It is the forefiture [sic] of the bliss of divine favor. Not a cessation of conscious existence, but an alienation from God, whose favor is the normal sphere of the soul's happiness. Sinners are now dead yet live. They are cut off from God's favor. Just so in the future. They will be cut off from union with God eternally—dead—yet have a conscious existence and be tormented forever and ever in the lake of fire, which is the second death. Rev. 21:8. Rev. 20:10.

2. Eternal life is only promised to the righteous through Jesus Christ. Dom. [sic] 6:22. Rom. 6:22.

    (a) Eternal life is not only eternal conscious existence, but a blessed union with God, enjoyment in his service and favor without end. A blessed knowledge of his salvation. John 17:3.

    (b) Eternal life given by the word and Spirit of God reunites the soul to God and makes it alive to his glory. This blessed life is now attainable in this life. Eph. 2:1, 5, 6; 1 John 3:14. John 5:24. John 6:47. 1 John 6:47. 1 John 5:11, 13.

    (c) If we prove faithful until death, the same blessed union with God and eternal life we here enjoy in the world to come. Mark 10:30.

    (d) At the second coming of Christ, death, will be destroyed, the righteous will be raised to eternal life, and the wicked to shame and everlasting contempt. 1 Cor. 15:22–26. John 5:28, 29. Dan. 12:2.

3. The wicked shall be destroyed. 2 Thes. 1:7–10. Psa. 37:38.

    (a) Destroy does not always necessarily mean to annihilate. It also means to ruin, to render utterly useless for the purpose for which it was made. Floods may destroy cities and not annihilate them. Storms may destroy crops and not annihilate them.

    (b) Examples of its use in the Scripture.

        1. Israel destroyed herself, but not blotted out of existence as nation. Hos. 13:9.

2. A hypocrite with his mouth destroyeth his neighbor, but does not annihilate him. Prov. 11:9.
   3. We may destroy our brother by eating meat, yet he will have a living existence. Rom. 14:15.
   4. Destroy—to trouble. Psa. 78:45.
   5. Destroy—to pervert. Eccl. 7:7.
   6. Paul destroyed God's people by putting them in prison. They were not annilated [*sic*]. Acts 9:21; Acts 8:3.
   7. Faith was destroyed, yet lived. Gal. 1:23.
   8. Moral destruction, but conscious existence. 2 Chr. 26:16.
   9. Destroy—to spoil. Jer. 4:20.
(c) From all these scripture texts we learn that destroy does not imply anhihilation [*sic*]. So with the destruction of the wicked. It will not be a blotting out of existence as the heathen vainly hope; but an eternal separation from God, a depriviation [*sic*] of his approving smile and favor. Since man was created to enjoy God, love and serve Him, when etrnally [*sic*] disqualified by sin for that lofty end, he is ruined, destroyed, from the fact that he will never answer the exalted object of his creation. Being still conscious he will suffer an endless punishment. Rev. 20:10.
  4. The wicked shall perish. Luke 13:1–5.
   (a) The word perish not imply annihilation for the following resons [*sic*].
     1. The righteous perish as well as the wicked. Eccl. 7:15. Isa. 57:1. Mich. E:2 [*sic*].
  2. Truth may perish, but still live. Jer. 7:28.
   (b) The sense in which the wicked shall perish is that their doom is inredeemable [*sic*], and eternal, and there will be no hope of recovery from the state of torment.

THE STATE OF MAN BETWEEN DEATH AND THE JUDGMENT

I. Natural Death.
  1. Separates the soul from the body. Gen. 35:18. Luke 12:20.
  2. Is the time when the soul leaves the body. Gen. 35:18.
  3. Does not involve the soul in its ruin. 2 Cor. 4:16. Mat. 10:28.
II. At Natural Death.
  1. The body returns to dust. Gen. 3:19. Psa. 104:29. Eccl. 12:7.
   (a) It sleeps. Dan. 12:2. Mat. 7:52.
   (b) It knows nothing. Eccl. 9:5, 6.
  2. The spirit goes to God. Eccl. 12:7. Act 7:59. Luke 23:46.

III. The State of the Soul After Death.
  1. The righteous
     (a) Are in a heavenly realm called
  1. Paradise.

FUTURE STATE

I. Man will not Receive his full reward and punishment until after the Resurrection, beyond the Judgment. 2 Tim. 4:1, 8. Eccl. 12:14. Rev. 20:11–15. 2 Cor. 5:10. Rom. 14:10–12. 2 Pet. 2:9. Mat. 16:26, 27. 2 Thes. 1:7–10. Mat. 25:31–46.

II. The Reward of the Righteous.
  1. Will be in heaven. Mat. 5:11, 12; Mat. 6:19, 20; Mat. 19:21; Luke 6:22, 23.
  2. Heaven will be our future and eternal home. Heb. 10:34. 1 Pet. 1:4, 5. Col. 1:5; 2 Tim. 4:18.
  3. Heaven is a prepared place. John 14:2, 3. 2 Cor. 5:1.
     (a) Like the "Lamb slain from the foundation of the world," heaven was prepared in the mind of God, in his divine plan, from the beginning. Rev. 13:8. Mat. 25:34.
     (b) Christ in reality had to be slain, also went and really prepared our future place of abode. John 14:2, 3. Rev. 7:9–17.
  4. Heaven is termed
     (a) A city. Heb. 13:14. Rev. 22:14.
     (b) A country. Heb. 11:16.
     (c) New heavens and new earth. 2 Pet. 3:7–13. Rev. 20:11–15. Rev. 21:1.

III. The Punishment of the Wicked.
  1. The future punishment of the wicked will be in hell, which is a place prepared for the everlasting punishment of demons. Matt. 25:41. 2 Pet. 2:4, 9. Jude 6.
     (a) Hell is a place. Luke 12:4, 5.
     (b) Hell is a place prepared. Mat. 25:41.
     (c) The wicked shall Psa. 9:17.
  2. The place and state of future punishment is termed outer darkness, and in that darkness the wicked shall weep, wail, and gnash their teeth forever.
     (a) Outer darkness. Mat. 8:11, 12. Mat. 25:30.
     (b) There shall be wailing and gnashing of teeth. Matt. 24:50, 51.
     (c) The wicked shall remain there forever. 2 Pet. 2:9, 13–17. Jude 13.
  3. The place and state of future punishment is termed a lake of fire, which will be everlasting fire, and in this everlasting fire the wicked will suffer an everlasting punishment.

(a) A lake of fire. Rev. 20:15. Rev. 21:8.
(b) Hell fire. Mat. 18:19. Mark 9:47.
(c) Fire that never shall be quenched. Mark 9:43–48.
(d) Everlasting fire. Mat. 18:8. Mat. 25:41.
(e) Suffering the vengeance of eternal fire. Jude 7.
(f) Everlasting punishment. Mat. 25:46. Rev. 20:10.
4. The future punishment of the wicked consists in torment, and that torment will last forever and ever.
(a) Torment. Mat. 8:28, 29. Rev. 14:10.
(b) Forever and ever. Rev. 14:10, 11. Rev. 20:10.
5. The future punishment of the wicked consists in damnation.

GOD

I. Is a spirit. John 4:24. 2 Cor. 3:17.
II. Is declased [*sic*] to be
1. Invisible. Job 23:8, 9. John 1:18. John 5:37. (Invisible.) Col. 1:15. 1 Tim. 1:17; 1 Tim. 6:16
2. Eternal. Deut. 33:27. Psa. 90:2. Rev. 4:8–10.
3. Immortal. 1 Tim. 1:17.
4. Incorruptible. Rom. 1:23.
5. Omnipotent. Gen. 17:1. Rev. 19:6.
6. Omnipresent. Psa. 139:7–10; Jer. 23:23.
7. Omniscient. Psa. 139:1–6. Prov. 5:21
8. Immutable. Psa. 102:2, 6, 27; Jas. 1:17.
9. Only-wise. Rom. 16:27. 1 Tim. 1:17.
10. Incomprehensible. Job 36:26. Job 37:5. Isa. 40:18. Micah 4:12.
11. Unsearchable. Job 11:7. Job 26:14. Job 37:23. Isa. 40:28. Rom. 11:33.
12. Most High. Acts 7:48. Psa. 83:18.
13. Love. 1 John 4:8, 16.
14. Perfect. Mat. 5:48.
15. Holy. Psa. 99:9. Isa. 5:16.
16. Just. Deut. 32:4. Isa. 45:21.
17. True. Jer. 10:10. John 17:3.
18. Upright. Psa. 25:8. Psa. 92:15.
19. Righteous. Ezra 9:15. Psa. 145:17.
20. Good. Psa. 25:8. Psa. 119:68.
21. Great. 2 Chir. 2:5. Psa. 86:10.
22. Gracious. Ex. 34:6. Psa. 116:5.
23. Faithful. 1 Cor. 10:13. 1 Pet. 4:19.
24. Merciful. Ex. 34:6, 7. Psa. 86:5.

THE SAVED SOULS ARE AT REST

1. Luke 23:43.
   (a) Abraham's bosom. Luke 16:22.
   (b) Are dwelling with Christ. Phil. 1:21–24.
   (c) Are absent from the body and present with the Lord. 2 Cor. 5:19.
   (d) Are dwelling with their people. Gen. 49:33. Gen. 50:1–13.
   (e) Are in a state of blessedness. Rev. 14:13.
   (f) Are at rest. Job 3:17.
   (g) Are comforted. Luke 16:25.
   (h) Are conscious. 1 Thes. 5:10. Rev. 6:9, 10. Luke 16:22, 25, 26.
2. The wicked
   (a) Are in conscious suffering. Luke 16:22–24.
   (b) Are reserved in chains of darnkness [sic] unto the judgment day, when they will be punished.

THE NATURE OF MAN IN HIS PRESENT STATE.

I. When God Created Man.
  1. He made him but a little lower than the angels. Psa. 8:4–7.
  2. He made him in his own image and exact likeness. Gen. 1:26, 27.
     (a) God is a Spirit. John 4:24.
     (b) A spirit hath not flesh and bones. Luke 24:39.
     (c) God is invisible. Col. 1:15; 1 Tim. 1:17. Heb. 11:27.
     (d) God is immortal. 1 Tim. 1:17.
     (e) To create man in God's likeness and image would be to create him a spirit being, immortal, and immaterial. Job 32:8. Eccl. 12:7.
  3. He formed a spirit in man. Zech. 12:1.

Our doctrine on Justification and Sanctification, as definite works of grace cannot be changed. Our work shall be carried on by Conference, as the Bishop shall appoint. No Conference shall have any power to change any of our Doctrines or revoke any of our Doctrines and General Rules. We shall have quarterly Conference and General Conferences.

THE LORD'S SUPPER NIGHT

On the Lord's Supper night or day, the minister may preach the Lord's Supper sermon and, after he has preached the sermon, he can read 1 Cor. 11:23–32, to his people and give the supper. We always have the supper on Sunday night, and the Feet Washing on Thursday night before the Lord's Supper.

CONSECRATION AND ORDINATION OF OUR ELDERS AND BISHOPS

Elder and Bisho [*sic*] pare [*sic*] of the same rank, only differ in their office work.

(This service is not to be understood as an ordination to a higher Order in the Christian Ministry, beyond and above that of Elders or Presbyters, but as a solemn and fitting Consecration for the special and most sacred duties of Superintendency in the Church.)

The Elder need not be confined to this prayer according to form, but let him pray it in the spirit.

CONSECRATION AND ORDINATIONS

The Form of Consecrating

THE COLLECT.

Almighty God, who by thy Son Jesus Christ didst give thy holy Apostles, Elders, and Evangelists many excellent gifts, and didst charge them to feed thy flock: give grace, we beseech thee, to all the Ministers and Pastors of thy Church, that they may diligently preach thy word and duly administer the godly discipline thereof; and grant to the People that they may obediently follow the same, that all may receive the crown of everlasting glory, through Jesus Christ our Lord. Amen.

Then shall be read by one of the Elders: The Epistle. Acts xx, 17–35. . . .

From Miletus Paul sent to Ephesus, and called the elders of the Church. And when they were come to him, he said unto them, Ye know, from the first day that I came to Asia, after what manner I have been with you at all seasons, serving the Lord with all humility of mind, and with many tears, and temptations, which befell me by the lying in wait of the Jews: and how I kept back nothing that was profitable unto you, but have showed you, and have taught you publicly, and from house to house, testifying both to the Jews, and also to the Greeks, repentance toward God, and faith toward our Lord Jesus Christ. And now, behold, I go bound in the spirit unto Jerusalem, not knowing the things that shall befall me there: save that the Holy Ghost witnesseth in every city, saying that bonds and afflictions abide me. But none of these things move me, neither count I my life dear unto myself, so that I might finish my course with joy, and the ministry, which I have received of the Lord Jesus, to testify the Gospel of the grace of God. And now, behold, I know that ye all, among whom I have gone preaching the kingdom of God, shall see my face no more. Wherefore I take you to record this day, that I am pure from the blood of all men. For I have not shunned to declare unto all the counsel of God. Take heed therefore unto yourselves, and to all the flock, over the which Holy Ghost hath made you overseers, to feed the Church of God, which he hath purchased with his own blood. For I know this, that after my departing shall grievous [sic] wolves enter in among you, not sparing the flock. Also of your own selves shall men arise, speaking perverse things, to draw away disciples after them. Therefore watch, and remember, that by the space of three years I ceased not to warn everyone night and day with tears. And now, brethren, I commend you to God, and to the word of his grace, which is able to build you up, and give you an inheritance among all them which are sanctified. I have coveted no man's silver, or gold, or apparel. Yea, ye yourselves know, that these hands have ministered unto my necessities, and to them that were with me. I have showed you all things, how that so laboring ye ought to support the weak, and to remember the words of the Lord Jesus, how he said, It is more blessed to give than to receive.

Then another shall read:

The Gospel. St. John xxi, 15–17.

Jesus saith to Simon Peter, Simon, son of Jonas, lovest thou me more than these? He saith unto him, Yea, Lord; thou knowest that I love thee. He saith unto him, Feed my lambs. He saith to him again the second time, Simon, son of Jonas, lovest thou me? He saith unto him, Yea, Lord; thou knowest that I love thee. He saith unto him, Feed my sheep. He saith unto him the third time, Simon, son of Jonas, lovest thou me? Peter was grieved because he said unto him the third time, Lovest thou me? And he said unto him, Lord, thou knowest all things; thou knowest that I love thee. Jesus saith unto him, Feed my sheep.

Or this: St. Matthew xxviii, 18–20.

Jesus came and spake unto them, saying, All power is given unto me in heaven and in earth. Go ye therefore, and teach all nations, baptizing them in the name of the Father, and of the Son, and of the Holy Ghost: teaching them to observe all things whatsoever I have commanded you: and, lo, I am with you always, even unto the end of the world.

After the Gospel and the Sermon are ended, the Electer [sic] Person shall be presented by two Elders unto the Bishop, saying:

We present unto you this holy man to be consecrated a Bishop.

Then the Bishop shall move the Congregation present to pray, saying thus to them:

Brethren, it is written in the Gospel of Saint Luke that our Saviour Christ continued the whole night in prayer before he did choose and send forth his twelve Apostles. It is written also in the Acts of the Apostles that the disciples who were at Antioch did fast and pray before they laid hands on Paul and Barnabas, and sent forth on their first mission to the Gentiles. Let us therefore, following the example of our Saviour Christ, and his Apostles, first fall to prayer before we admit and send forth this person presented to us to the work whereunto we trust the Holy Ghost hath called him.

As the Holy Spirit shall move to Pray then shall the following prayer be offered:

Almighty God, Giver of all good things, who by thy Holy Spirit hast appointed divers Offices in thy Church: mercifully behold this thy servant now called to the Work and Ministry of a Bishop, and replenish him so with the truth of thy doctrine, and adorn him with innocency of life, that both by word and deed he may faithfully serve thee in this Office, to the glory of thy name, and the edifying and well governing of thy Church, through the merits of our Saviour Jesus Christ, who liveth and reigneth with thee and the Holy Ghost, world without end. Amen.

Then the Bishop shall say to him that is to be Consecrated:

Brother, forasmuch as the Holy Scriptures command that we shall not be hasty in laying on hands and admitting any person to government in the Church of Christ, which he hath purchased with no less price than the sedding [*sic*] of his own blood; before you are admitted to this administration, you will, in the fear of God, give answer to the questions which I now propound:

Are you persuaded that you are truly called to this Ministration, according to the will of our Lord Jesus Christ?

Ans. I am so persuaded.

The Bishop: Are you persuaded that the Holy Scriptures contain sufficiently all doctrines required of necessity for eternal salvation, through faith in Jesus Christ? And are you determined out of the same Holy Scriptures to instruct the people committed to your charge, and to teach or maintain nothing as required of necessity to eternal salvation but that which you shall be persuaded may be concluded and proved by the same?

Ans.: I am so persuaded and determined, by God's grace.

The Bishop: Will you then faithfully exercise yourself in the same Holy Scriptures, and call upon God by prayer for the true understanding of the same, so that you may be able by them to teach and exhort with wholesome doctrine, and to withstand and convince the gainsayers? Titus 1:9.

Ans.: I will do so, by the help of God.

The Bishop: Are you ready with faithful diligence to banish and drive away all erroneous and strange doctrines contrary to God's word, and both privately and openly to call upon and encourage others to the same?

Ans.: I am ready, the Lord being my helper.

The Bishop: Will you deny all ungodliness and worldly lust, and live soberly, righteously, and godly in this present world, that you may show yourself in all things an example of good works unto others, that the adversary may be ashamed, having nothing to say against you?

Ans.: I will do so, the Lord being my helper.

The Bishop: Will you maintain and set forward, as much as shall lie in you, quietness, love, and peace among all men; and such as shall be unjust, disobedient, and criminal, correct and punish according to such authority as you have by God's word, and as shall be committed unto you?

Ans.: I will do so, by the help of God.

The Bishop: Will you be faithful in Ordaining, or laying hands upon and sending others, and in all the other duties of your office?

Ans.: I will so be, by the help of God.

The Bishop: Will you show yourself gentle, and be merciful, for Christ's sake, to poor and needy people, and to all strangers destitute of help?

Ans.: I will so show myself, by God's help.

Then the Bishop shall say:

Almighty God, our heavenly Father, who hath given you a good will to do all these things, grant also unto you strength and power to perform the same, that he accomplishing in you the good work which he has begun, you may be found blameless at the last day, through Jesus Christ our Lord. Amen.

That ended, the Bishop shall say:

Lord, hear our Prayer.

Ans.: And let our cry come unto thee.

The Bishop shall then say:

Let us pray.

Almighty and Most Merciful Father, who of thine infinite goodness has given thine only and dearly beloved Son Jesus Christ to be our Redeemer, and the author of everlasting life; who, after he had made perfect our redemption by his death, and was ascended into heaven, pouring down his gifts abundantly upon men, making some Apostles, some Prophets, some Evangelists, some Pastors and Teachers, to the edifying and making perfect of his Church: grant, we beseech thee, to this thy servant, such grace that he may evermore be ready to spend abroad thy Gospel, the glad tidings of reconciliation with thee, and use the authority given him, not to destruction, but to salvation; not to hurt, but to help; so that as a wise and faithful servant, giving to the family their portion in due season, he may at last be received into everlasting joy, through Jesus Christ our Lord, who, with thee and the Holy Ghost, liveth and reigneth, one God, world without end. Amen.

Then the Bishop and Elders present shall lay their hands upon the head of the Elected Person, kneeling before them, the Bishop saying:

The Lord pour upon thee the Holy Ghost for the Office and Work of a Bishop or Elder in the Church of God now committed unto thee by the authority of the Church through the imposition of our hands, in the name of the Father, and of the Son, and of the Holy Grost [*sic*]. Amen. And remember that thou stir up the grace of God which is in thee; for God hath not given us the spirit of fear, but of power, and love, and of a sound mind.

Then shall the Bishop deliver to him the Bible, saying:

Give heed unto reading, exhortation, and doctrine. Think upon the things contained in this book. Be diligent in them, that the increase coming thereby may be manifest unto all men. Take heed unto thyself, and to thy doctrine; for by so doing thou shalt both save thyself and them that hear thee. Be to the flock of Christ a shepherd, not a wolf; feed them, devour them not. Hold up the weak, heal the sick, bind up the broken, bring again the outcast, seek the lost; be so merciful that you may not be too remiss; so minister discipline that you forget not mercy; that when the chief Shepherd shall appear, you may receive the never-fading crown of glory, through Jesus Christ our Lord. Amen.

(Then the Bishop shall administer the Lord's Supper to the newly Consecrated Bishop and other persons present.)

Then shall be offered the following Prayers:

Most Merciful Father, we beseech thee to send down upon this thy servant thy heavenly blessing, and to so endow him with thy Holy Spirit that he, preaching thy word, and exercising authority in thy Church, may not only be earnest to reprove, beseech, and rebuke with all patience and doctrine, but also may be, to such as believe, a wholesome example in word, in conversation, in love, in faith, and in purity; that faithfully fulfilling his course, at the last day he may receive the crown of righteousness laid up by the Lord, the righteous Judge, who liveth and reigneth, one God with the Father and the Holy Ghost, world without end. Amen.

Prevent us, O Lord, in all our doings with thy most gracious favor, and further us with thy continual help, that in all our works, begun, continued, and ended in thee, we may glorify thy holy name; and finally, by thy mercy, obtain everlasting life, through Jesus Christ our Lord. Amen.

The peace of God, which passeth all understanding, keep your hearts and minds in the knowledge and love of God, and of his Son Jesus Christ our Lord: and the blessing of God Almighty, the Father, the Son, and the Holy Ghost, be among you, and remain with you always. Amen.

The Form of Ordaining Elders.

(When the day appointed by the Bishop is come, there shall be a Sermon or Exhortation, declaring the Duty and Office of such as come to be admitted Elders; how necessary that Order is in the Church of Christ, and also how the People ought to esteem the Elders in their Office.)

After which, one of the Elders shall present unto the Bishop all them that are to be Ordained, and say:

I present unto you these persons to be ordained as Elders.

Then their names being read aloud, the Bishop shall to the People:

Brethern, these are they whom we purpose, God willing, this day to ordain Elders. For after due examination, we find not to the contrary, but that they are lawfully called to this function and ministry, and that they are persons meet for the same. But, if there be any of you who knoweth any crime or impediment in any of them, for the which he ought not to be received into this holy Ministry let him come forth in the name of God, and show what the crime or impediment is.

(If any crime or impediment be objected, the Bishop shall surcease from ordaining that person until such time as the party accused shall be found clear of the same.)

Ordination of Elders.

Then shall be said the Collect, Epistle, and Gospel, as followeth: Now prayer can be offered as the spirit give utterance in the Holy Spirit.

THE COLLECT.

Almighty God, Giver of all good things, who by thy Holy Spirit hast appointed divers Orders of Ministers in thy Church: mercifully behold these thy servants now called to the Office of Elders, and replenish them so with the truth of thy doctrine, and adorn them with innocency of life, that both by word and good example they may faithfully serve thee in this Office, to the glory of thy name, and the edification of thy Church, through the merits of our Saviour Jesus Christ, who liveth and reigneth with thee and the Holy Ghost, world without end. Amen.

The Epistle. Ephesians iv, 7–13.

Unto every one of us is given grace according to the measure of the gift of Christ. Wherefore he saith. When he ascended up on high, he led captivity captive, and gave gifts unto men. Now that he ascended, what is it but that he also descended first into the lower parts of the earth? He that descended is the same also that ascended up far above all heavens, that he might fill all things. And he gave some, Apostles; and some, Prophets; and some, Evangelists; and some, Pastors and Teachers; for the perfecting of the saints, for the work of the ministry, for the edifying of the body of Christ: till we all come in the unity of the faith, and of the knowledge of the Son of God, unto a perfect man, unto the measure of the stature of the fullness of Christ.

After this shall be read for the Gospel part of the tenth chapter of St. John: St. John x, 1–16.

Verily, verily, I say unto you, He that entereth not by the door into the sheepfold, but climbeth up some other way, the same is a thief and a robber.

But he that entereth in by the door is the shepherd of the sheep. To him the porter openeth; and the sheep hear his voice: and he calleth his own sheep by name, and leadeth them out. And when he putteth fouth [sic] his own sheep, he goeth before them, and the sheep follow him; for they know his voice. And a stranger will they not follow, but will flee from him; for they know not the voice of strangers. This parable spake Jesus unto them; but they understood not what things they were which he spake unto them. Then said Jesus unto them again, Verily, verily, I say unto you, I am the door of the sheep. All that ever came before me are thieves and robbers: but the sheep did not hear them. I am the door: by me if any man may enter in, he shall be saved, and shall go in and out, and find pasture. The thief cometh not but for to steal, and to kill, and to destroy: I am come that they might have life, and that they might have it more abundantly. I am the good shepherd: the good shepherd giveth his life for the sheep. But he that is a hireling [sic], and not the shepherd, whose own the sheep are not, seeth the wolf coming, and leaveth the sheep, and fleeth; and the wolf catcheth them, and scattereth the sheep. The hireling fleeth, because he is a hireling, and careth not for the sheep. I am the good shepherd, and know my sheep, and am known of mine. As the Father knoweth me, even so know I the Father: and I lay down my life for the sheep. And other sheep I have, which are not of this fold: them also I must bring, and they shall hear my voice; and there shall be one fold and one shepherd.

And that done, the Bishop shall say unto the Persons to be Ordained Elders:

You have heard, brethren, in your private examination, and in the holy lessons taken out of the Gospel and the writings of the Apostles, of what dignity and of how great importance this Office is whereunto ye are called. And now again we exhort you, in the name of our Lord Jesus Christ, that ye have in remembrance into how high a dignity and to how weighty an Office ye are called: that is to say, to be Messengers, Watchmen, and Stewards of the Lord; to teach and to permonish, to feed and provide for, the Lord's family; to gather the outcasts, to seek the lost, and to be ever ready to spread abroad the Gospel, the glad tidings of reconciliation with God.

Have always therefore printed in your remembrance how great a treasure is committed to your charge. For they are the sheep of Christ, which he bought with his body. And if it shall happen, the same Church, or any member tereof [sic], do take any hurt or hindrance by reason of your negligence, ye know the greatness of the fault, and also the fearful punishment that will ensue. Wherefore consider with yourselves the end of the ministry toward the children of God, toward the spouse and body of Christ; and see that you never cease your labor, your care and diligence, until you have done all that lieth in you, according to your bounden [sic] duty, to bring all such as are or shall be committed to your charge unto that agreement in the faith and knowledge of God, and to that ripeness and perfectness of age in Christ, that there be no place left among you either for error in religion or for viciousness in life.

Forasmuch then as your Office is both of so great excellency and of so great difficulty, ye see with how great care and study ye ought to apply yourselves, as well that ye may show yourselves dutiful and thankful unto that Lord who hath placed you in so high a dignity; as also to beware that neither you yourselves offend, nor be occasion that others offend. Howbeit ye cannot have a mind and will thereto of yourselves, for that will and ability are given of God alone: therefore ye ought, and have need, to pray earnestly for his Holy Spirit. And seeing that ye cannot by any other means compass the doing of so weighty a work, pertaining to the salvation of man, but with doctrine and exhortation taken out of the Holy Scriptures, and with a life agreeable to the same; consider how studious ye ought to be in reading and learning the Scriptures, and in framing the manners, both of yourselves and of them that specially pertain unto you, according to the rule of the same Scriptures; and for this selfsame cause, how ye ought to forsake and set aside, as much as you may, all worldly cares and studies.

We have good hope that you have all weighed and pondered these things with yourselves long before this time: and that you have clearly determined, by God's grace, to give yourselves wholly to this Office, whereunto it has pleased God to call you: so that, as much as lieth in you, you will apply yourselves wholly to this one thing, and draw all your cares and studies this way, and that you will continually pray to God the Father, by the meditation of our only Saviour Jesus Christ, for the heavenly assistance of the Holy Ghost; that by daily reading and weighing of the Scriptures ye may wax riper and stronger in your ministry; and that ye may so endeavor to sanctify the lives of you and yours, and to fashion them after the rule and doctrine of Christ that ye may be wholesome and godly examples and patterns for the people to follow.

And now, that this present Congregation of Christ here assembled may also understand youd [*sic*] minds and wills in thes [*sic*] things, and that this your promise may the more move you to do your duties, ye shall answer plainly to these things which we, in the name of God and his Church, shall demand of you touching the same:

Do you think in your heart that you are truly called, according to the will of our Lord Jesus Christ, to the Order of Elders?

Ans.: I think so.

The Bishop: Are you persuaded that the Holy Scriptures contain sufficiently all doctrine required of necessity for eternal salvation through faith in Jesus Christ? And are you determined out of the said Scriptures to instruct the people committed to your charge, and to teach nothing as required of necessity to eternal salvation but that which you shall be persuaded may be concluded and proved by the Scriptures?

Ans.: I am so persuaded, and have so determined, by God's grace.

The Bishop: Will you then give your faithful diligence always so to minister the Doctrine, and Sacraments and Discipline of Christ, as the Lord hath commanded?

Ans.: I will so do, by the help of the Lord.

The Bishop: Will you be ready with all faithful diligence to banish and drive away all erroneous and strange doctrines contrary to God's word, and to use both public and private monitions and exhortations, as well to the sick as to the whole within your charge, as need shall require and occasion shall be given?

Ans.: I will, the Lord being my helper.

The Bishop: Will you be diligent in Prayers, and in reading of the Holy Scriptures, and in such studies as help to the knowledge of the same, laying aside the study of the world and the flesh?

Ans.: I will nedeavor [sic] so to do, the Lord being my helper.

The Bishop: Will you be diligent to frame and fashion yourselves, and your families, according to the doctrine of Christ; and to make both yourselves and them, as much as in you lieth, wholesome examples and patterns to the flock of Christ?

Ans.: I will apply myself thereto, the Lord being my helper.

The Bishop: Will you maintain and set forward, as much as lieth in you, quietness, peace, and love, among all Christian people, and especially among them that are or shall be committed to your charge?

Ans.: I will so do, the Lord being my helper.

The Bishop: Will you reverently obey your chief Ministers, unto whom is committed the charge and government over you, following with a glad mind and will their godly admonitions, submitting yourselves to their godly judgments?

Ans.: I will so do, the Lord being my helper.

Then shall the Bishop, standing up, say:

Almight [sic] God, who hath given you this will to do all these things, grant also unto you strength and power to perform the same; that he may accomplish his work which he hath begun in you, through Jesus Christ our Lord. Amen.

(After this the Congregation shall be desired secretly in their Prayers to make their humble supplications to God for all these things: for the which Prayers there shall be silence kept for a space.)

After which shall be said by the Bishop, the Persons to be ordained Elders, all kneeling, the Bishop beginning, and the Elders and others that are present answering by verse, as followeth:

> Come, Holy Ghost, our souls inspire,
> **And lighten with celestial fire.**
> Thou the anointing Spirit art,
> **Who dost thy sevenfold gifts impart.**
> Thy blessed unction from above
> **Is comfort, life, and fire of love.**
> Enable with perpetual light
> **The dullness of our blinded sight;**
> Anoint and cheer our soiled face
> **With the abundance of thy grace;**
> Keep far our foes, give peace at home;
> **Where thou art Guide, no ill can come.**
> Teach us to know the Father, Son,
> **And Thee of both to be but ONE;**
> That through the ages all along
> **This may be our endless song:**
> Praise to thy eternal merit,
> **Father, Son, and Holy Spirit.**

That done, the Bishop shall pray in this wise, and say:
Let us pray.
Pray in the Holy Spirit.

Almighty God and heavenly Father who of thine infinite love and goodness stoward [sic] us hast given to us thine only and most dearly beloved Son Jesus Christ to be our Redeemer, and the author of everlasting life: who, after he had made Perfect our redemption by his death, and was ascended into heaven, sent abroad into the world his Apostles, Prophets, Evangelists, Teachers, and Pastors, by whose labor and ministry he gathered together a great flock in all parts of the world, to set forth the eternal praise of thy holy name: for these so great benefits of thy eternal goodness, and for that thou has vouchsafed to call these thy servants here present to the same office and ministry appointed for the salvation of mankind, we render unto thee most hearty thanks; we praise and worship thee; and we humbly beseech thee by the same, thy blessed Son, to grant unto all who either here or elsewhere call upon thy name, that we may continue to show ourselves thankful unto thee for these, and all other thy benefits, and that we may daily increase and go forward in the knowledge and faith of thee and thy Son, by the Holy Spirit. So that as well by these thy Ministers, as by them over whom they shall be appointed thy Ministers, thy holy name may be forever glorified, and thy blessed kingdom enlarged, through the same, thy Son Jesus Christ our Lord, who liveth and reigneth with thee in the unity of the same Holy Spirit, world without end. Amen.

When this Prayer is done, the Bishop and the Elders present shall lay their hands severally upon the head of every one that receiveth the Order of Elders; the Receivers humbly kneeling, and the Bishop saying:

The Lord pour upon thee the Holy Ghost for the Office and Work of an Elder in the Church of God, now committed unto thee by the authority of the Church, through the imposition of our hands. And be thou a faithful dispenser of the word of God, and of his Holy Sacraments; in the name of the Father, and of the Son, and of the Holy Ghost. Amen.

Then the Bishop shall deliver to every one of them, kneeling, the Bible into his hands, saying:

Take thou authority as an Elder in the Church to preach the word of God, and to administer the Holy Sacraments in the Congregation.

These prayers are good let God lead. It must be from the heart and through the Holy Spirit.

Then the Bishop shall offer the following Prayer:

Most Merciful Father, we beseech thee to send upon these thy servants thy heavenly blessings, that they may be clothed with righteousness, and that thy word spoken by their mouths may have such success that it may never be spoken in vain. Grant alos [sic] that we may have grace to hear and receive what they shall deliver out of thy most holy word, or agreeably to the same, as the means of our salvation; and that in all our words and deeds we may seek thy glory, and the increase of thy kingdom, through Jesus Christ our Lord. Amen.

Prevent us, O Lord, in all our doings, with thy most gracious favor, and further us by thy continual help; that in all our works, begun, continued, and ended in thee, we may glorify thy holy name, and finally, by thy mercy, obtain everlasting life through Jesus Christ our Lord. Amen.

The peace of God, which passeth all understanding, keep your hearts and minds in the knowledge and love of God, and of his Son Jesus Christ our Lord: and the blessing of God Almighty, the Father, the Son, and the Holy Ghost, be among you, and remain with you always. Amen.

***(If on the same day the Order of Deacons be given to some, and that of Elders to others, the Deacons shall be first presented, and then the Elders. The Collect shall both be used; first that for Deacons, then that for Elders. The Epistle shall be Ephesians iv, 7–13, as before in this Office: immediately after which, they who are to be ordained Deacons shall be examined and ordained as is below prescribed. Then one of them having read the Gospel, which shall be St. John x, 1–16, as before in this Office, they who are to be ordained Elders shall likewise be examined and ordained, as in this office before appointed.)

THE FORM OF ORDAINING DEACONS.

When the day appointed by the Bishop is come, there shall be a Sermon or Exhortation, declaring the Duty and Office of such as come to be admitted to the Order of Deacons.

After which one of the Elders shall present unto the Bishop the Persons to be ordained Deacons, and their names being read aloud the Bishop shall say unto the People:

Brethren, if there be any of you who knoweth any crime of impediment in any of these persons presented to be ordained Dacons [sic], for the which he ought not to be admitted to that Office, let him come forth in the name of God, and show what the crime or impediment is.

The Elder can use the Prayer or let the Lord give him one as he may be led.

(If any crime of impediment be objected, the Bishop shall surcease from ordanining [sic] that persons until such time as the party accused shall be found clear of the same.)

Then shall be read the following Collect and Epistle:
The Collect.

Almighty God, who by thy divine providence hast appointed divers Orders of Ministers in thy Church, and dist [sic] inspire thy Apostles to chose [sic] into the Order of Deacons thy first martyr, Saint Stephen, with others: mercifully behold these thy servants, now called to the like Office and Administration; replenish them so with the truth of thy doctrine, and adorn them with innocency of life, that both by word and good example thy may faithfully serve thee in this Office to the glory of thy name, and the edification of they Church, through the merits of our Saviour Jesus Christ, who liveth and reigneth with thee and the Holy Ghost, now and forever. Amen.

The Epistle: 1 Timothy iii, 8–13.

Likewise must the Deacons be grave, not double-tongued, not given to much wine, not greedy of filthy lucre; holding the mystery of the faith in a pure conscience. And let these also first be proved; then let them use the Office of a Deacon, being found blameless. Even so must their wives be grave, not slanderers, sober, faithful in all things. Let the Deacons be the husbands of one wife, ruling their children and their own houses well. For they that have used the Office of a Deacon well purchase to themselves a good degree, and great boldness in the faith which is in Christ Jesus.

Then shall the Bishop, in the presence of the People, examine every one of those who are to be ordained, after this manner following:

Do you trust that you are inwardly moved by the Holy Ghost to take upon you the Office of the Ministry in the Church of Christ, to serve God for the promoting of his glory and the edifying of his people?

Ans.: I trust so.

The Bishop: Do you unfeignedly believe all the canonical Scriptures of the Old and New Testaments?

Ans.: I do believe them.

The Bishop: Will you diligently read or expound the same unto the people whom you shall be appointed to serve?

Ans.: I will.

The Bishop: It appertaineth to the Office of a Deacon to assist the Elder in divine service, and especially when he ministereth the Holy Communion, to help him in the distribution thereof; to read and expound the Holy Scriptures; to instruct the youth; and to baptize. And furthermore, it is his office to search for the sick, poor, and impotent, that they may be visited and relieved. Will you do this gladly and willingly?

Ans.: I do so, by the help of God.

The Bishop: Will you apply all your diligence to frame and fashion your own lives and the lives of your families according to the doctrine of Christ; and to make both yourselves and them, as much as in you lieth, wholesome examples of the flock of Christ?

Ans.: I will do so, the Lord being my helper.

The Bishop: Will you reverently obey them to whom the charge and government over you is committed, following with a glad mind and will their godly admonitions?

Ans.: I will endeavor so to do, the Lord being my helper.

Then the Bishop, laying his hands severally upon the head of every one of them, shall say:

Take thou authority to execute the office of a Deacon in the Church of God; in the name of the Father, and of the Son, and of the Holy Ghost. Amen.

Then shall the Bishop deliver to every one of them the Holy Bible, saying:

Take thou authority to read the Holy Scriptures in the Church of God, and to preach the same.

Then one appointed by the Bishop shall read the Gospel:

Luke xii,35–38.

Let your loins be girdled about, and your lights burning; and ye yourselves like unto men that wait for their lord, when he will return from the wedding; that, when he cometh and knocketh, they may open unto him immediately. Blessed are those servants, whom the Lord when he cometh shall find watching: verily I say unto you, that he shall gird himself, and make them to sit down to meat, and will come forth and serve them. And if he shall come in the second watch, or come in the third watch, and find them so, blessed are those servants.

The Elder may use this prayer if he desire, or pray as the Holy Spirit move him.

Immediately before the Benediction shall be said these Collects following:

Almighty God, Giver of all good things, who of thy great goodness has vouchsafed to accept and take these thy servants into the Office of Deacons in thy Church: make them, we beseech thee, O Lord, to be modest, humble, and constant in their ministration, and to have a ready will to observe all spiritual discipline; that they, have always the testimony of a good conscience, and continuing every stable and strong in thy Son Christ, may so well behave themselves in this inferior office that they may be found worthy to be called into the higher Ministries in thy Church, through the same, thy Son our Saviour Jesus Christ; to whom be glory and honor, world without end. Amen.

Prevent us, O Lord, in all our doings, with thy most gracious favor, and further us with thy continual help; that in all our works, begun, continued, and ended in thee, we may glorify the holy name, and finally, by thy mercy, obtain everlasting life, through Jesus Christ our Lord. Amen.

The peace of God, which passeth all understanding, keep your hearts and minds in the knowledge and love of God, and of his Son Jesus Christ our Lord: and the blessing of God Almighty, the Father, the Son, and the Holy Ghost, be among you, and remain with you always. Amen.

CHAPTER VII.

SOLEMNIZATION OF MATRIMONY.

First, the bans of all that are to be married together, must be published in the congregation three several Sundays in the time of divine service, unless they be otherwise qualified according to law, the minister saying, after the accustomed manner:

I publish these bans of marriage between M of _____ and N of _____. If any of you know just cause or impediment why these two persons should not be joined in holy matrimony, you are to declare it. This is the first, (second, or third) time of asking.

At the day and time appointed for the solemnization, the persons to be married standing together, the man on the right side and the woman on the left, the minister shall say:

Dearly beloved, we are gathered together in the sight of God, and in the presence of these witnesses, to join together this man and this woman in holy matrimony; which is an honorable estate, instituted by God in the time of man's innocency, signifying to us the mystical union which is between Christ and his Church; which holy estate Christ adorned and beautified with his presence, and first miracle that he wrought at Cana of Galilee, list. and is commended of St. Paul to be honorable among all men, and therefore not by any to be entered upon or taken in hand unadvisedly, but reverently, discreetly, advisedly, and in the fear of God.

Into which holy estate these persons come now to be joined. Therefore if any can show any just cause why they may not lawfully be joined together, let him now speak, or else hereafter forever hold his peace.

And also speaking to the persons that are to be married, he shall say:

I require and charge you both, as you will answer at the dreadful day of judgment, when the secrets of all hearts shall be disclosed that if either of you know any impediment why you may not be lawfully joined together in matrimony, you do now confess it; for be ye well assured that so many as are coupled together otherwise than God's word shall allow, are not joined together by God, neither is their matrimony lawful in the sight of God. For God's word forbids marrying to another while the first party of the first covenant are living. Machi [*sic*] 2:14–16; Mark 10:11–12; Luke 16:18; Rom. 7:1–3.

If no impediment shall be alleged, then shall the minister say unto the man:

M Wilt thou have this woman to be thy wedded wife, to live together after God's ordinance, in the holy state of matrimony? Wilt thou love her and cherish her and nurse her? Wilt thou love her, comfort her, honor and keep her, in sickness and in health, and forsaking all others, keep thee only unto her, as long as ye both shall live?

The man shall answer, I will.

Then shall the minister say unto the woman:

N Wilt thou have this man to be thy wedded husband, to live together after God's ordinance in the holy state of matrimony? Wilt thou obey him, serve him, love him, and honor him, and reverence him and keep him, in sickness and in health; and forsake all others, keep thee only unto him so long as ye both shall live? The woman shall answer, I will.

I, M, take thee N, to be my wedded wife, to have and to hold, from this day forward, for better, or for worse, for richer, for poorer, in sickness and in health, to love and to cherish till death do us part, according to God's holy ordinance; and thereto I plight thee my faith.

Then they shall loose their hands, and the woman with her right hand, taking the man by his right hand, shall likewise say after the minister:

I, N, take thee M, to be my wedded husband, to have and to hold, from this day forward, for better, for worse, for richer, for poorer, in sickness and in health, to love, cherish and to obey, till death do us part, according to God's holy ordinance; and thereto I plight thee my faith.

Then shall the minister say, let us pray.

O, Eternal God, Creator, Preserver of all mankind, giver of all spiritual grace, the author of everlasting life; send thy blessing upon these thy servants, this man and this woman, whom we bless in thy name; that as Isaac and Rebecca lived faithfully together, so these persons may surely perform and keep the vow and covenant betwixt them made, and may ever remain in perfect love and peace together, and live according to thy laws, through Jesus Christ our Lord, Amen.

If the parties desire it, the man shall here hand a ring to the minister, who shall return it to him and direct him to place it on the third finger of the woman's left hand. And the man shall say to the woman, repeating after the minister:

With this ring I thee wed, and with my worldly goods I thee endow, in the name of the Father, and of the Son, and of the Holy Ghost. Amen.

Then shall the minister join their right hands together and say:

Those whom God hath joined together, let no man put asunder.

Forasmuch as M and N have consented to live together in holy wedlock and have witnessed the same before God and this company, and thereto have pledged their faith to each other, and have declared the same by joining hands: I pronounce that they are man and wife together, in the name of the Father, and of the Son, and of the Holy Ghost. Amen.

And the minister shall add this blessing.

God the Father, God the Son, and God the Holy Ghost, bless, preserve and keep you; the Lord mercifully with his favor look upon you and so fill you with all spiritual benediction and grace, that you may so live together in this live [sic], that in the world to come ye may have life everlasting. Amen.

Then shall the minister say:

Our Father, who art in heaven, hallowed be thy name. Thy kingdom come. Thy will be done on earth, as it is in heaven. Give us this day our daily bread. And forgive us our trespasses, as we forgive those who trespass against us. And lead us not into temptation; but deliver us from evil: for thine is the kingdom, the power, and the glory, forever. Amen.

Then shall the minister say:

O God of Abraham, God of Isaac, God of Jacob, bless this man and woman, and sow the seeds of eternal life in their hearts, that whatsoever in thy holy word they shall profitably learn, they may indeed fulfill the same. Look, O Lord, mercifully upon them from heaven and bless them. And as thou didst send thy blessings upon Abraham and Sarah, to their great comfort, so vouchsafe to send thy blessings upon this man and this woman, that they obeying thy will, and always being in safety under thy protection, may abide in thy love unto their lives' end, through Jesus Christ our Lord. Amen.

O God, who by thy mighty power hast made all things of nothing, who also (after other things set in order,) didst appoint that out of man (created after thine own image and similitude,) woman should take her beginning; and knitting them together, didst teach that it should never be lawful to put asunder those whom thou, by matrimony, hast made one; O God who has consecrated the state of matrimony to such an excellant [*sic*] mystery, that in it is signified and represented the spiritual marriage and union betwixt Christ and his Church,—look mercifully upon this man and this woman; that both this man may love his wife according to thy word, (as Christ did love his spouse, the Church, who gave himself for it, loving and cherishing it even as his own flesh,) and also that this woman may be loving and obedient to her husband; and in all quietness, sobriety and peace, be a follower of holy and godly matrons. O Lord, bless them both, and grant them to inherit thy everlasting kingdom, through Jesus Christ our Lord. Amen.

Then shall the minister say:

Almighty God, who at the beginning didst create our first parents, Adam and Eve, and didst sanctify and join them together in marriage, pour upon you the riches of his grace, sanctify and bless you that ye may please him both in body and soul, and live together in holy love unto your lives' end. Amen.

BURIAL OF THE DEAD.

(We will on no account whatever make a charge for burying the dead.)

448. Form for the Burial of the Dead

Any of these Scriptures may be taken for the occasion.

The minister, going before the Corpse, shall say:

I am the resurrection, and the life: he that believeth in me, though he were dead, yet shall he live: and whosoever liveth and believeth in me shall never die. John xi,25, 26.

I know that my Redeemer liveth, and that he shall stand at the later [*sic*] day upon the earth: and though after my skin worms destroy this body, yet in my flesh shall I see God: whom I shall see for myself, and mine eyes shall behold, and not another. Job xix.25–27.

We brought nothing into this world, and it is certain we can carry nothing out. The Lord gave, and the Lord hath taken away; blessed be the name of the Lord. 1 Tim. vi,7; Job i,21.

In the House or Church may be read one or both of the following Psalms, or some other suitable portion of the Holy Scriptures:

We may read this at the unsaved but not at the saved.

I said, I will take heed to my ways, that I sin not with my tongue: I will keep my mouth with a bridle, while the wicked is before me. I was dumb with silence. I held my peace, even from good; and my sorrow was stirred. My heart was hot within me: while I was musing the fire burned: then spake I with my tongue, Lord, make me to know mine end, and the measure of my days, what it is; that I may know how frail I am. Behold, thou hast made my days as a handbreadth; and mine age is as nothing before thee; verily every man at his best state is altogether vanity. Surely every man walketh in a vain show: surely they are disquieted in vain: he heapeth up riches, and knoweth not who shall gather them. And now, Lord, what wait I for? my hope is in thee. Deliver me from all my transgressions: make me not the reproach of the foolish. I was dumb, I opened my mouth; because thou didst it. Remove thy stroke away from me; I am consumed by the blow of thine hand. When thou with rebukes does correct a man for iniquity, thou makest his beauty to consume away like a moth: surely every man is vanity. Hear my prayer, O Lord, and give ear to my cry; hold not thy peace at my tears: for I am a stranger with thee, and a sojourner, as all my fathers were. O spare me, that I may recover strength, before I go hence, and be no more.

PSALM XC:

Lord, thou has been our dwelling-place in all generations. Before the mountains were brought forth, or ever thou hadst formed the earth and the world, even from everlasting to everlasting, thou art God. Thou turnest man to destruction; and sayest, Return, ye children of men. For a thousand years in thy sight are but as yesterday when it is past, and as a watch in the night. Thou carriest them away as with a flood; they are as a sleep: in the morning they are like grass which groweth up. In the morning it flourisheth, and groweth up: in the evening it is cut down, and withereth. For we are consumed by thine anger, and by thy wrath are we troubled. Thou hast set our iniquities before thee, our secret sins in the light of thy countenance. For all our days are passed away in thy wrath: we spend our years as a tale that is told. The days of our years are threescore years and ten; and if by reason of strength they be four score years, yet is their strength labor and sorrow; for it is soon cut off, and we fly away. Who knoweth the power of thine anger? even according to thy fear, that we may apply our hearts unto wisdom. Return, O Lord, how long? and let it repent thee concerning thy servants. O satisfy us early with thy mercy; that we may rejoice and be glad all our days. Make us glad according to the days wherein thou hast afflicted us, and the years wherein we have seen evil. Let thy work appear unto thy servants, and thy glory unto their children. And let the beauty of the Lord our God be upon us: and establish thou the work of our hands upon us; yea, the work of our hands establish thou it.

Then may follow the reading of the Epistle, as follows: 1 Corinthians xv, 41–58:

There is one glory of the sun, and another glory of the moon, and another glory of the stars; for one star differeth from another star in glory. So also is the resurrection of the dead. It is sown in corruption, it is raised in incorruption: it is sown in dishonor, it is raised in glory; it is sown in weakness, it is raised in power; it is sown a natural body, and is raised a spiritual body. And so it is written, The first man Adam was made a living soul; the last Adam was made a quickening spirit. Howbeit that was not first which is spiritual, but that which is natural; and afterward that which is spiritual. The first man is of the earth, earthy; the second man is the Lord from heaven. As is the earthy, such are they also that are earthy, and as is the heavenly, such are they also that are heavenly. And as we have borne the image of the earthy, we shall also bear the image of the heavenly. Now this I say, brethren, that flesh and blood cannot inherit the kingdom of God; neither doth corruption inherit incorruption. Behold, I show you a mystery; We shall not all sleep, but we shall all be changed, in a moment, in the twinkling of an eye, at the last trump: for the trumpet shall sound, and the dead shall be raised incorruptible, and we shall be changed. For this corruptible must put on incorruption, and this mortal must put on immortality, then shall be brought to pass the saying that is written, Death is swallowed up in victory. O death, where is thy sting? O grave, where is thy victory? The sting of death is sin; and the strength of sin is the law. But thanks be to God, which giveth us the victory through our Lord Jesus Christ. Therefore, my beloved brethren, be ye steadfast, unmovable, always abounding in the work of the Lord, forasmuch as ye know that your labor is not in vain in the Lord.

At the grave, when the Corpse is laid in the Earth, the Minister shall say:

Man that is born of a woman hath but a short time to live, and is full of misery. He cometh up, and is cut down like a flower: he fleeth as it were a shadow, and never continueth in one stay.

In the midst of life we are in death: of whom may we seek for succor, but of thee, O Lord, who for our sins are justly displeased?

Yet, O Lord God most holy, O Lord most mighty, O holy and most merciful Saviour, deliver us not into the bitter pains of eternal death.

Thou knowest, Lord, the secrets of our hearts; shut not thy merciful ears to our prayers, but spare us, Lord most holy: O God most mighty, O holy and merciful Saviour, thou most worthy Judge eternal, suffer us not at our last hour for any pains of death to fall from thee.

Then, while the Earth shall be cast upon the Body by some standing by, the Minister shall say:

Forasmuch as it hath pleased Almighty God, in his wise providence, to take out of the world the soul of the departed, we therefore commit his body to the ground, earth to earth, ashes to ashes; dust to dust; looking for the general resurrection in the last day, and the life of the world to come, through our Lord Jesus Christ; at whose second coming in glorious majesty to judge the world, the earth and the sea shall give up their dead; and the corruptible bodies of those who sleep in him shall be changed and made like unto his own glorious body; according to the mighty working whereby he is able to subdue all things unto himself.

Then shall be said:

I heard a voice from heaven saying unto me, Write, From henceforth blessed are the dead who die in the Lord: Even so, saith the Spirit, for they rest from their labors.

Then shall the Minster say:

Lord, have mercy upon us.

Christ, have mercy upon us.

Lord, have mercy upon us.

This prayer only can be prayed at the save grave.

Then the Minister may offer this Prayer:

Almighty God, with whom do live the spirits of those who depart hence in the Lord, and with whom the souls of the faithful, after they are delivered from the burden of the flesh, are in joy and felicity: we give thee hearty thanks for the good examples of all those thy servants, who, having finished their course in faith, do now rest from their labors. And we beseech thee, that we, with all those who are departed in the true faith of thy holy name, may have our perfect consummation and bliss, both in body and soul, in thy eternal and everlasting glory, through Jesus Christ our Lord. Amen.

The Collect.

O Merciful God, the Father of our Lord Jesus Christ, who is the resurrection and the life; in whom whosoever believeth shall live, though he die, and whosoever liveth and believeth in him shall not die eternally: we meekly beseech thee, O Father, to raise us from the death of sin unto the life of righteousness; that when we shall depart this life we may rest in him; and at the general resurrection on the last day may be found acceptable in thy sight, and receive that blessing which thy well-beloved Son shall then pronounce to all that love and fear thee, saying, Come, ye blessed children of my Father, receive the kingdom prepared for you from the beginning of the world. Grant this, we beseech thee, O merciful Father, through Jesus Christ our Mediator and Redeemer. Amen.

Our Father who are in heaven, hallowed be thy name. Thy kingdom come. Thy will be done on earth, as it is in heaven. Give us this day our daily bread: and forgive us our trespasses, as we forgive them that trespass against us: and lead us not into temptation, but deliver us from evil: for thine is the kingdom, and the power, and the glory, forever. Amen.

The grace of our Lord Jesus Christ, and the love of God, and the fellowship of the Holy Ghost, be with us all evermore. Amen.

[AMENDED ARTICLES]

Article V, as an additional piece to the Constitution, covering doctrinal points and articles of faith.

The Apostolic Faith Mission, 312 Azusa Street, stands for the following Scriptural Doctrines, ordinances and truths, to-wit:

First, as amended: "Justification by faith, which we interpret as being the 'Forgiveness of Sins,' which is the 'New Birth,' spoken of in John 3:1–13; also Acts 10:42–43; Rom. 3:25. The Doctrine of Justification shall not be changed."

Second, as amended: "Sanctification by faith as a second definite work of Grace upon the heart, which represents entire cleansing, made Holy in heart." John 17:15–17; 1 Thess. 4:3–5; Thess. 4:3; Heb. 2:11–13; Heb. 10:10; Heb. 13:12. The doctrine of Sanctification cannot be changed.

Third, as amended: "The Baptism with the Holy Ghost as a gift of power upon the sanctified life, an anointing for service and work." Acts 2:1–4; Acts 10:45–46; Acts 19:6; 1 Cor. 4:21.

Fourth, as amended: "The speaking in tongues being one of the 'signs following' the baptised believers and other evidences of the Bible casting out devils, healing the sick and with the fruits of spirit accompanying the signs." 1 Cor. 13; Mark 16:16–19; Acts 2:2–3; Acts 10:44–45–46; Acts 19:6.

Fifth, as amended: "We believe and teach that God intended and Jesus taught that there could be no Holy union between man and woman after divorcement for any cause, so long as both parties to the first covenant lives." Mal. 2:14–17; Matt. 5:32; Matt. 19:3–9; Mark 10:11–12; Luke 16:18; Rom. 7:1–4; 1 Cor 7:39.

Sixth, as amended: "We believe in the ordinance of 'Water Baptism,' and teach that immersion is the only mode, in the name of the Father and of the Son, and of the Holy Ghost, only one dip, in the name of the Trinity."

Seventh, as amended: "We believe in the ordinance of the Lord's Supper as instituted by Jesus and followed by the Apostles, and teach that it, should be frequently observed in holy reverence."

We do not believe in Baptizing babies or children before they become to the age of accountability. A little child cannot believe.

Eighth, as amended: "We believe in feet washing as an ordinance, as it was established by our Master before the Lord's Supper, according to John

13:4–18, and believe it was practiced by the Apostles and disciples through the First Century." 1 Tim. 5:10.

To belong to this faith they must obey its teachings.

MARRIAGE.

*1. We do not prohibit our people from marrying persons who are not of our Church, provided such persons have the New Birth, and are seeking the power of godliness; but we are determined to discourage their marrying persons who do not come up to this description. Many of our Members have married unawakened persons. This has produced bad effects; they have been either hindered for life, or have turned back to perdition.

*2. To discourage such marriages, 1. Let every Minister publicly enforce the Apostle's caution. "Be ye not unequally yoked together with unbelievers" (2 Cor. vi,14). 2. Let all be exhorted to take no step in so weighty a matter without advising with the more serious of their brethren [sic].

*3. In general a woman ought not to marry without the consent of her pearents [sic]. Yet there may be exceptions. For if, 1. A woman believe it to be her duty to marry; if, 2. Her parents absolutely refuse to let her marry any Christian; then she may, nay ought to marry to marry [sic] without their consent. Yet even then a Minister ought not to be married to her.

SLAVERY.

We declare that we are as much as ever convinced of the great evil of Slavery. We believe that the buying, selling, or holding of human beings, to be used as chattles [sic], is contrary to the laws of God and nature, and inconsistent with the Golden Rule, and with that Rule in our Discipline which requires all who desire to continue among us to "do no harm," and to "avoid evil of every kind." We therefore affectionately admonish all our Ministers and people to keep themselves pure from this great evil, and to seek its extirpation by all lawful and Christian means.

EDUCATIONAL INSTITUTIONS

Our Preachers must take a caurse [sic] of studies as the Bishop shall prescribe later on.

*1. The educational institutions under the patronage of the Church shall be classified as follows:
    1. Primary Schools.
    2. Secondary Schools.

3. Colleges.
4. Universities.
5. Schools of Theology.
6. Apostolic Faith or Bible Schools.

In mission fields and other localities where inadequate provision has been made for elementary instruction, primary schools may be established.

THE ORDINANCE OF FEET WASHING

Then shall the minister say on the night or day when they gather to wash feet: Dear Beloved Brethren: We have gathered here in the name of our Lord Jesus Christ to partake in this holy and sacred Ordinance of Foot Washing which our Lord instituted on the same night he instituted the Lord's Supper, so we count it a happy night or day to carry it out. For our Lord said (John 13:13–17): "Ye call me master and Lord, and ye say well; for so I am. If I am then, your Lord and master have washed your feet; ye also ought to wash one another's feet. For I have given you an example, that ye should do as I have done to you. Verily, verily, I say unto you: The servant is not greater than his Lord; neither he that is sent greater than he that sent him. If ye know these things, happy are ye if ye do them." Then the minister shall say to his people this is the Master's saying, so we will obey it. Then shall he say Christ so loved the church, that he gave himself for it, that he might sanctify by the washing of water by the word, that he might present unto himself a glorious Church without spots or wrinkle, or any such thing; but that it should by Holy and without blemish. So when we wash each other [*sic*] feet we acknowledge that we are washed in the Blood of Jesus, and have pure hearts, and love each other. So Foot Washing gives every member a chance to examine himself before taking the Lord's Supper. So he can wash all the stripe like the Phil Jailer (Acts 16:21), that is to say if we wrong any we will be willing to Humble ourselves. The minister can read St. John 13 and comment on it as the Lord gave words to say in Harmony with the ordinance.

THE CHURCH AND ITS MISSION

The mission of the Church is to "Go Ye therefore and teach all nations, baptize them in the name of the Father, and of the Son, and the Holy Ghost. Teaching them to observe all things whatsoever I have commanded you; and lo, I am with you always, even unto the end of the world. Amen."

Now the church is to teach all that the Saviour commanded it to teach. Matt. 28:19–20; Matt. 10:1–14; Luke 9:1–6; Luke 10:1–20; Luke 22:35–37.

So the Church is to hold fast to Christ's teaching till he comes. Our children are to be instructed in their homes; the little babes are to be blessed by the church. Christ commanded to bring the little children to the church and have them blessed. And they brought young children to him, that he should teach them: and his disciples rebuked those that brought them.

But when Jesus saw it, he was much displeased, and said unto them, Suffer the little children to come unto me, and forbid them not: for of such is the kingdom of God.

Verily I say unto you, Whatsoever shall not receive the kingdom of God as a little child, he shall not enter therein.

And he took them up in his arms, put his hands upon them, and blessed them.

DUTY OF PARENTS

I. The duty of parents to their children.
    1. They should love them.
        Titus 2:4.
    2. They should train them up for God.
        Prov. 22:6.
        Eph. 6:4.
    3. They should instruct instruct [*sic*] them in God's word.
        Deut. 4:9.
        Deut. 11:19.
        Isa. 38:19.
    4. They should rule them.
        1 Tim. 3:4, 12.
    5. They should correct them.
        Prov. 13:24.
        Prov. 19:18.
        Prov. 23:13.
        Prov. 12:7.
II. Good parents.
    1. Pity their children.
        Psa. 103:13.
    2. Provide for their children.
        2 Cor. 12:14.
        1 Tim. 5:8.
    3. Pray for their children.
        1 Chr. 29:19.
        Job 1:5.
        John 4:46–49.

DUTY TO CHILDREN

I. Children are
   1. A blessing Prov. 10:1, Prov. 15:20.
       Prov. 17:6.
       Psa. 128:1–4.
   2. A gift from God.
       Psa. 127:3.
       Gen. 33:5.

II. The duty of children.
   1. They should obey God.
       Deut. 30:2.
   2. They should seek God early.
       Eccl. 12:1.
   3. They should attend to parental teaching.
       Prov. 1:8, 9.
   4. They should honor their parents.
       Heb. 12:9.
   5. They should obey their parents.
       Prov. 6:20–23.
       Eph. 6:1–3.
   6. They should take care of their parents.
       1 Tim. 5:4.

III. Good children.
   1. Observe the law of God.
       Prov. 28:7.
   2. Shall be blessed.
       Prov. 3:1–6.
   3. Show love to their parents.
       Gen. 46:29.

A CHRISTIAN HOME

A christian home is one of the sweetest places on God's green earth. It is a place where God is honored: a place where the Christ of God is worshipped! O how blessed it is to enter a Christian home where God is honored! God is mindful of our homes for we read in Gen. 18:17 and 19. God said, "Shall I hide from Abraham the destruction of Sodom and Gomorrah? Shall I hide from Abraham the thing which I do, seeing that Abraham shall surely become a great nation and all the nations of the earth shall be blessed in him: for I know him." Praise the Lord! God knows us. He knows our hearts, praise his name! Just listen what God said about Abraham? Can he say that about every home? This is a standard for us to go by. I know him that he will command his children and his household. Everything followed him: that is to say that the whole family would follow the example of Abraham in holiness and obedience to God's Word. It is so blessed when you can find a home saved. Father takes his place at the head of the home. Eph. 5:23. He rules it according to the word of God. Again God says, "And they shall keep the way of the Lord to do justice and judgment: that the Lord may bring upon Abraham that which he has spoken of him. We read again in 1 Tim. 3–4. To be a bishop he must have a home that will measure up to the word, he must be one that ruleth well his own house, having his children in subjection with all gravity, for if a man know not how to rule his own house how shall he take care of the Church of God. 1 Tim. 3, 4, 5. We read again in the Old Testament, Joshua 24:15. Joshua could speak for his whole family. When the Israelites were going astray after other Gods Joshua brought them together and he said: "If it seem evil unto you to serve the Lord, choose you this day whom you will serve whether the Gods which your fathers serve when you were on the other side of the flood, or the Gods of the Amorites in whose land ye dwelt but, as for me and my house, we will serve the Lord." And the people answered and said, "God forbid that we should forsake the Lord to serve other Gods." We can see that Joshua's home was a home for God. The promise is to you and your children. Acts 2:39. We see in another place in the word where God saves a whole home in one night. The Philippian jailer was saved and his whole household. Acts 16:32. This was a wonderful time in the prison. O how sweet it is to be a servant of God! We see that they had been beaten for this Gospel. But they were not discouraged. They prayed and sang at midnight and Heaven and Earth met together in that jail and God shook all those locks open so that they could carry on the meeting for souls. God awoke the jailer out of his sleep and he was saved that night and all his house was saved. Home is a place where characters are fashioned. If the Lord rules the home, all will be right. Home is a place where father and mother are found where children are born and reared. It is a community of persons, self-governed, or a kingdom within itself. It is an organization formed by God himself. The home is a sacred place which should be godly. Our preachers, statesmen, governors and president comes from the home. When Moses was found, Pharaoh's daughter said, "Take this child away and nurse it for me and I will give thee thy wages." The woman took the child and nursed it. Ex. 2:9. This was the great leader of Israel. O how sweet these words are! "Take this child away and nurse it for me and I will give thee thy wages." This is God's word to every mother. "Take this child and raise it for God and he will pay us in glory, for we don't know what he will be for God. We should be more careful in rearing our children. Although many homes have not children, they should be Christian homes just the same so that God would make them blessings to those who enter in them.

THE SOUL OF MAN

The soul is the real man. Matt. 16:26. For what is a man profited if he gain the whole world and lose his own soul or what shall a man give in exchange for his soul? And fear not them that kill the body but are not able to kill the soul; but rather fear him which is able to destroy both soul and body in hell. Matt. 10:28. The soul stands for the whole man. It is immortal and immaterial. But yet man himself is a trinity. He is a trinity like his maker. Consisting of spirit, soul and body. 1 Thess. 5:23. And the very God of peace sanctify you wholly; and I pray God your whole spirit and soul and body be preserved blameless unto the coming of our Lord Jesus Christ. Faithful is he that calleth you, who also will do it. So we see that we are spirit and soul and body.

The soul stands for the whole man because it will be required at the judgment. Thou fool, this night thy soul shall be required of thee. Luke 12:20.

Since man fell he has a perfect salvation granted him through Jesus Christ for spirit, soul and body. 1 Thess. 5:23. So, when speaking about the eternal existence of man, we say his soul.

The spirit, the higher nature of man is that which knows God, John 3:5–6. Jesus answered, "Verily, verily I say unto thee. Except a man be born of water and of the Spirit he cannot enter the Kingdom of God. That which is born of the flesh is flesh; that which is born of the Spirit is Spirit. Therefore it is through the Spirit that we know God. St. John 4:24. God is a spirit and they that worship him must worship him in Spirit and in truth. The Spirit is man's higher nature which knoweth God and commune with God by the Spirit. Before we can know God we must repent of our sins and accept Jesus and be born of the Spirit. Then we can know God for we have his Spirit to witness with our Spirit that we are the sons of God. The Spirit itself beareth witness with our Spirit, that we are children of God. Rom. 8:16. The Spirit is the higher nature of man which knows God, distinguishes between right and wrong and is capable of religious affections, emotions and exercises. This is Spiritual life.

MAN A TRINITY

The highest life a man can live is to commune with God, being born again and being filled with God's spirit.

Man, according to the Bible philosophy, is a trinity like his creator, consisting of spirit, soul and body. 1 Thess. 5:23. And the very God of peace sanctify you wholly: and I pray God your whole spirit and soul and body be preserved blameless unto the coming of our Lord Jesus Christ.

Faith is he that calleth you, who also will do it. Heb. 4:12.

The word of God is quick and powerful, and sharper than any two-edged sword, piercing even to the dividing asunder of soul and spirit and the joints and marrow, and is discerner of the thoughts and intents of the heart. Neither is there any creature that is not manifest in his sight. Heb. 4:12, 13. Man is a trinity. The spirit is his higher nature, that which knows God and distinguishes between right and wrong. Adam knew right from wrong because as soon as he did wrong he hid himself from the presence of God. Gen. 2:17; Gen. 3:7.

The spirit is the higher nature of man, capable of religious affections, emotions and exercise. The physical is the other extreme. It is the earthy part of man, material organism indewlt [sic] by the soul. They are tied together with spirit and the instrument of its desires, purposes and operations. Intermediate between these is the soul, the rational mind, the seat of the affections, the understanding, that which loves and hates, that which can discriminate, that which thinks, that which can be cultivated and which has at once its lower passion and its fined tastes.

The physical man is the man that is controlled by the physical nature. There are three conditions in which we may live. First, we may be controlled by our lower nature, our animal life or existence—our body and its gross appetites. This is pure sensuality, the real flesh life, the fruit of the flesh. Gal. 5:19–21.

Secondly, by our intellectual department, our tastes; by our intelligence and our affections and passions; the proud and haughty physical nature. If a man is controlled by his intelligence, it makes him proud many times. If he is controlled by his mind alone, he will be heady and high minded. He will be nice but in his heart he will be proud. Nothing can atone for him but the blood of Jesus Christ, the son of God.

Thirdly, he may be controlled by his spiritual nature. This will be quite different. The man that is controlled by his intellect will be worldly minded. His mind must be fed. How? By the material things—shows, picnics, card parties, dances, and big dinners. The natural man is controlled by his natural mind. He cannot help it because he was born after the fallen Adam. He must be born again. St. John 3:3. Behold I was shapen in iniquity and in sin did my mother conceive me. Psalms 51:5; Psalms 58:3.

Since all these departments of man's nature are fallen and under the curse, he needs the blood of Jesus Christ. When a man is born again he is a new cerature [sic]. 2 Cor. 5:17. Old things are passed away, all things have become new.

Since the three departments are fallen we need to turn the whole man over to God. 1 Thes. 5:23. All of these departments are tied together by the almighty God. His body is mortal, his spirit and soul are immortal.

It seems that the soul stands for the entire man or the whole of man. Heb. 10:39. Believing to the saving of the soul. "What will it profit a man if he gain the whole world and lose his own soul."

Temptations are great but the blood is sufficient for every trial. If we yield to the bodily appetites, we become sensual: if we yield to those of the mind, we become worldly-minded, and if we yield to an evil spirit we become devilish. May God help us to become strong and arm ourselves against the flesh. Eph. 6:10, 11.

We must remember that every man that is born in the world is lame in his intellect, will and affections. He must be born again and get sanctified and get filled with the Holy Ghost and go on to perfection. Heb. 6:1–4. That is the only safeguard for Christians.

Many churches today get a physical preacher to preach about Christ and many of them know nothing about Christ because they have not been born again. The Bible teaches that a man must be born again. St. John 3:3.

We learn from the Bible that a man must be holy to see God. Matt. 5:8. In Christ's first sermon on the mount, he preached holiness. Matt. 5:8; Matt. 5:20; Matt. 5:48; Heb. 12:14. Holiness, without which no man shall see the Lord. Many people today go to church and just hear a physical sermon and come back no better in their soul than they were before going. God help us. Amen.

PLAN OF SALVATION

The plan of salvation is already laid, so we can do nothing to improve it. It is fixed for all eternity. We are to accept it as it is. When we set up our own standard of holiness for God to work by, we dishonor God and set up an idol in our hearts. When we do this, also we tell God in the way we act that we won't hear his word without him coming to our terms. God wants us to have faith to take him at his word. So many people have made shipwreck of their faith by setting up a standard for God to respect or come to. When we set up tongues to be, the Bible evidence of Baptism in the Holy Ghost and fire only. We have left the divine word of God and have instituted our own teaching. But if we will take the divine word of God, it will lead us right. Ezekiel 14, says when a man set up any idols in his heart and seek the Lord, and if the prophet be deceived. He says he is the one that deceive the prophet. Ezekiel 14:9.

While tongues is one of the signs that follows God's spirit filled children, they will have to know the truth and de [*sic*] the truth. If not, grievous wolves will enter in among the flock and tear asunder the sheep. How will he get in? They will come in through the sign gift of speaking in tongues, and if God's children did not know anything more than that to be the evidence, they would not have no hard time to enter in among them and scatter them. The Holy Ghost gives men and women wisdom to execute the power of his word. 1 Cor. 4:20.

All ordination must be done by men not women. Women may be ministers but not to Baptize and ordain in this work.

THE APOSTOLIC FAITH

Stands for the restoration of the faith once delivered to the saints—the old-time religion, of camp meetings, revivals, missions, street and mission work and Christian unity everywhere. According to God's word, John 17:21, 25

Teaching on Repentance. Mark 1:14, 15.

Godly Sorrow for Sins—Examples: Matt. 9:13; 2 Cor. 7:9, 11; Acts 3:19; Acts 17:30.

Confession of Sin. Luke 15:21; Luke 18:13.

Forsaking Sinful Ways. Isa. 55:7; Jonah 3:8; Prov. 28:13.

Restitution. Ezek. 33:15; Luke 19:18, and Faith in Jesus Christ.

Jesus died for our sins and arose for our Justification. Rom. 4:25.

First Work: Justification is that act of God's free grace by which we receive remission of sins. Rom. 3:25; Acts 10:42, 43; Rom. 5:1, 10; John 3:3, 14; 2 Cor. 5:17.

The Holy Ghost call the second work the second benefit. The margin read second grace. And the Syriac read that you might receive the grace doubly. 2 Cor. 1:15.

Second Work: Sanctification is the second work of grace and is that act of God's grace by which He makes us holy in Doctrine and life. John 17:15, 17; Heb. 13:12:2:11; Heb. 12:14. Jesus opened the Bibye [Bible] to his disciples before he went back to Heaven. Luke 24:24–50. He taught his doctrine to them well before He went to Heaven so when we get sanctified Jesus will teach us the Bible also, bless the Lord.

Sanctification is cleansing to make holy. The disciples were sanctified before the day of Pentecost. By careful study of Scripture, you will find it is so now. "Ye are clean through the word which I have spoken unto you." John 15:3; John 13:10; and Jesus had breathed on them the Holy Ghost. John 20:21, 22. You know that they could not receive the Spirit if they were not all clean. Jesus cleansed and got all doubt out of His church before He went back to glory. The Disciples had the grace of the Spirit before the day of Pentecost. The Disciples had an infilling of the spirit before the day of Pentecost. For

Jesus had cleansed the Sanctuary and they had the witness in their hearts that he was their risen Lord and Savior and continually in the temple praising and blessing God. Luke 24:51, 53.

The baptism in the Holy Ghost and fire means to be flooded with the love of God and Power for Service, and a love for the truth as it is in God's word. So when we receive it we have the same signs to follow as the disciples received on the day of Pentecost. For the Holy Spirit gives us a sound mind, faith, love and power. 2 Tim. 1:7. This is the standard Jesus gave to the Church.

The greatest evidence of the Holy Spirit abiding in the believer is what Jesus Christ promised he would do. Jesus promised he would teach us all things, and bring all things to your remembrance, whatsoever I have said unto you, so he means what he says, whatsoever I have said so he means what he says. John 14:17–26. Also John 16:7–15. So when he comes he does that in the believer, for he does it for me.

Seeking Healing. We must believe that God is able to heal. Exodus 15:26. "I am the Lord that health thee." Jas. 5:14; Psa. 103:3; 2 Kings 20:5; Matt. 8:16, 17; Mark 16:16–18. "Behold I am the Lord, the God of all flesh; is there anything too hard for me?" Jer. 32:27; Luke 24:52, 53. With great joy.

God, Spirit and Word goes together. They are the two witnesses spoken of in Zech. 4:3–14; Rev. 11:3. When these two witnesses are not recognized all kinds of confusion will be manifested in the Church.

Too many have confused the grace of Santifcation [*sic*] with the Enduement of Power, or the Baptism with the Holy Ghost; others have taken "the annointing" [*sic*] (John 20:21–24) which we receive after we are sanctified for the Baptism, and failed to reach the glory and power of a true Pentecost. Act 2:3, 4.

We read in the second chapter of Colossians: "Beware lest any man spoil you through philosophy and vain deceit, after the tradition of men, after the rudiments of the world, and not after Christ." This chapter tells us about Christ blotting out the handwriting of ordinances that were against, and contrary to us, and I am glad he did nail these ordinances to the cross with Him, took them out of the way, nailing it to His cross. Bless the Lord. These were the old Jewish ordinances of divers washings, Sabbath days, new moons, circumcision and the Passover supper, and so on. But Jesus has ordinances in His church. Bless His dear Name.

Three ordinances Christ Himself instituted in His Church. First—He commands His ministers to baptise in water in the name of the Father and the Son and the Holy Ghost. Matt. 28:19; and it was practiced by the Apostles. Acts 2:38; Acts 22:16; Acts 8:12, 17. The enuch [*sic*], Acts 8:35, 38. The Apostle Paul was baptised. So many cases we can find in Acts where it was practised after John the Baptist had died. Second—Foot washing is an ordinance that Jesus Himself instituted in His Church, and we, His followers, should observe it. For He has commanded us to observe all things that He has commanded us to teach. So we find we will have to recognize these three ordinances.

We believe in the feet washing; we believe it to be an ordinance, John 13: Jesus said, in the 13th verse of the 13th chapter of John: "Ye call me Master and Lord, and ye say well, for so I am." Verse 14th: "If I then, your Lord and Master, have washed your feet, ye also ought to wash one another's feet." Verse 15: "Says, for I have given you an example, that ye should do as I have done to you. Verily, verily I say unto you, the servant is not greater than his Lord: neither is he that is sent greater than he that sent him. If ye know these things, happy are ye if ye do them." John 13:13–17.

We believe in the ordinance of the Lord's supper, as it is set forth in 1 Cor. 11:2, 23–34; Matt. 26:26–29. We believe in taking unfermented wine and unleavened bread.

We believe in water baptism. Our mode is immersion only, and single, in the name of the Father, and of the Son, and of the Holy Ghost. Matt. 28:19, 20; 2 Cor. 13:13; and as much light as the Holy Ghost will reveal to us by His word. We, the ministers, must be the husband of one wife. 1 Tim. 3:2; Tit. 1:6–9. We do not believe in unscriptural marriage. Rom. 7:2–4; 1 Cor. 7:39.

In Matt. 19:3–9; Matt. 5:32, and Mark 10:5–11, Jesus restored marriage back to the Edenic standard. Many are confused over the meaning of these passages. If either the husband or wife have defiled themselves in the sins mentioned Jesus does not give either recognition as being legally married, while the first husband or wife is still living. They must repent to God and be reconciled to each other (1 Cor. 7:11) "for as Christ forgives so must we forgive." If a man or woman marry and either one has a living husband or wife their continuing to live together as a committing of fornication or adultery and the party who has a living husband or wife should be put away by the other, leaving the man or woman who has no living companion free to marry again to some one who is also free. 1 Cor. 7:2; Matt. 19:9.

We do not believe in making a hobby of this doctrine of divorce, but we believe in the truth by comparing Scripture with Scripture, that no one in this work can marry the second husband or the second wife, while the first one is living. Rom. 7:2, 3, 4; 1 Cor. 7:10–11; 1 Cor. 7:39; 1 Tim. 3:9; Matt. 5:32; Luke 16:18; Mark ?:2–12.

Bishop Hurst says, in Church History, that the gift of tongues has appeared in communities under powerful religious stimulus, as among the Carnisards [sic], early Quakers, Lasare in Sweden in 1841–43, in the Irish Revival in 1859, and in the Catholic Apostolic (Irvingite) Church. (Vol. 1, page 90.)

I can say, through the power of the Spirit, that wherever God can get a people that will come together in one accord and one mind in the Word of God, the baptism of the Holy Ghost will fall upon them, like as a Cornelius' house (Acts 10:45, 46). It means, to be in one accord, as the Word says, Acts 2:42, 47.

The Blood of Jesus will never blot out any sin between man and man they can make right; but if we can't make wrongs right, the blood graciously covers. Matt. 5:24; Matt. 6:15; Matt. 18:35; 1 John 1:7–9.

Dear Loved Ones: God's promises are true. We read in Exodus 12:3, God commanded Moses to take a lamb for a house and a house for a lamb when he was about to bring the children out of Egypt. Bless His Holy Name, amen! They were to kill the lamb and take its blood and sprinkle it over the door overhead and the sides to save them from the destroyer. But in the very house they were instructed to eat the body. The blood saved them from the destroyer, but the body of the lamb saved them from disease and sickness. Glory to His Name! May we obey God's word and voice and we shall be saved through Jesus from sins, and feasting on His perfect body. Jesus is founder of His Church, the Christian Church, by His own precious Blood. Hallelujah! so [*sic*] Jesus is the Christian Passover? So when the Jews eat the passover they remember God bringing them out of Egypt, and point to His coming. So we eat the Christian passover and remember Calvary, how Jesus died and saved us, and we look forward to His coming again.

Moses' lamb was a type of Christ, the true Lamb, so Christ is our Lamb, bring health to our imperfect body. Moses was founder of the Jewis [*sic*] Church by God through the paschal lamb by the blood and body of the lamb. But Jesus is the Lamb of God, the founder of the Christian Church.

WILLIAM JOSEPH SEYMOUR.
Azusa Mission, 312 Azusa St.,
Los Angeles, Cal.
U.S.A.

C. AZUSA STREET REVIVAL ACCOUNTS IN THE *APOSTOLIC FAITH* (1906–08)

INTRODUCTION

The following reports from Seymour's *Apostolic Faith* are important because they provide firsthand accounts of the revival and his leadership. Seymour and his editorial team published thirteen editions from September 1906 to May 1908. Although he served as the Executive Editor, a former newspaper reporter named Glenn Cook managed the mission and ran the day-to-day operations of the newspaper for about a year until he left to pioneer the work in the Midwest and Clara Lum and others replaced him. Florence Crawford, Lucy Farrow, and others assisted. The first print run was five thousand copies and the last fifty thousand, distributed free of charge around the world. Although many of the editorials, testimonials, and sermons are signed, a large number were left unsigned, probably because it would look unbecoming for Seymour to author so many entries in a single issue.

Against the expressed wishes of Seymour and the Azusa Trustees, Lum moved the paper to Portland in May 1908 and kept it there, along with the state, national, and international mailing lists. She left behind only the mailing lists for people in the Los Angeles area. Although Seymour made several attempts to recover the paper and lists in 1908 and 1909, he was unable to secure them. He reportedly printed one final edition (October–November 1908) in Los Angeles before giving up the venture. Lum and Crawford continued to publish the paper from June 1908 to March–April 1910 and thereafter under a different format.

The newspaper was vital to Seymour and the revival for many reasons. It served as a vehicle through which to teach his followers Pentecostal doctrine around the world and enabled him and his supporters to respond quickly to criticisms, misunderstandings, myths, and rumors. He also used it to publish testimonies, letters, and editorials, which lured the curious, skeptical, and spiritually hungry. Finally, he used it to challenge Parham and promote his own vision and version of Pentecostalism. Lum's decision to take the paper and mailing lists made it impossible for Seymour to continue to significantly influence the American and global Pentecostal movements since he no longer had an inexpensive way to reach the masses. The following documents are a reproduction of the original texts, although most have been shortened due to space limitations. The date and page number in parentheses were not in the original and are included here for reference.

29. PENTECOST HAS COME

LOS ANGELES BEING VISITED BY A REVIVAL OF BIBLE SALVATION AND PENTECOST AS RECORDED IN THE BOOK OF ACTS

(September 1906, 1)

The power of God now has this city agitated as never before. Pentecost has surely come and with it the Bible evidences are following, many being converted and sanctified and filled with the Holy Ghost, speaking in tongues as they did on the day of Pentecost. The scenes that are daily enacted in the building on Azusa street [sic] and at Missions and Churches in other parts of the city are beyond description. . . .

The meetings are held in an old [AME] Methodist church that had been converted in part into a tenement house, leaving a larger unplastered, barn-like room on the ground floor. Here about a dozen congregated each day, holding meetings on Bonnie Brae in the evening. The writer attended a few of these meetings and being so different from anything he had seen and not hearing any speaking in tongues, he branded the teaching as third-blessing heresy, and thought that settled it. It is needless to say the writer was compelled to do a great deal of apologizing and humbling himself to get right with God.

In a short time God began to manifest His power and soon the building could not contain the people. Now the meetings continue all day and into the night and the fire is kindling all over the city and surrounding towns. Proud, well dressed preachers come into "investigate." Soon their high looks are replaced with wonder, then conviction came, and . . . in a short time wallowing on the dirty floor, asking God to forgive them and make them as little children.

It would be impossible to state how many have been converted, sanctified, and filled with the Holy Ghost. They have been and are daily going out to all points of the compass to spread this wonderful gospel.

30. THE OLD-TIME PENTECOST.

(September 1906, 1)
This work began about five years ago last January, when a company of people under the leadership of Chas. Parham, who were studying God's word tarried for Pentecost, in Topeka, Kan. After searching through the country everywhere, they had been unable to find any Christians that had the true Pentecostal power. . . . They had a prayer tower in which prayers were ascending night and day to God. After three months, a sister who had . . . all the carnality taken out of her heart, felt the Lord lead her to have hands laid on her to receive the Pentecost. So when they prayed, the Holy Ghost came in great power and she commenced speaking in an unknown tongue. This made all the Bible school hungry, and three nights afterward, twelve students received the Holy Ghost, and prophesied, and cloven tongues could be seen upon their heads. . . .

Now after five years something like 13,000 people have received this gospel. It is spreading everywhere, until churches who do not believe backslide and lose the experience they have. Those who are old in this movement are stronger, and greater signs and wonders are following them.

The meetings in Los Angeles started in a cottage meeting [on Bonnie Brae Street], and. . . . then transferred to Azusa Street, and since then multitudes have been coming. The meetings begin about ten o'clock in the morning and can hardly stop before ten or twelve at night, and sometimes two or three in the morning, because so many are seeking, and some are slain under the power of God. People are seeking three times a day at the altar and row after row of seats have to be emptied and filled with seekers. . . . Many are speaking in new tongues, and some are on their way to the foreign fields, with the gift of the language. . . .

31. THE SAME OLD WAY.

(September 1906, 3)
It has been said of the work in Los Angeles that it was "born in a manger and resurrected in a barn." Many are praising God for the old barn-like building on Azusa street [sic], and the plain old plank beside which they kneeled in the sawdust when God saved, sanctified and baptized them with the Holy Ghost. Those who know God feel His presence as soon as they cross the threshold. . . .

The work began among the colored people. God baptized several sanctified wash women with the Holy Ghost, who have been much used of Him. . . . Since then multitudes have come. God makes no difference in nationality, Ethiopians, Chinese, Indians, Mexicans, and other nationalities worship together.

32. THE PROMISE STILL GOOD.

(September 1906, 3)

The hundred and twenty on the day of Pentecost were baptized with the Holy Ghost according to promise. . . . That . . . Apostolic church had wonderful power. . . . We have the promise of the same power today . . . [at Azusa]. . . .

At the beginning of the Eighteenth century, among the French Protestants, there were wonderful manifestations of the Spirit power accompanied by the Gift of Tongues. The early Quakers received the same powerful religious stimulus and had the Gift of Tongues. The Irvingite church, about 1830, had the baptism with the Holy Ghost, and spoke in other tongues. In the Swedish revival in 1841–43 there were the same manifestations of the Spirit and also the Gift of Tongues. In the Irish revival of 1859 there is the record of the power of the Spirit in winning souls and the speaking in tongues by Spirit filled men and women. . . . Bishop Taylor left the record that he took a young lady to labor among a certain tribe in Africa, and . . . two months later and found her preaching fluently in the native language, without having learned it.

33. THE PENTECOSTAL BAPTISM RESTORED

THE PROMISED LATTER RAIN NOW BEING POURED OUT ON GOD'S HUMBLE PEOPLE.

(October 1906, p. 1)

All along the ages men have been preaching a partial Gospel. A part of the Gospel remained when the world went into the dark ages. God has from time to time raised up men to bring back the truth to the church. He raised up [Martin] Luther to bring back . . . justification by faith. He raised up . . . John Wesley to establish Bible holiness in the church. Then he raised up Dr. [Charles] Cullis who brought back . . . divine healing. Now He is bringing back the Pentecostal Baptism to the church.

God laid His hand on a little crippled boy [Charles Parham] seven years of age and healed him of disease and made him whole except his ankles. He walked on the sides of his ankles. Then, when he was fourteen years of age, he had been sent to college and God had called him to preach. One day as he was sitting reading his Bible, a man came for him to go and hold a meeting. He began to say to the Lord: "Father, if I go to that place, it will be necessary for me to walk here and vonder [*sic*], just put strength into these ankle joints of mine." And immediately he was made whole and leaped and praised God, like the man at the beautiful gate. He has since been in evangelistic work over the United States, seeing multitudes saved, sanctified and healed.

Five years ago, God put it into this man's heart (Bro. Charles Parham) to go over to Topeka, Kansas, to educate missionaries to carry the Gospel. It was a faith school and the Bible was the only text book. The students had gathered there without tuition or board, God sending in the means to carry on the work. Most of the students had been religious workers and said they had received the baptism with the Holy Ghost a number of years ago. Bro. Parham became convinced that there was no religious school that tallied up with the second chapter of Acts. Just before the first of January, 1901, the Bible School began to study the word on the Baptism with the Holy Ghost to discover the Bible evidence of this baptism that they might obtain it.

The students kept up continual prayer in the praying tower. A company would go up and stay three hours, and then another company would go up and wait on God, praying that all the promises of the Word might be wrought out in their lives.

On New Year's night, Miss Agnes N. Ozman, one who had had for years "the anointing that abideth," which she mistook for the baptism, was convinced of the need of a personal Pentecost. A few minutes before midnight, she desired hands laid on her that she might receive the gift of the Holy Ghost. During prayer and invocation of hands, she was filled with the Holy Ghost and spoke with other tongues as the Spirit gave utterance.

This made all hungry. Scarcely eating or sleeping, the school with one accord waited on God. On the 3rd of January, 1901, Bro. Parham being absent holding a meeting at the time, while they all waited on God to send the baptism of the Spirit, suddenly twelve students were filled with the Holy Ghost and began to speak with other tongues, and when Bro. Parham returned and opened the door of the room where they were gathered, a wonderful sight met his eyes. The whole room was filled with a white sheen of light that could not be described, and twelve of the students were on their feet talking in different languages. . . .

[Later Parham] knelt in one corner and . . . the Lord took his vocal organs, and he was preaching the Word in another language. . . . He was surely raised up of God to be an apostle of the doctrine of Pentecost.

This Pentecostal Gospel has been spreading ever since, but on the Pacific coast it has burst out in great power and is being carried from here over the world. We are expecting Bro. Parham to visit Los Angeles in a few days and for a mightier tide of salvation to break out.

34. BIBLE PENTECOST

GRACIOUS PENTECOSTAL SHOWERS CONTINUE TO FALL

(November 1906, 1)
The news has spread far and wide that Los Angeles is being visited with a "rushing mighty wind from heaven." The how and why . . . is . . . the very opposite of those conditions that are usually thought necessary for a big revival. No instruments of music are used. . . . No choir . . . No collections are taken. No bills have been posted to advertise the meetings. No church or organization is back of it. . . .

But here you find a mighty Pentecostal revival going on from ten o'clock in the morning till about twelve at night. . . .

I bless God that it did not start in any church in this city, but out in the barn, so that we might all come and take part in it. If it had started in a fine church, poor colored people and Spanish people would not have got it, but praise God it started here. . . .

It is noticeable how free all nationalities feel. If a Mexican or German cannot speak English, he gets up and speaks in his own tongue and feels quite at home for the Spirit interprets through the face and people say amen. No instrument that God can use is rejected on account of color or dress or lack of education. This is why God has so built up the work. . . .

35. PENTECOST WITH SIGNS FOLLOWING.

SEVEN MONTHS OF PENTECOSTAL SHOWERS, JESUS, OUR PROJECTOR AND GREAT SHEPHERD.

(December 1906, 1)
Many are asking how the work in Azusa Mission started and who was the founder. The Lord was the founder and He is the Projector of this movement. A band of humble people in Los Angeles had been praying for a year or more for more power with God for the salvation of lost and suffering humanity. . . .

Then [the saints in Los Angeles] felt led of the Lord to call Bro. Seymour from Houston . . . and [sent] his [train] fare. . . . He told them he did not have the Pentecost but was seeking it and wanted all the saints to pray with him till all received their Pentecost. Some believed they had it, and others believed they did not have it because the signs were not following. Hardly anyone was getting saved.

There was a great deal of opposition, but they continued to fast and pray for the baptism with the Holy Spirit, till on April 9th the fire of God fell in a cottage on Bonnie Brae. Pentecost was poured out upon workers and saints. Three days after that, Bro. Seymour received his Pentecost. . . .

Hundreds of souls have received salvation and healing. . . . This revival has spread through . . . the United States . . . and across the ocean. . . .

Some are asking if Dr. Chas. F. Parham is the leader of this movement. We can answer, no he is not the leader of this movement of Azusa Mission. We thought of having him to be our leader and so stated in our paper, before waiting upon the Lord.

We can be rather hasty, especially when we are very young in the power of the Holy Spirit. We are just like a baby—full of love and were willing to accept anyone that had the baptism with the Holy Spirit as our leader. But the Lord commenced settling us down, and we saw that the Lord should be our leader. So we honor Jesus as the great Shepherd of the sheep. He is our model. . . . There is no pope, Dualism, or Sanfordism. . . .

Bro. Seymour is simply a humble pastor of the flock over which the Holy Ghost has made him overseer, according to Acts 20.28. . . . ,

We believe in old time repentance, old time conversion, old time sanctification, healing of our bodies and the baptism with the Holy Ghost. . . .

We do not believe in any eighth day creation, as some [i.e., Charles Parham] have taught, and we do not believe in the annihilation of the wicked.

We stand on Bible truth without compromise. We recognize every man that honors the blood of Jesus Christ to be our brother, regardless of denomination, creed, or doctrine. But we are not willing to accept any errors. . . . If they do not tally with the Word of God, we reject them. . . .

God is sending the latter rain, and the refreshing times have come. . . .

36. BEGINNING OF WORLD WIDE REVIVAL

(January 1907, 1)

Pentecost first fell in Los Angeles on April 9th. Since then the good tidings has spread in two hemispheres. . . . Wherever the work goes, souls are saved. . . . Hundreds have been baptized with the Holy Ghost . . .

It is a continual upper room tarrying at Azusa Street. It is like a continual camp meeting or convention. All classes and nationalities meet on a common level. . . .

The Lord is graciously healing many sick bodies . . . almost every day. . . . Handkerchiefs are sent in to be blest, and are returned to the sick and they are healed in many cases. One day nine handkerchiefs were blest, another day sixteen. . . . The mission people never take medicine . . . They have taken Jesus for their healer and He always heals.

There is a very sweet spirit of unity among Pentecostal missions in Los

Angeles and workers in suburban towns. Every Monday morning, the misiners [ministers] and workers from these different points meet together for prayer and counsel.... All are in one accord.... [and] in perfect harmony....

37. PENTECOSTAL MISSIONARY REPORTS

(October–January 1908, 1)

Since the last paper, Spirit-filled missionaries have gone out from Los Angeles [sic] to Monrovia, Liberia, Africa, two sisters to South China and a band of nine missionaries to North China. Also a band of fourteen missionaries went from Spokane, Wash., to Japan and China. They were able to talk to the Chinese and Japanese at the dock and on the ship in their native languages. The "Apostolic Light" is now published by Brother [M.L.] Ryan in Tokyo, Japan.

Our dear Brother A.H. Post... is on his way to South Africa... [and]... a Spirit-filled band of [12] missionaries... left Los Angeles for North China. ... Brother [Bernt] Bernstein [sic], Brother and Sister Hess and six workers from the Swedish Mission, made up the company from here.... Address B. Bernsten, Taiming fu, Chih-li, North China.

38. WHO MAY PROPHESY?

(January 1908, 2)

It is the privilege of all the members of the bride of Christ to prophesy, which means testify or preach....

Before Pentecost, the woman could only go into the "court of the women" and not into the inner court. The anointing oil was never poured on a womans head but only on the heads of kings, prophets and priests. But when our Lord poured out Pentecost, He brought all those faithful women with the other disciples into the upper room, and God baptized them all in the same room and made no difference. All the women received the anointed oil of the Holy Ghost and were able to preach the same as the men.

The woman is the weaker vessel and represents the tenderness of Christ, while the man represents the firmness of Christ. They both were co-workers ... in the Gospel. (I. Cor. 11:8,9.) No woman that has the Spirit of Jesus wants to usurp authority over the man. The more God uses you in the Spirit, the more... meek and tender you are and... filled with the... Holy Spirit.

It is contrary to the Scriptures that woman should not have her part in the salvation work to which God has called her. We have no right to lay a straw in her way, but to... encourage the woman in her work, and God will honor and bless us as never before. It is the same Holy Spirit in the woman as in the man.

D. HISTORICAL OVERVIEWS AND TESTIMONIES OF SEYMOUR AND THE AZUSA REVIVAL

INTRODUCTION

The following sources are historical overviews and testimonies about Seymour and the Azusa Revival and their influence around the world. These sources have been culled from histories, autobiographies, testimonies, diaries, reports, newspapers, books, and journals. The following testimonies reveal the influence that Seymour and Azusa had on some of the most important pioneer Pentecostal leaders around the world. They also help to explain why Seymour's vision and version of Pentecostalism had so quickly—in the words of Parham—supplanted his own "the true Apostolic work."

HISTORICAL OVERVIEWS

INTRODUCTION

Although none of the following documents were written by academically trained historians, most provide a broader overview of how and/or why change took place over time in the Azusa Street Revival, in Seymour's ministry, and in particular conflicts at Azusa. Shumway's thesis is arguably one of the most important sources on Seymour because it is based on interviews with Seymour and Parham and three hundred people (friends and foes) across the United States and around the world. Bartleman's *Azusa Street* was one of the first historical overviews of the rise, decline, and influence of Azusa. Vanzandt, Cook, Osterberg, and the obituary provide more partisan but still important firsthand insights and interpretations of Seymour's life, actions, and influence.

39. CHARLES SHUMWAY

Shumway's (1886–1934) 1914 AB thesis at the University of Southern California is one of the earliest and most important critical sources on Seymour,

Parham, and the Azusa revival. It is based on personal interviews with Seymour, Parham, and key leaders and critics. He also sent out more than three hundred letters of inquiry, including nearly one hundred of them to persons living overseas. His Boston University PhD dissertation, "A Critical History of Glossolalia," surveyed the practice of glossolalia throughout Christian history, though it provides less important material than his 1914 thesis.

"A CRITICAL STUDY OF 'THE GIFT OF TONGUES'"

(AB thesis, USC 1914, 172–80, 191–93)

The colored believers held Monday night meetings in the home of Mr. and Mrs. Richard [and Ruth] Asbery [sic—Asberry], 216 North Bonnie Brae Street . . . in the center of a large section of negro homes. . . .

No recognized leader was engaged for these meetings. . . . It was thought best to get a man from a distance since he, being a stranger, would be more likely than an acquaintance to command respect and to maintain discipline. One of the women. . . . presented the name of William Joseph Seymour [based on her previous meeting with him in Houston] as the best man for the place. . . .[a] [I]t was decided, after prayer, to send for him.

We will recall that Seymour had been a frequent visitor in Parham's mission [in Houston]. According to the custom of the section, colored people were allowed to visit meetings of white people under some circumstances, but they must remain in the rear and keep silent. Thus it was that although Seymour had heard much preaching from Parham on the subject of "speaking in tongues" and kindred doctrines . . . he had not been privileged to go to the altar and seek it [the Holy Spirit baptism] for himself.

---

a. Seymour, as a young man, was a waiter in an Indianapolis restaurant. He was converted in a colored Methodist Episcopal Church there. After claiming the grace of instantaneous sanctification in Cincinnati, he felt the call to preach. He refused to obey the call and says that God sent him the small-pox which robbed him of one of his eyes. He then consented to preach. He was (and is) quite uneducated. He has always been an earnest pre-millennialist, very literal in his interpretation and a student of un-fulfilled prophecy. Soon after recovering from the small-pox he went into Texas to look for some relatives lost through slavery. In the winter of 1904–1905 he went "by special revelation" to Jackson, Miss., to receive spiritual advice from a well known colored clergyman [Charles Price Jones] there. There he was grounded more firmly in his millenarianism and he came away a more firm believer than ever in the value of "special revelations." Finding some of his relatives in Houston, Seymour made his home there. Although converted in a Methodist Episcopal Church and for a time a member of that communion, he early left it for the very good reason that the Church does not endorse either premillennialism or special "revelations."

He arrived in Los Angeles in April and took immediate charge of the meetings at 9th and Santa Fe. He preached regeneration, sanctification, the baptism of the Spirit, "the anointing of the Spirit," and the gift of tongues *as a sign that the baptism of the Spirit had taken place*. Much attention was given to faith healing.

On the fifth night the company found the door locked against them. Mrs. Hutchinson [Julia Hutchins] declared that she would not permit such extreme teaching in a mission if she could help it. Mrs. Asbery [*sic*—Asberry] offered the use of her home for the meetings and on Friday April 6th the company began a ten day fast, with nightly meetings, much heart-searching, and above all else a firm determination to "hold on to God" until he should send the baptism of the Spirit, which they had schooled themselves to believe would be recognized by the coming of the gift of tongues. Almost exclusive attention was devoted to the first four verses of the second chapter of Acts, where Luke describes the Pentecostal scene and the appearing of the tongues. . . .

On Monday evening at six, Seymour was calling by special request, upon a colored brother named [Edward] Lee. . . . [He] had been in Houston, had heard Parham and had sought "the baptism with tongues" for two years. On this Monday he was indisposed and asked Seymour to come and pray for his recovery in time to attend the evening meeting at Asbery's [*sic*], a few blocks away. Seymour laid his hands on Lee's head as requested and prayed for his recovery. Lee then asked him to pray that at that moment he might be given the gift of tongues. This prayer was offered and Lee burst forth into utterance in "the unknown tongue." He and Seymour were overjoyed.

The meeting at 216 North Bonnie Brae began a little before 7:30 since the larger double parlor and the rooms and halls adjoining were already filled with eager colored people. Seymour took charge. A song was sung. Three prayers were offered. Several personal testimonies were given. Seymour then arose to speak, announcing Acts 2:4 as his text. In his introduction he told the company of Lee's experience of an hour previous. No sooner had he made the statement than somebody broke out "in tongues." The whole company was immediately swept to their knees as by some mighty power. Many of them spoke "in tongues." Jennie Moore . . . was the first woman thus to speak. She ran to the piano and improvised a melody. . . . Seymour did not finish his sermon that night. The company remained until about ten o'clock, giving thanks for what they believed to be "Pentecost restored," and then broke up, carrying the news . . . to the entire neighborhood. . . .

A few days after "Pentecost fell." . . . Many white people began to come. Crowds filled the yard . . . Some of the colored brethren had been members of the First African Methodist Episcopal Church when that society built the building at 312 Azusa Street in 1888 . . . and had long been used as a storeroom. A lease was negotiated for eight dollars a month and on April 20th [actually April 14th] . . .

The missionary zeal of these enthusiasts was enormous. They carried their message everywhere. Churches were deprived of members who caught the enthusiasm. . . . On Easter Sunday Miss Jennie Moore attended morning service in the "New Testament Church . . ." Pastor [Joseph] Smale was in charge.[b] After . . . [Jennie's testimony] he was drawn into sympathetic study of the new faith, which he soon endorsed [for a short while] as genuine. . . .

Very quickly Seymour and his co-workers saw the necessity of publishing a paper of their own, which should set forth their doctrines and defend them against the attacks made by the newspapers. . . . This was sent broadcast over the land, without money and without price . . .

[Daughter] [b]ranches of the Azusa Street mission were early established in many places. . . . By the middle of July a "Pentecostal" mission was . . . in New York City . . . [and] was visited by Dr. Thomas Ball Barratt of Norway. . . . He . . . received his "baptism with the tongues," and a few weeks later had a mission of his own going night and day in Christiania, Norway. . . .

Parham heard of the work and in October came out to Los Angeles to take charge of it. He felt that the place of leadership was his since he had begun the work over five years previously.

When he approached the Azusa mission he heard chatterings, jabberings, and screams. When he entered, he saw shaking and "falling under the power." He is no believer in noise of physical demonstration of any kind and was disgusted with what he saw and heard.

Working his way to the front, he greeted Seymour, who was in charge, stepped upon the platform and declared in his characteristic fashion, "God is sick at his stomach!" he then proceeded to show that he would not be a self-respecting God if he could stand for any such animalism as was in progress there. His addressed secured for him the cordial dislike of many of the "saints."

Finding himself unable neither to secure the place of leadership nor correct the things which he felt were excesses and works of evil spirits, he opened a Los Angeles mission of his own, making also a vigorous campaign against the conduct of the Azusa devotees. From that day to this [1914] he cannot say anything too strong in condemnation of these who claim to be in the Apostolic Faith Movement. . . .

Late in the summer of 1906 [actually 1911] Seymour left Los Angeles for

---

b. Pastor Joseph Smale of the First Baptist Church, Los Angeles, had visited Wales at the time of the great revival there. He returned to his congregation full of evangelistic fire and enthusiasm and began a series of protracted meetings. These were conducted along deeply spiritual lines for ninteen [sic] weeks....

a brief season during which he preached his new doctrine among his old friends in Indianapolis, Cincinnati, Chicago, and Texas. When he returned to Azusa Street he found William Durham obtaining something of ascendancy over the opinions and doctrines he himself had been teaching before his eastern trip. Durham denied that sanctification is a second definite work of grace. Seymour taught that it is.

When Seymour demanded that Durham cease such teaching in his mission . . . Durham refused to cease and withdrew with about two thirds of the Azusa mission workers.

He [Durham] was a man of impressive personality, of intense dogmatic zeal, and of a firm determination to rule or ruin. Seymour's personality is not such as can easily command a situation such as he faced, and he had to sit quietly and see his following dwindle. Those who withdrew began to circulate stories which reflected upon the moral tone of the Azusa work, and this made matters worse.

[By late 1911, Elmer Fisher and George Studd] . . . and soon Durham's mission . . . were the leading centers of the work in the city. Seymour and Azusa Street were pretty nearly deserted. At the present time (February 1914) the Azusa work is supported by less than twenty people, most of whom were in the Asbery [sic] home when "Pentecost fell." Some whites still adhere to the work there.

The [Azusa] building, which was purchased for $15,000 and paid for in full in the first year, is therefore now almost deserted. Mr. Seymour and his wife, Jennie Moore, live in a few of the rooms on the upper floor. They have an adopted daughter, aged nine.

Added to his early troubles. . . . Miss Clara Lumm [Lum] . . . took "French leave" from Azusa Street, leaving the mission without a paper, which she began publishing for the "saints" in a northern city [Portland] . . .

Since April 9 [1906] . . . the movement has spread over the earth, so well prepared for it coming by the many similar local movements. . . .

I have traced the course of all things accurately from the beginning, using only such materials as were gained from the persons actually concerned, from answers to special inquiries[f] or from the files of the periodicals of the "Pentecostal" people themselves. . . .

Extent of the "Pentecostal" Movement and the Present Outlook

Although the Los Angeles revival of "speaking in tongues" only took place April 9, 1906, it is probably quite safe to say that there is not a town of three

---

f. Replies have come from over three hundred special letters of inquiry, nearly a hundred of them coming from abroad.

thousand population in the United States where the movement is not represented. In addition to that, its literature is printed in thirty languages, and it has missions in both hemispheres from Tasmania to Iceland . . . Arthur S. Booth-Clibborn . . . places the number of those who "speak in tongues" today at 70,000. He says that there are about as many who are identified with the movement, but who do not "speak in tongues. . . ."

Many earnest people are snared by the zeal and sincerity of those in this movement. These people are honest; they are prayerful . . . they are zealous. . . . They are best described by the word *"restless."* . . . This partly explains why the "Pentecostal" movement has attracted such a large following of the ignorant, the literal, the visionary, the unsettled, the "floaters," the eccentric and the discontented. . . .

The lines of division among the churches these days are not so much doctrinal as tempermental . . . [However, many] can be found who would not be in the Kingdom at all were it not that they can find a church among the "Pentecostal" people. . . .

40. J. C. VANZANDT

Vanzandt was converted to Pentecostalism in Oregon. He was a critic of Florence Crawford and M. L. Ryan. Although no friend of Seymour, he defended his right to recover the Azusa newspaper and mailing lists. He claimed that Lum and Crawford tried—at first—to cover up their decision to take Seymour's paper and lists. Vanzandt's testimony is important because it mentions that Seymour published one more issue of the *Apostolic Faith* (October–November 1908) and was the newspaper's "editor." He also notes that the trustees warned Lum not to take the newspaper since it was the "property" of the Mission—a word used by Seymour's followers.

SPEAKING IN TONGUES

(Originally 1911, reprinted with revisions 1926, 31–38)

Crookedness in Portland

W.J. Seymour opened up the Apostolic Faith work in Los Angeles, and he and his people were publishing a paper called "The Apostolic Faith," which carried his name as editor. I . . . was taking the paper.

Contrary to Seymour's wish, the leaders [Lum and Crawford] at Portland decided to move the paper to Portland. By some means they secured two copies of Seymour's mailing lists, and published their first issue of the paper here, labeled "Vol. 2, No. 15," from which I quote the following: "We have moved the paper which the Lord laid on us to begin at Los Angeles to Portland, Oregon, which will now be its headquarters."

Whoever wrote the above note says God laid upon them to begin the paper in Los Angeles, and that they had MOVED it to Portland. The Los Angeles paper carried Seymour's name as the editor . . . , but "The Apostolic Faith" of Portland has never carried the name of any one as editor, nor . . . any information that would keep its readers from believing that Seymour had moved his paper from Los Angeles to Portland; indeed it was conclusively designed to leave the impression that he [Seymour] had done so, and that those who had been sending donations to him at Los Angeles would hence-forth be sending them to Portland, thinking that he [Seymour] was there.

Well, it was not all easy sailing at Portland, for Seymour resented such treatment and printed another issue of the paper, exposing the hypocrisy of the Portland leaders. Having been exposed they were forced to do something. An editorial in the issue of May and June 1909, contained the following carefully veiled explanation: "This paper would be No. 21 from the beginning in Los Angeles, but it is No. 7 of Portland. We said it was moved from Los Angeles when we should have stated we were starting a new "Apostolic Faith" of Portland, as nothing was moved except two lists of subscribers, leaving twenty complete lists of all subscribers in Los Angeles. We ask the forgiveness of any souls that have been grieved over the mistake."

MISTAKE? No, indeed. As they had not moved the paper from . . . Los Angeles . . . [and] they certainly knew it. The first announcement, later termed a "mistake," is therefore *prima facia* evidence that they knowingly, wilfully [*sic*] and intentionally misrepresented the facts when they said they had. The truth is, having obtained Seymour's mailing lists, they could send their paper to all who had been receiving his, and to make it more deceptive they dated, volumed and numbered theirs, in apparent conformity with his, so that those who did not personally know of the trick would send their donations to them in Portland, instead of to Seymour in Los Angeles. . . .

Please note. They say that nothing was moved but the subcription [*sic*] lists. I understand Seymour had no presses, no types, no fixtures, hence had nothing but subscription lists. They say they left "twenty complete lists of all subscribers in Los Angeles." Left lists of all subscribers that were in, but not outside of, Los Angeles. Taking them at what they say, they did not leave any lists of subscribers that were outside of Los Angeles, hence those outside of Los Angeles, unless they lived near there, were not liable to find out about it. . . .

Note, will you, they did not confess that they had intentionally misrepresented the facts when they tried to smooth things over by calling it a mistake, for which they, in pious language asked "souls that have been grieved" to forgive them. . . . Their so-called confession contradicts itself. . . .

In the October-November [1908] issue of the Los Angeles paper, and over his signature, W.J. Seymour speaks thus concerning the deception and duplicity of the people using the name of his publication for an enterprise of their own in Portland: "I must for the salvation of souls let it be known that the editor is still in Los Angeles, . . . and will not remove 'The Apostolic Faith' from Los Angeles, without letting subscribers and field workers know."

[Seymour wrote:] "This was a sad thing to our hearts for a worker to attempt to take the paper which is the property of the Azusa Street Mission to another city without consent, after being warned by the elders not to do so."

Seymour says they had been warned by the leaders not to take the paper. In their first issue they said plainly that they had moved the paper, but when Seymour's exposé came out they said they had NOT moved it. It is very evident that one or the other of these statements is a positive, wilful [sic], intentional misrepresentation of the truth. . . .

I am very conscious of the fact that if the foregoing statements are false I have laid myself liable to a term in prison, but I defy the head of the Apostolic Faith Mission in Portland, Ore., to bring suit against me. I published these same truths in 1911, and the action they took was to forbid me to attend their meetings.

41. FRANK BARTLEMAN

Bartleman (1871–1936) was from Philadelphia. He attended Russell Conwell's Grace Baptist Church, where he was converted in 1893. After receiving his call to preach, he studied briefly at Temple University and Moody Bible Institute. In 1897 he left the Baptist ministry for Alma White's Pillar of Fire Holiness movement in Denver. He also ministered with the Salvation Army, the Wesleyan Methodists, and Peniel Mission. He preached across the United States. A self-described "lone wolf," he and his Bulgarian-born wife, Anna Ladd, and their four children moved to Los Angeles in December 1904, where he followed with great interest Evan Roberts' Welsh revival throughout 1905. He pastored a small Holiness mission, regularly attended Azusa Street, and spread Pentecostalism around the world during his travels from 1910 to 1911 and 1912 to 1914. He documents his accounts in *Azusa Street* (1925) and global travels in *Around the World* (1925).

AZUSA STREET

(*Azusa Street*, 1925 [1980], 47–59, 63, 81–82, 89, 145)

All classes began to flock to the [Azusa Street Revival] meetings. Many were curious and unbelieving. There was much persecution, especially from the press. They wrote us up shamefully, but this only drew the crowds. Some gave the work six months to live. Soon the meetings were running day and night. The place was packed out nightly. . . .

There were far more white people than colored coming. The "color line" was washed away in the blood . . . A high standard was held up for a clean life. . . . Divine love was wonderfully manifest in the meetings. They would not even allow an unkind word said against their opposers, or the churches. The message was the love of God. . . .

Friday, June 15 . . . the Spirit dropped the "heavenly chorus" into my soul. I found myself suddenly joining the rest who had received this supernatural "gift." It was a spontaneous manifestation and rapture no earthly tongue can describe. In the beginning this manifestation was wonderfully pure and powerful. We feared to try to reproduce it. . . .

[F]resh revival brings in its own hymnology. And this one surely did. In the beginning in "Azusa" we had no musical instruments. In fact we felt no need of them. There was no place for them in our worship. All was spontaneous. . . . All the old and well known hymns were sung from memory, quickened by the Spirit of God. "The Comforter Has Come," was possibly the one most sung. We sang it from fresh, powerful heart experience. Oh, how the power of God filled and thrilled us. . . .

Brother Seymour was recognized as the nominal leader in charge. But we had no pope or hierarchy. We were "brethren." We had no human programme [*sic*]. The Lord Himself was leading. We had no priest class, nor priest craft. These things have come in later, with the apostatizing of the movement. We did not have a platform or pulpit in the beginning. All were on the same level. The ministers were servants, according to the true meaning of the word. We did not honor men for their advantage, in means or education, but rather for their God-given "gifts." . . .

Brother Seymour generally sat behind two empty shoe boxes, one on top of the other. He usually kept this head inside the open one during the meeting, in prayer. There was no spiritual pride there.

The services ran almost continuously. Seeking souls could be found under the power almost any hour, night and day. The place was never closed nor empty. The people came to meet God. He was always there. . . .

The meeting did not depend upon a human leader. God's presence became more and more wonderful. In that old building, with its low rafters and bare floors, God took strong men and women to pieces, and put them together again, for His glory. It was a tremendous overhauling process. Pride and self-assertion, self-importance and self-esteem, could not survive there. The religious ego preached its own funeral sermon quickly.

No subjects or sermons were announced ahead of time, and no special speakers for such an hour. No one knew what might be coming, what God might do. All was spontaneous, ordered of the Spirit. We wanted to hear from God, through whoever he might speak. We had no "respect of persons." The rich and educated were the same as the poor and ignorant, and found a much harder death to die. We only recognized God. All were equal. No flesh might glory in His presence. He could not use the self-opinionated. . . .

All came down in humility together, at His feet. . . . The rafters were low, the tall must come down. . . . We were delivered right there from ecclesiastical hierarchism and abuse. We wanted God. . . .

One reason for the depth of the work at "Azusa" was the fact that the workers were not novices. . . . They were largely seasoned veterans. . . . These were pioneers, "shock troops," the Gideon's three hundred, to spread the fire around the world. . . .

In the early days the "tarrying room" [on the 2nd floor] was held sacred, a kind of "holy ground. . . ." There men sought become quiet from the activities of their own too active mind and spirit, to escape from the world for the time, and get alone with God. There was no noisy, wild, exciting spirit there . . . It was a sort of "city of refuge" from this sort of thing, a "haven of rest," where God could be heard, and talk to their souls. Men would spend hours in silence there, searching their own hearts in privacy, and securing the mind of the Lord for future action. . . .

[P]latforms and pulpits were . . . removed. . . . We were all "brethren . . ." He had poured out His Spirit "on all flesh," even on His servants and handmaidens.—Act 2. We honored men for their God-given "gifts" and offices only.

As the movement began to apostatize platforms were built higher, coat tails were worn longer, choirs were organized, and string bands came into existence to "jazz" the people. The kings came back once more, to their thrones, restored to sovereignty. We were no longer "brethren." Then the divisions multiplied, etc. While Brother Seymour kept his head inside the empty box in "Azusa" all was well. They later built for him a throne also. Now we have, not one hierarchy, but many. . . .

Old Azusa Mission became more and more in bondage. The meetings now had to run just in appointed order. The Spirit tried to work through some poor, illiterate Mexican, who had been saved and "baptized" in the Spirit. But the leader deliberately refused to let them testify, and crushed them ruthlessly. It was like murdering the Spirit of God. Only God knows what this meant to those poor Mexicans. Personally I would rather die than to have assumed such a spirit of dictatorship. Every meeting was now programmed from start to finish. Disaster was bound to follow, and it did so. . . .

42. ARTHUR OSTERBERG

Born to Swedish immigrants, Louis and Emma Osterberg, Arthur (ca. 1886–1970) was a key eyewitness of Seymour and Azusa. He attended the Bonnie Brae prayer meetings, cleared the Mission of debris the day before the revival began, reportedly witnessed a number of miraculous events, and merged his mission with Seymour's Revival. He later served as Superintendent of the Southern California–Arizona District of the Assemblies of God.

ORAL HISTORY OF THE AZUSA STREET REVIVAL

(Oral History Interview with Jerry Jensen & Jonathan Perkins, 17 March 1966, 4–14)

I was pastoring a full gospel church before the Azusa street revival came. . . . Half of the people who were in those Bonnie Brae prayer meetings were colored. . . . The result was the Bonnie Brae meetings took fire almost over night . . . the colored people spread the word around among their friends, white and black . . . and invited everyone into the prayer meeting . . .

Mother [Emma Osterberg] got up in the [Full Gospel] church and talked about that [Bonnie Brae Street prayer] meeting and . . . had our whole congregation excited. . . . [and] suggested we all attend one of those meetings. . . .

The four of us [Osterberg and deacons Worthington, Weaver, and Dodge] . . . [and] [m]y mother and a lot of the other folks went also.

That meeting . . . on Bonnie Brae convinced me . . . [that] they were spiritual people and there was no nonsense going on. [However,] I couldn't quite understand the "tongues. . . ." But . . . I realized it could revolutionize our whole theory, because we . . . didn't even have the baptism of the Holy Spirit. So . . . I said . . . I'm going to go to my Bible and find out for myself. . . .

I spent the rest of the week . . . studying my Bible . . . and going through the concordance for anything pertaining to the baptism of the Spirit. I became convinced, aside from the Bonnie Brae meetings and the folks there, that our theology was on the wrong side of the second work of grace. . . .

I became convinced that the baptism of the H.S. was connected with tongues. . . . I went back to Bonnie Brae several times in the next couple of weeks. Then one night . . . they announced that they had found a place on . . . Azusa St. . . .

The first meeting I would say at Bonnie Brae . . . was about doubled— about 75 to 100 people. Then after that we had meetings every night and they would double every night until the end of the week the place was packed full . . . every inch big enough for a chair jammed full . . . they would stand two and three deep around the walls.

When the place was full Sunday morning I would be save [*sic*] in saying there was 750 to 800 people inside. On the outside for several months, windows were taken out and they stood on the outside all around the building—another four or five hundred people . . . on Sunday, from 7:00 in the morning, there would be 1500 people there all day. That's an estimate. . . .

We had very few loudly speaking tongues . . . Seymour taught from the very beginning, "Let him who speaketh in tongues pray that he may interpret." That had a restricting influence upon these many women who wanted to get up and talk in tongues in every Pentecostal meeting. He [Seymour] didn't have that. . . .

There was very little of the interpreter speaking in the place of god in the first person . . . as though they were talking for God . . . [Seymour] stopped that . . . they didn't attempt to speak to the congregation as an oracle and tell the congregation what they should do. . . .

43. GLENN COOK

Cook (1867–1948) was raised a Baptist in Indianapolis, Indiana, before moving to Los Angeles to work for a newspaper, where he was ordained in the Burning Bush Holiness movement. Cook was one of Seymour's staunchest defenders. He not only edited the *Apostolic Faith* and handled all incoming mail for the first year, but also he was one of the two elders that asked Parham to leave the Mission because of his harsh denunciation of the Azusa revival in October 1906. In 1907, Cook spread Pentecostalism to Indiana, Oklahoma, Arkansas, Missouri, and across the United States. He became a Oneness leader and returned to Los Angeles in the 1920s, where he pastored Belvedere Christian Mission.

THE AZUSA STREET MEETING: SOME HIGHLIGHTS OF THIS OUTPOUTING

(ca. 1920)

The writer of this tract was made business manager by the laying on of hands by Bro. Seymour and others. The duties of his office made him familiar not only with the Work . . . [at] Azusa Street, but all over the world. He opened all the mail and handled all the correspondence for over a year after the power fell. . . .

In the early spring of 1906, Bro. Seymour arrived here from Houston, Texas. He had been a hotel waiter in Indianapolis, Indiana. . . . While there [in Houston] he attended [Parham's] meetings for some time. . . . Bro. Seymour did not receive his baptism at the Houston meeting. The doctrines preached by this people were very confusing and there was a lack of love and power in the meetings. . . . The leader [Parham] became puffed up, declared himself the progenitor of the movement and would strut around with a high silk hat like a dictator. The result that followed . . . [was] great confusion in doctrine and the absence of the spirit of love.

When Bro. Seymour arrived in Los Angeles he . . . [received] the baptism . . . [and later] gathered together a small group of people, black and white, and started a meeting in the old [AME] church building. A few benches and chairs with a packing case for a pulpit was the equipment. Every time he preached he would quote from Mark 16 and Acts 2:4, insisting that no one had received the baptism of the Holy Ghost unless they spoke in tongues. This caused a great deal of opposition by the Holiness people who began to attend the meetings. The writer . . . went to the meeting thinking he might be able to straighten the people out in their doctrine. . . .

But the contention was all on our part. I never have met a man who had such control over his spirit. The scripture that reads, "Great peace have they that love thy law, and nothing shall offend them," was literally fulfilled in this man. No amount of confusion and accusation seemed to disturb him. He would sit behind that packing case and smile at us until we were all condemned by our own activities.

Although most all of the Holiness people who attended continued to reject the preaching, all had a secret reverence and admiration for this man [Seymour] who really lived what we had been preaching for years, a sanctified life. It was the wonderful character of this man [Seymour] . . . that attracted the people to keep coming to this humble meeting. . . .

After asking forgiveness of Bro. Seymour and all the rest for all my hard sayings I fell on my face and began to pour out my soul in prayer, but could not receive the Holy Ghost. Then followed a period of about five weeks of repenting and prayer. My eyes were seldom dry during this time. . . . When I had just about given up all hope, the Holy Ghost fell on me as I lay in bed at home. I seemed to be in a trance for about twenty-four hours and the next day in the meeting began to speak in tongues.

The crowds kept increasing until the people could not get in the building . . . and soon the street was filled with people from every walk of life and every nationality. . . .

I was working on a daily newspaper at the time, but my work had lost all interest . . . the Lord spoke to me and told me to quit my work, as He had something for me to do. I resigned my position, and a few days afterwards Bro. Seymour made me his business manager without salary. . . .

One of the great features of the meetings was the singing of heavenly anthems in the Spirit. I was seldom away from that old building for nearly a year, except to go home to sleep, and much of the time slept in the building in a room adjoining Bro. Seymour. We all seemed to live in an atmosphere that was separated from the rest of the world. Evil speaking and even evil thinking was departed. We were saturated with the spirit of love and prayer and the days passed all too swiftly.

The Apostolic Faith paper was soon published. . . . The first issue was 5,000 copies and soon 50,000 was the number. People began to pour in from all over the United States . . . and . . . different parts of the world. The place was packed from morning until far into the night. . . . Over twenty nationalities were present, and they were in all perfect accord and unity of the Spirit. . . .

44. SEYMOUR OBITUARY

Seymour died of a heart attack while dictating a letter to his secretary on September 28, 1922. Approximately two hundred people attended his funeral. He was buried in Evergreen Cemetery in East Los Angeles. This obituary describes his last moments and ministry.

BROTHER SEYMOUR CALLED HOME

(*Pentecostal Herald*, 1 October 1922, 1–2, 4)

Dearly Beloved in the Lord . . .

We write you to let you know that our father in the Gospel Rev. W.J. Seymour, was called home to be with the Lord, Sept. 28, 1922, after a most active life of consecrated service to the God he knew and loved so well. He answered the call with a radiant smile, without a struggle, with the words, "I love my Jesus so" after spending the day with his wife in much prayer, praise and song and in planning for the work which was so dear to his heart.

His departure is a grief and loss to many a heart that remembers how often his great understanding and loving heart had comforted and advised them and brought them to see Christ in a deeper way. His travel [*sic* —travail] of soul was that the children of God everywhere might live in the Word, to obey it in its precepts, to follow on in the faith once delivered to the saints, to be preserved and led by this unerring guide, and to know that "love to all and malice to none, and holiness without which no man shall [serve] the Lord."

His life was a crowning example of the believer in word and deed, self-denial and whole consecration to God. He was true to the end, never failing in faith or lowering the standard, but standing against every tide in firm allegiance to God and the Truth. He so often said, "Never doubt your God and never disappoint Him." He walked in closest communion and fellowship, looking unto Jesus, his never failing source of comfort and strength. Never was there one more conscientious in standing between God and man "as one that must give account" for revealing Christ to their souls and establishing them in the way. He was an exceptional teacher because of the illumination of his mind through the word.

Brother Seymour was our father. . . . The world was his parish. He lived the life, a man of God, strong in he Lord, holy, pure and bodly [*sic* —boldly] standing against everything defiling in life or worship. And because of it his life was one of power with God in rebuking evil spirits and setting men free. He was the Paul of this age. When asked so often the secret of his power he would say, "Living free from sin and in the Word of God."

His memory shall be revered among all who have the Spirit's work in their own lives since the outpouring in 1906 when Brother Seymour was so chosen of God to present to the people the light concerning the great office work of the Comforter for this age, and was so wondrously used in the administration of the Word in power from on high. He has stood in old Azusa as her pastor these years in true adherence to the full Gospel. His last message was a plea for love among the brethren everywhere.

His great plans for the work will be carried on by his beloved wife, Sister Jennie M. Seymour, who is herself an evangelist of power and note greatly loved by all, and into whose hands, Bishop Seymour placed his work before his decease [*sic*]. Azusa's original high standard of holiness and power shall never be effaced, but shall ever be a call to stablish [*sic* —establish] your hearts for the coming of the Lord draweth nigh.

The grace of the Lord be with you all, as you grow in grace and the knowledge of the Lord Jesus Christ.

The Azusa Street Apostolic
Faith Mission
312 Azusa Street.

EURO-AMERICAN TESTIMONIES

INTRODUCTION

Seymour had a significant impact on Euro-Americans. They played a key role in spreading Seymour's vision and version of Pentecostalism and in his emphasis on racial equality. Many of the leaders in this section contributed to the origins of Pentecostal denominations in the Pacific Northwest, the Midwest, and South and those like Durham created vitally important centers around the world. Seymour had a significant impact on Euro-Americans.

They played a key role in spreading Seymour's vision and version of Pentecostalism and his emphasis on racial equality. Many of these people below became key leaders in global Pentecostalism.

45. WILLIAM DURHAM

Durham was a Kentucky Baptist who pastored in Michigan for several years before taking over Chicago North Avenue Mission in 1901. He first heard about Azusa from ministers in Chicago and Louis and Emma Osterberg, former Michigan friends. They paid Durham's train fare and room and board to visit Azusa on February 10, 1907. Durham was immediately struck by Seymour's deep spirituality and gentle spirit. His North Avenue Mission soon became one of the leading centers of global Pentecostalism and sent out Aimee Semple McPherson, A. H. Argue (Canada), E. N. Bell, Howard Goss, Daniel Berg (Brazil), Adolf Gunner Vingren (Brazil), and Luigi Francescon (Argentina, Brazil). After 1911, he promoted his "Finished Work of Calvary" views on sanctification and repudiated the traditional Pentecostal position that sanctification was a second work of grace. He maintained fraternal relations with Seymour until he attempted to take over the Azusa mission in February 1911. He was expelled in May and set up a rival mission in Los Angeles before he died of tuberculosis in July 1912.

A CHICAGO EVANGELIST'S PENTECOST.

(*AF*, February–March 1907, 4)
Chicago, Ill., March 19.

Dear Readers of the Apostolic Faith . . .

Nine years ago I was deeply convicted of sin. . . . Five years ago I was called into the ministry . . . I traveled as an evangelist from coast to coast . . . speaking to as high as 1,000 people at a time. . . . And many were saved, sanctified, and many healed.

But in some way all this did not satisfy me, and for a year the heart hunger has increased . . . I kept praying for love, [and] power . . .

Finally I heard of the . . . Azusa Street Mission . . . Later . . . the Lord impressed me to go . . . and attend the meetings, and seek the baptism in the Holy Ghost. Finally on Feb. 8, [1907] I arrived there. . . .

The first thing that impressed me was the love and unity that prevailed in the meeting, and the heavenly sweetness that filled the very air that I breathed . . . I never felt the power and glory that I felt in Azusa Street Mission, and when about twenty persons joined in singing the "Heavenly Chorus," it was the most ravishing and unearthly music that ever fell on mortal ears ... I know it came direct from heaven....

But on Friday evening, March 1, His mighty power came over me, until I jerked and quaked under it for about three hours. It was strange and wonderful and yet glorious. He [Holy Spirit] worked my whole body ... and finally at 1 a.m. Saturday, Mar. 2, after being under the power for three hours, He ... spoke through me in unknown tongues....

Almost three weeks have passed.... My soul is melted over and over again, and many times I feel as if there were, and I believe there is a dynamo of power in me; there is nothing selfish about this, but it is fathomless, real, literal, blessed, grand....

[Since that time] the Spirit falls like rain wherever I preach His word, and it seems there is no effort on my part....

Now just a word concerning Bro. Seymour, who is the leader of the movement under God: He is the meekest man I ever met. He walks and talks with God. His power is in his weakness. He seems to maintain a helpless dependence on God and is as simple-hearted as a little child, and at the same time is so filled with God that you feel the love and power every time you get near him.

–W.H. Durham

46. GASTON BARNABAS CASHWELL

Cashwell (1862–1916) served as a minister in the Methodist Episcopal Church, South, in his native Dunn, North Carolina, before switching over to the Pentecostal Holiness Church (PHC) in 1903. After hearing about Azusa, he traveled there in November 1906, where he received the Spirit baptism and "crucified" his racial prejudice. Seymour raised money for a dress coat and his return trip to the South. Cashwell conducted a revival at his home church in Dunn on December 31, 1906, and from there he conducted services throughout the South, sweeping in Holiness leaders and movements like G. F. Taylor, H. H. Goff, F. M. Britton, J. H. King, M. M. Pinson, H. G. Rodgers, Ambrose J. Tomlinson and the Fire Baptized Holiness Church, the Pentecostal Free-Will Baptist Church, and the Church of God (Cleveland, TN). He began publishing the *Bridegroom Messenger* in 1907 and claimed that he was leading the "Azusa Street" of the South. He is called the "apostle of Pentecost in the South." He left the PHC in 1909 after not being elected its leader and for other reasons.

CAME 3,000 MILES FOR HIS PENTECOST.

(*AF,* December 1906, 3)
About two months ago, I began to read in the *Way of Faith* the reports of the meetings in Azusa Mission, Los Angeles. I had been preaching holiness for nine years, but my soul began to hunger and thirst for the fullness of God. ... My wife prayed and wept with me till we both got the witness that it was the will of God for me to go. ...

I was six days on the road, was fasting and praying to the Lord continually. As soon as I reached Azusa Mission, a new crucifiction [*sic*] began in my life and I had to die to many things, but God gave me the victory.

The first altar call I went forward in earnest for my Pentecost. I struggled from Sunday till Thursday. While seeking in an upstairs room in the Mission, the Lord opened up the windows of heaven and the light of God began to flow over me in such power as never before. I then went into the room where the service was held, and ... before I knew it, I began to speak in tongues and praise God ... He filled me with His Spirit and love. ...

The Lord also healed my body. I had been afflicted with rheumatism for years, and at a healing service held here, I was anointed and prayed for and was immediately healed of rheumatism and catarrh, and have a sound body and clothed in my right mind.

–G.B. Cashwell, Dunn, N.C.

47. F. M. BRITTON

Francis Britton (1870–1937) was a leader in the Fire Baptized Holiness Church in North Carolina. He received his Spirit baptism through Cashwell in January 1907, persuaded his denomination to embrace Pentecostalism, and in 1911 merged it with J. H. King's Pentecostal Holiness Church.

"IN ALVIN, S.C."

(*AF,* February–March, 3)
In Alvin, S.C.
Alvin, S.C., Mar. 2.—

In January we heard of Bro. G.B. Cashwell of Dunn, N.C., that had been to [the Azusa Revival in] Los Angeles and received the Holy Ghost and spoke with tongues. So our hearts began to hunger more and more, and after praying over it, my wife and I decided to invite him to come to our Pentecostal meeting which was to begin the 8th of February. He came to us and stayed three days, and in those three days, there were about twenty-three saints that received the baptism of the Holy Ghost, and all of them spoke with other tongues as the Spirit gave them utterance. I am glad to tell you, dear saints, that I am one of the twenty-three. As soon as He came into my soul, He spoke with my tongue in an unknown language. . . . We have had several short meetings since . . . and all speak with other tongues. Demons have been cast out in the name of Jesus.

—F.M. Britton.

48. A. E. ROBINSON & [J. H. KING]

Albert Robinson (1877–1950) was a leader in the Pentecostal Holiness Church (PHC). He developed a lifelong friendship with J. H. King and served as the first general secretary of the PHC. Below, he describes Cashwell's ministry and ability to persuade leaders in the Fire Baptized Holiness Church to become Pentecostal. He also mentions his influence on J. H. King and contact with Glenn Cook. King (1869–1946) was the founder and first bishop of the PHC and was persuaded by Cashwell to bring his denomination into the Pentecostal movement in January 1907.

REPORT ON THE FIRE BAPTIZED HOLINESS CHURCH

(*AF,* May 1907, 2)

Pentecost has swept across the country, and through the instrumentally [*sic*] of Brother Cashwell a great number of the officials and members of the Fire Baptized Holiness Church have given up their man-made theories about Pentecost, and gone down and received the genuine Pentecostal baptism, with the Bible evidence following.

As far as we can learn, the general overseers, ruling elders, and evangelists are swept in, with a few exceptions. . . .

Our editor, Brother J.H. King, will probably be in Oklahoma in May, with Brother [Glenn A.] Cook, and he may go to visit you.

—A.E. Robinson, Royston, Ga.

49. A. W. ORWIG

Orwig wrote one of the first essay-length histories of Azusa for the Assemblies of God, published as *Weekly Evangel*. It was based on firsthand experiences and interviews with participants. He acknowledged Seymour as the leader and that some people fought against Azusa because of the "malignant demon of prejudice."

"'TONGUES' THE GREAT STUMBLING BLOCK"

(*The Weekly Evangel*, April 8, 1916, 4–5)
I heard W.J. Seymour, an acknowledged leader, say, "Now don't go from this meeting and talk about tongues, but try to get people saved." Again I heard him counsel against all unbecoming of fleshly demonstrations, and everything not truly of the Holy Spirit. . . .

Bro. Seymour constantly exalted the atoning work of Christ and the Word of God, and very earnestly insisted on thorough conversion, holiness of heart and life and the fullness of the Holy Spirit. . . .

MY FIRST VISIT TO THE AZUSA STREET PENTECOSTAL MISSION

(*The Weekly Evangel*, March 18, 1916, 4–5, 7)
It was . . . September 1906. I had heard of the meetings. . . . The daily papers . . . characterized them as scenes of wild fanaticism, enacted by ignorant and crazy people . . . tongues [was] bitterly denounced as a fraud, and was sacrilegiously caricatured. . . . some declaring them to be of the devil. . . .

I began to read it [*The Apostolic Faith*] with considerable interest, and . . . said to my wife, "I am going to Azusa Street Mission on Sunday and see and hear for myself."

I . . . [attended Azusa] six solid hours on that one day. And I was more than ever persuaded that the movement was of God. . . .

The sermons, testimonies, prayers and songs . . . were usually attended with divine unction to such as a degree as to move and melt hearts in every direction. The altar of prayer was generally crowded. . . .

Not all . . . fully . . . accepted this teaching. . . .

The subject . . . of divine healing received special attention and many cases of deliverance from various diseases and infirmities were more or less continually reported. Likewise was the doctrine of the premillenial [*sic*] coming of Christ ardently promulgated.

One thing that somewhat surprised me . . . [was] the presence of so many persons from the different churches, not a few of them educated and refined. Some were pastors, evangelists, foreign missionaries and others of high position in various circles, looking on with seeming amazement and evident interest and profit . . . many nationalities were also present . . . representing all manner of religious beliefs. Sometimes these, many of them unsaved, would be seized with deep conviction for sin under the burning testimony of one of their own nationality, and at once heartily turn to the Lord. . . .

Further from Los Angeles about the Pentecostal Work

.... Not a few of the so called "Holiness People . . ." found the meetings a great blessing . . . [while others] stood aloof for different reasons . . . some from more or less prejudice. . . . Oh, the loss and injury often sustained by some persons because of the malignant demon of prejudice possessing them! . . .

50. RACHEL SIZELOVE

Sizelove (1864–1941) and her husband Josie were credentialed Free Methodist evangelists by the time they attended Azusa in April 1906. She received the Spirit baptism along with R. J. Scott in July. They organized the First Azusa Camp Meeting on June 1, 1907. She spread Seymour's message to Springfield, Missouri, in May 1907 and (with Lucy Farrow) to Texas. After starting a work in Springfield she returned to Los Angeles. She conducted revivals throughout the South, Midwest, and along the West Coast.

PENTECOST HAS COME

("The Temple," *Word and Work,* May 1936, 1, 2, 12; "A Sparkling Fountain for the Whole Earth," *Word and Work,* June 1934, 1, 11, 12)

In . . . April, 1906. . . . [my] dear husband and I . . . entered the old [Azusa Mission] building [and] somehow I was touched by the presence of God. It was such a humble place with its low ceilings and rough floor . . . [and] cob webs . . . I thought of Jesus when He came to earth and was born in a manger . . . I thought of the fine church houses in Los Angeles, but the Lord had chosen this humble spot to gather all nationalities. . . .

Brother Seymour stayed behind that box on his knees before the Lord, hid away from the eyes of the world so much of the time. O! How God used that old colored brother and gave him wisdom as he did to Moses to lead and teach the people. . . .

My very soul cried out, O! Lord the people have something I do not have.

Brother Seymour gave out the Word and made an altar call and said anyone wanting to seek the Lord for pardon or sanctification or the baptism of the Holy Ghost and fire to come and bow at the altar. I thought, well praise God, he is not doing away with any of my experience or belief, but just adding to my experience that of the baptism of the Holy Ghost. . . .

I went home and began to search the Word of God. I saw it was in the Bible. I was again in the mission in [In] July, 1906. . . .

When Brother Seymour gave the altar call, I with many others went to the altar, raising my hands towards heaven. I said Lord I want my inheritance, the baptism of the Holy Ghost and fire. . . . There was a great open space in my heart and He just came in and took up His abode. . . .

We felt all flesh should keep silent before the Lord, and upon entering the building we would kneel at our seats or the altar, with tears dripping on the seats. . . .

[W]hen some one would begin to pound the seat, with their hand or fist while they were praying, Brother Seymour would go to them gently and tap them on the shoulder, and say, "Brother that is the flesh," and a holy hush and quietness would settle upon those tarring for the baptism of the Holy Ghost. . . .

Brother [Seymour] would get up and say, "Dear lubbed on' these met'ns ah difent from any you ebber saw in all your born days. These ah Holy Ghost met'ns and no flesh can glory in the presence of God" (He had the colored brogue in his speech).

No one seemed to get offended at him. My dear husband used to say the Lord gave Brother Seymour wisdom to rule the people as He did to Moses. No one dared to get up and sing a song or testify except under the anointing of the Spirit. They feared lest the Holy Ghost would cut them off in their song or testimony. . . .

No one dared say, 'We will now have a song by Brother or Sister so and so," and then as they would come to the front to sing, for the congregation to clap their hands and laud them . . . O no! . . . .

While the Holy Ghost was having His way at the Azusa Street Mission money was not spoken of. They had a small mail box nailed to a post that was in the center of the mission with the words printed above it "Free Will Offering. . . ."

But alas, how well I remember the first time the flesh began to get in the way of the Holy Ghost, and how the burden came upon the saints that morning when Brother Seymour stood before the audience and spoke of raising money to buy the Azusa Street Mission. The Holy Ghost was grieved. You could feel it all over the audience . . . and the Holy Ghost power began to leave, and instead of the Holy Ghost heavenly choir, they brought in a piano. . . .

51. FLORENCE CRAWFORD

Crawford (1872–1936) was a key Azusa leader before she founded The Apostolic Faith, Portland, Oregon, denomination in 1908. She was converted to Methodism and moved to Los Angeles, where she became active in the Women's Christian Temperance Movement (WCTU). A woman of considerable intellectual and financial means, she married Frank Crawford, a builder.

She was appointed director of the Azusa work throughout California and parted company with Seymour in 1907.

TESTIMONY

(*AF,* October 1906, 3)

Sister Florence Crawford says: "There is no spot on earth so dear to me as this place [Azusa Mission], but I must go out and tell this story. Souls are perishing far and near. The Lord told me yesterday to go into all the world and preach His Gospel. . . . He has anointed me [at Azusa] to tell the story of Jesus and I can go alone for Jesus is with me. O, glory to God!"

–Florence Crawford

A CHEERING TESTIMONY.

(*AF,* October to January 1908, 4)
I bless and praise God that the Holy Ghost fell in dear Los Angeles. Oh, and it took me in. Oh, how hungry I was, and how the glory of heaven flooded my soul as I sat and listened to dear Brother Seymour expound the Word of God. . . . O how I love Jesus. I never loved Him as I do now. . . . How can I ever praise Him enough or do enough or suffer enough for what He's done for me! What a privilege to suffer a little with Jesus. This awful power and prince of the air is our worst enemy. . . .

–Florence Crawford.

52. CLARA LUM

Lum (1869–1946) was a Wisconsin native, seasoned Christian worker, and former schoolteacher in Artesia, California. She was also a lay preacher in the World's Faith Missionary Association, had served as associate editor of Missionary World, and worked with Phineas Bresee in the Pentecostal Church of the Nazarene. After Glenn Cook left Azusa, Lum ran the newspaper. She also stenographically recorded many of the testimonies and probably all of Seymour's published sermons.

MISS CLARA LUM WRITES WONDERS.

(The Missionary World, August 1906, 2)
June 18th

Dear Bro. and Sister Hanley . . .

The Lord is . . . pouring out Pentecost in old time power. . . . I have never seen the power of God manifest in so many people, nor have I ever seen such manifestations of his power . . . I first went to the meeting three weeks ago [late May], and knew that God was there.

He . . . gave me the baptism of the Holy Ghost. . . . It came in power thrilling me and remaining upon me in a power like electricity. He also gave me the gift of healing and casting out devils. He has used me to heal a few sick since then. He shows me he is going to use me to write in a different way than before. He also will not take this power from me. . . .

The Lord is saving souls, sanctifying believers and baptizing them with the Holy Ghost. . . . They have spoken in Spanish, Chinese, Japanese, African dialects, Indian dialects, Esquimaux language is spoken by one; deaf mute language is spoken by one; Hebrew, Greek, Latin, a language of India, French, by others. . . .

The Lord is giving the gift of prophecy . . . that a revival of the pure Gospel is to sweep over the land . . . I feel the power of God as I am writing. . . . He wants me to preach the Gospel. He also wants me to write for Him. . . .

The leader is a humble colored man [William Seymour]. He has true wisdom and gentleness in conducting the meetings. All realize that he is called of God and anointed for this work. . . .

Yours in Him, Clara E. Lum

AFRICAN-AMERICAN TESTIMONIES

INTRODUCTION

African Americans made up the core of Seymour's Mission. They served as pastors, worship leaders, and on the Board of Trustees. Despite not being well documented, the following accounts capture the impact that Seymour and the Revival had on future leaders like Charles H. Mason and G. T. Haywood, who helped organize the Church of God in Christ (COGIC) and Pentecostal Assemblies of the World (PAW). While most of the testimonies discuss their Spirit baptism or evangelistic calling, Emma Cotton offers a more female-centered interpretation of the Azusa Revival that points to their important contributions.

53. JENNIE EVANS MOORE (SEYMOUR)

Jennie Evans Moore (Seymour) (1883–1936) was born in Texas. She moved to Los Angeles where she worked as a maid for white women and attended Joseph Smale's First New Testament Church and the Bonnie Brae prayer meetings, where she was the first woman to receive the Spirit baptism on Monday, April 9. She served as the music leader, an evangelist, and on the ordination committee. Observers described her as attractive, intelligent, feisty, and deeply spiritual. On May 13, 1908, she married Seymour and became his "backbone" and "put Bro. Seymour in his place" as leader of the Azusa Mission.

MUSIC FROM HEAVEN.

(*AF,* May 1907, 3)

For years before this wonderful experience came to us, we as a family, were seeking to know the fullness of God. . . . On April 9, 1906 . . . we attended the [Bonnie Brae] meeting [and] the power of God fell and I was baptized in the Holy Ghost and fire, with the evidence of speaking in tongues . . . when the power came on me . . . it seemed as if a vessel broke within me and water surged up through my being, which when it reached my mouth came out in a torrent of speech in the languages [I had not learned] . . . French, Spanish, Latin, Greek, Hebrew, Hindustani, and . . . interpretation of each message followed in English. . . . I sang under the power of the Spirit in many languages . . . [and] the Spirit led me to the piano, where I played and sang under inspiration, althought [*sic*] I had not learned to play . . . I praise Him for the privilege of being a witness for Him under the Holy Ghost's power.

–J.M., 312 Azusa St., Los Angeles.

54. EMMA CUMMINGS

Emma married William Cummings and came from Atlanta, Georgia, to Los Angeles in 1903. They participated in the Bonnie Brae meetings and Azusa Revival. They had six children (Ardell, Bessie, Frank, Ida, Mae Mattie Belle, John). Prior to joining Seymour's ministry, they attended an African Methodist Episcopal Church and Emma attended Clark University in Atlanta, but decided to become a missionary. In May 1907, Seymour sent them to evangelize Liberia, West Africa.

YE ARE MY WITNESSES

(*AF,* May 1907, 4)

I was justified when 12 years old . . . I had a call to go to Africa. I was going to Clark's University and was encouraged by the missionaries from the north that when I got old enough I could go, as I was a good M.E. Methodist. As years advanced I began to get careless . . .

My oldest child began to question and watch my life, and, oh, how I tried to walk right before her, and, praise God, He kept me, and when I came to California from Atlanta, Ga., June 1903, I . . . began seeking until the Lord really sanctified me. . . .

When I heard of the baptism of the Holy Ghost with Bible evidence I thought it impossible for the Lord to do anything more for me, yet I was seeking for more power. I would go up to [the Bonnie Brae altar to] be prayed for, and tell the people I did not have power with God to win souls. The second time I went . . . I received a high anointing. . . .

[On] July 5, 1906, [I] received the baptism of the Holy Ghost with the Bible evidence, and since that time my husband and five children have been saved, sanctified, and baptized with the Holy Ghost.

We are now getting ready to go to Africa, a family of nine. . . . My all is on the altar . . . I could tell of wonderful things God has done in my family since the Comforter has come. Glory to our King. I will praise Him forever.

–Mrs. Emma Cummings, 312
Azusa Street, Los Angeles, Calif.

55. "MOTHER" EMMA COTTON

"Mother Cotton" (1877–1952) was born in Louisiana and married Henry Cotton (1879–1959). She was reportedly healed of cancer and weak lungs at Azusa. She became an evangelist, pastor, church planter, and magazine editor. She conducted divine healing services in 1916 and helped organize a number of independent missions in Bakersfield, Oakland, and Fresno. She co-organized with her husband the Thirty-Ninth Anniversary Celebration of the Azusa revival. They copastored Azusa Pentecostal Temple (Crouch Memorial Temple today) in Los Angeles. In April 1939, she published *The Message of the "Apostolic Faith"* magazine, in which she provided an eyewitness account of the Bonnie Brae prayer meetings, the Asuza Revival, and important details about Seymour's life.

INSIDE STORY OF THE OUTPOURING OF THE HOLY SPIRIT

Azusa Street April 1906
(*Message Of The "Apostolic Faith*," April 1939, 1–3)
Brother Seymour, the one whom God used to bring the message that stirred the world, was born in Louisiana. He was saved and sanctified under the "Evening Light Saints," a Holiness group. Later, he came to Houston, Texas, where he met Sister Farrar [Farrow], who had a small Holiness mission. She was led to go to Kansas to attend Bible School and Brother Seymour, who was not one of the congregation, was asked to act as pastor during her absence. . . .

It was at this time that a Sister Terry [Neely] . . . heard of a group of Nazarene colored saints in Los Angeles . . . [led by] pastor Julia Hutchins . . . [After] Sister Terry finally arrived in Houston that summer . . . she met Brother Seymour.

Sister Terry later returned to Los Angeles . . . and told Sister Hutchins about the "very godly man" she had met in Houston . . . [T]he group invited . . . Brother Seymour, to their little church.

Just before Brother Seymour received this invitation to the Coast Sister Farrar [i.e., Lucy Farrow] had returned from Kansas to her little mission . . . [and] made it known to the preacher [Seymour], that she had received the Baptism with the Holy Ghost . . .

Brother Seymour began asking the Lord to empty him of false ideas, and when he was emptied of every false thought and idea that he had, the Lord then made plain to him Acts 2:4, as a personal experience.

By this time, the fare from Los Angeles had reached him, and when he arrived here . . . Everybody was happy to see him, but on Sunday morning, when Brother Seymour preached on Acts 2:4, as a personal experience . . . they were told by the preacher they did not have the Holy Ghost; they were only sanctified.

When the meeting was dismissed, Brother [Edward] Lee . . . invited Brother Seymour to his home for dinner. When they returned to the mission to the afternoon service, the lock was on the door, because the saints thought he had a false doctrine, and they would not permit him in the mission any more. So then, Brother Lee, out of courtesy for the stranger, (not that he believed that he was right) had to take him back to his home. He could not leave the stranger in the street.

Brother Seymour had not money to get out of town and the saints did not believe in him and he did not know anybody, so he stayed in his room and prayed. Brother and Sister Lee did not feel so good toward him, but they just could not invite him to leave. They had the unwelcome guest on their hands.

After a few nights in the home, Brother Seymour asked them if they would pray when Brother Lee would come in from his work, so they did. In a few nights . . . they felt differently toward the stranger. Then in a few days more, the saints from the little mission began to come around to see if the stranger was still in town or had gone.

They found such a wonderful spirit of prayer in that home. . . . The news began to spread among the people about that praying man. They would not receive his doctrine, but they would pray with him.

Then came a neighbor into the home, a Baptist sister, Sister Asbury [Ruth Asberry] of 214 North Bonnie Brae, and invited the stranger, Brother Seymour, to hold the prayer meeting in her home. So they began the prayer meeting. . . .

One evening he came in from work, and he [Ed Lee] said to Brother Seymour, "If you will lay your hands on me, I will receive my baptism." And Brother Seymour said, "No, the Lord wants me to lay hands suddenly on no man." Later on in the evening, Brother Seymour said to Brother Lee, "Brother, I lay my hands on you in Jesus' name," and when he laid his hands on him Brother Lee fell under the power, like dead, and Sister Lee was so frightened that she screamed and said, "What did you do to my husband?"

In a few minutes, Brother Lee rose up and sat in a chair. Brother Seymour . . . told about Sister Farrar, whom he had met in Texas, who had given him the light on Acts 2:4, so after Brother Lee had this experience with the Lord. . . .

They went on over to the prayer meeting at Sister Asbury's home. When Brother Lee walked into the house, six people were already on their knees praying. As he walked in the door, he lifted his hands and began to speak in tongues and the Power fell on them and all six of them began to speak in tongues. . . .

The people came from everywhere . . . the whole city was stirred. . . .

Then they . . . found Old Azusa . . . and there began that great world-wide revival, where the people came from all over the world by the hundreds and thousands. That meeting lasted for three years, day and night, without a break. . . .

56. JULIA HUTCHINS

Hutchins was the interim leader of a black Holiness mission in Los Angeles until Seymour arrived in April 1906. She wanted Seymour to become pastor so she could fulfill her dream to travel to Africa as a missionary. She was surprised by Seymour's view on tongues and locked him out of the mission. Later she changed her mind and became Pentecostal. She, her husband Willis, and niece Leila McKinney traveled to Monrovia, Liberia, for a short time before she returned to Los Angeles with an adopted African girl.

TESTIMONIES OF OUTGOING MISSIONARIES

(*AF*, October 1906, 1)

A company of three missionaries left Los Angeles September 13, en route for the west coast of Africa. Sister Hutchins has been preaching the Gospel in the power of the Spirit . . .

Sister Hutchins' Testimony.

I was justified on the 4th of July, 1901, and at that time, I felt that the Lord wanted me in Africa, but I was not then at all willing to go. But on the 28th of July, 1903, the Lord sanctified me . . . From that time on, I have felt the call to Africa. . . .

On the sixth of last month, while out in my back yard one afternoon, I heard a voice speaking to me these words: "On the 15th day of September, take your husband and baby and start out for Africa." And I looked around and about me to see if there was not someone speaking to me, but I did not see anyone, and I soon recognized that it was the voice of God. I looked up into the heavens and said: "Lord, I will obey. . . ."

After hearing the voice . . . , I went to one of my neighbors and testified to her that the Lord had told me to leave for Africa on the 15th of September. She looked at me with a smile. I asked her what she was smiling about. She said: "Because you have not got street car fare to go to Azusa Street Mission tonight, and [now you're] talking about going to Africa." But I told her I was trusting in a God that could bring all things to pass that He wanted us to do. He has really supplied all my needs. . . .

It is now ten minutes to four o'clock in the afternoon on the 15th day of September. I am all ready and down to the [Azusa] Mission with my ticket and everything prepared, waiting to have hands laid on and the prayers of the saints. . . . We expect to go to Mt. Coffee, Monrovia, Liberia. . . . [with] my niece and my husband . . . I want the prayers of the saints that I may stay humble.

–Mrs. J.W. Hutchins

57. CHARLES H. MASON

Mason (1866–1961) probably met Seymour through black Holiness leader Charles Price Jones in Louisiana in the 1890s. He arrived at Azusa along with John Jeter and David Young in March 1907 and received the baptism of the Holy Spirit on March 19. Mason was already a leader in a Holiness denomination and, as a result of a conflict with Price Jones over tongues, started the Church of God in Christ (COGIC) in September 1907. That same year he also began propagating Seymour's message through *The Whole*

Truth. After 1910, Mason allowed three white Pentecostal fellowships led by Howard Goss, Mack Pinson, and H. G. Rodgers to join COGIC. By 1913, they and almost 350 other whites left Mason's interracial fellowship and formed the General Council of the Assemblies of God. Mason kept in regular contact with Seymour until his death in 1922 and afterwards kept alive Seymour's interracial message.

TENNESSEE EVANGELIST WITNESSES.

(*AF*, February–March 1907, 7)
I had a false interpretation in my heart concerning the speaking in tongues. . . .

I had a great desire in my heart to come to Los Angeles. I had preached the Pentecost to my people and they were hungry for it. When I came, it was not strange to me for the Lord had showed it to me in a vision. . . .

As I arose from the altar and took my seat, I fixed my eyes on Jesus, and the Holy Ghost took charge of me. I surrendered perfectly to Him and consented to Him. Then I began singing a song in unknown tongues, and it was the sweetest thing to have Him sing that song through me. He had complete charge of me. I let Him have my mouth and everything. After that it seemed I was standing at the cross and heard Him as He groaned, the dying groans of Jesus, and I groaned. It was not my voice but the voice of my Beloved that I heard in me. When He got through with that, He started the singing again in unknown tongues. When the singing stopped I felt that complete death, it was my life going out, but it was a complete death to me.

When He had finished this, I let Him hold my hands up, and they rested just as easily up as down. Then He turned on the joy of it. He began to lift me up. I was passive in His hands . . . I could hear the people but did not let anything bother me. . . . He lifted me to my feet and then the light of heaven fell upon me and burst into me filling me.

Then God took charge of my tongue and I went to preaching in tongues. . . . The gestures of my hands and movements of my body were His . . . Such an indescribable peace and quietness went all through my flesh and into my very brain and has been there ever since.

–C.H. Mason, 609 Stephens Ave.,
Memphis, Tenn.

TESTIMONIES

(*AF*, January 1908, 4)
Dear ones [at Azusa Street], it is sweet for me to think of you all and your kindness to me while I was with you. . . . I was put out [of my denomi-

nation], because I believed that God did baptize me with the Holy Ghost among you all. Well, He did it and it just suits me. . . . The Lord is casting out devils, healing the sick, and singing the sweetest songs . . . I sit under His shadow with great delight. His banner over me is love.

–C.H. Mason, Lexington, Miss.,
Nov. 28.

58. D. J. YOUNG

Young, and J. A. Jeter traveled with Charles Mason to Azusa in February 1907. He received the Spirit baptism along with Mason and became a key leader in the Church of God in Christ. When Jeter and Charles Price Jones broke fellowship with Mason over tongues, Young stayed with Mason.

PENTECOSTAL MEETINGS IN LITTLE ROCK, ARK.

(*AF*, May 1907, 1)

Pentecostal Meetings.

In Little Rock, Ark.

May 7. I thank God that I am able to report victory through Jesus Christ our Lord. . . . The fire is falling and the people are getting the baptism right along. The Holy Ghost is working in our midst as never before. The Lord has made known to us that the speaking in tongues is the Bible evidence of the baptism with the Holy Ghost. Bro. Jeter and I are holding the meeting here with some others of the brethren. The Holy Ghost has charge. Pray much that we may get out of the way of the Holy Ghost, so that He can run things to suit Himself.

–D.J. Young, 212 N. Hickory St.,
Pine Bluff, Ark.

59. MACK JONAS

Jonas (1885–1973) received the Spirit baptism at Azusa on April 20, 1906. On October 23, he received a divine call to spread Seymour's message to Georgia. He attended Mason's COGIC Convention and was ordained by him on June 11, 1909. In December 1917, he pioneered the work among African Americans and whites in Cleveland, Ohio. He later served as the COGIC Overseer in Georgia and as a bishop.

TESTIMONY

(*AF*, February—March 1907, 8)
I went to Azusa Mission to make fun, but a little girl about eight years old got up and testified to the saving power of Jesus, and while she spoke, the Holy Ghost convicted me of my sins. I went to the altar and cried out to the Lord to save me from sin. Now I can witness His saving power and His cleansing power and His keeping power. O how I praise Him for saving, cleansing and baptizing me with the Holy Ghost. He has given me six languages. Now God has called me out into His work and O how I delight in His service.

–Mack E. Jonas, Long Beach, Cal.

60. GARFIELD HAYWOOD

Haywood (1880–1931) was an African-American cartoon illustrator who was raised in Indiana. After his conversion, he resigned his position and held a Pentecostal prayer meeting in a Freemason Lodge, where blacks were converted and spoke in tongues. Haywood preached throughout Indianapolis and the Midwest and became one of the most eloquent leaders in Pentecostalism. In July 1908, he noted in Seymour's *Apostolic Faith* that over two hundred people had received the Spirit baptism in the past year. In 1911, Haywood obtained credentials from the Pentecostal Assemblies of the World (PAW) and by 1913 his interracial congregation numbered more than four hundred. Under the influence Glenn Cook, in June 1915 Haywood joined the Oneness movement.

NOTICE ABOUT G. T. HAYWOOD

(*AF,* May 1908, 1)
The leading man [G.T. Haywood] among the colored Freemasons in Indianapolis and who was also cartoonist for two newspapers, was sanctified and baptized with the Holy Ghost speaking in divers new tongues. He resigned and had prayer with his members in the [Masonic] lodge room, and they were much touched. Some of his brethren have since received their Pentecost also.

EURO-AMERICAN IMMIGRANT TESTIMONIES

INTRODUCTION

Glenn Cook stated that twenty nationalities attended the Azusa Revival, including Mexicans, Portuguese, Swedes, Danes, Germans, Russians, Armenians, English, Irish, Indians, and Jews. They likened the national and racial-ethnic diversity to the outpouring of the Holy Spirit at Pentecost (Acts 2) where almost every nation on earth was reportedly represented. Many of these immigrants spread Seymour's message among their co-ethnics and then to their native countries, which was the case with both Andrew Johnson and Owen "Irish" Lee—who spread Pentecostalism to Sweden and Ireland. Immigrants were particularly attracted to Seymour's message because he promoted equality irrespective of class, education, language, and nationality.

61. LOUIS OSTERBERG

Louis and Emma Osterberg immigrated from Sweden to Chicago before moving on to Benton Harbor, Michigan, where they raised their children, attended a Baptist church, and served as lay evangelists. Emma met Seymour at the Bonnie Brae meetings. She brought her skeptical son Arthur and husband to Azusa. Arthur was so moved that he merged his mission into Azusa's. Louis became an Azusa Trustee and Emma conducted evangelistic-social work with Susie Villa Valdez—mother of A. C. Valdez.

[SWEDISH IMMIGRANT] FILLED WITH GOD'S GLORY.

(*AF,* April 1907, 4)
Up to the time of my first visit to the Azusa Street Mission . . . I was at the time hungering for the deeper things of God . . . I knew that my experience fell short of the Pentecostal life. . . . I concluded that on the following Lord's day, June 10, [1906] I would attend and see for myself.

From the first time I entered I was struck by the blessed spirit that prevailed in the meeting, such a feeling of unity and humility among the children of God . . . I was fully satisfied and convinced that it was the mighty power of God that was working. . . .

Tuesday, March 5 . . . Bro. [Hiram] Smith remarked that probably the Lord would send me my Pentecost . . .

Little by little I felt the power fall. I was soon speaking in other tongues, and the blessed experience gained then I cannot tell in words, for they would fail to express the divine meaning which it has to my soul. I spoke in tongues for nearly three hours and glorified God in them . . . I did not think it possible for a human being to be so filled with God's glory . . . I now begin to comprehend . . . the love of Christ which passeth knowledge [and] . . . the fullness of God.

–Louis Osterberg.

62. OWEN "IRISH" LEE

Lee (ca. 1880s–1930s) was one of the most colorful characters at Azusa and one of the first non-Mexican Catholics to receive the Spirit baptism. A former bartender in Ireland, he immigrated to the United States where he became a street brawler and womanizer in New York. He traveled to Los Angeles, where he knocked out the Santa Monica police chief who tried to arrest him and later "battered" four police officers who were mistreating a drunken man, an effort that landed him in jail. Written off by most as a violent man given to wine, women, and song, he reportedly found redemption at Azusa, which he began attending in 1906. He spread Seymour's message to Ireland for a short period before returning to Los Angeles.

A CATHOLIC THAT RECEIVED PENTECOST.

(*AF*, November 1906, 4)

Bro. Lee, whom God so wonderfully saved from darkness and a life of sin, and baptized him with the Holy Ghost, testified, "I praise God for this old barn. This is my confession box right here. My priest was Jesus Christ. I praise God for justifying me and sanctifying me wholly, and baptizing me with the Holy Ghost. Jesus Christ is the head of my church. It was Jesus who did the work for me. When the Holy Ghost comes in He speaks for Himself and sings His own songs. Friends, I did not go to college to get this language. It is the Holy Ghost that speaks. He can talk the languages of the nations.

It makes no difference what judges or policemen say, this Irishman is saved by the grace of God. Glory to God. It settles a man when he gets the baptism. It gives you a sound mind. This salvation keeps me out of the saloons and jails and red light districts. Jesus Christ gave his life for us that we might be saved. Glory to God for a salvation that keeps me night and day. This means persecution. Hallelujah."

MEXICAN-AMERICAN AND NATIVE-AMERICAN TESTIMONIES

INTRODUCTION

Although twenty nationalities attended Azusa, most scholars have focused on the revival's black-white origins. Mexican Americans and Mexican immigrants also attended the first week it opened until at least 1909. At least three were ordained by Seymour. They were involved with the first supernatural manifestation of the Spirit, conversion, and healing of the revival. Arthur Osterberg stated that "hundreds" of Catholics came into Azusa, "many" of whom were Spanish (Mexican American) or Mexican (Mexican immigrant). He noted they were the quickest to get their Spirit baptism and that Spanish, Mexican, and other Catholics "became quite prominent" in the Revival. This is probably why Seymour published Abundio and Rosa López's bilingual testimony in English and Spanish in the *Apostolic Faith*. Mexican Indians also attended and prayed for white men and women to receive healing. Azusa evangelist A. C. Valdez spent six years preaching in northern California at various places like the Hoopa Valley Indian reservation and Thomas Hezmalhalch preached among the Indians at Needles, California. They and their converts helped spread Pentecost throughout Native America.

63. ARTHUR OSTERBERG

MEXICAN CONVERSION AND HEALING AT THE AZUSA STREET REVIVAL

(Oral History, 17 March 1966)
They announced that they had found a place on . . . Azusa St. . . . [The downstairs] was now occupied by a lot of building material. . . . My mother asked if I couldn't help them [clear the debris]. I said, "Yes. . . ."

When I got the three men to Azusa St. there were some colored ladies [from Bonnie Brae] already working around there. And the first thing they wanted to do . . . was to have a prayer meeting. One of the colored women got to talking to one of my [Mexican] workmen and found out he was a Catholic, but his mother was a Protestant.

And she said to the [Mexican who spoke to her in a mocking tone], "You ought to be ashamed of yourself! You ought to kneel down there right now and ask God to forgive you for ever doing a think [*sic*] that like, and then go home and tell your mother what happened to you."

And that colored woman stuck to him during that whole night while I and the other two men were working. She had this one [Mexican] man off in one corner. He was trying to get out of it, and got to acting and talking a little bit smart to her to make her let him alone [*sic*]. And she said, "Now don't you start giving me that kind of language. I want you to listen to me because you are going to have to give an account to God Almighty on the Day of Judgment for what you say, so don't you say one thing that you are going to have to give an account for in Judgment."

Finally, we notice[d] that he was off in the corner with that woman and he had pulled out his handkerchief and was wiping his eyes. Whatever she had said to him, we didn't know; but the next thing we knew she had him down on his knees in the corner and I think that was the first conversion in Azusa Street, which took place [the night] before we even opened it up . . . a Roman Catholic, too. . . .

My mother [Emma Osterberg] used to go with Sister [Susie Villa] Valdez to Riverside and hold Pentecostal meetings. . . .

The . . . [Mexican Roman Catholic] folks . . . were the quickest to get their baptism, sometimes before we even knew they were converted. . . . They had sat in the meetings and . . . undoubtedly their hearts were changed, but we were too prejudiced to see that. . . .

Hundreds of them [Roman Catholics] came into Azusa St. and got the baptism. Many of them were Spanish or Mexican Catholics. . . . So in the beginning the Catholics got into Azusa Street through the Spanish people, but finally it spread out to others and [Owen] Irish Lee, being a former Roman Catholic, brought in other Catholics too. So they became quite prominent.

The first miracle I saw—the first week Azusa Street was opened up—the following Sunday I went down with the family . . . and a Spanish family [husband, wife and two daughters from San Bernardino] came in and filled in the rest of the row. From the very beginning we had prayer in the services for almost everything. I noticed that every time Brother Seymour said . . . "Let's stand and pray," this Spanish brother always crossed himself and I figured he was Catholic. So after the service and we got down to the prayer service, they always got down on their knees, and he got down with the rest of the folks and watch what everyone else did. And he was kneeling next to me and I saw him cross himself before he prayed. . . .

And lo and behold . . . all at once . . . [this Mexican] who had come in walking haltingly with a club foot, got up and went out into the aisle and he was clapping his hands and his face was uplifted. His wife looked at him and pretty soon she followed him. They walked toward the back and then back toward the front, and by this time they were walking arm in arm and he was clapping his hands and his face uplifted. That must have taken place for four or five minutes, then it quieted down, then he came down [to the altar] with his wife. I noticed when he came up the aisle he wasn't stumbling like he was when he walked into the meeting. I knew something had happened to his foot, that he was no longer stumbling.

Afterward, I took him by the hand and shook it. I wanted him to know that I was friendly to him. After the meeting [and altar call] was over I said to him: "Your foot—did something happen to your foot?"

For the first time he noticed—he stood there moving it and then started to walk—then he started to shout "Hallelujah." Then I told him "the Lord has healed your foot." But he didn't understand much English.

The Spanish folks had explained to him all about the baptism, and afterward when he came to the altar, the first time he kneeled down at the altar he got the Baptism. And here I had been praying for years and I was still seeking....

64. ABUNDIO AND ROSA LÓPEZ

Abundio López (July 11, 1870—ca. 1945) immigrated from Guadalajara, Mexico, to Los Angeles. After being ordained by the Presbyterians in July 1902, he later attended the Azusa Revival on May 29, 1906. He and his wife Rosa became lay leaders at Azusa. They preached in the Mexican Plaza District on Olvera Street in Los Angeles and throughout California. Abundio was ordained by Seymour in 1909. Abundio ministered at the Spanish Apostolic Faith Mission (1909–1914), Central Pentecostal Assembly (1914), Victoria Hall (1943), and with the Latin American Council of Christian Churches (1944).

SPANISH RECEIVE THE PENTECOST.

(*AF,* October 1906, 4)
[There are a good many Spanish-speaking people in Los Angeles. The Lord has been giving the language, and now a Spanish preacher [Abundio López], who, with his wife, are preaching the Gospel in open air meetings on the [Mexican] Plaza have received their Pentecost. They are very happy, and God is using them. The following is their testimony and the translation.]—Ed.

Los Angeles, Cal., September 14.

Soy testigo de el poder del Espiritu Santo, en perdon, en sanctificacion, y bantismo en fuego. Acts 1:8; Mark 16,17, 18. Doy gracias a Dios por esta combicsion y poder. Recibibo de Dios comforme a sus promesas el os giara. John 16:13–14. Gracias a Dios por la ordenacion de ir a la Calle de Azusa a la Mission Apostolic Faith. Old time religion Ho y mi Ezpoza el dia, 29th of May, 1906.

Por sanctificacion en verdad y gracias a Dios por la dadiba del baptismo del Eptu Santo en fuego, 5th de Junc. 1906. No podemos expresar en nuestros corazones dia tras dia y momento tras momento usandonos el Sr como instrumentos para la salvacion y sanidad de almas y de cuerpos y de cuerpos tomos tes tizo de estas permosas marabillas y miligros, en el Espiritu Santo y son promesas para cada uno de los que a Dios, se lleguen por medio del Sr. J. Cristo, San John 7:37-39; Rev. 22:17; Acts 2:37-39; James 1:5–7. Due Dios os Vendiga a todos. Acts 10, 34, 35; I John 1:1–3; Rev. 1:6, 7.

Abundio L. López an [sic] Wife,
Rosa de Lopez.

The translation of the above into English is as follows:

We testify to the power of the Holy Spirit in forgiveness, sanctification, and the baptism with the Holy Ghost and fire. We give thanks to God for this wonderful gift which we have received from Him, according to the promise. Thanks be to God for the Spirit which brought us to the Azusa Street Mission, the Apostolic Faith, old-time religion, I and my wife, on the 29th of last May. I came for sanctification, and thank God also for the baptism with the Holy Ghost and fire which I received on the 5th of June, 1905. We cannot express the gratitude and thanksgiving which we feel moment by moment for what He has done for us, so we want to be used for the salvation and healing of both soul and body. I am a witness of His wonderful promise and marvelous miracles by the Holy Ghost, by faith in the Lord Jesus Christ. May God bless you all.

65. BRIGIDO PÉREZ

Pérez (ca. 1880s—1900s) attended Azusa in late August, received the Spirit baptism on September 3, and preached throughout southern California. Seymour and the Mission sponsored his evangelistic work among the Spanish-speaking population.

PREACHING TO THE SPANISH.

(*AF*, November 1906, 4)

Bro. and Sister Lopez, Spanish people, who are filled with the Holy Ghost, are being used of God in street meetings and in helping Mexicans at the altar at Azusa street.

Bro. Brigido Perez is another young Spanish boy who has received the Pentecost. He is now in San Diego. He writes his testimony in Spanish, which being translated reads, "Through the grace of Almighty God and faith in Jesus Christ, I can testify to sanctification and the baptism with the Holy Spirit and fire of love in my heart. How good He has been to me. On September 3rd, while I was praying, I felt in my heart that Christ our Savior wanted me to go and testify in His precious name in different parts of the country." The Holy Ghost shines out of this brother's face.

66. *APOSTOLIC FAITH* EDITORIAL

Mexican Indian Prays for White Woman's Healing
(*AF*, September 1906, 2–3)

On Aug. 11th, a man from the central part of Mexico, an Indian, was present in the meeting and heard a German sister speaking in his tongue which the Lord had given her. He understood, and through the message that God gave him through her, he was most happily converted so that he could hardly contain his joy. All the English he knew was Jesus Christ and Hallelujah.

He testified in his native language, which was interpreted by a man who had been among that tribe of Indians. This rough Indian, under the power of the Spirit was led to go and lay his hands on a woman in the congregation who was suffering from consumption, and she was instantly healed and arose and testified.

Los Angeles, Aug. 12th, 1906. This will certify that my daughter, Mrs. S. P. Knapp, of Avenue 56 and Alameda street, was healed of consumption by God on the above date, God's Spirit working in answer to prayer and through a poor Mexican Indian. . . .

67. ADOLFO C. VALDEZ

A. C. Valdez (1896–1988) was a Mexican-American Catholic who attended and converted at Seymour's Revival in the spring of 1906. He, his mother (Susie), Father (José), and siblings attended Azusa for three years. Valdez was ordained in an independent mission (Long Beach) in 1916. He preached among Euro-Americans, Latinos, and Native Americans and later conducted evangelistic-healing crusades in Australia, New Zealand, India, China, Japan, Hawaii, the South Sea Islands, and Latin America. He is one of the founders of Pentecostalism in Australia and New Zealand due to his 1920s campaigns.

MEXICAN-AMERICAN ACCOUNT OF AZUSA STREET

(*Fire on Azusa Street*, 1980, 1–12, 40)

When I was fast asleep, my mother came into my dark bedroom after a service at the Azusa Street Mission. She bent over and touched my shoulder. As I brushed the sand out of my eyes to wake up, she began talking fast in some language I had never heard before.

I was frightened.... What had come over her?

Then the other language stopped, and she said: "Son, I have had a most glorious experience! I have just been baptized in the Holy Ghost and have been given the gift of tongues!"... "The Holy Ghost is here on earth—like at the Pentecost...." The Bible in Joel 2:28 tells us: "... I will pour out my Spirit upon all flesh; and your sons and your daughters shall prophesy ... your young men shall see visions...."

On the platform, a black man—mother said it was Pastor W.J. Seymour—sat behind two wooden boxes, one on top of the other. They were his pulpit. Now and then he would raise his head and sit erectly his large lips moving in silent prayer....

As I looked out over the congregation ... Wave after wave of the Spirit went through the hall, like a breeze over a corn field ... And prayers began to buzz through the hall....

Everything about the Azusa Street Mission fascinated me especially the prayer or "tarrying room" on the second floor. Usually one hundred or more black, brown, and white people prayerfully waited there for the Holy Spirit to come upon them. Dozens of canes, braces, crutches and blackened smoking pipes leaned against the barnlike walls....

Meetings used to go past midnight and into the early hours of the morning. Hours there seemed like minutes. Sometimes after a wave of glory, a lot of people would speak in tongues. Then a holy quietness would come over the place, followed by a chorus of prayer in languages we had never before heard.

Many were slain in the Spirit, buckling to the floor, unconscious, in a beautiful Holy Spirit cloud, and the Lord gave them visions.... During the tarrying, we used to break out in songs about Jesus and the Holy Spirit.... heavenly music would fill the hall, and we would break into tears. Suddenly. ... Out of their mouths would come new languages and lovely harmony that no human beings could have learned....

Old-line churches frowned on the Azusa Street Mission's Bible teachings, "so-called miracles," and "noisy meetings...."

A sure way to get kicked out of an established church in the early twentieth century was to admit having been baptized in the Holy Spirit. I learned this from experience, as did thousands of others ... so we had to go it without the establishment. This is why many Pentecostal churches got started.

My parents were overjoyed when, after my baptism in the Holy Spirit, I informally started ministering. They had still another reason for joyousness. For some years, my father had had a steadily enlarging malignant growth on his back, which, doctors feared, would spread to every critical part of his body and take his life. After he had been born again and baptized in the

Holy Spirit, his condition improved steadily. One day the growth dissolved completely and disappeared from his body. . . .

Now I had a little more time to spread the gospel . . . carrying my small, cane suitcase full of tracts, I sang and preached on street corners . . . I [peddled my bicycle] all the way to Los Angeles, Riverside, San Bernardino, and even to San Diego—100 miles away—to carry on my ministry.

I was set afire by preaching under the skies and inviting people to visit their nearest Pentecostal mission—especially by introducing them to Jesus. . . .

MEXICAN-AMERICAN MINISTRY
AMONG NATIVE AMERICANS

(*Fire on Azusa Street*, 59–66, 97–98)

My northern California crusades were . . . exciting and soul-satisfying. I shall never forget the miraculous events in Eureka and then Willow Creek [at the Indian Reservation] in the Humboldt Mountains . . . [where] many souls were saved and . . . crippled people were made whole. . . .

"Aunt" Fanny Lack . . . was 100 years old, almost totally blind and struggled to walk. . . . She asked to receive the Lord and then be baptized in the Holy Spirit. I immersed her in the river, and she came out of the water, dripping, speaking in an unknown tongue, glorifying the Lord Jesus Christ . . . Aglow with the Spirit, Fanny Lack briskly walked to the Hoopa Indian Reservation thirteen miles away to visit relatives.

She told them what God had done in her life, but they could not believe it was Fanny. One relative said, "It looks like her, but it is not her, because Aunt Fanny Lack can't walk without canes and can hardly see."

Fanny began to clap hands and dance in the Spirit. "Praise the Lord," she sang. "Jesus saved me and filled me with the Holy Ghost, and I feel like a young girl again."

Aunt Fanny Lack lived on to work with us and others in that area for another twenty years—a walking miracle who served as an example to bring others to a saving knowledge of Jesus Christ. . . .

On numerous visits to the Hoopa Reservation . . . the Indians asked and received help from the Lord in circumstances beyond their control. Never did they fail to give Him the glory and praise. . . .

Like God's miracles of protection, His miracles of healing during and after Azusa Street days were numerous.

68. THOMAS HEZMALHALCH

After immigrating to the United States from England in 1880, Hezmalhalch (1848–1934) attended Azusa in 1906. He spread Pentecostalism around the world and helped found the work in South Africa. Before he left, he also spread Seymour's message among Indians in Needles, California.

AMONG THE INDIANS AT NEEDLES, CALIFORNIA.

(*AF,* January 1907, 3)
Jan. 8th.

I reached the Needles on Saturday, Jan. 1 [1907]. Found dear old friends there, working in their beautiful little mission house among the Mojave Indians. . . .

On Sunday afternoon, we had over thirty Indians in the Mission besides the white people. It was a blessed time. While the Indians were testifying in their own language, and some in English. . . . The interpretation by some of the Indians is as marvelous as the Holy Spirit speaking through others in tongues.

The evening meeting was a wonderful demonstration of the Holy Spirit's leading, to all present. The converted Indians have a better knowledge of what the baptism with the Holy Ghost is, than their teachers do. Our Indian brother George rose and interpreted into their own language what we had said. It was a wonderful manifestation of the Holy Spirit. . . .

The Indian preacher in his own language said, "When God-Father forgive you all your wrong doing, through God—Jesus, you have first make Indian (yourself) all naked from wrong. Then God—Father forgive. But you no naked in heart. God-Holy Ghost no occupy till Jesus make naked in heart, (pointing to a picture of Jesus on the wall, every time he mentioned His name.) Then (going through an imaginary performance of stripping himself naked, beginning at the head and ending with his feet), he said, "As you make naked outside, God—Jesus make Indian naked inside . . . from the devil, (slapping his side . . . the hand fist and fingers spread apart. God—Holy Ghost no live where devil live. God—Holy Ghost talk through us to all the Indians in the mountains, like Holy Ghost talk through that brother, (for the Holy Ghost had spoken through me in three languages, giving the interpretation after each one.) And God—Jesus make all Indians in mountains, and us, and these, and these all big Holy Ghost tribe."

There are thousands of Indians of different tribes in the mountains, and he meant they . . . and . . . the white people, and a colored brother, pointing to each of us, would, by the Blood of Jesus Christ, be made one great spiritual family. . . .

One of the Indians came to me and said, "Bro. Tom . . . we want you to pray for us every day, that we may have the baptism of the Holy Ghost . . . forever. . . ."

[T]he cry . . . from these different tribes among the mountains has gone up to our Heavenly Father, and He will answer it . . . God will satisfy the longing of these precious souls. . . .

Yours, T. Hezmalhalch

AFRICA MISSIONARY TESTIMONIES

INTRODUCTION

Africa was one of the first continents Seymour and Azusa missionaries targeted for conversion. Lucy Farrow, Julia Hutchins, S. J. and Ardella Mead, Daniel Awrey, Ansel Post, John Lake, H. M. Turney, the Frank Cummings family, and others led groups to Liberia, Egypt, South Africa, and elsewhere from 1906 to 1911. There is little doubt that they targeted these countries and colonies because they spoke English and were part of the British or American overseas colonial empire, which provided a measure of political protection, religious freedom, and personal safety.

69. LUCY FARROW

Farrow was born into slavery in Norfolk, Virginia, prior to 1865. She was the niece of abolitionist Frederick Douglass and served as Charles Parham's governess. She attended Parham's meetings, pastored a black holiness mission in Houston where she met Seymour, and asked him to serve as interim pastor while she traveled with Parham's family to Kansas. Seymour later invited her to attend Bonnie Brae and then Azusa, where she was known for her ability to lead people into the Spirit baptism. She spent seven months preaching in Johnsonville, Liberia, before returning in 1908 and preaching throughout the American South.

REPORT ON LUCY FARROW'S MINISTRY IN LIBERIA

(*AF,* October to January 1908, 1)
Our dear Sister Farrow, who was one of the first to bring Pentecost to Los Angeles, went to Africa and spent seven months at Johnsonville, 25 miles from Monrovia, Liberia, in that most deadly climate. She has now returned and has a wonderful story to tell. Twenty souls received their Pentecost, numbers were saved sanctified and healed. The Lord had given her the

gift of the Kru language and she was permitted to preach two sermons to the people in their own tongue. The heathen some of them after receiving the Pentecost, spoke in English and some in other tongues. Praise God. The Lord . . . brought her home safely, and used her in Virginia and in the South along the way.

70. GEORGE AND DAISY BATMAN

The Batmans were inspired by the Meads and Seymour to spread the fires of Pentecost to Monrovia, Liberia. They journeyed with Farrow, the Hutchins, and others in the fall of 1906. The Batmans and a Mrs. Cook and Lee died of pestilence and were buried in Monrovia shortly after they arrived.

EN ROUTE TO AFRICA.

(*AF*, December 1906, 4)
Bro. and Sister G.W. Batman . . . are tried and true workers and have the enduement of power from on high and the fitness of the gift of tongues. . . . They have the gift of healing and we believe God will wonderfully use them among those darkened souls.

Bro. G.W. Batman's Testimony.

I was converted nine years ago, and got a know-so salvation . . . After that, I received the baptism with the Holy Ghost and fire and now I feel the presence of the Holy Ghost . . . and at times I am shaken like a locomotive steamed up and prepared for a long journey . . . I also speak in six foreign tongues given me at God's command. God has called me to Africa as a missionary, and told me to go to Monrovia, Liberia. . . .

Mrs. Daisy Batman's Testimony.

At the age of fourteen, the Lord saved me from my sins . . . when the Pentecost came to Los Angeles, I found that was just what I wanted. . . . One day the Lord told me to stop everything and go to the meeting. I said, Lord, I have three small children and no way to support them. He said, I will supply your needs . . . Three years ago last April, the Lord gave us the call to Africa. At first I thought I would stay and let my husband go, but He said, "No, you must go too. . . ." And three months after we received our baptism, He said, "Now go to Africa." O glory to God, I am so glad I got to the place where the blessed Lord's will is my will."

71. EDWARD AND MOLLY MCCAULEY

Molly received the Spirit baptism on November 30, 1906. Edward was a flamboyant preacher. He followed Seymour's ministry and pastored a multiracial congregation in Long Beach before traveling to Liberia. They, along with Rosa Harmon, arrived in Monrovia in November 1907 and began preaching at a makeshift hall around December 1, where they organized a mission with a large sign that read: "Apostolic Faith Mission." They held services until March 26, 1907, when they began a ten-day revival in a school. On the tenth day, the Spirit reportedly fell and ten were sanctified and five Spirit baptized, including a Liberian man and his household. Harmon wrote that by July 1908 God had saved a number of "heathens" that had formerly walked around almost naked with "their gods" "tied . . . around their necks, arms, and waists." By June 1909 they reported having saved and baptized 154 members of the Kru tribe. Their ministry set the stage for Liberian evangelist William Wade Harris, who was probably influenced by people who attended these meetings. Harris preached to an estimated 100,000 people from 1913 to 1914.

MOLLY MCCAULEY TESTIMONY

(*AF,* February-March 1907, 8)
I was justified about 35 years ago. . . . Last August [1906] my husband went through the South preaching holiness. When he came back, he heard about the meetings in Los Angeles where the people had the baptism with the Holy Ghost and speaking in tongues. He said if it was of God, he wanted it, and if not he wanted nothing to do with it. He went up to Los Angeles and came back and said to me, "Darling that work is of God, and I am going back to Los Angeles and stay at the Azusa Mission until I get the baptism with the Holy Ghost." He paid no attention to me but went to the Mission and came back with the baptism and speaking in tongues . . . and on the 30th of November, God baptized me with the Holy Ghost. . . . O, glory to God for this wonderful salvation.

—Mollie McCauley, Long Beach, Cal.

72. JOHN LAKE

Lake (1870–1935) was a pioneer Pentecostal missionary to South Africa. He was influenced by the Methodist Church, Alexander Dowie, and Seymour. In 1907, he reportedly received a divine calling to South Africa, where he traveled along with his wife, seven children, and four other adults in the spring of 1908. His wife died that December due to malnutrition and exhaustion. Four years later he returned to the United States. He spent six years conducting a healing ministry in Portland beginning in 1920 and later in Spokane. However, before he returned to the United States, he organized the Apostolic Faith Church in South Africa. He brought South Africans such as P. E. LeRoux and E. M. Letwaba into the movement, and they and others in turn splintered into other traditions. Lake placed great emphasis on divine healing and supernatural power encounters.

ORIGIN OF THE APOSTOLIC FAITH MOVEMENT

(*The Pentecostal Outlook,* September 1952, 3; originally published in June 1911.)

Soon the fire began to fall at the Azusa Street Mission . . . which became known world-wide as a great centre of Holy Ghost power.

After considerable time the work spread throughout the whole country and world, until every land has its representatives of . . . [Seymour's] Apostolic Faith Mission, and Pentecost is a household word. . . .

The work in Africa took a still deeper phase of spiritual power, especially along the line of miraculous healing of the sick. From careful investigation we are free to state that in no land had such a demonstration of healing of the sick occurred as in South Africa. We rejoice in this . . . deepening of spiritual power over the whole world, as the fire has spread from place to place, and country to country. . . .

73. THOMAS HEZMALHALCH

PENTECOST IN DENVER.

(*AF,* November 1906, 1)

E. 18th ave., Denver, Colo.

What I received on that memorable Sunday night in Los Angeles [at the Azusa Mission] has never left me for one moment. . . .

Dear Bro. Seymour, God surely sent me here [to Denver]. These dear, hungry people, when they learned I came from the meeting at Los Angeles, received me with open arms. . . . Dear Bro. G.F. Fink, the brother in charge, was coming to Los Angeles to Azusa Street to learn and get a better understanding of the baptism with the Holy Ghost . . . You little know how the people have been praying for you and the [Azusa] meetings in Los Angeles in the midst of their own struggles. Give my love in Jesus to all the saints.

—T. Hezmalhalch.

74. SAMUEL AND ARDELL MEAD

Samuel (1849–1936) and Ardell (1843–1934) Mead were veteran Methodist Episcopal Church missionaries to Angola, Central Africa. They left their native Vermont in 1885 and worked under the auspices of Bishop William Taylor in Malange, where they preached, opened up a school, and supervised a large communal farm. In 1904, they journeyed to Los Angeles, where they later met Seymour and reported that some of the tongues at Azusa were real African languages. Seymour sent them back to Africa, where they served until 1909, after which time they returned to Los Angeles.

NEW-TONGUED MISSIONARIES FOR AFRICA.

(*AF*, November 1906, 3)

Our dear Brother and Sister Mead, who have spent twenty years in missionary work in Africa have received their Pentecost in Los Angeles, and as the Lord leads and opens the way they will be on their way to the dark continent again with the divine fitness for missionary work.

Bro. Mead's Testimony of Pentecost.

I went to the [Azusa] meetings when I first heard of the manifestation of the Spirit, speaking in tongues, healing of the body, etc. . . .

The first night at the meetings, my heart went out for the baptism. I went forward to be prayed for, and hands were laid on me, and prayer was made, that I might receive the baptism of the Holy Spirit. I continued praying and fasting . . . and. . . . One evening, in complete abnegation of self . . . my soul was flooded with Divine love; and I commenced to speak as I would sing a new song. . . .

Many ask, "Do you think these tongues will be used in a foreign field?" As for myself I cannot say. My God is able, this I know. The Pentecost or baptism of Divine love, that would enable a missionary to say to the poor Africans, as the Spirit did through Peter and John, to the poor cripple at the gate of the Temple, "Silver and gold have I none, but such as I have give I thee. In the name of Jesus Christ of Nazareth, rise up and walk," would mark a grand epoch in the history of foreign missions. I believe God is about to repeat many of the miracles and wonders wrought in the early history of the church.

—S.J. Mead.

Sister Mead's Baptism.

Two years before we left Africa, the Holy Spirit began to speak to us in an especial way. We felt the lack of the power and love in the service of our

Master, and we commenced seeking that power from Him . . . in our little mission home in Africa. . . .

Just before our return to America, we believe it was the Spirit of God, who said to us very plainly. "Los Angles, California, is the end of your journey. . . ."

[At Azusa]. . . . Bro. Seymour, Sister Crawford and another Sister laid their hands upon me that I might receive the Holy Ghost. As they prayed, I felt the power go through my body, but did not receive then the full baptism.

We waited on God daily in our home for three weeks, searching the Scriptures, confessing our faults. . . . Then the enemy tried to get me discouraged, telling me that this baptism was not for me. . . . So we sang and testified, and then fell on our knees in prayer . . .

On Saturday morning. . . . the Holy Ghost fell upon me in great sweetness and power . . . Jesus was real to me.

I was under the power from early morning till about five at night, prophesying in the Scriptures, and then began to speak in tongues, as the Spirit gave me utterance. . . . Since then I have been shown that what I speak is an African dialect. . . .

—Ardell K. Mead.

75. HENRY TURNEY

Turney (1850–1900s) was born in Louisville, Kentucky, and raised Catholic. He heard about Azusa through Seymour's newspaper. He received the Spirit baptism in October 1906, and preached along the Pacific Coast and in Hawaii, Japan, China, and especially South Africa.

ALASKA BROTHER PROVES ACTS 1.8.

(*AF,* December 1906, 3)

I was born at Louisville, Ky., on May 17, 1850. My parents were Irish Catholics so of course I was brought up in that faith. . . .

Two months ago, a paper was given me, telling of the wonderful outpouring of the Holy Spirit in Los Angeles. Just as soon as I could, I packed my grip and left Alaska for Los Angeles, arriving there Oct. 5th. The night following found me at the altar seeking the baptism with the Holy Ghost and fire. (Matt. 2.11.) Praise God . . . I received my Pentecost and the gift of tongues, and am speaking in many different languages. I am soon expecting to start around the world preaching full salvation. . . . Glory to God.

–H.M. Turney, San Jose, Cal., Gen. Del.

76. ANSEL POST

Post (d. 1931) was a Baptist minister for thirty years before attending Azusa and receiving the Spirit baptism in June 1906. He spread Seymour's message around the world, starting in 1907, to England, Wales, South Africa, India, and Sri Lanka. In 1910, he and his wife, Etta, organized the work in Egypt, where they spent the next thirty years. They joined the Assemblies of God in 1916 and conducted evangelistic work, planted churches, conducted revivals among Coptic Christians, and supported Lillian Thrasher's (1887–1961) orphanage in Assiout, Egypt. The Posts died and were buried in Egypt.

TESTIMONY OF A MINISTER.

(*AF*, January 1907, 4)

For more than thirty years, I was a minister in one of the leading denominations . . . I had been seeking for a deeper fullness of God's love, conscious that . . . we needed a greater anointing in order to be made adequate to the work to be done. . . .

About the middle of June [1906], without any planning of my own, I was led for the first time into those meetings at Azusa St., Los Angeles. . . .

In the altar service, I quietly presented myself before the Lord. On the second day, while at the altar, as distinct to my inner consciousness as a clear voice to my ear, Jesus said, "receive ye the Holy Spirit. . . ." I did not feel any overflow of joy or emotion, but rather a deeper calm and quiet, and in my mission work on the Lord's Day following, I had more liberty and a clear knowledge of my Lord's presence.

On the Monday following [at Azusa]. . . . the Holy Spirit fell upon me and filled me literally, as it seemed to lift me up, for, indeed, I was in the air in an instant, shouting, praise God, and instantly I began to speak in another language.

Two of the saints quite a distance apart, saw the Spirit fall upon me. One of them sprang towards me, also talking in an unknown language. Oh, how God did indeed fill my whole being in a way indescribable. I could not have been more surprised if at the same moment some one had handed me a million dollars. I had not been seeking the gift of tongues, or any other gift; but, oh how I did long for God Himself to completely fill me, and in His great love surely He did. . . .

God has come into my life, in a fuller and more profound sense than ever before, and He makes all things spiritual much more real, and His love completely permeates my whole being. . . .

In these few months . . . this work has spread till its influence has reached half round the world. Many of all ages and races . . . has received a definite baptism of the Spirit. . . .

—Yours in Jesus, A.H. Post Pasadena, Cal.

EUROPE AND MIDDLE EAST MISSIONARY TESTIMONIES

INTRODUCTION

By spring 1906, Seymour had sent missionaries to Africa, Europe, Scandinavia, and the Middle East. England, Norway, and Sweden became launching points for Pentecostal evangelism across Europe to Germany, Italy, France, and Russia. Many who were Spirit baptized were veteran Christian leaders. They used their denominational ties and newspaper to spread Seymour's message and revival. The testimony by Johnson, Boddy, and Leatherman reveals the deep and personal influence Seymour had on their lives and ministries and other future national leaders like Barratt.

77. ANDREW JOHNSON

Johnson was a Swedish immigrant who attended Azusa in the spring of 1906. Seymour raised funds to send him to the Middle East, but he changed plans and went to his native Sweden. There he laid the foundation for its most famous leader, Lewi Petrus (1884–1974), who received the Spirit baptism through the ministry of T. B. Barratt of Norway. Johnson's letters reveal a deep love and appreciation for Seymour and his desire to replicate Azusa's paradigmatic experience throughout Sweden. This love was reciprocated; Seymour published seven of Johnson's letters in his *Apostolic Faith* newspaper—more than any other missionary, black or white.

LETTER FROM BRO. JOHNSON.

(*AF*, October 1906, 3)
. . . Aug., 31st.
Peace be unto you. I am, God willing, going to leave New York [for Sweden] in a few days. . . .

Tell Bro. Seymour that I am one with him and all the other saints in Los Angeles. I love my dear Bro. Seymour so much. He has been a good help to me. May God bless him in his work. My love to all the saints. . . .

Andrew Johnson. Address Care of Soldiers' and Sailors' Home, Gibraltar, Spain,

"IN SWEDEN"

(*AF,* April 1907, 1)
Viby, April 2. . . .
I am happy in Jesus Christ and glad for what He has been doing in Sweden. . . . There are now about twelve preachers who have received the Holy Ghost with signs following, and a few hundred have been saved, many getting a clean heart. Some have been healed, and many of God's children have received the Holy Ghost. I am called to many places and the cry for help comes from all over Sweden. . . . There is strong opposition and talking about me, and writing in the papers even. . . .

Tell the saints [at Azusa Street] to love one another and keep united in love, and under the Blood every day, and humble. I am with you every day in the Spirit and praying for you all . . . God's people are going to be one soon. Glory!

"SALVATION IN SWEDEN"

(*AF,* June-September 1907, 1)
Stockholm, Sweden, many souls are filled with the Holy Ghost and have the Bible evidence. The tidal wave is sweeping on, [and] on to victory. Hundreds of souls are at the feet of Jesus. . . . "I have Eric Hollingsworth and his wife here with me [from Azusa] now in this city, and hope we shall have a house like Azusa Mission. The church in Skofde [Skövde] is growing. I think there are about 40 now who are baptized with the Holy Ghost and speaking and singing in new tongues. . . ." [Since the last report, two Spirit-filled sisters [from Azusa], Sister Anderson and Sister Jacobson, have gone to help in the work in Sweden].

"SWEDEN"

(*AF*, October-January 1908, 1)
Nov. 19
"I am very glad to hear from the old Azusa Mission, my home. I have victory through the dear, cleansing Blood of Christ. . . . The fire is falling in 'Norrland. . . . This work will go on till Jesus our Lord comes. . . .

"SWEDEN"

(*AF,* May 1908, 1)
The Holy Ghost is falling on the humble in Gottenberg. . . . Many sick have been healed, sinners saved and backsliders coming to the Lord. . . . Many are seeking the power of God day and night. . . .

Many sinners have come to God in different parts of Sweden. . . . A number of workers who received their baptism in Los Angeles are there being used of God.

> Address Brother Andrew G.
> Johnson, Backevick,
> 3 Hisingstad, Sweden.

78. THOMAS BALL BARRATT

Barratt (1862–1940) pioneered Pentecostalism in Norway and around the world. Born in Cornwall, England, his parents moved to Norway in 1867. He became a deacon (1889) and an elder (1891) in the Methodist Episcopal Church of Norway. He pastored Oslo City Mission (1902) and founded and edited the Christian periodical *Byposten* in 1904. On a fundraising and subscription trip to the United States in 1906, in New York City he met Azusa missionaries Lucy Leatherman, Andrew Johnson, and Louise Condit. They prayed for him to receive the Spirit baptism. He helped spread Seymour's message throughout Norway, Sweden, Finland, Denmark, Iceland, England, Poland, and Estonia, and visited India. He was expelled from the Methodist Church in 1909 for his views on tongues and related matters. He organized international conferences and authored more than three hundred publications.

BAPTIZED IN NEW YORK.

(*AF*, December 1906, 3)
Dear [Azusa] Friends in Los Angeles:—Glory to God! Tongues of fire . . . fell on the 7th of October [1906]. Since then I have been seeking the full Bible evidence,—the gift of tongues . . . O Glory! . . . .

At about half past twelve I asked a brother there and Sister Leatherman to lay their hands on my head again. And just then she says she saw a crown of fire and cloven tongues over my head. The brother saw a supernatural light.

Immediately I was filled with light and such a power that I began to shout as loud as I could in a foreign language . . . I must have spoken seven or eight languages. . . . I stood erect at times preaching in one foreign tongue after another, and I know from the strength of my voice that 10,000 might easily have heard all I said. Nine persons remained till three o'clock and are witnesses of the whole scene . . . I sang several times later on. . . . Oh it was wonderful. Glory! Hallelujah!

That night will never be forgotten by any who were there. . . . I felt strong as a lion and know now where David and Sampson got their strength from. Today I have been speaking and singing in tongues wherever I have been. Glory to God. Go on praying.

"IN NORWAY"

(*AF,* February to March 1907, 1)
Solfies, Pl. 2, Christiania, Norway, Jan. 29.

God is wonderfully demonstrating His power here in the Norwegian capital. It is about ten days since I held the first meeting in the large gymnasium that will take when crowded from 1,500 to 2,000 people. People from all denominations are rushing to the meetings.

Over twenty have received their Pentecost and are speaking in tongues. Several have been in trances and had heavenly visions. Some have seen Jesus at our meetings, and the tongues of fire have been seen again over my head by a freethinker, convincing him of the power of God. . . . The fire is spreading very rapidly. Glory to God!

I received word from the country districts that the fire is falling there. . . .

The account of God's work for my soul has been inserted in many religious papers, and has caused a stir. . . . Several preachers are seeking their Pentecost. . . .

Yours in Christ Jesus, T.B. Barratt.

79. ALEXANDER A. BODDY

Boddy (1854–1930), parish minister of All Saints Anglican Church in Sunderland, England, was one of the first Pentecostal converts in Great Britain and Europe. He was an eyewitness to Evan Roberts's Welsh Revival in 1904–5. Boddy heard about Seymour and Azusa in May 1906 through Seymour's *Apostolic Faith* and T. B. Barratt. He became convinced that Seymour's Revival was of God. In the summer of 1908, Boddy organized an international Pentecostal convention that attracted workers from Holland, Italy, Norway, Scotland, Wales, and elsewhere and edited *Confidence* from 1908 to 1926. Boddy visited Azusa in 1912.

A MEETING AT THE AZUSA STREET MISSION, LOS ANGELES

(*Confidence,* November 1912, 224–25)
A week after my first visit [in 1912] . . . I came back to the Azusa Street Mission . . . and saw [that evening] the light of the now historical Mission beaming out from the window. A transparency over the door said: "You shall know the truth, and the truth shall make you free."

Though the regular gatherings are not what they were, yet "Azusa Street" is a sort of "Mecca" still to Pentecostal travelers. They like to kneel in the place "where the Fire fell."

As I pushed open the side door of fine mosquito wire, I found a large company of white and coloured people assembled. Sister Jennie (Mrs. Seymour) a colored sister was leading in hymn-singing, and giving exhortations between. [William Seymour was traveling back east.] The assembly went to prayer, and she led very earnestly, as one who knew God.

Soon she welcomed "Brother Boddy, of England," in the name of the Lord, and placed the meeting in my charge.

I . . . looked around on the bright, dark faces, and on the white friends . . . I tried to realize that I was really worshipping in the Azusa Street Mission, of Los Angeles, at last, and I thanked God sincerely. The Lord graciously gave me liberty in speaking from heart to heart in that place where He had so wonderfully blessed.

A Season of Blessing

At the close of the long address hearts being moved, many seekers thronged the penitent form, and we had a wonderful season of blessing. . . .

The meeting was very orderly, but Spirit-possessed. The hymn-singing was very earnest, and unaccompanied by any instrument. It was good to hear these coloured people freely praising God.

An aged coloured sister sat near to me. It was most encouraging to hear her continued ejaculations of "Praise God," and "That is so," and "Hallelujah to the Lamb! . . ."

So at the late hour the meeting ended, and friends thronged around to shake hands with Brother Boddy, of England. Many of them are readers of "Confidence." It seemed like meeting old acquaintances as one looked into their faces and heard how they valued our paper, and I received a warm embrace from one brother. The old wooden walls of the Azusa Street Mission were brightly lit up. All seemed clean and comfortable. At last I said "Goodbye" to the friends, and came home . . . with some blessed things to treasure in my memory.

I am greatly drawn to these dear coloured people. There are some true children of God amongst them. . . . They are so simple, and so open to God.

80. LUCY LEATHERMAN

Leatherman attended A. B. Simpson's Nyack Bible College (NY), where she received her calling to reach the Arab population in Jerusalem. In August 1906, Seymour sent Leatherman, Andrew Johnson, and Louise Condit to the Middle East. She reported to Seymour in May 1908 that a Lebanese

Christian accepted the Pentecostal baptism in Jerusalem. She also reported "the 'latter rain' is falling" in Israel and that a Christian and Missionary Alliance missionary named Miss Elizabeth Brown (d. 1940) accepted the Spirit baptism and joined the work.

"PENTECOSTAL EXPERIENCES"

(*AF,* November 1906, 4)
While seeking for the Baptism with the Holy Ghost [at the Azusa Mission] in Los Angeles, after Sister Ferrell [Lucy Farrow] laid hands on me, I praised and praised God and saw my Savior in the heavens . . . I found that rest that passeth all understanding, and He said to me, you are in the bosom of the Father . . . I said, Father, I want the gift of the Holy Ghost, and the heavens opened and I was overshadowed, and such power came upon me and went through me. He said, Praise Me, and when I did, angels came and ministered unto me. I was passive in His hands, and by the eye of faith I saw angel hands working on my vocal cords, and I realized they were loosing me. I began to praise Him in an unknown language. . . .

ASIA: INDIA MISSIONARY TESTIMONIES

INTRODUCTION

The Pentecostal message found a receptive audience on the Indian subcontinent, which was then a colony of the British Empire. Many veteran missionaries from the United States, Great Britain, and Europe were looking for personal spiritual renewal and a Christian theology that transcended some of the racial and nationalistic provincialism prevalent in their day. Seymour's message filled the gap in caste-conscious India. Alfred and Lillian Garr and others helped spread Pentecostalism, especially in Protestant mission schools. By July 1908, fifteen missionary societies and twenty-eight mission stations experienced Pentecost. Some like the Mukti Mission were run and led by foreign missionaries and native workers like Minnie Abrams and Pandita Ramabai who had already witnessed pre-Azusa manifestations of the Spirit in their students. This helped set the stage and receptivity for Seymour's message, which eyewitnesses state brought them into a fuller and deeper understanding of the global Pentecostal outpouring.

81. FLORENCE CRAWFORD AND CLARA LUM

Crawford and Lum's report reveals the proto-Pentecostal manifestations of the Spirit at several mission schools led by Minnie Abrams and Pandita

Ramabai prior the first Azusa missionaries' (Garrs) arrival in 1906. The Garrs led many seasoned missionaries into the Pentecostal baptism, and they along with native youth evangelists led by Abrams and Ramabai played a key role in Pentecostalism's growth in India.

"HOW INDIA RECEIVED PENTECOST"

(*AF,* Portland, Oregon, July and August, 1908, 3)
India is a ripe field. About 1,000 have received the baptism of the Holy Ghost in that land already. Shortly after Pentecost fell [at Azusa Street] in Los Angeles, the Lord baptized and called some [i.e., Alfred and Lillian Garr] to India.

They arrived in Calcutta at the opening of the Winter season there. The missionaries . . . were holding meetings for the deepening of the Spirit, and were praying for the baptism of the Holy Ghost. . . .

In this meeting our missionaries were asked if they knew about the Pentecostal Movement in Los Angeles. They told them, Yes, and that God had given them the blessing, and the Spirit came on them to speak in tongues. They were invited to come back, and that night the brother [Garr] spoke on the outpouring of the Spirit. At the close a Baptist minister [Rev. C. H. Hook], pastor of the oldest Baptist church [Carey Baptist Chapel] in Calcutta, offered his church for them to hold meetings.

Tarrying in the Baptist Church

The following Sunday they opened meetings in the Baptist Church, and nearly all from the other meeting came over in a body and closed their services to tarry in the Holy Ghost. The work went on for two months, people getting saved and sanctified and straightening their lives under the mighty hand of God. Then the Lord laid it on one to open up a house for tarrying . . . Nearly all the missionaries were baptized. . . .

Little Indian Girls Baptized With the Holy Ghost.

One of the missionaries who was at the head of a native school for girls in Calcutta received her baptism. . . . and in a short time 45 were baptized with the Holy Spirit and speaking in tongues. . . .

The Lord's Way of Humbling.

Brother [Max Wood] Moorhead, who now edits, "The Cloud of Witnesses to Pentecost in India," was one who received his Pentecost there. While seeking, he prayed one night that the Lord would humble the proud Europeans. . . .

Hundreds of Native Girls Baptized.

Pentecost had fallen in great power in Panditta [*sic*] Ramabai's work at Mukti, India. Sister Ramabai had written to the Pentecostal missionaries when they first went to India, asking them to come and preach this truth in her school. . . . But before any came to Mukti, there were about 400 girls baptized with the Spirit and speaking in tongues. Sometimes as many as 1,000 would be praying at the same time, and the power could only be compared to the roar of Niagara. . . . Some were much used in laying on of hands for the healing of the sick. They also had the interpretation of tongues.

The power also fell in Brother Norton's school of boys, just a few miles from Mukti, where 65 boys were baptized with the Spirit and a number had the interpretation.

In a Baptist mission of India there were two girls that were baptized with the Spirit and spoke in tongues in the Hindustani language, a language to them unknown. They were taken to the market place, where the people all congregate, and preached the Cross of Christ in great power. In Bombay, in a Church of England School, a girl came through speaking in tongues and prophesized.

A Late Report from Bombay.

India has ceased to be a pioneer field as touching Pentecost. Sixty missionaries are baptized and 15 missionary societies have witnesses to Pentecost in 28 stations scattered through Punjab, Bombay Presidency, Bengal and Madras Provinces, the Northwest and Nizams Dominion. The natives of India who have received represent various races, kindreds and tongues. Hallelujah! There are witnesses in the following missions:

Church Missionary Society,
English Baptist Mission,
American Baptist Mission,
The Mukti Mission,
Penial Mission,
The Open Brethren,
Salvation Army,
Scandinavian Alliance,
Christian and Missionary Alliance,
American Presbyterians,
Women's Foreign Missionary,
Thibetan Mission,
Poona and India Village,
Latter Rain Mission,
Industrial and Evangelical Mission . . .

God is bestowing power to prophesy, the sick are healed, demons cast out, and the saints are pressing on for more of God. . . .

82. LILLIAN GARR

Alfred (1874–1944) and Lillian Garr left the Burning Bush Holiness denomination after receiving the Spirit baptism at Azusa in June 1906. They pioneered the Azusa work in India, Sri Lanka, China, and elsewhere. They joined forces with Minnie Abrams (1859–1912) and Pandita Ramabai (c. 1858–1922), who had already witnessed Pentecostal-type experiences among their students. Some missionaries in India had read copies of Seymour's *Apostolic Faith* and followed the revival in Los Angeles prior to the Garrs' arrival. The Garrs also read excerpts from Seymour's paper in their services. They continued their work until 1911, then returned to their evangelistic ministry in the United States.

"TESTIMONY AND PRAISE TO GOD"

(*AF,* June To September 1907, 4)

When the Comforter first came my heart was so overflowing with the joy, I had not time to prove thereality [*sic*], the blessed reality of the experience received in dear old Azusa Street Mission, but as persecution arose in India I have proved day by day, hour by hour that He abides and reveals Jesus to my soul in wonderful ways. . . .

There are several hundred natives baptized with the Holy Ghost and speaking in tongues today in India. . . .

Our hearts are knit with the dear Saints at Azusa street [*sic*] and we think with love of all. How often I think of the times the Spirit sang through Sister Crawford and me:

Jesus, Savior, pilot me
Over life's tempestuous sea.

That testified to my own heart that much would arise for which the Spirit was preparing me . . .

—Mrs. Lillian Garr, Bethany,
Slave Island, Colombo, Ceylon.

"IN CALCUTTA, INDIA."

(*AF*, April 1907, 1)
Calcutta, India.
55 Creek Row—God is spreading Pentecost here in Calcutta, and thirteen or fourteen missionaries and other workers have received it. The Spirit is giving the interpretation, song and writing in tongues, and other wonderful manifestations of His presence among us . . . [and among] Bible teachers . . . which is wonderful to behold. . . .

We enjoy the [Azusa] paper very much, in fact, much of it is read in the meetings, and all rejoice. The little [Azusa] paper was a forerunner for us. We came to find that its contents had made God's children hungry . . . [and] waiting for their Pentecost. We found India ripe for this light, in fact the revival had already broken out among the natives, and some were speaking in tongues.

Miss Easton, the head of the American Women's Board of Missions, the oldest woman's missionary board in India, has been baptized and is a power for God. . . .

—Sister A.G. Garr.

83. MAX WOOD MOORHEAD

Moorhead (1862–1937) decided to become a missionary at one of Dwight Moody's Northfield Conferences in 1886. He joined the Student Volunteer Movement for Foreign Missions in 1891 and traveled to India as a Presbyterian missionary, where he worked with youth at the YMCA and prayed for revival for a year before meeting the Garrs in Calcutta in January 1907. He received the Spirit baptism and helped spread Pentecostalism through his preaching and newspaper *Cloud of Witnesses to Pentecost in India* (1907–1910). He worked closely with Abrams and Ramabai and wrote that Seymour's teaching (through Garr and the *Apostolic Faith*) brought them into a "deeper fullness of the outpouring of the Holy Ghost accompanied with the gift of tongues which had not yet been received."

PENTECOST IN MUKTI, INDIA

(*AF,* September 1907, 4)
"Mukti," which means Salvation, is a community . . . [of schools] in whose various departments useful trades are taught, a printing office employing 30 men, and a hospital. About 1,400 girl students are enrolled (inclusive of 300 rescued women in the Krupa Sadan) and there is a separate institution for boys. The great majority of the girls have been admitted to "Mukti" in times

of famine during the past ten years. . . . [Today] more than 800 of the girls are Christians in the saving sense of that word.

Both Pandita Ramabai and Miss [Minnie] Abrams were deeply impressed by the truth contained in the reports which came from [the Azusa newspaper from] Los Angeles concerning Pentecost, and believing that God was willing to send like Pentecostal blessings to Mukti which up to that time had not been received, after the manner described in Acts 2, they exhorted all the Christian boys and girls to begin to tarry for the promised baptism of the Holy Ghost.

In taking this step, Pandita Ramabai fully acknowledged all that God had bestowed through His Spirit in the past; but she discerned there was the deeper fullness of the outpouring of the Holy Ghost accompanied with the gift of tongues which had not yet been received. Before Christmas 1906, the seekers assembled in the Church daily at 6 o'clock in the morning for a time of waiting on God.

About this time a band of 20 girls were sent to the station of K—attended by two English Missionaries, and before much preaching had been done, J–, a native girl, began to speak in a new tongue and magnify God. Within a few days every member of the party, including the two lady missionaries, received the Pentecostal baptism of the Holy Ghost and all were speaking in new tongues . . . and held the people spell bound.

The joyful news of Pentecost at K—stirred the seekers at Mukti with fresh zeal. A worker from Mukti visited the band at K—and in a few days she herself returned full of joy and the Holy Ghost. . . .

Mukti is the glad scene of a continuous Pentecost, as day after day seekers come into fullness of blessing. . . .

Some have received the gift of healing . . . and in answer to their prayers the sick are healed. . . .

As in other countries so in Mukti, the girls and women are . . . believing for the restoration to the Church of all the lost gifts of the Spirit. Those baptized have been filled with a new and burning desire for lost souls. . . . Their joy is unbounding. . . .

Address Max Wood Moorhead,
Publisher, Colombo, Ceylon.

ASIA: CHINA MISSIONARY TESTIMONIES

INTRODUCTION

After spreading Seymour's message to India, in October 1906 Alfred and Lillian Garr felt called to China, a country carved up by Western powers and still simmering with internal conflict. They arrived in the British port of

Hong Kong in early October 1907. As they had done in India, they preached and worked through preexisting missionary organizations. M. L. Ryan, another Azusa participant, left Portland, Oregon, in September for China with a group of fifteen missionaries, many of whom eventually made contact with the Garrs. The Garrs were joined by May Law and Rosa Pittman. They began preaching at the American Board of Commissioners for Foreign Missions (ABCFM), a Congregationalist operation. The Garrs persuaded a key Chinese leader named Mok Lai Chi and nine Christian and Missionary Alliance (CMA) missionaries and a hundred other Chinese Christians to receive the Spirit baptism. In the fall of 1907, Mr. and Mrs. McIntosh, A. E. Kirby, Mabel Evans, and S. C. Todd joined the Garrs. They were joined by a stream of other Azusa veterans like Anna Deane in 1909 and Paul and Nelly Bettex in 1911. Below, Crawford sketches the origins of Pentecostalism in China and Bernsten and Moomau talk about the influence of Seymour's Azusa Revival on their lives and ministries.

84. FLORENCE CRAWFORD AND CLARA LUM

"HOW PENTECOST CAME TO CHINA"

(*AF,* Portland, Oregon, July and August 1908, 4)

Pentecost Has Fallen on the Dear Chinese People—Praise God.

Then the Lord sent Pentecostal missionaries [Garrs] from Los Angeles, who had been in India, over to Hong Kong, China. And He opened the way the same day they arrived for them to hold meetings in a missionary church. The meetings continued every night for several weeks. A revival broke out and the Chinese began making restitution and getting really saved.

The interpreter [Mok Loi Chi]. . . . was the first man to get his baptism. . . .

In Hong Kong 25 Were Baptized.

Pentecost fell and 25 were baptized with the Holy Ghost. God baptized a printer and a Chinese scholar. And the Lord laid it on a brother [T. J. McIntosh] in Macao that they should have a Chinese paper to send into the interior of China . . . And God laid it on Brother Mock [Mok Loi Chi], the Chinese scholar, and the printer. They have never missed an issue. It is published free. They send it to every missionary in China. They are asking for it in the interior of China. In a province in the Northwest of China they received word that the missionaries of the province were seeking the baptism. . . .

Two sisters came from the South and took the Pentecost to Canton. One missionary received her baptism there and was preaching twice a day on the streets. . . . China is a ripe field. . . .

85. BERNT BERNSTEN

Bernt and Magna Bersten were missionaries who heard about Azusa in December 1906 after reading Seymour's newspaper circulating among missionaries in China. They sailed to the United States in August 1907, met M. L. Ryan and Azusa missionaries in Seattle, and then visited Seymour and received the Spirit baptism on Sunday, September 15. They returned to China with the Hess and Hanson families and six others from the Swedish Pentecostal mission in Los Angeles, one of Azusa's daughter missions. They also conducted evangelistic-social work by giving away food to people suffering from the famine. In 1912, Bernt founded China's second Pentecostal paper, *Popular Gospel Truth*.

CAME FROM CHINA TO AMERICA FOR PENTECOST.

(*AF*, January 1908, 3)
As I am on my way back to China, I feel led to leave my testimony for the glory of God . . .

Five years ago a burden came on me for more of Him. . . . and in 1904 I started for China. When I got there the burden became stronger yet. . . .

About December, 1906, I received the [Asuza] *Apostolic Faith* paper; and as I read it through in the spirit of prayer, I saw it was the thing that I had been looking for. . . .

After that [January 1, 1907] I went to Shanghai with the intention of finding some one in the Centennial Missionary Conference that had the baptism of the Holy Ghost who could help me out. Instead of that I met opposition from every side, and one from Los Angeles that had attended the meetings denounced the whole thing as of the devil. . . .

A desire came into my heart to go to America . . . I . . . landed in. . . . Los Angeles and [at Azusa on] the third day, on Sunday, Sept. 15th, He baptized me. I was under the power of God on the floor for more than two hours, and it seemed that every nerve in my body was charged. . . . A short time after, the Holy Ghost . . . began to speak through me in an unknown tongue, and I rose up under the power, going back and forth before the people preaching. I had no control of my body.

I praise God for His manifestation and for the wonderful sweetness and joy that is growing stronger every day. I will advise anyone to get rid of all that you have and gain that "pearl of great price. . . ."

Yours for lost souls in China.
B. Berntsen. Tai-ming-fu,
Chih-li, North China.

86. ANTOINETTE MOOMAU

"Nettie" Moomau (1872–1937) was born in Davis City, Iowa, on December 1, 1872. She attended the Moody Bible Institute and became a Presbyterian missionary to Suzhou from 1899 until October 1906, after which while on furlough she attended Azusa and met Seymour. Although originally believing that the spiritual gifts ceased with the death of the apostles, she was persuaded that the revival and gifts were of God and received the Spirit baptism at Azusa. Seymour sent her to Shanghai, where she worked among women and Chinese elites. Leola Phillips and several other missionaries established a mission and other works. Smallpox took Philips's life in October 1910. In February 1911, Moomau took a furlough to the United States before returning to China, where she ministered until her death on March 25, 1937.

CHINA MISSIONARY RECEIVES PENTECOST.

(*AF*, October to January 1908, 3)

On leaving China, October, 1906, I was asked to investigate the Apostolic Faith Movement in Los Angeles, where they claimed to have manifested the same gifts of the Holy Ghost as of old. (I Cor. 12: 8–10.) . . . I had no rest until I went and heard and saw for myself.

It only took a short time after the beginning of the first meeting, to know it was of God. And when the altar call came, I went forward. . . .

When I had left for the foreign field seven years before this, I thought I had died to everything; but . . . the Spirit began to deal with me . . . [since] I . . . had been taught the suppression [i.e., cessationist]. . . .

After some of the saints had prayed for me, one of them asked me if I had the witness of the Spirit to my sanctification according to Heb. 10: 14, 15 . . . I then began to praise God audibly, and in a few minutes I was flooded with billows of glory, and the Spirit sang through me praises unto God. . . .

To sum it up, the baptism of the Spirit means to me what I never dreamed it could this side of Heaven: victory, glory in my soul, perfect peace, rest, liberty, nearness to Christ, deadness to this old world, and power in witnessing. Glory to His name forever and forever!

—Antoinette Moomau, Eustice, Nebr.

E. CRITICS OF SEYMOUR AND THE REVIVAL

INTRODUCTION

Seymour and his Azusa Revival were criticized by both the secular and religious press. The *Los Angeles Daily Times* ripped into Azusa as nothing less than the latest brand of charlatanism tramping its way into Los Angeles to steal hard-won sheep from other Protestant churches. The *Indianapolis Star* luridly reported on the interracial nature of Seymour's services at Glenn Cook's mission in Indianapolis.

Protestant and Holiness leaders like A. Sulger of Alma White's Pillar of Fire holiness denomination and devotional writer Oswald Chambers capture the range of criticism from satanically inspired to a wait-and-see Gamiliel approach (Acts 5:34–40). Chambers argued that divine love and the fruit of the spirit are the true evidence of the Spirit baptism—a view that Seymour and Alexander Boddy later affirmed in their writings, perhaps reflecting his influence. Sulger's criticism is particularly important because he offers an insider-turned-critic perspective of Seymour. Durham's letter provides his side of the Durham-Seymour schism and explains why he believes Seymour lost his following.

87. *LOS ANGELES TIMES*

"WEIRD BABEL OF TONGUES"

New Sect of Fanatics is Breaking Loose

Wild Scene Last Night on Azusa Street

Gurgle of Wordless Talk by a Sister

(*Los Angeles Daily Times,* 18 April 1906, 1)
Breathing strange utterances and mouthing a creed which it would seem no sane mortal could understand, the newest religious sect has started in Los Angeles. Meetings are held in a tumble-down shack on Azusa Street, near San Pedro Street, and devotees of the weird doctrine practice the most fanatical rites, preach the wildest theories and work themselves into a state of mad excitement in their peculiar zeal. Colored people and a sprinkling of whites compose the congregation, and night is made hideous in the neighborhood by the howlings of the worshippers who spend hours swaying forth and back in a nerve-racking [*sic*] attitude of prayer and supplication. They claim to have "the gift of tongues;" and to be able to comprehend the babble.

Such a startling claim has never yet been made by any company of fanatics, even in Los Angeles, the home of almost numberless creeds. Sacred tenets, reverently mentioned by the orthodox believer, are dealt with in a familiar, if not irreverent, manner by these latest religionists.

STONY OPTIC DEFIES.

An old colored exhort, blind in one eye, is the major-domo of the company. With his stony optic fixed on some luckless unbeliever, the old man yells his defiance and challenges an answer. Anathemas are heaped upon him who shall dare to gainsay the utterances of the preacher.

Clasped in his big fist the colored brother holds a miniature Bible from which he reads at intervals one or two words—never more. After an hour spent in exhortation the brethren [*sic*] present are invited to join in a "meeting of prayer, song and testimony." Then it is that pandemonium breaks loose, and the bounds of reason are passed by those who are "filled with the spirit," whatever that may be.

"You-oo-oo gou-loo-loo come under the bloo-oo-oo boo-loo;" shouts an old colored "mammy;" in a frenzy of religious zeal. Swinging her arms wildly about her, she continues with the strangest harangue ever uttered. Few of her words are intelligible, and for the most part her testimony contains the most outrageous jumble of syllables, which are listened to with awe by the company.

LET THE TONGUES COME FORTH

One of the wildest of the meetings was held last night [April 17], and the highest pitch of excitement was reached by the gathering, which continued to "worship" until nearly midnight. The old exhorter urged the "sisters" to let the "tongues come forth" and the women gave themselves over to a riot of religious fervor. As a result a buxom dame was overcome with excitement and almost fainted.

Undismayed by the fearful attitude of the colored worshipper, another black women [*sic*] jumped to the floor and began a wild gesticulation, which ended in a gurgle of wordless prayers which were nothing less than shocking.

"She's speaking in unknown tongues;" announced the leader, in ah [*sic*] awed whisper, "keep on sister." The sister continued until it was necessary to assist her to a seat because of her bodily fatigue.

GOLD AMONG THEN

Among the "believers" is a man who claims to be a Jewish [*sic*] rabbi [Gold]. . . . Gold claims to have been miraculously healed and is a convert of the new sect.

88. A. SULGER

"DELIVERED FROM THE 'TONGUE' HERESY"

(*Rocky Mountain Pillar of Fire*, 27 March 1907)
Recently, there began in Los Angeles, California, a soul destroying work called the "Apostolic Faith Movement," better known as the "Tongues," whose awful heresy has already spread throughout the country and deceived thousands.

Because of disobedience to God, the writer was turned over for a short time to this awful delusion from which the Lord in His infinite mercy delivered him. . . .

I . . . went on to Los Angeles, where the devil soon led me to the well-known snake's nest on Azusa Street. I had heard that A.G. Garr, in whose meetings I had been converted, had received this "baptism of tongues," which strengthened my confidence in this Babylonian mess. In the very first meeting I attended, I felt a strange power take hold of me, and being in a state where I had no spiritual discernment, I thought this to be the power of God. I was perfectly honest and went into the thing with great sincerity.

Before realizing it, I found myself at the altar trembling under this demon power. . . . The next evening . . . Glenn Cook . . . laid hands on me, claiming the Holy Ghost had told him to do this, and said, "Receive yet the Holy Ghost." Instantly this (know now) hypnotic, demon power took possession of me and I shook until it seemed impossible for me to hold together. . . . All at once I began jabbering off in a so-called foreign language, which was the "Bible evidence," as they claim, that I had receive the baptism of the Holy Ghost. I somehow felt happy and strange at the same time . . .

In Azusa Mission

For some time after receiving these "Tongues," I remained in the Azusa mission.... When strangers came in, almost everyone ... said they felt a lack of power and were not satisfied with their [prior] experiences.

The truth is, these people were backsliders ... from the ... Methodists, Baptists, etc., members of labor unions and lodges, all were accepted, and all got the "tongues...."

Most of the strangers are drawn to Los Angeles through ... *The Apostolic Faith*.... Some people claim to be healed through their hypnotic or demoniacal power, but the writer has seen people hanging around ... for weeks without receiving any help....

The members of the true Church are baptized by one Spirit into one body, and all have the same mind. This is not the case at Azusa Street ... the whole thing is utter confusion. Some believe in annihilation, some in eternal punishment....

On a Missionary Trip

[Since] I had received various "tongues" ... I ... thought I was called as a missionary to my native land, Denmark. Everybody thought I had great power and was going to be used mightily. I received my credentials and was to go ... when the Lord in His great mercy ... changed my thoughts and I went to Oakland, California....

My Resignation

While in Oakland I had a dream. I was standing by a sea, and up out of the sea came a tremendous serpent, trying to devour me.... Someone handed me a hammer and I hit the serpent in the forehead. Immediately it was killed. ... Praise God, He showed me how I was going to conquer this enemy ...

I told Mr. Seymour ... about what I had discovered and how I felt about it. He said he was very much surprised as he and everyone had perfect confidence in my experience, and thought the Lord was going to work miracles through me in Denmark.

I stood by my convictions and expressed my desire to resign. Then his [Seymour] countenance quickly changed and I never saw a more bitter and hateful look in any person's face.

Then he told me I would sin against the Holy Ghost and lose my soul. When this did not affect me, he said I would lose my mind and the next time he saw me, be full of the devil.

These people claim to have power to bind people by the word of God, so they will either have to do what they want them to do, or go to hell....

The next day Seymour denounced me before his followers, and remarked something about my having committed the unpardonable sin.

Nevertheless, a few days later, he sent me word that he wanted me to go to Orange, California and hold meetings . . . but I was out of the whole thing, and of course refused this offer . . .

The "Tongue" delusion is throughout, the work of the devil. . . . May God in His great mercy . . . use the writer's experience to prevent others from being devoured of Satan in his delusion.

89. *INDIANAPOLIS STAR*

NEGRO BLUK KISSED: FOUNDER IS WARMLY GREETED, BROTHER SEYMOURE, ERSTWHILE INDIANAPOLIS HOTEL WAITER, MADE WELCOME BY WHITE FOLLOWERS.

(*Indianapolis Star*, June 3, 1907, 3)
The much looked for leader of the Bluks . . . [and] negro founder [is] Brother W.J. Seymore. . . . [A]s he mounted the platform [of the mission] in front, Brother Glenn Cook, pro tem leader, threw both arms about his neck and kissed him.

"Why its Brother Seymour," shouted a hundred Bluks, and "glories" mingled with "hallelujahs" as the other ten members of the leader's party flocked to the front.

"Let's sing de comfortah hab come," said Brother Seymore, in a voice that shook the church . . .

"Oh, that white fellow kissed the negro," said one astonished little girl who had witnessed the osculating ceremony. . . .

This founder [Seymour] of the sect stands full six feet in height.* He wears a rubber collar, decorated by no sign of necktie. Adorning his mouth is open massive gold tooth, flanked by rows of other teeth, perfectly straight and white. . . .

His voice is like the roaring of a cannon, and . . . he has but one eye. Time was when Brother Seymore was a table waiter . . . but since then he has been a religious founder.

"I hab cum to spread the gospel ovah Indianapolis," he said after he had been introduced to the audience by Cook, as "my brother, Seymore. . . ."

The negroes who accompanied Brother Seymore were appointed . . . temporary accommodations . . . [last night with] white members of the flock being eager to do some part in entertaining the negro leader and the [W.H.] Cummings family.

[* Seymour was actually 5'9.]

90. OSWALD CHAMBERS

"GIFT OF TONGUES"

(God's Revivalist and Bible Advocate, Martin, 263–266)
Paul . . . emphasizes the use and abuse of *tongues* . . . Paul . . . says, all these gifts must be guarded and guided by the grand principle of love.

Today when this *gift of tongues* is being over-rated, we do well to remember two things, (1.) Don't *underrate,* and (2) Don't *overrate* . . . Paul urges all such to pray for interpretation or to keep quiet, and to use the gift only before God in prayer. . . . But Paul never hinted that it was from the devil . . .

Gifts of the Spirit are not the *fruit* of the Spirit. *Gifts* are irrespective of the person's character . . . we must judge a servant of God by *fruit* (John 15) not by gifts. I may have all *gifts* (gifts of tongues of men and angels) but if I have not love, I am nothing. . . .

The greatest [unwise thing being said today] is that . . . no one is really baptized in the Holy Spirit who does not speak with tongues. This gives the devil an excellent occasion to [imitate] . . . tongues. . . .

Fruit means character, gifts simply indicate God's sovereignty. . . . An instrument of God is not necessarily a servant of God. Fruit in character is the living witness to the *baptism in the Holy Ghost,* but do remember, gifts are the sign that God is working. You can never have a great awakening without extraordinary manifestations. . . .

Another important matter is that the *gift of another tongue,* as at Pentecost, is a distinctly other matter than the gift of *spiritual ecstasy tongues.* The baptism in the Holy Ghost and new tongues . . . means . . . God . . . gives the gift of a new language immediately, as at Pentecost . . .

Keep every avenue . . . open towards God. Be suspicious of nobody that has tongues unless they want to teach . . . a private interpretation of the Word of God. Do not grieve the Holy Spirit. *Keep firm to the Word.* . . .

91. WILLIAM DURHAM

"THE GREAT REVIVAL AT AZUSA STREET MISSION— HOW IT BEGAN AND HOW IT ENDED"

(Pentecostal Testimony, 1911, 3–4)
On February 14th [1911], we began meetings in Azusa Mission. From the first day the power of God rested upon the meetings in a wonderful way. The altar was crowded at every service. . . .

The work in Los Angeles was in a sad condition . . . [T]he leaders . . . had proven so incompetent that the saints had lost all confidence in them. . . .

Scores were really in a backslidden state, and . . . others were . . . crying to God to send some one who could preach the truth and lead His people on. The suffering of many had been great indeed. . . .

[I]nside of a few days the place was crowded to the doors, and many turned away. Sometimes there would be more than a hundred at the altar at a single service. . . . Week after week . . . the power increased, till the glory of God literally filled the place. . . . As many as twenty-two were baptized in the Holy Spirit in one week. Some of the hardest sinners were saved. I believe that literally hundreds . . . were restored, and many [healed] . . .

[W]e were condemned and denounced. . . . up and down this [West] Coast . . . my teaching has been denounced as from the pit [of hell], and . . . the most bitter persecution and opposition has raged against me. . . .

I preach the finished work of Calvary, that we come into Christ and are fully saved in conversion, and that the next step is to be baptized in water, and then in the Holy Spirit. . . .

[P]eople on all sides began to ask what Brother Seymour would probably do, when he returned from the East. . . .

The Spirit . . . showed me clearly that he [Seymour] was trying to get home to get possession of the [Azusa] work, and that if he could not do so, he would do all in his power to stop it. . . .

Brother Seymour came, and instead of making the honest confession he owed the people, for the way he had compromised and denied the truth, and then taking a humble place, till such time as he had regained the confidence of the people, he attempted to push himself on the people, and preach to them against their will, and a little later, notified me that this was his work, and that he wanted his place.

I tried to reason with him, telling him that it would ruin the work to place him in charge at that time, but he showed a very bitter spirit and condemned and judged the people, saying that if the people did not want to hear him they could leave. When he said this I knew that it was useless to try to reason with him further.

I saw plainly that. . . . He does not care in the least for the work of the Lord, but wants a place in it. If he can not have the place, he will not hesitate to tear down the work.

The next day I asked for an expression from the congregation, as to whether they wanted him to take charge of the work, or me to continue. With the exception of ten, or less, the congregation, consisting of several hundred people, voted that the meetings should continue, as they were. The glory and power of god continued to rest mightily upon the meetings. . . . This was Sunday.

When we came to the Mission Tuesday we found that Seymour had influenced a few of the officers of the Mission, men of his own color, to stand with him, and they had locked and bolted the door. . . .

While we were preaching, praying and seeking God in the Mission, Seymour had been scheming and planning . . . how he could get possession of the building, if he could not get the work. This last move was necessary to let all men see what manner of man he has come to be.

Many of us who knew him when the power and glory of God was so mightily upon him years ago, could never have turned away and left him with God, [but] . . . he had gotten into such a condition that the power of God had entirely left him . . . he [Seymour] was no longer worthy of the confidence and respect of the saints.

I have been the last of all the brethren, that I know of, to give him up, and have always found an excuse for his failures and blunders; but now I am compelled to acknowledge that the brethren have been right, and that, though once a mighty man, he is such no longer. Sadly do I pen these lines, and I hope every reader will pray that the Lord will restore him.

We all saw in this move a tremendous effort on the part of Satan to force us into a compromise. Failing in this, he succeeded in having us turned out of the place that was paid for with consecrated money for a place of worship. Thus we were turned into the street in the very midst of one of the greatest revivals we ever saw.

It took some little time to see that this was really God's way of separating us from an element who were not loyal to Him, and into a . . . large, airy hall at the corner of Seventh and Los Angeles streets. . . . By the help of the Lord we had it ready for the Sunday services, and from the first meeting the power and glory of God has been mightily upon us. . . .

With joy I have told of the beginning of the great revival at dear old Azusa St. Mission, and with real grief I have told how it ended, and why. Let none of the saints condemn me, or think I have desired to condemn Mr. Seymour or Mr. Fisher or anyone else. The circumstances have forced this most unpleasant duty upon me. The news of the outpouring at Azusa brought rejoicing wherever it went; and so many letters of inquiry have reached me, that I feel it my duty to tell the saints everywhere just what happened, and who is responsible for it.

F. WRITINGS OF CHARLES FOX PARHAM

INTRODUCTION

In addition to founding the *Apostolic Faith* (Baxter Springs) newspaper and editing it for three decades, Parham also wrote *Kol Kare Bomidbar: A Voice Crying in the Wilderness* (1902, 1912) and *The Everlasting Gospel* (ca. 1919/1920). Parham's writings are important for a number of reasons. They reveal Parham's Pentecostal theology; thinking on white supremacy, annihilation, and the British-Israelism theory—all positions that Seymour later rejected as unbiblical; why Parham rejected Seymour and Azusa; why Parham blamed Seymour for his loss of influence; Parham's claim that Glenn Cook led Azusa into fanaticism; Parham's view that Azusa was infiltrated by spiritualists, hypnotists, and that people there engaged in sexually inappropriate contact; and Parham's conviction that anyone who accepted or propagated Seymour's teaching and the Revival would fall from grace.

92. PARHAM'S THEOLOGICAL, SOCIAL, AND RACIAL VIEWS

(*Kol Kare Bomidbar: A Voice Crying In The Wilderness,*
1902 [1910], 82–85, 94–100, 105–107)
During the sixth day, (age or thousand years) . . . God said: "Let us make man in our image, male and female." Here were *created* the first inhabitants of the earth . . . whose fall was the most pitiful, whose destruction most complete.

[On] the opening of the eighth day . . . Adam [was] formed, from whose rib Eve was made . . . [and] for whose benefit God *formed* a second and different class [of people] . . . placing them in the garden [of Eden], a portion of the earth not then inhabited [by people from the sixth day]. . . .

After Adam had sinned, he was driven from this Paradise, but received the promise of a Redeemer, which the created [sixth day] race never obtained.

When Cain killed his brother, he fled to the land of Nod, there took unto himself a wife, one of the sixth day creation. Thus began the woeful inter-marriage of races for which cause the flood [of Noah] was sent in punishment, and has ever been followed by plagues and incurable diseases upon the third and fourth generation, the offspring of such marriages.

Were time to last and inter-marriage continue between the whites, the blacks, and the reds in America, consumption and other diseases would soon wipe the mixed bloods off the face of the earth. . . .

The reason for the flood is plainly seen. God intended to destroy man whom He had created, with all the half-breeds resulting from inter-marriages. Yet having made a promise to Adam of a Savior, was compelled to preserve the Adamic race.

For this reason Noah was chosen, not only because he was a just man and walked with God, but was perfect in his generation; a pedigree without mixed blood in it, a lineal descendant of Adam.

The flood destroyed not only the human part of the sixth day creation but man and beast. . . . [except for] Noah. . . .

Aryan[s]. . . . [migrated] into Western Europe . . . [Scholars] never put two and two together and discovered that the cradle of the Aryan race was the exact country where previously the 10 lost tribes of Israel were colonized . . . Pushing their way westward into what is now Germany. . . . they became Anglo-Saxons! . . .

These are the nations [High Germans, English, Scottish, Welsh, Irish, High German, Scandinavian] who have acquired and retained experimental salvation and deep spiritual truths; while the Gentiles,—the Russians, the Greek, the Italian, the low German, the French, the Spanish and their descendants in all parts are formalists, scarce ever obtaining the knowledge and truth discovered by Luther,—that of justification by faith or of the truth taught by Wesley, sanctification by faith. . . .

While the heathen,—the Black race, the Brown race, the Red race, the Yellow race, in spite of missionary zeal and effort are nearly all heathen still; but will, in the dawning of the coming age be given to Jesus for an inheritance.

Just where the tribes are located has not been fully determined, except in the case of the Danes (the tribe of Dan); England who stands for Ephraim; and of the United States for Manassah. . . .

The stone of Scone on which the Kings of Ireland, Scotland and England have been crowned was brought to Ireland, and was the stone on which the Kings of Judah were crowned, and is a memorial stone of Israel belonging to Joseph's sons. (Gen. 49:24.)

93. LETTER FROM BRO. PARHAM [TO AZUSA MISSION]

(*AF*, Los Angeles, September 1906, 1)

I rejoice in God over you all, my children, though I have never seen you; but since you know the Holy Spirit's power, we are baptized by one Spirit into one body. Keep together in unity till I come, then in a grand meeting let all prepare for the outside fields I desire, unless God directs to the contrary, to meet and see all who have the full Gospel when I come.

Charles Parham

94. LETTER FROM CHARLES PARHAM TO MRS. SARAH PARHAM / APOSTOLIC FAITH

(Parham, Letter, Fall 1906,
Reprinted in *The Life of Charles Fox Parham*, 1930 [1977], 163–164)
I hurried to Los Angeles, and to my utter surprise and astonishment I found conditions even worse than I had anticipated. Brother Seymour came to me helpless, he said he could not stem the tide that had arisen. I sat on the platform in Azusa Street Mission, and saw the manifestations of the flesh, spiritualistic controls, saw people practicing hypnotism at the altar over candidates seeking the baptism; though many were receiving the real baptism of the Holy Ghost.

After preaching two or three times, I was informed by two of the elders, one [i.e., Glenn Cook] who was a hypnotist (I had seen him lay his hands on many who came through chattering, jabbering and sputtering, speaking in no language at all) that I was not wanted in that place.

With workers from the Texas field we opened a great revival in the W.C.T.U. building on Broadway and Temple Streets in Los Angeles. Great numbers were saved, marvelous healings took place and between two and three hundred who had been possessed of awful fits and spasms and controls in the Azusa Street work were delivered, and received the real Pentecost teachings and man spake with other tongues.

95. "A NOTE OF WARNING"

(*AF* [Zion City, IL], December 1 1906)
Throughout the summer [of 1906] I was greatly encouraged, and truly rejoiced at the reports of the work that was sweeping the California field . . . it seemed as if the whole Pacific Coast would be taken for God. . . .

For some time I had been in touch with many friends who knew the extremes that had crept into the [Azusa] meetings in California. . . . [They] wrote me repeatedly to come quickly to the rescue. . . .

[At Azusa], I found hypnotic influences, familiar-spirit influences, spiritualistic influences, mesmeric influences, and all kinds of spells, spasms, falling in trances, etc. All of these things are foreign to and unknown in this movement outside of Los Angeles, except in the places visited by the workers sent out from this city. . . .

The speaking in tongues is never brought about by any of the above influences. In all our work the laying on of hands is practiced only occasionally, and then for the space of only a minute or two. No such thing is known among our workers as the suggestion of certain words and sounds . . . Nonsense! The Holy Ghost needs no help! . . .

The falling under the power in Los Angeles has, to a large degree, been produced through a hypnotic, mesmeric, magnetic current.

The Holy Ghost does nothing that is unnatural or unseemingly, and any strained exertion of body, mind, or voice is not the work of the Holy Spirit, but of some familiar spirit. . . .

How vastly important it is that we try the spirits. . . .

I feel that it is still my duty to stand against anything and everything that will in any way prove a hindrance to . . . the advancement of the work. . . .

96. "THE SEALING"

(*AF,* Baxter Springs, December 1910)
This movement utterly repudiates the doctrine of Inherent Immortality, perpetuated by the Roman Catholic church and perpetuated by Protestants . . . Catholics and orthodoxy [i.e., Protestants] continue to teach "Dante's Inferno" and "Milton's Paradise Lost" instead of the Word of God. . . . It is a marvel that every verse used to prove Eternal Torment teaches "Death," "Destruction, " "Perish" and the annihilation of the wicked. It has been charged that this editor is a "No Hellite, " which we deny. We believe in a literal Lake of Fire, but deny that the wicked are eternally tormented.

97. HELL

(*AF,* Baxter Springs, January 1912, 7)
The most important tenet before the Christian world today is Conditional Immortality. On it hangs the whole fabric of Christian doctrine—the Divinity of Christ and authenticity of the Scriptures. . . . We believe in hell, but that it means destruction instead of torment, and death instead of life . . . ignorant benighted people still cling to the lie concocted by Augustine and adopted by Protestants—hell (eternal torment) for all who will not join us and our church.

98. SOURCE OF DISEASE

(*AF,* Baxter Springs, August 1912, 1–5)
Sickness arises from three causes/ . . . sources. The first is hereditary disease. . . . [The] next . . . is from allowing conditions, climate, food, over-eating, under-eating and over-exertion to bring on disease. The third and last is

where people disobey God or break vows. . . . It is an absolute fact that the mass of Christians are sick because of disobedience to the known will of God. . . .

Lots of you people coming here for healing never get it; you need to have the demons cast out of you. Many of these diseases—so called by Materia Medica—are not diseases, but are [demonic] torments. . . .

At the age of twenty-four, I found the power of God to sanctify the body from inbred disease as well as from inbred sin. . . .

A sanctified body is as much provided for in the atonement of Jesus as is sanctification for the soul. . . . Epilepsy, fits, insanity, drunkenness and abnormal passions are demon controls. . . .

99. BAPTISM OF THE HOLY GHOST

(*AF,* October 1912, 8–10).
The purpose of the Pentecost is four-fold.

First—the 'sign of a believer.' Mark 16:16–20, one of God's credentials to those engaged in His work.

Second—a 'sign to unbelievers.' Scores of infidels have been converted on hearing the workers speak in real languages, seeing this latter-day proof of the authenticity of the Bible . . .

Third—it is the power of witness; not only to prophesy by inspiration in native tongue, but any language of the world. . . .

Fourth—it constitutes the sealing power. . . .

Speaking in tongues is the only legitimate evidence of the baptism of the Holy Ghost, and no one can feel assured they have the second chapter of Acts experience unless they talk freely in a real language as the Sprit gives utterance.

Any one going to a foreign field should seek the gift of the language of that country and should be able to use it and understand it when spoken by others. . . .

O, how many have been deceived by the Azusa mess. . . .

100. CRITICISMS OF AZUSA STREET

(*AF,* Baxter Springs, January 1912, 6–7)
A Happy New Year To All

May this be a year of mighty purification from wild-fire, fanaticism, flesh, sin, disease and death. . . .

[T]his counterfeit Pentecost (a cross between the Negro and Holy Roller form of worship) that had its origination in Los Angeles and spread all over the country. . . .

We do not doubt that some have received a genuine baptism in these fanatical meetings, but two thirds of the so called baptisms are only a worked up animal spiritism with chattering and jabbering and no language at all.

The so called Heavenly Choir [singing in the spirit] was only a modification of the Negro chanting of the Southland, and was not the result of the Pentecostal baptism.

One is driven to distraction in some Missions by emitting of all kinds of animal sounds . . . that proves a state of animalism and developing of spiritistic mediums, rather than the power of the Holy Spirit. When in Los Angeles five years ago, I begged the leaders not to send certain workers of this kind to the foreign fields, knowing they would disgrace the cause, but heedless of advice they were sent out, and the result—world-wide shame. . . .

101. "LEADERSHIP"

(*AF,* Baxter Springs, June 1912, 7–9)
My reason for writing this article is to . . . warn honest men to fight the spirit of leadership that has . . . destroyed so many able men in this movement. . . .

The first man who sought leadership was a Mr. Carothers [Faye Warren Carothers], of Texas. . . .

Next came Seymour of Azuza [*sic*] St., Los Angeles; instructed and carefully trained in our Bible School in Texas, he held the work in Azuza [*sic*] in bounds for four months. Then came the Holly Rollers under a confessed hypnotist by the name of [Glenn] Cook, whose hypnotic work, assisted by all kinds of fanatics, soon made Azuza [*sic*] a hotbed of wildfire; religious orgies outrivaling scenes in devil or fetish worship, took place in the Upper Room where deluded victims by the score were thrown into hypnotic trance, out of which they chattering and jabbering.

While up to the advent of this man [Glenn] Cook, many received the Pentecost and spoke in real languages [at Azusa], very little real was known afterward, but barking like dogs, crowing like rooster, etc., trances, shakes, fits and all kinds of fleshly contortions with windsucking and jabbering resulted, until I exposed him. . . .

Seymour, in his first paper, gave a true account of the origins of the work but after he was made Pope by his followers, and I refused to acknowledge the fanaticism of Azuza [*sic*] as the work of the Holy Ghost, he [Seymour], drunken with power and flattery, used all his papers to prove that Azuza [*sic*] was the original "crib" of this Movement and a Negro the first preacher.

I went to him and plead with him to repent to God and man of the lies he [Seymour] had printed to the world and to reject leadership or God would humble him; I told him plainly that if he did not repent in one and one-half years, he would be pastor of a dead Mission and no followers in Azuza [*sic*]. Let all who know, judge between us. . . .

I want to say as a messenger of God, and the senior preacher of this

Movement, that all... who now accept or propagate the wildfire, fanatical, wind-sucking, chattering, jabbering, trance, body-shaking originating in Azuza [*sic*], as the true work of Pentecost, will fall. . . .

102. "UNITY"

(*AF*, Baxter Springs, June 1912, 9–11)
In the early days of this Movement. . . . Reporters, professors of languages, interpreters and foreigners stood amazed at the manifestations of healings and speaking in tongues.

After the fanaticism broke out at Azuza [*sic*] St., Los Angeles, a chattering, jabbering, wind-sucking and body-shaking superceeded [*sic*] the true work.

I went in great concern to Mr. Seymour and begged him not to send any workers to the field until they were proven, for I heard but few in all that wilderness of religious prostitution who really spoke in tongues; but I did see spiritism, hypnotism and unconscious cerubration as taught in psychic phenomena.

Seymour, drunken with power and swollen to bursting, sent forth a hundred or more of this kind of worker to fill the earth with the worst prostitution of Christianity I have ever witnessed; in shame we have had to hang our heads, as fanatics and fools have returned from foreign fields in disgrace and shame, with only a monkey chattering; bring a just criticism and condemnation from the Christian press and public.

This kind of work has well-nigh destroyed the true Pentecostal power. . . .

The so called Apostolic papers [published by Seymour] have so lied and exaggerated about the work, till there will certainly have to come a reckoning. . . .

We have invested too much . . . to see this work captured by the imps of the devil, in fanaticism, flesh and wildfire, and not make a desperate fight; and now is the time since God has laid low men-leaders, self-seekers and the propogators [*sic*] of Azuza-Durham [*sic*] counterfeits and false teachings. . . .

[The movement I founded] was bidding fair to capture the world, when men-leaders arose to draw a following to themselves and fanaticism broke out in Azuza [*sic*], until his work was well-nigh wrecked; but thanks be to God . . . true hearts . . . have weathered the gale [and] are now fully armored for liberty and power. . . .

103. "FREE-LOVE"

(*AF*, Baxter Springs, December 1912, 4–5)
Free-love is an animalism which has arisen in the Holiness and Apostolic work . . .

One of the fruitful sources of this cancerous condition is the promiscuous gathering of men and women around he altars of prayer . . .

For instance, in the Azuza [*sic*] mission in Los Angeles (where all this counterfeit Pentecost power was born) in the Upper Room, men and women, whites and blacks, knelt together or fell across one another; frequently, a white woman, perhaps of wealth and culture, could be seen thrown back in the arms of a big "buck nigger," and held tightly thus as she shivered and shook in freak imitation of Pentecost.

Horrible, awful shame! Many of the missions on the Pacific cost are permeated with this foolishness, and, in fact, it follows the Azuza [*sic*] work everywhere. . . .

For instance, in a meeting in Oakland, Cal., where the leader (a lady) took great pains to tell how "they loved each other, SO MUCH!"

In speaking of a Negro who was visiting them, she told how "they all loved him so, and just made him love them; in fact, we will not let anyone stay in our house unless [they] love us all, and we just love each other more and more all the time, etc., etc."

This lovey dovey talk went on until it was actually sickening. An outsider would have said that this was another bunch of nigger-lovers and free-lovers; but they were not, oh no, but were a very esteemable class of Christians. "Avoid the very appearance of evil."

I thank God we are gaining ground and victory against these forces and the true Apostolic Faith is arising from this muck and mire. Let . . . us humble ourselves under the mighty hand of God, that He may lift up a standard for the people, and that this BLIGHT be removed.

Chas. F. Parham

104. E. N. BELL

NOTICE ABOUT PARHAM.

(*Word and Witness,* Malvern, Arkansas, October 1912, 3)

Chas. F. Parham, who is claiming to be the head and leader of the Apostolic Faith Movement, has long since been repudiated. He has refused to "hear the church" and we are obeying the command of Christ, the Head of the church by letting him be unto us as a "heathen and a publican." We are sorry it is so, but until he repents and confesses his sins we cannot obey God and do otherwise. Let all Pentecostal and Apostolic Faith people of the church of God take notice and be not misled by his claims.

NOTES

PREFACE

1. Martin, *Life and Ministry of William J. Seymour*, 11–12.
2. Eliade, *The Quest*, Preface, 4–10; Olsen, *Theory and Method in the Study of Religion*, 156.

INTRODUCTION. DEFINITIONS AND ONE HUNDRED YEARS OF HISTORIOGRAPHY ON SEYMOUR

1. As late as 1912, Seymour and the Azusa Street mission were still hailed as the single most important leader and center of early Pentecostalism. This is based on a number of facts, the two most important being: (1) Parham wrote that Seymour and Azusa were the most important rival leader and center of global Pentecostalism in 1912 and (2) Boddy wrote that same year that Azusa was a "Mecca" of global Pentecostalism. Durham died that year, before he could patch up his differences with Seymour over his summer 1911 schism. This left Seymour without one of his most famous white friends and one who promoted Seymour and the Azusa revival throughout the larger white Pentecostal movement from 1907 until the summer of 1911.
2. These data were provided by Peter Crossing and Todd Johnson from the *World Christian Database*, Leiden, Brill Online, 2012. Gastón Espinosa, e-mail exchange with Peter Crossing, March 5 and April 15, 2012.
3. John T. Maempa, "Keeping the flame alive—an Azusa Street Centennial Report," AG.org News & Information, May 3, 2006, http://rss.ag.org/articles/detail.cfm?RSS_RSSContentID=3938&RSS_OriginatingRSSFeedID=1034
4. For the nineteenth-century and early twentieth-century roots of Pentecostalism see Dayton, *Theological Roots of Pentecostalism*; Wacker, *Heaven Below*; Blumhofer, *Assemblies of God*, Vol. 1; Goff, *Fields White unto Harvest*; Robeck, *Azusa Street Mission and Revival*; Alexander, *Black Fire*; Synan, *Holiness-Pentecostal Tradition*; Nelson, "For Such a Time as This"; Jacobsen, *Thinking in the Spirit*; Hollenweger, *The Pentecostals*; Mapes Anderson, *Vision of the Disinherited*; Anderson, *Spreading Fires*.
5. Bergunder, "Introduction: Constructing Indian Pentecostalism," 10; McGee, "Initial Evidence," 784–90.
6. Warfield, *Counterfeit Miracles*; Scofield, *Scofield Reference Bible*; MacArthur, *Charismatic Chaos*; Hanegraaff, *Counterfeit Revival*.
7. Synan, *Holiness-Pentecostal Tradition*, 207–11; Robeck, "National Association of Evangelicals," 922–25.

8. Reed, "Aspects of the Origins of Oneness Pentecostalism," 144–68; Synan, *Holiness-Pentecostal Tradition*, 156–63.

9. Marsden, *Fundamentalism and American Culture;* Synan, "Fundamentalism," 657–58.

10. Marsden, *Fundamentalism and American Culture;* Synan, "Fundamentalism," 657–58.

11. Bennett, *Nine O'Clock in the Morning;* Christenson, *Speaking in Tongues;* McDonnell, *Catholic Pentecostalism;* O'Connor, *Pentecostal Movement in the Catholic Church;* Hamilton, *Charismatic Movement,* 220–78; Synan, *Twentieth-Century Pentecostal Explosion,* 10.

12. Donald Miller, *Reinventing American Protestantism.*

13. Miller, *Global Pentecostalism: The New Face of Christian Social Engagement,* 1–12, 34–38, 211–24.

14. Alex Murashko, "Greg Laurie Seeks Churches, Venues to Host 'Harvest America' Event."

15. For statistics and cautions about them see Jenkins, *The Next Christendom* and Anderson, *An Introduction to Pentecostalism.* Also see Yong, *Spirit Poured Out on All Flesh.*

16. Espinosa, "*Righteousness and Justice,*" chapters 1, 10; Dias, "Revealed: President Obama's Daily Email Devotional."

17. Espinosa, *Religion and the American Presidency,* 482–85; Miller and Yamamori, *Global Pentecostalism;* Feston, *Evangelicals and Politics in Asia, Africa, and Latin America.*

18. Parham, "Lest We Forget"; Parham, Editorial (October 1912): 6; Parham, "Free-Love." Seymour and some followers also downplayed Seymour's role by pointing to divine origins. Seymour, *D&D.*

19. Sarah Parham, *Life of Charles F. Parham,* 142, 161.

20. Lawrence, *Apostolic Faith Restored,* 52–56; Bartleman, *Azusa Street,* 57–58, 69; Frodsham, *With Signs Following,* 105; Kendrick, *Promise Fulfilled,* 37, 64–68; Brumback, *Suddenly . . . From Heaven,* 37–38, 41–42, 48–63; Menzies, *Anointed to Serve,* 34–52.

21. Lawrence, *Apostolic Faith Restored,* 56.

22. Bartleman, *Azusa Street,* 57, 69.

23. Frodsham, *With Signs Following,* 105.

24. Kendrick, *Promise Fulfilled,* 64–67; Guillén, *La Historia del Concilio Latino Americano de Iglesias Cristianas,* 26–48, 345; Golder, *History of the Pentecostal Assemblies of the World,* 25–31.

25. Brumback, *Suddenly . . . from Heaven,* 37–63.

26. Italics added. Menzies, *Anointed to Serve,* 1, 34, 41, 48–49.

27. Hollenweger, *The Pentecostals,* 9, 15–24; Nelson, "For Such a Time as This," 126.

28. Synan, *Holiness-Pentecostal Tradition,* 18–24, 89, 102–3, 170.

29. Tinney, "Black Origins of the Pentecostal Movement," 4–6; Tinney, "William J. Seymour: Father of Modern-Day Pentecostalism," 34–44.

30. Lovett, "Black Origins of the Pentecostal Movement," 135–40.

31. Anderson, *Vision of the Disinherited,* 47, 82–89, 140, 190, 195–96, 240, 257.

32. Nelson, "For Such a Time as This," 9–13.

33. Goff, *Fields White unto Harvest,* 11, 15, 110–11.

34. Blumhofer, *Assemblies of God,* 67–92, 109, 389–96, 399.

35. Robeck, *Colorline Was Washed Away in the Blood,* 12–18.

36. Cox, *Fire from Heaven*, 57–64, 81–121.
37. Creech, "Visions of Glory," 405–24.
38. Espinosa, "Borderland Religion," 81–116, 92–93, 139, 117–40; Espinosa, "Ordinary Prophet," 29–60; Espinosa, *Latino Pentecostals in America*.
39. Martin, *Life and Ministry of William J. Seymour*, 267–71.
40. Sanders, *William Joseph Seymour*, VIII, 1–8, 12.
41. Wacker, *Heaven Below*, 10–14, 227–33.
42. Goff, *Fields White unto Harvest*, 10–11, 107–10, 157; Blumhofer, *Assemblies of God, Vol. 1*, 91; Wacker, *Heaven Below*, 226–35; Cerillo and Wacker, "Bibliography and Historiography," 401–3.
43. Robeck, *Azusa Street Mission and Revival*, 89, 129.
44. Robeck, *Azusa Street Mission and Revival*, 4, 47–48, 89, 110, 128–29, 139–41, 310.
45. Borlase, *William Seymour*, xi, 236–37.
46. Anderson, *Spreading Fires*, 4–6, 52–54.
47. Rosenior, "Toward Racial Reconciliation," 119–20.
48. Omenyo, "William Seymour and African Pentecostal Historiography," 244–58; Kalu, *African Pentecostalism*, 13, 20, 22, 47, 75.
49. Dove, "Hymnody and Liturgy in the Azusa Street Revival, 1906–1908," 242–63.
50. Fox, "William J. Seymour," 3, 161–66, 180–87.
51. Brathwaite, "Tongues and Ethics," 203–5, 217–22.
52. Campbell, "'The Newest Religious Sect Has Started in Los Angeles,'" 16–21.
53. Foxworth, "Raymond T. Richey," 255, 270.
54. Alexander, *Black Fire*, 157–60.
55. Synan and Fox, *William J. Seymour: Pioneer of the Azusa Street Revival*, 11–13. Unfortunately, I was not able to secure this book far enough in advance to offer up a more thorough analysis of it.
56. Bergunder, *South Indian Pentecostal Movement in the Twentieth Century*, 2–11; Anderson, *Spreading Fires*, 6–7, 52–54
57. Creech selected 1912 because he holds up Durham (who died that year) and his mission as the premier alternative leader and center of Pentecostal origins that not only matched but perhaps even superseded Seymour and Azusa's influence and because he argues that almost all of the other points of origin were active by this date. Creech, "Visions of Glory," 405–24. Osterberg said the Azusa Revival ran from 1906 to 1911. Osterberg, "Oral History."
58. Bartleman, *Azusa Street*, 13–24, 57, 69, 103–4, 120–23, 132–33, 143–58.
59. Synan, *Holiness-Pentecostal Tradition*, 107–25.
60. See the photo "P10156—Azusa" of S. D. Paige and F. M. Britton in front of the Azusa Mission, ca. early 1920s, in the Flower Pentecostal Heritage Center Archives.
61. Durham, "The Great Revival at Azusa Street—How it Began and How it Ended," 3–4.
62. Apostolic Faith, Portland, *The Apostolic Faith*, 19, 28, 43–46.
63. Bergunder, *South Indian Pentecostal Movement in the Twentieth Century*, 6–11; Creech, "Visions of Glory," 407–16.
64. Bergunder, *South Indian Pentecostal Movement in the Twentieth Century*, 6–11; Creech, "Visions of Glory," 407–16.
65. Anderson, *Spreading Fires*, 12.
66. Bergunder, *South Indian Pentecostal Movement*, 6–11.

67. Bartleman, *Azusa Street*, 9–42, 69.

68. Turney, "Missionaries to Johannesburg, South Africa," 4; Moorhead, "Pentecost in Mukti, India," 4; Frodsham, *With Signs Following*, 121.

69. Turney, "Missionaries to Johannesburg, South Africa"; Moorhead, "Pentecost in Mukti, India"; Frodsham, *With Signs Following*.

70. Vinson Synan, "George Floyd Taylor: Conflicts and Crowns," in *Portraits of a Generation: Early Pentecostal Leaders*, eds., James R. Goff Jr. and Grant Wacker (Fayetteville, AR: The University of Arkansas Press, (2002), 335.

71. Anderson, *Spreading Fires*, 85, 88, 98; italics in original. Blumhofer, *Assemblies of God*, Vol. 1, 188–89.

72. The language in Abrams's booklet *The Baptism of the Holy Ghost and Fire* (December 1906), 3–4, 7, 22, and 27, and Ramabai's summer 1907 description of a "Holy Ghost revival" bears an uncanny resemblance to language in the first four issues of Seymour's *Apostolic Faith* (September–December 1906). Anderson, *Spreading Fires*, 79–81; Taylor, "Publish and be Blessed."

73. This number was tallied from the publication figures and estimates published in the Mast section of each of Seymour's *Apostolic Faith* newspapers.

74. For the rapid spread and importance of Seymour's newspaper, see Taylor, "Publish and be Blessed."

75. Parham, No title, *AF* (Baxter Springs) (January 1912): 6–7; Parham, "Unity," 9–11; Parham, "Free-Love," 4–5.

76. Parham, *Kol Kare Bomidbar*, 91–108; Seymour, *D&D*, 10, 12–13.

77. My view is not necessarily opposed to Grant Wacker's aforecited theory but rather emphasizes different elements in his metaphor. In fact, he is correct with respect to many early Pentecostal leaders—just not Seymour and Parham, though they were not the primary focus of his comment. See the next endnote for the data source. Wacker, 1–17.

78. These data were provided by Peter Crossing and Todd Johnson from the *World Christian Database*, Leiden, Brill Online, 2012. Gastón Espinosa, e-mail exchange with Peter Crossing, March 5 and April 15, 2012.

79. Seymour, *D&D*, 92.

80. Burns, *Leadership*, 3–5, 12–22.

81. Bass and Riggio, *Transformational Leadership*, 3–5, 12–22.

82. Synan, "Cashwell, Gaston Barnabas," 457–58; Riggio, Murphy, and Pirozzolo, *Multiple Intelligences and Leadership*, 1–5, 9–11, 105–18.

83. James, *The Varieties of Religious Experience*, 15–31; Shumway, "A Study of 'The Gift of Tongues,'" 190–93.

84. James, *The Varieties of Religious Experience*, 15–31.

85. Conger, *The Charismatic Leader: Behind the Mystique of Exceptional Leadership*, 137–58.

CHAPTER 1. AMERICAN PENTECOSTAL ORIGINS

1. Valdez and Scheer, *Fire on Azusa Street*, 3–4.

2. *Los Angeles Daily Times*, "Weird Babel of Tongues," 1. All references to Seymour's, Parham's (Baxter Springs, KS), Crawford's (Portland, OR), and Carother's (Houston, TX) *Apostolic Faith* newspapers will be abbreviated *AF*. Unless stated otherwise, all references to *AF* will refer to Seymour's Los Angeles newspaper. I will distinguish all other *AF* editions by noting the editor's name and/or city.

3. Wiebe, *Search for Order*, viii, 56, 76–83.
4. Shumway, "A Study of 'The Gift of Tongues,'" 192–93; Bartleman, *Azusa Street*, 73–74.
5. Marsden, *Fundamentalism and American Culture*, 15–16, 62, 215–21.
6. Warfield, *Counterfeit Miracles*, 143–53, 233–34; Sharpe, *Comparative Religion*, 48–56, 94–95, 166; Gaustad and Noll, *A Documentary History of Religion in America Since 1877*, 322–51.
7. Frankiel, *California's Spiritual Frontiers*.
8. Braude, *Radical Spirits*.
9. Dayton, *Theological Roots of Pentecostalism*; Blumhofer, *Assemblies of God, Vol. 1*; Goff, *Fields White unto Harvest*, 62ff; Synan, *Holiness Pentecostal Tradition*, 1–84; Nelson, "For Such a Time as This," 184–87; Hollenweger, *Pentecostals*, 1–28; Tinney, "Black Origins of the Pentecostal Movement," 4–6; Tinney, "William J. Seymour: Father of Modern-Day Pentecostalism," 34–44; Lovett, "Black Origins of the Pentecostal Movement," 123–41; Jacobsen, *Thinking in the Spirit*; Anderson, *Spreading Fires*, 17–42; Parham, *Kol Kare Bomidbar* (hereafter *KKB*), 29; Seymour, *Doctrines and Disciplines* (hereafter *D&D*), 95; *Apostolic Faith* (Portland), *A Historical Account of The Apostolic Faith*, 35–42; Lawrence, *Apostolic Faith Restored*, 71–73; Bartleman, *Azusa Street*, 1–42.
10. For the nineteenth-century contributions to Pentecostal origins see the sources cited in the previous endnote.
11. Hollenweger, *Pentecostals*, 22–28; Anderson, *Vision of the Disinherited*, 28–78; Wacker, *Heaven Below*; Jacobsen, *Thinking in the Spirit*; Robeck, *Azusa Street Mission and Revival*; Alexander, *Black Fire*.
12. The best books on Parham, Seymour, and Azusa are the aforecited books by Goff, Nelson, and Robeck.
13. Shumway was quite critical of Parham. Goff wrote: "Approval by the hierarchy meant a loss of spiritual freedom. He could obey God or man, but he could no longer obey both. In resigning [from the Methodist Church], he fashioned for himself a ministerial career that would be unhindered by human authority. Charles Parham received his orders directly from heaven." Shumway, "Study of 'The Gift of Tongues,'" 164–65; Shumway, "Critical History of Glossolalia," 112; Goff, *Fields White unto Harvest*, 16, 18–37, 183; Anderson, *Vision of the Disinherited*, 47–52.
14. Goff, *Fields White unto Harvest*, 16, 18–37, 183.
15. Goff, *Fields White unto Harvest*, 31–61, 186.
16. Parham, *KKB*, 83–100, 105–8; Goff, *Fields White unto Harvest*, 107–11, 131–32; Parham, *AF* (Baxter Springs, January 1912): 7.
17. Parham, *KKB*, 81–138; Goff, *Fields White unto Harvest*, 107–32.
18. Parham, *KKB*, 81–138; Goff, *Fields White unto Harvest*, 107–32.
19. Parham, *KKB*, 81–138; Goff, *Fields White unto Harvest*, 107–32.
20. Sarah Parham, *Life of Charles F. Parham*, 48; Shumway, "A Study of 'The Gift of Tongues,'" 167; Goff, *Fields White unto Harvest*, 51–74.
21. *Topeka State Journal*, "Hindoo and Zulu Both Represented in Bethel College"; Sarah Parham, *Life of Charles F. Parham*, 52; Shumway, "A Study of 'The Gift of Tongues,'" 164–67; Goff, *Fields White unto Harvest*, 38–39, 57–59, 69–79; Mapes Anderson, *Vision of the Disinherited*, 52–61, 161–65; Brumback, *Suddenly . . . from Heaven*, 58; Blumhofer, *Assemblies of God, Vol. 1*, 80–85, 393–94; Wacker, *Heaven Below*, 35–57; Synan, *Holiness-Pentecostal Tradition*, 164–65.
22. Parham, *KKB*, 32–35; Sarah Parham, *Life of Charles F. Parham*, 51–80; Shum-

way, "A Study of 'The Gift of Tongues,'" 164–69. For the debate over who spoke in tongues first, see Blumhofer, *Assemblies of God, Vol. 1*, 81–85, 392, 393–94; Goff, *Fields White unto Harvest*, 38–49, 57–59, 66–85, 90–98; Anderson, *Vision of the Disinherited*, 52–61, 161–65; Brumback, *Suddenly . . . from Heaven*, 58; Wacker, *Heaven Below*, 35–57, 289–90; Synan, *Holiness-Pentecostal Tradition*, 164–65; Seymour, "The Pentecostal Baptism Restored," *AF*, 1.

23. Shumway, "A Study of 'The Gift of Tongues,'" 168; Sarah Parham, *Life of Charles F. Parham*, 52–68.

24. Anderson argues the initial evidence theory was not crystallized until after 1915. Anderson, *Vision of the Disinherited*, 51–58, 253–54. Parham claimed that language interpreters corroborated their claims. Shumway was unable to find anyone who would corroborate Parham's claims. Parham, "History of the Apostolic Faith Movement," 5; Shumway, "A Study of 'The Gift of Tongues,'" 168.

25. Cook, *Azusa Street Meetings*.

26. Shumway, "A Study of 'The Gift of Tongues,'" 170; Sarah Parham, *Life of Charles F. Parham*, 101–45; Goff, *Fields White unto Harvest*, 87–105.

27. Nelson, "For Such a Time as This," 151–52; Martin, *Life and Ministry of William J. Seymour*, 31–59.

28. Nelson, "For Such a Time as This," 151–52; Martin, *Life and Ministry of William J. Seymour*, 31–59.

29. Du Bois, "The Talented Tenth," 33–75; Lewis, *W.E.B. Du Bois*.

30. Seymour, "River of Living Water," 2; Seymour, "Gifts of the Holy Spirit."

31. Shumway, "A Study of 'The Gift of Tongues,'" 173; Nelson, "For Such a Time as This," 153–66.

32. Lake, "Origins of the Apostolic Faith Movement," 3; Shumway, "A Study of 'The Gift of Tongues,'" 173; Nelson, "For Such a Time as This," 153–66.

33. Lake, "Origins of the Apostolic Faith Movement," 3; Shumway, "A Study of 'The Gift of Tongues,'" 173; Nelson, "For Such a Time as This," 153–66.

34. Lake, "Origins of the Apostolic Faith Movement," 3; Shumway, "A Study of 'The Gift of Tongues,'" 173; Nelson, "For Such a Time as This," 153–66; Irwin, "Charles Price Jones," 45.

35. Shumway, "A Study of 'The Gift of Tongues,'" 173; Goss, "Reminiscences of an Eyewitness"; Lawrence, *Apostolic Faith Restored*; Sarah Parham, *Life of Charles F. Parham*, 161–62.

36. Sarah Parham, *Life of Charles F. Parham*, 137, 142, 161–69, 237–43. Valdez stated Seymour asked Parham: "I was wondering . . . can I just sit in the doorway and listen to the lessons?" He implied Parham's consent. Valdez and Scheer, *Fire on Azusa Street*, 18. Shumway wrote that in Parham's revival services "colored people . . . must remain in the rear and keep silent." Shumway, "A Study of 'The Gift of Tongues,'" 173. Nelson, "For Such a Time as This," 35, 167; Sarah Parham, *Life of Charles F. Parham*, 137; Goss, "Reminiscences of an Eyewitness," 4–5; Goff, *Fields White unto Harvest*, 107, 210–12. That Parham was not merely following the social conventions of his day are evidenced by (1) his own views on white supremacy in *KKB*, (2) Parham's racialized criticisms of Seymour in his newspaper from 1910 to 1913, and (3) the fact that Parham did not normally allow interracial mixing at the altars. Mack Jonas as cited in Lovett, "Black Origins of the Pentecostal Movement," in Synan, *Aspects of Pentecostal-Charismatic Origins*, 133–34. Sarah Parham notes that Parham was in southern California from December 1911 to July 1912. He also returned again in February 1913. To his credit, Parham continued to carry out evangelistic work among blacks. Parham, *KKB*, 81–85.

37. Sarah Parham, *Life of Charles F. Parham*, 137, 142, 161.
38. Parham, *KKB*, 81–85; Parham, *Everlasting Gospel* (hereafter *TEG*), 71–73; Parham, "Leadership," 7–9; Parham, "Unity," 9–11; Parham, "Free-Love," 4–5; Parham, *Life of Charles Fox Parham*, 137, 142, 161. Seymour, *D&D*, Preface, 8, 12–13, 52–58, 91.
39. "Pentecost with Signs Following," *AF*, 1; Parham, *KKB*, 82–85, 91–108, 115–18; Seymour, *D&D*, 10, 12–13.
40. Carothers, "History of the Movement," 1–2.
41. Carothers, "History of the Movement," 1–2; Cotton, "Inside Story," 1–4.
42. Lawrence, *Apostolic Faith Restored*, 55, 64; Sarah Parham, *Life of Charles F. Parham*, 142; Carothers, "History of the Movement," 1–2; Seymour, "Bro. Seymour's Call," 1; Shumway, "A Study of 'The Gift of Tongues,'" 173–74; Cotton, "Inside story," 1–4; Nelson, "For Such a Time as This," 37, 55, 187–89; Bartleman, *Azusa Street*, 41.

CHAPTER 2. HOLY AWE AND INDESCRIBABLE WONDER

1. Shumway, "A Study of 'The Gift of Tongues,'" 173; Cotton, "Inside Story," 1–4; Nickel, *Azusa Street Outpouring*, 4; Nelson, "For Such a Time as This," 56.
2. Shumway, "A Study of 'The Gift of Tongues,'" 172–76; Lawrence, *Apostolic Faith Restored*, 73–75; Nickel, *Azusa Street Outpouring*, 4–6; Bartleman, *Azusa Street*, 43–63; Nelson, "For Such a Time as This," 55–58.
3. Sarah Parham, *Life of Charles F. Parham*, 154, 160–70; Seymour, "Letter to W. F. Carothers;" Carothers, "History of the Movement," 1–2; Bartleman, *Azusa Street*, 1–27; "The Promise Still Good," *AF*, 2.
4. Sarah Parham, *Life of Charles F. Parham*, 154.
5. Sarah Parham, *Life of Charles F. Parham*, 154, 161–64; Goss, "Reminiscences of an Eyewitness," 4; Nelson, "For Such a Time as This," 189; *AF* (September 1906): 1.
6. Bartleman, *Azusa Street*, 9–42; Lawrence, *Apostolic Faith Restored*, 70–73.
7. Moore, "Music From Heaven," 3; *AF*, "Pentecost Has Come," 1; *AF*, "Bro. Seymour's Call," 1; *AF*, "The Old-Time Pentecost," 1; *AF*, "The Pentecostal Baptism Restored," 1; Lawrence, *Apostolic Faith Restored*, 56, 73–75; Bartleman, *Azusa Street*, 41–47; Nelson, "For Such a Time as This," 187–92.
8. Shumway, "A Study of 'The Gift of Tongues,'" 171–76; Nelson, "For Such a Time as This," 191.
9. *AF* (December 1906): 1; *AF*, "The Same Old Way," 3; *AF*, "Bible Pentecost," 1; Bartleman, *Azusa Street*, 47, 54.
10. *AF*, "Bible Pentecost," 1; Seymour, *D&D*, 12, 95; Bartleman, *Azusa Street*, 45.
11. Shumway, "A Study of 'The Gift of Tongues,'" 179; Bartleman, *Azusa Street*, 13.
12. Seymour, *D&D*, 95; Lawrence, *The Apostolic Faith Restored*, 70–73; Bartleman, *Azusa Street*, 13.
13. Moorhead, "Pentecost in Mukti, India," 4; *AF*, "Pentecost in India," 1; *AF*, "Revival in India," 4; Shumway, "A Study of 'The Gift of Tongues,'" 180–86.
14. Seymour, *D&D*, 12; *AF*, "Tongues as a Sign," 2; *AF*, "Bible Pentecost," 1; *AF*, "Who May Prophesy," 2.
15. *AF* (September 1906): 1; *AF*, "The Same Old Way," 3; Franklin, *From Slavery to Freedom*, 324–25; Fillmer, "1906 Lynchings Grew from Tensions, Racism."
16. Nelson, "For Such a Time as This," 191.
17. *AF*, "The Same Old Way," 3; Shumway, "A Study of 'The Gift of Tongues,'" 175–76; Lawrence, *Apostolic Faith Restored*, 74; Nickel, *Azusa Street Outpouring*, 6–10.
18. Noll, *History of Christianity in the United States and Canada*, 201–3; Lincoln and Mamiya, *Black Church in the African American Experience*, 50–60.

19. Shumway, "A Study of 'The Gift of Tongues,'" 72–75; Nelson, "For Such a Time as This," 192; Lawrence, *Apostolic Faith Restored*, 73–74.

20. Louis Osterberg remained on Seymour's Board at least until Durham's revolt in 1911 and then later. Shumway, "A Study of 'The Gift of Tongues,'" 175–76.

21. Shumway, "A Study of 'The Gift of Tongues,'" 175–76; Lincoln and Mamiya, *Black Church in the African American Experience*, 54–56.

22. Osterberg, "Oral History of the Life of Arthur G. Osterberg and the Azusa Street Revival," 11; Espinosa, "The Holy Ghost Is Here on Earth," 118–26.

23. *AF*, "Pentecost Has Come," 1; Nelson, "For Such a Time as This," 196.

24. Espinosa, "The Holy Ghost Is Here on Earth," 118–26.

25. Osterberg, "Oral History," 12; Nickel, *Azusa Street Outpouring*, 12–15.

26. Osterberg, "Oral History," 11–12; Nickel, *Azusa Street Outpouring*, 12–13; Crayne, *Pentecostal Handbook*, 228.

27. Valdez and Scheer, *Fire on Azusa Street*, 27, 34, 39; López, "Spanish Receive the Pentecost," 4.

28. Bartleman, *Azusa Street*, 145.

29. Seymour, "Gifts of the Holy Spirit," 2; *AF* (February–March, 1907): 1; Lawrence, *Apostolic Faith Restored*, 78–80; Nickel, *Azusa Street Outpouring*, 8–9; Valdez and Scheer, *Fire on Azusa Street*, 9–10. Bartleman, *Azusa Street*, 57, 101, 145; *Apostolic Faith* (Portland Oregon), *A Historical Account of the Apostolic Faith*, 59. Seymour, *Azusa Street Mission Fourteenth Anniversary*, 1–12; *AF* (September 1906): 1.

30. *AF*, "At Azusa," 2; Cook, *Azusa Street Meetings*, 2; Orwig, "My First Visit to the Azuzu [sic] Street Pentecostal Mission," 4; Bartleman, *Azusa Street*, 55, 82; Valdez and Scheer, *Fire on Azusa Street*, 9–10.

31. McGee, "Garr, Alfred Goodrich, Sr.," 660; Mapes Anderson, *Vision of the Disinherited*, 15–20; Wacker, *Heaven Below*, 40–57; Goff, *Fields White unto Harvest*, 199–202.

32. Mead, "From a Missionary to Africa," 3; *AF*, "Russians Hear in Their Own Tongue," 4; *AF* (September 1906): 3; *AF*, "Missionaries to Jerusalem," 4.

33. Mapes Anderson, *Vision of the Disinherited*, 15–20; Wacker, *Heaven Below*, 40–57.

34. *AF*, "Good News from Danville, VA," 4. Shumway, "A Study of 'The Gift of Tongues,'" 180–86; McGee, "Garr, Alfred Goodrich, Sr.," *NIDPCM*, 660.

35. Bartleman, 57; Cook, *Azusa Street Meetings*, 2; Orwig, "My First Visit to the Azuzu [sic] Street Pentecostal Mission," 4. Some of the songs included "The Comforter Has Come," "Were You There, He's Coming Soon," "I Remember Calvary," "This Is Like Heaven to Me," "Where Jesus Is, Tis Heaven There," "The Hallelujah Song," "He Lifted Me Up," "I Want To Be Ready," "Lord, I Want To Be A Christian," "Since Jesus Came Into My Heart," and "I Couldn't Hear Nobody Pray." Seymour, *Azusa Street Mission Fourteenth Anniversary*, 1–12.

36. *AF*, "Two Works of Grace and the Gift of the Holy Spirit," 3; *AF*, "The Pentecostal Baptism Restored," 1; Seymour, *D&D*, 22, 27–31, 92; Bartleman, *Azusa Street*, 45–46, 102, 151, "The Old-Time Pentecost," 1; Cook, *Azusa Street Meetings*, 3; Bartleman, *Azusa Street*, 55, 63, 70, 82, 90; Valdez and Scheer, *Fire on Azusa Street*, 10.

37. Bartleman, *Azusa Street*, 70, 47, 53–55, 82, 90.

38. This literacy is evident in Seymour's articles and minister's manual. Orwig, "Additional Highlights from Los Angeles," 4; *AF*, "Two Works of Grace and the Gift of the Holy Spirit," 3; *AF*, "The Pentecostal Baptism Restored," 1; Seymour, *D&D*, 22, 27–31, 92; Bartleman, *Azusa Street*, 45–46, 102, 151, "Tongues as a Sign," 2; *AF*, "Two

Works of Grace and the Gift of the Holy Spirit," 3; *AF,* "The Pentecostal Baptism Restored," 1; Seymour, *D&D,* 22, 27–31, 92; Bartleman, *Azusa Street,* 45–46, 102, 151; "The Salvation of Jesus," 4.

39. David Daniels, "Charles Harrison Mason," 256–70; Goff and Wacker, *Portraits of a Generation.*

40. *AF,* "Two Works of Grace and the Gift of the Holy Spirit," 3; *AF,* "The Pentecostal Baptism Restored," 1; Seymour, *D&D,* 22, 27–31, 92; Bartleman, *Azusa Street,* 45–46, 102, 151.

41. *AF,* "The Pentecostal Baptism Restored," 1; *AF,* "Two Works of Grace and the Gift of the Holy Spirit," 3; *AF,* "The Pentecostal Baptism Restored," 1; Seymour, *D&D,* 22, 27–31, 92; Bartleman, *Azusa Street,* 1–42, 45–46, 65–66, 102, 151, "Bible Pentecost," 1; Seymour, *D&D,* 95.

42. Orwig, "Additional Highlights from Los Angeles," 4; *AF,* "Tongues as a Sign," 2; *AF,* "Two Works of Grace and the Gift of the Holy Spirit," 3; *AF,* "The Pentecostal Baptism Restored," 1; Seymour, *D&D,* 22, 27–31, 92; Bartleman, *Azusa Street,* 45–46, 102, 151; "The Salvation of Jesus," 4. Seymour and his colleagues cite church historians like John Fletcher Hurst, J. H. Merle, D'Aubigne, and Philip Schaff to promote Protestant doctrines over against "Romanism" and to argue that pneumatic outpourings had taken place throughout history. Seymour, *D&D,* 28–35, 95; Bartleman, *Azusa Street,* 45, 77, 102, 110, 151, 160–73.

43. Seymour, *D&D,* 13, 43, 83–95.

44. One Azusa editorial stated: "The Lord has taken Spirilualism [*sic*] and Christian Science out of people in this mission, and filled them with the Spirit, and they are sitting at the feet of Jesus. We teach against Theosophy, Christian Science, Magnetic Healing, Spiritualism, Hypnotism and all works of the devil." *AF,* February–March 1907): 1; *AF,* "Pentecost with Signs Following," 1: Seymour, "Counterfeits," 2; *AF,* "Demons Cast Out," 3; Seymour, "Impure Doctrine," 3; Seymour, *D&D,* 8, 12–13, 52; Bartleman, *Azusa Street,* 81.

45. See the *AF* newspaper masthead for October 1906, 4. Seymour and his colleagues warned: "You cannot win people by abusing their church or pastor . . . The main thing is, Are [*sic*] you in Christ?" *AF,* "The Church Question," 2.

46. *AF,* "God is His Own Interpreter," 2; *AF* (February–March 1907): 1.

47. Bartleman, *Azusa Street,* 61, 70, 81; Shumway, "A Study of 'The Gift of Tongues,'" 176; Lawrence, *Apostolic Faith Restored,* 79.

48. Goff argued tongues were key to Seymour's ministry, Anderson argued it was eschatology, and Martin a call to biblical holiness. This author argues Seymour's primary goal was to convert the lost to a born-again, Spirit-filled relationship with Jesus Christ—something cited six times in the first three pages in his minister's manual. Goff, *Fields White unto Harvest,* 9, 15–16; Anderson, *Vision of the Disinherited,* 4, 43, 229–32, 240; Martin, *Life and Ministry of William J. Seymour,* 197, n84; Seymour, *D&D,* 10, 88–95; *AF,* "Tongues as a Sign," 2; Shumway, "A Study of 'The Gift of Tongues,'" 173; Lawrence, *Apostolic Faith Restored,* 64; Valdez and Scheer, *Fire on Azusa Street,* 10–11.

49. Bartleman, *Azusa Street,* 27, 32, 43, 59, 92; Osterberg, "A Revival and A Revolution," 6–7; Brumback, *Suddenly . . . from Heaven,* 42; Valdez and Scheer, *Fire on Azusa Street,* 91–92.

50. Lawrence, *Apostolic Faith Restored,* 81–83; Bartleman, *Azusa Street,* 63; Nickel, *Azusa Street Outpouring,* 14.

51. *AF,* "Two Works of Grace and the Gift of the Holy Spirit," 3; *AF,* "The Pentecostal Baptism Restored," 1; Seymour, *D&D,* 22, 27–31, 92; Bartleman, *Azusa Street,* 45–46, 102, 151; (September 1906): 4; *AF,* "Fire Still Falling," 1.

52. Bartleman, *Azusa Street,* 81; *AF,* "One Church," 3–4; *AF,* "Spreads the Fire," 4; *AF,* "Pentecost With Signs Following," 1; Bresee, "The Gift of Tongues;" Bridwell, "Fanatical Sect in Los Angeles Claims Gift of Tongues;" Shumway, "A Study of 'The Gift of Tongues,'" 176; Apostolic Faith, *A Historical Account of The Apostolic Faith,* 56–57.

53. Washburn, *History and Reminiscences,* 384–89; *AF,* "Ascension Robes," 4; Shumway, "A Study of 'The Gift of Tongues,'" 176; Martin, *Skeptics and Scoffers.*

54. *AF* (September 1906): 1; *AF,* "Pentecost Has Come," 1; *AF,* "Shall We Reject Jesus' Last Words?" 3; *AF,* "Back to Pentecost," 4.

55. Seymour, "The Holy Ghost is Power," 3.

56. *Los Angeles Daily Times,* "Weird Babel of Tongues;" Nickel, *Azusa Street Outpouring,* 10.

57. Bartleman, *Azusa Street,* 52; David Daniels, "Charles Harrison Mason," 256–70.

58. Cook, *Azusa Street Meetings,* 3; Nelson, "For Such a Time as This," 37.

59. Johnson, "Missionaries to Jerusalem," 4; Mead, "Sister Mead's Baptism," 3; Post, "Testimony of a Minister," 3; Johnson, "From Our Brother in Sweden," 3; Bartleman, *Azusa Street,* 61.

CHAPTER 3. MOSES AND MECCA

1. Cook, "The Azusa Street Meeting"; Bartleman, *Azusa Street,* 143–58; Sizelove, "Pentecost Has Come"; Durham, "The Great Revival at Azusa Street," 3–4.

2. Shumway, "A Study of 'The Gift of Tongues,'" 191.

3. Robeck, *Azusa Street Mission and Revival;* Anderson, *Spreading Fires.*

4. Boddy, "A Meeting at the Azusa Street Mission," 244; Brumback, *Suddenly . . . from Heaven,* 41.

5. Shumway, "A Study of 'The Gift of Tongues,'" 171–75; Lawrence, *Apostolic Faith Restored,* 75–76.

6. Bartleman, *Azusa Street,* 63, 70, 82. Contrary to Creech, he doesn't say it was the "sole" origin and center of global Pentecostalism, but "a" center.

7. Creech, "Visions of Glory," 406; Nelson, "For Such a Time as This," 279–80; Anderson, *Spreading Fires,* 12.

8. *AF,* "This is a world-wide revival, the last Pentecostal revival to bring our Jesus," 4; *AF,* "The Millennium," 3; *AF,* "Jesus Is Coming," 4.

9. Kessel, "The Tongues Delusion."

10. Parham, *KKB,* 29; Lake, "Origin of the Apostolic Faith Movement," 3; Seymour, *D&D,* 95; Henke, "The Gift of Tongues," 193–206; Nelson, "For Such a Time as This," 72n46.

11. Moorhead, "Pentecost in Mukti, India," 4; Frodsham, *With Signs Following,* 121.

12. Robert, *Converting Colonialism.*

13. *AF* (Portland), "How India Received Pentecost," 3; *AF* (Portland), "How Pentecost Came to China," 4; *AF* (Portland), "A Late Report from Bombay," 3.

14. Frodsham, *With Signs Following,* 253–62.

15. *AF,* "Tongues as a Sign," 2.

16. Robert, *American Women in Mission.*

17. Hastings, *A World History of Christianity,* 499–502; Sindima, *Drums of Redemption,* 70–80.

18. Hastings, *A World History of Christianity*, 499–502; Sindima, *Drums of Redemption*, 70–80.
19. Henke, "The Gift of Tongues," 195; Cox, *Fire from Heaven*, 213–41.
20. Hastings, *History of World Christianity*, 443–49, 505–8; Anderson, *Vision of the Disinherited*, 162–67; Sindima, *Drums of Redemption*, 85–88.
21. Shumway, "A Study of 'The Gift of Tongues,'" Preface, 180; Anderson, *Spreading Fires*, 232–56.
22. Kalu, *African Pentecostalism*; *AF*, "Latest Report from our Missionaries to Africa," 3; Batman, "En Route to Africa," 4.
23. *AF*, "In Africa," 1.
24. Harmon, "West Africa," *AF*, 1.
25. Mead, "From a Missionary to Africa," 3; *AF*, "A Message of His Coming," 3; Mead, "New-Tongued Missionary for Africa," 3; Mead, "Sister Mead's Baptism," 3; Mead, "On the Way to Africa," 5; McGee and Gitre, "Mead, Samuel J. and Ardella (Knapp)," 867–68.
26. *AF*, "Received Her Pentecost," 2.
27. *AF*, "From Los Angeles to Foreign Fields," 4; Batman, "En route to Africa," 4; Batman, "Bro. G.W. Batman's Testimony," 4; Batman, "Mrs. Daisy Batman's Testimony," 4.
28. Boddy, "Mission Day at Stouffville Camp Meeting," 147.
29. Ward, "Africa," in Hastings, *History of World Christianity*, 222, also see 335–36, 449–72, 489–90, 505–7; Spickard and Craig, *God's People*, 308–10; Sindima, *Drums of Redemption*, 85–86.
30. *AF*, "Missionaries to Johannesburg, South Africa," 4; Hexham and Poewe-Hexham, "South Africa," 227–28; Ziegler, "Lake, John G.," 828; Warner, "Hezmalhalch, Thomas," 712.
31. Lake, "Brother Lake's Letter."
32. Schwede, "Letter from South Africa."
33. Hastings, *History of World Christianity*, 499–501.
34. Turney, "Came from Alaska," *AF*, 2; Turney, *AF*, "Alaska Brother Proves Acts 1.8," 3; *AF*, "Missionaries to Johannesburg, South Africa," 4; Hexham and Poewe-Hexham, "South Africa," 227–28; McGee and Pavia, "Turney, Henry Michael," 1155; Ziegler, "Lake, John G.," 828; Warner, "Hezmalhalch, Thomas," 712.
35. Studd, *Diary*, 1.
36. Turney, "Came from Alaska," *AF*, 2; Turney, *AF*, "Alaska Brother Proves Acts 1.8," 3; *AF*, "Missionaries to Johannesburg, South Africa," 4; Hexham and Poewe-Hexham, "South Africa," 227–28; McGee and Pavia, "Turney, Henry Michael," 1155.
37. *AF* (Portland), "Pentecost in South Africa," 1.
38. *AF* (Portland), "South Africa," 1.
39. *AF* (Portland), "The Dead Raised," 1; *AF* (Portland), "Pentecost among the Zulu and Basuto People in South Africa," 1; *AF* (Portland), "Cape Colony, South Africa," 4; *AF* (Portland), "Johannesburg, S. Africa," 4; *AF* (Portland), "Pretoria, Transvaal, S. Africa," 4.
40. *AF* (Portland), "The Dead Raised," 1; *AF* (Portland), "Pentecost among the Zulu and Basuto People in South Africa," 1; *AF* (Portland), "Cape Colony, South Africa," 4; *AF* (Portland), "Johannesburg, S. Africa," 4; *AF* (Portland), "Pretoria, Transvaal, S. Africa," 4.
41. *AF* (Portland), "The Dead Raised," 1; *AF* (Portland), "Pentecost among the Zulu and Basuto People in South Africa," 1; *AF* (Portland), "Cape Colony, South

Africa," 4; *AF* (Portland), "Johannesburg, S. Africa," 4; *AF* (Portland), "Pretoria, Transvaal, S. Africa," 4.

42. *AF* (Portland), "Signs and Wonders Following the Work in South Africa," 1; *AF* (Portland), "Missionary Life among the Natives," 1; *AF* (Portland) (March-April 1910): 2; Brand, "Brandenburg, Lady Brand, O.R.C., South Africa," 3.

43. Boddy, "Across the Atlantic," 176.

44. *AF*, "Missionaries to Jerusalem," 4; Leatherman, "Jerusalem," 1; Booze, "Africa, North, and the Middle East," 8; *AF* (Portland), "Poured Out on the Humble People of God All Over the World," 1; Leatherman, "Syria," 1.

45. *AF*, "Missionaries to Jerusalem," 4; Leatherman, "Jerusalem," 1; Booze, "Africa, North, and the Middle East," 8; *AF* (Portland), "Poured Out on the Humble People of God All Over the World," 1; Leatherman, "Syria," 1; Anderson, *Spreading Fires,* 152–53.

46. *AF* (Portland), "Assiout, Egypt," 1.

47. *AF* (Portland), "Egypt"; Post, "Testimony of a Minister," 4; Gitte, "Post, Ansel Howard," 994; Booze, "Africa, North, and the Middle East," 6–7; *AF*, "Pentecostal Missionary Report," 1; Post, "Los Angeles to Ceylon, India," 4.

48. *AF* (Portland), "Assiout, Egypt," 1; *AF* (Portland), "Egypt"; Post, "Testimony of a Minister," 4; Gitte, "Post, Ansel Howard," 994; Booze, "Africa, North, and the Middle East," 6–7; *AF* "Pentecostal Missionary Report," 1; Post, "Los Angeles to Ceylon, India," 4.

49. Post, "Testimony of a Minister," 4; Gitte, "Post, Ansel Howard," 994; Booze, "Africa, North, and the Middle East," 6–7; *AF,* "Pentecostal Missionary Report," 1; Post, "Los Angeles to Ceylon, India," 4; Brelsford, "Missionaries to Egypt," 4; McIntosh, "Missionaries to Palestine," 4.

50. Louis Osterberg told Arthur how much was collected and given away that day. Osterberg, "Oral History of the Life of Arthur G. Osterberg and the Azusa Street Revival," Reel #4, page 11.

51. Johnson, "Letter from Bro. Johnson," 3.

52. Johnson, "From Our Brother in Sweden," 3; Johnson, "Sweden," 1; Ahonen with Johannesson, "Sweden," 255.

53. Johnson, "From Our Brother in Sweden," 3; Johnson, "Sweden," 1; Ahonen with Johannesson, "Sweden," 255.

54. Johnson, "From Our Brother in Sweden," 3; Johnson, "Sweden," 1; Ahonen with Johannesson, "Sweden," 255; Alvarsson, "Scandinavian Pentecostalism."

55. Johnson, "Salvation in Sweden," *AF* (June-February 1906): 1; *AF* (December 1906): 1; *AF* (January 1907): 4; Hollingsworth, "In Stockholm," 1.

56. Johnson, "Sweden," 1.

57. Johnson, "Gottenberg, Sweden," *AF* (Portland): 1; *AF* (Portland), "Germany," 1; *AF* (Portland), "Baptismal Service in Sweden," 3.

58. Barratt, "In Norway," 1; Barratt, *Work of T. B. Barratt,* 103–9, 123–29, 140.

59. Bundy, "Barratt, Thomas Ball," 365; Nilsen and Ahonen, "Norway," 193.

60. Iverson, *AF* (Portland), 2; Alvarsson, "Scandinavian Pentecostalism."

61. Hook, "In London," 1; Hook, *AF* (January 1908): 4; Hook, "Baptized in the Little Vestry of All Saints, Sunderland," 3.

62. Boddy, "Pentecost in England," 1.

63. Hinmers, "In London," 1; Boddy, "Reports from England," 1; Barratt, "Witnesses in England, Children Receive Pentecost," 1; Boddy, "Testimony of a Vicar's Wife," 1; *AF,* "Testimony of a Sunday School Teacher," 1; *AF,* "Testimony of a Yorkshire Farmer," 1.

64. Tomlinson, "In Wales," 1; Bundy, "Boddy, Alexander Alfred," 436–37; *AF,* "Pentecostal Outpouring in Scotland," 1; Sister Barratt, "All These Cannot Be Hypnotized," 3; *AF* (Portland), "Grovesend, Wales," 1; *AF* (Portland), "Wales," 1.

65. Valdez and Scheer, *Fire on Azusa Street,* 12; Nickel, *Azusa Street Outpouring,* 13.

66. *AF* (Portland), "Germany," 1; *AF* (Portland), "The Promised Latter Rain, Poured Out on the Humble People of God All Over the World," 1; *AF* (Portland), "Amsterdam, Holland," 1; *AF* (Portland), "Scotland, England and Ireland," 1; *AF* (Portland) (August and September 1908): 3; *AF* (Portland) (August and September 1908): 4; *AF* (Portland), "Amsterdam," 1; Hollenweger, *Pentecostals,* 218–87; Steelberg, "Impressions of Pentecost 35 Years Ago," 2–3; Henke, "The Gift of Tongues," 196.

67. *AF,* "Pentecost in India," 1.

68. *AF,* "Pentecost in India," 1; *AF,* "Revival in India, Wonderful Pouring Out of God's Spirit among the Natives of the Khassia Hills," 4; Norton, "Natives in India Speak in Tongues," 2.

69. *AF,* "A Late Report from Bombay," 3.

70. Garr, "Good News from Danville, VA," 4; Garr and Wife, "Pentecost in Danville, VA," 2.

71. Garr, "In Calcutta, India," 1; *AF* (Portland), "How India Received Pentecost," 3.

72. Garr, "In Calcutta, India," 1.

73. Shumway, "A Study of 'The Gift of Tongues,'" 180–82; "The Work in India, *AF* (June–September 1907): 1; Garr, "In Calcutta, India," 1; Bridwell, "Fanatical Sect in Los Angeles Claims Gift of Tongues"; "The Gift of Tongues," *The Burning Bush;* "Bubbles," *The Burning Bush;* "Garr in India," *The Burning Bush;* Harvey, "Given Over to Believe a Lie"; "Tongues Mix-Up," *The Burning Bush.*

74. Garr, "Good News from Danville," 4; McGee, "Garr, Alfred Goodrich, Sr.," *NIDPCM,* 660–61; Shumway, "A Study of 'The Gift of Tongues,'" 180–81.

75. Shumway, "A Study of 'The Gift of Tongues,'" 182–84; Moorhead, "Pentecost in Mukti, India," *AF* (September 1907): 4. Garr, "In Calcutta, India"; "How India Received Pentecost," *AF* (Portland) July-August 1908: 3.

76. McGee and Rodgers, "Abrams, Minnie F.," 305–6; Shumway, "A Study of 'The Gift of Tongues,'" 182–84; Moorhead, "Pentecost in Mukti, India," *AF* (September 1907): 4. Garr, "In Calcutta, India"; "How India Received Pentecost," *AF* (Portland) July-August 1908: 3.

77. Anderson, *Spreading Fires,* 79–98.

78. McGee and Rodgers, "Abrams, Minnie F.," 305–6.

79. Johnson, "In Calcutta, India," 1; *AF,* "India," 1; Shumway, "A Study of 'The Gift of Tongues,'" 182–83; *AF,* "Manifestations of the Spirit in India," 4; Knight, "Heavenly Visitations in India," 4; *AF* (Portland), "Pentecostal Revival in India," 4.

80. *AF,* "God Heals in India," 4; *AF* (Portland), "India," 1.

81. Moorhead, "Tribes in India That Have Received Pentecost," 3.

82. *AF* (Portland), "A Late Report from Bombay," 3.

83. Though the paper was controlled by Lum and Crawford by this time, most still believed they were writing to Seymour and Azusa because they hadn't been notified of the change in ownership. Norton, "Natives in India Speak in Tongues," 2; Shumway, "A Study of 'The Gift of Tongues,'" 180.

84. Garr, "Testimony and Praise to God," 4.

85. Todd, "China," 1; *AF* (Portland) (July and August 1988): 1; McGee and Burgess, "India," 118–26; McGee and Rodgers, "Abrams, Minnie F.," 305–6; McGee, "Garr, Alfred Goodrich, Sr.," 660–61; *AF,* "How India Received Pentecost," 3.

86. *AF* (Portland), "In Hong Kong 25 Were Baptized," 4.
87. *AF,* "China," 1; *AF,* "In Hong Kong 25 Were Baptized," 4.
88. Bro. Mok Lai Chi, "Hong Kong, China," 1.
89. Bays and Johnson, "China," 58–60.
90. *AF,* "China," 1; *AF,* "In Hong Kong 25 Were Baptized," 4.
91. Boddy, "Mission Day at Stouffville Camp Meeting," 147.
92. *AF,* "Chinese Want the Gospel of the Bible," 3; Bays and Johnson, "China," 58–60; McGee, "Garr, Alfred Goodrich, Sr.," 660–61.
93. Todd, "China," 1.
94. Todd, "China," 1; *AF,* "Chinese Filled with the Holy Spirit," 4.
95. Bernsten, "Came from China to America For Pentecost," 3.
96. See Bernsten's note in "Pentecostal Missionary Reports," 1; Berntsen, "Came from China to America For Pentecost," 3; Bernsten, "Cheng Ting Fu, North China," 1; *AF,* "Cheng Ting, Fu, Chih-li, North China, B. Bernsten and R. Hess," 4; *AF* (Portland), "A Chinese Brother Writes of the Plague," 4.
97. Bernsten, "Pentecostal Missionary Reports," 1; Berntsen, "Came from China to America For Pentecost," 3; Bernsten, "Cheng Ting Fu, North China," 1; *AF,* "Cheng Ting, Fu, Chih-li, North China, B. Bernsten and R. Hess," 4; *AF* (Portland), "A Chinese Brother Writes of the Plague," 4.
98. *AF,* "China Missionary Receives Pentecost," 3; Anderson, *Spreading Fires,* 54–55, 114, 128, 131–37, 142, 152.
99. Bays and Johnson, "China," 58–63.
100. Anderson, *Spreading Fires,* 138–41.
101. *AF,* "Pentecost in Australia," 1; Barclay, "A Policeman Receives Pentecost," 1; Hutchinson, "Australia," 26–27.
102. Studd, *Diary,* 13.
103. Valdez, "Letter to Brother Williams"; Valdez, "Letter to J. R. Flower"; Johnson, "The Impact A. C. Valdez Had on My Life"; Hutchinson, "02 Second Founder: A. C. Valdez, Sr. and Australian Pentecostalism"; Menzies, *Anointed to Serve,* 149–50.
104. Espinosa, *Latino Pentecostals in America.*
105. Espinosa, *Latino Pentecostals in America;* Shumway, "A Study of 'The Gift of Tongues,'" 186.
106. Shumway, "A Study of 'The Gift of Tongues,'" 186; Bundy, "Hoover, Willis Collins," 770; Colletti, "Berg, Daniel," 370.

CHAPTER 4. GOD MAKES NO DIFFERENCE IN COLOR

1. *AF,* "The Same Old Way," 3; *AF* (February–March 1907): 7.
2. White, *Demons and Tongues,* 67–70, 82, 108.
3. Parham, *Life of Charles F. Parham,* 163.
4. Shumway, "A Study of 'The Gift of Tongues,'" 178–79.
5. Shumway, "A Study of 'The Gift of Tongues,'" 178–79; Parham, "A Happy New Year to All," *AF* (January 1912): 6–7.
6. Parham, "Unity."
7. Parham, *Life of Charles F. Parham,* 161–64; Shumway, "A Study of 'The Gift of Tongues,'" 179; Parham, "Leadership"; Parham, "Unity"; Messenger, "The 'Tongues' in Zion City."
8. Shumway, "A Study of 'The Gift of Tongues,'" 179; Martin, *Skeptics and Scoffers,* 70, 121–22, 195–97, 227–29.
9. Sarah Parham, *Life of Charles F. Parham,* 163–64. Carothers stated Parham, not Seymour, caused the first schism. Carothers, "History of the Movement," 1–2.

10. Parham, "Leadership."
11. Messenger, "The 'Tongues' in Zion City"; Parham, "Leadership."
12. Shumway, "A Study of 'The Gift of Tongues,'" 178; Parham, *Everlasting Gospel* (hereafter *TEG*), 118–19; Parham, "Leadership"; Parham, "Unity"; Parham, "Lest We Forget," 6; Parham, *AF* (October 1912): 6; *The Burning Bush*, "Modern Tongues"; *The Burning Bush*, Messenger, "Schism and Tongues"; Messenger, "The 'Tongues' in Zion City."
13. Parham, *TEG*, 72; Messenger, "The 'Tongues' in Zion City."
14. Parham, *AF* (January 1912): 6–7; Parham, *AF* (August 1912): 6; Parham, *KKB*, 82–85, 91–97, 115; Parham, *TEG*, 92–95, 111–17; *AF*, "Annihilation of the Wicked," 2; *AF*, "Pentecost With Signs Following," 1
15. "Modern Tongues," *The Burning Bush*.
16. Parham, "Leadership."
17. Parham, "A Happy New Year To All," *AF* (January 1912): 6; Parham, "Unity."
18. Parham, *AF* (August 1912): 6; Parham, "Lest We Forget"; Parham, "Baptism of the Holy Ghost."
19. Williams reported that Parham made Seymour "conscious of color." Williams, "Black Involvement at Azusa Street Revival"; Parham, *TEG*, 118–19; Parham, "Leadership"; Parham, "Unity"; Parham, *AF* (October 1912): 6; Parham, "Lest We Forget"; Parham, "Free-Love."
20. Parham, *TEG*, 72–73.
21. Emphasis added. Parham, "Leadership"; Parham, "Free Love"; Parham, *AF* (October 1912): 6.
22. Emphases in original. Parham, "Free-Love."
23. Williams, "Black Involvement at Azusa Street Revival."
24. Sarah Parham, *Life of Charles F. Parham*, 147–60, 171–79, 203.
25. Sarah Parham, *Life of Charles F. Parham*, 147–60, 171–79, 203.
26. *AF*, "Pentecost with Signs Following."
27. *AF*, "Pentecost with Signs Following."
28. *AF*, "Pentecost with Signs Following;" *AF* (December 1906): 1. Parham's racial views led Goff to conclude that although, "Parham had demonstrated sensitivity to the spiritual needs of blacks . . . he was hardly an advocate of racial equality . . . he assumed white supremacy and feared miscegenation. The Anglo-Israel theory convinced him that . . . miscegenation could only weaken the bloodlines of this chosen race." He also noted that the "sin of intermarriage" had been the chief cause of Noah's flood and was the "root of all inherited disease and abnormalities up to the present time. When confronted with the lack of racial distinction at Azusa, Parham was personally revolted." See Goff, *Fields White unto Harvest*, 103–4, 130–32; Parham, *KKB*; Parham, *TEG*.
29. *AF*, (December 1906): 1.
30. *AF*, "Annihilation of the Wicked," 2.
31. *AF*, "Beginning of Worldwide Revival," 1; *AF* (February–March 1907): 7.
32. Shumway, "A Study of 'The Gift of Tongues,'" 178; Parham, "Free-Love."
33. Sarah Parham, *The Life of Charles F. Parham*, 142, 161–64; Parham, "Leadership"; Parham, "Unity."
34. Sarah Parham, *The Life of Charles F. Parham*, 142, 161–64; Parham, "Leadership."
35. Parham, "Leadership"; Parham, "Unity."
36. Bartleman, *Azusa Street*, 69; Brumback, *Suddenly . . . from Heaven*, 59.
37. *AF*, "Pentecost with Signs Following," 1.
38. *AF*, "Letter from Bro. Parham," 1; *AF*, "The Old-Time Pentecost," 1.

39. *AF,* "Pentecost Has Come," 1; *AF,* "Letter from Bro. Parham," 1.

40. Goff described Parham's organization as a "kind of loose, freewheeling evangelism program which was ultimately tied to the charismatic personality of Parham himself." He also believes Seymour "officially remained an Apostolic Faith minister in the Texas state division under W. F. Carothers' jurisdiction." Carothers and the Houston Apostolic Faith faction expelled Parham for his alleged moral failings. Parham called Carothers and his followers "driveling, spiritual idiots." Parham, *AF* (November 1912): 7; Parham, "Leadership"; Goff, *Fields White unto Harvest,* 48, 117, 119, 136–40.

41. Seymour, *D&D,* Preface, 8, 12–13, 52.

42. *Los Angeles Herald,* "Zion City Has a New Leader"; *Waukegan Gazette,* "Viola Wants to 'Be Shown'"; *Waukegan Sun,* "Parham Skips Again"; Blumhofer, *Assemblies of God, Vol. 1,* 396n104; Goff, *Fields White unto Harvest,* 223–28.

43. *Los Angeles Herald,* "Zion City Has a New Leader"; *Waukegan Gazette,* "Viola Wants to 'Be Shown'"; *Waukegan Sun,* "Parham Skips Again"; Goff, *Fields White unto Harvest,* 223–28.

44. Carothers, "History of the Apostolic Faith," 1–2; Bell, *Word and Witness,* 3; Parham, "Leadership," 7.

45. Parham, "Free-Love," 4.

46. Goff, *Fields White unto Harvest,* 159.

47. *AF,* "Who May Prophesy?" 2.

48. Seymour, *D&D,* 91; Valdez and Scheer, *Fire on Azusa Street,* 25; *AF,* "Preaching to the Spanish," 4.

49. *A Historical Account of the Apostolic Faith,* 58, 63; "Bubbles," *The Burning Bush.*

50. Crawford, "San Francisco and Oakland," 4; Seymour, "The Marriage Tie," 3; Seymour "To the Married," 3; *AF,* "Questions Answered," 2; Seymour, *D&D,* 83, 86–87; Crayne, *The Mailing List Controversy,* 8–17; Robeck, "Florence Crawford," 224–35; Osterberg, "Oral History."

51. Apostolic Faith, Portland, *A Historical Account of the Apostolic Faith,* 58, 63.

52. Blumhofer, *Assemblies of God, Vol. 1,* 396n104; Goff, *Fields White unto Harvest,* 223–28.

53. *AF,* "Bible Teaching on Marriage and Divorce," 3.

54. *AF,* "Bible Teaching on Marriage and Divorce," 3.

55. *AF,* "Bible Teaching on Marriage and Divorce," 3.

56. Seymour, *D&D,* 91.

57. *AF,* "Fire Falling at Hermon," 3.

58. Bartleman, *Azusa Street,* 58.

59. Jeffries as cited in Orwig, "My First Visit to the Azuzu [sic] Street Pentecostal Mission," 7.

60. Nelson, "For Such a Time as This," 62–64, 213.

CHAPTER 5. WRECKING THE SPIRIT OF AZUSA

1. Bernsten, "Came from China to America for My Pentecost," 3; Studd, *Diary,* 1—entry for Sunday, February 2, 1908; *AF* (October–January 1908): 1; Parham, "Unity;" Parham, "Leadership."

2. Seymour, *D&D,* 47; Bartleman, *Azusa Street,* 57, 68; Studd, *Diary,* entry for February 2, 1908; *AF* (October–January 1908): 1.

3. Seymour, *D&D,* 47; Bartleman, *Azusa Street,* 57, 68; Studd, *Diary,* entry for February 2, 1908; *AF* (October–January 1908): 1.

NOTES FOR CHAPTER 5

4. Bartleman, *Azusa Street*, 68.
5. Bartleman, *Azusa Street*, 57, 68; *AF* (February–March 1907): 2.
6. Studd, *Diary*, January 7–February 2, 1908.
7. Studd, *Diary*, January 7–February 2, 1908.
8. Bundy, "G. T. Haywood," 242–43.
9. Crawford, "San Francisco and Oakland," 4; Cook, "Receiving the Holy Ghost," 2; Cook, "Pentecost in Lamont, Oklahoma," 1; Cook, "Pentecostal Power in Indianapolis," 3.
10. Cook, "Pentecostal Power in Indianapolis," 3.
11. Cook, "Pentecostal Power in Indianapolis," 3.
12. *AF*, "Los Angeles Campmeeting of the Apostolic Faith Missions," 1.
13. Cook, *The Azusa Street Meeting*, 3; Seymour, *Doctrines & Discipline*, 10, 92.
14. *AF* (October–January 1908): 1; Nelson, "For Such a Time as This," 63.
15. Osterberg, "Oral History."
16. Osterberg, "Oral History."
17. Osterberg, "Oral History."
18. Notes from A. G. Osterberg, May 24, 1956; Osterberg, "Oral History"; Nelson, "For Such a Time as This," 64, 216–18.
19. Clemmons, *Bishop C. H. Mason*, 50.
20. Ithiel Clemmons stated Mason told him in 1948, "Seymour told him [Mason] that Clara Lum had privately made it clear that she fell in love with Seymour and wanted him to propose marriage to her. Seymour had tentatively considered the possibility and discussed the matter in its early stages with Mason who advised him not to even think about the idea." Clemmons believes that Seymour had a private ceremony to avoid making Lum feel bad. Lum never married. Clemmons, *Bishop C. H. Mason*, 50. See also David Daniels, "Charles Harrison Mason," 256–70.
21. There are three different dates given for Moore's birthday: see Jennie's marriage and death certificates. Nelson, "For Such a Time as This," 217–18; Blumhofer and Wacker, "Who Edited the Azusa Mission's Apostolic Faith?" 15–21.
22. Osterberg, "Oral History." See Williams, interview by Tinney. This interview was also cited in *Agora*, Winter, 1979.
23. Vanzandt, *Speaking in Tongues*, 37; Nelson, "For Such a Time as This," 217.
24. Sulger, "Delivered from the 'Tongue' Heresy."
25. Williams, interview by James Tinney.
26. Hills, *Hero of Faith and Prayer*, 155, 403–4; Nelson, "For Such a Time as This," 218.
27. Nelson, "For Such a Time as This," 253, 255; Espinosa, "The Holy Ghost Is Here on Earth," 122.
28. Eldridge, *Personal Reminiscences*, 40–41; Nelson, "For Such a Time as This," 219.
29. Lugo, *Pentecostés en Puerto Rico*, 12.
30. Espinosa, "Your Daughters Shall Prophesy," 25–28; Espinosa, "'The Holy Ghost Is Here on Earth," 118–25.
31. The alternative leader and date for the conflict could be Durham, 1911. However, this is unlikely because this passage appears in Bartleman's book before he talks about his trip around the world, which began on March 17, 1910. Notwithstanding this, what's the evidence for 1911? A. C. Valdez wrote that Durham preached at Azusa in 1908–9 and that the revival came to an end (for him) in 1909. This is incorrect. Durham first preached at Azusa in April 1911, though the Second Azusa Revival (as it was called) he led did come to an end that summer. Around 1911 other missions

experienced an upswing in Mexican attendance and around 1911–12 Genaro Valenzuela founded the Spanish Apostolic Faith Mission. Finally, it may help explain why Seymour did not include Mexicans in the leadership of the mission after he revised the Constitution and Articles of Incorporation in 1914. Perhaps he thought they were loyal to Durham rather than himself since some like Valdez's family sided with Durham. Espinosa, "The Holy Ghost Is Here on Earth," 118–25; "Our Spanish Meeting," *The Upper Room,* 1; Pisgah Mission, "Work among Spanish," 11–12; Valdez and Scheer, *Fire on Azusa Street,* 2–26.

32. Fox argues that "Espinosa, Alvarez, and [Daniel] Ramírez all suggest that Seymour rejected the Hispanic contingency [sic], either by not permitting them to speak, or through blatant discrimination" against Latinos. Fox inaccurately implies that Espinosa argued in his article (a) that Seymour was the leader in question in that particular passage of Bartleman's history (145), and (b) that Seymour engaged in "blatant discrimination" against Latinos. However, this is inaccurate and misleading because Espinosa doesn't believe either view. Instead, Espinosa contends that the identity of the leader in question is *unclear* and that Seymour never discriminated against Latinos. This is also why, as a precaution, Espinosa never mentions Seymour by name in the article cited by Fox. Rodgers similarly misrepresents Espinosa's and Ramírez's views when he claims that they described the conflict between Seymour and Latinos as a "racial conflict" driven by possible "racial motives." As already noted, Espinosa never made these claims. Rodgers, "The Assemblies of God and the Long Journey toward Racial Reconciliation," 52. Wood, "This Pentecostal River," 133–34; Robeck, *Colorline Was Washed Away in the Blood,* 13; Klaus, *We've Come This Far,* 130–52, 184–90; Fox, "William J. Seymour," 165; Synan and Fox, Jr., *William J. Seymour,* 144–45.

33. *AF,* January 1907.

34. Nelson, "For Such a Time as This," 269; Sizelove, *A Sparkling Fountain for the Whole Earth,*" 1, 11–12.

35. *The Upper Room,* "Our Spanish Meeting," 1; Pisgah Mission, "Work among Spanish," 11–12; Valdez and Scheer, *Fire on Azusa Street,* 2, 26.

36. Espinosa, "'The Holy Ghost Is Here on Earth," 118–25; *The Upper Room,* "Our Spanish Meeting," 1; Pisgah Mission, "Work among Spanish," 11–12; Valdez and Scheer, *Fire on Azusa Street,* 2, 26.

37. Espinosa, "'The Holy Ghost Is Here on Earth," 118–25.

38. Shumway, "A Study of 'The Gift of Tongues,'" 179; Bartleman, *Azusa Street,* 155; Nelson, "For Such a Time as This," 246–52; Blumhofer, "William H. Durham," in Goff and Wacker, *Portraits of a Generation,* 138–39.

39. Shumway, "A Study of 'The Gift of Tongues,'" 179; Bartleman, *Azusa Street,* 155; Nelson, "For Such a Time as This," 246–52; Blumhofer, "William H. Durham," in Goff and Wacker, *Portraits of a Generation,* 138–39; Durham, "The Great Revival at Azusa Street," 3.

40. Shumway, "A Study of 'The Gift of Tongues,'" 179; Bartleman, *Azusa Street,* 155; Nelson, "For Such a Time as This," 246–52; Blumhofer, "William H. Durham," in Goff and Wacker, *Portraits of a Generation,* 138–39; Durham, "The Great Revival at Azusa Street," 3.

41. Durham, "The Great Revival at Azusa Street," 3.

42. Shumway, "A Study of 'The Gift of Tongues,'" 179; Bartleman, *Azusa Street,* 155; Nelson, "For Such a Time as This," 246–52; Blumhofer, "William H. Durham," in Goff and Wacker, *Portraits of a Generation,* 138–39; Durham, "The Great Revival at Azusa Street," 3.

43. Osterberg, "Oral History"; Nelson, "For Such a Time as This," 252–53.

44. Bartleman, *Azusa Street*, 150–51.
45. Nelson, "For Such a Time as This," 253–55.
46. Nelson, "For Such a Time as This," 253–55.
47. Nelson, "For Such a Time as This," 253–55.

CHAPTER 6. RACE WAR IN THE CHURCHES

1. Nelson, "For Such a Time as This," 241.
2. Seymour, *D&D*, 12, 49.
3. Blumhofer, *Assemblies of God, Vol. 1*, 91.
4. Brathwaite, "Tongues and Ethics."
5. Seymour, *D&D*, 49.
6. *Random House Webster's College Dictionary*, 1040.
7. Sue, *Overcoming Our Racism*, 25, 29.
8. Seymour, *D&D*, 49.
9. Italics added. Seymour, *D&D*, 13.
10. Seymour, *D&D*, 12.
11. Parham, *TEG*, 72–73; Parham, "Leadership"; Parham, *AF* (October 1912): 6; Parham, "Free-Love."
12. Parham, "Greeting: Backward—Forward."
13. Parham, "Free-Love."
14. Seymour, *D&D*, 12.
15. Seymour, *D&D*, 12.
16. Parham, "Leadership."
17. Bartleman, *Azusa Street*, 101, 156; Nelson, "For Such a Time as This," 254.
18. Parham visited southern California in: (1) the winter of 1907; (2) January 12 to around April 16, 1908—he began meetings and possibly a church plant—in Los Angeles at the same WCTU building where he set up a rival Azusa Mission in October 1906; (3) December 10, 1911, to January 31, 1912—he held revival services in Perris and then Los Angeles in February until right before July 14; and (4) January until at least February 20, 1913. Parham, "Fanaticism: Flesh and Familiar Spirits"; Parham, "The Sealing"; Parham, "A Happy New Year To All"; *AF (Baxter Springs)*, "Meeting in the Apostolic Faith Mission," 1–2; Parham, "Leadership"; Parham, "Unity"; Parham, "Lest We Forget"; Parham, "The Pentecostal Baptism Restored"; Parham, *AF* (August 1912): 6; Parham, "Camp Meeting Snap Shots"; Parham, *AF* (October 1912): 6; Parham, "Baptism of the Holy Ghost," *AF* (October 1912): 9–10; Parham, "Free-Love," 4–5; Parham, "Greeting: Backward—Forward"; Sarah Parham, *Life of Charles F. Parham*, 203, 237–45, 293.
19. Seymour, *D&D*, 5.
20. Boddy, "A Meeting at the Azusa Street Mission, Los Angeles," 244.
21. Seymour, *D&D*, 10–12, 47.
22. Seymour, *D&D*, 10–12, 47.
23. Nelson, "For Such a Time as This," 264–73.
24. Nelson, "For Such a Time as This," 256–58; Goff, *Fields White unto Harvest*, 157; Katz, *Eyewitness*, 389–90; Bernstein, *First Waco Horror*.
25. Goff, *Fields White unto Harvest*, 157; Katz, *Eyewitness*, 389–90; Bernstein, *First Waco Horror*.
26. Voogd, *Race Riots and Resistance*; Franklin, *From Slavery to Freedom*, 354–67.
27. Gerstle, "Race and Nation in the Thought and Politics of Woodrow Wilson," 93–113; Goff, *Fields White Unto Harvest*, 157.

28. Seymour, *D&D*, 10.
29. Wacker, *Heaven Below*, 227, 234–35.
30. Parham, *AF* (October 1912): 6.
31. Jacobsen, *Thinking in the Spirit;* Hollenweger, *Pentecostals;* Nelson, "For Such a Time as This"; Goff, *Fields White unto Harvest;* Blumhofer, *Assemblies of God, Vol. 1.*
32. Lawrence, *Apostolic Faith Restored;* Brumback, *Suddenly . . . from Heaven;* Menzies, *Anointed to Serve;* Synan, *Holiness-Pentecostal Tradition,* 167–86.
33. Nelson, "For Such a Time as This," 161–66.
34. Blumhofer and Wacker, "Who Edited the Azusa Mission's Apostolic Faith?" 15–21.
35. Seymour, *D&D*, 40.
36. *AF*, "The Same Old Way," 3.
37. Jennie Seymour, Marriage Certificate.
38. Bauerlein, *Negrophobia;* Burns, *Rage in the Gate City.*
39. *AF*, "Bible Pentecost," 1.
40. *AF*, "Bible Pentecost," 1.
41. Emphasis added; *AF* (December 1906): 1; Parham, *KKB*, 83–85.
42. Nelson, Interview with Ms. Mattie Cummings; Nelson, "For Such a Time as This," 234.
43. Du Bois, "The Talented Tenth."
44. *AF* (December 1906): 1.
45. As cited in Nelson, "For Such a Time as This," 235.
46. *AF*, "Beginning of World Wide Revival," 1.
47. Emphasis added, *AF* (February-March 1907): 7.
48. *AF*, "Pentecost with Signs Following," 1; Seymour, *D&D*, 52.
49. Seymour, *D&D*, 12, 47–50.
50. Seymour, *D&D*, 10–12.
51. Seymour, *D&D*, 10–13, emphasis added.
52. Seymour, *D&D*, 12, 29.
53. Bartleman, *Azusa Street*, 54.
54. Orwig, "My First Visit to the Azuzu Street Pentecostal Mission," 7.
55. Cashwell, "Came 3,000 Miles for His Pentecost," 3; Nelson, "For Such a Time as This," 51, 198; Synan, *Holiness-Pentecostal Tradition*, 123–29.
56. Robeck, *Azusa Street Mission and Revival*, 125–26; *Los Angeles Daily Times*, "Weird Babel of Tongues."
57. *Indianapolis News*, 5 June 1907; *Indianapolis Star*, "Negro Bluks Blow: Why? Husband May Know"; *Indianapolis Star*, "Oddy Asks Divorce Because of Bluks."
58. *Indianapolis News*, 5 June 1907; *Indianapolis Star*, "Negro Bluks Blow: Why? Husband May Know"; *Indianapolis Star*, "Oddy Asks Divorce Because of Bluks."
59. Parham, "Free-Love."
60. Parham, *TEG*, 118; Parham, "Leadership"; Parham, "A Happy New Year to All," 6.
61. Parham, "Leadership."
62. Parham, "The Pentecostal Baptism Restored."
63. Parham, "Leadership"; Parham, "Unity"; Nelson, "For Such a Time as This," 208.
64. Parham, *TEG*, 72–73; Parham, "Leadership"; Parham, "Unity"; Parham, "Free-Love."
65. Seymour, *D&D*, 52, 82.

66. Seymour, *D&D*, Preface.
67. Seymour, *D&D*, 92.
68. Seymour, *D&D*, 10–12.
69. Seymour, *D&D*, 40–43.
70. Seymour, *D&D*, 40–41.
71. Synan, *Holiness-Pentecostal Tradition*, 173–86.

CHAPTER 7. WE DON'T BELIEVE IN RELICS

1. Shumway, "A Study of 'The Gift of Tongues,'" 178–79; Nelson, "For Such a Time as This," 262.
2. A cross-burning delegation of the KKK walked down the aisle of Raymond Richie's tent revival—Flower Pentecostal Heritage Archives: P8707-Richey. Du Bois, *The Crisis* (January 1915): 119–20; Nelson, "For Such a Time as This," 262–63.
3. Nelson, "For Such a Time as This," 262–63.
4. Driver and Bryant, Minutes of the 12th General Convocation of the Church of God in Christ; Nelson, "For Such a Time as This," 262–63.
5. Nelson, "For Such a Time as This," 262–63.
6. Nelson, "For Such a Time as This," 267.
7. Driver and Bryant, Minutes of the 12th General Convocation of the Church of God in Christ; Nelson, "For Such a Time as This," 267.
8. Nelson, "For Such a Time as This," 268–70.
9. Nelson, "For Such a Time as This," 269–70.
10. Nelson, "For Such a Time as This," 268–70.
11. *The Bridegroom's Messenger*, "Home-Going of Rev. W. J. Seymore [sic]," 4; *The Pentecostal Herald*, "Brother Seymour Called Home," 1.
12. Nelson, "For Such a Time as This," 270.
13. Goff, *Fields White unto Harvest*, 159.
14. *Pentecostal Herald*, "Brother Seymour Called Home," 1.
15. *Voice in the Wilderness*, "Death of W. J. Seymour," 7.
16. Nelson, "For Such a Time as This," 270.
17. *Pentecostal Herald*, "A Great Unity Conference," 1.
18. Nelson, "For Such a Time as This," 272–73.
19. Nelson, "For Such a Time as This," 272–73.
20. Bloch-Hoell, *The Pentecostal Movement*, 39.
21. Nelson, "For Such a Time as This," 273–74.
22. Nelson, "For Such a Time as This," 273–74.
23. Nelson, "For Such a Time as This," 273–74.

CONCLUSION. HOLY RESTLESSNESS AND CRACKING BOTTLES

1. Shumway, "A Study of 'The Gift of Tongues,'" 191–92.
2. See also David Daniels, "Charles Harrison Mason," 256–70; Synan, *Holiness Pentecostal-Movement*.
3. Parham, "Leadership"; Seymour, *D&D*, 12.
4. Seymour, *D&D*, 10.
5. Parham, "Leadership"; Seymour, *D&D*, 12.
6. Lewis, *W.E.B. Du Bois, 1868–1919: Biography of a Race*, 406, 468–70.
7. Cone, *Martin and Malcolm*, 125, 214.
8. Du Bois, "The Talented Tenth."

BIBLIOGRAPHY

ABBREVIATION FOR COMMONLY USED PUBLICATIONS

AF	*Apostolic Faith*, published by William J. Seymour in Los Angeles from 1906 to 1908.
AF (Baxter Springs)	*Apostolic Faith*, published by Charles Parham in Baxter Springs, Kansas.
AF (Houston)	*Apostolic Faith*, published by W. F. Carothers in Houston, Texas.
AF (Portland)	*Apostolic Faith*, published by Clara Lum in Portland, Oregon, 1908–12.
NIDPCM	Stanley M. Burgess and Eduard M. Van Der Maas, eds., *New International Dictionary of Pentecostal and Charismatic Movements*. Grand Rapids, MI: Zondervan, 2002.

All abbreviated *AF* entries refer to Seymour's Los Angeles–based newspaper unless otherwise noted.

SOURCES

Abrams, Minnie. *The Baptism of the Holy Ghost and Fire,* 2nd edition. Pandita Ramabai Mukti Mission, December 1906.

Ahonen, L., with J. E. Johannesson. "Sweden." *NIDPCM*, 255.

Alexander, Estrelda. *Black Fire: One Hundred Years of African American Pentecostalism.* (Downers Grove, IL: IVP Academic, 2011).

Alvarsson, Jan-Åke. "Scandinavian Pentecostalism." In William K. Kay and Anne E. Dyer, eds., *European Pentecostalism*, 19–39 (Leiden: Academic Brill, 2011).

Anderson, Allan. "The Dubious Legacy of Charles Parham: Racism and Cultural Insensitivities among Pentecostals." *Pneuma* 27, no. 1 (spring 2005): 51–64.

Anderson, Allan. *Spreading Fires: The Missionary Nature of Early Pentecostalism.* Maryknoll, NY: Orbis Books, 2007.

Anderson, Allan. *An Introduction to Pentecostalism: Global Charismatic Christianity*, 2nd ed. Cambridge, UK: Cambridge University Press, 2013.

Anderson, Robert Mapes. *Vision of the Disinherited: The Making of American Pentecostalism* (Peabody, MA: Hendrickson Publishers, 1979).

Apostolic Faith (Los Angeles)—Paper edited by William Seymour, Glenn Cook, Clara Lum, and others.

Apostolic Faith (Los Angeles). "Pentecost Has Come." *AF* (September 1906): 1.
Apostolic Faith (Los Angeles). "The Old-Time Pentecost." *AF* (September 1906): 1.
Apostolic Faith (Los Angeles). "Bro. Seymour's Call." *AF* (September 1906): 1
Apostolic Faith (Los Angeles). "Letter from Bro. Parham." *AF* (September 1906): 1.
Apostolic Faith (Los Angeles). Editorial. *AF* (September 1906): 1.
Apostolic Faith (Los Angeles). *AF* (September 1906): 1.
Apostolic Faith (Los Angeles). "Tongues as a Sign." *AF* (September 1906): 2.
Apostolic Faith (Los Angeles). "The Promise Still Good." *AF* (September 1906): 2.
Apostolic Faith (Los Angeles). "Los Angeles, Aug. 12, 1906." *AF* (September 1906): 2.
Apostolic Faith (Los Angeles). *AF* (September 1906): 3.
Apostolic Faith (Los Angeles). "The Millennium." *AF* (September 1906): 3.
Apostolic Faith (Los Angeles). "Fire Falling at Hermon." *AF* (September 1906): 3.
Apostolic Faith (Los Angeles). "The Same Old Way. *AF* (September 1906): 3.
Apostolic Faith (Los Angeles). "Jesus Is Coming." *AF* (September 1906): 4.
Apostolic Faith (Los Angeles). "Russians Hear in Their Own Tongue." *AF* (September 1906): 4.
Apostolic Faith (Los Angeles). "Missionaries to Jerusalem." *AF* (September 1906): 4.
Apostolic Faith (Los Angeles). "Good News from Danville, VA." *AF* (September 1906): 4.
Apostolic Faith (Los Angeles). "Ascension Robes." *AF* (September 1906): 4
Apostolic Faith (Los Angeles). "The Ten Virgins." *AF* (September 1906): 4.
Apostolic Faith (Los Angeles). "The Pentecostal Baptism Restored: The Promised Latter Rain Now Being Poured Out on God's Humble People." *AF* (October 1906): 1.
Apostolic Faith (Los Angeles). "Fire Still Falling." *AF* (October 1906): 1.
Apostolic Faith (Los Angeles). "Shall We Reject Jesus' Last Words?" *AF* (October 1906): 3.
Apostolic Faith (Los Angeles). "A Message of His Coming." *AF* (October 1906): 3.
Apostolic Faith (Los Angeles). "Chinese Want The Gospel of the Bible." *AF* (October 1906): 3.
Apostolic Faith (Los Angeles). "One Church." *AF* (October 1906): 3–4.
Apostolic Faith (Los Angeles). "Back to Pentecost." *AF* (October 1906): 4.
Apostolic Faith (Los Angeles). "Apostolic Faith, 312 Azusa Street" [Masthead], *AF* (October 1906): 4.
Apostolic Faith (Los Angeles). "Spreads the Fire." *AF* (October 1906): 4.
Apostolic Faith (Los Angeles). "Pentecost in India." *AF* (November 1906): 1.
Apostolic Faith (Los Angeles). "Bible Pentecost." *AF* (November 1906): 1.
Apostolic Faith (Los Angeles). "Came from Alaska." *AF* (November 1906): 2.
Apostolic Faith (Los Angeles). "The Lord Led Her." *AF* (November 1906): 3.
Apostolic Faith (Los Angeles). "Sanctification and Power." *AF* (November 1906): 4.
Apostolic Faith (Los Angeles). "Preaching to the Spanish." *AF* (November 1906): 4.
Apostolic Faith (Los Angeles). "Pentecost with Signs Following." *AF* (December 1906): 1.
Apostolic Faith (Los Angeles). "Pentecost in San Jose." *AF* (December 1906): 1.
Apostolic Faith (Los Angeles). *AF* (December 1906): 1.
Apostolic Faith (Los Angeles). "Started for Africa." *AF* (December 1906): 3.
Apostolic Faith (Los Angeles). "From Los Angeles to Foreign Fields." *AF* (December 1906): 4.
Apostolic Faith (Los Angeles). "Revival in India, Wonderful Pouring Out of God's Spirit among the Natives of the Khassia Hills." *AF* (December 1906): 4.

Apostolic Faith (Los Angeles). "Beginning of World Wide Revival." *AF* (January 1907): 1.
Apostolic Faith (Los Angeles). "Behold the Bridegroom Cometh!" *AF* (January 1907): 1.
Apostolic Faith (Los Angeles). "God Is His Own Interpreter." *AF* (January 1907): 2.
Apostolic Faith (Los Angeles). "The Church Question." *AF* (January 1907): 2.
Apostolic Faith (Los Angeles). "Received Her Pentecost: Testimony of Mrs. Myrtle K. Shideler written in New York on her way to Africa." *AF* (January 1907): 2.
Apostolic Faith (Los Angeles). "Annihilation of the Wicked." *AF* (January 1907): 2.
Apostolic Faith (Los Angeles). "Latest Report from our Missionaries to Africa." *AF* (January 1907): 3.
Apostolic Faith (Los Angeles). "Bible Teaching on Marriage and Divorce." *AF* (January 1907): 3.
Apostolic Faith (Los Angeles). *AF* (January 1907): 3.
Apostolic Faith (Los Angeles). *AF* (January 1907): 4.
Apostolic Faith (Los Angeles). "The Salvation of Jesus." *AF* (January 1907): 4.
Apostolic Faith (Los Angeles). *AF* (February–March 1907): 1.
Apostolic Faith (Los Angeles). *AF* (February–March 1907): 2.
Apostolic Faith (Los Angeles). "Demons Cast Out." *AF* (February–March 1907): 3.
Apostolic Faith (Los Angeles). *AF* (February–March 1907): 7.
Apostolic Faith (Los Angeles). "In Africa." *AF* (April 1907): 1.
Apostolic Faith (Los Angeles). "Los Angeles Campmeeting of the Apostolic Faith Missions." *AF* (May 1907): 1.
Apostolic Faith (Los Angeles). "At Azusa Mission." *AF* (May 1907): 2.
Apostolic Faith (Los Angeles). "Manifestations of the Spirit in India." *AF* (June–September 1907): 4.
Apostolic Faith (Los Angeles). "Questions Answered." *AF* (October 1907–January 1908): 2.
Apostolic Faith (Los Angeles). "Testimony of a Sunday School Teacher." *AF* (October 1907–January 1908): 1.
Apostolic Faith (Los Angeles). "Testimony of a Yorkshire Farmer." *AF* (October 1907–January 1908): 1.
Apostolic Faith (Los Angeles). *AF* (October 1907–January 1908): 1.
Apostolic Faith (Los Angeles). "Two Works of Grace and the Gift of the Holy Spirit." *AF* (September 1906): 3.
Apostolic Faith (Los Angeles). "Good Tidings of Great Joy: Pentecostal in Many Lands—News of Salvation—Jesus Son Coming." *AF* (October 1907–January 1908): 1.
Apostolic Faith (Los Angeles). "Pentecostal Missionary Reports." *AF* (October 1907–January 1908): 1.
Apostolic Faith (Los Angeles). "Germany." *AF* (October 1907–January 1908): 1.
Apostolic Faith (Los Angeles). "China Missionary Receives Pentecost." Apostolic Faith (October 1907–January 1908): 3.
Apostolic Faith (Los Angeles). "Bible Pentecost." *AF* (November 1906): 1.
Apostolic Faith (Los Angeles). "From the Bible School in Mukti, India." *AF* (January 1908): 2.
Apostolic Faith (Los Angeles). "Pentecostal Outpouring in Scotland." *AF* (May 1908): 1.
Apostolic Faith (Los Angeles). "India." *AF* (May 1908): 1.
Apostolic Faith (Los Angeles). "Pentecost in Australia." *AF* (May 1908): 1.

Apostolic Faith (Los Angeles). "Cheng Ting, Fu, Chih-li, North China, B. Bernsten and R. Hess." *AF* (May 1908): 4.
Apostolic Faith (Los Angeles). "God Heals in India." *AF* (May 1908): 4.
Apostolic Faith (Los Angeles). "Chinese Filled with the Holy Spirit." *AF* (May 1908): 4.
Apostolic Faith (Los Angeles). "Missionaries to Johannesburg, South Africa." *AF* (May 1908): 4.
Apostolic Faith (Portland)—Paper edited by Florence Crawford and Clara Lum
Apostolic Faith (Portland). "Who May Prophesy." *AF* (January 1908): 2.
Apostolic Faith (Portland) "Other Manifestations." *AF* (July–August 1908): 1.
Apostolic Faith (Portland). *AF* (July–August 1908): 1.
Apostolic Faith (Portland). "Poured Out on the Humble People of God All Over the World." *AF* (July–August 1908): 1.
Apostolic Faith (Portland). "The Promised Latter Rain, Poured Out on the Humble People of God All Over the World." *AF* (July–August 1908): 1.
Apostolic Faith (Portland). "How India Received Pentecost." *AF* (July–August 1908): 3.
Apostolic Faith (Portland). "A Late Report from Bombay." *AF* (July–August 1908): 3.
Apostolic Faith (Portland). "How India Received Pentecost." *AF* (July–August 1908): 3.
Apostolic Faith (Portland). "Hundreds of Native Girls Baptized." *AF* (July–August 1908): 3.
Apostolic Faith (Portland). "How Pentecost Came to China." *AF* (July–August 1908): 4.
Apostolic Faith (Portland). "In Hong Kong 25 Were Baptized." *AF* (July–August 1908): 4.
Apostolic Faith (Portland). "A Chinese Brother Writes of the Plague." *AF* (July–August 1908): 4.
Apostolic Faith (Portland). *AF* (August–September 1908): 3.
Apostolic Faith (Portland). "Pentecost in South Africa." *AF* (September 1908): 1.
Apostolic Faith (Portland). "South Africa." *AF* (January 1909): 1.
Apostolic Faith (Portland). "Germany." *AF* (January 1909): 1.
Apostolic Faith (Portland). "Assiout, Egypt." *AF* (January 1909): 1.
Apostolic Faith (Portland). "Amsterdam, Holland." *AF* (January 1909): 1.
Apostolic Faith (Portland). "Scotland, England and Ireland." *AF* (January 1909): 1.
Apostolic Faith (Portland). "India." *AF* (January 1909): 1.
Apostolic Faith (Portland). "Baptismal Service in Sweden." *AF* (May–June 1909): 3.
Apostolic Faith (Portland). "The Dead Raised." *AF* (August–September 1909): 1.
Apostolic Faith (Portland). "Pentecost among the Zulu and Basuto People in South Africa." *AF* (August–September 1909): 1.
Apostolic Faith (Portland). "Cape Colony, South Africa." *AF* (October 1909): 4
Apostolic Faith (Portland). "Johannesburg, S. Africa." *AF* (October 1909): 4.
Apostolic Faith (Portland). "Pretoria, Transvaal, S. Africa." *AF* (October 1909): 4.
Apostolic Faith (Portland). "Signs and Wonders Following the Work in South Africa." *AF* (March–April 1910): 1.
Apostolic Faith (Portland). "Missionary Life among the Natives." *AF* (March–April 1910): 1.
Apostolic Faith (Portland). *AF* (March–April 1910): 2.
Apostolic Faith (Portland). "Egypt." *AF* (March–April 1910): 1.

Apostolic Faith (Portland). "Grovesend, Wales." *AF* (March–April 1910): 1.
Apostolic Faith (Portland). "Wales." *AF* (March–April 1910): 1.
Apostolic Faith (Portland). "Amsterdam." *AF* (March–April 1910): 1.
Apostolic Faith (Portland). "Pentecostal Revival in India." *AF* (March–April 1910): 4.
Apostolic Faith (Portland). "Meeting in the Apostolic Faith Mission." *AF* (March 1912): 1–2.
Apostolic Faith (Portland). *A Historical Account of The Apostolic Faith: A Trinitarian—Fundamental Evangelistic Organization*. Portland, OR: Apostolic Faith, 1965.
Barclay, John. "A Policeman Receives Pentecost." *AF* (May 1908): 1.
Barratt, David B., George Thomas Kurian, and Todd M. Johnson, eds. *World Christian Encyclopedia: A Comparative Survey of Churches and Religions in the Modern World*. New York: Oxford University Press, 2001.
Barratt, Sister. "All These Cannot Be Hypnotized." *AF* (July–August 1908): 3.
Barratt, Sister. "Witnesses in England, Children Receive Pentecost." *AF* (October–January 1908): 1.
Barratt, T. B. *The Work of T.B. Barratt*. New York: Garland, 1985.
Barratt, T. B. "In Norway," 1.
Bartleman, Frank. *Azusa Street: The Roots of Modern-day Pentecost*. S. Plainfield, NJ: Bridge, [1925] 1980.
Bass, Bernard M. and Ronald E. Riggio, *Transformational Leadership*. 2nd Ed. New York: Taylor & Francis Group Psychology Press, 2006.
Batman, Daisy. "En Route to Africa." *AF* (December 1906):4.
Batman, Daisy. "Mrs. Daisy Batman's Testimony." *AF* (December 1906): 4.
Batman, G. W. "Bro. G.W. Batman's Testimony." *AF* (December 1906): 4.
Bauerlein, Mark. *Negrophobia: A Race Riot in Atlanta, 1906*. New York: Encounter Books, 2002.
Bays, D. H., and T. M. Johnson, "China." *NIDPCM*, 58–64.
Bell, E. N. *Word and Witness*. (Malvern, Arkansas) (October 20, 1912): 3.
Bendroth, Margaret Lamberts, and Virginia Lieson Brereton. *Women and Twentieth-Century Protestantism*, eds. Chicago: University of Illinois Press, 2002.
Bennett, Dennis J. *Nine O'Clock in the Morning*. Alachua, FL: Bridge Logos Foundation, 1970.
Bergunder, Michael. *The South Indian Pentecostal Movement in the Twentieth Century*. Grand Rapids, MI: Eerdmans, 2008.
Bernstein, Patricia. *The First Waco Horror: The Lynching of Jesse Washington and the Rise of the NAACP*. College Station: Texas A&M Press, 2006.
Bernsten, B. "Came From China to America for Pentecost." *AF* (January 1908): 3.
Bernsten, B. "Cheng Ting Fu, North China." *AF* (P) (January 1909): 1.
Bloch-Hoell, Nils. *The Pentecostal Movement*. Oslo, Norway: Universitetsforlaget, 1964.
Blumhofer, Edith L. *The Assemblies of God: A Chapter in the Story of American Pentecostalism, Volume 1–To 1941*. Springfield, MO: Gospel Publishing House, 1989.
Blumhofer, Edith L. "William H. Durham: Years of Creativity, Years of Dissent." In James R. Goff and Grant Wacker, eds., *Portraits of a Generation: Early Pentecostal Leaders*, 123–42. Fayetteville: University of Arkansas Press, 2002.
Blumhofer, Edith L., and Grant Wacker, "Who Edited the Azusa Mission's Apostolic Faith?" *A/G Heritage* (summer 2001): 15–21.
Boddy, Alexander A. "Pentecost in England." *AF* (May 1907): 1.

Boddy, Alexander A. "Reports from England." *AF* (June to September 1907): 1.
Boddy, Alexander A. "Mission Day at Stouffville Camp Meeting." *Confidence* (July 1909): 147.
Boddy, Alexander A. "Across the Atlantic (Pentecostal Experiences): From Canada to the States." *Confidence* (August 1909): 176.
Boddy, Alexander A. Editorial. *Confidence* (September 1912): 209–12.
Boddy, Alexander A. "At Los Angeles, California." *Confidence* (October 1912): 232–34.
Boddy, Alexander A. "A Meeting at the Azusa Street Mission, Los Angeles." *Confidence* (November 1912): 244–45.
Boddy, Mrs. A. A. "Testimony of a Vicar's Wife." *AF* (October to January 1908): 1
Booze, J. "Africa, North, and the Middle East." *NIDPCM*, 6–7.
Borlase, Craig. *William J. Seymour: A Biography*. Lake Mary, FL: Charisma House, 2006.
Brand, Lady. "Brandenburg, Lady Brand, O. R. C., South Africa." *AF* (Portland) (March and April 1910): 3.
Brathwaite, Rene. "Tongues and Ethics: William J. Seymour and the 'Bible Evidence': A Response to Cecil M. Robeck, Jr." *Pneuma* 32 (2010): 203–22.
Braude, Ann. *Radical Spirits: Spiritualism and Women's Rights in Nineteenth-Century America*. Boston, MA: Beacon Press, 1989.
Brelsford, G. S. "Missionaries to Egypt." *AF* (May 1908): 4.
Bresee, Phineas. "The Gift of Tongues." *Nazarene Messenger*, 13 December 1906.
Bridegroom Messenger, "Home-Going of Rev. W. J. Seymore." No. 21 (Atlanta, GA, 1922): 4.
Bridwell, C. W. "Fanatical Sect in Los Angeles Claims Gift of Tongues." *Rocky Mountain Pillar of Fire*, 13 June 1906.
Brumback, Carl. *Suddenly . . . from Heaven*. Springfield, MO: Gospel Publishing House, 1961.
Bundy, David. "Bibliography and Historiography of Pentecostalism Outside of North America." In Stanley M. Burgess and Eduard M. Van Der Maas, eds., *The New International Dictionary of Pentecostal and Charismatic Movements*, 405–17. Grand Rapids, MI: Zondervan, 1992.
Bundy, David. "G. T. Haywood: Religion for Urban Realities." In James R. Goff and Grant Wacker, eds., *Portraits of a Generation: Early Pentecostal Leaders*, 237–53, 410–11. Fayetteville: University of Arkansas Press, 2002.
Bundy, David. "Barratt, Thomas Ball." *NIDPCM*, 365.
Bundy, David. "Boddy, Alexander Alfred." *NIDPCM*, 436–37.
Bundy, David. "Hoover, Willis Collins." *NIDPCM*, 770.
Burgess, Stanley M., and Gary B. McGee, eds. *The New International Dictionary of Pentecostal and Charismatic Movements*. Grand Rapids, MI: Zondervan, 1992.
Burning Bush. "The Gift of Tongues." 13 September 1906.
Burning Bush. "Bubbles." 15 November 1906.
Burning Bush. "Garrs in India." 4 April 1907.
Burning Bush. "The Tongues." 2 May 1907.
Burning Bush. "Modern Tongues." 23 May 1907.
Burning Bush. "Tongues Mix-Up." 21 November 1907.
Burns, James MacGregor. *Leadership*. New York: HarperPerennial, 1978.
Burns, Rebecca. *Rage in the Gate City: The Story of the 1906 Atlanta Race Riot*. New York: Emmis Books, 2006.

Butler, Anthea. *Women in the Church of God in Christ: Making a Sanctified World*. Charlotte: University of North Carolina Press, 2007.
Campbell, J. G. "History of the Apostolic Faith Movement: Origin, Projector, etc." *The Apostolic Faith* (Goose Creek, TX) (May 1921): 7.
Campbell, Marne. "'The Newest Religious Sect Has Started in Los Angeles': Race, Class, Ethnicity, and the Origins of the Pentecostal Movement, 1906–1913." *Journal of African American History* 95, no. 1 (winter 2010): 1–25.
Cantú, Ernesto S., and José Ortega. *Historia de la Asamblea Apostólica de la fe en Cristo Jesús, 1916–1966*. Mentone, CA: Sal's Printing Service, 1966.
Carothers, W. F. "History of the Movement: A Brief Statement of the Origin and Spread of the Present Pentecostal and Accompanying Movement." *AF* (Houston) (October 1908): 1–2.
Carothers, W. F. "Church Government." *AF* (Houston) (1909): 61–63.
Cashwell, G. B. "Came 3,000 Miles for His Pentecost." *AF* (December 1906): 3.
Cerillo, Gus, and Grant Wacker, "Bibliography and Historiography of Pentecostalism in the United States." *NIDPCM*, 382–402.
Chi, Bro. Mok Lai. "Hong Kong, China." *AF* (Portland) (January 1909): 1.
Christenson, Larry. *Speaking in Tongues*. Minneapolis, MN: Bethany House, 1987.
Clark, Otis G., and Gwendolyn Williams. *The Azusa Mission*. Bixby, OK: Holiness Mission Publishing, 1993.
Clemmons, Bishop Ithiel C. *Bishop C. H. Mason and the Roots of the Church of God in Christ*. Bakersfield, CA: Pneuma Life Publishing, 1996.
Colletti, J. "Berg, Daniel." *NIDPCM*, 370–71.
Cone, James. *Martin & Malcolm & America: A Dream or a Nightmare*. 2nd Ed. Maryknoll, New York: Orbis Books, 1993.
Conger, Jay. *The Charismatic Leader: Behind the Mystique of Exceptional Leadership*. San Francisco: Jossey-Bass Publishers, 1989.
Cook, Glenn A. "Receiving the Holy Ghost." *AF*, (LA) (November 1906): 2.
Cook, Glenn A. "Pentecost in Lamont, Oklahoma." *AF* (LA) (January 1907): 1.
Cook, Glenn A. "Pentecostal Power in Indianapolis." *AF* (February–March, 1907): 3.
Cook, Glenn A. *The Azusa Street Meetings: Some Highlights of this Outpouring*. Belvedere, CA: Belvedere Christian Mission, ca. 1920.
Cornelius, Lucille J. *The Pioneer: History of the Church of God in Christ*. San Francisco, CA: privately published, 1975.
Corum, Fred T., and Hazel Bakewell. *The Sparkling Fountain*. Windsor, OH: Corum & Associates, [1983] 1989.
Cotton, "Mother" Emma. "Inside Story of the Outpouring of the Holy Spirit, Azusa Street, 1906." *Message of the Apostolic Faith* 1, no. 1 (April 1939): 1–4.
Cox, Harvey. *Fire from Heaven: The Rise of Pentecostal Spirituality and the Reshaping of Religion in the Twenty-First Century*. Reading, MA: Addison-Wesley, 1995.
Crawford, Florence. "San Francisco and Oakland." *AF* (December 1906): 4
Crayne, Richard. *Pentecostal Outpouring*. Morristown, TN: Richard Crayne, [1963] 1994.
Crayne, Richard. *The Mailing List Controversy*. Morristown, TN: Richard Crayne, 2004.
Creech, Joe. "Visions of Glory: The Place of the Azusa Street Revival in Pentecostal History." *Church History* (September 1996): 405–24.
Crossing, Peter, and Todd Johnson, *World Christian Database*. Leiden: Brill Online, 2012.

Daniels, David. "Charles Harrison Mason: The Interracial Impulse of Early Pentecostalism." In James R. Goff and Grant Wacker, eds., *Portraits of a Generation: Early Pentecostal Leaders,* 254–70, 411–13. Fayetteville: University of Arkansas Press, 2002.

Dayton, Donald. *Theological Roots of Pentecostalism.* Metuchen, NJ: The Scarecrow Press, 1987.

De Leon, Victor. *The Silent Pentecostals: A Biographical History of the Pentecostal Movement among Hispanics in the Twentieth-Century.* Taylors, SC: Faith Printing, 1979.

Dias, Elizabeth. "Revealed: President Obama's Daily Email Devotional," TIME *Swampland blog,* October 20, 2013, http://swampland.time.com/2013/10/20/revealed-president-obamas-daily-email-devotionals/.

Dove, Stephen. "Hymnody and Liturgy in the Azusa Street Revival, 1906–1908." *Pneuma* 31 (2009): 242–63.

Driver, E. R., and J. E. Bryant, *Minutes of the 12th General Convocation of the Church of God in Christ, Memphis, Tennessee* (December 10, 1919).

Du Bois, W.E.B. "The Talented Tenth." In *The Negro Problem: A Series of Articles by Representative American Negroes of To-day,* 33. New York: James Pott, 1903.

Du Bois, W.E.B. *The Crisis.* (January 1915): 119–20.

Dupree, Sherry Sherrod. *Biographical Dictionary of African-American Holiness—Pentecostals, 1880–1990.* Moorestown, NJ: Middle Atlantic Regional Press, 1989.

Durham, William H. "A Chicago Evangelist's Pentecost." *AF* (February–March 1907): 4.

Durham, William H. "The Great Revival at Azusa Street—How it Began and How it Ended." *Pentecostal Testimony* (ca. 1912): 3–4.

Eldridge, George N. *Personal Reminiscences,* 1931: 40–41.

Eliade, Mircea. *The Quest: History and Meaning in Religion.* Chicago: University of Chicago Press, 1984.

Espinosa, Gastón. "Borderland Religion: Los Angeles and the Origins of the Latino Pentecostal Movement in the U.S., Mexico, and Puerto Rico, 1900–1945." Ph.D., diss., University of California, Santa Barbara, 1999.

Espinosa, Gastón. "Francisco Olazábal: Charisma, Power, and Faith Healing in the Borderlands." In James R. Goff and Grant Wacker, eds., *Portraits of a Generation: Early Pentecostal Leaders,* 177–97, 400–404. Fayetteville: University of Arkansas Press, 2002.

Espinosa, Gastón. "'Your Daughters Shall Prophesy': A History of Women in Ministry in the Latino Pentecostal Movement in the United States." In Margaret Lamberts Bendroth and Virginia Lieson Brereton, eds., *Women and Twentieth-Century Protestantism,* 25–48. Urbana and Chicago: University of Illinois Press, 2002.

Espinosa, Gastón. "The Pentecostalization of Latin American and U.S. Latino Christianity." *Pneuma: The Journal of the Society for Pentecostal Studies* 26, no. 2 (fall 2004): 262–92.

Espinosa, Gastón. "Ordinary Prophet: William J. Seymour and the Azusa Street Revival." In Cecil M. Robeck and Harold Hunter, eds., *The Azusa Street Revival and Its Legacy,* 29–60. Cleveland, TN: Pathway Press, 2006.

Espinosa, Gastón. "'The Holy Ghost Is Here on Earth': The Latino Contributions to the Azusa Street Revival." *Enrichment Journal* 11, no. 2 (spring 2006): 118–26.

Espinosa, Gastón. ed. *Religion and the American Presidency: George Washington*

to George W. Bush with Commentary and Primary Sources. New York: Columbia University Press, 2009.
Espinosa, Gastón. ed. *Religion, Race, and the American Presidency*. Lanham, MD: Rowman & Littlefield, 2011.
Espinosa, Gastón, ed. *Religion, Race, and Barack Obama's New Democratic Pluralism*. New York: Routledge, 2013.
Espinosa, Gastón. *Latino Pentecostals in America: Faith and Politics in Action*. Cambridge, MA: Harvard University Press, 2014.
Feston, Paul. *Evangelicals and Politics in Asia, Africa, and Latin America*. Cambridge, UK: Cambridge University Press, 2004.
Fidler, Richard L. "Historical Review of the Pentecostal Outpouring in Los Angeles at the Azusa Street Mission in 1906." *International Outlook* (January–March 1963).
Fillmer, Jenny. "1906 Lynchings Grew from Tensions, Racism." *News-Leader* (Springfield, Missouri), 14 April 2006.
Fox, Charles R. Jr. "William J. Seymour: A Critical Investigation of his Soteriology, Pneumatology, and Ecclesiology." Ph.D., diss., Regent University, 2009.
Foxworth, John David. "Raymond T. Richey: An Interpretive Biography." Ph.D., diss., Regent University, 2011.
Frankiel, Sandra Sizer. *California's Spiritual Frontiers: Religious Alternatives in Anglo-Protestantism, 1850–1910*. Berkeley: University of California Press, 1988.
Franklin, John Hope. *From Slavery to Freedom: A History of Negro Americans*. New York: Alfred Knopf, 1974.
Fredericks, C. H. "Is Speaking in Tongues Scriptural?" *AF* (Baxter Springs) (October 1912): 7–8.
Frodsham, Stanley H. *With Signs Following: The Story of the Pentecostal Revival in the Twentieth Century*. Springfield, MO: Gospel Publishing House, [1926] 1946.
Garr, A. G., and Sister. "Good News from Danville, VA." *AF* (September 1906): 4.
Garr, A. G., and Sister. "The Work in India." *AF* (June to September 1907): 1.
Garr, A. G., and Wife, "Pentecost in Danville, VA." *AF* (October 1906): 2.
Garr, Mrs. Lillian. "In Calcutta, India." *AF* (April 1907): 1.
Garr, Mrs. Lillian. "Testimony and Praise to God." *AF* (June to September 1907): 4.
Gaustad, Edwin S and Mark A. Noll, eds., *A Documentary History of Religion in America since 1877*. Grand Rapids: William B. Eerdmans Publishing, 2003.
Gerstle, Gary. "Race and Nation in the Thought and Politics of Woodrow Wilson." In John Milton Cooper, Jr., ed. *Reconsidering Woodrow Wilson: Progressivism, Internationalism, War, and Peace*, Baltimore, MD: Johns Hopkins University Press, 2008.
Gibson, Robert A. "The Negro Holocaust: Lynching and Race Riots in the United States, 1880–1950." Report. Yale–New Haven Teachers Institute, 2005.
Gitte, E. J. "Post, Ansel Howard." *NIDPCM*, 994.
Goff, James R. Jr. *Fields White unto Harvest: Charles F. Parham and the Missionary Origins of Pentecostalism*. Fayetteville: University of Arkansas Press, 1988.
Goff, James R. Jr., and Grant Wacker, eds. *Portraits of a Generation: Early Pentecostal Leaders*. Fayetteville: University of Arkansas Press, 2002.
Gohr, Glenn. "Jennie Seymour: Azusa Street Leader." *Spirit Led Woman* (December–January 2004).
Golder, Morris E. *History of the Pentecostal Assemblies of the World*. Indianapolis, IN: privately printed, 1973.

Goss, Howard A. "Reminiscences of an Eyewitness." *The Weekly Evangel*, 5 March 1916.
Guillén, Miguel. *La Historia Del Concilio Latino Americano De Iglesias Cristianas*. Brownsville, TX: Latin American Council of Christian Churches, [1982] 1991.
Hamilton, Michael, ed. *The Charismatic Movement*. Grand Rapids, MI: Eerdmans, 1975.
Hanegraaff, Hank. *Counterfeit Revival*. Nashville, TN: W. Publishing Group, 2001.
Harmon, Rosa. "West Africa." *AF* (May 1908): 1.
Harvey, Mrs. E. L. "Given Over to Believe a Lie." *Burning Bush*, 27 June 1907.
Hastings, Adrian, ed. *A World History of Christianity*. Grand Rapids, MI: Eerdmans, 1999.
Henke, Frederick G. "The Gift of Tongues and Related Phenomena at the Present Day." *American Journal of Theology* 13 (April 1909): 193–206.
Henretta, James A., W. Elliot Brownlee, David Brody, and Susan Ware. *America's History*. New York: Worth, 1993.
Hexham, I., and K. Poewe-Hexham. "South Africa." NIDPCM, 227–28.
Hill, Robert A., and Barbara Bair, eds. *Marcus Garvey Life and Lessons: A Centennial Companion to the Marcus Garvey University Negro Improvement Association Papers*. Berkeley: University of California Press, 1988.
Hills, A. M. *A Hero of Faith and Prayer, or Life of Rev. Martin Wells Knapp*. Jamestown, NC: Newby Book Room, 1973.
Hinmers, J. "In London." *AF* (April 1907): 1
Hollenweger, Walter J. "Black Pentecostal Concept." *Concept* 30. Geneva, Switzerland: World Council of Churches, June 1970.
Hollenweger, Walter J. *Pentecost between Black and White*. Belfast, Ireland: Christian Journals, 1974.
Hollenweger, Walter J. *The Pentecostals*. Peabody, MA: Hendrickson, [1972] 1988.
Hollenweger, Walter J. *Pentecostalism: Origins and Developments Worldwide*. Peabody, MA: Hendrickson, 1997.
Hollingsworth, Eric. "In Stockholm." *AF* (February–March 1907): 1.
Hook, C. H. "In London." *AF* (February–March 1907): 1.
Hook, C. H. "Testimonies." *AF* (January 1908): 4.
Hook, C. H. "Baptized in the Little Vestry of All Saints, Sunderland." *AF* (P) (June 1908): 3.
Hutchins, Julia. "Report of Chattanooga meetings." *AF* (December 1906): 3.
Hutchins, Julia. "Meetings in Chattanooga." *AF* (December 1906): 1.
Hutchinson, Mark. "Australia." NIDPCM, 26–27.
Hutchinson, Mark. "'02 Second Founder': AC Valdez Sr and Australian Pentecostalism." *Australian Pentecostal Studies* 11 (January 2009), available at webjournals.alphacrucis.edu.au, http://webjournals.ac.edu.au/journals/aps/issue-11/02-second-founder-a-c-valdez-sr-and-australian-pen.
Indianapolis News. 5 June 1907.
Indianapolis Star. "Negro Bluks Blow. Why? Husband May Know." 5 June 1907, 20.
Indianapolis Star. "Oddy Asks Divorce Because of Bluks." 6 June 1907, 3.
Irvin, Dale T. "Charles Price Jones: Images of Holiness." In Goff and Wacker, eds., *Portraits of a Generation: Early Pentecostal Leaders*, 36–50, 380–82.
Iverson, Marie. *AF* (Portland) (September 1908): 2.
Jacobsen, Douglas. *Thinking in the Spirit: Theologies of the Early Pentecostal Movement*. Indianapolis: Indiana University Press, 2004.

Jacobsen, Douglas. *A Reader in Pentecostal Theology: Voices from the First Generation.* Indianapolis: Indiana University Press, 2006.
James, William. *The Varieties of Religious Experience.* New York: Vintage Books, 1990.
Jenkins, Philip. *The Next Christendom: The Coming of Global Christianity.* New York: Oxford University Press, 2003.
Johnson, Andrew. "Missionaries to Jerusalem." *AF* (September 1906): 4.
Johnson, Andrew. "Letter from Bro. Johnson." *AF* (October 1906): 3.
Johnson, Andrew. "From Our brother in Sweden." *AF* (January 1907): 3.
Johnson, Andrew. "In Sweden." *AF* (April 1907): 1.
Johnson, Andrew. "Salvation in Sweden." *AF* (June to September 1907): 1.
Johnson, Andrew. "Gottenberg, Sweden." *AF* (January 1909): 1.
Johnson, Ian. "The Impact A. C. Valdez Had on My Life." Post by Ian Johnson, July 22, 2011, available at http://www.facebook.com/note.php?note_id=208146569232913.
Jones, Lawrence Neale. "The Black Pentecostals." In Michael P. Hamilton, ed., *The Charismatic Movement,* 145–58. Grand Rapids, MI: Eerdmans, 1975.
Kalu, Ogbu. *African Pentecostalism: An Introduction.* New York: Oxford University Press, 2008.
Katz, William Loren. *Eyewitness: The Negro in American History.* New York: Pitman, 1967.
Kendrick, Claude. *The Promise Fulfilled.* Springfield, MO: Gospel Publishing House, 1961.
Kessel, G. G. "The Tongues Delusion." *The Free Methodist,* 26 November 1906.
Klaus, Byron D. *We've Come This Far: Reflections on the Pentecostal Tradition and Racial Reconciliation.* Springfield, MO: Assemblies of God Theological Seminary, 2007.
Knapp, Mrs. *AF* (September 1906): 2.
Knight, Kate. "Heavenly Visitations in India." *AF* (May 1908): 4.
Kydd, Ronald A. N. *Charismatic Gifts in the Early Church.* Peabody, MA: Hendrickson, 1984.
Lake, John G. "Brother Lake's Letter." *The Upper Room* (June 1909): 2.
Lake, John G. "Origin of the Apostolic Faith Movement." *The Pentecostal Outlook* ([June 1911] September 1932): 3.
Lawrence, Bennett F. *The Apostolic Faith Restored.* Springfield, MO: Gospel Publishing House, 1916.
Lake, John G. "Syria." *AF* (Portland) (January 1909): 1.
Lake, John G. "Houston, Texas and W. J. Seymour." *Pentecostal Evangel* (February 19, 1916): 4–5.
Leatherman, Lucy M. "Jerusalem." *AF* (May 1908): 1.
Lewis, David Levering. *W.E.B. Du Bois: Biography of a Race.* New York: Henry Holt & Company, 1993.
Lincoln, C. Eric, and Lawrence H. Mamiya. *The Black Church in the African American Experience.* Durham, NC: Duke University Press, 1990.
López, Abundio, and Rosa López. "Spanish Receive the Pentecost." *AF* (October 1906): 4
Los Angeles Daily Times. "Weird Babel of Tongues." 18 April 1906, 1.
Los Angeles Daily Times. "Queen 'Gift' Given Many." 23 July 1906, 7.
Los Angeles Daily Times. "Baba Bharati Says Not a Language." 19 September 1906, 1.

Los Angeles Herald. "Zion City Has a New Leader." 27 September 1906, 8.

Lovett, Leonard. "Perspective on the Black Origins of the Contemporary Pentecostal Movement." *Journal of the Interdenominational Center* 1 (fall 1973): 36–49.

Lovett, Leonard. "Black Origins of the Pentecostal Movement." In Synan, ed., *Aspects of Pentecostal-Charismatic Origins,* 123–41.

Lovett, Leonard. "Black Holiness-Pentecostalism: Implications for Ethics and Social Transformation." Ph.D. diss., Emory University, 1978.

Lovett, Leonard. "The Present: The Problem of Racism in the Contemporary Pentecostal Movement." *Cyberjournal for Pentecostal-Charismatic Research* 14 (May 2005).

Lovett, Leonard. "William J. Seymour: Peril and Possibilities for a New Era." *Enrichment Journal* 11, no. 2 (spring 2006): 46–54.

Lugo, Juan L. *Pentecostés en Puerto Rico O La Vida de un Misionero.* San Juan, Puerto Rico: Puerto Rico Gospel Press, 1951.

MacArthur, John F. *Charismatic Chaos.* Grand Rapids, MI: Zondervan, 1993.

MacRobert, Iain. *The Black Roots and White Racism of Early Pentecostalism in the USA.* New York: St. Martin's Press, 1988.

Maempa, John T. "Keeping the flame alive—an Azusa Street Centennial Report," AG.org *News & Information,* May 3, 2006: http://rss.ag.org/articles/detail.cfm?RSS_RSSContentID=3938&RSS_OriginatingRSSFeedID=1034

Marsden, George. *Fundamentalism and American Culture: The Shaping of Twentieth-Century Evangelicalism, 1870–1925.* New York: Oxford University Press, 1980.

Martin, Larry. *The True Believers: Eye Witness Accounts of the Revival that Shook the World, Vol. 2.* Pensacola, FL: Christian Life Books, 1998.

Martin, Larry. *The Life and Ministry of William J. Seymour, Vol. 1.* Joplin, MO: Christian Life Books, 1999.

Martin, Larry, ed. *Azusa Street: The True Believers Part 2, Vol. 3.* Joplin, MO: Christian Life Books, 1999.

Martin, Larry, ed. *Azusa Street Sermons by William J. Seymour, Vol. 5.* Joplin, MO: Christian Life Books, 1999.

Martin, Larry, ed. *The Doctrines and Discipline of the Apostolic Faith Mission of Los Angeles, California, Vol. 7.* Joplin, MO: Christian Life Books, 2000.

Martin, Larry, ed. *Skeptics and Scoffers, Vol. 8.* Pensacola, FL: Christian Life Books, 2004.

Martin, Larry, ed. *Saved and Sanctified: Holy Ghost Revival on Azusa Street.* Pensacola, FL: Christian Life Books, 2005.

Mason, Mary. *The Life and Work of Bishop C. H. Mason and His Co-laborers.* Memphis, TN: privately published, 1931.

McClymond, Michael J., ed. *Embodying the Spirit: New Perspectives on North American Revivalism.* Baltimore, MD: Johns Hopkins University Press, 2004.

McDonnell, Kilian. *Catholic Pentecostalism: Problems in Evaluation.* Pecos, NM: Dove, 1970.

McGee, Gary. "William J. Seymour and the Azusa Street Revival." *Enrichment* (fall 1999): 26–33.

McGee, G. B. "Garr, Alfred Goodrich, Sr." NIDPCM, 660.

McGee, G. B., and S. M. Burgess. "India." NIDPCM, 118–26.

McGee, G. B., and E. J. Gitre. "Mead, Samuel J. and Ardella (Knapp)." NIDPCM, 867–68.

McGee, G. B., and B. A. Pavia. "Turney, Henry Michael." NIDPCM, 1155.

McGee, G. B., and Darrin Rodgers. "Abrams, Minnie F." NIDPCM, 305–6.

McIntosh, T. J. "Missionaries to Palestine." *AF* (May 1908): 4.
McKinney, Leila. "A Girl's Consecration for Africa." *AF* (October 1906): 1.
Mead, Ardell K. "Sister Mead's Baptism." *AF* (November 1906): 3
Mead, Samuel J. "From a Missionary to Africa." *AF* (September 1906): 3.
Mead, Samuel J. "New-Tongued Missionary for Africa." *AF* (November 1906): 3.
Mead, Samuel J. "On the Way to Africa." *AF* (February–March 1907): 5.
Menzies, William W. *Anointed to Serve: The Story of the Assemblies of God, Vol. 1.* Springfield, MO: Gospel Publishing House, 1971.
Messenger, F. M. "The 'Tongues' in Zion City." *Burning Bush,* 24 January 1907.
Messenger, F. M. "Schism and Tongues." *Burning Bush,* 24 January 1907.
Messenger, F. M. "Garrs in India." *Burning Bush,* 18 April 1907.
Messenger, F. M. "Counterfeit Gifts of Tongues." *Burning Bush,* 19 September 1907.
Miller, Donald. *Reinventing American Protestantism: Christianity and the New Millennium.* Berkeley: University of California Press, 1997.
Miller, Donald and Tetsunao Yamamori. *Global Pentecostalism: The New Face of Christian Social Engagement.* Berkeley: University of California Press, 2007.
Moore, Jennie Evans. "Music from Heaven." *AF* (May 1907): 3.
Moorhead, Max Wood. "Pentecost in Mukti, India." *AF* (September 1907): 4.
Moorhead, Max Wood. "Tribes in India that Have Received Pentecost." *AF* (Portland) (January 1909): 3.
Murashko, Alex. "Greg Laurie Seeks Churches, Venues to Host 'Harvest America' Event," *The Christian Post,* March 21, 2012, http://www.christianpost.com/news/greg-laurie-seeks-churches-venues-to-host-harvest-america-event-71863/
Nelson, Douglas J. Interview with Ms. Mattie Cummings, Los Angeles, 1979.
Nelson, Douglas J. "For Such a Time as This: The Story of Bishop William J. Seymour and the Azusa Street Revival." Ph.D., diss., University of Birmingham, England, 1981.
Nichol, John Thomas. *The Pentecostals.* Plainfield, NJ: Logos International, 1966.
Nickel, Thomas R. *Azusa Street Outpouring: As Told To Me by Those Who Were There.* Handford, CA: Great Commission International, 1956.
Nilsen, O., and L. Ahonen. "Norway." *NIDPCM,* 193.
Noll, Mark A. *A History of Christianity in the United States and Canada.* Grand Rapids, MI: Eerdmans, 1992.
Norton, Albert. "Natives in India Speak in Tongues." *AF* (April 1907): 2.
O'Connor, Edward D. *The Pentecostal Movement in the Catholic Church.* Notre Dame, IN: Ave Maria Press, 1971.
Olsen, Carl. *Theory and Method in the Study of Religion.* New York: Oxford University Press, 2005.
Omenyo, Cephas. "William Seymour and African Pentecostal Historiography: The Case of Ghana." *Asian Journal of Pentecostal Studies* 9, no. 2 (July 2006): 244–58.
Orwig, A. W. "My First Visit to the Azuzu [*sic*] Street Pentecostal Mission, Los Angeles, California." *Weekly Evangel,* 18 March 1916, 4.
Orwig, A. W. "Additional from Los Angeles Covering the Early Pentecostal Work." *Weekly Evangel,* 8 April 1916, 4.
Osterberg, Arthur G. "A Revival and a Revolution." *Gull Gospel Men's Voice* (October 1956): 6–7.
Osterberg, Arthur G. "Oral History of the Life of Arthur G. Osterberg and the Azusa Street Revival." Interview by Jerry Jensen and Jonathan Ellsworth Per-

kins, March 1966 (4 tapes), Transcription by Mae Waldron, Tapes 1-4, Flower Pentecostal Heritage Center.

Owens, Robert R. *Speak to the Rock: The Azusa Street Revival, Its Roots and Its Message*. Lanham, MD: University Press of America, 1998.

Owens, Robert R. *The Azusa Street Revival*. Maitland, FL: Xulon Press, 2005.

Ozman, Agnes. "A Witness to First Scenes: As Told by the One Who First Received The Baptism In Bible School in Topeka." *Apostolic Faith* (Baxter Springs) (January 1913): 4-5.

Parham, Charles Fox. *Kol Kare Bomidbar: A Voice Crying in the Wilderness* [KKB]. Baxter Springs, KS: Apostolic Faith Bible College, [1902] 1910.

Parham, Charles Fox. "Fanaticism: Flesh and Familiar Spirits." *AF* (Baxter Springs) December 25, 1910): 4-6.

Parham, Charles Fox. "The Sealing." *AF* (Baxter Springs) (December 25, 1910): 10.

Parham, Charles Fox. *The Everlasting Gospel* [TEG]. Baxter Springs, KS: Charles Fox Parham, [1911] 1919, 1920, 1942.

Parham, Charles Fox. Editorial. *AF* (Baxter Springs) (January 1912): 7.

Parham, Charles Fox. "A Happy New Year to All." *AF* (Baxter Springs) (January 1912): 7-9.

Parham, Charles Fox. "Leadership." *AF* (Baxter Springs) (June 1912): 7-8.

Parham, Charles Fox. "Unity." *AF* (Baxter Springs) (June 1912): 9-11.

Parham, Charles Fox. "Lest We Forget." *AF* (Baxter Springs) (July 1912): 6.

Parham, Charles Fox. "The Pentecostal Baptism Restored." *AF* (Baxter Springs) (July 1912): 10.

Parham, Charles Fox. "The Source of the Disease: Sanctification of Spirit, Soul and Body Only Real Antidote for Sickness." *AF* (Baxter Springs) (August 1912): 1-4.

Parham, Charles Fox. "Camp Meeting Snap Shots." *AF* (Baxter Springs) (September 1912): 9-10.

Parham, Charles Fox. "Hell." *AF* (Baxter Springs) (September 1912): 11.

Parham, Charles Fox. "Prophetic Symbols." *AF* (Baxter Springs) (September 1912): 1-13.

Parham, Charles Fox. Editorial. *AF* (Baxter Springs) (September 1912): 6.

Parham, Charles Fox. "Camp Meeting Snap Shots." *AF* (Baxter Springs) (September 1912): 9-10.

Parham, Charles Fox. "Baptism of the Holy Ghost." *AF* (Baxter Springs) (October 1912): 8-9.

Parham, Charles Fox. *AF* (Baxter Springs) (October 1912): 6.

Parham, Charles Fox. *AF* (Baxter Springs) (November 1912): 7.

Parham, Charles Fox. "Free-Love." *AF* (Baxter Springs) (December 1912): 4-5.

Parham, Charles Fox. "Greeting: Backward—Forward." *AF* (Baxter Springs) (January 1913): 8-9.

Parham, Charles Fox. "History of the Apostolic Faith Movement. Origine [sic], Projector & C." *AF* (Baxter Springs) (May 1921): 5.

Parham, Mrs. Sarah (Charles) Fox. *The Life of Charles F. Parham: Founder of the Apostolic Faith Movement*. 3rd Printing. Birmingham, AL: Commercial Printing Company, [1930] 1977.

Paris, Arthur E. *Black Pentecostalism: Southern Religion in an Urban World*. Amherst, MA: University of Massachusetts Press, 1982.

Patterson, J. O., German Ross, and Julia Atkins, eds. *History and Formative Years of*

the Church of God in Christ. Memphis, TN: Church of God in Christ Publishing House, 1969.
Pentecostal Herald. "Brother Seymour Called Home." 1 October 1922, 1.
Pentecostal Herald. "A Great Unity Conference." 1 October 1922, 1.
Pisgah Mission. "Work among Spanish." *Pisgah* (January 1909): 11–12.
Post, A. H. "Testimony of a Minister." *AF* (January 1907): 3.
Post, A. H. "Los Angeles to Ceylon, India." *AF* (May 1908): 4.
Ramírez, Daniel. "Borderlands Praxis: The Immigrant Experience in Latino Pentecostal Churches." *Journal of the American Academy of Religion* 67, no. 3 (September 1999): 573–96.
Ranaghan, Kevin, and Dorothy Ranaghan. *Catholic Pentecostals.* New York: Paulist Press, 1969.
Rangel, Nellie. *Historia de la Confederación Nacional de Sociedad Femeniles "Dorcas."* Rancho Cucamonga, CA: Apostolic Assembly of the Faith in Christ Jesus, 1984.
Reed, Daniel. "Aspects of the Origins of Oneness Pentecostalism." In Vinson Synan, ed., *Aspects of Pentecostal-Charismatic Origins,* 143–168.
Riggio, Ronald E., Susan E. Murphy, and Francis J. Pirozzolo. *Multiple Intelligences and Leadership.* Mahwah, NJ: Lawrence Erlbaum Associates, Publishers, 2002.
Robeck, Cecil M. Jr. *The Colorline Was Washed Away in the Blood: A Pentecostal Dream for Racial Harmony.* Costa Mesa, CA: Christian Education Press, Newport-Mesa Christian Center, 1995, 1–25.
Robeck, Cecil M. Jr. *"Azusa Street Revival."* NIDPCM, 344–50.
Robeck, Cecil M. Jr. "National Association of Evangelicals." NIDPCM, 922–25.
Robeck, Cecil M. Jr. *"William Joseph Seymour."* NIDPCM, 1053–58.
Robeck, Cecil M. Jr. "Florence Crawford: Apostolic Faith Pioneer." In Goff and Wacker, eds., *Portraits of a Generation: Early Pentecostal Leaders,* 219–35, 406–10.
Robeck, Cecil M. Jr. "The Past: Historical Roots of Racial Unity and Division in American Pentecostalism." *Cyberjournal for Pentecostal-Charismatic Research* 14 (May 2005), available at http://www.pctii.org/cyberj/cyber14.html.
Robeck, Cecil M. Jr. "Azusa Street: 100 Years Later." *Enrichment Journal* 11, no. 2 (spring 2006): 26–42.
Robeck, Cecil M. Jr. "Azusa Street Revival Timeline." *Enrichment Journal* 11, no. 2 (spring 2006): 65–70, 103–8.
Robeck, Cecil M. Jr. *The Azusa Street Mission and Revival.* Nashville, TN: Thomas Nelson, 2006.
Robert, Dana Lee. *American Women in Mission: A Social History of their Thought and Practice.* Macon, GA: Mercer University Press, 1997.
Robert, Dana Lee. *Converting Colonialism: Visions and Realities in Mission History, 1706–1914.* Grand Rapids, MI: Eerdmans Publishing, 2008.
Rodgers, Darren J. "The Assemblies of God and the Long Journey toward Racial Reconciliation." *Assemblies of God Heritage* 28 (2008).
Roof, Wade Clark, and William McKinney. *American Mainline Religion: Its Changing Shape and Future.* New Brunswick, NJ: Rutgers University Press, 1987.
Rosenior, Derrick Rodney. "Toward Racial Reconciliation: Collective Memory, Myth and Nostalgia in American Pentecostalism." Ph.D., diss., Howard University, 2005.
Sánchez-Walsh, Arlene. *Latino Pentecostal Identity: Evangelical Faith, Self, and Society.* New York: Columbia University Press, 2003.

Sanders, Rufus G.W. *William Joseph Seymour: Black Father of the 20th Century Pentecostal/Charismatic Movement.* Sandusky, OH: Alexandra Publications, 2003.
Schwede, L. T. "Letter from South Africa." *The Upper Room* (June 1909): 7.
Seymour, William J. "Impure Doctrine." *AF* (October–January 1905): 3.
Seymour, William J. Letter to W. F. Carothers, July 12, 1906.
Seymour, William J. "Bro. Seymour's Call." *AF* (September 1906): 1.
Seymour, William J. "The Precious Atonement." *AF* (September 1906): 1.
Seymour, William J. "River of Living Water." *AF* (November 1906): 2.
Seymour, William J. "Counterfeits." *AF* (December 1906): 2.
Seymour, William J. "Gifts of the Holy Spirit." *AF* (January 1907): 2.
Seymour, William J. "The Marriage Tie." *AF* (September 1907): 3.
Seymour, William J. "To The Married." *AF* (January 1908): 3.
Seymour, William J. "The Baptism of the Holy Spirit." *AF* (May 1908): 3.
Seymour, William J. "The Holy Ghost is Power." *AF* (May 1908): 3.
Seymour, William J. [D&D] *The Doctrines and Discipline of the Azusa Street Apostolic Faith Mission of Los Angeles, Cal.* Los Angeles, CA: Apostolic Faith Mission, 1915.
Seymour, William J. *Azusa Street Mission Fourteenth Anniversary of the Out-pouring of the Holy Spirit In Los Angeles, California.* Los Angeles, CA: W. H. Giles (Gospel Printer), 1920.
Sharpe, Eric. *Comparative Religion: A History.* London, UK: Duckworth, [1975] 2009.
Shumway, Charles W. "A Study of 'The Gift of Tongues,'" A.B. thesis, University of Southern California, 1914.
Shumway, Charles W. "A Critical History of Glossolalia." Ph.D. diss., Boston University, 1919.
Sindima, Harvey. *Drums of Redemption: An Introduction to African Christianity.* New York: Praeger Books, 1999.
Sizelove, Rachel. "Pentecost Has Come." *Word and Work* (May 1936): 1, 2, 12.
Sizelove, Rachel. "A Sparkling Fountain for the Whole Earth." *Word and Work* (June 1934): 1, 11, 12.
Smith, Otis J., and Oree Keyes, eds. *Manual of the Apostolic Faith Church of God.* nd, np.
Spickard Paul R., and Kevin M. Craig. *God's People: A Social History of Christians.* Grand Rapids, MI. Baker Books, 1995.
Steelberg, Mrs. Wesley. "Impressions of Pentecost 35 Years Ago." *The Pentecostal Evangel,* 24 February 1945, 2–3.
Stephens, Randall J. "Assessing the Roots of Pentecostalism: A Historiographic Essay." Available at http://are.as.wvu.edu/pentroot.htm.
Stock, Jennifer. "George S. Montgomery: Businessman for the Gospel." *A/G Heritage* (Summer 1989): 12–14.
Stokes, Melvyn. *D.W. Griffith's The Birth of a Nation: A History of the Most Controversial Motion Picture of All Time.* New York: Oxford University Press, 2008.
Studd, George B. *Diary.* Typed for the Assemblies of God Archives from original diary, January 1988, by Maranatha Studd Michael, daughter of George Studd.
Sue, Derald. *Overcoming Our Racism.* New York: Jossey-Bass, 2003.
Sulger, A. "Delivered from the 'Tongue' Heresy." *Rocky Mountain Pillar of Fire* (March 27, 1907).
Synan, Vinson. *The Holiness-Pentecostal Tradition: Charismatic Movements in the Twentieth-Century.* Grand Rapids, MI: Eerdmans, [1971] 1997.

Synan, Vinson. ed. *Aspects of Pentecostal-Charismatic Origins*. Plainfield, NJ: Logos International Press, 1975.
Synan, Vinson. *The Twentieth-Century Pentecostal Explosion*. Altamonte, FL: Creation House, 1987.
Synan, Vinson. "The Future: A Strategy for Reconciliation." *Cyberjournal for Pentecostal-Charismatic Research* 14 (May 2005).
Synan, Vinson. "Cashwell, Gaston Barnabas." *NIDPCM*, 457–58.
Synan, Vinson. "Fundamentalism." *NIDPCM*, 655–58.
Synan, Vinson and Charles R. Fox, Jr. *William J. Seymour: Pioneer of the Azusa Street Revival*. Alachua, FL: Bridge Logos Foundation, 2012.
Taylor, Malcolm John. "Publish and be Blessed: A Case Study in Early Pentecostal Publishing History." Ph.D. diss., University of Birmingham, England, 1994.
Tinney, James S. "Black Origins of the Pentecostal Movement." *Christianity Today* 16, no. 1 (October 8, 1971): 4–6.
Tinney, James S. "William J. Seymour: Father of Modern-Day Pentecostalism, *Journal of the Interdenominational Theological Center* 4:1 (fall 1976): 34–44.
Tinney, James S. "Who Was William J. Seymour?" *Spirit* 2, no. 2 (1978): 10–20.
Tinney, James S. "Competing Theories of the Historical Origins for Black Pentecostalism." AAR unpublished paper (16 November 1979).
Todd, "China," *AF* (Portland) (July and August 1988): 1.
Tomlinson, W. J. "In Wales." *AF* (October–January 1908): 1.
Topeka State Journal. "Hindoo and Zulu Both Represented in Bethel College: Students Suddenly Begin Talking in Strange Languages." 9 January 1901.
Townsend-Gilkes, Cheryl. "The Role of Women in the Sanctified Church." *Journal of Religious Thought* 43, no. 1 (Spring-Summer 1986): 24–41.
Trask, Thomas. "The Azusa Street Revival: Celebrating the Past, Anticipating the Future." *Enrichment Journal* 11, no. 2 (spring 2006): 16–18.
Turney, H. M. "Alaska Brother Proves Acts 1.8." *AF* (December 1906): 3.
Turney, H. M. "Apostolic Faith Mission in San Jose." *AF* (January 1907): 1.
Turney, H. M. "Missionaries to Johannesburg, South Africa." *Apostolic Faith* (Los Angeles) (September 1908): 4.
Turney, H. M., and A. E. Turney. "In Honolulu, Hawaii." *AF* (April 1907): 1.
Turney, H. M., and wife. "In Honolulu." *AF* (February–March 1907): 1.
Upper Room. "Our Spanish Meeting." (January 1911): 1.
Valdez, A. C. "Letter to Brother Williams." 21 February 1940, 1–2.
Valdez, A. C. "Letter to J. R. Flower." 29 March 1940.
Valdez, Adolfo C., and James F. Scheer. *Fire on Azusa Street*. Costa Mesa, CA: Gift Publications, 1980.
Vanzandt, J. C. *Speaking in Tongues*. Portland, OR: J. C. Vanzandt, [1911] 1926.
Villafañe, Eldin. *The Liberating Spirit: Toward an Hispanic American Pentecostal Social Ethic*. New York: University Press of America, 1992.
Voice in the Wilderness. "Death of W. J. Seymour." Vol. 2, no. 13 (1922): 7.
Voogd, Jan. *Race Riots and Resistance: The Red Summer of 1919*. New York: Peter Lang, 2008.
Wacker, Grant. "Pentecostalism." In Charles H. Lippy and Peter W. Williams, eds., *Encyclopedia of the American Religious Experience*, 935. New York: Scribner, 1988.
Wacker, Grant. *Heaven Below: Early Pentecostals and American Culture*. Cambridge, MA: Harvard University Press, 2001.
Walling, Aaron. "The 1906–1908 Azusa Revival Paper: An Evaluation of the Apostolic Faith." *A/G Heritage* (summer 1999): 10–15.

Ward, Kevin. "Africa." In Adrian Hastings, eds., *A World History of Christianity*, 222. Grand Rapids, MI: Eerdmans, 1999.
Warfield, B. B. *Counterfeit Miracles*. Carlisle, PA: Banner of Truth Publications, 1918.
Warner, Wayne. *The Azusa Street Newspapers: A Reprint of the Apostolic Faith Mission Publications Los Angeles, California (1906–1908). William J. Seymour, Editor*. Foley, AL: Harvest Publications, 1997.
Warner, W. E. "Hezmalhalch, Thomas." *NIDPCM*, 712.
Washburn, Josephine M. *History and Reminiscences of the Holiness Church Work in Southern California and Arizona*. New York: Garland Publishers, [1912] 1985.
Washington, James R. *Black Sects and Cults*. Garden City, NY: Doubleday/Anchor Books, 1973.
Waukegan Gazette. "Viola Wants to 'Be Shown.'" 26 January 1907.
Waukegan Sun. "Parham Skips Again." 28 January 1907.
White, Alma. *Demons and Tongues*. Zarephath, NJ: Alma White, [1910] 1949.
Wiebe, Robert H. *The Search for Order, 1877–1920*. New York: Hill and Wang, 1967.
Williams, Ernest S. Interview by James S. Tinney, "Black Involvement at Azusa Street Revival." Cassette Tape, November 8, 1978.
Williams, George H., and Edith Waldvogel, "A History of Speaking in Tongues and Related Gifts." In Michael Hamilton, ed., *The Charismatic Movement*, 61–113. Grand Rapids, MI: Eerdmans, 1975.
Williams, Juan, and Quinton Dixie, *This Far by Faith: Stories of the African American Religious Experience*. New York: William Morrow, 2003.
Wood, George O. "This Pentecostal River: Azusa, the Originating Effluence." *Enrichment Journal* 11, no. 2 (spring 2006): 128–38.
Wuthnow, Robert. *The Struggle for America's Soul: Evangelicals, Liberals and Secularism*. Grand Rapids, MI: Eerdmans, 1989.
Wuthnow, Robert, and John H. Evans, eds. *The Quiet Hand of God: Faith-Based Activism and the Public Role of Mainline Protestantism*. Berkeley: University of California Press, 2002.
Yong, Amos. *The Spirit Poured Out on All Flesh: Pentecostalism and the Possibility of Global Theology*. Grand Rapids, MI: Baker Academic, 2005.
Yong, Amos, and Estrelda Alexander. *Afro-Pentecostalism: Black Pentecostal and Charismatic Christianity in History and Culture*. New York: New York University Press, 2010.
Ziegler, J. R. "Lake, John G." *NIDPCM*, 828.

INDEX

Abrams, Minnie, 25, 56, 84, 87, 88, 95
Adams, A. D., 69
Adultery, 107, 168, 191–205, 222, 228, 229, 230, 231, 299
Africa, xvii, xix, 1, 6, 7, 16, 23, 34, 54, 56, 73–78, 154, 161, 223, 304, 308, 332, 337, 355
Alexander, Estrelda, 10, 17
Allen, Richard, 57
American Baptists, 5
American Baptist Mission, 84
American Board of Commissioners for Foreign Missions, 89
American Presbyterian, 84, 365
American Women's Board of Missions, 367
Anderson, Alan, 16, 22, 23, 27, 73, 87
Anderson, Robert Mapes, 10, 11, 389n4, 390n31, 393n11, 393n13, 393n21, 394n22, 394n24, 396n31, 396n33, 397n48, 399n20
Anderson, Tom, 111
Annihilation, 10, 51, 64, 98, 103, 105, 141, 151, 216, 261–64, 307, 375, 380, 383
Angels, Doctrine of, 262, 267, 363, 377
Apostle Paul, xiii–xvii, 3; and Galatians, 2:11–12, 134, 138, 153, 239
Apostolic Assembly of the Faith in Christ Jesus, 4
Apostolic Faith, The, xvii, xxiii, 22–34, 45, 56, 57, 72–77, 83–95, 102, 113, 216, 301, 328
Apostolic Faith, Doctrine of, 218, 297
Apostolic Faith Mission, 256–61, 297
Apostolic Faith Mission of South Africa, 76

Apostolic Faith Movement, 46, 47, 104, 211, 312
Argue, A. H., 324
Arguinzoni, Sonny, 5
Articles of Incorporation of the Azusa Mission, 46–48; Amended Articles of Incorporation, 82–83
Articles of Religion, 216, 217, 233, 248
Asbery, Richard and Ruth, 53, 257, 310, 336
Ashcroft, John, 8
Asia, 6, 21, 23, 71, 72, 73, 88, 89, 363, 368; and Middle East, 34, 78, 80, 106, 112, 358, 362
Assemblies of God, 2, 3; and formation, 126, 130; and Oneness, 124
Atchison, Robert, 92
Atonement, Doctrine of, 165, 166, 167, 384
Australia, 72, 92, 93, 94, 95, 347
Awrey, Daniel, 75, 88, 91
Ayers, Mary, 93
Azusa Mission, xxiii, 57, 68, 316–62; and first Pentecostal camp meeting, 111; and white takeover, 126
Azusa Street Apostolic Faith Mission, 32, 37, 109, 128, 257, 389n1
Azusa Street Revival, xix, 2, 8, 11, 26, 32, 55–72, 157, 309, 319–22, 343–45; criticisms of, 372–84; and Latino response, 59, 60, 152; and spread, 69

Bailey, Gerald A., 94
Baptism in the Holy Ghost and Fire, The, 87

Barratt, T. B., 22–29, 81–95, 312, 358, 360
Bartleman, Frank, 13, 18, 19, 21, 24, 53–71, 91, 104, 108, 109, 118, 119, 120, 121, 139, 146, 151, 309, 316; and first generation, 8, 9; and Seymour's marginalization with Durham, 121–24, 130
Batman, George and Daisy, 74, 352
Bell, E. N., 106, 124, 324; and Parham, 387
Bennett, Dennis, 5
Bernsten, Bernt, 90, 91, 308, 370
Berg, George and Mary, 26, 88, 95, 324
Berrnauer, Estella, 92
Beth-el Bible School, 45, 46
Bethel Temple (Los Angeles), 117
Bettex, Paul, 91
Bible, Infallible, 219–20, 233
Birth of a Nation, The, 126
Bishop, 185, 186, 268–80
Blake, Charles, 7
Blessitt, Arthur, 7
Blood of Jesus, 165, 173, 176, 181–200, 211, 212, 219
Blumhofer, Edith, 12, 13, 15, 389n4, 390n34, 391n42, 392n71, 393n9, 393n21, 394n22, 404n42, 404n52, 405n21, 406n38, 406n39, 406n40, 406n42, 407n3408n31, 408n34
Boddy, Alexander, 22–29, 83, 95, 123, 361; and Azusa Mission as Mecca, 25, 70, 151, 389n1. *See also* Seymour, William
Bonnke, Reinhard, 7
Borlase, Craig, 15
Born Again, 1, 2, 4, 5, 6, 8, 35, 49, 64, 66, 105, 220, 294–96, 397n48
Bosworth, F. F., 2, 69
Braide, Garrick, 73
Brathwaite, Rene, 17, 128, 391n51, 407n4
Brelsford, George, 79
Bridegroom Messenger, 325
British Israelism, 31, 44, 45, 51, 64, 98, 150, 151, 216, 380
Britton, F.M., 3, 19, 65, 325, 326
Brown, Elizabeth, 79
Bruce, H. H., 93

Brumback, Carl, 9, 10
Bryant, Daniel, 76, 92
Burns, James MacGregor: and transformational leadership, 33, 153
Bush, George W., 7
Butler, A.H., 26, 65

Call to Preach, 217, 250, 310
Calvary Chapel, 5
Calvin, John, 4, and Calvinism, 242
Campbell, Marne, 17
Carothers, Warren Faye, 9, 47, 51, 54, 106, 161, 385, 395n40, 395n41, 395n42, 395n3, 402n9, 404n40, 404n44
Carpenter, Mr., 112, 113
Cashwell, Gaston Barnabas, 13, 19, 29, 65, 69, 111, 325, 326, 327
Catechism of Faith, 217
Cerillo, Augustus, 15, 391n42
Cessationist View on Tongues, 3, 4
Chambers, Oswald, 372, 377
Charismatics and Neo–Charismatics: and colonialism, 73; and dark side, 36; and fragmentation, 35; and Great Commission, 64, 72; and holy restlessness, 153; and maintenance of movement orthodoxy, 10; movement and, 2–7; origins of, 8, 23, 41–46; and secular histories, 23; as third way, 42, 73
Chi, Mok Lai, 29, 89, 91, 369
China, xvii, 1, 24–34, 54, 70, 72, 83–94, 110, 161, 308, 347, 356, 366–71
Christenson, Larry, 5
Christian and Missionary Alliance, 84, 87
Christian Home, Doctrine of, 292, 293
Christian Science, 64, 171, 397n44
Christian Unity, 56, 57, 64, 134, 143, 163, 164, 253, 297
Church, Doctrine of, 221, 222, 235, 290
Church Membership, 217, 222
Church, mission of, 218, 290, 291
Church Missionary Society, 84
Church of God (Cleveland), 2, 3
Church of God in Christ, 3, 7, 67, 68, 126, 143, 150, 156, 166, 332, 337, 339. *See also* Charles Mason

Church of God Reformation Movement, 49
Condit, Louise, 78, 81
Cone, James, 154
Confidence, 71, 84, 361, 362
Conger, Jay, 36
Consecration and Ordination of Elders and Bishops, 218, 268
Conservative Baptists, 4
Cook, G.A., 2, 68, 69, 81, 97, 110, 301, 320–41, 374–77; and Oneness, 124
Cook, Robert and Anna, 88
Cotton, Emma, 332, 334
Cox, Harvey, 10, 12, 13, 391n36, 399n19
Counterfeits, 8, 31, 42, 62, 86, 97, 100, 105, 117, 133, 140, 141, 149, 151, 152, 170, 171, 199, 384–87
Crawford, Florence, 14, 20, 66, 106, 301, 314–16, 330, 356, 369, 401n83; and Clara Lum, 114, 363, 369; and differences with Seymour, 107
Creech, Joe, 18, 20, 24, 391n57; and multiple centers theory, 13, 14
Cullis, Charles, 304
Cummings, Frank, 110, 351
Cummings, Emma, 333

Daniels, David, 10, 397n39, 398n57, 405n20, 409n2
Daughtry, Leah, 7; and Barack Obama, 7
Dayton, Donald, 13, 389n4, 393n9
Deacons, 72–74, 198, 218, 259, 278, 279
Deane, Anna, 91, 92, 369
Death, doctrine of, 264, 284–87
Demons, Doctrine of, 61, 88, 165, 169, 171, 200, 180–219, 222, 239, 265, 327, 332, 339, 350, 370–77, 386; and Satan, 162, 171, 174, 196, 199, 201–12, 376, 379
Denmark, 81, 84, 360, 375
Disciples of Christ, 5
Discrimination, racial, 17, 31, 119, 121, 128, 129, 131, 133, 138, 150, 152, 154, 155, 216, 224, 406n32
Doak, Edward, 58
Doney, C.W., 79
Dove, Stephen, 16
Dowie, John Alexander, 45, 76, 101, 353

DuBois, Joshua, 7, 157; and Barack Obama, 7; and "Talented Tenth," 48, 136, 155, 156
Du Bois, W.E.B., 48, 131–36, 154–56
Durham, William, 13, 14, 18–36, 69, 95, 115, 119, 144, 149, 150–53, 313, 323–25, 372, 377, 378, 386, 405n31; differences with Seymour, 121–33; and Second Azusa Revival, 121, 405n31
Duty of Parents, 218, 291
Duty to Children, 218, 292

Ecumenism, 163–64, 197, 249, 253
Educational Institutions, 218, 289, 290
Egypt, 78, 79, 171, 190, 351, 357
Eldridge, George N., 94, 117
Eliade, Mircea, xix
England, xix, 1, 22–30, 44, 70–83, 181, 223, 357, 358, 360, 361
English Baptist Mission, 84
Episcopalians, 5
Espinosa, Gastón, xv, xvi, xvii, 14, 119, 390n16, 390n17, 391n38, 396n22, 396n24, 406n31, 406n32
Ethiopians, 135, 304
Europe, xiv, xv, 16, 22, 23, 34, 71, 72, 79, 83, 84, 112, 358, 361, 363, 381
Evangelical Covenant, 4
Evangelical Free, 4
Evangelical Mission, 84
Evangelical Protestants: definition of, 4, 6, 9, 11, 26, 42, 56, 73
Evans, Mable, 90

Farrow, Lucy, xxiii, 49, 69, 74, 106, 301, 329, 335, 351; and "back to Africa" movement, 73
Faulkner, Cora Fritsch, 90
Feet Washing, 290, 299
Finney, Charles, 56, 64
First African Methodist Church, 311; and Seymour Minister Manual, xx, 37, 108, 129, 130, 133, 134, 141, 151, 152, 154, 216–300
Fisher, Elmer, 29, 64, 313; and Upper Room Mission, 94, 113, 117
Foursquare Church, 2, 3
Fox, Charles, 17, 119
Foxworth, John, 17

France, 84, 358
Francescon, Luigi, 324
Freewill Baptists, 4
Freemasons, 340
Free Methodists, 4
Frodsham, Stanley, 8
Fundamentalists: definition of, 4
Future State (Eschatology, End Times, Last Days), 218, 265

Garr, Alfred and Lillian, 26, 62, 64, 84–89, 366
Gifts of the Holy Spirit, xiv, xx, 2–5, 14–16, 25–36, 45, 64, 87, 99, 119, 174, 175, 197, 250, 253, 268, 271, 273, 277, 317, 318, 368, 371, 377
Glad Tidings Mission, 26
Godbey, W.B., 117
Goff, H.H., 325
Goff, James, 10–15, 389n4
Gold, Rabbi, 67
Gordon, A.J., 64
Goss, H.A., 19, 124, 324, 338
Great Depression, 147
Griffith, D.W., 126

Hanegraaff, Hank, 3
Hansen, George, 91
Harmon, Rosa, 74
Harris, William Wade, 73, 75, 353
Hawaii, 94, 347, 356
Haywood, G.T., 3, 68, 69, 124, 146, 332, 340; and Oneness, 124
Healing, 164, 165, 298; and medicine, 196
Hebden Mission, 26
Hell, doctrine of, 43, 44, 51, 103, 170, 265, 266, 294, 375, 383
Hess, Roy, 91
Hezmalhalch, Thomas, 69, 76, 350, 354
Holiness movement, 2, 43, 48, 316, 320
Holland, 84, 361
Hollenweger, Walter, 10, 11, 13, 23, 393n9, 401n66, 408n31
Holy Ghost, 161–207, 212–21, 233; baptism of, 164–95, 211, 219, 261, 288, 297–308, 334, 350, 352–56
Holy Spirit, 162–94, 223, 224, 261, 262, 307

Hook, C.H., 83, 85
Hoopa Reservation, 349
Hoover, Willis, 95
Hope Chapel, 5
Houston Bible School, xxiii, 32, 47, 50
Howard, Ansel, 79
Howell, Clark, 136
Huh, Heong, 92
Huntington, Mr., 67
Hurst, John Fletcher, 397n42
Hutchins, Julia, 53, 73, 74, 104–6, 311, 335–37, 351

Immoral Conduct, 254–56
India, xix, 1, 21–34, 54–63, 70–95, 112, 161, 223, 364–68
Initial Evidence Theory, 2, 5, 27, 46, 87, 141
International Pentecostal Holiness Church, 3, 91, 92
Italy, 84, 358, 361
Ireland, 44, 72, 83, 84, 341, 342, 381
Iverson, Maries, 83

Jakes, T.D., 7
James, Hanna, 77
James, William, 34; and Pentecostal movement, 35
Japan, 22, 29, 70, 89, 90, 92, 94, 223, 308, 347, 356
Jesus Movement, 5
Jim Crow segregation, xvi, 45–50, 101, 125, 135, 136, 155
Johnson, Andrew, 78, 79, 80, 81, 84, 95, 341, 358
Johnson, Berger, 83
Jones, Absalom, 57
Jones, Charles Price, 49, 103, 337, 339
Jonas, Mack, 144, 339, 340, 394n36
Junk, Thomas, 91
Justification, 163, 164, 176, 267, 297; and justified, 161, 166, 184, 235, 237

Kendrick, Klaude, 9
Keswick movement, 2
Keyes, Henry S., 66
Kimbangu, Simon, 73
King, J.H., 3, 19, 65, 88, 91, 325–27
King, Martin Luther, 146, 155, 156

Kirby, A.E., 90
Knapp, Martin Wells, 49, 103
Kol Kare Bomidbar, 45, 46, 136, 380, 381, 382
Korea, 89, 92
Ku Klux Klan, 127, 128, 131, 143

Lake, John, 69, 76, 143, 351, 353
Lamb of God, 166, 167, 168, 172, 174, 177, 183, 211, 265
Latin America, 6, 94, 95, 345, 347. *See also* Bailey, Gerald A.
Latino: and Pentecostalism, 9, 14, 59, 60, 94, 95, 117, 118–21, 150–55, 306, 347
Latter Rain, xiv, 56, 79, 184, 214, 304, 307, 363; and the Latter Rain Mission, 84, 365
Lawler, Emma, 90
Lawrence, B.F., 8, 9, 71
Leatherman, Lucy, 78, 79, 81, 84, 88, 106, 362
Lee, Edward, 53, 311, 335, 336, 342
Lee, Owen, 84, 341, 342
LeRoux, P.E., 76, 354
Letwaba, E.M., 354
Liberia, xix, 1, 16, 22, 30, 70–76, 110, 308, 333, 334, 351–53
Lightfoot, J.B., 84
Lion, Eduard, 76
López, Abundio and Rosa, xxiii, 59, 94, 106, 118, 343, 345; and birth of Latino Pentecostalism, 118
López, Luís, 59, 94
Los Angeles Ministerial Association, 66
Lovett, Leonard, 10, 11
Lugo, Juan, 94, 117
Lum, Clara, 106, 111, 113, 114, 301, 313, 314, 331, 332, 401n83, 405n20
Lupton Mission, 26
Lutherans, 5
Luther, Martin, xiii–xvii, 4, 56, 64, 304

Mabilitsa, Paul, 76
MacArthur, John, 3
Mainline Protestants: definition of, 4
Man, doctrine of, 218, 264, 267
Mason, Charles, 2, 3, 24, 25, 31, 49, 64–69, 113, 124, 130, 143–56, 332–39, 405n20

Marriage, 190–215, 226–36, 281–89. *See also* Seymour, William; Crawford, Florence; and Lum, Clara
Martin, Larry, xix, 14, 15
Martínez, Juan Navarro, 59, 94, 118
Mayo, Mae, 111
McAlister, Robert, 124
McCain, John, 7
McCauley, Edward and Molly, 74, 353
McDonnell, Kilian, 5
McIntosh, T.J. and Annie, 78, 90
McLean, Hector and Sigrid, 91
McNutt, Francis, 5
McPherson, Aimee, xxiii, 93, 143, 144, 324
Mead, Samuel and Ardella, 74, 351, 355
Membership, 217, 222, 246, 247, 248, 249, 260
Menzies, Willliam, 10
Merle, J.H., 397n42
Mexico, xxi, 59, 94, 345, 347
Mhlangu, Elias, 76
Michael, May Law, 90
Middle East, 34, 78, 80, 106, 112, 358, 362
Miller, Don, 6
Minister's Qualifications and Ordination via Seymour, 250–54, 268–81, 297, 308
Mishler, Jennie: and Puerto Rico, 94
Money, 169–70
Montgomery, George and Carrie, 88, 94
Moody, Dwight, 56, 64; and Moody Bible Institute, 72, 91, 316
Moomau, Antionette, 91, 371
Moore, Jennie Evans, 55, 110, 311, 312, 333; and Seymour marriage, 113
Moorhead, Max, 25, 29, 86, 87, 367
Morgan, Campbell G., 64
Mott, John: Student Volunteer Movement for Foreign Missions, 72
Mukti Mission and Revival, 16, 26–28, 56, 72, 84–88, 363, 365–68

National Association of Evangelicals (NAE), 3, 9
Neely, Terry, 51, 335
Nelson, Douglas 10, 11, 12, 13, 15, 119, 120, 389n4, 393n9, 393n12, 394n36, 405n21

Neo-Charismatics, xix, 1; definition of, 5, 6
New Birth, 176, 187, 220, 236, 288, 289. *See also* Born-Again
New Zealand, 92, 93, 94, 347
Nkonyane, Daniel, 76
North Bonnie Brae Street, 53, 104, 152, 302, 303, 307, 319; and womb of black church, 58
North Carolina, 13, 18, 19, 26, 34, 69, 111, 325, 326. *See also* Cashwell, Gaston Barnabas
Norway, xix, 1, 22, 25, 29, 30, 70, 79–83, 312, 358–61
Nuzum, Cornelia, 94

Obama, Barack, 7, 390n16
O'Connor, Edward, 5
Olazábal, Francisco, 94, 95
Omenyo, Cephas, 16
Oneness Pentecostals: definition of, 3; movement, 68; and controversy, 124
Ongman, John, 80
Open Brethren, 84
Oppong, Samson, 73
Original Sin, 165, 166, 169, 177, 178, 189, 196, 234, 239
Ortiz Sr., Francisco, 94
Orwig, A.W., 327
Osterberg, Louis, Anna, Emma, and Arthur, 53, 58, 59, 66, 106, 341, 319, 343
Ozman, Agnes N., 46, 305

Palin, Sarah, 7
Palmer, Phoebe, 43
Parents, Duty of and Christian Home, 291–94
Parham, Charles Fox, xix, xx, 2, 3, 42–51, 303–21, 380–89n1; and differences with Seymour 8, 30, 31, 62, 95–105, 129, 140, 149, 152; and ironies with Seymour, 150; and race, 31, 44–51, 133, 304–5, 307, 394n36, 403n28
Peniel Mission, 84, 316
Pentecost, 163, 164, 168, 171, 175, 195–98, 205, 211, 297, 302
Pentecostal Assemblies of the World, 2, 3, 68

Pentecostals, xix, 1; characteristics of and influences on, 2–4; commonalities with Charismatics, xix, 1; definition of, 5
Pentecostal Truth, The, 89
Pérez, Brigido, 59, 346
Petrus, Lewi, 81, 82, 358
Pierson, A.T., 64
Pinson, M. M., 19, 325, 338
Pittman, Rose, 90
Plan of Salvation, 218, 232, 296
Polhill, Cecil, 91; and Azusa Street Mission, 110; and Cambridge Seven, 72
Poona and India Village Mission, 84
Popular Gospel Truth, 91
Portland (Oregon), 107, 114–16, 130, 149, 301, 313–16
Post, Henrietta and Ansel, 79, 88, 351, 357
Potter's House, 7
Preaching, call to, 250–54
Prentiss, Henry, 68
Presbyterian (EPC and PCA), 4
Presbyterians (PCUSA), 5
Probation, 246–49
Protestant Reformation, xiv, xv, 4
Puerto Rico, xxi, 94, 117

Quakers, 56, 299, 304

Race, 15, 17, 31, 32, 44, 45, 51, 56, 57, 66, 73, 96, 99, 101, 108, 111, 126–42, 152, 154, 157
Racism, xv, 11, 15, 48, 137
Ramabai, Pandita, 16, 22, 27, 56, 84, 363–68
Ramírez, Dan, 119, 406n32
Randall, H.E., 79
Reception of Members, 217, 246
Red Summer, 131
Revival: *See* Azusa, Mukti, Topeka, and Welsh
Richey, Raymond T., 143
Robeck, Cecil M., 12, 15
Robert, Evans, 42, 54, 56, 84; and Welsh Revival of 1904, 42, 54, 56, 84, 103, 316, 361
Robinson, A.E., 327
Rodgers, Darren, 406n32

Rodgers, H.G., 19, 325, 338
Rosenior, Derrick, 16
Ross, James, 257
Rumsey, Mary, 92
Russia, 24, 84, 358
Ryan, M.L, 29, 89, 90, 308, 314

Salvation Army, 84, 316
Sanctification, 163–77, 189, 194, 196, 210, 267, 288, 297; and sanctified, 161–84, 212, 219
Sanders, Rufus, 14
Sanford, Frank, 45
Scandinavia, 84, 91, 358, 365, 381
Scandinavian Alliance, 84
Schaff, Philip, 397n42
Scheppe, John, 124
Schideler, Myrtle, 74
Scofield, Cyrus, 3
Scot, R.J., 111, 124, 329
Second Worldwide Pentecostal Camp Meeting, 124
Seymour, Jennie Evans (Moore), 55, 110, 114, 147, 154, 333
Seymour, William, 3, 7, 47–53, 306–54, 389n1; and Afrocentrism, 154, 155; and Apostle Paul, xiii–xvii; and Azusa's decline, 36; and common theological grammar, 20, 27, 28, 29; criticisms of 66; and decline, 116; and differences with Parham, 50, 51, 98, 99, 102, 105, 109, 140, 141, 149, 151, 301; and family and early years, 47–51; and ironies of ministry, 150; and irony of global spread, 37, 95; and loss of *The Apostolic Faith*, 115; and love, 111; and Luther, xiii–xvii; and missionaries, 69–95; and primary impact, 22, 23, 28, 30; and race, 31, 49, 133–55, 223, 224; and reconciliation, 134, 135; and revision of Constitution and Articles of Incorporation, 128; and socially liberative message, 8; and spiritual race war, 126; and theology, 64, 65; and tours, 144, 145; and transformational leadership, 34; and whites, 129–31; and women in ministry, 106, 308
Shakarian, Demos, 61
Shumway, Charles, 71, 86, 87, 309–14; and Seymour biography, 310
Simpson, A.B., 45, 64
Sin, doctrine of, 165, 166, 169, 177, 178, 189, 196, 239
Sizelove, Josie and Rachel, 69, 109, 329
Slavery, 218, 289
Smale, Joseph, 54, 312, 333
Smart, Ninian, xix
Smith, Chuck, 5
Smith, Hannah Whitall, 43
Smith, Hiram, 58, 111, 112, 341
Smith, Hoke, 136
Smith, Rodney, 76
Soul of Man, 218, 262, 294
Sound Doctrine, 64, 217, 224, 247
South Africa, xix, 1, 22–30, 70, 76–79, 83, 308, 350–54
Southern Baptists, 4
Spanish Apostolic Faith Mission, 121, 345, 406n31
Spencer, James, 257
Spiritualists, 171, 219
Spurgeon, Charles, 64
Sri Lanka, 79, 86, 357, 366
Stevens African Methodist Episcopal Church, 57, 58, 109
Studd, George, 92, 313
Sulger, A., 372, 374, 375
Swatson, John, 73
Sweden, xix, 1, 22, 30, 70–81, 95, 299, 341, 358–60
Synan, Vinson, 10, 11, 17, 18

Taylor, G.F., 19, 325
Taylor, Hudson: China Inland Mission, 72, 91
Taylor, Williams, 355
Thistlethwaite, Sarah, 43
Tibet Mission, 84
Tinney, James, 10, 11
Todd, S.C., 90
Tomlinson, A.J., 3, 19, 65, 150, 325
Tongues 180: speaking in, 163, 171, 181–84, 197, 198, 235, 304, 311–14, 320, 357
Topeka Bible School, 2, 9, 103
Topeka Revival, 10, 28, 56

Transgressive space, xvi, 14, 32–36, 56–58, 62, 70, 96–101, 155, 156; loss of, 119
Trasher, Lillian, 79, 357
Trinitarian Pentecostals: definition of, 3
Trinity, doctrine of, 3, 214, 218, 233, 288, 294–96
Turney, Henry, 77, 351, 356

United Church of Christ, 5
United Methodists, 5, 19, 43, 51, 58, 66, 84, 91
United Pentecostal Church, 3
Upper Room Mission, 88, 94, 99, 106, 113, 117, 120, 121. *See also* Fisher, Elmer

Valdez, Susie, José, and Adolfo, 41, 59–66, 93–106, 341–47, 405n31
Valenzuela, Genaro and Romanita Carbajal, 59
Vanzandt, J.C., 115, 309, 314
Venezuela, 94
Victory Outreach International, 5
Vineyard Christian Fellowship, 5
Vingren, Adolf Gunnar, 95, 324

Wacker, Grant, 13–15, 391n42, 392n77, 405n21
Wales, 21, 24, 63, 72, 79, 84, 86, 312, 357, 361
Warfield, Benjamin, 3, 42
Warner, Daniel S., 49, 103
Washington, Booker T., 131, 154
Welch Revival. *See* Evans, Robert
Wesley, Charles and John, 56, 64, 245, 304
White, Alma, 96, 316, 372
White supremacy, 10–17, 31, 45, 51, 101, 129, 133, 150, 380, 394n36, 403n28; and black supremacy, 131
Whole Truth, The, 337
Widney, Joseph, xiii–xvii
Wigglesworth, Smith, 92
Wiley, Ophelia, 69
Williams, Ernest, 69, 99
Williams, F.W., 69, 146
Wilson, Woodrow, 131
Wimber, John, 5
Women, 73–74, 85–92, 106–8, 113–16, 153, 177–80, 215, 308, 344; and Abrams, Minnie, 56, 86–88, 363–65, 367–68; and Cotton, "Mother" Emma, 334–36; and Crawford, Florence, 66, 106–8, 314–16, 331; and Deane, Anna, 91; and Cummings, Emma, 333–34; and Farrow, Lucy, 49–50, 73–74, 351–52; and Garr, Lillian, 84–86, 366–67; and Hutchins, Julia, 53, 73–74, 311–13, 336–37; and interracial mixing, 99–100, 139, 373, 376, 381, 386–87; and Leatherman, Lucy, 78–79, 362–63; and López, Rosa, 59–60, 345–46; and Lum, Clara, 106, 111, 113–16, 313, 331–32; and marriage and divorce, 190–94, 199–200, 207–10, 226–31, 281–84, 289, 299; and McPherson, Aimee Semple, 143; and Mead, Ardella, 75, 355–56; and Montgomery, Carrie Judd, 88, 94; and Moomau, Antionette, 91, 371; and Moore (Seymour), Jennie Evans, 55, 110, 121, 146–48, 153, 333; and Osterberg, Emma, 106; and prophesy, 308; and Ramabai, Pandita, 56, 86–88, 367–68; and Rumsey, Mary, 92; and Sizelove, Rachel, 69, 109, 329–30; and Valdez, Susie Villa, 41, 59; and White, Alma, 96; and Women's Christian Temperance Union, 98, 330, 382; and women evangelists across the U.S., 69, 73, 352–53; and women in ministry and ordination, 106–8, 297, 308; and women missionaries to Asia, 90–92, 363–65
Wood, George O., 7
World Christian Fundamentalist Association, 4
World's Faith Missionary Association, 331

Yamamori, Tetsunao, 6
Young, D.J., 339

Zion City, 45, 54, 76, 101, 105, 106, 184, 382. *See also* Dowie, Alexander; Parham, Charles

www.ingramcontent.com/pod-product-compliance
Lightning Source LLC
Chambersburg PA
CBHW061341300426
44116CB00011B/1936